ENGLISH-LATIN DICTIONARY;

OR

DICTIONARY OF THE LATIN TONGUE,

WITH THE

ENGLISH WORDS RENDERED INTO THE LATIN;

TOGETHER WITH

AN APPENDIX OF FRENCH AND ITALIAN WORDS,

WHICH HAVE THEIR ORIGIN FROM THE LATIN;

COMPILED FROM THE BEST AUTHORITIES.

BY

THOMAS GOODWIN, A.B., T.C.D.

HEAD MASTER OF THE
GREENWICH PROPRIETARY SCHOOL.

London:
JOHN WEALE, 59, HIGH HOLBORN.
MDCCCLV.

LONDON:
GILBERT AND RIVINGTON, PRINTERS,
ST. JOHN'S SQUARE.

ENGLISH-LATIN DICTIONARY.

ABO

A, *an indefinite particle, signifying one, as* liber, a book
To abandon, derelinquo, desero
Abandoned (wicked), perditus, flagitiosus [tutio
Abandonment, derelictio, desti-
An abandoning, derelictio
To abase, humilio, dejicio
An abasement, dejectio
To abash, pudefacio, confundo
To abate, remitto, decresco
An abatement, detractio
An abbacy, cœnobiarchia
An abbess, abbatissa
An abbey, cœnobium
An abbot, cœnobiarcha
To abbreviate, contraho
An abbreviation, abbreviatio
To abdicate, abdico, resigno
An abdication, abdicatio
To abet, adjuvo, instigo
An abetting, instigatio
An abettor, instigator
To abhor, detestor, abominor
To be abhorred, detestandus
Abhorrence, detestatio, execratio
An abhorring, detestatio
To abide (continue), moror, duro
To abide by, defendo
An abiding, commoratio
An abiding by, tuitio
An abiding in, perseverantia
Abject, abjectus, vilis
Abjectly, abjectè, humilitèr
Abjectness, abjectio
Abilities (of mind), peritia
Ability (power), facultas
Ability (strength), robur
Abjuration, abdicatio
To abjure, abjuro, renuncio
An abjuring, ejuratio
Able, capax, potens, valens
To be able, possum, queo, valeo
To be very able, prævaleo
Ableness (skill), peritia
Ablution, ablutio
Abode, habitatio, domicilium, sedes
To abolish, abrogo, rescindo
To abolish (destroy), perdo, deleo
An abolishing, abolitio
Abominable, execrabilis, odiosus
Abominably, turpitèr, odiosè
To abominate, detestor, fugio
Abomination, detestatio, odium
Abortion, abortio, abortus
Abortive, abortivus, frustratus
Abortively, infeliciter
Above, *prep.* (not below), super, supra; (beyond, *or* more than), ante, præter, ultra; (upward), sursum
Above, *adv.* plùs, amplius, magis
[1]

ABS

Above, *adj. comp.* superior, major, præstantior
Above that, insupèr
From above, desupèr, supernè
Over and above, extra, insuper
Above-board, apertè
Above-mentioned, supradictus
To be above, emineo, antecedo
To abound, abundo, redundo
Abounding, abundans, affluens
An abounding, affluentia
About, *prep.* ad, apud, circa, circum, circiter, de, ferè, fermè, in, instar, quasi, sub, super, versus
To be about, *or* employed, occupor
To go about (attempt), aggredior
To abridge, privo, contraho
Abridged, of, privatus
An abridging, contractio
An abridging of, privatio
An abridgment, compendium
Abroach (tapped), terebratus
Abroad (from home), foris; (out of doors), foris; (in foreign parts), peregrè; (in sight), in propatulo; (here and there), latè, passim, undiquè
To abrogate, rescindo
An abrogating, abolitio
Abrupt, abruptus, præruptus
Abruptly, abruptè, raptim
Abruptness, abruptio
An abscess, abscessus
Abscision, abscissio
To abscond, abscondo, lateo
Absconded, absconditus
An absconding, occultatio
Absence, absentia, desiderium
Absent, absens
To be absent, absum, desum
To absolve, absolvo, libero
An absolving, absolutio
Absolute, absolutè, prorsùs
Absoluteness, dominatio
Absolution, absolutio
Absolutory, absolutorius
To absorb, absorbeo
Absorbed, absorptus [nere
To abstain, abstineo, sese continAn abstaining, abstinentia
Abstemious, temperatus, sobrius
Abstemiously, temperatè, sobriè
Abstemiousness, temperantia
Abstergent, *or* abstersive, abstergens
Abstinence, abstinentia
To abstract, centraho, sejungo
An abstract, compendium
Abstracted, abstractus, contractus
Abstractedly, separatìm [tus
Abstruse, occultus, abditus
Very abstruse, perreconditus

ACC

Abstrusely, occultè, abditè
Abstruseness, obscuritas
Absurd, absurdus, ineptus
Somewhat absurd, subabsurdus
Very absurd, perabsurdus
An absurdity, res inepta
Absurdly, absurdè, ineptè
Abundance, copia, abundantia
Abundant, copiosus, uber, plenus
Abundantly, copiosè, abundè
To abuse, abutor; (deceive), decipio; (pollute), polluo, vitio, stupro; (to one's face), scurror; (with the tongue), convicior; (in action), malefacio
An abuse (wrong use), abusus; (injury), injuria, fraus; (with the tongue), convicium, contumelia
Abused (in words), conviciis lacessitus; (in facts), violatus, læsus
An abuser, conviciator
An abusing, convicium, injuria, fraus
Abusive, scurrilis, dicax, petulans
Abusive language, convicium
Abusively, scurrilitèr, contumeTo abut, adjaceo [liosè
Abutting, conterminus, confinis
An abyss, abyssus, profundum
An academic, academicus
Academical, academicus
An academy, academia
To accede, accedo
To accelerate, accelero, festino
An accent, accentus
To accent (a word), accentum appingere; (to pronounce), pronunciare accuratè
To accept, accipio
Acceptable, carus, gratus
Acceptably, aptè, gratè
Acceptance, acceptio
Acceptation, sensus, significatio
Accepted, acceptus
An accepter, acceptor
An access, accessio, accessus, aditus
To have access, admittor
Accessible, affabilis, comis
Accession, accessio, accessus
An accessory, particeps
The accidence, grammatices introductio
An accident, casus fortuitus
Accidental, fortuitus, adventitius
Accidentally, casu, fortuitò
An acclamation, acclamatio
Acclivity, acclivitas
To accommodate, accommodo, apto, instruo [datio
An accommodation, accommo-
B

ACH

To accompany (go with), comitor, deduco, perduco; (keep company with), consocior
Accompanied, comitatus, perductus
An accomplice, particeps [tus
To accomplish, consummo, impleo, exequor, perago
Accomplished, completus
An accomplishing, peractio
An accomplishment, dos animi
To accompt (account), computo
An accord, consensus, concordia
To accord, assentio, convenio, concordo
Of his own accord, ultrò, sponte
Accordant, consentiens, assentiens [situs
Accorded, reconciliatus, compositus
According as, prout, perinde ut, uteunque; According to, ad, de, ex, secundum, pro
Accordingly, ideo, paritèr, sic
To accost, aggredior, adeo, compello
Accosted, compellatus [pello
An accosting, compellatio
To account, numero, computo
An account (reckoning), ratio; (esteem), reputatio, pretium
An accounting, computatio
Of little account, vilis
Accountable, obnoxius
A caster of accounts, calculator
An accountant, arithmeticæ peritus
To account (esteem), æstimo, habeo, pendo, facio
To account for, rationem reddere
To turn to an account, prosum
Of great account, carus, gratus
Of no account, vilis
Of some account, aliquo pretio
An account (cause), causa, ratio
Accounted, æstimatus, habitus
To accoutre, apparo, instruo
Accoutred, armis instructus
Accoutrements, arma, orum
An accoutring, apparatio
Accretion, accretio
To accrue, accresco, orior
To accumulate, accumulo
An accumulating, coacervatio
Accuracy, accuratio
Accurate, accuratus, exactus
Accurately, accuratè, exactè
To accurse, devoveo, execror
Accursed, devotus, execratus
Accusable, accusandus
Accusatory, accusatorius
To accuse, accuso, criminor
To accuse, or blame, reprehendo
To accuse falsely, calumnior
To be accused, in jus vocari
Accused, accusatus, postulatus
Accused falsely, falso delatus
An accuser, accusator, delator
A false accuser, calumniator
An accusation, accusatio
A secret accusation, delatio
A false accusation, calumnia
Accusing falsely, calumniosus
By false accusing, calumniosè
To accustom, assuefacio
To accustom one's self, assuesco
To be accustomed, soleo, solitus sum [tus
Accustomed to do a thing, assuetus
Accustomed to be done, solitus
Not accustomed, insolitus, insuetus
Accustomarily, usitatà, frequentèr
Accustomary, usitatus, assuetus
An accustoming, assuefactio
Acerbity (severity), duritia, rigor
An ache, dolor [dolor
Head-ache, cephalalgia, capitis

ADA

Belly-ache, tormina ventris
To ache, doleo
An achebone, os coxendicis
To achieve, perago, patro
To be achieved, geror, conficior
Achieved, confectus, actus, gestus
An achiever, confector, victor
An achieving, confectio
Achievements, res gestæ
Acid, acidus
Acidity, acrimonia
To acknowledge, agnosco, recognosco, confiteor, fateor, profiteor [nitus
Acknowledged, agnitus, recognitus
An acknowledgment, recognitio
Aconite, aconitum
An acorn, glans
Full of acorns, glandulosus
Bearing acorns, glandifer
To acquaint, indico, admoneo, certiorem aliquem facere
Acquaintance (the thing), notitia, consuetudo; (the person), familiaris, notus
Acquainted, familiaris, cognitus
Acquainted before, præcognitus
To be made acquainted, certior
An acquainting, indicium [fieri
To acquiesce, acquiesco, pareo
An acquiescence, assensus
Acquiesced in, comprobatus
To acquire (get), acquiro, consequor, lucror; (learn), disco
Acquired, acquisitus, adscitus
An acquiring, adeptio
Acquisition, accessio, lucrum
To acquit, solvo, libero
Acquittal, absolutio
An acquittance, acceptatio
Acquitted, liberatus, absolutus
An acquitting, liberatio
An acre, jugerum
Acre by acre, jugeratim
Acrid, or acrimonious, acer, acidus
Acrimony, acrimonia
Across, obliquè
To act (do), ago, facio
To act, or imitate, gesticulor
To act plays, ludos agere
An act, or deed, factum, gestum
An act, or decree, decretum; (of the commons), plebiscitum; (in a play), actus; (exploit), facinus; (wicked), flagitium, scelus
Acts registered, acta, orum
An acting, or mimicking, gesticulatio
An action, actum; (fight), pugna; (in speaking), actio, gestus; (in law), actio forensis, formula
To enter an action, in jus vocare
Actionable, judicio obnoxius
Actions (in commerce), sortes
Active, agilis, promptus, strenuus
Actively (in grammar), activè
Activity, agilitas
An actor (in a play), histrio, mimus; (a doer), actor, auctor
An actress, mima
Actual, ipso facto
Actually, reverà, re ipsâ
To actuate, incito, animo
Acute, or sharp, acutus; (in judgment), sagax, subtilis; (in reply), salsus
Acutely, acutè, subtilitèr, salsè
Acuteness, subtilitas, sagacitas
An adage, adagium, proverbium
Adamant, magnes; (a diamond), adamas
Adamantine, adamantinus
To adapt, accommodo, apto
An adapting, accommodatio

ADM

Adapting, accommodans, aptans
To add (put to), addo, appono, adjicio; (join to), adjungo, subjicio; (over and over), superaddo; (fuel to fire), incendo; (together), coaddo; (in speaking), superdico
Added to others, conscriptus
An adding, accessio, adjectio
An addition, appendix
Addition, or ornament, ornamentum
Addition (in arithmetic), additio
An adder, coluber, vipera
Like an adder, viperinus
An addice, or adze, harpago, dolabra
To addict one's self to something, se applicare ad aliquid; (to some art), artem aliquam colere
Addicted, addictus, devotus, deditus [taneus
Addle, vacuus, inanis, subventaneus
Addle-headed, fatuus, stultus
To address (direct unto), inscribo; (speak to), alloquor
An address (direction), forma directionis; (petition), libellus supplex; (subtle speaking), calliditas, comitas, dexteritas; (a speaking to), compellatio
Addressing, inscribens, supplicans, alloquens
Addressed unto, inscriptus
Adequate, adequatus
An adept, peritus, usu promptus
To adhere, adhæreo, adhæresco
Adherent, adhærens
An adherent, particeps, socius
An adhesion, adhæsio
Adjacent, adjacens, contiguus
An adjective, adjectivum
Adjectively, adjectivè
Adieu, vale
To bid adieu, valedico, renuncio
To adjoin, adjaceo; (add to), adjungo, addo, adjicio
Adjoining, adjacens, conterminus
To adjourn, differo
Adjourned, dilatus
An adjournment, dilatio
To adjudge, adjudico, addico
Adjudged, adjudicatus, addictus
An adjudication, adjudicatio
An adjunct, adjunctum
Adjunction, adjunctio
To adjure, adjuro
To adjust, apto, accommodo, compono, orno [tus
Adjusted, accommodatus, exæquatus
An adjusting, accommodatio
Admeasurement, mensura
To administer (serve), procuro, dispenso; (an oath, &c.), administro; (physic), medicinam adhibere [ratus
Administered, administratus, curatus
An administration, administratio
An administrator, administrator
Administratorship, munus procuratoris
An administratrix, administratrix
An admiral, classis præfectus
High-admiral, summus classiarius
Vice-admiral, summi classiarii legatus
The admiralship, navis prætoria
The admiralty-court, curia maritima [fectus
Rear-admiral, extremæ classi præfectus
Admirable, insignis, mirandus, mirus
Admirably, insignitèr, egregiè
Admiration, Admiring, admiratio
To admire, admiror, miror

[3]

ADV

Admired, carus, amatus
An admirer, amator
Admission, admissio
To admit, admitto, ascisco
Admittable, Admissible, admittendus
Admitted, admissus, ascitus; (into college), in collegium cooptatus; (into orders), sacris initiatus
Admittance, accessus, admissio
To admix, admisceo, immisceo
To admonish, admoneo, hortor
Admonished, monitus, admonitus
An admonisher, monitor, admonitor
An admonition, admonitio
Ado (stir), tumultus, turba; (with much ado), difficultèr, ægrè; (without much ado), facilè
Adolescence, adolescentia
Adonic, adonicus
To adopt, adopto, coopto, ascisco
An adopter, adoptator
An adopting, Adoption, adoptio
Adoptive, adoptivus
Adorable, adorandus
Adoration, adoratio, cultus
To adore, adoro, veneror, colo
An adorer, cultor
To adorn, orno, excolo
An adorning, ornamentum
An adorner, qui ornat
Adroit, solers, callidus
Adscititious, adscitus, acquisitus
To advance (forward), procedo, progredior; (lift up), attollo, exalto; (money), pecuniam deponere
Advanced (jutting out), prominens
Advanced in age, ætate provectus
Advance-guard, stationes priores
Advancement, promotio
Advancing, promovens, provehens
Advantage, lucrum, emolumentum, commodum, fructus
To have an advantage of, præsto, superior esse
To advantage, conduco, prosum
To make advantage of, lucror
With advantage (interest), fœnerato
Advantaged, adjutus
Advantageous, lucrativus, utilis, commodus
Advantageously, utilitèr, commodè
Advantageousness, utilitas
Advent, adventus
Adventitious, adventitius
To adventure (attempt), audeo; (hazard), periclitor
An adventure, casus, fors
An adventurer, periclitator
Adventurous, audax, fortis
An adverb, adverbium
Adverbial, adverbialis
An adversary (he), adversarius, inimicus; (she), adversatrix, inimica, antagonista
Adverse, adversus, diversus, infestus
Adversity, infelicitas, res adversæ
To advert, adverto, considero
Advertency, cura, consideratio
To advertise, commonefacio, edoceo
Advertised, edoctus, certior factus
An advertisement, monitum
An advertiser, monitor
An advertising, admonitio, renunciatio
Advice, consilium
Advice (intelligence), nuncium
Advisable, commodus, utilis
To advise, suadeo, hortor; (with),

AFF

consulo; (of), certiorem facere; (beforehand), præmoneo; (to the contrary), dissuadeo
To be well-advised, sapio
Well-advised, sapiens, circumspectus
Ill-advised, incautus, temerarius
Advisedly, cogitatè, cautè
Advisedness, cautela, prudentia
An adviser, consultor
Advising, nuncians, suadens, monens [berans
Advising, or deliberating, deliAdulation, adulatio, assentatio
Adulatory, adulatorius
Adult, adultus, maturus
To adulterate, adultero, commisAdulterated, adulterinus [ceo
An adulterator, interpolator
An adulterating, commixtio
An adulterer, adulter, mœchus
An adulteress, mœcha, adultera
Adulterous, adulterinus, stuprosus
Adultery, adulterium, stuprum
To commit adultery, adultero
Taken in adultery, stupro compertus
To adumbrate (shadow), adumbro
An advocate, advocatus, causidicus
An advowee, patronus ecclesiæ
An advowson, advocatio
Aerial, or airy, aërius, æthereus
Æstival, æstivus
Ætherial, æthereus
From afar, à longinquo
Affable, affabilis, comis
Affableness, Affability, urbanitas, comitas
Affably, comitèr, urbanè
An affair, res, negotium
To affect (accustom), affecto; (love), diligo; (make a show of), ostento, jacto; (with joy, &c.), gaudio afficere
Affectation, Affectedness, affectatio [tus
Affected, affectatus, delectus, moAffected person, homo putidus; (thing), nimis accuratus; (with diseases), morbo laborans
Maliciously affected, malignus
Affectedly, putidè, exquisitè, odiosè
Affection (love), amor, gratia, benevolentia; (passion of the mind), impetus, affectus, motus, desiderium, animi affectio, cupiditas; (disorder), affectio
Without affection, affectibus carens
Evil affection, cacozelia
Affecting the soul, patheticus
Affectionate, amans, benevolus
Affectionately, amantèr, benevolè
To affiance, spondeo, despondeo
Affiance (betrothing), sponsalia; (trust), fiducia, confidentia
To have affiance in, alicui confidere
Affianced, desponsus, desponsatus
An affiancing, desponsatio
An affidavit, testificatio cum jure jurando
Affinity, affinitas, similitudo
To affirm, affirmo, assero, assevero
An affirmation, affirmatio
Affirmative, affirmans, afferens
Affirmatively, affirmativè, affirmatè
Affirmed, affirmatus [matè
To affix, affigo, annecto
To afflict, affligo, premo, pungo, excrucio; (to afflict one's self), se macerare

AGE

Afflicting, Afflictive, acerbus, tristis
Affliction, afflictio, cruciatus
An affluence, copia, abundantia
Affluent, affluens, abundans
To afford, præbeo; (yield), reddo, fero; (in selling), vendo
Afforded, præbitus, suppeditatus
Affording, ferens, præbens, vendens
To affright, terreo [deus
An affright, timor, consternatio
Affrighted, territus, metu percussus [reor
To be affrighted, consternor, terTo affront, irrito, provoco
An affront, injuria, contumelia
Affronted, contumeliis lacessitus
Affronting, contumeliosus
Affusion, affusio
Afloat, fluitans, fluctuans
Afoot, pedestris
Afore, præ, ante
Aforegoing, præcedens
Aforehand, antè
To be aforehand, prævenio
Aforesaid, prædictus, supradictus
Aforetime, quondàm, olim
Afraid, timidus, pavidus, trepidus
Not afraid, impavidus, intrepidus
To be afraid, paveo, timeo, vereor, metuo, formido; (much), exhorreo, pertimeo, expavesco; (beforehand), præformido, prætimeo; (a little), subtimeo, subterreo
To make afraid, terrefacio, perterreo, horrifico
Made afraid, territus, exanimatus
Afresh, iterùm, denuò
Aft, à puppi, or puppe
After, à, ab, ex, post; (for after that), quàm, posteàquam, ubi, cum, ut, posthæc; (referring to proximity of degree, order, or succession), juxtà, proximè, secundum, sub; (for afterwards), exindè, posteà, post, posteriùs, postmodò; (for according to), ad, de, in; (behind), pone, à tergo
A little after, paulò post
The day after, postridiè
The after-birth, fecunditas
An after-clap, ictus iteratus
Afternoon, post meridiem
An afternoon's luncheon, merenda
Again, iterùm, rursùs, denuò, de integro, deindè; (for hereafter), pòst, posteà, posthàc
Again (after verbs), is often expressed by re prefixed; as, to come again, re-deo, re-peto
Again and again, iterùm atque iterùm
Back again, retrò
Over again, de novo, denuò
Against (denoting defence, or preservation), à, ab, adversùs, adversum; (referring to time), ante, dum, in; (for contrary), contra, adversùs, præter; (to the prejudice of), adversum; adversus; (signifying over against), contra, è regione
Against, adversus, à, um
To be against, adversor, oppugno
To be against an enemy, contra hostem incedere
To go against, or be nauseous, ingratum esse
Aghast, consternatus, attonitus
Age of a person, &c., ætas
An age (100 years), sæculum, ævum
Old age, senectus, senecta

AIM — ALL — ALL

One under age, impubis
Great age, longævitas, senectus
Of the same age, æquævus
Of the first age, primævus
In this age, hoc sæculo, hodiè
Aged, grandis, ætate provectus
An aged man, senex
An aged woman, anus
Of full age, adultus, maturus
Agency, *or* action, actio
Agency (acting for another), curatio, procuratio
An agent, curator
To agglutinate, agglutino
To aggrandize, promoveo, augeo
To aggravate, exaggero, accumulo; (provoke), incendo, provoco
An aggravation, exaggeratio
To aggregate, aggrego
The aggregate, aggregatum
Aggression, aggressio
An aggressor, aggressor
To aggrieve, dolore afficere
Aggrieved, mœstus, dolore affectus
Ague, agilis, vegetus
Agility, agilitas, dexteritas
To agitate, agito, concito
Agitation, agitatio, commotio
Ago (before this time), abhinc, antè; (long ago), jampridèm, jamdudùm; (a while ago), haud ita pridèm; (how long ago), quamdudùm? (so long ago), tamdiù
Agony, cruciatus, agonia
To agree (assent), assentior, assentio; (reconcile), reconcilio, compono; (in one mind), convenio, concordo; (hang together), cohæreo; (make a bargain), paciscor; (with one), in pace vivere; (answer to), respondeo, quadro; (be pleasing to), placeo
Agreeable, gratus, acceptus, aptus; (very agreeable), pergratus
Agreeableness, gratificatio
Agreeably, gratè, jucundè, aptè
Agreed, pactus, reconciliatus
Agreeing, consentiens, concors
Not agreeing, discrepans, disjunctus
An agreement, *or* agreeing, consensus; (bargain), conditio; (covenant), pactum, fœdus, stipulatio; (reconciling), reconciliatio; (proportion), symmetria; (in tune), concentus; (according to agreement), ex compacto
Agriculture, agricultura
Agrimony, agrimonia
Aground, humi jacens
To run aground, in terram navem appellere, *or* impingere
An ague, febris intermittens; (quotidian), quotidiana; (tertian), tertiana; (quartan), quartana; (consumptive), pertica, febriculosus [petus
Aguish, febriculosus
Ah! ah!
Aid, auxilium, subsidium
To aid, adjuto, succurro, juvo
An aide-de-camp, ducis adjutor
An aider, adjutor, auxiliator
Aiding, adjuvans, opem ferens
To ail, doleo
An ailment, morbus, malum
To aim (at a mark), ad metam dirigere; (design), designo, conor
An aim (mark), album; (design), propositum

[4]

Aimed at, designatus, petitus
Air, aër, aura, cœlum, æther
In the open air, sub dio
To air (abroad), aëri exponere; (by the fire), ad ignem exiccare
An air-hole, spiramentum
An air-pump, machina ad aërem exhauriendum
To take the air, deambulo
To take, *or* get air, evulgor
Aired (abroad), soli expositus; (at the fire), ad ignem expositus; (on the fire), calefactus
Airiness (of place), amœnitas; (of person), lepor, festivitas
An airing, deambulatio
To take an airing, deambulo
An airy place, locus apricus
An airy person, lepidus, levis
Airy, aërius, amœnus
Airy (thin), tenuis
Alabaster, alabastrum
Alack! hei mihi!
Alacrity, alacritas, lætitia
Alamode, more novo et eleganti
An alarm, *or* alarum (in war), classicum; (sudden fright), trepidatio, pavor; (of a clock), suscitabulum
To sound an alarm, bellicum, classicum canere
To alarm, bellicum canere; (fright), perterrefacio
Alarmed, territus, trepidus
Alarming, perturbans, terrens
Alas! heu! hei mihi misero! ah!
Alate, nupèr
An alb, alba
Albeit, tametsi, etsi, etiamsi, quamvis, quanquam
Alcaic, alcaicus
An alchemist, alchymista
Alchemy, alchymia, chymia
An alcove, locus fornicatus
An alder, alnus
Made of alder, alneus
An alderman, senator urbanus
Like an alderman, senatoriè
Ale, cerevisia; (strong), prima; (small), tenuis; (stale), vetula; (new), mustum
An alehouse, cerevisiarium; (belonging to an alehouse), popinalis
An alehouse-keeper, caupo
An alembic, alembicus
Alert, alacris, vegetus
Algebra, algebra
An algebraist, algebræ peritus
An alien, alienus, alienigena
Alienable, quod alienari potest
To alienate (take from), alieno; (sell away), abalieno
Alienated, alienatus, proscriptus
An alienation, alienatio
To alight (as a bird), subsido; (from a horse), desilio
Alighted (slid down), delapsus
An alighting, descensus ab equo
Alike, *adj.* par, similis, æquus; *adv.* æquè, pariter
Aliment, nutrimentum, pabulum
Alimentary, alimentarius
Alimony, alimentum
Alive, vivus, superstes
To be alive, vivo
All, omnis, cunctus; (the whole), totus, integer, universus; (every one in particular), singuli; quisque, unusquisque; (in general), universi; (only), unus, unicus
All in all (familiar), perfamiliaris
All about, undiquè, passim

All alone, solus, solitarius
All along, perpetuò, usquè
All along, (prostrate), prostratus, pronus
All one, perindè, idem
All the while, per totum tempus
All together at once, omnes simùl
Altogether (wholly), omninò, prorsùs
By all means, quoquomodò
On all sides, undiquè, quaquaversus
All over (throughout), passim
All this while, usquè adhùc
All the better, tantò meliùs
All to one, eodem
All to no purpose, nihil agis
To all intents, omninò, penitùs
All our own, noster
For all that, neque eo seciùs; (for good and all), omninò; (this is all), tantum est; (at all), prorsùs, omninò, unquàm; (most of all), præsertim, præcipuè; (not at all), ne omninò quidem
Allknowing, omnisciens
Allseeing, omnituens
Allwise, omnisapiens
To allay (lessen), mitigo, lenio; (abate), resedo; (mingle), diluo, tempero
To be allayed, defervesco, diluor, temperor
Allayed (lessened), lenitus; (mingled), dilutus, temperatus
An allayer, delinitor, temperator
An allaying, lenimen
An allegation, allegatio; (false allegation), calumnia
To allege, allego, cito, causor
Alleged, allegatus, citatus
Allegiance, fides, fidelitas
Allegorical, allegoricus
An allegory, allegoria
Allelujah, alleluja
To alleviate, allevo, levo
An alleviating, alleviation, levatio
An alley (walking-place), ambulacrum; (narrow street), angiportum, *and* angiporta
Alliance (by blood), consanguinitas; (by marriage), affinitas; (of states), fœdus
Allied, propinquus, conjunctus, cognatus
Alligation (tying), alligatio
An alligator, crocodilis
To allot, assigno, delego
An allotment, sortitio
To allow (approve), approbo, confirmo; (give), exhibeo, præbeo; (grant), concedo, do; (to allow expenses), sumptus suppeditare; (permit), permitto, patior
To allow in accounts, decido, deduco
Allowable, laudabilis, justus
An allowance (approbation), approbatio; (gift), donum; (permission), licentia, permissio; (deduction), deductio; (portion of meat, &c.), portio
Allowed (approved), ratus; (permitted), permissus; (deducted), deductus; (given) præbitus
An allowing (approving), approbatio; (permitting) permissio; (giving), donatio; (deducting), deductio
Alloy, *or* allay, mistura
An alluding, Allusion, allusio
To allure, allicio, seduco, lacto

AMA   ANA   ANO

Allured, allectus, illectus
Allurement, allectatio, illecebra
An allurer, seductor
An alluring, solicitatio
An allusion, parodia
Allusion to a name, agnominatio
An ally, socius, amicus
An almanack, calendarium
An almanack-maker, fastorum scriptor
Almightiness, omnipotentia
Almighty, omnipotens
An almond, amygdala
Almonds of the ears, aurium glandulæ
An almoner, eleemosynarius
Almost, *adv.* ferè, fermè, penè, propè, propemodùm, modò non tantùm, non, quasi (*followed by a dative*), usquè, juxtà; *adj.* proximus, a, um
Alms, eleemosyna
An alms-house, perontocomium
Belonging to alms, eleemosyparius   (nignus
An almsgiver, erga pauperes benignus
To ask alms, stipem rogare
To give alms, stipem porrigere
An almsman, pauper orator
An almsger, mensor ad ulnam
Aloes, aloë
Aloft, sublimis, altus, supernus; *adj.* suprà, sursùm, sublimè; *adv.* (from aloft), desupèr
Alone, *adj.* solus, solitarius, unicus, unus; *adv.* solùm
All alone, persolus
To leave alone, desero
Left alone, desertus, desolatus
To let alone, omitto, mitto
Along, per, secus, secundum; *or by an ablative case: as, I went along the highway*, publicâ ibam viâ; (along with), una cum; (all along, *adv.*) ubiquè (*adv.*), prostratus; (extended), extensus
Aloof, de longinquo, longè
Aloud, clarè, clarâ voce
The alphabet, alphabetum
Alphabetical, alphabeticus
Alphabetically, alphabeticè
Already, jam, dudum, pridèm
Also, itèm, etiàm, quoquè, necnòn, paritèr, itidèm; (moreover), quinetiàm, præterea, autèm, insupèr, adhæc
An altar, altare, ara
To alter, muto, vario, verto, commuto, immuto, permuto
Alterable, variabilis, mutabilis
Alteration, mutatio
Altercation, altercatio, jurgium
Alternate, Alternative, alternus
Alternately, alternè, vicibus
Although, licèt, quantumlibèt, quanquam, quamvis, quamlibèt, etiamsi, tametsi, et-i
Altitude, altitudo, sublimitas
Altogether, prorsùs, omninò
An alveary, alvearium
Alum, alumen
Always, sempèr, perpetuò, jugitèr, nunquàm non, in æternum
Am *is frequently only the sign of a verb passive or neuter*
Am (signifying to exist), sum
Amain, strenuè, valdè
To amass, accumulo, congero
Amassed, accumulatus, congestus
An amassing, accumulatio
To amaze (astonish), obstupefacio; (daunt), perterrefacio
Amazement, animi stupor
Amazing, mirabilis, mirandus
[5]

Amazingly, mirabilitèr
An ambassador, legatus
An ambassage, legatio
Amber, succinum
Made of amber, succineus
Ambergris, ambra
An ambidexter, ambidexter
Ambient, ambiens
Ambiguity, ambiguitas
Ambiguous, ambiguus, dubius
Ambiguously, ambiguè, dubiè
Ambit, ambitus
Ambition, ambitio
Ambitious, ambitiosus, cupidus
To be ambitious, honores ambire
Ambitiously, ambitiosè
To amble, gressus glomerare
Amblingly, tolutim
Ambrosia, ambrosia
Ambulatory, ambulatorius
An ambuscade, Ambush, insidiæ
To lie in ambush, insidias struere
Laid in ambush, in insidiis positus
A lier in ambush, insidiator
Amen, amen, ita fiat, esto
To amend, emendo, corrigo, convalesco
Amendment, correctio, castigatio
Amends, compensatio
To make amends, compenso, rependo
Amenity, amœnitas
To amerce, mulcto, punio
Amerced, mulctatus
An amercement, mulcta, pœna
An amercing, mulctatio
Amiable, amabilis, pulcher, venustus
Amiableness, venustas, decor
Amiably, venustè, decorè, pulchrè
Amicable, benevolus, amicus
Amicably, benevolè, amicè
Amidst, inter, in medio
Amiss, *adj.* pravus, vitiosus; *adv.* pravè, malè, perperàm, vitiosè
To do amiss, offendo, pecco
Amity, amicitia
Ammunition, *subst.* apparatus bellicus
An amnesty, lex oblivionis
Among, *or* Amongst, apud, inter, in; (from among), è, ex
Amorous, amatorius, mollis, lascivus
Amorous potions, philtra, orum
Amorously, amatoriè, blandè
To amount, summa, totum
Amours, amores, um
Amphibious, amphibius, ancepe
Amphitheatre, amphitheatrum
Ample, amplus, copiosus, largus
Amplified, exaggeratus
An amplifier; amplificator
To amplify, amplifico, exaggero
An amplifying, amplificatio
Amplitude, amplitudo
Amply, amplè, abundè, copiosè
To amputate, amputo
Amputation, amputatio
An amulet, amuletum
To amuse, oblecto, detineo
Amused, detentus, occupatus
An amusement, detentio, oblectatio
An anabaptist, anabaptista
Anacreontic, anacreonticus
An anagram, anagramma
Analogous, Analogical, analogus
Analogy, analogia, comparatio
Analysis, analysis
Analytic, Analytical, analyticus
Anarchy, anarchia
Anathema, anathema

To anathematize, anathematizo
An anatomist, anatomicus
Anatomical, anatomicus
To anatomize, anatomiso
An anatomizing, anatome
Anatomy, anatomice
Ancestors, antecessores, priores, majores
Ancestry, prosapia, stirps
An anchor, anchora
To ride at anchor, ad ancheras stare   [vero
To weigh anchor, anchoram solAncient, antiquus, vetustus
An ancient (ensign), signifer
Anciently, olim, quondam
The ancle, talus, sura
And, et, ac, atque, que
Anew, de integro, de novo
An angel, angelus
Angelic, angelicus
Anger, ira, iracundia
To anger, irrito, acerbo
Angry, iratus
To be angry, irascor, succenseo
An angle, angulus
An angler, piscator
To angle, piscor
An angling-rod, arundo
Anguish, ægor, solicitudo
To animadvert (correct), castigo; (remark), animadverto
An animadverter, animadversor
An animal, animal, animans
Belonging to animals, animalis
An animalcule, animalculum
Animal life, anima
To animate (encourage), cohortor, excito; (give life), animo
An animating, cohortatio
An anker (measure), doliolum
Animosity (heat), ardor; (grudge), simultas, odium
Anise-seed, anisum
An annalist, annalium conditor
Annals, annales, ium, fasti, orum
Annates, primitiæ, arum
To annex, annecto, appono, adjungo, adjicio
Annexed, addictus, adjectus
To annihilate, ad nihilum redigere
Annihilated, funditùs extinctus
An annihilating, extinctio
Anniversary, anniversarius, annuus
An anniversary, festum annuum
Annotation, annotatio, nota
An annotator, annotator
To announce, denuncio
To annoy, incommodo, lædo
An annoying, noxa, offensio
Annoyed, læsus, offensus
Annoyance, noxa, damnum, offensio
Annual, annuus, solemnis
Annually, quotannis
An annuity, reditus annuus
To annul, abrogo, rescindo
Annular, annularis
Annulled, abrogatus, rescissus
An annulling, abrogatio, abolitio
To annunciate, annuncio
The annunciation, annunciatio
To anoint, ungo, inungo; (about), circumungo, circumlino; (all over), perlino; (often), unctito; (upon), superinungo
An anointing, unctor
An anointing, unctio, inunctio
Anomalous (irregular), enormis
Anon, confestim, illicò, mox, statim; (ever and anon), identidèm
Anonymous, anonymus

B 3

APO   APP   AQU

Another, alius; (one another), alter alterius, se invicem; (one after another), alternis vicibus; (another man's), alienus; (way), aliorsum
To answer, respondeo; (correspond), congruo, convenio; (excuse), excuso; (for), apbudeo, rationem reddere; (again), responseo; (impudently), obloquor, proterve respondere; (as an echo), resono; (at law), restipulor; (objectious), dissolvo
An answer, or answering, responsio, responsum
Answerable, congruens, consonus
To be answerable, praesto
Answerable to, or for, obligatus
Answerably, congruenter, proprie
An answerer, responsor
An ant, formica
An ant-hill, caverna formicosa
An antagonist, adversarius
An antarctic, australis
Antecedent, antecedens
An antechamber, antithalamus
To antedate, tempus antequum adscribere [natus
Antedated, prochronismo signatus
An anthem, antiphona
St. Anthony's fire, erysipelas
Antichrist, antichristus
Antichristian, antichristianus
To anticipate, anticipo, praevenio
Anticipated, praeoccupatus
An anticipating, anticipatio
Anticipating, praeoccupans
An antic, histrio, mimus
An antidote, antidotus
Antimonarchical, monarchiae adversarius
Antimony, stibium
Antipathy, odium, fastidium
Antipodes, antipodes, um
An antiquary, antiquarius
To antiquate, abrogo, aboleo
Antiquated, antiquatus, abrogatus
Antique, antiquus, exoletus
Antiquity, antiquitas, vetustas
Antlers, cornu
An anvil, incus
Anxiety, anxietas, solicitudo
Anxious, anxius, solicitus
Anxiously, anxie, solicite
Any, unus, quilibet, quisquam, quivis, ecquis, ecquisquam; (any thing), quicquam, quidpiam, quippiam, quodvis; (any further), alterius, amplius; (any how), quoquomodo; (any longer), diutius; (any more), amplius; (any where), usquam, alicubi, ubivis, ubilibet, uspiam; (at any time), unquam, quandocunque; (any whither), quoquam, usquam, quopiam; (any while), aliquandiu
Any man, or one, quispiam, quivis
Aorist (a Greek tense), indefinitum
Apace, celeriter, propere, cito
Apart, seorsum, separatim
To stand apart, disto, distito
An apartment, domus pars
Apathy, apathia
An ape, simia
To ape, imitor
Aperture, apertura
An aphorism, aphorismus
An apiary, apiarium
Apiece, singula, singuli
Apish (mimicking), mimicus
Apish tricks, ineptiae
Apocryphal, apocryphus
To apologise, excuso, defendo

An apology, defensio, purgatio
An apologue, apologus, fabula
Apoplectic, apoplecticus
An apoplexy, apoplexia
Apostacy, defectio, apostatia
An apostate, apostata
To apostatise, deficio, desero
An apostome, abscessus, apostema
An apostle, apostolus
Apostleship, apostoli munus
Apostolic, apostolical, apostolicus
An apothecary, pharmacopola
An apothecary's shop, pharmacopolium
An aposem, decoctum
To appal, consterno, percello
Apparel, vestis, vestimentum
Apparel (utensils), apparatus
Apparelled, amictus, vesitus
Apparent, evidens, conspicuus
An apparent crime, crimen flagrans
To be apparent, pareo, consto
Apparently, manifeste, aperte
An apparition, spectrum
An apparitor, lictor [voco
To appeal, appello, defero, proAn appeal, Appealing, appellatio
Appealed, appellatus, delatus
An appealer, Appellant, appellator
To appear, appareo pareo; (above water), exto; (above others), emineo; (against), accuso; (for), faveo, tutor; (seem), videor; (become visible), illuceo, effulgeo
To begin to appear, patesco
To make to appear, demonstro, ostendo
It appears, constat, patet
An appearance, or appearing (outward show), species; (concourse of people), concursus, frequentia; (likelihood), similitudo; (above water), emersio; (vision), visio, spectrum; (figure), persona
A first appearance, exortus
A day of appearance, dies status
Appearing, apparens
To appease, compesco, compono, comprimo, sedo, placo; (by sacrifice), expio
An appeaser, placator
An appeasing, placatio
An appellant, appellator
An appellation, appellatio
Appellative, appellativus
Appendent, appendens
To append, appendo, adhaereo
An appendix, appendix
To appertain, pertineo, respicio, specto
It appertaineth, interest, refert
Appertaining, pertinens, spectans
An appetite, appetitus, cupiditas
An insatiable appetite, ingluvies
To have an appetite, esurio
To applaud, applaudo, laudo
An applauder, laudator
An applause, or applauding, plausus, applausus, laus
Deserving applause, plausibilis
An apple, pomum, malum; (summer), malum praecox; (winter), malum serotinum; (oak), galla; (pine), nux pinea
The apple of the eye, oculi pupilla, acies
An apple-loft, pomarium
An apple-seller, pomarius
An apple-tree, malus
Bearing apples, pomifer, malifer

Full of apples, pomosus
An applier, accommodator
An applying, Application, applicatio
Application (diligence), diligentia, cura, studium, attentio
To apply (put unto), applico, apto, accommodo, appono; (addict one's self to), se ad aliquid applicare; (his mind unto), animum applicare; (lay out money), pecuniam impendere; (address, or entreat), aliquem adire, or accedere, ab aliquo opem petere
To appoint, statuo, constituo; (name), nomino; (order, or design), designo, assigno; (by law), lege praescribere; (set), praestituo, praescribo; (in another's place), substituo
An appointing, assignatio, designatio, praescriptio
An appointment, compactum; (assignation), dici et loci constitutio; (order), mandatum; (without appointment), injussu
To appo. tion, divido, distribuo
Apposite, aptus, idoneus
Apposition, appositio
To appraise, pretium imponere, aestimo
An appraiser, aestimator; (sworn), jurejurando constitutus
An appraisement, or appraising, aestimatio
To apprehend (understand), deprehendo, intelligo; (fear), timeo; (suspect), suspicor; (seize), prehendo, capio; (take unaware), intercipio
An apprehension (capacity), ingenium, facultas, intelligentia; (fear), timor, metus; (suspicion), suspicio; (seizing), captura, prehensio
Apprehensive, sagax, acutus, perspicax
An apprentice, tyro, discipulus; (girl), discipula
An apprenticeship, tyrocinium
To apprise, certiorem aliquem facere
To approach, appropinquo, accedo, adeo, immineo
An approach, accessus, aditus
Approached to, prope admotus
An approaching, appropinquatio
Approaching, appropinquans, imminens, instans
Approbation, approbatio
To appropriate, ascisco, assero
Appropriated (fit, or proper), aptus, idoneus, proprius
An appropriation, vindicatio
To approve, approbo, comprobo, applaudo, addico
An approver, approbator
An approving, approbatio
An appurtenance, appendix
An apricot, malum persicum
April (month), Aprilis
An apron, praecinctorium
Apt (fit), aptus, idoneus; (inclined), pronus, propensus; (active), agilis, dexter
Aptness, habilitas, propensio, ingenium, docilitas
Aptly, apte, idonee
An aptote, aptoton
Aquatic, Aquatile, aquatilis
An aqueduct, aquaeductus
Aqueous, aquosus
Aquiline, aquilinus

[6]

ARM — ART — ASK

Arabian, Arabicus
An Arabian, Arabs
In Arabic, Arabicè
Arable, arabilis
Arbitrarily, pro libitu, imperiosè
Arbitrariness, dominatio
Arbitrary, imperiosè dominans, imperiosus
An arbitrary prince, princeps sui arbitrii, *or* juris
To arbitrate, quæstionem decidere
An arbitration, *or* arbitrement, litis arbitrium, arbitratus
An arbitrator, *or* arbiter, arbiter
An arbour, pergula
Arch, vafer, astutus
Archness, astutia
An arch, arcus, fornix
To arch, arcuo, fornico
An arched roof, laquear
Arched, arcuatus, laqueatus
Archwise, arcuatim
An archangel, archangelus
An archbishop, archiepiscopus
Archbishopric, archiepiscopatus
An archdeacon, archidiaconus
Archdeaconry, archidiaconatus
Archducal, archiducalis
An archduke, archidux
An archduchess, archiducissa
An archdukedom, archiducatus
An archetype, archetypum
An archer, sagittarius
Archery, ars sagittandi
An arch-heretic, hæresiarcha
Archiepiscopal, archiepiscopalis
An architect, architectus
Architecture, architectura
Of architecture, architectonicus
An architrave, epistylium
Archives, archiva, orum, tabularium
An archpriest, archipresbyter
Arctic, arcticus, *or* borealis
Ardency, ardor, fervor, æstus
Ardent, ardens, candens, acer
Ardently, fervidè, vehementèr
Ardour, æstus
Arduous, arduus, difficilis
An area, area, superficies
Argent, argenteus, candidus
To argue (dispute), argumentor, disputo; (show, *or* prove), evinco, probo
An arguer, disputator
An arguing, disceptatio
An argument, argumentum, ratio, thema, lemma
Argumentation, argumentatio
Argumentative, argumentalis
Arid, aridus
Aright, rectè
To arise (get up), surgo; (again), resurgo; (proceed from), nascor, procedo; (as the sun), exorior, orior; (as waves), undo; (together), consurgo [patus
Aristocracy, optimatum principium
Arithmetic, arithmetica
Arithmetical, arithmeticus
Arithmetician, arithmeticæ peritus
An ark, navis, navigium, arca
An arm, brachium, lacertus; (of the sea), sinus, fretum; (of a tree), ramus; (of a vine), palmes
A little arm, brachiolum
An armpit, ala, axilla
To take in the arms, amplector
To arm (*or* take up arms), armo; (put on arms), arma, induere, *or* sumere; (furnish with arms), arma suppeditare
An armada, classis armata
[7]

An armament, bellicus apparatus
Armed, armatus, armis indutus; (all over), perarmatus; (with a buckler), scutatus, clypeatus; (with darts), pilatus; (with a sword), ense *or* gladio instructus; (with a coat of mail), loricatus
An arming, armatura
Armorial, ad arma pertinens
Armour, arma, orum
An armourer, faber armorum
An armoury, armarium
Arms, arma, orum
To be in arms, in armis esse
To lay down arms, arma ponere
Fire-arms, scloppus, scloppetum
By force of arms, vi et armis
To bear arms, arma ferre
An army (in a state of training), exercitus; (in line of march), agmen; (in battle array), acies
To marshal an army, aciem instruere. To muster an army, exercitum lustrare. To raise an army, milites conscribere
Aromatic, aromaticus
Around, circumquaquà, undiquè
To arraign, in jus vocare, postulo
Arraigning, in jus vocans
Arraignment, accusatio, actio
Arrangement, digestio, series
Arrant, merus
Array, vestis, vestimentum
To array, vestio
To set an army in array, aciem instruere
In battle-array, acie instructâ
Arrearage, Arrears, reliqua, orum; (one in arrears), qui aliquid insolutum reliquit
To arrest, prehendo, rapio
An arrest, Arresting, prehensio
Arrested, prehensus, in jus tractus
An arrival, accessus, appulsus
To arrive (at a place), accedo, advenio; (as a ship), appellor, pervenio
Arrogance, arrogantia, fastus
Arrogant, arrogans, fastosus
Arrogantly, arrogantèr, superbè
To arrogate, arrogo, assumo
Arrogated, sibi assumptus
An arrow, arundo, sagitta; (broad *and* barbed), tragula; (head), mucro, cuspis
Of arrows, sagittarius
An arsenal, armarium
Arsenic, arsenicum
An art, ars; (cunning), artificium; (black), magicè
An artery, arteria
An artichoke, cinara
Artful, subtilis, callidus; (made by art), artificialis
Artfully, subtilitèr, elegantèr
An article, articulus, caput, conditio, conventa, orum
Articles of marriage, pactio nuptialis
Article by article, articulatim
To article with, cum aliquo paciscì; (branch into articles), articulatim dividere; (break), pacta convellere; (against one), accuso; (to keep), stare conventis; (to surrender upon articles), sub conditionibus dedere
Articled, conventus, pactus
Articular, articularis
Articulate, distinctus [tinctè
Articulately, articulatim, disAn article, artificium, ars, fraus
An artificer, artifex
Artificial, factitius, concinnus

Artificially, artificiosè
Artillery, tormenta bellica; (a train of), series, *or* apparatus tormentorum bellicorum
The artillery-yard, palæstra militaris
An artist, opifex, artifex [taris
Artless, *adv.* insulsè; *adj.* insulsus
As, dum, ut, cum. As, *signifying* accordingly, *or* proportionably as, ut, uti, sicùt, pro, proùt, ità ut, pro eo ac, pro eo atque, perindè ut, perindè atque, proindè, proindè ac, utcunque, &c.
As (which, *or* which thing), quod, id quod; (used for if), si
As for, *or* as to, de, quatenus, quantùm, quod ad, ad [licèt
As being, ut, utpotè, quippè, sciAs far as, qua, quantùm, quoad, usquè, usquè ad, usquè eo
As if, as though, quasi, perindè quasi, perindè ac si, tanquam, ut si [quàm
As it were, ut, ceu, quasi, tanAs long as, quamdiù, tamdiù, tantisper dum, quoad, usquè dum, dum
As big as, as bad as, instar, *with a genitive case*
As big again, duplo major
As many as, tot, totidem, quotquot, quodcunque
As much, tantùm, tantundem
As much as ever, ut cum maximè, quantus maximè [quoties
As often as, quotiescunquè, totiès
As soon as, ubi, cum, cùm primùm, ut, simùl ac, simùl ut, simùl atque
As soon as ever, ubi primùm, ut primùm, cum primùm, simùl ac primùm, statim ut
As well as, ut tam, quàm, æquè ac
As yet, adhuc. Not as yet, nondum
As rich as he is, qualibet dives. Such as it is, qualis qualis
To ascend, ascendo, scando
Ascendant, auctoritas; (of a nativity), horoscopus
An ascending, Ascension, ascensio, ascensus
An ascent, locus altus
To ascertain, stabilio, confirmo
Ascertained, certus, confirmatus
An ascertaining, confirmatio
Ascetic, asceticus
To ascribe, imputo, arrogo, tribuo
An ash, fraxinus
Ash-coloured, cinereus
Ashen, fraxineus, fraxinus
Ash-Wednesday, dies cinerum
Ashamed, verecundus, pudore suffusus
To be ashamed, erubesco. To make ashamed, pudore aliquem afficere
Shameful, pudendus, turpis
Ashes, cinis [gere
To burn to ashes, in cineres rediPale as ashes, cinereus
Ashore, in tellure, super terram. To come ashore, è navi descendere. To put ashore, in terram deponere
Aside, seorsùm, obliquè
To call aside, sevoco
To lay, *or* set aside, sepono
To set aside an order, *or* decree, rescindo, antiquo
Asinine, asinarius
To ask (a question), interrogo, rogo; (again), reposco; (advice), consulo, *followed by an accusative of the person consult*-

B 4

ASS   AST   ATT

ed; (require), requiro; (boldly), postulo; (earnestly), oro; (with success), exoro; (the price, as a buyer), licitor; (as a seller), indico; (frequently), requirito; (humbly), supplico; (industriously), perquiro; (mournfully), imploro; (secretly), suppeto; (as a lover), proco
An asker, postulator, percontator
Askew, transversè
An asking, postulatio, petitio; (of advice), consultatio; of a question), rogatio; (humbly), supplicatio; (inquiring), inquisitio; (entreating), obsecratio, petitio, supplicatio; (demanding), postulatio
Aslant, obliquè
Asleep, somno oppressus, sopitus
To sleep, dormio, obdormisco; (fall asleep), dormito; (lull asleep), soporo, somnum inducere
To be asleep, torpeo, dormio
A lulling asleep, somni inductio
Sleepy, semisopitus, semisomnis
Aslope, obliquè
An asp, aspis
Asparagus, asparagus
An aspect, aspectus, prospectus, vultus
Asperity, asperitas
To asperse, infamo, defamo
Aspersed, infamatus, defamatus
An aspersion, aspersio, infamia
An aspirate, spiritus asper
An Aspiring, ambitus, cupiditas
To Aspire (breathe), aspiro; (strive), annitor; (unto honour), honores ambire; (at, to, *or* after), magna affectare
Asquint, obliquè, transversè
An ass, asinus, asina
A wild ass, onager
Belonging to an ass, asininus
An ass-driver, asinarius
An ass, *or* fool, stultus
To assail, incesso, oppugno
An assassin, sicarius
To assassinate, ex insidiis interimere
An assassination, cædes ex insidiis
To assault, aggredior, adorior, invado, oppugno
An assaulting, Assault, impetus
To take by assault, expugno
Won by assault, vi captus, expugnatus
Assaulted, oppugnatus
An assaulter, aggressor
An assay, *or* Assaying, tentamen
To assay, probo, tento; (again), retento ; (beforehand), prætento; privily, subtento
An assayer, tentator, inspector
An assemblage, coacervatio
To assemble, convoco, congrego, cogo, convenio, confido
Assembled, collectus, conjunctus
An assembling, congregatio, convocatio, conventus, concilium
An assembly, cœtus, synodus
To assent, comprobo, assentior
An assent, assensus
To assert (affirm), affirmo, assero ; (vindicate), defendo, tueor
An assertion, assertio, affirmatio
An asserting, affirmatio
An assertor, assertor, vindex
To assess, tributum imponere
Assessed, census
An assessment, census, tributum

[8]

An assessor (of taxes), censor; (in an assembly) assessor
Assets, bona restantia
An asseveration, asseveratio
Assiduity, assiduitas, sedulitas
Assiduous, assiduus, sedulus
To Assign (time), præstituo; (place), indico ; (any thing), assigno ; (a pension), statuo; (a lease), assigno; (a reason), reddo, do
An assign, *or* assignee, assignatus [tus
Assignable, quod assignari potest
Assigned, assignatus, addictus
An assignment, assignatio, denunciatio, distributio
To assimilate, assimilo
Assimilation, assimilatio
An assise, *or* assises, *or* assizes, comitia judicum provincialia
To hold assizes, jus pro tribunali dicere
To assise weights and measures, ponderum et mensurarum jura præscribere
An assiser, ædilis, signator
To assist (aid), adjuvo, optitulor, subvenio, opem alicui ferre ; (stand by), assisto
Assistance, auxilium, opis
An assistant, adjutor, collega, adjutrix
Assisted, adjutus
Assisting, adjuvans
An associate, socius, familiaris
To associate, familiaritatem contrahere, se conjungere, consocio
Associated, fœdere conjunctus
An association, consociatio
As soon, cum, ubi, postquam
To assume, assumo, arrogo
An assuming person, nimis arrogans
An assumption, assumptio
Assurance (warrant), cautio ; (certainty), certa notitia ; (confidence), audacia ; (security), securitas ; (pledge), pignus, fides ; (of great assurance), audax
To assure (affirm), assero, affirmo; (protect), protego, tueor, defendo ; (a thing), firmo ; (by promise), polliceor
Assured, certus, securus
To be assured, exploratum habere, certò scire
Assuredly, certò, fidentèr, certè
To assuage, mitigo, lenio, placo; (to be assuaged), subsido, detumeo
Assuaged, mitigatus, lenitus
An assuager, mitigator
Assuaging, mitigatorius
An assuaging, mitigatio, lenimen
An asthma, asthma
Asthmatic, asthmaticus
To astonish, stupefacio, terreo
To be astonished, miror, obstupesco
Astonished, attonitus, percussus
An astonishing, Astonishment, consternatio, stupor, pavor
To go astraddle, varico
To ride, *or* sit astraddle, divaricatis cruribus sedere, *or* æquitare
Astray, errans, errabundus
To go astray, vagor, erro ; to lead astray, a viâ rectâ abducere
A going astray, erratio, error
Astringency, astrictio
Astringent, Astringing, comprimens

An astrologer, astrologus
Astrological, astrologicus
Astrology, astrologia
An astronomer, astronomus
Astronomy, astronomia
Asunder, separatim, seorsùm
To cut asunder, disseco
To pull asunder, separo, dissolvo
At, à, ab, ad, ante, apud, de, cum, ex, in, inter, sub, super, pro
To achieve, conficio
A notable achievement, facinus præclarum, egregium, *or* illustre
Atheism, atheismus
An atheist, atheus
Atheistical, atheisticus
To be athirst, sitio
Athletic, athleticus
Athwart, transversè, obliquè
The atmosphere, vaporum sphæra
An atom, atomus, corpusculum
To atone, propitio, expio
Not to be atoned for, inexpiabilis
An atonement, expiatio, piamentum, compensatio
Atrocious, atrox
Atrociously, atrocitèr
Atrocity, atrocitas
To attach (detain), detineo; (take prisoner), prehendo, comprehendo, pignoror
To be attached to, adhæreo
Attached, prehensus, addictus
An attaching, Attachment, alligatio, retentio, prehensio, adhæsio
An attack, aggressio, impetus, oppugnatio, tentatio
To attack (quarrel), provoco ; (an enemy), aggredior, irruere in hostem; (a town) oppugno
An attacker, provocator
To attain unto, potior, attingo
Attainable, assequendus, obtinendus [tus
Attained unto, impetratus, potiAn attainment, *or* Attaining, impetratio; of good attainments, eruditus, exornatus
To attaint, accuso, evinco, inficio
To attemper, misceo, commisceo
To attempt, conor, audeo
An attempt, ausum, conatus
An attempter, inceptor, molitor
Attempted, inceptus, molitus
To attend, præstolor, comitor, curo, servio ; (unto), ausculto
Attendance, *or* attending, obsequium, expectatio, ministerium
Attendance on business, diligentia, cura
An attendance (retinue *or* train), comitatus, pompa
An attendant, assecla, comes
Attendant on, præstolans
Attended, curatus, deductus
Attended by, *or* with, concomitatus
Attention, attentio, intentio
Attentive, attentus, intentus
Very attentive, perattentus
Attentively, attentè
Attentiveness, attentio
To attenuate, attenuo
To attest, testor, testificor
An attestation, testificatio
Attested, consignatus, confirmatus
Attire, ornatus
Attitude, corporis positio, *or* situs
An attorney (at law), procurator rerum forensium ; (of the king), procurator regiarum causarum, cogitor regis

To attract (draw to), attraho; (allure), illicio; (the eyes), rapio, allicio
Attraction, *or* Attracting, attractio; (by fair words), blanditiæ, arum; (alluring), illecebra
Attractive, attrahens, blandus
An attribute, attributum
To attribute, attribuo, assumo
Attributed, attributus, vindicatus
An attributing, attributio
Attrition, attritio, attritus
To attune, modulationem dare
To avail, valeo, prosum, confero
Available, valens, efficax, utilis
Availment, emolumentum
It availeth, conducit, refert, juvat
Avant! abi! apage!
Avarice, avaritia, sordes
Avaricious, avarus; (niggardly), parcus, sordidus
Avariciously, avarè, parcè, sordidè
Avariciousness, avaritia
An auction, auctio
To sell by auction, auctionor
An auctioneer, auctionarius
Audacious, audax, improbus
Audaciously, audactèr, improbè
Audaciousness, audacia, improbitas
Audible, audiendus, sonorus
Audience (act of hearing), audientia; (auditory), cœtus, conventus
To audit, examino
An audit, rationum examinatio
An auditor, auditor; (of accompts), calculator; (of the exchequer), fisci procurator
An auditory, concio
To avenge, ulciscor, vindico
Not avenged, inultus
An avenger, ultor, ultrix
An avenging, ultio, vindicta
An avenue, aditus, introitus
To aver, assero
An average, æqua distributio
An averring, Averment, confirmatio
Averse, aversus, alienus, abhorrens
Aversion, aversatio, fastidium: to have an aversion to, alieno animo esse
Deserving aversion, aversabilis
To avert, averto, abduco, deprecor
To augment, augeo, amplio
An augmentation, accessio
An augmenter, amplificator
An auger, terebra
An augur, augur
Auguration, Augury, augurium
Of an augur, auguralis
August (the month), augustus
August (the month), augustus
An aviary, aviarium
Avidity, aviditas
Aulic, aulicus
An aunt, amita, matertera
Avocation, avocatio
To avoid (shun), devito, fugio, vito; (quit), discedo; (a blow), declino
Easily avoided, evitabilis
Not to be avoided, inevitabilis
An avoiding, evitatio, devitatio
Avoirdupois-weight, libra sexdecim unciarum
To avouch, assevero, constantèr affirmare; (for another), spondeo
Avouchable, quod affirmari potest
An avoucher, sponsor
An avouching, sponsio
To avow, assero, profiteor
[9]

An avowed enemy, hostis declaratus
Avowedly, apertè, ex professo
An avower, affirmator
Avowry, purgatio, justificatio
Auricle, auricula
Auricular, auricularis
Auspice, auspicium
Auspicious, faustus, auspicatus, felix
Auspiciously, faustè, auspicatò
Auspiciousness, felicitas
Austere, austerus, severus, durus
Austerely, austerè, severè, duritèr
Austereness, Austerity, austeritas, severitas, asperitas
Authentic, Authentical, certæ fidei [tus
Authentic papers, auctoritates,
To make authentic, facere ratum
Authenticity, certa rei cognitio
Made authentic, auctoritate comprobatus, ratificatus
An author (writer), auctor, scriptor; (inventor), conditor, molitor; (of a report), anctor; (of a law), legislator [tus
Authoritative, auctoritate firmaAu:horitatively, auctoritate
Authority, auctoritas, jus; (leave), licentia; (chief), primatus; (quotation), auctoritas
Of great authority, præpollens; (of small authority), parùm pollens; (in authority), auctoritate valens; (with authority), cum privilegio
To excel in authority, præpolleo
To put in authority, auctoritatem dare alicui
To speak with authority, cum potestate loqui
To authorize, auctoritate munire aliquem [tio
Autography, propria manuscrip-
Autumn, autumnus
Of autumn, autumnalis
Avulsion, avulsio
Auxiliary, auxiliaris
To await, expecto, maneo
Awake, vigilans, vigil
To awake, excito, suscito, expergiscor: to be, *or* keep awake, vigilo: to lie awake, insomnis cubare
Awaked, experrectus, commotus
Half awake, semisomnis
To award, adjudico, addico
An award, litis adjudicatio
Awarded, adjudicatus
Aware, sciens, præscius: not aware, ignarus, nescius, *followed by a gen. of the thing not known*
To be aware, caveo, prævideo
Away! (fy!) vah!
To away (go away), abeo; (take away), aufero, tollo
To be away, absum
Awe, reverentia, metus
To stand in awe, timeo, metuo
To keep in awe, coerceo, deterreo
Awed, deterritus
Awful, verendus, horrendus
Awfully, venerandè, terribilitèr
Awfulness, veneratio, horror
Awkward, inhabilis, ineptus, perversus
Awkwardly, ineptè, minùs aptè
Awkwardness, ineptia
An awl, subula
An awning, velorum prætentura
Awoke, expergefactus
Awry, obliquus, inclinatus
Awry, obliquè

To go awry, oberro: to look awry, obliquè tueri: to tread awry, distortis calceis incedere: to turn, *or* set awry, torqueo, distorqueo
An axe, securis; (broad axe), dolabra; (poll axe, *or* battle axe), bipennis; (chip axe), dolabella; (pick axe), bipennis
An axle-tree, axis
An axiom, axioma
Ay, imò, maximè, sanè, immò
Ay me! hei mihi! eheu!
An azimuth, circulus verticosus
Azure, cæruleus, cyaneus
An azure stone, lapis lazuli
An ayry, nidus accipitrum

B.

To baa like a sheep, balo
To babble, garrio, deblatero
A babbler, garrulus
A babbling, garrulitas
A babe, *or* baby, infans
Babish, puerilis
A baboon, cynocephalus
A baby (doll), pupus, pupa
Babylonian, Babylonius
Bacchanals, Bacchanalia, um
Bacchus, Bacchus
A bachelor, cœlebs, baccalaureus
To back, adjuvo, faveo, succurro
A back, tergum, dorsum
To backbite, vituperare clam
A backbiter, obtrectator
A backbiting, obtrectatio
The backbone, spina dorsi
Of the backbone, spinalis
The back parts, posteriora, um
A back room, camera interior
A back shop, officina postica
Back-stairs, scalæ posticæ
A backside (yard), chors postica
The backside, podex
Back, *or* backside, aversus
On the backside, pone
A back-sword, machæra
A backslider, desertor
A backsliding, desertio, defectio
Backed, adjutus, levatus
Backwards, retrò
Backward, *or* averse to, alienus; (negligent, slow), remissus
To be backward, cunctor
To go backward and forward, obambulo
Backwardness, remissio, tarditas
Bacon, laridum
A flitch of bacon, succidia
Bad, malus, pravus
Bad (sick), æger, ægrotus
Bad hours, multâ nocte, serò
To be very bad, *or* sick, ægroto
A badge, tessera, insigne
A badger, taxus, melis
Badly, malè, pravè, ægrè, improbè
Badness, pravitas; (of roads), viarum asperitas; (of weather), cœli intemperies
To baffle, fallo, decipio
Baffled, deceptus, delusus
A baffling, deceptio, dolus
Baffling, fallens, decipiens
A baffler, deceptor, delusor
A bag, saccus, crumena, pera
A little bag, loculus
A cloak-bag, mantica
A bag-bearer, saccarius
Bag and baggage, impedimenta
A baggage, mulier improba
Baggage, scruta, orum

B 5

BAN   BAR   BAS

A bag-net, reticulum subtilius
A bagnio, balneum, fornix
A bagpipe, tibia utricularis
A bagpiper, utricularius
A bag-pudding, massula
Bail, vadimonium
Bail, or surety (in criminal matters), vas; (for debt), præs
To give bail, vadem dare
To bail one, vadem sistere
Bailable, vadimonio interponi potest
Bailed, vadimonio liberatus
A bailiff (magistrate), prætor; (serjeant), lictor, apparitor; (steward), dispensator; (of a hundred), villicus; (water), aquilex
Bailiwick, jurisdictio
A bait, esca, incitamentum
To bait (lay a bait), inesco, illicio
To bait (at an inn), diversor
To bait a hook, escâ hamum obducere
To bait (tease), lacesso
To bait a bull, taurum canibus committere
A baiting-place, diversorium
To bake, pinso, torreo, coquo
Baked, pistus, coctus, coctilis
Easy to be baked, coctibilis
A bakehouse, pistrinum
A baker, pistor
A balance, libra, statera, trutina
A balance (even weight), æquipondium, trutina
To balance, pondus æquare
To balance accounts, rationes æquare
A balancer, libripens
A balcony, podium, pegma
Bald, calvus, glaber
A bald discourse, sermo insipidus
To be bald, calveo, calvesco
Balderdash, farrago
Baldness, calvities
A bale, farcina, fascis
A little bale, fasciculus
Baleful, tristis, mœstus, noxius
A balk of wood, trabs, tignum
A balk of land, porca, lira
To balk, frustror, decipio
A ball to play with, pila
Ball-playing, pililudium
A ball-player, pilarius
A foot-ball, pila pedalis
The ball of the hand, palma
The ball of the eye, oculi pupilla
The ball of the foot, planta pedis
A ball, or bullet, globulus
The ball of a pillar, scotia
A wash-ball, smegma
A printer's ball, tudes
A ball (in dancing), celebres choreæ   [rea
A ballad, canticum
Ballast, saburra
Ballasted, saburratus
A ballot-box, cista   [tere
To ballot, suffragia in cistam mittere
Balsam, opobalsamum
A baluster, clathrus
Balmy, Balsamic, balsaminus
A ban, edictum, execratio
To ban, execror, devoveo
A band (tie), vinculum
A band, or ward, tribus
A hat-band, spira
A band of soldiers, caterva, grex
A band under one captain, manipulus
By bands, turmatim
A bandage, ligatura, fascia
A band-box, cistellula
Banditti, latrones

[10]

To bandy, in partes trahere, conspiro, pello
Bandy, or crooked, valgus
Bane, ruina, mors
Baneful, noxius, pestiferus
To bang, verbero, pulso
A bang, ictus
To banish, in exilium mittere
To be banished, exulo, pellor
Banished, exulans, ablegatus
A banished person, exul, extorris
A banishing, relegatio   [tio
A banishment, exilium, proscriptio
A banister, clathrus
A bank (hillock), tumulus; (of a river), ripa; (shelf in the sea), arenaria moles; (of oars), remigum subsellium; (of money), pecuniæ acervus, collybus
A bank bill, syngrapha publica pecuniaria
A banker, nummularius
A bankrupt, conturbator
To be a bankrupt, foro cedere
Bankruptcy, rationum conturbatio
A banner, vexillum, signum
Banns of matrimony, futurarum nuptiarum solennis denunciatio
A banquet, convivium, epulæ
To banquet, or feast, convivor
A banqueter, conviva, epulo
A banqueting, epulatio
A banqueting-house, epularium
Of a banquet, convivialis
A banter, jocatio, lusus scurrilis
To banter, derideo, irrideo
By way of banter, jocosè
To turn to banter, in ridiculum convertere
A banterer, homo jocularis
A bantling, puerulus, puerula
Baptism, baptisma
Baptismal, baptismalis
The day of baptism, dies lustricus
To baptise, baptizo
A baptistry, fons baptismi sacer
Baptised, baptizatus
A baptising, baptisatio
A bar, vectis; (for a fence), repagula curiæ; (of a door), obex, pessulus; (of a haven), repagulum; (hindrance), impedimentum, mora; (of a public-house), abacus
To bar (keep from), excludo; (a door), pessulum foribus obdere
Barred, pessulo firmatus; (from), exsectus
A barb, spiculum
Barbarian, barbarus
Barbarity, barbaries, inhumanitas, truculentia
Barbarous, barbarus, truculentus
Barbarously, immanitèr, inhumanè
To barb, tondeo
Barbed, barbatus, phaleratus
A barber, tonsor, tonstrix
Belonging to a barber, tonsorius
A barbican, promurale
A bard, bardus, vates
Bare, *adj.* (naked), nudus; (of grass, *or* hair), glaber; (of clothes), pannosus; (of money), inops; (lean), macer; (threadbare), tritus; (barefaced), impudens; (barefooted), discalceatus; (bareheaded), capite aperto; *adv.* (only), solùm, tantummodò
To make bare, nudo, denudo
A place bare of grass, &c., glabretum
Barely (scarcely), vix

Bareness (nakedness), nuditas; (of hair), calvities; (of money), tenuitas
A bargain (agreement), pactum, ludificatio
To bargain, paciscor, stipulor
To stand to a bargain, pactis manere
A bargain-maker, pactor
Bargained, pactus, contractus
A bargaining, pactio
A barge, linter, navigium
A bargeman, naviculator
Bark of a tree, cortex; inner bark, liber
To bark a tree, decortico
A bark (ship), navigiolum
To bark (as a dog), latro; (as a fox), gannio; (at), allatro; (against), oblatro
A barker, latrator
A barking, latratus
Barley, hordeum; (flour), polenta; (water), ptisanarium; (broth), jusculum hordeaceum
Belonging to barley, hordeaceus
Barm (yeast), cerevisiæ cremor
A barn, horreum
A barn-floor, area horrei
A barn-owl, alucus
A barometer, instrumentum ad gravitatem incumbentis aëris metiendam
A baron, baro
Baronage, baronatus
A baronet, baronettus
A barony, baronia, satrapia
A barrack, casa militaris
A barrel, dolium, cadus; (of a gun), tormenti fistula; (of a jack, *or* clock), fusus   [dere
To barrel (as a dog), doliis, *or* cadis recondere
Barren, sterilis, effœtus
To grow barren, sterilesco
Barrenness, sterilitas
A barricade, munimentum
To barricade, viæ aditus occludere
Barricaded, munitus, præseptus
Barriers, limites, fines
A barrister, causidicus
A barrow (sepulchre), tumulus; (to carry dung), vehiculum
Barter, merx
To barter, merces commutare
Bartered, commutatus, permutatus   [tatio
A bartering, mercium commutatio
A base (in architecture), basis, fundamentum; (in music), sonus gravis
Base (inferior), inferior; (servile), servilis; (mean, low), humilis, obscurus, ignobilis; (child), nothus; (metal), adulterinus; (knavish), fallax; (shameful), infamis; (vile), vilis, turpis; (cowardly), ignavus, timidus
A base wretch, nebulo
A base action, res turpis
A base trick, versutia, stropha
O base! O facinus indignum!
Basely, abjectè, timidè, improbè, fœdè, turpitèr
Baseness (of birth), ignobilitas; (cowardliness), timiditas; (knavishness), fallacia; (vileness), vilitas, turpitudo
A bashaw, præses provinciæ, homo fastosus
Bashful, modestus, verecundus
Bashfully, modestè, verecundâ
Bashfulness, modestia, pudor
A basis (foundation), basis
To bask in the sun, apricor

A basket, corbis, cophinus, panarium
A basket maker, cophinarius
A basin, pelvis, crater
A bastard, nothus, spurius
Bastardised, adulterinus
To baste (meat), carnem hamectare; (beat), verbero; (a garment with thread), filo raro consuere
A basting (beating), fustigatio
To bastinade, fuste cædere
A bastinado, fustuarium
A bastion, agger
A bat (bird), vespertilio; (stick to play with), clava, fustis, baculus [cocti
A batch of bread, panes simul
To bate, or abate, diminuo
Bate (strife), lis
Bating some few, paucis exceptis
Bating that, nisi quòd
A bath, balneum; (hot), thermæ, arum; (cold), cella frigidaria
To bathe, balneo uti; (soak), macero; (wash), lavo
Bathed, balneo lotus, maceratus
A batoon, baculus, fustis
A battalion, agmen, phalanx
To batter, pinguesco, sagino
To batter, obtundo, concutio, verbero, diruo, everto
A battering, concussio
A battering-ram, aries
A battery (breach), ruina; (besieging), oppugnatio; (to raise), tormenta disponere
A battle, pugna, prælium, acies
To give battle, acie congredi
To gain a battle, vinco, supero
To lose a battle, vincor
In battle array, acie instructâ
A sea-battle, prælium navale
To battle with one, contendo
Belonging to a battle, præliaris
A battle-axe, bipennis
A battledore, palmula lusoria
Battlements, pinnæ murorum
Baubles, tricæ, arum [lena
A baud (male), leno; (female),
Bawdry (in speech), spurcities
Bawdy, impudicus, spurcus
A bawdy-house, lupanar
To bawk, frustror
To bawl, vociferor, exclamo
A bawler, vociferator
A bawling, vociferatio, convicium
Bawling, vociferans, clamitans
Belonging to bawling, clamosus
A bay (of water), sinus; (road for ships), statio; (dam), moles; (tree), laurus
Bearing bays, laurifer
Crowned with bays, laureatus
Bay-coloured, badius, fulvus
A bayonet, sica
Bayes (cloth), pannus villosus
Be, in *composition, set before verbs*, *as* to bedaub, *signifies* all over, *and is rendered in Latin by* con; *as*, conspergo
To be *is rendered variously in Latin, according to the word following it*; *as*, to be (exist), sum, fio, existo; (against), adversor, aspernor, abhorreo ab; (present), adsum, intersum; (doing), ago; (away), absum; (by), adsum; (for one), stare cum aliquo, faveo; (mad), insanio; (quiet), quiesco; (sick), ægroto; (of no authority), parûm valere; (in danger), periclitor; (mistaken), erro, fallor; (without), careo, egeo
[1i]

A beach (shore), littus; (tree) fagus
A beacon, specula
Of a beacon, speculatorius
A bead, pilula, sphærula
A pair of beads, rosarium [tor
A beadsman, eleemosynarius, ora-
A beadle, anteambulo, lictor
A beadle, catulus venaticus
A beak, rostrum; (of a ship), rostra, orum; (the beak head), extremitas proræ
Beaked, rostratus
A beaker, cantharus, cyathus
A beal (pimple), pustula
To beal (gather matter), suppuro
A beam, trabs; (principal), lacunar; (weaver's), jugum textorium; (of a carriage), temo; (of a balance), scapus, statera; (of the sun), jubar
Like a beam, trabalis
Compassed with beams, radiatus
Beamy, radians
A bean, faba [seolus
A French, or kidney bean, pha-
Belonging to a bean, fabalis
A bean cod, siliqua, valvulus; (stalk), folabe; (straw), stipula fabalis; (podden), puls fabacea, (meal), lomentum; (chaff), palingo; (plat), fabetum
To bear (carry), porto, gesto, bajulo; (suffer), fero, patior; (away), aufero; (bring forth, as animals), pario; (as trees), fructum edere; (one company), comitor; (a grudge), simultates exercere; (in mind), reminiscor, recordor
A bearer, gestator, portitor; (of a corpse), vespillo
A bearing down, oppressio
A bearing out, prominentia
Bearing date, datus
Past bearing, effoetus
A bear, ursus, ursa
The bear (constellation), aretos
Of, or like a bear, ursinus
A beard, barba; (of a goat), spirillum; (of a cat), genobarbum; (of corn), spica, arista
To beard, barbesco
Bearded, barbatus, spicatus
Beardless, imberbis
A bearn, or child, infans
A beast, bestia; (a wild), fera; (of burden), jumentum; (for sacrifice), victima
To become a beast, brutesco
Bestial (belonging to beasts), belluinus; (lewd), turpis, obscoenus
Beastliness (brutishness), feritas; (lewdness), impudicitia; (nastiness), immunditia, bestialitas
Beastly, immundus, lascivus
To beat, or Walk, ambulatio
Beat of drum, sonus tympani
The beat of a pulse, arteriæ pulsus
To beat, verbero, cædo; (bruise), tero; (conquer), vinco; (against), allido, impingo; (an alarm), bellicum canere; (back), repello; (the breast), plango; (a drum), pulsare tympanum
To be beaten, vapulo, cædor; (to the ground), collabefio, eri
A beater (rammer), fistuca
A beating, verberatio, pulsatio, pulsus; (back), repercussio; (on the breast), plangor; (with a cudgel), fustuarium; (down), demolitio; (against another), collisio, contusio

To beatify, beo, beatifico
Beatified, beatis ascriptus
Bearific, Beatifical, beatificus
Beatification, beatificatio
Beatitude, beatitudo
A beaver (beast), castor; (oil), castoreum; (hat), pileus castoreus; (meal), merenda
Of a beaver, castoreus
Beautiful, formosus, pulcher, venustus
Beauty, pulchritudo, forma, nitor, elegantia, venustas; (of a place), amoenitas
To beautify, decoro, illustro
Beautified, decoratus, ornatus
A beautifying, decoramen, ornatus
To be beautiful, niteo, nitesco
Beautifully, decorè, nitidè
To becalm, paco, sedo
Because, quia, quòd, quoniam, proptereà quòd; (of), ob, propter, gratiâ, ergò
A beck (rivulet), rivulus, rivus; (nod), nutus
To beckon, nuto, innuo
A beckoning, nutatio
To become (be fit, fitting, or becoming), decere; (grow, or be made), evado, fio
Becoming (decent), decens; (convenient), conveniens; (graceful), decorus
Become, factus
A bed, lectus, torus, cubile; (of state), pulvinar; (in a garden), areola; (of a river), alveus, canalis; (of sand), stratum; (of leeks), cepetum
A bed's head, cubitale; (feet), lecti pedes; (tester), lecti umbella; (stead), sponda, lecti fulcrum; (post), lecti columna; (maker), lecti strator; (tick), culcita; (curtains), lecti vela, ductilia; (chamber), cubiculum; (clothes), stragula
Abed, i. e. in bed, lecto affixus
To make a bed, lectum sternere
Bed-time, hora somni
To be brought to bed, parturio
To keep one's bed, lecto affigi
To bed with, concumbo
A bride-bed, lectus genialis
Of a bedchamber, cubicularia
A lying in bed, decubitus
Bedrid, clinicus
A bedfellow, consors lecti
To bedaub, conspurco
Bedded, in lectum receptus
Bedding, lecti stragula
To be bedewed, roresco
A bedewing, roratio, aspersio
Bedlam, hospitium insanorum
A bedlamite, insanus, maniacus
Bedlam-like, furibundus
To bedung, stercoro
To bedust, pulvere conspergere
A bee, apis; (gad-bee), asilus; (humble-bee), bombilius; (drone-bee), fucus; (swarm of bees), apum examen
A bee-master, apiarius
Of, or belonging to bees, apianus
A beech-tree, fagus
Beechen, fagineus, fageus
Beef, caro bubula, *or* bovilla; (powdered), bubula salita; (hung), bubula infumata
A beef, bos
Beer, cerevisia; (strong), cerevisia generosa; (small), cerevisia tenuis; (dead), vappa; (new), mustum

B 6

BEH BEN BER

A beetle (fly), scarabæus; (fish), cantharus piscis
Beetle-browed, superciliosus; (headed), fatuus, plumbeus
To befal, contingo, evenio, accido
Befitting, conveniens, idoneus
To befool, alicui illudere
Before, antè, apud, coram, in, ob, palam, præ, præter, pro, sub, supra
Before that, antè, antequàm, citiùs, priusquàm, potiùs
Before, prior
A little before, paulò antè
Long before, jamdudùm
Before all things, imprimis
Before all men, palàm, in propatulo
Before now, antehàc
Before then, anteà
Beforetime, olim, dudùm
To befoul, coinquino [levo
To befriend, alicui favere, sub-
Befriended, fautus
To beg, mendico; (entreat), oro; (humbly), supplico; (earnestly), obsecro
To beget (as a father), gigno, genero; (procure), produco
A begetting, generatio, procreatio
Begged, mendicatus; (entreated), oratus, rogatus
A beggar, mendicus, mendicula
To beggar, ad inopiam redigere
Beggared, ad inopiam redactus
Beggarly, inops, pauper
Beggarly (mean), vilis, abjectus
Beggary, paupertas, mendicitas
A begging, mendicatio
To begin, incipio; (take rise), orior, nascor; (again), repeto; (design), instituo; (a journey), ingredi iter; (a battle), prælium inire; (an office), magistratum inire; (a thing), rem tentare, or aggredi; (war), bellum suscipere; (the world), quætum occipere
A beginner, inceptor, auctor
A young beginner, tiro
Beginning, incipiens, exorsus
A beginning, initium, principium, exordium; (rise or source), origo, primordium
A good or bad beginning, bonum, or malum auspicium
To begird, cingo, obsideo, obsepio
To begrime, denigro
To beguile, fraudo, fallo
Beguiled, deceptus, fraudatus
A beguiling, dolus, fallacia
In behalf, vice, loco, causâ
To behave, gero, se præbere
Ill-behaved, male moratus
Well-behaved, benè moratus
Behaviour, morum gestus
Good behaviour, urbanitas
Ill behaviour, inurbanitas
To behead, decollo, obtrunco
Beheaded, decollatus
A beheading, decollatio
A behest (promise), promissum; (commands), jussa
Behind (not before), ponè, pòst, à tergo; (remaining), porrò, reliquus
To be behind (left), relinquor
Behold ! ecce ! en !
To behold, auspicio, inspicio; (afar off), speculor; (look about), perlustro
Beholden, obligatus, devinctus
To be beholden to, obligor, obstringor
[13]

A beholder, spectator, contemplator
A beholding, spectatio
Behoof, commodum, gratia
It behoveth, oportet, expedit, convenit, decet
A being (essence), essentia, natura, existentia, ens; (habitation), habitatio, domus; (here, there, or by), præsentia
Beistinga, colostrum
To belabour, cædo, verbero
A belch, ructus
To belch, ructo, eructo
Belched, ructatus
A belching, ructatio
Given to belching, ructuosus
A beldame, vetula, bellona
To beleaguer, or besiege, obsideo
A beleaguerer, obsessor
A belfrey, campanarum locus
Belgic, Belgicus
To belie, calumnior, ementior
Belief, fides
Past belief, incredibilis; (easy of belief), credulus; hard of belief), incredulus; (wrong belief), erroneus
Easiness of belief, credulitas
Hardness of belief, incredulitas
The belief (creed), symbolum fidei
To believe (assent to), credo; (trust to), confido; (think), existimo, opinor
To make one believe, persuadeo
A believer, fidelis, credens [mulo
To make believe (pretend), si-
Belike, verisimilis
A bell, campana
A little bell, tintinnabulum
A bell-founder, campanarius
A bellman, præco nocturnus
A bellwether, dux gregis
To bellow, mugio, emugio
A bellowing, mugitus
Bellows (a pair of), follis
Belluine, belluinus
A belly, venter, alvus
A little belly, ventriculus
Belly-ache, tormina ventris; (troubled with it), alvi dolore laborans
Great-bellied, ventricosus
Big-bellied (as a woman with child), gravida, prægnans
A belly-god, belluo
A belly-friend, parasitus
A bellyfull, satietas
Full-bellied, satur
To belong to, pertineo, attineo
Belonging, pertinens, attinens
Beloved, dilectus, carus, gratus
Dearly beloved, carissimus
Below, infernus, inferus, inferior
Below, infrà, subtèr, deorsùm
Below, sub, subter, infra
From below, infernè
A belt, cingulum, balteus
A belying, calumnia
To bemire, se inquinare
Bemired, inquinatus
To bemoan, deploro, lugeo
To be bemoaned, flebilis, dolendus
Bemoaned, deploratus
A bemoaning, planctus, luctus
Bemoaning, deplorans, lugens
A bench, scamnum, sedile; (of justice), tribunal; (of justices), concessus
The King's bench, bancus regius
A bencher, assessor
Benches (in a ship), transtra, orum; juga, orum

To bend, flecto, curvo, intendo, inclino; (the mind to), animum adjungere; (back), reclino, reflecto; (of a bow), arcum tendere; (round), in urbem flectere; (the brows), frontem corrugare; (the fist), pugnum complicare; (a course), cursum tendere; (forwards), inclino; (from), reclino, declino; (inwards), incurvo; (towards), acclino, vergo; (his study), annitor
To bend, vergo; (under, or shrink), succumbo
To begin to bend, incurvesco
Easy to bend, flexilis
Bending (down), inclinans; (downwards), declivis; (upwards), acclivis; (forwards), vergens; (as the heavens), concavus; (like a bow), arcuatim; (inwards), acclivis; (to), acclinans; (leaning), innitens
A bending (bowing), flexio, inclinatio; (about), circumflexio; (archwise), sinuatio; (down), declivitas [cula
Bendings and turnings, diverti-
Beneath, infra, sub
Benediction, benedictio
A benefaction, largitio
A benefactor, patronus
A benefice, beneficium
Beneficed, præfectus gregi
Beneficence, beneficentia
Beneficent, benignus, liberalis
Beneficial, commodus, utilis
A benefit, beneficium, gratia
To benefit (to do good), prosum, proficio, progredior
A benevolence, largitio
Benevolence, benevolentia
Benevolent, benevolens, benevolus
Benighted, nocte preventus
Benign, benignus, clemens
Benignity, benignitas, clementia
Benignly, benignè, clementèr
Bent (bowed), flexus, tenuus; (ready), promptus, pronus; (against), adversus alicui; (backwards), recurvus; (bloodily), flagrans odio, sanguinem sitiens; (many ways), sinuosus; (resolutely), obstinatus; (unto, or on), addictus, deditus; (easily), flexilis
Bent of mind, inclinatio
To benumb, stupefacio
To be benumbed, obstupeo; (with cold), algeo, frigeo
Benumbed, torpidus
A benumbing, stupor, torpor
To bequeath, testamento relinquere
Bequeathed, legatus
A thing bequeathed, legatum
A person to whom a thing is bequeathed, legatarius
A bequeather, legator
A bequeathing, legatio
To bereave, orbo, spolio
Bereaved, Bereft, orbatus
A berlin, currus Berliniensis
A berry, bacca; (bayberry), bacca aurea; (bilberry), vaccinium nigrum; (blackberry), morum; (cranberry), vaccinium palustre; (elderberry), sambuci bacca; (ivyberry), corymbus; (gooseberry), grossulariæ acinus; (raspberry), idæi rubi bacca; (strawberry), fragum; (wild strawberry), arbutus;

BET   BIL   BIT

(service-berry), unbum; (white thorn-berry), mea
Bearing berries, baccifer
Having berries, baccatus
To beseech, supplico, imploro
Beseeching, supplicans, obsecrans
A beseeching, supplicatio
To beseem, decet, convenio
To beset, circumdo, obsideo; (on all sides), circumsideo
To beshrew, maledico, imprecor
A beshrewing, maledictio
Beside, or Besides, adv. præh, præterea, præterquam, ad hæc, tum, simul; prep. à, ab, abs, ad, extra, juxta, præter, prope, propter, secundum, &c.
To be beside one's self, deliro
Beside the mark, à scopo aberrans
To besiege, obsideo, obsidione cingere
Besieged, obsessus
A besieger, obsessor
A besieging, obsidio, obsessio
To besmear, illino, inquino
Besmeared, delibutus, illitus
A besmearing, inunctio
A besom, scopæ, arum
To besot, infatuo, inebrio
Besotted, stupidus, inebriatus
Besought, imploratus, oratus
To be besought, exorandus
Bespangled, bracteatus
To bespatter, luto conspergere; (defame), calumnior
Bespattered (with dirt), luto conspersus; (by a bad tongue), infamia aspersus
To bespawl, conspuo
To bespeak, compello, allicio, jubeo, procuro
To bespeckle (or bespot), maculo
To besprinkle, aspergo, conspergo
Best, optimus, præstantissimus
Best of all, optimè, maximè
Bestial, bellainas, turpis
To bestir, diligenter agere, moveo
To bestow (give), largior, dono; (lay out), expendo, erogo; (place), loco, colloco; (time in), tempus terere; (lay up), repono, recondo
A bestower, largitor, dator
To bestride, inequito, insideo
To bet, pignus deponere
A bet, pignus, depositum
To betake, conferre, or recipere se
To bethink, cogito, reputo
To betide, evenio, accido
Woe betide you! væ tibi!
Betimes, citò, temporì; (in the morning), multo mane
To betoken, indico, portendo
To betray, prodo, trado, profero
Betrayed, proditus, traditus
A betrayer, proditor, traditor
A betraying, proditio, traditio
To betroth, despondeo
A betrothing, sponsalia
Betted, oppigneratus [sponsor
A better, qui pignus deponit,
A betting, sponsio, pigneratio
Better, melior, potior, præstantior, satior, superior, carior
Better, adv., meliùs, satiùs, potiùs, præstantiùs, rectiùs
To better, amplifico, augeo
To be better, præsto
To get the better, supero, vinco
To grow better, melioresco; (in health), convalesco
It is better, præstat
Never the better, nihilo melior
Betters, superiores, um [medio
Between, or Betwixt, inter, in
[13]

Lying between (as a mediator), interjaceno
To go between, intercedo
Put between, interpositus
Between whiles, interim
Beverage, nutrenda
A bevy, grex
To bewail, ploro, defleo, lugeo
Bewailable, plorandus, flebilis
Bewailed, deploratus, defletus
A bewailing, lamentatio
To beware, caveo, video; (of), vito, devito
To bewarez, consummo
To bewilder, seduco
Bewildered, errabundus, devius
To bewitch (enchant), fascino; (charm, or please), demulceo
Bewitched, incantatus, territus
A bewitcher, incantator
A bewitching, incantamentum
Bewitching beauty, forma eximia
To betray (disclose), prodo; (defile), fœdo, contamino
Bewrayed, inquinatus, fœdatus; (with blood), cruore pollutus
A bewrayer, proditor   [supra
Beyond, extra, ultra, præter, trans,
Beyond sea, transmarinus
The bezel of a ring, pala
A bias, præponderatio, inclinatio, momentum
To bias one, seduco, traho, inclino
A biassing, inclinatio
A bib, infantis pectorale
A bibber, bibax, potator
A bibbing, potatio, ebrietas
The bible, biblia, sanctæ literæ
To bicker, discepto, litigo, altercor
A bickerer, altercator
A bickering, altercatio
To bid, jubeo, impero, mando; (invite), invito, voco, rogo; (adieu), valedico; (battle, or defiance), provoco; (banns), matrimonium promulgare; (good morrow), saluto; (money for wares), licitor
Bidden (commanded), jussus; (invited), invitatus, vocatus
Not bidden, injussus, invocatus
A bidder, jussor, vocator; (of money), licitator
A bidding, jussum, invitatio; (of a price), licitatio; (of banns), denunciatio matrimonii
Biennial, biennis
A bier, feretrum, sandapila
Big, magnus, grandis; (in bulk), crassus; (in authority), potens; (with child), gravida, prægnans; (with pride, &c.), inflatus, tumidus
To grow big, tumeo, turgeo; (with child), adolescere in partum
A bigamist, qui duas uxores duxit
Bigamy, bigamia
Bigger, major, grandior
To make bigger, extendo
To grow bigger (in bulk), cresco; (in stature), adolesco
Bigness, amplitudo
A bigot, superstitiosus homo
Bigotted, superstitione afflatus
Bigotry, superstitio
A bile, tuber, ulcus
Bile (choler), bilis, cholera
Fall of biles, ulcerosus
Bilious, biliosus
To bilk, fraudo
Bilked, fraudatus
A bilker, fraudator
A bilking, fraudatio

A bill, or scroll, scheda; (of debt), syngrapha; (bills of exchange), tesseræ nummariæ; (bank bills), tesseræ argentariæ; (bills of sale), tabulæ auctionariæ; (of costs), tabula impensarum; (of entry), tabula mercium inscriptarum; (of divorce), repudium uxori missum; (of fare), ciboriorum tabella; (catalogue), catalogus; (indictment), libellus accusatorius; (of lading), tabella rerum vectarum; (of parcels), tabella rerum singularium; (of record), libellas memorialis; (in parliament), lex roganda; (over a door), programma, mercer; (book), falx; (or beak), rostrum
Bills of mortality, tabulæ mortuorum
To bill (as doves), rostrum rostro inserere; (or lop), falco
A billet-doux, epistola amatoria
A billet, fasciculus, bacillum
Soldier's billets, tesseræ militares
Having a bill, rostratus
Billiards, lusus rudicularis
A billing, basiatio, suavium
A billow, fluctus ingens maris
A bin, panarium, cista
To bind, ligo, obligo; (about), circumligo; (back), restringo; (before), præligo; (books), libros compingere; (a bargain), pactum confirmare; (fast), constringo; (a garment), prætexo; (himself to appear), vador; (himself to pay), judicatum solvere; (the legs), præpedio; (by oath), jurejurando obstringere; (over to sessions), vador; (an apprentice), tironem artifici tradere ad artem discendam; (with osiers), vieo; (by promise), stipulor; (with rushes), scirpo; (to), alligo; (together), conjungo; (underneath), subligo; (upon), superalligo; (up a wound), vulnus obligare; (up in bundles), fasciculis constringere; (hand and foot), quadrupedem constringere [nator
A bookbinder, librorum concin-
A binding, ligatura, ligatio
Binding (costive), alvum astringens
A biographer, vitarum scriptor
Biography, biographia
Bipartite, bipartitus
A birch-tree, betula
A bird, avis, volucris
A bird-cage, cavea
A bird-call, fistula
To go a birding, aucupor
Birdlime, viscus
Birth, ortus, partus
Birth-day, dies natalis
Birth-hour, hora natalis
A birth (parentage), genus
Belonging to one's birth, natalis
Birth-right, jus majori debitum
Birth-place, natale solum
New birth, regeneratio
The after-birth, secundæ
The birth, partio, ortus
To give birth, exordium dare
Biscuit, panis nauticus
To bisect, disseco
A bishop, episcopus
Of a bishop, episcopalis
A bishopric, episcopatus
Bissextile, bissextilis
A bit, frustum, bucca
A little bit, frustulum

BLA

The bit of a bridle, lupatum
A bitch, canis fœmina, canicula
A bitch fox, vulpes fœmina
A bite, morsus
A bite (cheat), homo fallax, veterator
To bite, mordeo; (again), remordeo; (off), demordeo; (the lips), labia corrodere; (the nails), ungues arrodere; (to the quick), admordeo; (round), ambedo; (often), morsito; (cheat), decipio; (as pepper, &c.), uro
A biting, morsus
A biting, or stinging, mordacitas
Biting, mordax, asper
Bitingly, mordacitèr, mordicùs
Bitten, demorsus, morsus
Frost-bitten, gelatus
Bitter (in taste), amarus; (severe), acerbus, aculeatus, intensus
Bitterly, amarè, acerbè
A bittern, ardea
Bitterness, amaritudo, asperitas
Bitumen, bitumen
Bituminous, bituminosus
To blab, garrio, deblatero
A blab, garrulus, loquax, futilis
Blabbed, deblateratus
Black (in colour), ater, niger, (as soot), fuligineus; (as pitch or a coal), nigerrimus; (wicked), scelestus, improbus
To be black, nigreo, nigresco
To black, denigro, obfusco
Clothed in black, pullatus, atratus
Black and blue, lividus
Made black and blue, sugillatus
To be black and blue, liveo
A black, Æthiops
A blackbird, merula
Blacked, atratus, denigratus
To die black, nigro colore inficere
To blacken, denigro, infamo
A blackguard, pannosus, balatro
Blacking, atramentum
Blackish, fuscus, nigellus
To be blackish, nigreo
Blackness, nigrities, nigritudo
A bladder, vesica
A blade (of grass, &c.), caulis; (of an oar), remi tonsa; (of a sword), ensis lamina; (of the shoulder), scapula; (of a knife), cultri lamina
A blade, juvenis alacer, bellus [homo
A blain, ulcus
Full of blains, ulcerosus
Blame, culpa, crimen
To blame, culpo, incuso; (chide), increpo, reprehendo
Blameable, vituperabilis
Blamed, culpatus, incusatus
To be blamed, culpor, incusor
Blameless, innoxius, integer
A blaming, incusatio
To blanch, candefacio, decortico
Blanched, dealbatus, decorticatus
Blandishment, blanditiæ
Blank, albus, candidus; (pale), pallidus; (confounded), confusus
A blank, tessera pura; (bad business), res cassa; (in a lottery), sors cassa [nind
Point-blank, planè, penitùs, omnino
To look blank, confundor
A blanket, stragulum, torale
To blare (as a candle), liquando scintillare; (like a cow), mugio
To blaspheme, blasphemo, execror
A blasphemer, homo blasphemus
Blasphemous, in Deum contumeliosus, impius

[14]

BLI

Blasphemously, blasphemè, impiè
Blasphemy, blasphemia
A blast, or blasting, sideratio; (of corn, &c.), rabigo; (of wind), venti flatus; (sound), flamen
To blast (corn, &c.), uro; (with lightning), fulgure percuti; (a design), frustror; (reputation), infamo, famam violare
Blasted, sideratus, frustratus
A blaze, flamma
To blaze (as fire), flagro; (abroad), divulgo, pervulgo
To blazon (display), enarro; (arms), insignia depingere
To bleach, dealbo, candefacio
Bleached, dealbatus
Bleak, frigidus, algidus, pallidus
To grow bleak, frigesco
Bleakly, pallidè
Bleakness, rigor, pallor
Blear-eyed, lippus, lippiens
To be blear-eyed, lippio
To bleat (as a sheep), balo; (as a goat), caprisso
A bleating, balatus
To bleed, sanguine fluere
To bleed (let blood), venam incidere
A bleeder, qui venam incidit
A bleeding, sanguinis fluxus
A bleeding heart, cor vulneratum
To stop bleeding, sanguinem sistere
A blemish, macula, labes; (of credit), dedecus, infamia, probrum
To blemish, maculo, inquino; (one's reputation), famam lædere
Blemished, læsus, aspersus
Full of blemishes, maculosus
To blend, admisceo, commisceo
A blending, mixtio, mixtura
To bless, benedico; (consecrate), consecro; (wish good success), aspiro, secundo
To bless God, Deum laudare
The blessed, cœlites
Blessedness, felicitas, beatitudo
A blessing, benedictio; (good wish), fausta precatio; (benefit), beneficium, munus
A blight, rubigo, uredo
To blight, uredine percutere
Blind, cæcus, oculis captus; (dark), tenebricosus; (uncertain), obscurus [aus
Purblind, myops, luscus, lusciosus
A blind (false pretence), prætextum, species; (for windows), velum fenestris prætextam
To blind (deceive), fallo; (make blind), cæco, excæco [lippio
To be blind, cæligo; (purblind),
Stark-blind, luminibus orbatus
To be half blind, cæcutio
To blindfold, oculos obvolvere
Blinded, cæcatus, exæcatus
Blindly, cæcè; (rashly), temerè
Blindness, cæcitas, caligo
To blink, conniveo
Blink-eyed, strabo, pætulus, luscus
Bliss, beatitudo, felicitas
A blister, pustula
Blister flies, cantharides
To blister, vesicatorium applicare; (rise in blisters), in vesiculas inflari
A blister-plaister, vesicatorium
Blistered, vesicatorio laceratus
Full of blisters, pustulosus
Blithe, lætus, hilaris, alacer

BLU

To bloat, tumeo, turgeo
Bloated, tumidus, inflatus
A block, truncus, stipes; (for a hat), forma pilearis
A blockade, urbis circumclusio
To block up, aditus præcludere
Blocks, orbiculi volubiles
A blockhead, hebes, stipes
A blockhouse, arx, propugnaculum
Blocked, or blocked up, obsessus
A blocking up, obsessio
Blockish, fatuus, stupidus, insulsus
Blood, sanguis; (gore), cruor; (corrupted), sanies
Belonging to blood, sanguineus
To blood, sanguine fœdare
Blood-letting, venæ sectio
To daub with blood, sanguine inquinare
Of noble blood, illustri familiâ
The blood royal, stirps regia
Blood of the grape, vini succus
Blood-warm, tepidus
Blood-thirsty, sanguinis sitiens
A bloody-flux, hemorrhoia
Bloody, sanguineus, cruentus
Bloodied, sanguine oblitus
Bloodily, cruentè, sævitèr
Full of corrupt blood, saniosus
Next in blood, consanguineus
Blood (kindred), prosapia
Bloody-minded, sanguinarius, cruentus
A bloom, or blossom, flos
To bloom, or blossom, floreo
Bloomed, or blossomed, floridus
A blooming, germinatio
A blot, macula, litura; (in reputation), labes, dedecus
To blot, maculo; (out), deleo, expungo, oblitero, tollo
To take out a blot, maculam tollere
A blotch, pustula
Blotted, maculatus; (out), deletus, erasus, expunctus
A blotting-paper, chartula bibula
A blow, ictus, colaphus, plaga; (with a club), fustuarium; (on the cheek), alapa; (side), ictus obliquus
To blow, flo, sufflo; (breathe), spiro, aspiro; (against), reflo; (away), dissipo; (up), sufflo; (into), inflo; (the nose), emungere nasum; (out), efflo; (and puff), anhelo; (together), conflo; (a bladder), inflo; (up, or ruin), funditùs evertere; (vehemently), perflo; (a trumpet), buccinum inflare; (a fire), ignem sufflare; (as a flower), effloresco
A blower of a horn, cornicen
A blower, ignis suscitabulum
A blowing, sufflatio; (on), afflatus; (of the nose), naris emunctio
Blown, flatus; (down), eversus; (away), dissipatus; (upon, or despised), contemptus; (puffed), inflatus, turgidus
Blubber, adeps cetacea
To blubber, lachrymas effundere
One blubber-lipped, labeo
A bludgeon, baculum curtum
Blue, subst. cæruleum
Blue, adj. cæruleus
To blue, cæruleo inficere
Blued, cæruleo infectus
Blueness, livor
Bluff, rusticus
A blunder, error
To blunder, hallucinor

BOI   BOO   BOT

A blunderbuss, sclopus grandior; (blunderer), stupidus, bardus
A blundering, hallucinatio
Blunt, obtusus, hebes; (in speech), asper, rudis
To blunt, hebeto, obtundo, lenio
To be blunt (as a tool), hebeo; (in behaviour), rusticis esse moribus
Blunted, hebetatus
Bluntly, obtusè, asperè, liberè
Bluntness (dullness), hebetudo; (clownishness), rusticitas morum; (of speech), libertas loquendi
A blur, macula, labes
To blur, maculo, lædo
To blush, erubesco, rubeo
A blush, or blushing, rubor
To bluster, fremo, strepo
A blusterer, thraso
Blustering, turpidus, procellosus
A blusterous, or blustering, fremitus
A boar, aper, setiger
A wild boar, aper sylvestris
A young boar, verres
Boarish, aprugnus, crudelis
A board (plank), assis, tabula; (of commissioners), concilium, or conventus delegatorum
To board (or lay a floor), contabulo
Boarded with boards, tabulatus
Overboard, è nave
To board a ship, in navem insilire
A sideboard, abacus
Aboveboard, candidè, apertè
Board, or boarding, convictus
A boarder, convictor, hospes
A boarding-house, contubernium
A boarding-school, convictio literaria
To boast, glorior, jacto
Boasted, jactatus, ostentatus
A boasting, jactatio
A boaster, jactator
Boastingly, jactantèr, gloriosè
A boat, cymba, navicula; (long boat), scapha; (passage-boat), ponto; (fisher-boat), navigium piscatorium; (packet-boat), navis actuaria
To sail in a boat, navigulor
A boatman, remex
A boatswain, proreta
To bob (mock), ludificor; (strike), ferio, percutio, cædo; (jog), succutio
A bob (joke), dicterium; (of an ear-ring), inauris
Bob (short), curtus
A bobbing, calamus textilis
To bode, præsagio, portendo
Bodily, corporeus, in personâ
A bodkin, subula
A body, corpus; (dead), cadaver; (of a tree), truncus; (of foot-soldiers), peditatus; (of horse), equitatus; (company), societas; (of divinity, or law), corpus
Every body, unusquisque, singuli
Nobody, nemo
Somebody, aliquis, quidam
Big-bodied, corpulentus, immanis
Bodiless, incorporeus
A bog, palus
A bog-house, forica, latrina
To boggle, hæsito, dubito
Boggling, hæsitans, dubitans
Boggy, paludosus, palustris
A boil, ulcus
To boil, bullio, ebullio; (meat), cibos coquere
Boiled, coctus, elixus

[15]

A boiler (kettle), lebes
Boisterous, violentus, turbidus
Boisterously, violentèr, turbidè
Bold, audax, impavidus; (free), liber; (rash), temerarius; (saucy), insolens, impudens; (stout), intrepidus
To be bold, audeo
A bold face, perfrictæ frontis
Boldly, audactèr, impavidè; (freely), liberè; (rashly), temerè; (saucily), impudentèr; (stoutly), fortitèr
Boldness, audacia, temeritas, impudentia, procacitas; (in speech), libertas loquendi
Boiled, habens calmum
A bolster (of a bed), cervical, pulvinar; (to fill up a part), farcimentum
To bolster up, suffulcio
Bolstered up, suffultus, sustentus
A bolt (of a door), pessulus, obex; (dart), jaculum, pilum; (fetter), manicæ, arum; (thunder-bolt), fulmen
To bolt, oppessulo; (out upon), subitò egredi; (or shut in), includo; (out), excludo; (or bump out), extubero
Bolted, oppessulatus; (as meal), cribratus; (rashly), temerè dictus
A bolter (sieve), incerniculum
Bolting-house, pistrinum
A bolus, bolus
A bomb, bomba
To bombard, bombis oppugnare
Bombast, ampullæ, arum
A bond (for debt), syngrapha; (tie), vinculum; (for appearance), vadimonium; (of arbitration), compromissum
To give bond, satisdo
Bondage, servitus, servitium
To be in bondage, servio
A bondman, verna, mancipium
A bondwoman, serva
Bonds (fetters), compedes, um
A bone, os; (of contention), litis occasio; (of the back), spina dorsi
Belonging to bones, osseus
Bone by bone, ossiculatim
To bone, exosso
Boney (full of bones), osseus
A bonnet, rediminculum
Bonny, bellus, lepidus
A booby, bardus, antronus
A book, liber, codex
To book down, in codicem referre
A book of accounts, codex rationarius
A day-book, diarium
A news-book, novellæ literæ
A note-book, libellus portandus
A school-book, liber scholasticus
A shop-book, mercium commentarius
Books of record, tabulæ publicæ
Statute-book, capitularia
A book-worm, blatta
Bookish, helluo librorum, studiis addictus
A bookbinder, bibliopegus
A book-keeper, qui mercium rationes curat
A bookseller, bibliopola
A bookseller's shop, taberna libraria
A boon (of a ship), malus; (bar to a harbour), repagulum
A boon (favour), donum
Boon (agreeable), facetus, bellus
A boor (clown), rusticus

Boorish, rusticus, agrestis
Boosy, temulentus
Boot (advantage), emolumentum
A boot, ocrea
To boot, ocreas induere
Booted, ocreatus
Bootless, incassum, frustrà
A booth, tabernaculum [bis
A booty, præda, spolium, manubiæ
To get booty, prædor, prædam facere
To play booty, colludo
The border, margo, ora; (of a garment), fimbria; (brim), crepido; (of a country), finis, terminus, confinia
To border upon, adjaceo
Bordered with, fimbriatus
A borderer, accola [gnus
Bordering upon, vicinus, contiI bore, or did bear, tuli
To bore, terebro, penetro, perfodio, pertundo
The bore, or hole made, foramen
Bored, perforatus, perterebratus
A borer, perforator
Boring, terebrans, perforans
A boring, terebratio
To be born, nascor, orior; (again), renascor; (of), enascor; (before its time), abortivus nasci
Born, natus, ortus, satus; (after a father's death), posthumus; (again), renatus; (of good parents), loco honesto natus; (of mean parentage), humili loco natus; (together), congenitus [primogenitus
The first-born, natu maximus,
Base-born, natus adulterinus
Still-born, natus mortuus
Born of such a stock, oriundus
Borne down, oppressus, depressus
To be borne down, opprimor; (up), fulcior; (to be borne), portor [rendus
To be borne with (tolerable), feNot to be borne, intolerabilis
A borough, municipium
To borrow, mutuor, mutuo sumere; (upon use), fœneror
Borrowed, mutuatus, conductus
A borrower, mutuator
A borrowing, mutuatio
The bosom, gremium, sinus; (of a shirt), fissura
A bosom-friend, intimus amicus, charissimus
A boss, bulla; (of a book), umbilicus; (of a buckler), umbo; (in the body), gibbus
To boss, prominso, exto
Bossed, gibbosus, gibbus
Botanic, botanicus
Botany, herbarum scientia
A botanist, herbarum peritus
A botch, ulcus, bubo, carbunculus, aphtha
A botch (patch), pannus
To botch, resarcio; (bungle), ineptè, or infabrè facere
Botched, resartus, sartus
A botcher, sartor imperitus
Both, adj. ambo, uterque
Both, conj. cum, tum, et—et, quà —quà, vel—vel
Both-handed, ambidexter
Both sides, utrinquè
Both ways, bifariàm
The bots (in horses), ascarides
A bottle, uter, ampulla; (of hay), fasciculus; (maker), ampullarius
Smelling-bottle, olfactorium
To bottle, in ampullas infundere

BOX — BRA — BRE

Bottled, in ampullis conservatus
Bottle-nosed, nasutus
The bottom, fundus; (of a ship), carina; (dregs), fæx, sedimentum; (depth of a thing), profundum; (of a mountain), radix; (of the belly), hypogastrium
A bottom (ship), navis; (valley), vallis; (of thread, &c.), glomus; (to wind thread on), gyrgillus
To bottom, fundo munire
At the bottom, in imo
To the very bottom, funditùs
Bottomless, fundo carens, immensus
Bottomless pit, vorago, abyssus
Without bottom, immensus
A bough, ramus
Full of boughs, ramosus
To be bought, emor
A bounce (noise), crepitus; (boasting), jactatio
To bounce, crepo, strepo; (often), crepito; (up), resilio, prosilio
Bouncing, pinguis, valens, pugil
To bound, finio, limito; (or border upon), adjaceo; (back, or again), resilio
A bound, meta, terminus
To be bound, obligor, teneor
Bound, ligatus, obligatus; (beholden), devinctus, astrictus; (by covenant), pactione obligatus; (by duty), necessitudine astrictus; (restrained), vinetus; (with an oath), jurejurando obstrictus; (as an apprentice), artifici traditus; (as a bond), compactus; (to), alligatus; (together), colligatus; (under), substrictus
Bounded, circumscriptus, confinis
Bounding upon, conterminis, contiguus, confinis
A bounding, limitatio, confinium
Boundless, immensus, infinitus
Bounden, debitus, obvinctus
Bountifully, benignè, liberalitèr
Bountifulness, benignitas, liberalitas, munificentia
Bounty, benignitas, largitas
A bourn, torrens
To bouse, poto   [potatio
A bout, vicis; (drinking), combow, arcus; (case), corytos; (man), sagittarius; (string), arcûs nervus, or chorda; (sprit), malus anterior
Like a bow, arcuatus
Bowlegged, valgus, varus
To bow, flecto, inclino; (backwards), reclino; (down), incurvo; (round), circumflecto; (bend), acclino
Bowed, curvatus, flexus
To bowel, eviscero, exentero
The bowels, intestina; (of compassion), miseratio
A bower, or arbour, pergula
A bowl (for drink), acyphus; (to wash in), labrum; (to play with), globus, sphæra
To bowl, globum mittere
Bowled, missus, jactatus
Bowling, sphæromachia
A bowling-green, sphæristerium
A box, cista, arca, pyxis
A Christmas-box, strena
A coach-box, currûs sedile
A dice-box, orca, fritillus
A snuff-box, pyxidicula pulveris
A tobacco-box, pyxidicula tabaci
The poor's box, arca paupercu- lorum

[16]

Boxes in a shop, locelli, nidi
A box on the ear, alapa
To box (fight), pugnis certare; (on the ear), alapam, or colaphum alicui infligere
A boxer, pugil
A box-tree, buxus
Of box, buxeus
A boy, puer; (soldier's), calo, lixa; (servant), famulus
A schoolboy, ludi discipulus
A little boy, puerulus
Boyish, puerilis
Boyishly, puerilitèr
Boyishness, puerilitas
To brabble, altercor, purgo
A brabble, rixa, lis
A brabbler, altercator
A brace (couple), par; (in building), fibula; (ship's rope), rudens; (in printing), uncus; (hook), uncus; (to join things together), copula
To brace, alligo, ligo
A bracer, alligator
A bracing, alligatio
A bracelet, armilla
Brachygraphy, stenographia
A bracket, mutulus
Brackish, salsus
Brackishness, salsitudo
To brag (boast), jacto, glorior
A bragger, jactator
A braid of hair, cincinnus
To braid, complico, implico
Braided, plexus, cirratus
The brain, cerebrum; (hinder part), cerebellum
To brain, excerebro
Brainless, inconsultus, stultus
Hair-brained, temerarius
Brake (fern), filix
A brake (for flax), lini frangibulum; (thicket), dumetum; (horse-bit), epistomium
Braky (thorny), dumosus
A bramble, rubus, sentis
Bran, furfur
A branch (of a tree), ramus; (of a discourse), caput; (of a pedigree), stemma
To branch (as a tree), germino; (as a discourse), distinguo
Branched, ramosus, distinctus
Branching, germinans, frondens
Branchy, frondosus
A brand, stigma, nota; [of fire), torris, fax
To brand, noto   [tatus
Branded, stigmate inustus, noBranded with a crime, infamis
A brand-iron, cauterium
Brand-new, omninò novus
To brandish, vibro, corusco
Brandy, vini spiritus
To brangle, lixor, litigo
Branny, furfuraceus
Brass, æs
Made of brass, æneus, aheneus
Covered with brass, æratus
Brass-work, ærificium
A brat, infans
A bravado, insultatio
Brave (fine), nitidus; (excellent), præstans; (skilful), peritus; (valiant), fortis; (learned), eruditus; (to behold), præclarus, pulcher
To brave, lacesso
Bravely, concinnè, scitè, eximiè, peritè, fortitèr, animosè
Bravery, decor, excellentia, fortitudo, magnanimitas
A braving, insultatio
A bravo, sicarius, thraso

A brawl, rixa, jurgium
To brawl, jurgo, rixor
A brawler, rabula, rixator
A brawling, jurgium, rixa
Brawling, contentiosus, jurgans
Brawn, callum aprugnum
Brawny, callosus
Brawniness, callositas
To bray (pound), tero, tundo; (as an ass), rudo; (as an elephant), barrio; (cry out), fremo
A braying, tritura, barritus, rugitus, mugitus
To braze, ære inducere
Brazed over, ære inductus
Brazen (made of brass), æreus, aheneus; (impudent), impudens, effrons
A brasier, faber ærarius
A breach, ruina; (between two), simultas; (of friendship), alienatio; (of promise), violatio fidei; (made by water), inundatio; (of a treaty of peace), violatio
Bread, panis; (leavened), panis fermentatus
Bread-corn, frumentum
Breadth, latitudo, amplitudo
To break, frango, infringo, rumpo; (with age), defloresco; (asunder), diffringo; (bruise), contero; (a covenant), violare fœdus; (down), demolior
A break, intervallum, interstitium; (of day), diluculum
To break fast, jento
A breakfast, jentaculum
A breaker, ruptor; (down), demolitor; (through), perfossor; (of the laws, &c.), violator; (of horses), equorum domitor
A breaking, infractio, fractura; (down), demolitio; (asunder), diruptio; (in), irruptio; (out), eruptio; (off), abruptio, intermissio; (of a horse), equi domitura; (small), tritura; (violation), violatio
The breast, pectus; (of a woman), uber; (bone), sternum
Abreast, æquâ fronte   [laris
Of the breast, pectoralis, mamilA breast-work, lorica lapidea
A breast-plate, lorica, thorax
Having a breast-plate, thoracatus
Breath, spiritus, halitus, flatus; (of air), aura
To breathe, spiro, respiro, anhelo; (after), cupio, desidero; (between), interspiro; (into), inspiro; (one's last), expiro; (on, or upon), aspiro, inspiro; (out, or exhale), exhalo; (through), perspiro
A breathing, respiratio; (on), afflatus; (hole), spiraculum; (sweat), sudor parvus
Breathing, spirans
Breathless, ægrè anhelans
Bred (born), generatus; (brought up), educatus; (in), ingenitus; (with), congenitus; (well), benè moratus; (ill), malè moratus
The breech, podex, clunes
Breeches, braccæ
Wearing breeches, braccatus
Breeched, braccis indutus
To breed, gigno, pario; (cause), produco; (be bred), gignor; (or bring up), alo, educo
A breed, genus; (teeth), dentio
A breeder (father), generator; (mother), genitrix; (of cattle), nutritor

BRI   BRO   BUG

A breeding, generatio; (of teeth), dentitio; (good manners), urbanitas; (education), educatio
A breeze, aura
Brethren, fratres, um
A brevet, or brief, rescriptum
A breviary (book), breviarium
A breviate, compendium
Brevity, brevitas
To brew (mingle), misceo, confundo; (beer, &c.), coquere, or concoquere potum
Brewed, coctus, mixtus
A brewer, cerevisiæ coctor
A brewhouse, sythepsarium
A brewing, coctio
A briar, sentis, rubus
Where briars grow, rubetum
A bribe, munus, repetundæ
To bribe, corrumpere munere
Bribed, corruptus, subornatus
A briber, corruptor muneribus
Bribery, ambitus, corruptio, repetundæ
A bribing, subornatio
A brick, later
Brick-coloured, figulinus
Belonging to brick, lateritius
A bricklayer, laterum structor
A brick-maker, laterum confector
A brick-wall, murus coctilis
To lay with bricks, lateribus sternere
A bride, sponsa, nupta
A bridechamber, thalamus
A bridegroom, sponsus
A bridemaid, pronuba
A bridal song, epithalamium
Bridewell, pistrinum
A bridge, pons
A bridge-master, pontis curator
A bridle, frænum, habena
To bridle, freno, frænum imponere; (one's passion), iræ moderari
A brief (writ), schedula juridica; (letters patent), diploma; (for asking charity), literæ petitoriæ; (for a counsellor), litis summa; (sentence), sententiola; (account), summarium; (discourse), concisa oratio
Brief, brevis, concisus; (rife), frequens
Briefly, breviter, concisè
Briefness, brevitas
A brier, vepres; (sweet), cynosbatos
Briery, spinosus
A brigade, turma, manipulus
A brigadier, turmæ ductor
A brigantine (ship), phaselus
Bright, splendens, lucidus, nitidus; (of bright character), integer vitæ; (of bright parts), sagacissimus; (very bright), perlucidus, pellucidus
To be bright, clareo, niteo, inclaresco, laceo, lucesco
To brighten, lucesco; (make bright), polio, limo
Brightly, clarè, nitidè
Brightness, fulgor, splendor; (of character), morum integritas; (of understanding), ingenii sagacitas; (of the sun), lumen
The brim, labrum, margo
Having a brim, marginatus
Brimful, ad summum impletus
To brim (as a sow), subo
A brimmer, calix potu coronatus
Brimstone, sulphur
Done with brimstone, sulphuratus
Brindled (streaked), variegatus

[17]

Brine, salsugo, alex
A brine-pit, salina
Salt as brine, salsissimus
Brinish, salsus
To bring, fero, affero, adduco: (about), efficio, perduco; (by force), traho; (to an end), perficio, ad exitum perducere; (an action), dicam impingere; (away), aufero; (back), reduco; (to bed), obstetricor; (forth), pario; (down, or lessen), diminuo; (down, or weaken), attenuo; (down, or demolish), demolior; (forth before time), aborto; (forth plenteously), effundo; (forth flowers), floresco; (abroad), profero; (forth, or produce), produco; (from), defero; (from far), aveho; (in), infero; (in guilty), condemno; (one's hand in), operi assuescere; (into an office), promovere ad; (into debt), æs alienum contrahere; (into question), examino; (into subjection), redigo, subigo; (into fashion), in morem inducere; (low), dejicio
A bringer, portitor; (back), reductor; (up), educator, educatrix; (of tidings), nuncius; (down), dejector
A bringing, advectio; (back), reductio; (forth), prolatio; (forth of young), fœtus; (over), traductio; (in), inductio, introductio; (to pass), effectio; (down), diminutio; (together), collatio; (under), subjectio; (up), educatio
A brink, extremitas, margo
Brisk, agilis, vividus, lætus
To be brisk, vigeo
Briskly, alacriter, acriter, agiliter
Briskness, alacritas, vigor
The brisket, pectus animalis cæsi
A bristle, seta
To bristle up, horreo, setas erigere
Having bristles, setiger, hirsutus
Bristly, setoeus, hirsutus
Britain, Britannia
British, Britannicus
A Briton, Britannus, Brito
Brittle, fragilis, caducus, vitreus
Brittleness, fragilitas
A broach (spit), veru, obolus
Abroach (as beer), terebratus
To broach (a cask), vas terebrare
Broad, latus, largus, amplus
To make broad, dilato
Brogue, mala pronunciatio
A broil, ria, turba
Full of broils, turbulentus
To raise broils, tumultuor, turbas ciere
To broil, carnem torrere; (be broiled), torresco, torreor
Broiled, tostus
Brokage, versura
A broker (agent), transactor, mango; (of clothes, &c.), interpolator; (exchange), proxeneta argentarius; (pawn), pignerator; (in old goods), scrutarius
Bronze, frons perfricta
A bronze, numisma æreum
A brooch (necklace), monile, gemma
A brood, proles; (of chickens), pullities
To brood, or set brooding, incubo
A brooding, incubatio

A brook, rivulus
To brook (bear), fero, tolero
A broom, spartum, genista
A broom, scopæ, arum
Broth, jus, jusculum, muria
A brothel, lupanar, ganea
A brother, frater
A half-brother, germanus
A brother-in-law, frater mariti
A foster-brother, collectaneus
Brotherhood, sodalitium
Brotherly, adj. fraternus; adv. fraternè; (love), mutua amicitia
The brow, frons; (of a wall), corona muri; (eye-brow), supercilium
Brown, fuscus, pullus
To make brown, fusco
To be in a brown study, meditor
To browse, depasco, carpo
To bruise, contero, quasso; (in a mortar), pinso; (small), comminuo, confringo
A bruise, contusio
Bruised, contusus, contritus; (black and blue), sugil, sugillatus, lividus
A bruising, contusio, pinsatio
A bruit (report), rumor
A brunt (assault), impetus
A brush, scopula, verriculum; (or running against), occursus; (debate), aggressio; (for painters), penicillus
To brush, verro, purgo
Like a brush, verriculatus
To brush away, festinè fugere
Brushed, scopulâ purgatus
To bristle, crepito, se erigere
A brute, animal brutum
Brutish, ferinus, fœdus, impudicus, fatuus, stupidus, brutus
Brutishly, ferociter, fœdè, fatuè
Brutality, ferocitas, sævitia, impudicitia, stultitia
A bubble, bulla, fraus
To bubble (cheat), dolis fallere; (in seething), ferveo; (as water), ebullio, scateo
A bubbling, ebullitio
A buck, cervus, dama
A bucket, situla, sipho
Buck's horn, cornu cervinum
A buckle, fibula, spinther; (of hair), cincinnus; (of a shoe), fibula calcearia
To buckle, fibulâ colligare
A buckler, clypeus, scutum
Buckram, pannus cilicinus
Buckskin, pellis cervina
Bucolics, bucolica
A bud, germen, gemma; (of a rose), calyx; (of a vine), oculus, gemma
To bud, germino; (again), repullulasco; (out), egermino; (together), congermino
A budding, germinatus
To budge, pedem ciere
A budget, saccus, bulga
Buff (leather), pellis bubula
A buffet, colaphus, alapa; (for china, &c.), abacus
To buffet, colaphum dare
Buffeted, colaphis cæsus
A buffeting, colaphis verberatio
A buffalo, bubalus
A buffle-head, stolidus, bardus
A buffoon, sannio, scurra
Buffoonery, scurrilitas
A bug, cimex, bruchus
A bugbear, larva, terriculum
Buggy, cimicibus abundans
A bugle, segmenta vitrea; (horn), cornu venatorium

BUR   BUT   CAK

To build, ædifico, condo; (about), circumstruo; (again), reædifico; (before), præstruo; (in), inædifico; (under), substruo; (by, or near unto), astruo; (up), perædifico; (upon), inædifico; (or rely upon), nitor
A builder, ædificator, conditor
A master-builder, architectus
A building, ædificium, structura
Art of building, architectura
A bulb, bulbus
Bulbous, bulbosus
To bulge (as a ship), vacillo
To be bulged, scopulis illidi
A bulk (projection before a shop), appendix; (bigness), amplitudo, moles; (of a body), statura corporis; (of a ship), navis capacitas
To bulk out, propendeo; (to break bulk), navem exonerare
Bulkiness, magnitudo
Bulky, corpulentus, crassus, ingens, gravis, solidus, onerosus
A bull, taurus; (blunder), atribligo; (Pope's), bulla
Bull-baiting, certamen inter canes et taurum
Bull-baiters, bubetii
A bull-dog, canis laniensis
A bull-finch, rubicilla
A bullet, glans plumbea
Bullion, aurum, &c. in massâ
A bullock, juvencus
To bully, insulto
A bully, thraso
A bulrush, juncus, scirpus
A bulwark, agger, præsidium
A bumbailiff, lictor
A bumkin, rusticus
A bump (swelling), tuber; (thump), plaga
To bump out, turgeo, promineo
A bumper, calix repletus
A bun (cake), collyra
A bunch (swelling), scirrus, gibbus; (bundle), fasciculus; (of grapes), racemus
To bunch out, promineo, exto
A bundle, fascia, fasciculus, sarcinula; (of rods), fasces
To bundle up, consarcino
A bung, obturamentum; (hole), spiramentum
To bung up, obturo
To bungle, imperitè conficere
A bungler, imperitus, rudis
Bunglingly, infabrè, crassè
A buoy, index anchoræ jactæ
To buoy up, attollo, sustineo
A burden, onus; (of a song), scrupulus
To burden, onero, sarcino
Burdensome, gravis, onerosus
A bur, lappa
A bureau, scrinium
A burr (of a deer's horn), tuberculum; (of the ear), lobus auris
A burgess (magistrate), burgensis; (senator), senator, pater conscriptus; (freeman), civis, municeps
Burglary, parietum perfossio
Buriable, sepelibilis
A burial, funus, exequiæ, sepultura
Belonging to burials, funebris
To bury, sepelio, humo, condo
A burying, humatio, sepultura
A burying-place, sepulcretum, calvaria
Burlesk, or burlesque, jocularis, ludicrus
[18]

To burlesque, jocularitèr illudere
A burn, vulnus ex ustione factum
To burn, uro, cremo, incendo, ardeo, candeo, flagro; (sear), cauterio urere
To burn to ashes, in cineres redigere
To burn with anger, irâ ardere
To be burned, uror; (down), deflagro
Burned, or burnt, ustus, exustus; (to ashes), in cineres redactus; (in roasting), retorridus; (in the hand), stigmate innatus; (before, or at the end), præustus; (half), seminustus
Burning, exurens, ardens, flagrans
A burning, combustio, deflagratio; (in sores), uredo; (iron), cauterium; (coal), pruna; (shame) res pessima
To burnish, expolio, defrico
A burnisher, politor
A burnishing, expolitio
A burnt-offering, holocaustum
A burrow, cuniculus
To burrow, in cavum subire, cuniculos agere
The burse, excambium
A burser, collegii dispensator
To burst, rumpo, disrumpo; (in pieces), dissilio; (out), prosilio; (with laughing), risu emori; (into laughter), in risum prorumpere; (into tears), in lachrymas effundi; (with envy), invidiâ commoveri
A bursting, ruptio; (out), eruptio
A burthen (burden), onus
To burthen, onero, gravo
To bury, tumulo, sepelio   [ries
A bush, rubus; (of hair), cæsaries
Bushy, dumosus; (hair), cæsaries comatæ; (place), dumetum
A bushel, modius, medimnus
Busied, occupatus, districtus
Busily, solicitè, studiosè
Business (bustle), tumultus; (employment), negotium res; (to mind), rei operam dare; (to come into), in foro florere; (to manage), res gerere
Full of business, occupatissimus
A buskin, cothurnus, pero
A buss, basium, suavium
To buss, osculor, basio
A buss (ship), navigiolum
A bussing, basiatio
A bust, statua trunca
Bustard, otis, idis
A bustle, turba, tumultus
To bustle about, diligentèr rem administrare
Bustling (diligent), diligens, alacer
Busy, occupatus; (meddling), curiosus, impertinens, molestus
To busy, occupo, solicito
To be busy, satago
A busybody, ardelio
But (an adversative), ast, at, atqui, autem, cæterùm, nisi, sed, sin, verò, verum; (but for), ni, absque; (before, or before that), cùm; (except), extra, nisi, præter, præterquàm, modò, solùm, tantùm
A butcher, lanius
To butcher, macto, lanio
A butcher's shop, macellum
Butcherly (adj.), crudelis; (adv.), crudelitèr, truculentè
Butchery, cædes, stragea
A butler, promus

A butt (vessel), amphora, dolium; (mark), meta; (bank), agger
To butt, arieto, cornu petere
Butted, or bounded, finitus
Butter, butyrum
Buttered, butyro illitus
A butterfly, papilio
Buttermilk, lac serosum
A buttery, cella promptuaria
A buttock, clunis, nates
A button, fibula
To button, fibulo
A buttress, fulcrum
To buttress, suffulsio
Buxom, alacer, hilaris, lætus
To be buxom, hilaritate perfundi
To buy, emo, mercor; (again), redimo; (a bargain), benè emere; (dear), pluris emere; (often), emptito; (meat), obsonor; (upon trust), fide data emere; (up), emercor
A buyer, emptor
A buying, emptio
To buzz (as a bee), bombilo; (in the ear), insusurro; (abroad), rumorem spargere
A buzzing, bombus, murmur
A buzzard, buteo
By, à, ab, ad, apud, cum, de, e, ex, juxta, ob, per, præ, præter, pro, prope, propter, secundum, sub
By itself, separatim, seorsim; (by heart), memoritèr; (by stealth), furtim; (by-and-by), confestim, continuò; (by-the-bye), obitèr, in transitu; (by course), vicissim; (by chance), casu, fortè, ut fit; (by degrees), paulatim; (by myself), per me, ego solus; (by day), interdiù; (by night), noctu; (by what place, or way?) quâ? (hard by), in proximo; (by much), multo; (by how much), quantò; (by so much), tantò

C.

A cabal, conciliabulum
To cabal, occultè agere
The cabala, cabala, traditio
Cabalistical, cabalisticus
A cabbage, brassica, caulis
Cabbaged (headed), capitatus; (stolen), suppilatus
A cabin (in a ship), stega; (little place to dwell in), tugurium
A cabinet, cistula, scrinium
A cabinet council, concilium secretius
A cable, rudens
A sheet-cable, rudens sacra
To cack, caco
To cackle, glocio, deblatero
A cackling, glociratio
A cacodemon, malus genius
Cadaverous, cadaverosus
Cadence, clausura periodi numerosa
A cadet, frater minor
A cag, testa
A cage, cavea, aviarium; (for criminals), carcer clathratus
Caged, inclusus
To cajole, inesco, illicio, lacto
A cajoling, blandimentum
A cajoler, sycophanta
A caitiff, nefarius, captivus
A cake, placenta, libum

CAN   CAP   CAR

Calamine-stone, lapis calaminaris
Calamity, calamitas, infortunitum, res adversæ
Calamitous, calamitosus
A calash, carpentum, pilentum
To calcine, exuro
Calcination, exustio
To calculate, rationem putare; (a nativity), futura prædicere
Calculated (computed), computatus; (adapted), accommodatus
A calculation, computatio
A calculator, calculator, computator, ratiocinator
A caldron, lebes, ahenum
A calendar, calendarium, fasti
A calender (of cloth), politor
Calendered, politus, lævigatus
Calends, calendæ, arum
A calf, vitulus; (sea-calf), phoca; (of the leg), sura
Of a calf, vitulinus
Calico, tela Indica
To calk, stupâ rimas farcire
A calker, rimarum stipator
To call, voco, compello; (aloud), exclamo; (aside), sevoco; (back), revoco; (back one's word), retracto, denego; (by name), nomino; (for), arcesso; (for help), imploro; (out, or forth), evoco; (for a thing), posco; (in), introvoco; (at a place), compello; (in money), pecuniam exigere; (often), vocito; (out of bed), suscito; (over), recito; (to mind), recordor; (to arms), classicum canere; (to an account), ad rationem reddendam vocare; (together), convoco; (unto), inclamo; (upon), invoco; (upon for witness), appello; (to witness), testor
A call, vocatio; (at a call), ad nutum
A calling, vocatio; (profession), artificium; (to remembrance), recognitio; (together), convocario; (by name), compellatio; (back), revocatio; (for), accitus; (out), evocatio; (from), avocatio; (upon), invocatio
Callosity, callus, callositas
Callous, callosus
Calm, sedatus, tranquillus, placidus
A calm (sea), maris tranquillitas; (weather), serenitas
To calm, paco, placo, mulceo
To becalm, mitesco, placor
Calmy, lenitèr, tranquillè
Calmness, tranquillitas, serenitas
To calumniate, calumnior, infamo
Calumnious, contumeliosus
Calumniously, contumeliosè
Calumny, calumnia
Cambric, sindon
A camel, camelus
Of a camel, camelinus
Camlet, pannus camelinus
Camomile, chamæmelum
A camp, castra, orum
A standing-camp, stativa
To pitch a camp, castra ponere
Belonging to a camp, castrensis
Followers of a camp, calones
A campaign (flat country), planities; (taking the field), expeditio militaris; (coat), sagum
Camphire, camphora
Camphorated, camphorâ mixtus
I can, possum, queo
I cannot, nequeo
[19]

A canal, canalis
Of the Canaries, Canarius
Canary-wine, vinum Canariorum
To cancel (a writing), deleo, expungo; (make void), abrogo
A cancelling, deletio, abolitio
A cancer, cancer, gangrena
Candid, candidus, ingenuus
A candidate, candidatus
To stand a candidate, munus ambire
Candidly, candidè, ingenuè
Candied, saccharo conditus
A candle, candela, lucerna
A wax-candle, cereus
A watch-candle, lucubra
Candle-light, lucerna
To study by candle-light, lucubro
A candlestick, candelabrum
Candlemas-day, purificatio virginis Mariæ
Candour, candor
To candy, saccharo condire
A cane, canna Indica, calamus; (sugar-cane), canna saccharata
To cane, fuste cædere
Like a cane, arundineus
Caned, fuste cæsus
Made of cane, canneus
A caning, fustuarium
Canine, caninus, insatiabilis
A canister, canistrum
A canker, ulcus; (in the mouth), aphthæ; (in the nose), polypus
Canker (rust), rubigo, ferrugo; (a worm), oruca
A cann, cantharus
A cannibal, anthropophagus
A cannon, tormentum bellicum
To cannonade, tormentis verberare
A cannoneer, bombardarius
A canon (rule), regula; (law), canon; (in a cathedral), canonicus
Canonical, canonicus
To canonise, in divos referre
Canonized, in divos ascriptus
A canonising, canonisatio
A canopy, canopeum
To cant (cast away), abjicio; (talk gibberish), uti fictitio sermone; (whine), verba trahere; (wheedle), dictis ducere; (chirp), cantillo
A cant, auctio, sermo fictitius
A canting fellow, homo subdolus
A canting, fictio, conjectus
A canticle, Canto, canticum
A canton, distribuo, divido
A canton, tribus, pagus
Canvas, cannabum
To canton (for preferment), ambio; (sift for business), inquiro, vestigo
A cap, pileus, calyptra
Capped, præpilatus
To cap a person, caput nudare; (in verses), alternis versibus contendere
Wearing a cap, pileatus
Cap-à-piè, à capite ad calcem armatus
Capable, capax, idoneus, potens
Capacious, capax, amplus
Capaciousness, capacitas, mensura; (of a place), amplitudo
Capacity (ability), facultas, ingenium
A caparison, lorica
To caparison, loricâ munire
A cape (at sea), promontorium; (of a garment), collare
A caper, saltus; (fruit), capparis
To caper, tripudio, assilio

Capillary, capillaris
Capital, capitalis, præcipuus
A capital (in architecture), capitulum; (letter), litera majuscula
A capitation, capitum exactio
The capitol, capitolium
To capitulate, de deditione agere
Capitulated, pacto constitutus
Capitulating, paciscens
A capitulation, pactio de deditione
A capon, capo, capus
A capouch, cucullus
A caprice (fantastical humour), repentinus animi motus; (obstinate humour), pertinacia
Capricious, inconstans, pertinax
Capriciously, levitèr, morosè
Capriciousness, inconstantia
A captain, dux; (in-chief), summus dux; (of the guards), prætorii præfectus; (of a company), ordinum ductor; (of horse), hipparchus; (of 10 men), decurio; (of 50), pentæcontarchus; (of 100), centurio; (of 1000), chiliarchus, tribunus; (of a ship), dux nauticus; (of a castle), arcis præfectus
A captainship, centuriatus
Captious, argutus, morosus, fallax
A captious fellow, cavillator
Captiously, captiosè, argutè
Captiousness, cavillatio, captio
To captivate (enslave), in servitutem redigere; (the affections, &c.), mulceo, teneo, capto
A captive, captivus, mancipium
Captivity, captivitas, servitus
To carry, or lead away into captivity, in captivitatem abducere
A captor, qui captivum facit
Capture, captura, comprehensio
A carat, unciæ triens
A caravan, mercatorum caterva peregrè euntium; (carriage), vehiculum oblongum
A caravansera, diversorium
Caraway (seed), carua
A carbine, sclopeta velitaris
A carbineer, veles [torrere
To carbonade, carnem in prunâ
A carbuncle, carbunculus
A carcase, cadaver
A card, charta lusoria; (written), charta epistolica; (sea-card), tabula nautica; (for wool), ferreus pecten; (court), charta picta; (plain), charta simplex
To play at cards, chartis pictis ludere [carpere
To card wool, carmino, lanam
Carded, carminatus, pexus
A carding, carminatio
A cardinal, cardinalis, pater purpuratus; adj. præcipuus
Care (diligence), diligentia; (heed), cautio; (regard), cura; (trouble), onus, anxietas, solicitudo; (tuition), tutela
To care, or take care of, curo; (for), provideo; (for diligently), invigilo, solicitus esse
To have a care, caveo
To careen, purgo
A career, anfractus, gyrus
A career, cursus incitatus
Careful, diligens, sedulus, cautus, solicitus, circumspectus
To be careful, satago, angor a-horo, attendo
Carefully, anxiè, cautè, sedulò
Carefulness, diligentia, consideratio, solicitudo, cautio

CAR — CAT — CEN

Careless (not thinking), improvidus; (at ease), securus; (neglectful), negligens, inconsideratus
To be careless, negligo
Carelessly, negligentè, securè
Carelessness, incuria, negligentia
To caress, indulgeo, amantèr accipere, adblandior
Caresses, blanditiæ, blandimenta
Caressed, comitèr acceptus
A cargo, navis onus
A caring for, provisio
Carious, cariosus
A carle (churl), silicernium
Carnage, internecio, cædes
Carnal, carnalis, pravus
Carnally, carnalitèr, pravè
To enjoy carnally, coeo
Carnality, voluptatum appetitus
A carnation, caryophyllon
Carnival, bacchanalia
Carnivorous, carnivorus
A carol, carmen, hymnus
To carouse, pergræcor
A carousing, potatio intemperans
A carp, carpio, caprinus
To carp, carpo, vellico
Carped at, vellicatus
A carper, criticus, captor
A carping, vellicatio
A carpenter, faber lignarius
Belonging to a carpenter, fabrilis
Carpentry, ars fabrilis
A carpet, tapes, gausape
A cart, carrus
Carriage (behaviour), gestus; (good), urbanitas; (of a burthen), bajulatio; (cartage), vectura; (money), vectiva; (on horseback), hippagium; (for artillery), lignea compages
A carriage, currus, vehiculum
A carrier, portator, bajulus; (of letters), tabellarius; (of tales), rumigerus
Carrion, caro morticina
A carrot, pastinaca, daucus
Carrot-pated, rutilus
To carry, gero, porto, fero; (or behave), se gerere; (about), circumfero; (all before one), vinco, supero; (away), aufero; (away by force), rapio; (the prize), palmam ferre; (before), præfero; (beyond), præterfero; (into slavery), in servitutem abducere; (in a carriage), veho, conveho; (a burden), bajulo; (conduct), duco; (forth), effero; (down), deveho; (from place to place), transporto; (in), importo; (news), nuncio; (on a war), bellum producere; (on a building), continuare ædificium; (to a place), adveho; (together), comporto; (privately), subveho; (water), aquor; (wood), lignor
A carrying, gestatio, portatio; (away), asportatio; (over), trajectio; (to a place), advectio; (by a cart, &c.), vectio
A cart, cartus, plaustrum, curriculum, biga, triga, quadriga; (child's), plostellum; (covered), capsus, covinus
To cart, in vehiculo portare
A carter, auriga
A cartilage, cartilago
A cartouch, capsula
To carve, sculpo, exartuo, seco
A carver, sculptor, carptor
A carving, sculptura, cælatura
A carving-knife, culter structoris

[20]

A cascade, præceps æquæ lapsus
A case (in law), causa; (matter), res; (of conscience), scrupulus; (cover), theca; (for a bow), corytos; (for a comb), pectinarium; (for needles), acuarium; (for pins), acicularium; (of instruments), capsula; (of a noun), casus; (state), conditio, status [quàm
In no case, haudquaquàm, nequa-
A casement, fenestra
Cash, pecunia numerata, census
To cashier, exauctoro
A cask, testa, cadus, dolium; (headpiece), galea
A casket, scrinium, cistula
A cassock, sagum
To cast, jacto, jacio; (about), circumjacio; (abroad), spargo; (again), rejicio; (back), rejicio; (away), abjicio; (along), prosterno; (against), objicio; (between), interjicio; (a bowl), mitto; (a skin), exuo; (condemn), condemno; (in one's dish), exprobo; (devise), conjicio; (down), dejicio; (down from), deturbo; (headlong), præcipito; (under foot), pessundo; (forth), emitto; (in), injicio; (in one's mind), recolo, meditor; (in a suit), vinco; (metals), liquo, conflo; (off a garment), exuo; (off, or renounce), repudio; (off, as a printer), lineas computare; (over, or beyond), trajicio; (over, or upon), superinjicio; (out), ejicio; (out, or expose), expono; (a smell), redoleo; (to and fro), agito; (up), computo; (up, as the sea), expuo; (up, or vomit), evomo
A cast, jactus; (of the eye), oculorum distortio
A casting, jactatus, jactus; (about), respersio; (at), petitio; (off, or away), abjectio; (down), dejectio; (between), interjectus; (in), injectio; (upon), superjectio; (out), ejectio; (beyond, or over), trajectus; (under), subjectio; (in one's teeth), exprobratio; (in the mind), cogitatio; (of a dart, &c.), jaculatio; (of a skin, &c.), exuvium; (of metals), fusura; (calculation), calculatio; (vomiting), rejectio
Castinets, crepitacula
A castle, castellum, arx
A castor, jaculator; (a counter), calculus [matilo
To castrate, castro; (a book),
Casual, contingens, fortuitus
Casually, fortuitò, casu
A casualty, casus
A casuist, casuista
A cat, felis
A catalogue, catalogus
A cataract, cataracta
A catarrh, catarrhus
A catastrophe, eventus, exitus
A catch (song), cantilena; (prize), captio, præda; (hawk's lure), palpum; (of a door), obex
To catch (lay hold), arripio, capio; (overtake), assequor; (at unawares), prehendo; (snatch), rapio; (at), appeto; (hold of), apprehendo; (with a bait), inesco; (in a net), illaqueo [sus
Catching (infectious), contagio-
A catching hold of, apprehensio

To catechize, catechizo
A catechism, catechismus
A catechumen, catechumenus
Categorical, categoricus
To cater, obsono
A caterer, obsonator
A catering, obsonatus
A caterpillar, volvox
A cathedral, ecclesia cathedralis
Catholic, catholicus, universalis
Cattle (small), pecus; (great), pecus; (labouring), jumenta, orum
Belonging to cattle, pecuarius
A cavalcade, pompa equestris
Cavalry, equiratus
A caudle, sorbitio
A cave, spelunca, antrum
A caveat, cautio
Caught, apprehensus
A cavil, cavillatio, captio
To cavil, altercor, litigo
A caviller, litigator
Cavilling, rixosus, litigiosus
Cavillingly, captiosè, pertinacitèr
Cavity, concavitas, cavum
The caul, omentum; (for a woman's cap), reticulum
A cauldron, lebes
A caulker, stipator
A cause, causa; (occasion), occasio; (action in law), dica
To cause, facio, concito, gigno, incito, infero
For what cause? quamobrèm? quapropter?
For this, or that cause, idcirco, ideo
Causeless, sine causâ
A causer, effector, auctor
Caustic, causticus
To cauterize, cauterio inurere
A cautery, cauterium
Caution, cautio, prudentia, circumspectio, monitio
To caution, moneo, admoneo
Cautious, cautus, prudens, providus
Cautiously, cautè, prudentèr
To cease, cesso, intermitto, quiesco, desisto, desino
Ceaseless, perpetuus, continuus
A ceasing, cessatio, intermissio
Without ceasing, continentèr
A cedar-tree, cedrus
Made of cedar, cedrinus
To ceil, laqueo, laqueari ornare
A ceiling, laquear, lacunar
To celebrate, celebro, laudo
Celebrated (famous), celebris, illustris; (solemnized), celebratus, solennis
Celerity, celeritas
Celestial, coelestis
Celibacy, cœlibatus
A cell, cella; (friar's), mandra
A cellar, cellarium, cella
Cement, cæmentum
To cement, conjungo, consolido, coalesco
Cemented, coagmentatus
A cenotaph, cenotaphium
A censer, thuribulum, acerra
A censor, censor
Censorious, maledicus, mordax
Censoriousness, maledictio
A censure, censura, reprehensio
To censure, reprehendo, animadverto, carpo, noto
Censured, reprehensus, notatus
A censurer, animadversor
A censuring, reprehensio
A centaur, centaurus
Belonging to a centre, centralis
To center (or centre), termino

CHA — CHA — CHI

A sentinel, speculator, excubitor
A centurion, centurio
A century, centuria, seculum
A cerecloth, ceratum
Ceremonial, ceremonialis, ritualis
Ceremonious, officiosus, urbanus
Ceremoniously, officiosè, religiosè
Ceremony, cæremonia; (pomp), pompa, solemnitas; (complaisance), urbanitas
Certain, certus, compertus; (person), quidam, nonnullus; (others), alii
It is certain, constat, liquet
For certain, certè, pro certo
A certainty, certitudo
A certificate, testificatio scripta
To certify, certiorem facere
Certified, certior factus
To cease, cesso, desino
A cess, census
Cessation, cessatio; (of arms), induciæ, arum
A cession, cessio
To chafe (warm), calefacio; (vex), iram movere; (be vexed), stomachor, succenseo; (be galled), cutem atterere; (with the hand), tero, frico
A chafing, calefactio, indignatio, cutis attritus
Chafing, irâ exardescens, fricans
A chafing-dish, ignitabulum
Chaff, palea, acus
Chaffy, paleatus, acerosus
To chaffer, mercor, licitor
Chagrin, molestia, dolor
To chagrin, molestiâ afficere
A chain, catena, catenula
To chain, cateno, concateno
A chair, sella, cathedra; (easy), sella supina; (of state), thronus; (to carry one), lectica; (with elbows), solium
A chairman, lecticarius; (of a club, &c.), præses
A chaise, currus levior
A chalice, calix
Chalk, creta, calx; (pit), cretarum
To chalk, cretâ notare
Of chalk, cretaceus
Chalked, cretatus, cretâ notatus
Chalky, cretosus, cretaceus
A challenge, provocatio
To challenge, provoco; (a juryman), rejicio; (accuse), accuso
Challenged, provocatus [catio
A challenging, vindicatio, provo-
Chalybeate, chalybe mixtus
A chamber, cubiculum, camera, cubile, triclinium, thalamus
An antechamber, antithalamus
A chamberlain, cubicularius
A chamber-maid, ancilla cubicularia
A chamber-pot, matula
To champ, mando, mordeo
A champion, pugil; (of a party), antesignanus

To change (act), muto, commuto; (pass), mutor, vacio; (as the moon), renovor; (one's place), demigro
Changeable, mutabilis, instabilis, varietas, mixtus, versicolor
Changeableness, inconstantia
A changeling, ineptus, idiota
A changing, variatio, mutatio
A channel, canalis; (of a river), alveus; (narrow sea), fretum
A chanter, præcentor
A chaos, chaos
To chap, hio
A chap, rima, hiatus
The chaps, fauces
A chapel, sacellum
A chapiter, capitulum
A chaplain, capellanus
A chaplet, corona, sertum
A chapman, emptor, licitator
A chapter (of a book), caput; (in a cathedral), capitulum
A chapter-house, exedrium
A character (note), character; (description), descriptio; (letter), litera, typus; (reputation), existimatio, fama
A good character, bona fama
A bad character, mala fama
To characterise, ad vivum describere
Charcoal, carbo lignarius
A chare-woman, mercenaria
A charge (accusation), accusatio; (assault), impetus; (burden), onus; (command), mandatum
To charge (accuse), accuso; (assault), adorior; (burden), onero; (command), impero; (with, or entrust), committere fidei; (fix a price), pretium imponere; (a gun), sclopetum instruere
Chargeable (costly), sumptuosus; (burdensome), gravis, onerosus
Charged, jussus, impugnatus, accusatus, oneratus
A charger, patina; (of a gun), infundibulum
A charging, exprobratio, præceptio
A chariot, rheda, carpentum
A charioteer, auriga
Charitable, benignus, candidus
Charitably, liberalitèr, benignè
Charity (alms), eleemosyna; (love), caritas; (children), liberalitate educati liberi
A charm, incantamentum, carmen, illecebra
To charm, incanto, delecto, permulceo, delinio
A charmer, fascinator delinitor
Charming, fascinans, permulcens, eximius, suavis, jucundissimus
Charmingly, jucundissimè, blandissimè, amœnissime
A chart, charta, lineatio
A charter, charta, diploma
A chase, silva, saltus
To chase (pursue), venor, sector; (an enemy), pello; (plate, &c.), signis decorare; (forward), propello, propulso
A chasm, hiatus, chasma
Chaste, castus, pudicus, continens [nenter
Chastely, castè, pudicè, continTo chasten, castigo, punio
A chastising, castigatio
Chastity, castitas, continentia
Chat, loquacitas
To chat, garrio

Chattels (real), bona realia; personal, res personales
To chatter, garrio; (as a swallow), minurio; (with the teeth), dentibus crepitare
A chatterer, garrulus, loquax
Chattering, loquacitas, crepitus, garritus
Chartering, garrulus, crepitans
Cheap, vilis
Dog-cheap, vilissimus, pervilis
To cheapen, licitor, liceor
A cheapening, licitatio
Cheapness, vilitas
To cheat, fraudo, decipio
A cheat, fraudator, impostor
A cheat, dolus, fraus
A cheating, fraudatio
Cheatingly, subdolè, fallacitèr
To check, corripio; (restrain), cohibeo, submoneo
A cheek, reprehensio, coërcitio; (at chess), latrunculi; (of conscience), stimulus; (to prevent mistakes), cautio
Checkerwise, tessellatus; (work), opus tessellatum
A checking, objurgatio
The cheek, gena, bucca; (teeth), dentes maxillares; (bone), maxilla
Cheer, (countenance), vultus, facies; (courage), animus; (provision), dapes; (good), cœna opipara; (cheers), læti clamores
To cheer, exhilaro, lætifico; (encourage), animo, hortor; (comfort), solor
Cheerful, lætus, hilaris
Cheerfully, alacritèr, lætè
Cheerfulness, alacritas, hilaritas
Cheering, leniens, refocillans
Cheery, paulò hilarior
Cheese, caseus; (fresh), caseus recens; (cake), placenta; (monger), casei venditor
To cherish (nourish), alo; (keep warm), calefacio
A cherisher, fautor, nutritor
Cherishing, fovens, aleus
A cherry, cerasum; (stone), acinus; (tree), cerasus
Chess, ludus latrunculorum
To play at chess, latrunculis ludere
Chess-men, latrunculi
A chest, cista, arca; (of drawers), cistulæ tractiles; (for clothes), vestiarium; (for precious things), scrinium
The chest, pectus
A chesnut, castanea
A chevalier, eques
To chew, manduco, mando; (the cud), rumino
A chewing, manducatio, ruminatio
Chicane, chicanery, cavillatio
A chicken, pullus gallinaceus
To chide, objurgo, increpo
A chider, objurgator
Chiding, increpans, objurgatorius
A chiding, jurgium, objurgatio
Chief, primus, præcipuus, summus, supremus; (men), optimates, principes, primates
Chiefly, præcipuè, summè
A chieftain, imperator, coryphæus
A chilblain, pernio
A child, infans, puer, puella; (in the womb), embryo; (bastard), nothus; (nurse), alumnus [nans
Great with child, gravida, præg-

[21]

CHR

To bear a child, parturio
Childbirth, partus, nixus
Child-bearing, partus, nixus
Of a child, puerilis, ludicer
Childhood, pueritia, ætatula
Childish, puerilis, infantilis
Childishness, puerilitas
Childless, orbus
Children, liberi, proles, soboles
Chill, algidus, algosus
To chill, algeo, frigeo
Chilly, frigidè
Chilliness, algor
A chime, campanarum modulatio
To chime, modulatè pulsare
A chimera, chimæra, figmentum
Chimerical, futius
A chimney, caminus, focus; (sweeper), caminorum mundator; (piece), frons camini
A chin, mentum
The chine, vertebræ, spina; (of beef), tergum bovis; (of pork), tergum porcinum
A chink, rima; (money), pecunia
To chink, rimas agere, tinnio
A chip, segmen, assula
To chip, distringo; (with an axe), ascio, dædolo
A chipping, in frustula dissectio
Chippings, resegmina
Chips for a fire, fomes
To chirp (as a bird), minurio, pipilo; (as a cricket), strideo
Chirurgery, medicina chirurgica
A chirurgeon (surgeon), chirurgus
A chisel, scalper, celtis
Chit chat, garritus
A chattering h lla, omasum
Chivalry (knighthood), equitatus; prowess, virtus
A choice, elec io, delectus; (diversity), vari tas
Choice, adj. lectus, exquisitus
To make choice of, agere delectum
A choir, chorus
To choke, suffoco, præfoco, strangulo; (stop), obs ruo
Choked, suffocatus, strangulatus
Choler, cholera, bilis
Choleric, biliosus, morosus
The cholic, dolor cholicus
To choose, eligo, deligo, seligo, constituo, asciscao, coopto, substituo, eximo, malo, adopto
A choosing, electio
A chop, divisura, frustum; (of mutton), offula carnis ovinæ
To chop, concido; (change), permuto; (off), trunco, præcido; (about as wind), mutor
Chopped, concisus, truncus
Chopped off, truncatus, abscissus
A chopping and changing, permutatio
With chopping, cæsim
Choral, ad chorum pertinens
A chord, chorda, funis
A chorister, chorista
Chorography, chorographia
The chorus, chorus
To chouse, decipio, fraudo
Chrism, chrisma
CHRIST, CHRISTUS
To christen, baptizo
Christendom, orbis christianus
Christian, christianus
Christianity, Christianismus
Christmas, CHRISTI natale festum
Chronic, diuturnus, perpetuus
To chronicle, in annales referre
A chronicle, annales, chronica
A chronologist, chronologus

[22]

CLA

Chronology, temporum historia
A chub (clown), rusticus, villicus
Chubbed, crassus et curtus
A chuck, ictus levis
To chuck, levitèr percutere; (cast), jacio; (like a partridge), cacabo
A chuckle-head, capito
A chum, contubernalis
A chump, truncus
A church, templum, ecclesia
Church-lands, glebæ, arum
A church-warden, æditnus
A church-yard, cœmeterium
Of the church, ecclesiasticus
A churl, rusticus, sordidus
Churlish, illiberalis, truculentus
Churlishness, rusticitas, asperitas
A ch rn, cirnea
To churn, lac agitare
A churning, lactis agitatio
To chuse, eligo, seligo
The chyle, chylus
Chymical, chymicus
A chymist, alchymista
Chymistry, chymia, alchymia
Cider, succus è pomis expressus
A cincture, cingulum, zona
Cinder, cinis
Cinnamon, cinnamomum [tus
The cinque-ports, quinque portus, urbs maritima, stolo
A cipher, ciphra; (nought), nihil; (engraved), literæ inter se involutæ; (secret writing), notæ arcanæ
To cipher, arithmeticam discere
Ciphering, arithmetica
A circle, circulus, orbis; (about the moon), halo; (about the eye), iris
Half a circle, semicirculus
A circuit, circuitus, ambitus
Circular, circularis, orbicus
To circulate, circulor, terminor
Circulation, circulatio
Circulatory, circulatorius
Circumambient, circumambiens
To circumcise, circumcido
Circumcision, circumcisio
A circumference, circulus
A circumflex, circumflexus
Circumlocution, circumlocutio
To circumscribe, circumscribo
A circumscribing, or circumscription, circumscriptio [tus
Circumspect, consideratus, cauTo be circumspect, caveo, provideo
Circumspection, consideratio
Circumspectly, cautè, providè
A circumstance, circumstantia, res
Circumstantial, circumstantialis; (particular), singularis
Circumstances, res, conditio
To circumvent, circumvenio
A circumventing, deceptio
A circus, or cirque, circus
A cistern, cisterna
A citadel, arx, acropolis
A citation, citatio, prolatio
To cite, cito, accerso
A citizen, civis, municeps
A citron, malum Assyrium
A city (building), urbs, oppidum; (inhabitants), civitas
Of a city, urbanus
Civil, civilis, comis, urbanus
Civility, comitas, urbanitas
To civilize, mansuefacio
Civilly, comitèr, urbanitèr
A clack, crepitaculum; (long tongue), lingulaca, garrulitas

CLE

To clack, crepito, garrio
A clacking, crepitatio
Clad, vestitus, amictus
A claim, vindicatio
To claim, vindico, assero, arrogo, reposco
A claimant, vindicator
A claiming, vindicatio
To clamber, scando
Clammy, viscidus, viscosus
Clamminess, viscositas
Clamour, clamor
To clamour, clamo, exclamo
Clamorous, clamosus, importunus
A clan, tribus, clientela [tus
Clandestine, clandestinus, secreClandestinely, clàm, clanculùm, occultè
To clang, clango
To clank, tinnire
A clap (blow), ictus; (noise), crepitus; (of thunder), fragor; (with the hands), plausus
To clap (strike), percutio; (at a play), plaudo; (on the back), demulceo; (make a noise), strepo; (hands), plaudo; (up in prison), in custodiam tradere; (wings), alas quatere
Clap-boards, materia cadorum
A clapper, plausor; (of a bell, or door), malleus; (of a mill), crepitaculum
A clapping, plausus
To clarify, purgo, despumo, claresco
A clarion, lituus
To clash (disagree), discrepo; (make a noise), clango; (beat against), collido
A clashing, discrepatio, clangor
Clashing, collidens, dissidens
A clasp, fibula, clavicula
To clasp, infibulo, amplector; (hands), manus conjungere
A class, classis, series
Classical, classicus
To clatter, strepo, garrio, altercor, litigo
A clattering, strepitus, garritus, altercatio
A clause, clausula, sententia
A claw, unguis, ungula
To claw (scratch), scalpo; (flatter), demulceo
Clawed, unguibus laceratus
A clawing, laceratio
Claws of a fish, chelæ, arum
Clay, lutum, argilla
To clay, luto oblinere
Clayey, lutosus, argillaceus
Clean, mundus, nitidus, purus
Very clean, permundus
To clean, or cleanse, mundo, expurgo, diluo, elimo
To clean entirely, niteo
Cleanliness, mundities, nitor
Cleanly, mundè, purè
To cleanse, mundo. See to Clean
A cleansing, purificatio
Clear (bright), lucidus, perlucidus; (fair), serenus; (manifest), conspicuus; (calm), imperturbatus; (pure), limpidus; (in sound), clarus, sonorus; (without infection), integer; (without mixture), merus; (out of debt), solutus ære alieno; (in the head), sagax; (innocent), innoxius
Clear (quite), prorsùs, omninò
To clear (acquit), absolvo; (a doubt), explano; (a crime), purgo; (from), libero; (an account), rationes exæquare

CLO — COC — COL

To be clear, clareo, niteo
To clear up, claresco
Clearly, clarè, perspicuè, planè, purè, omninò, prorsùs
Clearness, nitor, serenitas, perspicuitas, claritas, sinceritas, innocentia, integritas
To cleave, findo, dehisco ; (unto), adhæreo
A cleaver, clunaculum [fissio
A cleaving (to), adhæsio; (of),
Cleaving to, adhærens
A cleft, rima, fissura
That may be cleft, fissilis
Cleft in two, bifidus
Clemency, clementia, lenitas
Clement, clemens, mitis
To clench, retundo
The clergy, clerus
Of the clergy, sacerdotalis
A clergyman, clericus
Clerical, clericalis
A clerk (clergyman), clericus; (of a parish), sacrista; (to write), scriba; (of the peace), clericus pacis; (of the market), ædilis libripens; (of the rolls), scriniarius; (to a gentleman), scriba
Clever, dexter, agilis, solers
Cleverly, dextrè, agilitèr
The clew, (of a sail), pes veli; (of thread), glomus
To click, crepito, resono
A clicking, tinnitus
A client, cliens, clientela
A cliff, rupes, petra; (in music), clavis; (of wood), frustum ligni
Climacterical, climactericus
A climate, or clime, regio, tractus, plaga, clima
A climax, gradatio
To climb, scando, ascendo, conscendo, subeo
To clinch (as the fist), contraho; (a nail), repango, inflecto
A clinching, contractio, retusio
To cling, adhæreo, cohæreo
A clink, crepo, tinnio
A clinking, crepitus, tinnitus
To clip, tondeo, obscindo, circumtondeo, præcido, diminuo; (in speech), malè pronunciare, Oscè and Volscè loqui
Clipped, or clipt, tonsus
A clipping, tonsio, præcisio
Clippings, præsegmina
A cloak, pallium, sagum
A cloak-bag, mantica
A cloak (for a fault), prætextus
To cloak, velo, dissimulo
A clock (machine), horologium; (hour), hora; (insect), scarabeus
A clod, gleba, grumus
To clod, coagulor
Cloddy, glebosus
A clog (hindrance), impedimentum; (for horses), obex; (wooden), calones; (leather), sculponeæ ex corio confectæ
To clog, impedio, obstruo, onero, præpedio
A cloister, monasterium, porticus
Close (shut), occlusus; (secret), arcanus; (dark), tenebrosus; (fast), firmus; (narrow), angustus; (near to), contiguus; (reserved), taciturnus; (thick), densus; (covetous), avarus
Close by, vicinus, propinquus, juxta, prope, propter, secundum
Close together, confertus, continuus, confertim, conjunctè
[23]

To close, claudo, concludo; (conceal), celo, taceo; (keep in), coerceo; (hedge in), sepio; (together), conjungo; (with a proposal), paciscor
A close, or inclosure, septum
Closely, tectè, densè, confertim, clanculùm, simulatè
Closeness, angustia
A closet, conclave, cella
A clot, gleba, grumus
Cloth, pannus; (of state), conopeum; (for a horse), stragulum; (hair), cilicium; (linen), linteum
To clothe, vestio, amicio
Clothes, tectè, densè, vestimentum
Clothing, vestitus
Clotted, concretus, coagulatus
A cloud, nubes
To cloud over, nube tegere
To grow cloudy, nubilo
Cloudy, nubilus, subnubilus; (weather), cælum nubilum
Clouded, undulatus, nube tectus
A clove, caryophyllum
Cloven, fissus; (footed), bifidus
Clover, trifolium pratense
A clout, pannunculus
To clout, sarcio, assuo
A clown, rusticus, colonus
Clownish, agrestis, inurbanus
Clownishly, rusticè, inurbanè
Clownishness, rusticitas
To cloy, satio, exsaturo
Cloyed, satiatus, saturatus
A club, clava, fustis; (at cards), trifolium; (meeting), compotatio, societas; (towards a reckoning), collecta, symbola
To club, symbolam conferre
Club-footed, loripes
To cluck, glocito
A clue. See Clew
Clumsily, crassè, malè
Clumsiness, ruciditas
Clumsy, inhabilis, rusticus
A cluster (of grapes, &c.), racemus; (heap), acervus
The clutches, ungues, manus
To clutter, tumultuor, concurro
A clutter, tumultus, turba
A clyster, clyster
A coach, rheda, currus
A hackney-coach, currus meritorius
A coachman, auriga [rium
A coach-house, stabulum rhedaA coadjutor, collega
To coagulate, coagulo
A coal, carbo, pruna; (pit), carbonaria fodina; (merchant), carbonarius
Of coals, carbonarius
To coalesce, coalesco
Coalition, coalitio, conjunctio
Coarse, crassus, agrestis
Coarsely, crassè
Coarseness, crassitudo
A coast, ora, limes, littus
To coast along, oram legere
A coat, tunica, vestis; (of mail), lorica; (of arms), insigne gentilitium; (of armour), paludamentum; (of a horse), setæ equinæ; (of a child), vestis puerilis
Coated, tunicatus
To coax, adblandior, demulceo
To cobble, sarcio
A cobbler, sutor, cerdo; (cobbler's shop), sutrina
A cobweb, aranea
Full of cobwebs, araneosus
Cochineal, cochinilla

A cock, gallus; (of a dial), gnomon; (of hay), fœni meta; (of a cistern), epistomium, papilla; (of a gun), serpentina; (boat), scapha; (of an arrow), crena sagittæ
Cock's crowing, gallicinium
Of a cock, gallinaceus
To cock (a hat), attollo; (hay), fœnum, in cumulos struere; (a gun), serpentinum adducere; (a bow), arcum intendere
A cockatrice, basiliscus
A cockade, vitta rosæ formâ
Cocked (as a gun), adductus; (as hay), in cumulos structus
To cocker, nimis indulgere
Cockered, mollitèr, enutritus
A cockering, indulgentia
A cocket, schedula vectigalis
A cockle, cochlea
To cockle, corrugor
A cockney, vir urbanus
A cod (husk), siliqua; (fish), asellus
A code, codex
A codicil, codicillus
To coddle, coquo, elixo
Coddled, coctus, elixus
A codlin, pomum præcox
Coefficient, coefficiens
Coequal, coæqualis
Coercion, coërcitio
Coercive, coërceus
Coessential, coëssentialis
Coetaneous, ejusdem ætatis, æqualis
Coeternal, coæternus
Coëval, coævus, ejusdem ævi
Coexistent, coëxistens
Coffee, kupha
A coffee-house, kuphipolium
A coffer, arca, capsa
A cofferer, dispensator; (to the king), quæstor ærarius
A coffin, loculus, sandapila
To cog a die, aleam componere
The cog of a wheel, deus rotæ
A cog-wheel, rota denticulata
Cogency, vis, efficacia
Cogent, cogens, efficax
Cogently, efficacitèr, importunè
Cogitation, cogitatio
Cognisance, cognitio, notitia
To have cognizance, cognosco
To take cognizance, examino
To cohabit, simul habitare
A cohabitation, convictus
A coheir, cohæres
To cohere, cohæreo
A coherence, cohærentia
Coherent, cohærens, congruens
A cohort, cohors
A coif, capitale, mitella [rare
To coil a rope, rudentem glomeCoin, moneta, pecunia, nummus, forma
To coin, cudere nummum; (feign), fingo
Coinage, monetæ percussio
Coined, cusus, fictus, signatus
A coiner, nummi cusor
Coins, numismata; (of buildings), ancones
To coincide, congruo, convenio
Coincident, conveniens
A coincidence, concursus
A coit, discus
Cold, subst. frigus, algor; adj. frigidus, gelidus, algidus
A cold, gravedo
To have a cold, gravedine laborare
To be cold, frigeo, frigesco, rigeo, rigesco, horreo, deferveo

CON

Confirmation, confirmatio
To confiscate, confisco
Confiscated, confiscatus
A confiscation, confiscatio
A conflagration, incendium
A conflict, conflictus, contentio, controversia, certamen, impetus, pugna
Confluent, confluens
A conflux, or confluence, concursus, frequentia
To conform, conformo, accommodo, morigeror, obsequor
Conformable, conformis, congruens
Conformably, congruentèr
A conformist, qui conformat
Conformity, conformitas
To confound, confundo, pessundo, perdo, permisceo, evinco, pudorem incutere
A confounder, turbator
A confounding, confusio
To confront, coràm conferre
Confronted, coràm adductus
To confuse, confundo, perturbo
Confusedly, confusè, mistìm
Confusion, confusio, pudor, labes, pernicies
A confutation, refutatio
To confute, confuto, refello
To congeal, congelo, rigeo
A congealing, concretio
To conglutinate, conglutino
To congratulate, gratulor
Congratulation, congratulatio
To congregate, congrego
A congregation, congregatio, concio
A congress, congressus, coitio
Congruity, congruentia
Congruous, congruens
Conic, Conical, conicus
Conjectural, conjecturalis
A conjecture, conjectura
To conjecture, conjicio, auguror
Conjointly, Conjunctly, conjunctìm
Conjugal, conjugalis
To conjugate, declino, inflecto
A conjugating, inflectio
A conjugation, conjugatio
A conjunction, conjunctio
Conjuncture (state of affairs), rerum status
A conjuration, conjuratio; (enchanting), fascinatio
To conjure, conjuro, conspiro, obtestor
A conjurer, magus veneficus
A conjuring, fascinatio
To connect, connecto, alligo
A connexion, connexio, nexus
Connivance, dissimulatio
To connive, conniveo, dissimulo
Connubial, connubialis, conjugalis
To conquer, vinco, subigo, debello, supero, domo
A conqueror, victor, debellator
A conquest, victoria, triumphus
Consanguinity, cognatio
The conscience, conscientia, religio
Conscientious, æquus, integer
Conscientiously, religiosè, justè
Conscientiousness, æqui reverentia
Conscious, conscius
Consciousness, conscientia
To consecrate, consecro, sacro, dedico
A consecrating, consecratio
Consent, consensus, assensus
Against my consent, me invito

[28]

CON

Without my consent, me inconsulto
With one consent, uno ore
To consent, consentio, assensio, indulgeo, annuo
Consentaneous, congruens
A consenting to, assensio
Consequence, consequentia, consecutio, momentum, utilitas
By, or of consequence, ideò, ergò
Consequently, deincèps, necessariò
Conservation, conservatio
A conservator, conservator
A conservatory, repositorium
To conserve (keep), custodio, conserve ; (with sugar), condio
To consider, considero, præmeditor, revolvo; (requite), remuneror; (regard), æstimo
Considerable, clarus, eximius, illustris, spectatus, amplus
Considerably, maximè, multò
Considerate, prudens, consultus
Considerately, consultè, pensìm
Consideration, consideratio, prudentia; (requital), compensatio; (regard), respectus, ratio; (measure), modus; (on account of), causa
Without consideration, inconsultè
Considering, cogitans
Considering that, quandò, utpotè
To consign, consigno, assigno
A consigning, consignatio
To consist, consisto, convenio, congruo, cohæreo
Consistence, stabilitas, aptaxitas, congruentia
Consistent, consonus, congruens
Consistently, congruentèr
Consisting, constans, positus
A consistory, consilium
Consolable, consolabilis
Consolation, solamen, solatium
Consolatory, consolatorius
To console, consolor, solor
To consolidate, consolido, conglutino, solidesco, solidor
A consolidating, consolidatio
Consonance, congruentia
Consonant, consonans, consecutaneus
To be consonant, consto, congruo
A consonant, consonans
A consort (wife), conjux, uxor; (companion), socius, consors; (in music), concentus
To consort with, associo
Conspicuous, perspicuous, illustris, manifestus
Conspicuously, manifestè
A conspiracy, conspiratio, conjuratio
A conspirator, conspiratus, conjuratus
To conspire, conspiro, consentio, conjuro
A constable, irenarcha
Constancy, constantia, firmitas, fidelitas, tolerantia, perseverantia
Constant (even), æquabilis, certus; (steadfast), constans, stabilis; (faithful), fidus; fidelis; (in suffering), patiens; (lasting), perpetuus
Constantly (always), sempèr, constantèr
A constellation, sidus
Consternation, consternatio
To constipate, constipo, contraho
A constipation, stipatio, suppressio

CON

A constituent, constitutor, elector
To constitute, constituo, statuo
Constituting, constituens
A constitution, constitutio
To constrain, compello, cogo
Constraint, vis, necessitas, impulsus, coërcitio
By constraint, invitè, vi, nolens volens
Without constraint, sine vi, ultrò
To construct, construo
Construction, constructio; (construing), expositio; (meaning), interpretatio
To construe, expono, explico
Consubstantial, consubstantialis
Consubstantiation, consubstantiatio
A consul, consul
A consulship, consulatus
Consular, consularis
A consultation, consultatio
To consult, consulo, delibero, consulto, provideo
Consulting, consulens, perpendens
To consume, consumo, dissipo, abeo, extabesco
To consume (devour), devoro; (diminish), imminuo; (melt), excoquo; (spoil), spolio, vasto; (time), tero
A consumer, consumptor, profligator, dissipator, exesor
A consuming, dissipatio
To consummate, consummo, perficio [fectus
Consummate, consummatus, perA consummating, consummatio
A consumption, consumptio, tabes
Consumptive, tabidus, phthisicus
A contact, contactus
A contagion, contagio, tabes
Contagious, pestiferus, tabificus
Contagiousness, via tabifica
To contain, contineo, comprehendo, reprimo, coërceo
Containing, continens, capiens
To contaminate, inquino, polluo
To contemn, contemno, sperno
A contemner, contemptor, spretor
A contemning, contemptio
To contemplate, contemplor
A contemplation, contemplatio
Contemplative, contemplativus
A contemplator, contemplator
Contemporary, æqualis
Contempt, contemptus, despectus, odium, ignominia [us
Contemptible, contemnendus, vilis
Contemptibleness, vilitas
Contemptibly, contemptim
Contemptuous, fastidiosus
Contemptuously, fastidiosè
To contend, contendo, certo adversor, propugno
Contending, contendens
A contention, contentio
A contender, certator
To content, placeo, mulceo
The content, capacitas, ambitus
Contentedness, æquanimitas
Contentedly, æquanimitèr, lenitèr
A contention, contentio, lis
Contentious, litigiosus, morosus
Contentiousness, morositas
Contentment, oblectatio
Contents of a book, caput, argumentum; (of a vessel, &c.), res contenta
To contest, contendo, litigo
A contest, lis, disceptatio
Contestable, dubitabilis

CON

A contesting, contentio
The context, contextus
A contexture, contextum
Contiguity, propinquitas
Contiguous, contiguus, adjunctus
Contiguously, strictim, pressè
Continence, continentia, pudicitia
Continent, castus, pudicus
The continent, continens
Continently, castè, pudicè
A contingency, casus
Contingent, casu accidens
A contingent, pars fœderata
Contingents, contingentia
Contingently, casû, fortuitò
Continual, perennis, perpetuus
Continually, perpetuò, continentèr
Continuance, perpetuitas, perennitas; (in a place), commoratio; (perseverance), perseverantia; (of time), progressus
A continuation, continuatio
To continue (endure), duro, continuo; (stay), maneo; (as a custom), inveterasco; (go on), pergo; (prolong), produco, protraho
A continuing, permansio
Continuing, durans, diuturnus
Continuity, continuitas
A contortion, contortio, distortio
Contraband, prohibitus, interdictus
A contract, pactum, compactum
To contract, contraho, paciscor, spondeo
A contraction, contractio
A contractor, pactor, stipulator
To contradict, contradico, adversor
Contradicting, contradicens
A contradiction, contradictio
Contradictory, contrarius
Contrariety, repugnantia
Contrariwise, contrariè
Contrary, contrarius, aversus, oppositus
To be contrary, adversor, repugno
On the contrary, contrà
A contrast, oppositio
To contrast, diverso situ ponere
A contravention, violatio
Contributary, stipendiarius
To contribute, contribuo, confero
A contributor, collator
A contribution, collatio
Contrite, contritus, tristis
Contrition, resipiscentia
A contrivance, inventio, ars
To contrive, fingo; (design), statuo, machinor
Control, reprehensio
To control (disprove), redarguo, contradico; (examine), examino, observo
A controller, inspector, curator
Controversial, ad controversiam pertinens
A controversy, controversia, lis
To controvert, discepto
Contumacious, contumax, pertinax
Contumaciously, contumacitèr
Contumacy, contumacia
Contumelious, contumeliosus
Contumely, contumelia
A contusion, contusio
To convene, cito, convoco, convenio, congregor
A convenience, commoditas, opportanitas, convenientia
Convenient, commodus, idoneus, congruens, opportunus

[37]

COP

Conveniently, commodè, aptè, opportunè
Very convenient, peridoneus
A convent (meeting), conventus; (monastery), monasterium
A conventicle, conventiculum
A convention, conventus, conventio, cœtus
Conventual, ad monasterium pertinens
To converge, vergo, deflecto
Convergent, vergens, deflectens
Conversant, versatus, exercitus; (with), aliquo familiaritèr utens
Conversation, or converse, consuetudo, usus, commercium, colloquium
To converse, versor, utor, colloquor, congredior
A conversion, conversio, mutatio, transitus
A convert, ad fidem conversus
To convert, converto, reduco
Convertible, mutabilis
Convex, convexus, gibbus
Convexity, convexitas
To convey, deduco, asporto, abduco, eripio, conveho, transmitto, importo, exporto, abalieno
A conveyance, exportatio; (deed), abalienationis instrumentum; (of water), aquæ deductio
A conveyor, abalienator; (carrier), portitor, bajulus
A conveying (away), subductio; (an estate), abalienatio; (in), inductio; (over), trajectio; (out), exportatio
A convict, convictus, evictus
To convict, convinco, evinco
A conviction, convictio
To convince, convinco, coarguo
Convincing, convictio
Convincingly, manifestè
Convivial, convivialis
A convocation, convocatio
To convoke, convoco
A convoy (guide), deductor; (guard), præsidium
To convoy, deduco
Convulsed, convulsus
A convulsion, convulsio
Convulsive, ad convulsionem pertinens
A cony (rabbit), cuniculus
To coo, gemo
A cooing, gemitus
A cook, coquus; (maid), ancilla culinaris; (room), culina; (shop), popina
To cook, coquo
Cookery, ars coquinaria
A cooking, coctio
Cool, frigidulus, frigidus
To cool, refrigero, frigesco
To cool one's courage, animum frangere
Coolly, frigidè
A cooling, refrigeratio
Cooling medicines, refrigeratoria
Coolness, frigus, cautela
A coomb, mensura quatuor modiorum
A coop, cors, cavea
To coop in, or up, obsideo, circumcingo
A cooper, doliarius
To cooperate, cooperor
A cooperating, cooperatio
A cooperator, cooperator
Coordinate, æqualis
A coot, fulica
A cop, crista, apex
A copartner, particeps
Copartnership, societas

COR

A cope, læna, pallium, feralx
To cope, colluctor, committo
A coping, colluctatio, congressio
The coping (of a house), fastigium; (of a wall), projectura
Copious, copiosus, abundans, uber
Copiously, copiosè, affatim
Copiousness, abundantia
Copped, cacuminatus, cristatus
Copper, cuprum, orichalcum
A copper, caldarium, ahenum
Of copper, ærarius, æreus
Coppers, vitriolum
A coppice, sylva cædua
To copulate, copulo, necto
A copulation, conjunctio, cœitus
Copulative, copulativus
A copy, exemplar; (transcript), apographum
To copy after, imitor, transcribo
A copying (after), imitatio; (out) descriptio
A coquet, virgo petulans
Coquetry, petulantia
Coral (the plant), coralium
A cord, funis, restis; (of wood), strues; (maker), restio
Cordage, funes
To cord up, funibus succingere
A Cordelier, Franciscanus
Cordial, cordatus, sincerus
Cordially, ex animo, sincerè
Cordials, cardiaca
A cordwainer, calcearius, sutor
Core (of fruit), cicus, volva; (of a boil), sinus ulceris
A cork-tree, suber, cortex
A cork, operculum subereum
To cork, suber immittere
Of cork, subereus
A cormorant (bird), cervus aquaticus; (glutton), helluo
Corn, far, frumentum, seges, annona, sata; (field), arvum; (ear of), spica arista
Of corn, farreus, triticeus
To reap corn, frumentor
To corn, sale condire
A corn (of salt, &c.) gramma, mica; (on the toes, &c.) callus
A cornelian, sarda lapis
A corner, angulus; (lurking-place), latibulum, latebra, recessus; (of a house, &c.), versura; (of the eye), hirquus; (of a street, &c.), compitum; (in walls), ancones
In a corner, secreto, clanculàm
A cornet (horn), buccina; (of horse), vexillifer
He that bloweth a cornet, cornicen
A cornice, corona, projectura
A corollary, corollarium
The coronation, inauguratio
A coroner, cædis quæsitor
A coronet, sertum, corolla
A corporal (officer), decurio
Corporal, corporalis, corporeus
Corporally, corporalitèr, corporè
Corporate, corporatus
A corporation (town), municipium; (company), sodalitium
A corpse, cadaver
Corpulency, corpulentia, obesitas
Corpulent, obesus, crassus
Corpuscles, corpuscula
To correct, castigo, reprehendo; (amend), elimo, emaculo, recudo
Correct, accuratus
A corrector, corrector, castigator; (of manners), censor
A correcting, or correction, co-

C 2

COV | COU | CRA

, rectio; (punishment), supplicium
Correctly, correctè, emendatà
Correctness, accuratio
To correspond (suit), congruo; (by letter), literas transmittere
Correspondence (agreement), congruentia; (commerce, or familiarity), commercium, consuetudo
Correspondent, congruens, consentaneus
A correspondent (friend), intimus; (in trade), absentis negotiorum procurator
A corridor, lorica, cortina
A co-rival, competitor
To corroborate, confirmo, firmo, roboro, ratum facere
To corrode, corrodo
A corroding, corrosio, anxietas
Corrosive, rodens, exedens
To corrupt, corrumpo, vitio, perdo, polluo, stupro, inficio, depravo, putresco, tabesco
Corrupt, malus, pravus, vitiosus, morbidus, vitiatus, contagiosus, pestilens, mendosus
A corruptor, vitiator, violator
Corruptible, corruptibilis
Corruption (of manners), depravatio, corruptio; (bribery), repetundæ; (in the body), empyema; (infection), corruptela; (rottenness), putredo
Corruptly, sordidè, purulentè
A corsair, pirata
A corse (corpse), cadaver
A corset, perizonium
A corslet, lorica
Coruscant, coruscans, rutilans
A cosmographer, orbis descriptor
Cosmographical, cosmographicus
Cosmography, cosmographia
Cost, impensa, sumptus
To cost, consto, sto
Costive, constipatus, astringens
Costiveness, alvi astrictio
Costliness, caritas
Costly, carus, sumptuosus, splendidus, magnificus
Costly, lautè
Cot, or cottage, casa; (for sheep), ovile
Contemporary, æquævus, æqualis
Cotton, gossipium
Of cotton, gossipinus
To cotton (agree), consentio
A couch, grabatus
To couch, comprehendo; (lie down), procumbo, cubo
Couchant, cubans, jacens
A couching, cubatio
A covenant, pactum, fœdus
To covenant, paciscor, depaciscor
Covenanted, pactus, depactus
A covenanting, pactio
A cover, tegmen, operculum; (pretence), prætextus
To cover, tego, velo, celo, obduco; (a bed), sterno, compono; (a mare), ineo; (a table), instruo
A covering, tegumen, velamen; (of a bed), stragulum; (of a house), tectum, imbricium; (the action), obductio; (clothing), amictus, vestitus; (hiding), prætextus
A coverlet, stragula, teges
Covert, tectus
A covert, latibulum, latebra
Covertly (closely), tectè, secretò, clam
To covet, cupio, concupisco, sitio, appeto, aveo
[28]

Coveting, cupiens, appetens
A coveting, cupiditas, libido
Covetous, cupidus, avarus, avidus
Covetousness, avaritia, auri fames
A covey, grex, pullities
A cough, tussis
To cough, tussio
A coulter, culter
A council, concilium, senatus; (ecclesiastical), synodus
Of a council, comitialis
Counsel, consilium, monitum
To counsel, consulo, moneo
A counsellor, consiliarius; (at law), juris consultus; (privy), à consiliis regis arcanis
A count, comes
To count (number), numero, computo, pernumero; (esteem), existimo, deputo, duco
A countenance, vultus, aspectus; (credit), existimatio; (encouragement, favour), auxilium, suppetiæ, favor
A stately countenance, grande supercilium
Out of countenance, confusus
To countenance, faveo, adjuvo
A counter, calculus; (for a shop), abacus, loculus; (prison), carcer
Counter, adj. contrarius; adv. è contrario, contrà, aliorsum
To counterbalance, exæquo
Counterfeit, spurius, fictitius
A counterfeit, simulatio; (person), simulator, imitator
To counterfeit, imitor, simulo, dissimulo, obtego, adultero, fingo, adumbro, repræsento
A counterfeiting, simulatio, imitatio
Counterfeiting, simulans
A countermand, mandatum contrarium
To countermine, contrariò agere
A counterpane, stragulum superius
A counterpart, antigraphum
A counterpoise, equilibrium
To counterpoise, libro, propendeo
A counterscarp, lorica
To countervail, compenso
A countess, comitissa
Counting, numerans
A counting, numeratio
A country, terra, regio; (native), patria, natale solum
The country, rus
Proper to our country, vernaculus
Of your country, vestras
Of the country, agrestis
A countryman, ruricola; (or of the same country), indigena
A country life, vita rustica
Country-like, rusticatim
A county, comitatus, ager
A couple, bini, par, duo
To couple, copulo, conjungo, jungo; (unite), unio, coeo
A coupling, copulatio
Courage, magnanimitas, virtus
Courage! macte! age!
Courageous, fortis, strenuus
Courageously, fortitèr, strenuè
A courier, nuncius, cursor
A course (turn), vicissitudo; (way, or means), via, ratio; (running), cursus; (custom), mos; (order), series; (of water), ductus
To course (hunt), sector
A courser, veredus, sonipes
Courses (of the moon), invectiones; (of women), menses

A court (yard), area, atrium; (of law), curia; (of a prince), regia, palatium; (of equity), cancellaria; (roll), archivum; (days), dies fasti
To court, solicito, ambio
A courtier, aulicus
Courteous, urbanus, civilis, candidus, beneficus, affabilis
Courteously, comitèr, affabilitèr
A courtesan, meretrix, scortum
Courtesy, urbanitas, lenitas, comitas, benignitas
A courtesy, beneficium, officium
Courtliness, civilitas
Courtly, indulgens
Courtship, ambitus, solicitatio
A cousin, affinis, consanguineus
A cow, vacca, bos, juvenca
Of a cow, bovillus, vaccinus
A coward, timidus, ignavus
To cow, timorem injicere alicui
Cowed, timore affectus
Cowardice, timiditas
Cowardly, ignavè, timidè
To cower, se incurvare
A cowl, cucullus; (a tub), dolium
Coy, protervus, fastidiosus
To be coy, modestiæ studere
Coyly, fastidiosè, cautè
Coyness, fastus, fastidium
To cozen, decipio, fallo
Cozenage, fraus, dolus
A cozener, fraudator
A cozening, fraudatio, deceptio
A crab (fruit), arbutum; (fellow), morosus; (fish), cancer; (stick), fustis arbuteus
Crabbed, acerbus, torvus, morosus; (obscure), obscurus, difficilis
Crabbedly, austerè, morosè
Crabbedness, austeritas, torvitas
A crack (flaw), rima, fissura; (noise), crepitus; (boaster), jactator
To crack, collido, rumpo, findo, crepo, crepito; (flaw), fatisco; (one's credit), conturbo; (boast), glorior; (burst), dissilio
Crack brained, insanus, cerritus
Cracked, pertusus, comminutus
A cracker (boaster), jactator, gloriosus; (of gunpowder), sclopus, pyrobolum; (of nuts), nucifrangibulum
A cracking, crepitatio, crepitus, jactantia
A cracknel, collyra
A crackling, crepitus
A cradle, cunabula, cunæ; (of iron), craticula
Craft (cunning), astutia; (trade), ars; (trick), dolus
A handicraft, ars mechanica
A craftsman, artifex
Craftily, callidè, astutè
Craftiness, calliditas, astutia
Crafty (sly), vafer; (cunning) callidus; (deceitful), subdolus
A crag, petra, rubes
The crag (neck), cervix
Craggy, petrosus, inæqualis
To cram, farcio; (together), constipo; (poultry), sagino
Crammed, saginatus, fartus
A cramming, saginatio, fartura
The cramp, spasmus, torpor
To cramp (squeeze), contorqueo, convello; (restrain), coerceo
Cramp, adj. duriusculus
A cramp-iron, subacus ferrea
To cranch, dentibus frangere
A crane (bird), grus; (to raise

CRI   CRU   CUN

up goods), sucula, grus; (pipe to draw liquors), sipho
Crank (brisk), lætus; (of a wall), sucula
A cranny, fissura, rima
Crape, pannus camelinus tenuis
A crash, fragor, stridor
To crash, frango, strideo
Crassitude, crassitudo
A cravat, collare
To crave, rogo, postulo, efflagito, rogito, imploro
A craving, aviditas, rogatus
Craving, avidus, rabidus
Cravingly, avidè, cupidè
The craw, avis ventriculus
To crawl, serpo, repo; (with lice), vermino, vermiculor
Crawling, repens, reptilis
A crawling, reptatio
A cray-fish, cancer
Crazed (broken, or weak), fractus, confectus; (mad), insanus; (sickly), infirmus, imbecillis
Craziness, imbecillitas, debilitas
To creak, strideo, crepo
Creaking, stridulus
A creaking, crepitus, stridor
Cream, lactis flos; (of a jest), joci medullæ
A crease, plica
To crease, plico
To create, creo, condo
Creative, creans
A creating, or Creation, creatio
A creator, creator, procreator
A creature, creatura; (living), animal; (of a great man), cliens
Credence (belief), fides
To give credence, credo, fidem habere
Credentials, auctoritates
Credible, credibilis
Credibility, probabilitas
Credibly credibilitèr
Credit (authority), auctoritas; (reputation), fama; (belief), fides; (in traffic), fides
Of credit, honorificus
To credit, confido, credo, decoro
To grow in credit, innotesco
Creditable, honorificus
Creditableness, honor, decus
A creditor, creditor
Credulous, credulus
Credulity, credulitas
The creed, symbolum fidei
A creek, sinus, crepido
To creep, serpo, repo; (into favour), insinuo; (fawn), adulor; (unawares), subrepo
Creeping, repens, reptilis
A creeper, focarius
A creeping, reptatio, subreptio
Crept (in falsely), surreptitius
Cresses, nasturtium
A crest, crista, apex; (of an helmet), galeæ pinna; (of a horse), juba; (of a coat of arms), apex galeatus
Crested, cristatus
A crevice, fissura, rima
A crew, grex
A crib, præsepe
A crick, tetanus, spasmus
A cricket (insect), grillus; (stool), sella humilior; (play), ludus baculi et pilæ
A crime, crimen, delictum, flagitium, facinus
Criminal, criminalis; (person), noxius, sons, reus; (action), facinus, indignum, flagitium
Crimson, coccum
Of crimson, coccineus
[29]

To cringe, serviliter inclinare
Cringing, venerabundus
A cringing, veneratio servilis
A crinkle, ruga, sinus
To crinkle, corrugo, plico
Full of crinkles, flexuosus
A cripple, claudus, silicernium
To cripple, debilito
Crisis, crisis
Crisp (brittle), fragilis; (curled), crispatus, tortus
To crisp, crispo, torqueo
A crisping-iron, calamistrum
A critic, criticus, censor
Critical, criticus, censorius; (dangerous), periculosus
Critically, accuratè
Criticism, critice, notatio
To criticise, carpo, noto
To croak (as a raven), crocito; (as a toad), coaxo
Croaking, crocitans, murmurans
A croaking, crocitatio
A crock (earthen pot), olla fictilis; (soot), fuligo
A crocodile, crocodilus
Crocodile tears, fictæ lacrymæ
A croe, vectis ferreus
A crony, congerro, amiculus
A crook, harpago, hamus; (shepherd's), pedum
To crook, incurvo, inflecto, flecto; (become crooked), curvesco, curvor
Crookedness, curvitas, curvamen
A crop (of corn), messis; (boldness), audacia; (of a bird), ingluvies
To crop, carpo, decerpo
Cropsick, crapulâ gravis
A crosier, pedum episcopale
A cross, crux; (disappointment), infortunium; (monument in the way), stela
Cross (contrary), adversus, perversus; (athwart), transversus; (peevish), morosus; (untoward), pervicax
To cross (disappoint), frustror; (vex), exagito; (over), trajicio, transeo; (out), oblitero, deleo
A cross-bow, balista
A crossing, repugnantia, frustratio, trajectio, obliteratio
Crossly, perversè, morosè
Crossness, pervicacia
A crotchet (in music), semiminima; (in printing), hamulus quadratus; (idle), ineptiæ; (trick), techna
To crouch, succumbo, adulor
A crouching, demissio, adulatio
A crow, cornix, corvus; (iron), vectis ferreus
To crow (as a cock), cano, canto; (boast), glorior
Cock-crowing, gallicinium
A crowd (fiddle), fidicula
A crowd, frequentia, turba
To crowd, premo, arcto, stipo
A crowder, fidicen
A crowding, stipatio
A crown, corona, diadema; (of the head), vertex; (of money), coronatus, scutum; (kingdom), regnum
To crown, corono, coronâ ornare
A crucible, vas fusorium
A crucifix, Christi crucifixi imago
To crucify, crucifigo
A crucifixion, crucis supplicium
Crude, crudus, indigestus
Crudity, cruditas
Cruel, crudelis, dirus, atrox, sanguineus, cruentus

To be cruel, sævio, ferocio
Cruelly, crudelitèr, ferocitèr
Cruelty, crudelitas, sævitia
A cruet, ampulla, lecythus
A cruise (cup), pocillum
To cruise, circumnavigo
A cruiser, navis circumnavigans
A crum, mica
The crum, medulla panis
To cram, frio, comminuo
To crumble, frio, contero
Crummy, micis abundans
A crumple, ruga, plica
To crumple, corrugo
Crumpled, rugosus, tortilis
A crupper, postilena
The crupper, clunis
Crural, cruralis
A cruse, simpulum, phiala. See *Cruise*
A crush, contusio
To crush, contundo, comminuo, opprimo, everto
A crushing, contusio, oppressio
A crust, crusta, crustum
To crust, crusto, incrusto
Crusty (crabbed), tetricus, morosus
A crutch, scipio, fulcrum
Crutches, gralla
To cry, clamo, vociferor, exclamo, ejulo, vagio, clamito; (up), laudo; (down), diffamo; (for help), imploro; (against), objurgo; (lament), ploro; lamentor; (weep), lacrymor, fleo
A cry, clamor, ejulatus
Cryed, clamatus, publicatus
A cryer, præco, clamator
Crying, lamentans, flens
A crying, ploratus, fletus; (of infants), vagitus; (of hounds), canum fatratus
Crystal, crystallus
Crystalline, crystallinus
A cub, catulus, proles
To cub, catulos parere
A cube, cubus
Cubical, cubicus
A cubit, cubitus, ulna
A cuckold, curruca
A cuckoo, cuculus
A cucumber, cucumis
The cud, ruma, rumen
To chew the cud, rumino
A cudgel, fustis, baculus
To cudgel, fuste cædere
Cudgelled, fustigatus
A cue, occasio, ingenium
A cuff, ictus, plaga; (on the ear), colaphus; (on the face), alapa; (sleeve), manica
To cuff, pugnis cædere
A cuirass, lorica
A cuirassier, eques cataphractus
Culinary, culinarius
To cull (choose), eligo, deligo
A cullender, colum
A cully, delusus, fatuus
Culpable, culpandus, culpâ dignus
A culprit, culpa præstò est, reus
To cultivate, colo, foveo
A cultivation, or culture, cultus, cultura
A culver, columba
To cumber, onero, præpedio
Cumbersome, impediens, onerosus
Cumbersomeness, molestia
A cumbrance, impedimentum
To cumulate, accumulo
Cunning, peritia, versutia
Cunning (in a good sense), doc-

C 3

CUS   DAL   DAS

tus, peritus, expers; (crafty), astutus, vafer, versutus
A cunning man, augur; (trick), dolus, techna
Cunningly, vafrè, doctè, peritè
A cup, poculum, scyphus, crater; (of a flower), calyx
A cup-bearer, pincerna
A cupboard, abacus, cella
To cup, cucurbitulas imponere
In his cups, inter pocula
Cupid, Cupido, Amor
Cupidity, cupiditas, aviditas
A cupola, turricula rotunda
A cupping-glass, cucurbitula
Curable, sanabilis, medicabilis
A curate, sacerdos vicarius
A curacy, vicarii munus
To curb, fræno, reprimo, domo, cohibeo, coërceo
A curb, coërcitio; (of a well), margo; (for a horse), lupatum, frænum munitum
Curd, coagulum, lac pressum
To curdle, concresco, congelor
Curdling, coactio, coagulatio
A cure (remedy), remedium, medela; (of a wound), sanatio; (charge of souls), cura animarum; (benefice), beneficium ecclesiasticum [dire
To cure, sano; (fish), sale condio
A curing, sale conditura
Curiosity, curiositas, studiosa indagatio; (rarity), res rara
Curious, curiosus, accuratus, elegans, nitidus, anxius
Curiously, curiosè, nitidè, captiosè, ad amussim
A curl of hair, cirrus
To curl, crispo, torqueo
A curling-iron, calamistrum
A cur, canis vallaticus
Currants, uvæ Corinthiacæ
Currency, cursus, tenor
Current, genuinus, probus; (price), pretium commune; (year), annus vertens; (coin), probus nummus
A current, profluens, cursus
Currently, vulgò
Curried (as a horse), strigili defricatus; (as leather), maceratus, politus
To curry (a horse), defrico; (leather), macero; (favour), blandior
A curry-comb, strigilis
To curse, maledico, devoveo, execror, anathematizo
A curse, imprecatio; (of the church), anathema
Curses, diræ
Cursing, maledicens, maledicus, execrans
A cursing, maledictio
Cursorily, obitèr, perfunctoriè
Cursory, levis, præceps
Curst, dirus
To curtsy, poplitem flectere
To curtail, decurto, minuo
A curtailing, decurtatio
A curtain, velum ductile; (before a stage), cortina theatri; (in fortification), facies, or frons aggeris
A curvature, curvatura
A curve, linea curvata
A curvet, saltus, exultatio
A cushion, pulvinar; (for pins), spinularium
A cusp, cuspis, mucro
A custard, artolaganus
Custody, custodia, carcer; (ward), tutela

[30]

Custom (use), consuetudo, mos, usus; (fashion), præscriptum, institutum; (habit), habitus
Customable, usitatus, solitus; (tribute), vectigal; (trade), negotium, emptorum frequentia
Customary, consuetus, usitatus
Customarily, usitatè, assiduè
A custom-house, telonium; (officer), publicanus, portitor
A customer, emptor
To cut, seco, scindo, incido; (as the teeth), erumpo; (mangle), mutilo; (asunder), rescindo; (off), amputo; (the hair), tondeo; (the nails), reseco; (hew), diffindo; (away), execco; (with an axe), ascio; (capers), tripudio; (down), cædo; (corn), fruges metere; (geld), emasculo; (grave), cælo, sculpo; (in), incido; (off), abscindo; (off an heir), exhæredo; (off a speech), sermonem dirimere; (off a head), detrunco; (out), excindo, exseco, disseco; (the throat), jugulo; (in two), discindo
A cut, scissura; (blow), ictus; (slice), offula; (gash), plaga, vulnus
A cut-throat, sicarius
Cut, sectus, scissus
Cuticular, Cutaneous, cuticularis
A cutlass, sica, acinaces
A cutler, faber cultrarius
Cutleta, segmina
A cutter, sector, sculptor
A cutting, consectio
Cutting (in taste), asper, acer; (in words), mordax, acerbus
Cuttings, segmenta
The cycle, cyclus
A cylinder, cylindrus
Cylindrical, cylindricus
A cymbal, cymbalum
Cynical, cynicus
A cypress-tree, cupressus
Of cypress, cupresseus
A czar, imperator
A czarina, imperatrix

D.

A dab (blow), ictus; (of dirt), labecula; (of fat), frustulum
A dab (one skilful), peritus
To dabble, crebrò immergere manus aquæ; (one's clothes), vestes lutare; (meddle without skill), imperitè tractare
A dabbling, frequens ablutio
A dace, spua
A dactyl, dactylis
Dad, daddy, tata, papa
A daffodil, narcissus
A dagger, pugio, sica
To daggle, collutulo
Daggled, lutosus
Daily, adj. quotidianus
Daily, adv. quotidiè, indies
Dainty, delicatus; (brave), elegans; (costly), opiparus; (excellent), eximius; (squeamish), fastidiosus
Daintily, delicatè, lautè
Daintiness (of feeding), dapes; (loathing), expedia
A dairy, lactarium
A daisy, bellis
A dale, vallis
Of a dale, vallestris

Dalliance, lusus, lascivia
A dallier, nugator
To dally (be wanton), blandior, palpo; (trifle), nugor; (play the fool), ineptio, lascivio; (delay), cuncto; (with one), indiflcor, ludo
Dallying, blandus, lascivieus
A Dallying, nugæ, petulantia
A dam (mother), mater; (bank), agger, moles; (of planks), pila; (of a mill), stagnum, claustrum
To dam, oppilo, obstruo
Damage, damnum, incommodum, injuria, noxa, detrimentum, jactura
To damage, lædo, damnum inferre
Damageable, damnosus, noxius; (liable to receive damage), caducus, fluxus, obnoxius
Damask, sericum Damascenum
To Damask, calfacio
A dame, domina, hera
To damn, damno, explodo
Damnable, dirus, execrabilis
Damnation, damnatio
Damnably (very greatly), magnoperè
To damnify, damnum inferre
A damp (vapour), exhalatio tetra
To damp (moisten), humido, humesco; (discourage), animum frangere
Damp, humidus, mucidus
A dampness, humor
A damsel, puella, virgo
A dance, chorea, saltatio
To dance, salto, tripudio
A dancer, saltator, saltatrix
A dancing, saltatio, tripudiatio; (room), orchestra
To dandle, manibus gestare
Dandriff, furfures
Danger, discrimen, periculum
To be in danger, periclitor
Dangerous, periculosus, perniciosus
Out of danger, securus
Dangerously, periculosè
To dangle, dependeo, comitor
Dangling, pendulus
Dank, Dankish, humidus
Dapper, agilis, acer
To dare (venture), audeo; (challenge), lacesso, provoco
Daring, audax, intrepidus
A daring, provocatio
Daringly, audactèr, impavidè
Dark, tenebrosus, (blind), cæcus; (intricate), obscurus, ænigmaticus
Darkness, tenebræ, obscuritas; (of weather), caligo
To Darken, obscuro, caligo, obnubilo; (one's meaning), sensum turbare
Darkish, subobscurus, creperus
Darkly, obscurè, absconditè
A darling, deliciæ
Darling, gratus, amatus
To darn, reservio, reficio
A darning, sutura
Darnel, lolium
A dart, jaculum, telum
To dart, jaculor; (or come suddenly upon), subitò irruere
A darting, jaculatio
A dash (stroke with the pen), ductus; (mixture), mixtura
To dash (against), allido, incutio, illido, impingo; (sprinkle), aspergo; (mix), diluo, commisceo; (overthrow), everto; (or

DEA — DEC — DEF

strike out), exeutio, oblitero, deleo
Dashed against, allisus, illisus
A dastard, pusillanimus, timidus
Dastardly, timidè, ignavè
A date (of writing), tempus scribendi; (account of time), æra; (fruit), dactylus; (tree), palma
To date, diem subscribere, do
Out of date, exoletus
Dative, dativus
To daub (smear), oblino; (defile), inquino; (bribe), largitione corrumpere; (disguise), dissimulo; (flatter), adulor; (cover with), orno
A daubing, unctio, adulatio
A daughter, nata, filia; (in law), nurus; (god-daughter), filia lustrica; (step-daughter), privigna
To daunt, terreo, perterreo
Dauntless, impavidus, intrepidus
A daw, monedula
To dawn, illucesco, dilucesco
The dawn, diluculum
A day, dies; (light), lux, lumen
To-day, hodiè, hodierno die
Of this day, hodiernus
Every day (daily), quotidianus
Day by day, in singulos dies
The day before that, pridiè
The day after that, postridiè
In the day-time, luci
Of a day, diurnus, dialis
The day breaketh, lucescit
Before day, antelucanus
Sunday, dies Dominicus; (Monday), dies Lunæ; (Tuesday), dies Martis; (Wednesday), dies Mercurii; (Thursday), dies Jovis; (Friday), dies Veneris; (Saturday), dies Saturni
A holy-day, feriæ, festum
It is day, lucet
The space of two days, biduum; (three days), triduum; (four days), quatriduum
To dazzle, præstringo
Dazzled, præstrictus, attonitus
Dazzling, fulgidus, coruscans
A deacon, diaconus
A deaconry, diaconatus
Dead, mortuus, defunctus; (dull), segnis, iners; (numbed), torpidus; (senseless), exanimis; (flat), marcidus; (drink), vappa; (almost), semianimis; (drunk), vino sepultus
To be dead, diem obire
Deadly, lethaliter
Deadly, lethalis, funestus
Deadness, stupor, torpor
Deaf, surdus
To deaf, or deafen, surdum reddere, obtundo
To be deaf, surdeo, obsurdesco
Deafish, surdaster
Deafness, surditas
A deal-tree, abies
A deal (in number, or quantity), vis, numerus; (at cards), distributio
To deal, ago, distribuo; (falsely), prævaricor; (in business), mercor, negotior, paciscor, stipulor
By a great deal, multò
A dealer, mercator; (at cards), distributor; (falsely), prævaricator
Dealing (trade), occupatio; (doing), factum; (at cards), distributio; (treatment), tractatio
A dean, decanus
A deanery, decanatus

[31]

Dear (beloved), charus, dilectus; (costly), carus, pretiosus
Dearly, carè, quamplurimò
Dearness, caritas
A dearth, caritas, fames
Death, mors, interitus, lethum; (slaughter), nex, occisio, clades
A death-watch, ternes
Deathless, immortalis, æternus
To debar, privo, arceo
A debarring, privatio, exclusio
To debase, demitto, submitto, depravo, adultero
A debasing, depressio
A debate (in law), actio, lis; (friendly), colloquium; (strife), disceptatio, altercatio, contestio
To debate (discourse), arguo, dissero, disputo, discepto; (advise), delibero; (quarrel), contendo, altercor, litigo
A debating, disputatio, deliberatio
To debauch, vitio, stupro, corrumpo; (in drink), debacchor
A debauch, ingurgitatio vini
A debaucher, corruptor
Debauchery, nequitia
A debauchee, homo libidinosus
A debenture, tessera nummaria
To debilitate, debilito, enervo
Debilitation, debilitatio
Debility, debilitas
Debonair, comis, lætus, benignus
A debt, debitum, æs alienum
In debt, ære alieno premi, obæratus
A debtor, debitor
A decade, decas
The decalogue, decalogus
A decampment, castrorum motus
To decant, elutrio, transfundo
A decanter, lagena vitrea
To decay, declino, deficio; (grow obsolete), obsoleo; (with age), senesco; (in colour), defloresco; (as flowers), marcesco; (utterly), pereo
A decay, labefactio, ruina
Decaying, labens, caducus
A decease, decessus, mors
A deceit, fraus, dolus
Deceitful, subdolus, dolosus
Deceitfully, dolosè, ambiguè
Deceitfulness, fallacia
To deceive, fallo, decipio, fraudo, ludo, deludo, inesco, frustror
A deceiver, fraudator
Deceiving, fallens, fallax
December, December
Decemviral, decemviralis
The decemvirate, decemviratus
Decency, decor, decorum
Decennial, decennalis
Decent, decens, decorus
Decently, decenter, decorè
Deception, deceptio
Deceptive, fallax, dolosus
To decide, decido, decerno, dirimo
Decided, decisus, finitus, judicatus
A deciding, or Decision, decisio
Decimal, denarius
To decimate, decimo
To decipher, explico, describo
Decisive, decretorius, determinatus
The deck, transtra, fori
To deck, orno, exorno
A decking, ornatus, cultus
To declaim, declamo
A declaimer, declamator
A declamation, declamatio
Declamatory, declamatorius
A declaration, declaratio; (testi-

mony), testimonium; (at law), libellus; (of war), denunciatio
To declare, denuncio, nuncio, nuncupo, divulgo, narro; (one's mind), eloquor
A declension, declinatio
A decline, defectio, tabes
Declining, decrescens, restiuus
To decline (avoid), vito; (bend backwards), vergo; (a word grammatically), declino, inflecto; (decay), labasco, deficio
A declining, devitatio, declinatio, flexio
Declivity, declivitas
A decoction, apozema
To decorate, decoro, exorno
A decoration, ornamentum
A decorum, decorum, gratia
To decoy, illecebra, illex
To decoying, illecebratio
To decrease, decresco, minuo
Decreasing, decrescens
A decrease, diminutio
To decree (ordain), decerno, impero; (purpose), statuo
A decree (judgment), sententia; (of state), decretum, edictum; (of wise men), placitum; (act), consultum; (award), arbitrium; (purpose), propositum
Decrepit, decrepitus, incurvus
Decretal, decretorius
Decretals, decretalia
To decry, defamo, infamo
Decried, abrogatus, sugillatus
Decuple, decuplus
To dedicate, dedico, dico
A dedication, dedicatio
To deduce, deduco, colligo
Deducible, quod colligi potest
To deduct, subtraho, detraho
Deduction, deductio, illatio
A deed (action), factum, actum; (good), benefactum; (ill), flagitium; (instrument), instrumentum; (in war), res gesta
Indeed, sanè, manifestò
To deem, judico, existimo
Deep, altus, profundus; (close), reconditus; (cunning), versutus
The deep, profundum
To deepen, defodio, excavo
Deep, or Deeply, profundè, altè
Deepness, profunditas, altitudo
A deer, cervus, fera
To deface, deformo, expungo
A defacer, deletor, corruptor
A defacing, deformatio
A defalcation, defalcatio, deductio
A defamation, defamatio
Defamatory, famosus
To defame, calumnior, infamo
A defamer, calumniator
A defaming, calumnia
A default, culpa, defectus
To defeat, frustror, eludo, vinco, prosterno, rescindo
A defeat, clades, strages
A defeating, frustratio
A defect (want), defectus; (fault), mendum; (blemish), vitium; (in judgment), imprudentia
A defection, defectio
Defective, imperfectus, vitiosus
To be defective, deficio, desum
Defectiveness, defectus
A defence (guard), præsidium, tutamen; (protection), patrocinium, tutela; (in pleading), defensio
In the defence of, pro, a, ab
Defenceless, inermis, imparatus

C 4

DEL   DEM   DER

To defend, defendo, tueor, præmunio, patrocinor
A defendant (in law), reus
A defender, vindex, defensor, advocatus, patronus
Defensive, ad tegendum
To defer, differo, procrastino
Deference, cultus, honor
A deferring, dilatio, mora
Defiance, provocatio
A deficiency, defectus
Deficient, imperfectus, hiulcus
To defile, contamino, inquino, vitio, stupro, incesto, profano, conspurco, oblino ; (march troops), copias traducere
A defile, via angusta, or difficilis
A defiler, corruptor, temerator
A defiling, pollutio
To define, definio, describo
A definition, definitio
Definitive, definitus, decretorius
Definitively, definitè
To deflower, stupro, vitio
A deflowering, stupratio, violatio
A defluxion, defluxio
To deform, deformo, vitio, turpo
Deformity, deformitas
To defraud, defraudo, fraudo
A defrauder, defraudator
A defrauding, fraudatio
To defray, erogo, præbeo
A defraying, erogatio
Defunct (dead), mortuus
To defy, provoco
A defying, provocatio
To degenerate, degenero
Degenerated, degener
A degenerating, Degeneracy, decessio
Degradation, Degrading, dejectio
To degrade, dejicio, depono, exauctoro, abdico
A degree, gradus, ordo, status
By degrees, gradatim, sensim, paulatim
Dehortatory, dissuadens
To be dejected, doleo, mœreo
Dejectedly, mœstè, tristè
Dejection, Dejectedness, mœror
Deification, consecratio
To deify, deum facere, in divos referre
Deified, divus factus
A deifying, apotheosis
To deign, dignor
A deigning, dignatio
A deity, numen, deitas
A delay, Delaying, mora, tarditas, cunctatio, retardatio, dilatio
To delay, differo, procrastino, moror, produco
A delayer, cunctator
Delaying, morans, cunctabundus
Delectable, delectabilis, amœnus
Delectation, obiectatio
To delegate, delego
A delegate, delegatus
Deleterious, letalis, perniciosus
A deletion, deletio, expunctio
Delf (earthen), terreus ; (mine), fodina
To deliberate, delibero
Deliberate, cautus, circumspectus, consideratus, prudens, deliberatus
Deliberately, cautè, prudentèr
Deliberation, deliberatio
Deliberative, deliberativus
Delicacy, venustas, cupedia, elegantia, mollities
Delicate, pulcher, elegans, venustus, concinnus, eximius, exquisitus, acutus, delicatus, mollis, tener

[33]

Delicately, delicatè, exquisitè
Delicateness (delicacy), mollitia
Delicates, cupediæ, dapes, deliciæ, lautitiæ
Delicious, delicatus, suavis
Deliciously, delicatè, opiparè
Deliciousness, suavitas
Delight, voluptas, suavitas, delectatio, oblectatio
To delight, delecto, oblecto
To be delighted, oblector
Delightful, gratus, jucundus
Delightfulness, delectatio
Delightfully, jucundè, suavitèr
To delineate, delineo
A delineating, delineatio, adumbratio
Delinquency, delictum, culpa
A delinquent, delinquens, noxius
Delirious, delirus, mente captus
To deliver (to), trado ; (out of), libero ; (from), eripio ; (a speech), pronuncio ; (by tradition), trado ; (into one's hand), in potestatem dedere, or tradere ; (as a midwife), obstetricor ; (to memory), transmitto ; (up), resigno ; (betray), prodo
A deliverance, liberatio, redemptio, puerperium
To be delivered (of a child), pario
A deliverer, liberator, vindex
A delivery, or delivering, liberatio, vindiciæ ; (of goods), traditio ; (utterance), pronunciatio ; (of a woman), partus
A dell, fossa
To delude, deludo, irrideo, derideo, illudo, inesco
A deluder, illusor
A deluding, Delusion, delusio, irrisio, irrisus, derisus
Deluding, Delusive, Delusory, fallax, fraudulentus, irrisus
Delusions, præstigiæ, technæ
To delve, fodio, pastino
A deluge, inundatio, diluvium
A demagogue, antesignanus
A demain, Demesne, possessiones, patrimonium, reditus
A demand (claim), rogatum, postulatum ; (question), petitio
To demand (require), requiro, postulo, interrogo ; (claim), posco, vindico ; (a debt), exigere debitum
A demander, postulator
Demanding, postulans
A demanding, interrogatio
To demean, gero
A demeanour, habitus, mores
Demerit, meritum
A demi-god, semideus
Demise (death), mors, obitus
To demise (let), loco, eloco ; (give), dono, lego
Democracy, democratia
Democratical, democraticus
To demolish, demolior, diruo
Demolished, dirutus, eversus
A demolisher, eversor, subversor
A demolishing, Demolition, demolitio
A demon, dæmon
Demoniacal, dæmoniacus
Demonstrable, demonstrabilis
Demonstrably, manifestè, clarè
To demonstrate, demonstro, probo
Demonstration, demonstratio
A demonstrating, demonstrativus
Demonstratively, evidentissimè
A demonstrator, demonstrator
Demure, verecundus, taciturnus
Demurely, modestè, pudicè

Demureness, verecundia
A demur, Demurrer, exceptio, mora
To demur, demoror, cunctor
A demurring, judicii dilatio
A den, antrum, latibulum, specus, latebra, caverna, spelunca
A denial, repulsa, recusatio
A denizen, civis, civitate donatus
To denominate, denomino
A denominator, denominator
A denominating, or Denomination, denominatio
To denote, denoto, designo
To denounce, denuncio, edico
A denouncing, declaratio, indictio
Dense (thick), densus, cavernosus
Density, densitas
A dent (notch), crena
To dent, crenas incidere
Dental, dentatus
Dented, serratus
A denunciation, denunciatio
A dentifrice, dentifricium
To deny, nego, denego, abnego, abjuro, recuso, detrecto, dejero, pernego
To depart, discedo, abscedo, recedo, abeo, exeo, emigro, ucedo, digredior ; (die), morior, decedo
A departing, or Departure, discessus, abitus, demigratio, profectio
A department, munus
To depend upon, pendeo, nitor
Dependent, dependens, nixus
A dependent, cliens
A dependence (prop), fulcrum ; (trust), fiducia
To depict, depingo
Deplorable, deplorandus, flebilis
To deplore, deploro, lamentor
Deploring, deploratus
A deploring, ploratus
A deponent, testis juratus ; (verb), verbum deponens
To depopulate, depopulor, vasto
Depopulation, Depopulating, vastatio
A depopulator, vastator
To deport, gero
Deportment, gestus, mores
To depose, exauctoro ; (upon oath), jurejurando affirmare
To deposit (lay down), depono ; (give in trust), committo
A deposit, depositum
A deposition, testimonium
To deprave, depravo, corrumpo
Depravity, pravitas
To deprecate, deprecor
A deprecating, deprecatio
To depreciate, despicio, diminuo
Depreciated, despectus, vilis
Depredation, spoliatio, rapina
To depress, deprimo, reprimo
A depression, depressio, oppressio
To deprive, privo, spolio, orbo, eripio ; (of authority), abrogo ; (disinherit), exhæredo ; (of life), exanimo, animâ spoliare
A depriving, privatio, orbatio
Depriving, privans
Depth, profunditas, altitudo
Depurate (cleansed), depuratus, defæcatus
Depuration, depuratio
A deputation, legatio
To depute, assigno, delego
A deputy, legatus, vicarius ; (of a ward), tribunus populi ; (lord-deputy), prorex, proconsul
Dereliction, derelictio, desertio

DES   DEV   DIE

To deride, derideo, irrideo
A derider, derisor, irrisor, sannio, minus
Deriding, dicteria conjiciens
A deriding, derisio, irrisio
Derisive, scurrilus, ludicabilis
Derivation, derivatio, deductio; (of words), etymologia
Derivative, derivatus, dednctus
To derive, derivo, deduco; (from) procedo, orior
To derogate, derogo, detraho
Derogating, Derogatory, derogans
Derogation, derogatio, detractio
To descant, alludo, commentor
To descend, descendo; (from one), deducere genus ab; (to the bottom), subsido
Descendants, posteri
Descended (sprung), ortus, oriundus
Descending, descendens, declivis
A descending, descensus
A descent (offspring), progenies, prosapia; (invasion), invasio, descensio; (of a hill, &c.), declivitas, descensus
To describe, describo, delineo, depingo, exprimo
A describer, descriptor
A describing, description, descriptio
Descried, exploratus, repertus
To descry, speculor, exploro
A descrying, conspectus
A desert, deserta, eremus
To make desert, vasto, populor
To desert, desero, derelinquo
Desert (merit), meritum
A deserter, transafuga, desertor
Desertion, desertio
To deserve, mereo, mereor, promereor, commereor
Deservedly, meritò, dignè
A design (purpose), consilium; (first draught of), designatio, diagramma; (model), ichnographia; (plot), inceptum
To design, designo, machinor, constituo, assigno
Designedly, consultò, cogitatò
A designer, designator, delineator
A designing, designatio
Designing (craft), versutia
Desirable, desiderabilia, optandus
Desire (wish), desiderium; (request), rogatus, obsecratio
To desire (wish), desidero, cupio, opto; (request), oro, peto, supplico, expeto, imploro, flagito, obsecro
By desire, optatò, precariò
Desiring, expetens, cupiens
A desiring, obsecratio, cupiditas
Desirous, avidus, cupidus
With desire, avidè, cupidè
To desist, desisto, desino
A desk, abacus, pluteus
Desolate, desertus, afflictus
To make desolate, depopulor
Made desolate, devastatus
Desolately, moestè, lugubrè
Desolation, depopulatio, ruina
Desolateness, moeror, ægritudo
To despair, despero, despondeo
Despair, desperatio
Despaired of, desperatus
A despairing, desperratio
A desperado, vesanus, perditus
Desperate, temerarius, periculosus
Desperately, perditè, periculosè
Desperateness, audacia, desperatio
Despicable, aspernandus, vilis
Despicableness, vilitas

[23]

Despicably, cum contemptu
To despise, contemno, sperno
To be despised, contemnor
Despised, contemptus, spretus
A despiser, contemptor
A despising, despicientia
Despite, invidia, despectus
In despite, ingratiis, se invito
Despiteful, malignus, invidus
Despitefully, contumeliosè, malignè [dia
Despitefulness, malignitas, invi-
To despoil (spoil), spolio
To despond, animum demittere
Despondency, desperatio
Desponding, despondens
A despot, dominus, præses
Despotic, arbitrarius, summus
Despotically, imperiosè
The dessert, bellaria
To destine, destino, designo
Destination, destinatio
Destiny, fatum, sors
The destinies, parcæ
Destitute, inops, egens, derelictus, orbatus, orbus, egenus
Destitution, destitutio
To destroy, consumo, aboleo, deleo, extinguo, conficio, diruo, everto, destruo, perdo, corrumpo, subverto, vasto, populor, depopulor, deprædor, dilapido
A destroyer, vastator, deletor
Destroying, exitialis, exitiosus
A destroying, perditio, pernicies, excidium, demolitio
Destruction, strages, exitium, interitus, ruina, labes, internecio, populatio, clades, cædes
Destructive, exitiosus, exitialis
Destructively, perniciosè
Desultory, desultorius
To detach, mitto, seligo
A detachment, manus segregata
To detail, recito, enumero
A detail, enumeratio
To detain, moror, detineo, retineo, præpedio
To detect, detego, patefacio
A detecting, patefacio, indicium
Detention, retentio
To deter, deterreo
Detergent, detergens
Determinate, determinatus, certus
Determinately, præcisè, definitè
A determination, determinatio
To determine, statuo, constituo, decerno, decido; (end), definio, dirimo, concludo, compono, expedio; (be ended), cesso; (judge), dijudico; (beforehand), præfinio; (bachelor), gradum baccalaureatûs capessere [tivus
Determining, constituens, defini-
Detersive, detergens
To detest, detestor, abominor, fastidio, odi [lis
Detestable, detestabilis, execrabi-
A detestation, detestatio
Detesting, detestans, abominans
To dethrone, de solio deturbare, dejicere, or depellere
To detract from, detraho
Detracting, Detractive, maledicus
Detractingly, maledicè
Detriment, damnum
Detrimental, damnosus
Devastation, vastatio
To develope, patefacio
To devest, spolio, exuo
To deviate, devio, erro
A deviating, Deviation, error

A device, dolus, fabula, commentum, inventio
The devil, diabolus, dæmon
Devilish, diabolicus
Devious, devius, avius
To devise, excogito, machinor, fingo, formo, præmeditor; (imagine), hariolor; (bequeath), lego, do, relinquo
A devisee, legatarius
A deviser, inventor, testator
A devising (inventing), machinatio
Devoid, vacuus, inanis
Devoir, munus, officium
To devolve, devolvo; (a trust), committo
To devote, devoveo, addico
A devotee, nimis devotus
A devoting, devotio, addictio
Devotion, pietas, cultus
Devotional, ad caltum pertinens
To devour, devoro, prodigo; (oppress), opprimo
A devourer (of meat), helluo, gulosus; (of his fortune), prodigus
Devouring, devorans, edax, vorax; (flesh), carnivorus
A devouring, voracitas, edacitas
Devouringly, avidè, gulosiùs
Devout, pius, religiosus, sanctus
Devoutly, piè, religiosè, sanctè
Devoutness, pietas, sanctitas
Deuteronomy, deuteronomium
The dew, ros
To dew, irroro, roresco
Mildew, rubigo, melligo
Dewy, roscidus, rorulentus
Dew-falling, roratio
Dexterity, dexteritas, agilitas
Dexterous, expeditus, agilis, solers
Dexterously, expeditè, agiliter
Diabolical, diabolicus
A diadem, diadema, corona
Diagonal, diagonalis
A diagram, diagramma
A dial, horologium; (of the sun), sciothericum, solarium
A dialect, dialectos
A dialogue, dialogus
Diameter, diametros
Diametrical, diametricus
Diametrically, directè; (opposite), ex diametro oppositus
A diamond, adamas; (at cards), rhombus; (cut), angulatus
Of a diamond, adamantinus
Diaper, sindon variegata
Diaper-work, striatura
Diaphoretic, diaphoreticus
The diaphragm, diaphragma
A diarrhea, diarrhœa
A diary, diarium, ephemeris
A dibber, or dibble, pastinum
Dice, aleæ, tesseræ; (box), fritillus; (player), aleator
To dictate, dicto, præscribo
Dictates, dicta, præcepta
A dictator, dictator
Dictatorial, dictatorius
Dictatorship, dictatura
Diction, dictio
A dictionary, dictionarium, vocabularium, thesaurus linguarum, lexicon
To die, morior, obeo, intereo, occido, concido, occumbo, immorior, expiro; (away in a fit), animo linqui; (as liquors), vappesco
To die (colour), tingo.
Like to die, moribundus
A die (dice), alea

C 5

A diet (food), cibus, cibaria (course of food), victus, regimen, diæta; (of the empire), imperii conventus
To diet, diætam præscribere; (food), cibo aliquem sustinere; (board), pacto pretio in convictum admittere
To differ, differo, discrepo, disto dissideo, dissentio
A difference (unlikeness), differentia, discrepantia; (distance), distantia, discrimen; (controversy), lis, dissensio
Different, Differing, diversus, discrepans, dispar, dissimilis
To be different from, dissono
Differently, dissimiliter, variè
Difficult, difficilis, arduus; (person), morosus, fastidiosus
Difficultly, difficiliter, ægrè
Difficulty, difficultas, res angustæ, arduum; (of speech), linguæ balbuties, or titubantia
Diffidence, diffidentia
Diffident, diffidens, incredulus
Diffidently, diffidenter
To diffuse, diffundo, dispergo
Diffusive, largus, exundans
Diffusively, diffusè
Diffusiveness, diffusio, dispersus
To dig, fodio, confodio, effodio
To digest, digero, dispono; (meat), concoquo, digero
A digesting, digestio
Digestive, digestorius
Digged, fossus, pastinatus
A digger, fossor
A digging, fossio, effossio
A digit, digitus, pollex
Dignified, ornatus, nobilitatus
To dignify, orno, nobilito
A dignitary, dignitarius
Dignity, dignitas, honor
To digress, digredior, excurro
A digression, digressio
A dike, scrobs, fossa
To dilacerate, dilacero, dilanio
To dilapidate, dilapido, vasto
Dilapidations, damnum
To dilate, dilato, extendo, amplifico, produco
Dilatorily, cunctanter, tardè
Dilatoriness, cunctatio, mora
Dilatory, cunctans, dilatorius
A dilemma, dilemma. See *Difficulty*
Diligence, diligentia, solertia, cura, assiduitas, studium, obsequium, celeritas
Diligent, diligens, industrius, laboriosus, obsequiosus
To be diligent, satago, evigilo
Diligently, diligenter, sedulò
To dilucidate, dilucido, illustro
Dilucidation, explicatio
To dilute, diluo, tempero
Dim, obscurus, caliginosus
To dim, obscuro, præstringo
To grow dim, obscuror
Dimsighted, caligans, luscus
A dimension, dimensio, mensura
To diminish, diminuo, minuo
A diminishing, *or* Diminution, diminutio, extenuatio
Diminutive, parvus, diminutus
A diminutive, diminutivum
Diminutively, diminutivè
Dimissory, dimissorius
Dimly, obscurè, obtusè
Dimness, caligo, hebetudo
A dimple, gelasinus
A din, clamor, sonitus
To make a din, strepo
To dine, prandeo

A dining-room, cœnaculum
To ding, allido, obtundo
A dingle (vale), convallis
A diuner, prandium
A dint, impressio, vis
To dint, contundo
A diocesan, episcopus
A diocese, diocesis
To dip, tingo, mergo
Dipt, dipped, immersus; (as an estate), oppignoratus
A diphthong, dipthongus
A dipping, submersio, intinctus
Dire, dirus, horridus, atrox
Direct, directus, rectus
To direct, dirigo, moderor, ordino, inscribo, appello, tendo, ostendo, monstro, doceo, instruo, præcipio, jubeo, mando
Direction, directio, inscriptio, gubernatio, jussum
Directly, directè, expressè
A director, rector
A directory, directorium
Direful (dire), dirus, sævus
A dirge, nenia, carmen funebre
A dirk, mucro
Dirt, lutum cœsum
Dirtily, lutosè, fœdè, turpiter, sordidè, iniquè, indignè
Dirtiness, sordes, iniquitas
Dirty, cœnosus, fœdus, sordidus
To dirty, conspurco, inquino
To disable, debilito, mutilo
To disaccord, discordo
Disadvantage, incommodum
Disadvantageous, incommodus
Disadvantageousness, incommoditas
Disadvantageously, incommodè
To disaffect, improbo, alieno
Disaffection, offensio, aversatio
To disagree, dissideo, discordo, dissentio, non congruere
Disagreeable, dissentaneus, ingratus, inconveniens, injucundus
Disagreeableness, incongruitas
Disagreeably, injucundè, illepidè
Disagreeing, discors, diversus
A disagreeing, *or* disagreement, diversitas, discrepantia; (falling out), dissensio, discordia
To disallow, improbo, culpo
A disallowing, improbatio
To disannul, dissolvo, rescindo
A disannulling, abolitio, abrogatio
To disappear, evanesco
Disappearing, evanescens
To disappoint, frustror, fallo
Disappointment, frustratio
Disapprobation, improbatio
To disapprove, improbo
To disarm, exarmo, spolio
To disarray, exuo, prodigo
A disaster, infortunium, casus
Disastrous, infaustus, infelix
Disastrously, in faustè, infeliciter
To disavow, diffiteor, nego, rejicio, improbo
A disavowing, negatio
To disband, exauctoro, dimitto
A disbanding, dimissio
Disbelief, diffidentia
To disbelieve, diffido, non credere
Disbelieving, incredulus, diffisus
To disburden, exonero, levo
To disburse, impendo, erogo
A disbursing, erogatio [pensa
A disbursement, expensa, impensa
To discard, dimitto, rejicio
Discarded, exauctoratus, rejectus
To discern, discerno, distinguo, dignosco, conspicor, video

Discernible, dignoscendus
Discernment, dijudicatio, judicium
Discerning, perspicax, sagax
A discharge, absolutio, liberatio; (of humours), detractio; (of duty), functio
To discharge (money), acceptam pecuniam referre; (one's conscience), exonero, libero; (a gun), displodo; (a debt), solvo; (from a fault), absolvo; (exempt), eximo; (release), dimitto; (out of office), exauctoro; (one's duty), fungor, præsto, exequor; (an obligation), remuneror; (a ship), exonero; (the stomach), evomo; (itself, as a river), defluo
A discharging (from a fault), absolutio; (from service, &c.), dimissio; (paying), solutio; (of a gun), displosio
A disciple, discipulus
Discipline, disciplina, institutio
To discipline, doceo, instituo; (punish), punio, castigo
To disclaim, renuncio, abdico
To disclose, revelo, detego
To be disclosed, patesco, patesco
To discomfit, fundo, profligo
A discomfiture, strages, clades
To discommend, vitupero, culpo
To discommode, incommodo
Discommoded, incommodo affectus
To decompose, turbo, perturbo, confundo; (the mind), excrucio, inquieto, ango
Discomposure, perturbatio, confusio; (of mind), anxietas
To disconcert, concilia frangere
Disconcerted, fractus, perturbatus
Disconsolate, afflictus, tristis, mœstus
Discontent (sorrow), mœstitia; (disgust), offensio
To discontent, offendo, ango
Discontentedly, ægrè, molestè
Discontentment, anxietas
A discontinuation, *or* discontinuance, intermissio, desuetudo
To discontinue, intermitto
Discord, discordia, dissonantia
Discordant, discors, dissonus
To discover (reveal), detego; (accomplices), edo; (one's nakedness), pudorem profanare; (espy), conspicor; (find out), deprehendo, exploro; (*or* betray counsels), concilia enunciare
Discoverable, indagabilis
A discoverer, explorator, indagator
A discovery (invention), investigatio, inventio; (revealing), indicium, patefactio
To discount, detraho, remitto
Discount, subductio, detractio
To discountenance, inhibeo
To discourage, deterreo, frango
A discouragement, animi abjectio; (hindrance), impedimentum
To discourse, dissero, confabulor
A discourse, sermo, oratio, narratio, confabulatio; (idle), nugæ; (dry), loquela jejuna
Discredit, dedecus, ignominia
To discredit (disgrace), infamo; (not to believe), partum credere
Discreet, prudens, consultus
Discreetly, prudenter, consultò

[84]

DIS — DIS — DIS

Discreetness, prudentia, consilium, circumspectio
Discretionary (unlimited), interminatus
Discretion, arbitrium, jus. See also *Discreetness*
Discretive, discretivus
To discriminate, distinguo
To discuss, exploro, discutio, explico
A discusser, investigator
A discussing, discussio
Disdain, fastidium, contemptus
To disdain, dedignor, fastidio
A disdainer, contemptor
Disdainful, superciliosus, elatus
Disdainfully, contemptim, fastidiose
A disdaining, dedignatio
A disease, morbus
Diseased, æger, ægrotus
To disembark, è navi descendere
To disembogue, defluere in mare
Disencumbrance, liberatio
To disengage, extrico, libero
To disentangle, expedio, libero
Disesteem (disdain), fastidium
Disesteemed, contemptus, spretus
To disfavour, deformo
To disfigure, deformo, mutilo
A disfiguring, deformatio
To disfranchise, proscribo, privo
To disgorge, evomo, ejicio
A disgorging, evomitus, ejectio
Disgrace (shame), dedecus; (disfavour), offensa; (misfortune), infortunium, calamitas
To disgrace, dedecoro, deturpo
Disgraceful, dedecorus, turpis
A disgracing, calumnia, traductio
Disgracefully, turpiter
To disguise, celo, dissimulo
A disguise, larva, persona; (pretence), species, pretextus
Disguised, larvatus, ebrius
A disguising, dissimulatio
A disgust, fastidium, nausea
To disgust, displiceo, offendo
To be disgusted, indignor
A dish, patina, discus, lanx; (clout), peniculus; (of meat), ferculum, dapes
To dish (meat), patinis instruere; (out a table) mensas instruere
Dished up, patinis instructus
Dish-water, colluvies
A dishabille, vestis cubicularis
To dishearten, animum frangere
A disheartening, animi abjectio
Disherison, exhæredatio
To disherit, exhæredo
Dishevelled, passus
Dishonest, pravus, turpis, lascivus
Dishonestly, inhonestè, impurè
Dishonesty, fallacia, obscœnitas
Dishonour, dedecus, infamia
To dishonour, dehonesto, traduco
Dishonourable, inhonestus, turpis [piter
Dishonourably, inhonestè, turpiter
Disinclination, aversatio, odium
Disinclined, abhorrens
Disingenuity, illiberalitas [uus
Disingenuous, illiberalis, inurbanus
To disinherit, exhæredo
A disinheriting, exhæredatio
To disentangle, extrico, explico
Disinterested, incorruptus, integer [tegrè
Disinterestedly, incorruptè, integrè
To disjoin, disjungo, segrego
A disjunction, disjunctio
Disjointed, dissectus, deartuatus, disjunctus, luxatus
[35]

To disjoint (cut up, as a fowl), disseco; (separate), disjungo; (put out of joint), luxo
Disjunctive, disjunctivus
A disk, corpus apparens
A diskindness, noxa, injuria
To dislike, aversor, abhorreo
A dislike, fastidium
Disliked, fastiditus, rejectus
A disliking, aversatio
A dislocating, luxatio
To dislodge, hospitio aliquem expellere; (a camp), castra movere; (a deer), cervum excitare
Disloyal, perfidus, infidus
Disloyally, perfidiosè, impudicè
Disloyalty, perfidia, proditio
Dismal, dirus, horridus, atrox
Dismally, dirè, horridè
To dismantle, diruo, spolio
To dismay, territo, perterrefacio
A dismay, perturbatio
To dismember, deartuo, lacero
To dismiss, dimitto, exauctoro
A dismission, dimissio
To dismount (unhorse), equo aliquem excutere; (alight), ex equo desilire; (a cannon), tormentum rotis eximere [sio
A dismounting, dejectio, descensio
Disobedience, contumacia
Disobedient, contumax, inobsequens
Disobediently, contumaciter
To disobey, repugno, negligo
A disobeying, recusatio, neglectus
To disoblige, lædo, offendo
Disobliging, incivilis, acerbus
Disorder (confusion), confusio, perturbatio; (distemper), morbus, ægrotatio; (of mind), animi perturbatio
To disorder, confundo, conturbo, perturbo, turbo
Disorderly, inordinatè, inconditè
Disorderly, *adj.* confusus, infamis, dissolutus, immoderatus
Disorders (tumults), turbæ
To disown, nego, abnego, abdico, repudio
A disowning, abdicatio, negatio
To disparage (defame), obstrecto
A disparagement, dedecus
A disparager, obtrectator
A disparity, disparitas
Dispassionate, æquus, placidus
Dispatch, expeditio, properatio; (packet of letters), literarum fasciculus
To dispatch (accomplish), perficio, perago; (hasten), accelero, maturo; (send), mitto, ablego; (kill), occido, interficio; (out of the way), amando; (discharge), absolvo
A dispatcher, perfector
A dispatching, transactio
To dispel, dispello
A dispensation (distribution), administratio, dispensatio; (indulgence), exemptio, immunitas, licentia
A dispensatory, pharmacopœia
To dispense (distribute, *or* lay out), dispenso, erogo, distribuo; (with), indulgeo; (with the laws), leges relaxare
A dispenser, dispensator
A dispensing, dispensatio
A dispensing power, laxandi potestas
To dispeople, depopulor, vasto
To disperse, dispergo, spargo

A dispersion, dispersio
To dispirit, animum frangere
A dispiriting, animi debilitatio
To displace (a thing), dimoveo, submoveo; (a person), exauctoro
A displacing, amotio
To display (spread), expando; (declare), expono; (make a show of), jacto, ostento; (carve), disseco, deartuo
A displaying, explicatio
To displease, displiceo, offendo
To be displeased, indignor
Displeasing, ingratus, injucundus
Displeasure (distaste), offensa; (grudge), ira, simultas
To despoil, despolio, spolio
Disport, lusus, jocus
Disposal, dispositio, ordo, potestas, arbitrium
To be at one's own disposal, esse sui potens
To dispose (set in order), dispono, ordino, compono; (bestow), præsto; (lay out), expendo, insumo; (to some use), destino, assigno, utor; (by will), lego; (by gift), largior; (sell), vendo; (place out), eloco; (settle), constituo; (to another), alieno, transfero; (incline), præparo, paro
A disposer, ordinator, dispensator
A disposition (setting in order), dispositio, ordinatio; (inclination), indoles, animus, ingenium; (rule, *or* order), constitutum, decretum; (habit of body), habitudo; (of mind), affectus, affectio animi
To dispossess, detrudo, ejicio, dejicio, exuo
A dispossessing, ejectio
Disposure, potestas, arbitrium
Dispraise, vituperatio
To dispraise, vitupero, obtrecto
Disprofit, incommodum
A disproof, refutatio, confutatio
Disproportion, inæqualitas
Disproportionable, impar, dispar
Disproportionably, inæqualiter
Disproportioned, inæqualiter partitus
To disprove, refuto, confuto
A disproving, refutatio
Disputable, disputabilis
A disputant, disputator, dialecticus
A disputation, *or* Dispute (debate), disputatio, contentio; (quarrelling), jurgium, controversia
To dispute, disputo, ratiocinor, contendo, litigo, assero, vindico; (fondly), nugor
A disputing, disputatio
Disqualified, inhabilis, impar
To disqualify, inhabilem reddere
Disquiet, cura, solicitudo
To disquiet, inquieto, vexo
A disquisition, disquisitio
Disregard, despectus, contemptus
To disregard, negligo, sperno
To disrelish, improbo, nauseo
Disreputable, inhonestus
Disrepute, mala fama
Disrespectful, fastidiosus
Disrespectfully, fastidiosè
To disrobe, vestem exuere
Dissatisfaction, offensa, molestia
Dissatisfactory, molestus, gravis
Dissatisfied, offensus, dubius
To dissect, disseco, incido
A dissection, dissectio

C 6

To dissemble, dissimulo, simulo, tego, celo, obtendo
A dissembler, simulator, fictor
Dissembling, dolosus, fictus
A dissembling, simulatio
To disseminate, dispergo, spargo
A dissension, dissensio, discordia
To dissent, dissentio, dissideo
Dissentaneous, minimè conveniens [tista
A dissenter, dissentiens, separa-
A dissertation, discertatio
Disservice, damnum, noxa
Disserviceable, inutilis
To dissever, separo, sejungo
Dissimilar, dissimilis
Dissimilitude, dissimilitudo
Dissimulation, simulatio, dolus
Dissipable, dissipabilis
To dissipate, dissipo, disperdo
A dissipation, dissipatio
Dissoluble, dissolubilis
To dissolve, dissolvo, resolvo; (society), dissipo; (melt), liquefacio; (be dissolved), liquesco, liquefio
A dissolving, dissolutio
Dissolute, dissolutus, prodigus, remissus, negligens
Dissolutely, prodigè, remissè
Dissoluteness, luxuries, luxuria
A dissolution, dissolutio
Dissolution (death), obitus
Dissonance, discrepantia
Dissonant, dissonans, dissonus
To dissuade, dissuadeo, dehortor
A dissuader, dissuasor [sio
A dissuading, Dissuasion, dissua-
Dissuasive, dissuadens
A distaff, colus, penum
To distain, imbuo, inquino
A distance, intervallum, distantia; (discord), dissidium
At a distance, procul, longo intervallo
To distance, vinco, supero
Distant, distans, dissitus
Far distant, longinquus
To be distant, absum
To distaste, offendo, displiceo
A distaste, offensa
To take distaste, offendor
Distasteful, ingratus, molestus
A distemper, morbus, ægrotatio
Distempered, infirmus, morbidus, insanus, demens, languens
To distend, distendo [sio
A distending, Distension, disten-
A distich, distichon
To distil, stillo, elicio
A distilling, distillatio; (of rheum), defluxio, defluxus
Distilled, stillatus, expressus
A distiller, distillator
Distinct (different), distinctus, discretus, diversus ; (clear), distinctus, clarus, articulatus
Distinctly, distinctè, clarè
A distinction, distinctio
Distinctive, distinguens
Distinctness, pronunciatio distincta
To distinguish, discerno, intelligo, dignosco, eniteo
Distinguishing, distinguens, dignoscens
To distort, distorqueo, torqueo
A distorting, Distortion, distortio
To distract, turbo, furio
Distraction, confusio, dementia
To distrain, distringo
Distress, afflictio, angustiæ
To distress (distrain), arresto tenere ; (perplex), ango, premo
To be distressed, premor, laboro
[36]

Distressedly, miserè, calamitosè
Distressedness, miseria, calamitas
To distribute, distribuo, dispertio
A distributing, Distribution, distributio, partitio, dispensatio
Distributing, Distributive, distribuens
Distributively, divisè, partitè
A district, districtus, jurisdictio
Distrust, diffidentia
To distrust, diffido, suspicor
Distrustful, suspicax, suspiciosus
Distrustfully, diffidentèr, suspiciosè
Distrustfulness, diffidentia
To disturb, turbo, perturbo, impedio, moror, inquieto, excrucio, interpello
A disturbance, tumultus, turba
A disturber, interpellator
A disturbing, inquietatio
A disunion, separatio
To disunite, disjungo, dissocio ; (to be disunited), disjungor
A disuniting, disjunctio
Disusage, Disuse, desuetudo
To disuse, desuesco
A ditch, fossa, scrobs, lacuna, vallum, incile
To ditch, fossam ducere
A ditcher, fossor
A ditching, fossura
Dithyrambic, dithyrambicus
A ditty, cantilena, canticum
To divaricate, divarico
To dive (in water), demergo, urino ; (into business), scrutor, investigo, exploro
A diver, urinator
Divers, diversus, varius, multiplex ; (colours), multicolor, variegatus ; (shapes), multiformis ; (kinds), multigenus, multimodus ; (ways), multifariàm ; (humours), morosus
Diverse, diversus, absimilis
Diversified, variatus
To diversify, vario
A diversifying, variatio
A diversion (turning aside), digressio, digressus; (recreation), animi relaxatio, or oblectatio
Diversity, diversitas, varietas
Diversely, diversè, variè
To divert (turn aside), diverto, averto; (entertain), oblecto
A diverting, digressio
Diverting, jucundus, facetus
To divide, divido, partior, cerno, discedo, segrego
A dividend (in the stocks), pecunia, or summa dividenda; (in arithmetic), numerus dividendus
A divider, divisor
A dividing, divisio, partitio
A divination, divinatio, prædictio ; (the act), auguratio
Divine, divinus, cœlestis
A divine, theologus
Divinely, divinè, divinitùs, piè
A diviner, vaticinator
To divine, divino, vaticinor ; (enchant), incanto, fascino ; (guess), conjicio
A diving, urinatio
Diving, immergens in aquam
A divining, divinatio
Divinity, theologia
Of divinity, theologicus
The divinity, Deitas, Numen
Divisible, divisibilis, dividuus
Divisibility, divisabilitas
Division, divisio, partitio, distributio ; (of parties), factio,

seditio ; (strife), discordia, dissensio ; (in music), modulatio, cantillatio
A divisor, divisor
A divorce, divortium, repudium
To divorce, repudio, dimitto
A divorcer, repudiator
A divorcing, repudiatio
Diurnal, diurnus
A diurnal, diarium, ephemeris
To divulge, vulgo, pervulgo
A divulger, vulgator
A divulging, divulgatio
Divulsion, direptio
Dizziness, vertigo
Dizzy, vertiginosus, cerebrosus
To do, ago, facio, efficio ; (amissa), erro, pecco ; (accomplish), exequor, perago
Docile, Docible, docilis, capax
Docility, docilitas
A dock (for ships), navale, naupactum ; (herb), labathum, bardana, rumex, hippolapathum, hydrolapathum
To dock, or cut off, amputo
A doctor, doctor
A doctorship, doctoris gradus
Doctrinal, ad doctrinam pertinens
Doctrine, doctrina, eruditio
A document, documentum
To dodge, tergiversor
A dodger, prævaricator
A dodging, cunctatio
A dodkin, teruncius
A doe, dama femina
A doer, actor, effector
A dog, canis, catulus
Dog-cheap, vili pretio ; (dog-days), dies caniculares ; (kennel), canile
The dog-star, sirius
Of a dog, caninus
To dog one, à tergo sequi
A doge, dux
Dogged, doggish, caninus, morosus, cynicus, protervus
Dogged (followed), à tergo observatus
A dogger, navicula
Doggrel, ludicrus, inconditus
A dogma, dogma, placitum
Dogmatical, dogmaticus, fidens
Dogmatically, fidentèr
A doing (of something), actio ; (deed), factum
Doing, agens, moliens
A dole, donatio, largitio
Doleful, lugubris, tristis
Dolefully, lugubritèr
Dolefulness, luctus, tristitia
A doll, pupa
A dollar, thalerus
Dolorous, luctuosus, tristis
A dolphin, delphinus
A dolt, stipes, hebes
Doltish, stupidus, insulsus
Doltishness, stupor, stupiditas
A dome, basilica, fastigium
Domestic, domesticus, familiaris
Domination, dominium
To domineer, dominor, insulto
Domineering, insolens, arrogans
A domineering, insolentia
Dominical, dominicus
Dominion, dominium, ditio
To have dominion, dominor
A donation, donum, donativum
A donor, dator, donator
A doom, judicium, fatum
To doom, adjudico, condemno
Doomsday, dies novissimus
A door, ostium, janua, fores ; (back), posticum ; (folding),

DOW — DRE — DRO

valvæ; (case), hypothyrum; (poets), antea; (keeper), ostiarius, janitor
From door to door, ostiatim
Doric, Doricus
Dormant (sleeping), dormiens; (hidden), celatus, latens; (unimproved), servatus; (unactive), consopitus
To lie dormant, lateo, celor
A dormitory, dormitorium
A dormouse, glis
A dose, potio, dosis
A dot, punctiuncula
To dot, punctiunculis notare
Dotage, deliratio, delirium
Dotal, dotalis
A dotard, delirus, senecio
To dote, deliro, desippio; (upon, *or* love), depereo, deamo
Doted upon, deamatus
Doting, delirans, delirus, vecors
Dotingly, anilitèr, insanè
Dotish, delirabundus
Double, duplex, geminus
A double, *or* fold, plica
The double, duplum
To double, duplico, gemino; (cape), prætervehor; (one's fist), comprimere digitos
A double-dealer, velerator
Double-chinned, duplicato mento præditus; (hearted), fallax; (tongued), mendax, bilinguis, fallax
A doublet, subucula
A doubling, duplicatio, geminatio
Doubly, duplicitèr
A doubt, dubium, scrupulus
To doubt, dubito, hæsito, fluctuo, hæreo; (suspect), suspicor; (keep in suspense), suspendo
Without doubt, proculi dubio
Doubtful, dubius, anceps, incertus
Doubtfully, ambiguè, dubiè
Doubtfulness, ambiguitas, dubitatio
A doubting, dubitatio, hæsitatio
Doubtless, certè, certissimè
A dove, columbus, columba; (ring), palumbes; (stock), palumbus; (turtle), turtur; (house), columbarium
Like a dove, columbaris, columbinus
Dove-tail, compages, cardo
Dough, farina subacta
Doughty, fortis, validus
Dowager, vidua nobilis
Dowerless, indotata
Down, lanugo; (of flowers, &c.), pappus; (of feathers), lana
Of down, lanuginosus
A down (green hill), grumus; (plain), planities
The downs, tumuli arenarii
Down, *adv.* deorsùm
Down, *adj.* tristis, severus, nebulosus, mœstus, declivis, vergens, pronus, ad inopiam redactus
Right down, perpendicularis
Down to, usquè ad
Downright, simplex
Downward, deorsùm
Up and down, ultrò citròque
A downfall, casus, lapsus, ruina
Downhill, declivis, præceps
To bear down, prosterno, obruo
To bring down (humble), coërceo
Downy, mollis, tener
[37]

A dowry, dos, dotalitium
Given in dowry, dotalis
Having a dowry, dotata
Having no dowry, indotata
A dowse, alapa
A doxology, doxologia
A doxy, meretrix
To doze, sopio, soporor
A dozen, duodecim, duodeni
A drab, scortum, scrapta; (cloth), pannus crassior
Draff, siliquæ, segisterium
A drag, harpago; (net), tragula
To drag, traho, rapto
Dragging, trahens, raptans
To draggle, collutulo
Draggled, collutulatus
A draggle-tail, mulier sordida
A dragon, draco
A dragoon, eques sclopetarius
A drain, fossa, elicium
To drain, desicco
To be drained, exsiccor
A draining, exsiccatio
A drake, anas mas
A dram (in weight), drachma; (of spirits), haustus
A drama, drama, fabula
Dramatic, dramaticus
A dramatist, fabularum scriptor
A draper, pannarius; (woollen), lanarius; (linen), linteo
Drapery, panni textura; (in painting), voluta
A draught (first copy), exemplar; (of a will), formula; (pull), nisus, tractus; (of drink), haustus; (of a net), jactus; (privy), forica, latrina
Draughts, ludus latrunculorum
Draught, jugalis
Quick-draught, facilis, citus
To draw, traho, duco; (allure), allicio, pellicio; (a bill), chorographum mittere; (a circle), circulum ducere; (beer, &c.), promo; (*or* sweep along), verro; (asunder), detraho; (away), abstraho, subduco, averto; (back), retraho; (back), tergiversor; (back, *or* refuse), detrecto; (blood), detraho; (a bow), flecto, tendo; (breath), respiro; (lots), sortior; (in writing), describo; (as a painter), adumbro, delineo, pingo, depingo; (down forces), daco; (the eyes upon), converto
Drawers, subligacula
Drawing along, trahens
Drawing (with a pencil), adumbrans, delineans, describens
A drawing (away), secessio; (back), retractatio. See *to Draw*
A drawing, lineatio
To drawl, lentè proferre
Easily drawn, ductilis, ductitius
A dray, traha, tragula
A drayman, trahæ auriga
Dread, pavor, formido
To dread, metuo, expavesco
Dreaded, Dread, formidatus
Dreadful, horrendus, tremendus
Dreadfully, horrificè
Dreadfulness, horror
Dreadless, intrepidus
A dredging, timiditas, pavor
A dream, somnium; (idle fancy), nugæ, deliramentum
To dream, somnio, deliro
A dreamer, somniator
Dreaming, somnians, somniosus; (slow), tardus, tardigradus, tardipes, tardiloquus

Dreamingly, oscitantèr, somniculosè
Dreary, mœstus, horridus
Dregs, fæx, recrementum; (of oil), amurca; (of vinegar), oxygion; (of wine), floces; (of sugar), pargamenta; (of the people), sordes, sentina, fæx; (of a distemper), reliquiæ
Cleared from dregs, defæcatus
Dreggy, fæculentus
To drein (drain), eliquo
A drench, salivatum
To drench, potionem medicam dare; (dip in), immergo, repleo
Dress, ornatus, vestitus, cultus
To dress (adorn), orno, como; (put on), indao; (a horse), depecto; (hemp), carmino; (leather), macero; (cloth), polio; (a dead body), pollincio; (meat), coquo; (a tree), amputo; (a vine), colo; (a wound), emplastrum adhibere
A dresser, ornator, vestitor; (of meat), coquus; (board), mensa coquinaria
Dressing, ornans, exornans
Dressing (by a surgeon), curatio
A dressing, ornatio, ornatus; (of meat), coctio
To dribble (drip), stillo; (drivel), salivam emittere
A dribbler (driveller), ineptus
A dribblet, summula
Dribbling (small), parvus
A drift, propositum; (purpose), scopus; (of snow), procella, via; (of sand), cumulus
Adrift, solutus
A drill, terebra
To drill, terebro, perforo, ordino
Driness, siccitas, ariditas
Drink, potus, haustus
To drink, bibo, poto; (excessively), pergræcor; (in), imbibo; (up), absorbeo, exhaurio; (to), propino; (together), compono
A drinker, potator, potor; (excessive), bibax, temulentus, vinosus; (of water), aquæ potor
Drinking, potans, bibens
A drinking, potatio; (match), compotatio
To drip, stillo, distillo
Dripping, stillans, rorans
A dripping, stillatio
The dripping, liquamen
To drive, agito, pello, circumago, dispello; (at), molior, conor; (away), abigo, arceo; (away time), tero; (from pasture), dispesco; (a carriage), aurigor; (off, *or* delay), differo; (on), impello, urgeo, expello; (trade), exerceo; (to extremity), redigo; (force), compello, cogo; (toward), adigo; (under), subigo
Drivel, saliva, sputum
To drivel, salivam emittere
A driveller, ineptus, insulsus
A driver, auriga, agitator
A driving, agitatio; (of piles), fistucatio; (away), propulsatio; (out), expulsio
To drizzle, roro, irroro
A droll, mimus
Droll, lepidus, jocosus
Drollery, jocus, facetiæ
A dromedary, dromas
A drone (bee), fucus; (person), piger, segnis
To droop, langueo, consenesco

Drooping, languidus, tabescens, senescens, tristis, imbecilis
A drooping, languor
Droopingly, languidè
A drop, gutta, stilla
A little drop, guttula
By drops, guttatim
To drop, stillo; (let fall), dimitto; (let slip), omitto, prætereo; (down), cado, labor; (off, or die), decedo, morior; (with sweat), diffluo; (out, as water), emano; (as gum), lacrymo; (with wet), madeo
A dropping, stillicidium
Dropping (down), deciduus; (wet), malidus; (in), instillans
Dropsical, hydropicus
The dropsy, hydrops
Dross, scoria, fæx, apurcities
Drossy, scoriâ, or fæce abundans
A drove, armentum, agmen
A drover, pecoris agitator
By droves, catervatim
Drought, siccitas, sitis
Droughty, siccus, aridus
To drown, demergo, inundo, immergo; (a sound), obscuro
Drowsy, somnolentus
To be drowsy, torpeo, langueo
Drowsiness, torpor, stupor
To drub, cædo, verbero
A drubbing, fustuarium
A drudge, lixa, mancipium
To drudge, famulor, defatigo; (for oysters), piscari ostrea
Drudgery, servitus, famulitium
A drug, medicamen; (worth nothing), vile, nullius pretii
To grow a drug, vilesco
A druggist, seplasiarius
Druids, druides
A drum, tympanum
To drum, pulsare tympanum
A drummer, tympanista
Drunk, ebrius, vinolentus
To be drunk, inebrior
To make drunk, inebrio
A drunkard, ebriosus, temulentus
Drunkenness, ebrietas, crapula
Dry, aridus, siccus; (thirsty), siticulosus; (empty, flat), insulsus, jejunus; (reserved), taciturnus
A dry fellow, facetus
To dry, desicco, arefacio, exsicco, aresco
A drying, siccatio, insolatio
Dryly, siccè
Dryness, siccitas, ariditas
Dual, dualis
To dub, creo
Dubious, dubius, ambiguus
Dubiously, dubiè, incertè
Ducal, ducalis
A ducat, ducatus
The duce, dyas
A duchess, ducissa
A duchy, ducatus
A duck, anas
To duck, submergo
A ducking, submersio
A duct, ductus
Ductile, ductilis, sequax
Ductility, ductilitas
A dudgeon (half dagger), pugio
To take in dudgeon, gravor
Due, debitus, idoneus
A due, debitum, jus
To be due, debeor
A duel, pugna singularis
A dug, uber, mamma
A duke, dux, satrapes
A dukedom, ducatus

[38]

Dulcet, dulcis, suavis
To dulcify, edulco
A dulcimer, sambuca
Dull, hebes, insulsus, stupidus, nebulosus
To dull, hebeto, obtundo
To grow dull, hebesco, torpeo
Dulled, obtusus, contusus
Dully, tardè, insulsè
Dulness, segnities, inertia, tarditas, torpor, obscuratio, stupor, stupiditas
Duly, ritè, accuratè
Dumb, mutus, taciturnus
To be dumb, obmutesco
Dumbness, muti status
To be in the dumps, stupeo
In the dumps, mœstus, attonitus
Dun-coloured, fuscus
To dun, pecuniam exigere
A dun, or Dunner, exactor
A dunce, stipes, hebes
Dung, stercus, merda
To dung (as a horse), alvum exonerare; (land), stercoro
Of dung, stercorarius, stercoreus
Full of dung, stercorosus
A dunghill, sterquilinium
A dungeon, tullianum, barathrum
Dunned, efflagitatus, postulatus
A dunning, solicitatio, postulatio
Dunny, surdus, surdaster
A dupe, insulsus, stolidus
To dupe, fallo, illudo
A duplicate, exemplar alterum
Duplicity, duplicitas
Durable, perennis, firmus
Durableness, perennitas, firmitas
Durably, perennè, firmitèr, firmè
Durance (of time), duratio; (imprisonment), custodia, incarceratio
Duration, duratio, continuatio
Duress, custodia, afflictio
During, prep. per, inter, secundum; adv. dum
Dusk, Duskish, tenebrosus, obscurus
The dusk, crepusculum
Duskishness, tenebræ, caligo
Dust, pulvis; (mill-dust), molitura; (saw-dust), scobs; (file-dust), limatura, ramentum; (sweepings), quisquiliæ
Full of dust, pulverulentus
To make a dust, pulverem excitare
To throw dust, conspergo
To dust, abstergeo, detergeo
A duster, peniculum
Dusty, pulvereus
To grow dusty, pulvero
A reducing into dust, pulveratio
Dutch, Belgicus
A duchess, ducissa
A duchy, ducatus
Dutiful, obsequens, obediens
To be dutiful, obsequor
Dutifully, obedientèr
Dutifulness, obedientia, pietas
Duty, officium, munus; (tax), census, vectigal
Daumvirate, duumviratus
A dwarf, nanus, pumilio
Dwarfish, pusillus, exiguus
To dwell, habito, commoror, colo, incolo, inhabito, accolo; (in the country), rusticor; (insist upon), insisto
A dweller, incola, habitator, accola, vicinus
A dwelling, domus, domicilium
To dwindle, consumor, imminuor, tabesco
A dwindling away, consumptio

A dye, color; (or dyeing), tinctura
A dye. See Dice
To dye (colour), tingo, inficio; (red colour), mizio; (violet), conchylio
A dyer, tinctor, infector
Of a deep dye, atrox
Dying, moriens; (near death), moribundus
A dying away, animi deliquium
A dyeing colours, tinctura
Dynasty, dynastia, imperium
A dysentery, dysenteria

E.

Each, quisque, singuli; (of us), uterque nostrum
Eager (sharp), acer, acidus; (earnest), vehemens; (fierce), ferox; (ravenous), famelicus; (in desire), cupidus
To be eager, acrco, acesco; (after a thing), exardesco, ardeo
Eagerly, avidè, cupidè, acritèr
Eagerly bent upon, ardens
Eagerness (in taste), acor, acerbitas; (in temper), aviditas, cupiditas; (in fight), pugnacitas
An eagle, aquila
Like an eagle, aquilinus
An ear, auris; (of a pot), ansa
Of the ear, auricularis
To give ear, attendo, ausculto
Giving ear, attentus, auscultans
An ear-pick, auriscalpium
An ear-ring, inauris; (wig), fullo
Having ears (as a cup), ansatus
To ear, spicas emittere
Eared (as corn), spicatus
An earl, comes
An earldom, comitatus
Early, adj. maturus; (in the morning), matutinus, primâ luce, multo mane
Too early, præmaturus
Early, adv. maturè, tempori
To earn, lucror, mereor
Earned, labore quæsitus
An earning, stipendium, merces
Earnest (diligent), diligens, assiduus; (vehement), ardens, solicitus; (important), magnus, gravis
Earnest-money, arrha, arrhabo
In earnest, seriò, reverà, bonâ fide
To be earnest, urgeo, insto
Earnestly, diligentèr, instantèr
So earnestly, tantoperè
Earnestness, assiduitas, ardor
The earth, terra, tellus
To earth (as a fox), terram subire; (planta), terræ mandare
Earthen, fictilis, figlinus, testreus
Earthly, terrenus, terrestris
Born of the earth, terrigena
An earthquake, terræ motus
An earthing (of herbs), pulveratio
Earthy, terrenus, terrestris
Ease (rest), otium, quies, requies; (pleasure), voluptas, gaudium; (without pain), doloris vacuitas; (without trouble), facilitas
At ease, otiosè, facillimè
To ease (give ease), levo, relevo, lenio, sublevo; (a ship), laxo
With ease, facilè, promptè
A little ease, custodia arcta
An easement, or Easing, levamen
Easily, facilè, expeditè, lenitèr promptè, mollitèr

Easiness, facilitas; (of address), affabilitas; (of belief), credulitas; (of expression), celeritas
The east, oriens, ortus; (wind), eurus, subsolanus
Eastern, Easterly, orientalis, Eöus
Easter, pascha
Belonging to Easter, paschalis
Easy, facilis, expeditus, promptus; (of belief), credulus; (to be borne), tolerandus, ferendus, tolerabilis
To eat, edo, comedo, mando, vescor, manduco; (as cattle), depasco; (nibble), arrodo; (as aqua fortis), corrodo, exedo; (or wear away), tero, attero; (greedily), devoro; (immoderately), ingurgito; (as a sore), exulcero; (one's words), recanto
Eatable, esculentus, edulis
Eatables, cibaria, esca, cibus
A great eater, helluo, edax
An eating, comestura
Eating, *part.* edens, arrodens; *adj.* edax, corrosivus
An eating-house, popina, caupona
Eaves, colliquiae, suggrundia
An eaves-dropper (listener), eoryczus
To ebb (as the sea), recedo, refluo; (decrease), decresco
The ebb, recessus, refluxus
Ebbing and flowing, reciprocans
Ebony, ebenum
Ebullition, effervescentia
Eccentric, excentricus
Ecclesiastic, Ecclesiastical, ecclesiasticus
Ecclesiastics, ecclesiastici
An echo, echo, sonus repercussus
To echo, resono, repercutio
Echoing, resonans, repercutiens
An eclipse, eclipsis, deliquium
To eclipse, obumbro obscuro
To be in an eclipse, deficio
Ecliptic, eclipticus
An eclogue, ecloga
An ecstasy, ectasis
Ecstatic, maximus
An eddy, vortex; (wind), ventus retrocedens à vento
The edge (of any thing), margo, ora; (of a knife), acies, acumen; (of a fillet), taenia; (of a garment), fimbria; (of a place), extremitas
To set an edge, acuo, exacuo
To edge (in), intrudo, insinuo; (the teeth), dentes hebetare; (with lace), praetexo; (with gold), auro ambire
Edged, acutus, acuminatus; (bordered), fimbriatus
Edgeless, obtusus
An edging, fimbria, limbus
Edible, edulis, esculentus
An edict, edictum, decretum
Edification, instructio
An edifice, aedificium
To edify, instruo
Edifying, instruens, ad docendum utilis
An edile, aedilis
An edition, editio
An editor, editor
To educate, educo, instituo
An educating, Education, educatio
To eek, *or* eke out, produco, augeo
Eeked, productus, auctus
An eeking, productio, auctio

An eel, anguilla
To efface, oblitero, deleo
An effacing, obliteratio, deletio
An effect, effectum, summa
Effects, opes, facultates
To effect, efficio, exequor
Of no effect, cassus, irritus
To no effect, nequicquam, incassum
In effect, reverà, ferè
Effective, effectivus
Effectively, reverà, efficaciter
Effectual, efficax
Effectually, prorsus, omnino
Effeminacy, mollities muliebris
Effeminate, effeminatus, muliebris
Effeminately, muliebriter, molliter
Effervesce (to), efferveseo
Efficacious, efficax, valens
Efficaciously, efficaciter
Efficacy, efficacia, vis
Efficient, efficiens
An effigies, *or* effigy, effigies
An effort, conatus, impetus
Effrontery, impudentia, audacia
Effulgence, fulgor, splendor
Effulgent, fulgens, splendens
An effusion, effusio
An egg, ovum; (new), ovum recens; (addle), ovum urinum
To egg on, instigo, urgeo
An egger on, instigator, impulsor
Egregious, egregius, insignis
Egregiously, egregiè, valdè
An egress, egressus, exitus
Egyptian, Aegyptiacus, Aegyptius
To ejaculate, ejaculor
An ejaculation, ejaculatio
To eject, ejicio
An ejectment, ejectio
Eight, octo, octoni
Belonging to eight, octonarius
Eight times, octies
Eightfold, octuplex
Eight times as much, octuplus
Eight years old, octennis
Eighteen, octodecim
Eighteenth, decimus octavus
Eighteen times, octodecies
The eighth, octavus
Eighthly, octavùm
Eight hundred, octingenti
The eight-hundredth, octingentesimus
Eight hundred times, octingenties
Eight thousand, octies mille; (times), octies millies
Eighty, octoginta
Eighty times, octogies
By eighties, octogeni
The eightieth, octogesimus
An eilet-hole, ansula
Justice in eire, justitiarius itinerans
Either, *adj.* uter, alteruter, utervis, uterlibet
Either (*answering to* or), aut, vel
On either part, utrinque
Eke (also), etiàm, itidem
To eke out, produco. See Eek
Elaborate, elaboratus, accuratus
Elaborately, elaboratè, accuratè
To elapse, labor, praetereo
Elastic, resiliens
Elasticity, vis resiliendi
Elate, elatus, inflatus
To elate, superbum reddere, inflo
To be elated, superbio, inflor
The elbow, cubitus, ulna
Elbow-room, spatium laxum
Elder in age, senior; (elders), majores, proavi, veteres
An elder, presbyter

An elder-tree, sambucus
Eldership, major aetas; (in the church), presbyterium
Elderly, aetate provectior
Eldest, maximus natu
To elect, eligo, deligo
Election, electio, delectus; (day of), dies comitiorum
An elector, elector
Electoral, electoralis
An electorate, electoratus
Electricity, electricitas
An electuary, electuarium
Eleemosynary, eleemosynarius
Elegance, *or* Elegancy, venustas; (in dress), ornatus, munditiae
Elegant (in speech), elegans, eloquens; (in dress), comptus, nitidus
Very elegant, perelegans
Elegantly, eleganter, comptè
Elegiac, elegiacus
An elegy, elegia, elegus
An element, elementum; (elements, *or* grounds of an art), elementa, principia
The four elements, quatuor genitalia corpora
Elemental, elementarius
Elenchical, elenchticus
An elephant, elephas; (its trunk), proboscis
Elephantine, elephantinus
To elevate, levo, exhilaro; (the voice), vocem attollere
An elevating, *or* Elevation, elevatio, elatio; (of the host), sublatio, exhibitio; (of the pole), poli altitudo; (to honours), promotio
Eleven, undecim, undegeni
Of eleven, undenarius
Eleven times, undecies
The eleventh, undecimus
An elf, larva, pumilio
To elicit, elicio
Eligible, eligibilis, eligendus
Elision, elisio
Elixir, elixir
An elk, alce
An ell, ulna
An ellipsis, ellipsis
Elliptical, ellipticus, mancus
An elm-tree, ulmus
Elocution, elocutio
To elope, discedo, abscedo
An elopement, à marito discessus
Eloquence, eloquentia, facundia
Eloquent, eloquens, disertus, facundus
Eloquently, eleganter, disertè; (not eloquently), inornatè, incultè
Else (beside), praeterea; (with, *or answering to* whether), sive, an, utrum; (more), adhùc, ampliùs, porrò, praeterea; (other), aliùs; (otherwise), aliter, alioqui, alioquin, caeteroquin; (with, *or answering to* either), aut, vel; (or else), aut, vel, aliàs, aut secus
Elsewhere, alibi; (somewhere else), alicubi; (of somebody else), aliundè; (nowhere else), nusquàm alio
To elucidate, explico, elucido
An elucidation, explicatio
To elude, eludo, evado, effugio
An eluding, elusio, evitatio
Elves, larvae, lemures
An elusion, fraus, dolus
Elusive, fraudulentus, fallax
Elysian, elysius, laetus
To emacerate, macero, extenuo

EMP   END   ENS

To emaciate, emacio, macero
An emaciating, extenuatio
Emanation, emanatio
To emancipate, emancipo, libero
Emancipation, emancipatio
To emasculate (geld), castro; (weaken), enervo, debilito
To embalm, pollincio, condio
An embalming, pollinctura
An embargo, arrestum mercatorium
To embark, navem conscendere; (an army), imponere exercitum; (in an affair), rem agendam suscipere; (in the same design), particeps esse
An embarkation, in navem conscensio
Embarking, navem conscendens
To embarrass, impedio [tum
An embarrassment, impedimentum
To embase, depravo
An embassy, legatio
To embattle, aciem instruere
To embellish, polio, orno
An embellishment, ornatus
Embers, favilla, cinis
Of embers, cinereus
Ember-weeks, quatuor tempora jejunii; feriæ esuriales
To embezzle, interverto, surripio
Emblematic, emblematicus
To emboss, sculpo, cælo
To embowel, exentero
To embrace, amplector
An embrace, amplexus, complexus
An embrocation, fomentum
To embroider, acu pingere
An embroiderer, acupictor
An embroidering, intextus
Embroidery, opus Phrygium
To embroil, misceo
To embrue, tingo, imbuo
An embryo, embryo
An emendation, correctio
An emerald, smaragdus
To emerge, emergo
An emergency, casus, res natæ
Emergent (sudden), subitus, repentinus; (weighty), magni momenti
The emeroids, hæmorrhois
Emetic, emeticus, vomitorius
Emigration, migratio
Eminence (dignity), eminentia, dignitas; (height), altitudo, locus editus
Eminent, eximius, conspicuus, excellens, egregius
Eminently, eximiè, insignitèr
An emissary, emissarius
Emission, or Emitting, emissio
To emit, emitto
An emmet, formica
Emollient, emolliens
Emolument, lucrum, commodum
Emotion, agitatio, commotio
To empannel, designo
An empeachment, accusatio, criminatio
An emperor, imperator
An emphasis, energia, emphasis
Emphatical, emphaticus
Emphatically, emphaticè
An empire, imperium, summatus
An empiric, empiricus
An emplaster, emplastrum
To employ (bestow, *or* use), adhibeo, confero, impendo, impertio; (*or* set about an affair), committere negotium alicui; (occupy), occupo; (in study), literis versari
[40]

An employ, ars, quæstus
An employment, negotium
An empress, imperatrix
Emptily, levitèr, vanè
Emptiness, vacuum, inanitas
Empty (void), inanis, vacuus; (vain, unprofitable), vanus, inutilis, merus
To empty, vacuo, evacuo, exhaurio, exinanio; (into another vessel), transfundo, decapulo
To be empty, vaco
To grow empty, inanesco
An emptying, evacuatio
Empyreal, empyræus
To emulate (envy), invideo, æmulor; (imitate), imitor
An emulation, æmulatio
Emulgent, emulgens
Emulous, æmulus
An emulsion, lac medicinale
To enable, vires suppeditare
Enabled, potens, factus
To enact, sancio, decerno, fero
Enacting, sanciens, decernens
An enacting, sanctio
Enamel, encaustum
To enamel, encausto pingere
To enamour, amore accendere
Enamoured, amore captus; (desperately), perditè amans
To encamp, castra ponere
An encampment, castrametatio
To enchant, excanto. See Inchant
To encircle, cingo
To enclose, includo
An enclosure, septum
An encomiast, laudator
An encomium, laus
To encompass, cingo
To encounter, congredior, confligo
An encounter (meeting), congressus; (fight), certamen, dimicatio, pugna
To encourage, animo, instigo, hortor; (prefer), promoveo; (praise), plaudo
Encouraged, animatus, accensus
An encourager, hortator
An encouragement, hortatus
To encroach, usurpo, invado
To encumber, impedio
An end (extremity, *or* bound), finis, terminus, meta; (aim, *or* design), consilium, causa; (event, *or* issue), exitus, eventus; (an ill end), exitium; (end of a play), catastrophe
In the end, demum, deniquè
At the end of, extremò
To what end? quorsùm
To no end, frustrà
To the end that, eò ut
For this end, hujus rei causâ
Up on end, erectus
To end, finio, termino, concludo, desino
To make an end, perficio
To endamage, noceo
To endanger, periclitor
Endangering, periclitans
To endear, obligo, devincio
Endearment, caritas
An endeavour, conatus
To endeavour, conor, enitor, molior, expeto, contendo, aspiro
Endeavouring, conans, nixus
With great endeavour, enixè
Ended, finitus, perfectus
An ending (of a thing), exitus, eventus; (of a dispute), controversiæ diremptio
Endless, infinitus, perpetuus
Endive, intybum

To endorse, inscribo
To endow, doto, instruo
An endowment, dotatio, dos
To endue, imbuo, dono
To endure (bear, *or* suffer), fero, patior, tolero; (continue), duro, perduro, permaneo
Enduring, tolerans; (for ever), sempiternus, perennis
An enemy, inimicus, hostis
Of an enemy, hostilis
Like an enemy, hostilitèr
Energetical, energeticus
Energy, vis, efficacia
To enervate, enervo, debilito
To enfeeble, debilito, infirmo
To enfeoff, fidei alicujus credere
To enforce, cogo, confirmo
To enfranchise, manumitto; (make free), civitate aliquem donare
To engage (one), obligo, devincio; (pass one's word), spondeo, vador; (in battle), confligo, concurro; (one's honour), fidem interponere
To be engaged, occupor, devincior
An engagement (fight), pugna, prælium; (surety), vadimonium, sponsio; (promise), promissum
Engaging, jucundus, gratus
To engender, genero, gigno
An engine, machina; (device), artificium, stropha
An engineer, machinator
English, Anglus, Anglicanus
Englishmen, Angli
To English, Anglicè reddere
To speak English, Anglicè loqui
Engrailed, crenatus
To engrave, cælo, sculpo
An engraver, cælator, sculptor
An engraving, sculptura
To engross, coëmo, flagello; (a writing), latius exscribere
An engrosser, flagellator
To enhance, pretium augere
An enhancer, mercis corrogator
An enhancing, auctus
An enigma, ænigma
Enigmatical, ænigmaticus
To enjoin, injungo, jubeo
To enjoy, fruor, potior, possideo; (one's self), se oblectare
Enjoyed, perceptus
Having enjoyed, potitus
An enjoyer, possessor
An enjoying, *or* Enjoyment, possessio, fructûs perceptio
Enjoyments, voluptates
To enlarge (extend, *or* increase), extendo, dilato, distendo; (upon a subject), copiosè loqui; (set free), vinctum solvere, *or* ex custodiâ dimittere
An enlarging, *or* Enlargement, amplificatio, ex custodiâ emissio
To enlighten, illumino, illustro
An enlightening, illustratio
To enliven, animo
An enlivening, animatio
Enmity, simultas, inimicitia
To ennoble, nobilito, illustro
Enormity, atrocitas
Enormous, enormis, atrox
Enormously, enormitèr, nefariè
Enough, abundè, sat, satis
To enquire, inquiro
To enrage, stimulo, irrito
To enrich, locupleto, dito
To enroll, inscribo
An ensample, exemplum, typus

ENU   ERM   ETE

An ensign (colours), vexillum; (bearer), signifer
To enslave, in servitutem redigere
Enslaved, mancipatus
To ensue, sequor, succedo
Ensuing, sequens
To entail, hæreditatem tradere
To entangle, implico, irretio
To enter (go into), intro, ingredior; (as a sword, into the body), in corpus descendere; (by violence), irrumpo, intrudo; (by stealth), irrepo; (an action), dicam scribere; (into the merits), investigo, perscrutor; (into a treaty), consilia inire; (into conference), colloquium inire; (into strict friendship), hospitis jungere cum aliquo; (upon an office), magistratum occipere; (upon an estate), hæreditatem capessere; (upon a design), consilium capere; (into holy orders), sacris initiari
An enterprise, cœptum, inceptum, facinus
To enterprise, aggredior, conor
Enterprised, susceptus, gestus
An enterpriser, inceptor
An enterprising, susceptio
To entertain (believe, or admit), credo, admitto; (divert), oblecto; (lodge), hospitio aliquem accipere; (with stories), fabulas narrare; (treat), accipio, excipio; (keep), alo, sustento; (one kindly), benignè accipere; (hope), spem concipere
An entertainer, hospes
Entertaining, jucundus, gratus
An entertainment, convivium, epulæ, hospitium; (amusement), detentio, occupatio
To enthral, mancipo
Enthralment, servitus
To enthrone, in solio collocare
Enthroned, in solio collocatus
Enthusiasm, enthusiasmus
An enthusiast, enthusiasta
Enthusiastic, enthusiasticus
To entice, allicio, pellicio
An enticement, illecebra
Enticing, alliciens, blandus
Entire, integer, totus
Entirely, omninò, unicè
To entitle, appello, auctoro
An entity, res, ens
To entomb, tumulo
Entrails, exta, viscera
An entrance, ingressus, aditus
To give entrance, fores aperire
To deny entrance, januâ prohibere, sinibus arcere
Entrance-money, minerval
To entrap, irretio, inesco, illaqueo
To entreat, rogo, oro
Entreaty, rogatio, obsecratio, precatio, precis
An entering into, ingressus
An entry (into a house, or place), aditus, introitus, vestibulum; (in law), ingressus
To entwine, convolvo
To envenom, veneno inficere
Envenomed, venenatus
Envious, invidus, lividus
Enviously, invidiosè, invidè
To environ, circumdo, cingo
The environs, vicinitas
To enumerate, enumero, recenseo, stipo
An enumeration, recensio
An enunciation, enunciatio
[41]

An envoy, nuncius, legatus
Envy, invidia, livor
To envy, invideo
To be envied, invidiâ premi
The epact, epactæ
An ephemera, ephemeris
Ephemeral, diurnus
An ephod, ephod
Epic, epicus
An epicure, helluo, gulosus
Epicurism, ingluvies, gula
Epidemical, epidemicus, contagiosus
An epigram, epigramma
An epilepsy, epilepsia
Epileptic, comitialis
An epilogue, epilogus
The epiphany, epiphania
Episcopacy, episcopatus
Episcopal, episcopalis
An episode, episodium
An epistle, epistola, literæ
Epistolary, epistolaris
An epitaph, epitaphium [tiale
An ophthalmicum, carmen nuptiale
An epithet, epitheton
An epitome, epitome, compendium
To epitomise, in compendium redigere; (epitomised), in compendium redactus
An epoch, epocha, æra
Equal, æqualis, æquus, par
To equal, æquo, exæquo
Equal weight, æquilibrium
Equals, pares, consortes
Equality, æqualitas, paritas
To equalize, æquo, exæquo
An equalling, æquatio
Equally, æqualiter, æquè
Equanimity, æquanimitas
Equation, æquatio
The equator, æquator
An equerry, stabuli præfectus
Equestrian, equestris
Equiangular, equiangularis
Equidistant, ex æquo distans
Equilateral, æquis lateribus instructus, æquilateralis
Equilibrious, æquilibris
Equilibrium, æquilibrium
Equinoctial, æquinoctialis
Equinox, æquinoctium
To equip (with stores), necessaria suppeditare; (a fleet), classem adornare
Equipage, instrumentum, ornatus, pompa, comitatus, apparatus, cultus
An equipoise, æquilibrium
Equipped, ornatus, instructus
An equipment, apparatus
Equitable, æquus, justus
Equitably, ut æquum est
Equity, æquitas, æquum
Equivalence, par virtus
Equivalent, æquivalens, par
To be equivalent, æquivaleo, exæquo
Equivocal, æquivocus, ambiguus
Equivocally, æquivocè, ambiguè
To equivocate, callidè mentiri
An equivocation, ambiguitas
To eradicate, eradico, extirpo
An eradication, extirpatio
To erase, erado, deleo
An erasement, litura
Ere, antequam, priusquam; (ere long), modò, brevi; (ere now), ante hoc tempus
To erect (raise up), erigo; (build), ædifico, condo, struo
An erecting, erectio, ædificatio
An eremite, eremita
An ermine, mustela alba

Ermine-skin, mustelæ albæ pellicula
To err, erro, oberro, decipior, hallucinor
An errand, mandatum, nuncium
To carry an errand, mandata perferre
An errand-boy, nuncius
Errata, errata, menda
Erratic, erraticus
An erring, erratio
Erroneous, erroneus, falsus
Erroneously, falsè, falsò
Error (fault), erratum, delictum; (in opinion), error, hallucinatio; (in an error), deceptus
Erudition, eruditio
Eruption, eruptio
An escape, fuga, effugium
To escape, evado, effugio, aufugio, elabor; (by flight), evolo; (privily), subterfugio; (by struggling), eluctor; (danger), vitare periculum; (the memory), ex memoriâ excidere
An escar, cicatrix
An escheat, escæta
To escheat, ad fiscum recidere
To eschew, vito, devito, effugio
Eschewed, devitatus, evitatus
An eschewing, evitatio
To escort, deduco, comitor
Esculent, esculentus
An escutcheon, insigne gentilitium
Especial, præcipuus, specialis
Especially, præcipuè, specialiter, præsertim
Most especially, maximè
Espied, exploratus, visus
Espousals, sponsalia
To espouse, despondeo, desponso; (a cause), patrocinor
To espy, speculor, exploro; (by chance), aspicio, video; (an opportunity), tempus captare. *See* to Spy.
An esquire, armiger, scutiger
An essay, molimen, specimen, experimentum, periclitatio, conatus
To essay, tento, experior
An essence (being), natura, essentia; (in chymistry), extractio chemica
Essential, essentialis
Essentially, essentialiter, naturâ
To establish, stabilio, confirmo, constituo, sancio
An establishment, stabilimentum
An estate (means), res, res familiaris, census, bona, opes, divitiæ; (of life), status, conditio, ætas, ratio
Esteem, æstimatio
To esteem, æstimo, habeo, duco, pendo; (judge), existimo, reputo, statuo, opinor; (better), antehabeo; (greatly), magnifacio; (little), vili pendere, parvi ducere; (less), postpono; (as nothing), nihili facere; (worthy), dignor
To be esteemed, æstimor; (not to be esteemed), sordeo
To estimate, æstimo, pendo
An estimate, calculatio, pretium
Great estimation, dignitas
An estimator, calculator, æstimator
Estival, æstivus
To estrange, alieno, abalieno
An estreat, exemplum, extracta
To etch, aquâ forti corrodere
Eternal, æternus, sempiternus
Eternally, æternum

EVI   EXC   EXE

Eternity, æternitas
To all eternity, in æternum
To eternize, æterno, propago
Ethereal, æthereus
Ethic, ethicus
Ethics, ethica, mores
Etymological, etymologicus
An etymologist, etymologus
An etymology, etymon
To evacuate (empty), vacuo, evacuo, exhaurio; (a town), ab oppido cedere
An evacuation, evacuatio
Evacuative, purgans
To evade, evado, vito, illudo
Evangelical, evangelicus
An evangelist, evangelista
To evaporate, exhalo, exudo
An evaporation, exhalatio
An evasion, techna, vaframentum, effugium
Evasive, vafer, fallax
Evasively, vafrè, fictè
The eucharist, eucharistia
Eucharistical, eucharisticus
An eve, vigiliæ, pridiè diei
Even, adv. (also), etiàm, quoquè, omninò, vel; (namely), nempè, nimirùm, scilicèt; (even as), quemadmodùm, sicut, æquè atquè, perindè ac si; adj. (equal, &c.), æquabilis, æquus, par
To make even, adæquo; (smooth), polio, complano; (demolish), diruo, demolior
Even from, jam à, usque à; (even now), modò, jam nunc; (even then), jam tum; (even there), inibi
Even weight, æquilibrium
On even terms, æquali conditione
The even, Evening, or Even-tide, vespera vesper
Of the evening, vespertinus
At even, vesperi
Evenly, æqualitèr, constantèr
Evenness, æqualitas, lævor; (in temper), æquanimitas
An event, eventus, exitus
At all events, utcunquè ceciderit
Eventual, fortuitus
Eventually, forté, fortunâ
Ever (always), semper, æternùm; (any), ecquis, ecquisnam, nunquis; (at any time), ecquandò, siquando, unquàm, nuncubi; (after) inde; (ever and anon), subindè, (ever before), usquè antehac, (for ever), in æternum
Everlasting, sempiternus, æternus
Everlastingly, æternùm
An eversion, eversio, demolitio
Every, quilibet, quisque, singuli, quivis, 'body), unusquisque; (day), indiès, quotidiè; (occasion), ex omni occasione; (what), omninò, prorsùs; (side), undiquè; (way), quoquoversùm; (year), quotannis
Evidence (proof), testimonium; (witness), testis; (clearness), evidentia, perspicuitas
To evidence, probo, testor
Evident, evidens, manifestus
To be evident, consto, appareo
To make evident, illustro, patefacio
Evidently, manifestè, apertè
Evil, malus, pravus, improbus
An evil, malum, damnum
An evil-doer, sceleratus, scelestus
Evil-minded, malignus
To evince, evinco, probo

[42]

Evincibly, clarè, perspicuè
An evincing, evictio
To eviscerate, eviscero, exentero
Evitable, evitabilis, vitabilis
An eulogy, laus, encomium
An eunuch, eunuchus
To evolve, evolvo, explico
Evolution, evolutio
Euphony, euphonia
Evulsion, evulsio
An ewe, ovis fœmina; (lamb), agna
To ewe, agnum parere
An ewer, aqualis
Exact (accurate), accuratus, perfectus; (punctual), temporis, &c., observantissimus; (severe, or strict), rigidus, severus
To exact (demand), exigo, flagito; (upon), opprimo; (in price), nimis carè vendere
An exacter, exactor, oppressor
Exaction, exactio, oppressio
Exactly, exactè, ad unguem
Exactness (accuracy), accuratio; (neatness), concinnitas
To exaggerate, exaggero, aggravo
An exaggerating, exaggeratio
To exalt (lift up), exalto, eveho; (praise), extollo, celebro
An exaltation, exaltatio, elatio
Examination, inquisitio, examen, interrogatio; (of accounts), rationum comparatio
To examine (ask questions), interrogo; (weigh, or consider), expendo; (precisely), scrutor, inquiro
An examiner, inquisitor
An examining, examinatio
An example, exemplum, specimen; (as for example), exempli gratia [animo
To exanimate (discourage), exAn exarch, exarcha
To exasperate, exaspero, lacesso
To exceed, excedo, transcendo, supero, vinco, præsto, abundo, affluo, præpolleo; (the bounds), transire fines
Exceeding (surpassing), præstans, excellens; (excessive), nimius, immodicus; adv. valdè, vehementèr
An exceeding, excessus
Exceedingly, valdè, eximiè, egregiè [supero
To excel, excello, emineo, præsto, Excellence, excellentia, præstantia
Excellent, excellens, eximius
Excellently, egregiè, optimè
An excelling, antecessio
Excentricity, excentricitas
Except (unless), nisi, ni; (saving), præter, nisi, extra; (except that), nisi, quòd, nisi si
To except, excipio, eximo, excludo, secerno, oppugno, repudio, demo
An exception, exceptio
Exceptionable, exceptionibus obnoxius
Excess, excessus, intemperantia
Excessive, nimius, immodicus
Excessively, immoderatè, immodicè
Excessiveness, superfluitas
To exchange, permuto, commuto
An exchange, mutatio, commutatio; (to meet in), excambium, byrsa
An exchanger, nummularius
An exchanging, commutatio
The exchequer, ærarium, fiscus

Exciseable, tributum solvere debet
Excise, tributum, censas
Excision, excisio
To excite, excito, stimulo
An exciter, instigator, irritat
An exciting, provocatio, incitatio
Exciting, incitans, stimulans
To exclaim, exclamo; (against), declamitare in aliquem, oppugno
An exclaimer, clamator
An exclamation, exclamatio
To exclude, excludo, excipio
An excluding, exclusio
Exclusive, exclusorius; (of that), præter, extra
Exclusively, exclusivè
To excommunicate, excommunico
Excommunication, excommunicatio
To excoriate, excorio, deglubo
Excreation, excreatio
An excrement, excrementum
Excrementa, alvi purgationes
Exerementitious, excrementitius
An excrescence, tuber
Exeretion, excretio
To excruciate, excrucio, torqueo
Excruciating, excrucians
To exculpate, purgo, culpâ liberare
An excursion (in a subject, or discourse), digressio; (into a place), excursio, incursio, impetus, incursus
Excursive, errans, devius
Excusable, excusabilis
An excuse, excusatio, causa
To excuse (one's self), se excusare; (admit an excuse), excusationem accipere; (extenuate a fault), factum elevare
Excuseless, inexcusabilis
To make excuse, fingere causas
Execrable, execrabilis, dirus
Execrably, nefariè, odiosè
To execrate, execror, devoveo
An execration, execratio, diræ
To execute (perform), exequor; (a law), legem exercere; (a malefactor), capite plectere; (a will), testamentum curare; (orders), transigo; (conditions of peace), pacti conditiones implere
An executer, actor
An executing, or execution, executio; (of a malefactor), supplicii capitalis inflictio
A place of execution, furca
An executioner, carnifex
An executive power, administratio
An executor, testamenti curator
Executory, ad executionem pertinens
An executrix, testamenti curatrix
Exegetical, exegeticus
Exemplarily, insignitèr
Exemplary, exemplum præbens; (life), vita imitatione digna; (punishment), supplicium insigne
An exemplification, exemplar
To exemplify (copy), transcribo; (illustrate), explico
An exemplifying, descriptio, expositio
To exempt (free), eximo, libero
Exempt, exemptus, immunis
An exemption, exemptio, immunitas
Exequies, exequiæ, funus
An exercise, exercitium; (mili-

EXP — EXT — EYR

tary), exercitatio militaris; (of an office), muneris functio; (recreation), animi relaxatio; (task), pensum
To exercise, exerceo; (authority over), dominari alicui; (an office), fungor; (as a soldier), arma exercere; (in business), operi incumbere
To be exercised in, occupor, versor
Exercises, certamina, ludi
To exert, exero, exhibeo; (one's self), viribus eniti
To exhale, exhalo, expiro
An exhalation, exhalatio
To exhaust, exhaurio
An exhausting, exinanitio
To exhibit, exhibeo, ostendo
An exhibiting, or Exhibition, exhibitio; (allowance), stipendium
To exhilarate, exhilaro, lætifico
Exhilarating, lætans, lætabilis
To exhort, adhortor, suadeo
An exhortation, hortatio, monitum
Exhortative, suasorius
An exhorter, hortator
An exhorting, hortatio
An exigence, necessitas, angustia
An exigent (occasion), occasio; (expedient), ratio, commodum; (writ), exigenda
An exile, exul, extorris
Exile (banishment), exilium
To exile, relego, amando; (to be exiled), in exilium depelli
Exiled, relegatus
Exinanition, exinanitio
To exist, existo, sum
Existence, existentia
Existent, Existing, existens
An exit, exitus, eventus [rior
To make one's exit, discedo, moExodus, exodus
To exonerate, exonero, levo
An exonerating, oneris levatio
Exorable, exorabilis
Exorbitance, nimietas
Exorbitant, nimius
Exorbitantly, nimiò
To exorcise, exorcizo, adjuro
An exorcising, adjuratio
An exorcism, exorcismus
An exorcist, exorcista
An exordium, exordium, prologus
Exotic, exoticus, externus
To expand, expando, explico
The expanse, expansum, æther
An expansion, expansio
To expatiate, expatior, loquor
To expect, expecto, spero
Expecting, expectans
Expectation, expectatio, spes
To expectorate, expectoro
Expedient, commodus, utilis
An expedient, ratio, modus
To be expedient, expedit, prodest
Expediently, commodè, aptè
To expedite, expedio, accelero
Expedition, festinatio, properatio; (of soldiers), expeditio
Expeditious, impiger, strenuus
Expeditiously, expeditè, celeriter
To expel, expello, pello, arceo
An expelling, expulsio
Expense, impensa, sumptus
To expend, expendo, insumo
Expensive, carus, prodigus
Expensively, prodigè, effusè
Expensiveness, profusio
Experience, experientia, usus
To experience, experior
Of no experience, inexpertus
Experienced, expertus, experiens
[43]

An experiment, experimentum
Experimental, usu comparatum
Expert, expertus, peritus
Expertly, peritè, scienter
Expertness, peritia, scientia
Expiable, piabilis, placabilis
To expiate, expio, lustro
An expiation, expiatio, piatio
Expiatory, expiatorius
To expire, expiro, finior
Expired, mortuus, defunctus
An expiring, or Expiration, exitus, finis
To explain, explico, expono
An explainer, explicator
Explanation, explanatio, expositio
Expletive, expletivus
To explicate, explico
Explication, explicatio
Explicative, explanans
Explicit, explicitus, clarus
Explicitly, clarè, distinctè
To explode, explodo, rejicio
An exploding, explosio, exactio
An exploit, actum, facinus
Noble exploits, res gestæ
To explore, exploro, exquiro
An exploring, indagatio
An explosion, explosio, fragor
To export, exporto, transveho
Exportation, exportatio
To expose, expono, objicio; (to danger), periclitor; (to laughter), deridendum præbere; (to sale), venundo; (to view), exhibeo; (uncover), detego, nudo
An exposition, interpretatio
A short exposition, scholium
An expositor, interpres, expositor
To expostulate, expostulo, conqueror
An expostulation, expostulatio
To expound, expono, explico
An expounder, explicator, interpres
An expounding, expositio
To express, exprimo, narro; (one's mind), enuncio; (delineate), delineo; (joy), gaudium testari; (in numbers), numeros notis signare
Express, apertus, certus, clarus
An express, nuncius velox
Expressly, distinctè, planè
An expression (sentence), sententia; (word), dictio, dictum
Expressive, significans, denotans
Expressively, significanter
Expressiveness, significatio viva
To exprobrate (upbraid), exprobo
An expulsion, expulsio, exactio
An expunction, expunctio
To expunge, expungo, deleo
Exquisite, exquisitus, elaboratus, summus, acerrimus
Exquisitely, exquisitè, accuratè
Exsiccative, arescens
Extant, extans
To be extant, exto, supersum
An extasy, extasis
Extemporary, extemporalis
Extempore, haud præmeditatus
To extend, extendo, dilato, propago
An extension, extensio, prolatio
Extensive, latè patens
Extensively, latè, diffusè
Extensiveness, diffusio
Extent, spatium, amplitudo; (of capacity), captus; (of country), fines, tractus; (law term), extenta
To extenuate (lessen), extenuo, emacio, diminuo; (excuse), excuso, deprecor

Extenuation, extenuatio
Exterior, exterior, externus
To exterminate, extermino, extirpo
An extermination, extirpatio
External, externus, externè
Externally, extrinsecùs
Extinct, extinctus, defunctus
To be extinct, extinguor
An extinction, extinctio, interitus
To extinguish, extinguo, deleo
An extinguisher, suffocatorium
An extinguishing, extinctio
To extirpate, extirpo, eradico
An extirpating, extirpatio
To extol, laudo, prædico, laudibus efferre
An extoller, laudator
An extolling, laudatio
Extorsive, injustus, iniquus
To extort, extorqueo, diripio
Extortion, expilatio, direptio
An extortioner, extortor, expilator, exactor
To extract, extraho, exprome, exprimo, educo, excerpo
An extract (draught), exemplar, excerptum; (descent), genus, stirps; (epitome), compendium; (chymical), expressio
An extraction, prosapia, genus, origo
Extrajudicial, extrajudicialis
Extraneous, extraneus, externus
Extraordinarily, rarò, valdè [tus
Extraordinary, insolitus, inusitaExtraparochial, extra parœchiam positus [prodigentia
Extravagance, luxuria, profusio,
Extravagant, prodigus, effusus; (impertinent), ineptus, insulsus; (excessive), immodicus; (disorderly), perditus; (opinion), vaga opinio
Extravagantly, absurdè, profusè, immoderatè, perditè
Extreme, extremus, summus
Extremely, summè, valdè
Extremity (utmost part), extremum; (distress), miseria; (utmost extremity), rigor summus
To extricate, extrico, libero
Extrinsically, extrinsecùs
Extrusion, extrusio, expulsio
An exuberance, tumor
Exuberance, copia, redundantia
Exuberant, exuberans, redundans
To exulcerate, exulcero
To exult, exulto
An exulting, or Exultation, exultatio
An eye, oculus; (loop), ansula; (of a needle), foramen; (of a flower, or plant), gemma, germen; (in a doublet), ocellus; (witness), testis oculatus
Of the eye, ocularia
One-eyed, monoculus
Eye-lids, palpebræ
Hair of the eye-lids, cilium
Web in the eye, leucoma
Before one's eyes, in oculis
The eye-sight, acies oculi
Eye-service, perfunctorius
An eye-sore, odiosus
To eye, intueor, aspicio; (wantonly), oculis venari
Eyed, or Full of eyes, oculatus, fistulosus; (looked upon), intentè spectatus
Bleer-eyed, lippus
Grey-eyed, cæsius
An eyre, judicum itinerantium curia; (a justice in eyre), justitiarius in itinere

F.

A fable, fabula
Fabled, fictus, confictus
To fabricate, fabrico, struo
Fabrication, fabricatio
A fabric, ædificium, structura
Fabulosity, fabulositas
Fabulous, fabulosus, fictus
Fabulously, fabulosè, fictè
A face, facies, vultus, os; (confidence), fiducia; (of affairs), status; (appearance), species
Face to face, coràm, facie tenus
To face (look at), intueor, aspicio; (boldly), os induere, frontem explicare; (danger), periculum adire; (about), hosti frontem advertere; (a garment), orno; (one down), dictis protelare
In the face of the sun, palàm
Bare-faced, oris retecti
Double-faced, bifrons, simulator
Facetious, facetus, lepidus
Facetiously, facetè, lepidè
Facetiousness, lepor
Facile, facilis, affabilis
To facilitate, expedio
Facility, facilitas; (in speaking), sermo promptus
With facility, facilè, expeditè
A facing (about), in hostem conversio; (of danger), periclitatio
Facings, ornamenta vestis
The facion in horses, petimen
A fact, factum, gestum, facinus
In fact, reverà
A faction, factio, conspiratio
Factious, factiosus, seditiosus
Factiousness, partium studium
Factitious, factitius
A factor, negotiator, institor
Factorage, mercaturæ procuratio
A factory, procuratorum habitatio
A faculty, facultas, professio; (leave), licentia
To fade (wither), defloresco; (decay), debilitor, deficio
Faded, evanidus, flaccidus
To fadge, convenio, quadro
Fading, languidus, caducus
A fading, languor, marcor
To fag, cædo, laboro
The fag-end, extremitas posterior
A fagot, fascis; (amongst soldiers), miles supposititius
To fail (act), deficio, relinquo, succumbo, excido; (in promises), promissis non stare; (of duty), delinquo; (of expectation), fallere expectationem; (break as a tradesman), conturbo
Without fail, certò, planè
Failing, lapsus
A failing (ceasing), remissio; (deficiency), defectus; (disappointment), frustratio; (fault), culpa, delictum
A failure, culpa
Fain (desirous), cúpidus, avidus; (obliged), coactus
I would fain, cupio, gestio
Faint (weak), languidus, debilis; (slack), remissus; (weary), lassus; (fearful), timidus; (obscure), obscurus
A faint, dolus, dissimulatio
To make a faint, simulo; (to grow faint), deficio; (to make faint), labefacto, debilito; (to

[44]

make faint-hearted), exanimo; (to faint away), animo linqui
Faint-hearted, meticulosus
Faint-heartedness, timiditas ægre
Fainting, languens, fessus
A fainting-away, deliquium animi
Faintly, timidè, remissè
Faintness, languor
Fair (beautiful), pulcher; (clear), clarus, splendidus; (honest), justus, æquus; (fair-spoken), blandiloquus; (words), blanditiæ; (weather), cœlum sudum
To be, or look fair, niteo
To grow fair, sereno
To be fair in dealing, honestè agere
A fair, nundinæ; (of a fair), nundinalis, nundinarius
To keep a fair, nundinor
A fairing, strena, donum
Fairly, venustè, probè, aptè, æquè, justè, integrè
Fairness (in complexion), pulchritudo; (in dealing), æquitas
A fairy, lamia, nympha
Faith, fides
Of the right faith, orthodoxus
Of a wrong faith, heterodoxus
On my faith, mehercle
Faithful, fidelis, fidus
Faithfully, fidelitèr, fidè
Faithfulness, fidelitas, integritas
Faithless (not believing), incredulus; (not to be trusted), perfidus
A falchion, ensis falcatus
A falcon, accipiter, falco
A falconer, auceps
A fall, casus, lapsus
The fall (of Adam), delictum Adami; (of the leaf), autumnus
To fall, cado; (as hair), defluo; (in price), evilesco; (abate), decresco; (as wind), sileo; (asleep), obdormisco; (in love), amo; (into a passion), exardesco; (away), deficio; (back), recido, relabor; (down), concido, procido, procumbo; (down as a ship), delabor; (down together), corruo; (down under), succumbo; (from a horse), equo dejici; (in one's way), obviam occurrere; (into), illabor, ineido; (into poverty), ad inopiam redigi; (into a snare), in insidias cadere; (off), decido, deficio, declino; (on), aggredior; (out of), excido; (out with), inimicitias suscipere; (sick), morbo corripi
Ready to fall, caducus
A fall of rain, vis imbrium
Falling, labens, collabens; (down), prolapsus, ruinosus
A falling (away), defectio; (out with), dissidium; (of water), cataracta
Fallacious, fallax
Fallaciously, dolosè
Fallaciousness, dolus
A fallacy, fallacia, sophisma
Fallible, incertus, fallens
A fallow field, novale
Laid fallow, incultus
Fallow (in colour), fulvus
False, falsus, fallax, pravus, perfidus, vitiosus, spurius; (hearted), bilinguis, cordis infidi
Falsehood, mendacium, dolus
Falsely, falsò, subdolè

Falseness, perfidia
To falsify, suppono, corrumpo; adultero, depravo, commisceo; (one's word), fidem fallere; (wares), adultero
To falter, hæsito, deficio
Faltering, hæsitans, titubans
Fame (report), fama, rumor; (reputation), existimatio
Familiar, intimus, usitatus, facilis
Familiarity, familiaritas
Familiarly, familiaritèr
A family (household), familia; (stock), prosapia, genus
Of the family, domesticus, gentilis
A famine, fames, inedia
To famish, fame enecare, fame perire; (a town), famem oppidanis inferre
Famishing, fame moribundus
Famous, illustris, insignis, mirus, clarus
To make famous, celebro
To be famous, emineo, eniteo
Famously, insignitèr, præclarè, clarè
A fan, flabellum; (for corn), ventilabrum, vannus
To fan, ventilo
Fanatic, fanaticus   [cies
Fanaticism, vanæ religionis species
Fanciful, inconstans, levis
Fancifully, inconstantèr, levitèr
Fancifulness, levitas
A fancy, figmentum, arbitrium, opinio, imaginatio
To fancy, alicui rei studere; (imagine), imaginor, effingo
A fane, triton, fanum
Fangs (claws), ungues; (teeth), dentes incisores
Fanned, ventilatus
A fanning, ventilatio
Fantastical, inconstans, levis
Fantastically, affectatè, putidè
Fantasticalness, affectatio, levitas
Far, adj. longinquus, remotus; adv. longè, procùl; (and near), longè latèque
By far, multò, longè
Far within, penitùs, intimè
Far is it from me, longè absit
As far as, quantùm
So far, eousque
So far as, quatenus
Thus far, hactenùs
How far? quousque?
A farce, mimus, exodium; (hodge podge), farrago
A fardel, sarcina, fascis
Fare (victuals), victus; (chance), sors; (for carriage), vectura, portorium, naulum; (the person), qui vehitur
To fare, vietito; (well), lautè victitare; (late), communem casum sustinere
Farewell, vale, fac valeas
To bid farewell, valedico
Farrinaceous, farraceus
A farm, prædium, fundus
To farm, prædium conducere; (let a farm), prædium locare; (cultivate land), agrum colere
A farmer, agricola, villicus; (of revenues), publicanus
A farrier, hippocomus
Farther, adj. ulterior; adv. longius alterius, the comp. of far
Farthermore, præterea, porro
Farthermost, or farthest, adj. extremus, ultimus; adv. longissimè

FAU — FEE — FET

A farthing, quadrans; (to a farthing), ad assem
To fascinate (bewitch), fascino
Fascination, fascinatio
A fascine, virgultorum fascis
A fashion (form), figura, forma; (manner), mos, modus, ratio, consuetudo, usus, ritus
Fashion of work, artificis opera
In fashion, obtinens in usu; (out of fashion), exoletus
Of fashion, bono genere natus
For fashion-sake, perfunctoriè
Of the same fashion, similis
A fashion of clothes, habitus
To fashion, formo, fingo
Fashionable, concinnus
Fashionably, scitè, decentèr
Fashioned, formatus
Fast (bound), astrictus; (firm), stabilis; (in pace), celer
Fast, *adv.* celeritèr, tutò
A fast (from meat), jejunium
To fast, jejuno
To lay fast, includo
To make fast, affigo, claudo
Fast asleep, somno sopitus
To fasten, astringo; (about), circumpango; (to the ground), depango; (together), alligo; (under), subnecto; (unto), annecto; (upon, *or* seise), arripio; (eyes upon), intentè intueri; (a door), obdo
A fastening, astrictio
Faster, celerius
Fastidious, fastidiosus
Fastidiousness, fastidium
Fasting, jejunans
To be fasting, jejuno
Fasting days, jejunia
A fastness, munimentum, agger, vallum
Fat, *or* Fatness, pinguedo, adeps; (of a hog), lardum
Fat, pinguis, opimus, obesus; (plump), nitidus; (meat), adipatum; (wine), vinum spissum
To fat, sagino, pinguefacio; (grow fat), pinguesco
A fat, *or* Vat, dolium
Fatal, fatalis, feralis
Fatality, fatalis vis
Fatally, fatalitèr
Fate, fatum, sors
The fates, parcæ
Ill-fated, infaustus
A father, pater, genitor; (in law), socer
To father (adopt), adopto; (own), vendico; (upon), imputo
Fatherless, patre orbus, pupillus
Fatherly, *adv.* paternè; *adj.* paternus, patrius
A fathom, ulna
To fathom, exploro; (compass), ulnâ metiri
Fatidical, fatidicus
To fatigue, fatigo, delasso
Fatigue, fatigatio, labor
Fatiguing, fatigans, defatigans
Fatness, pinguedo
To fatten, sagino, incrasso
A fattening, saginatio
Fatty, pinguis, crassus
A fanchion, harpe
A fault (crime), culpa, delictum; (defect), vitium; (mistake), error; (great), scelus; (in writing), menda, erratum
Full of faults, mendosus, vitiosus
Without fault, insons, integer
To faulter in (speech), balbutio;
[45]

(stagger), vacillo; (stumble), titubo
Faultless, innocuus, insons
Faultily, vitiosè, mendosè
Faulty, culpandus, mendosus
Favour, favor, gratia; (of countenance), oris habitus; (of the people), popularis aura
A favour, beneficium; (for a wedding), lemniscus nuptialis
To favour, faveo, aspiro; (resemble), assimilo, refero
Favourable, benignus, propitius, opportunus, secundus
Favoured, carus; (well), speciosus, venustus; (ill), deformis
A favours, fautor, fortrix
Favouring, favens; (resembling), ore referens
A favourite, gratiosus, primus
To fawn upon, adulor, assentior
A fawner upon, adulator
Fawning, adulatorius, blandus
A fawning upon, adulatio
Fawningly, assentatoriè, blandè
Fealty, fidelitas, feudum
Fear, metus, timor; (reverence), reverentia; (great), horror, pavor
To fear, timeo, metuo; (greatly), horresco; (reverence), revereor
Fearful, timidus, terribilis
Fearfully, timidè, horridè
Fearfulness, metus, terror
Fearing, veritus, verens
Fearless, impavidus, intrepidus
Feasible, efficiendus
A feast, convivium, epulum [vator
The founder of a feast, convi-
To feast, epulor
Feasts, feriæ; (of Bacchus), baccanalia
A feaster, epulo
Feasting, epulans, comessans
A feasting, epulatio
A feat, facinus, gestum
A feather, pluma, penna
To feather, pluresco; (one's nest), opes accumulare
Of feathers, plumeus
Full of feathers, plumosus
Made of feathers, plumatilis
Bearing feathers, plumiger
Feathered, plumatus, pennatus
Featherless, implumis
A feature, lineamentum
Well featured, venustus; (ill), deformis
February, Februarius
Feculency, fæculentia
Feculent, fæculentus
Fecundity, fœcunditas
Fed, pastus, satur
A fee (reward), præmium; (simple), feudum simplex; (tail), feudum conditionale
To fee, præmio corrumpere
Feeble, debilis, infirmus
To make feeble, debilito
To grow feeble, languesco
Feebleness, debilitas, infirmitas
Feebly, infirmè, languidè
To feed, pasco, pascor; (grow fat), pinguesco; (upon), depascor; (with milk), lacto; (together), comedo
A feeder of cattle, armentarius
Finding (much), edax; (greedily), vorax
A feeding, nutritio; (eating), esus; (high), edacitas; (of cattle), depascio, saginatio
Feeing, honorarium solvens
To feel (handle), tango; (perceive), sentio; (gently), palpo

A feeling (handling), tactio; (pitying), miseratio
The feeling, tactûs sensus
To have feeling, persentisco
Without feeling, insensibilis
Fellow-feeling, sympathia
Feelingly (compassionately), compassione
Feet, pedes
To feign (invent), fingo; (pretend), assimulo; (lie), mentior
Feignedly, fictè, simulatè
A feigner, fictor, simulator
A feint, species simulata
Felicity, felicitas, beatitudo
Fell, atrox, dirus, trux
A fell (skin), pellis
To fell, sterno, cædo
A felling of wood, lignatio
A fellow (companion), socius; (equal), par; (good), comptor; (in office), collega; (in bed), concors thori
To fellow, adæquo
Fellowship, sodalitium, sodalitas
In fellowship, consociatus, consors
A felly, canthus
A felon, fur, latro
Felony, furtum, felonia
Felonious, sceleratus, nefarius
Feloniously, sceleratè
Felt, tactus, perceptus
Felt, lanæ coactæ
A felt-maker, lanarum coactor
Female, femineus, muliebris
A female, femina
Feminine, femininus
A fen, palus, locus palustris
A fence (inclosure), septum, lorica; (protection), tutamen
To fence, vallo, præsepio, defendo, ictum avertere; (with foils), obtusis gladiis dimicare
A fencer, lanista
A fencing, munitio
The art of fencing, ars gladiatoria
To fend, defendo, altercor
Fennel, fœniculum
Fenny, paludosus, palustris
To feoff, dono, feoffo
A feoffe, feoffarius, fidejussor
A feoffer, feoffator
A feoffment, feoffamentum
A ferment, fermentum
To ferment, fermento, ferveo
Fermentation, fermentatio
Ferocity, ferocitas
A ferret, viverra
To ferret, conquiro, exagito
A ferrule, annulus
A ferry, trajectus
A ferry-boat, ponto; (for horses), hippago
A ferryman, portitor
To ferry over, trajicio
Fertile, fertilis, fœcundus
To make fertile, fœcundo
Fertility, fertilitas, ubertas
Fervency, fervor, ardor
Fervent, fervid, fervidus, ardens
To be fervent, ferveo, ardeo
Fervently, fervidè, cupidè
A ferule, ferula
To ferule, ferulâ percutere
Fervor, fervor, ardor
To fester, exulcero, putreo [tus
Festered, suppuratus, exulcera-
A festering, suppuratio
Festival, Festive, festivus, festus
Festivity, festivitas, hilaritas
A fetch, dolus, fallacia

FIG — FIN — FIV

To fetch, affero, adduco; (to life), ad vitam revocare; (blood), sanguinem elicere; (breath), spiritum ducere; (back), reduco; (away), abduco; (a compass), circumeo; (from above), deveho; (down, or lessen), imminuo; (from far), aveho; (forth), educo; (a leap), salio; (out), depromo; (over), adveho; (over to a party), pertraho; (or go for one), accerso; (a sigh), suspirium trahere, suspiro; (up, or overtake), assequor
A fetcher of water, aquator
Fetching, adveheus, adducens
A fetching, comportatio
Fetid, fœtidus, putris
Fetlocks, cirri
Fetters, compedes
To fetter, compedio
A feud, simultas, odium, lis
A fever, febris
To have a fever, febricito
Feverish, febriculosus
Few, pauci, rari
Very few, perpauci
Fewer, pauciores
Fewness, paucitas
A fib (lie), mendacium
A fibber, mendax
A fibre, fibra
Fibrous, fibrosus
Fickle, inconstans, levis
Fickly, inconstantèr, levitèr
Fickleness, inconstantia
Fiction, fictio, figmentum
Fictitious, fictitius
Fictitiously, fictè
A fiddle, fides, fidicula
To fiddle, fidem pulsare; (trifle), nugor; (up and down), cursito
A fiddler, fidicen
A fiddle-string, chorda, nervus; (stick), plectrum
Fidelity, fidelitas, sinceritas
Fie, vah!
A fief, prædium, beneficiarium
A field, campus, ager; (of battle), prælii campus; (of a scutcheon), area, or solum acuti
Of the field, campestris
A field-officer, præfectus militaris; (marshal), castrorum præfectus; (piece), tormentum castrense
A fiend, malus genius
Fierce, ferox, acer, vehemens, sævus, ingens, atrox, ferus
To be fierce, ferocio, sævio
Fiercely, ferocitèr
Fierceness, ferocitas, feritas
Fiery, igneus, rutilans; (passionate), exardescens, ardens
Fifteen, quindecim, quindeni
Fifteenth, decimus quintus
A fifteenth, quindecima
Fifteen times, quindeciès
A fifth, quintus
Fifthly, quintò
Fiftieth, quinquagesimus
Fifty, quinquaginta
Fifty times, quinquagiès
Fifty years old, quinquagenarius
A fig, or fig tree, ficus
A fight, pugna, certamen
To fight, pugno, dimico; (in battle), prælior; (against), oppugno; (hand to hand), comminùs pugnare; (a duel), duello certare; (with swords), digladior
A fighter, pugnator

Fighting, pugnans
A fighting, conflictus
Figurative, figuratus
Figuratively, metaphoricè
A figure, figura, forma; (shape), imago, effigies; (delineation), diagramma; (appearance), species; (in speech), tropus, schema
To figure, delineo, depingo
A figuring, conformatio
Filaments, fibræ
A filberd, nux avellana; (tree), corylus
To filch, surripio, suffuror
A filcher, fur
Filching, furtivus, furax
A filching, surreptio
A file, lima, planula
To file, limo, abrado
To file (off), copias manipulatìm abducere; (up writings), filo suspendere scripta
Filial, filialis
A filing, limatura
Filings, scobs, ramenta
To fill, impleo, repleo; (up), expleo
The fill (fulness), satietas
A fillet, vitta, crinale; (of veal), coxæ vitulinæ pars crassior; (of a pillar), abacus
A filling, expletio
Filling, implens, replens
A fillip, talitrum
To fillip, talitro ferire
A filly, equula
A film, membrana, cutis
Filmy, membranaceus
To filter, or Filtrate, percolo
A filtering, or Filtration, purificatio facta percolando
Filth, sordes, colluvies
Filthy, sordidus, fœdus; (in speech), obscœnus; (action), turpe factu
To be filthy, squaleo
Filthily, sordidè, spurcè
Filthiness, squalor, fœditas
A fin, pinna
Final, extremus, ultimus, finalis
Finally, deniquè, demùm
The finances, fisci reditus
To find, invenio, reperio; (perceive), sentio; (fault), incuso; (maintain), sustento; (out), comperio
A finder, inventor
A finding, inventio, investigatio
Fine, elegans, eximius, venustus, mundus, ornatus, politus
Very fine, præclarus
To make fine, orno, polio
To fine, muleto, mulctam imponere; (purify), defæco, purgo
A fine, mulcta
To pay a fine, mulctam solvere
In fine (finally), deniquè
Fineable, mulctæ obnoxius
Finely, acitè, bellè
Fineness, elegantia, tenuitas
A finer (refiner), purgator
Finery, ornatus, ornamentum
A finger, digitus; (fore), index; (middle), verpus; (ring), digitus annularis; (little), digitus auricularis; (of a glove), digitale
Of a finger, digitalis
To finger, tracto, inuneo
Light-fingered, furax
At fingers' ends, ad unguem
Finical, mollis, nitidulus
A fining, mulctatio
To finish, finio, perficio

A finisher, perfector
A finishing, peractio, expletio
Finishing, ultimus
Finite, finitus, definitus
Finny, pinnatus
A fir-tree, abies
Made of fir, abiegnus
Fire, ignis; (heat), ardor, focus
A fire, incendium
To fire (set on fire), accendo, incendo; (be on fire), deflagro, ardeo; (be in a passion), excandesco
A fire (to strike), ignem excutere; (to make), ignem accendere
On fire, incensus, inflammatus
A setting on fire, incendium
A firebrand, torris
Fire-arms, arma ignivoma
A fire-lock, sclopetum
A fire-ball, glans ardens
For the fire, focarius
Fiery, igneus, ignitus
Firing (fuel), fomes
A firkin, amphorata
Firm, firmus, stabilis, ratus, confirmatus, constans
To make firm, firmo
The firmament, æther, cœlum
Of the firmament, æthereus
Firmly, firmitèr, firmè
Firmness, firmitas, constantia
The first, primus; (and foremost), princeps; (but one), à primo proximus
At first, primò, principio
First of all, imprimis
First-born, primogenitus
First-fruits, primitiæ
A fish, piscis
Full of fish, piscosus
Belonging to fish, piscatorius
To fish, piscor; (a pond), piscinam exhaurire; (out), exquiro
Fish-provision, opsonium
To treat with fish, opsonor
A fisherman, piscator
A fishery, piscaria
A fishing, piscatio, piscatura
A fishing-rod, arundo piscatoria
A fishmonger, piscarius
Shell-fishes, pisces testacei
Fishy, piscosus
To fisk, cursito, agito
A fissure, fissura, rima
A fist, pugnus
A fistula, fistula
Fit, accommodatus, congruens, idoneus; (becoming), decens; (capable), aptus; (convenient), tempestivus; (ready), paratus
It is fit, æquum est
To fit, or Be fit, accommodo; (make fit), adapto, accommodo; (match), socio; (retaliate), par pari referre; (up a house), domum ornare
A fit, paroxysmus, accessus; (whim), impetus animi; (of drunkenness), crapula; (of sickness), ægrotatio
Fitly, aptè, tempestivè
Fitness, habilitas, occasio
Fitting, congruens
A fitting, adaptatio
Five, quinque, quini
The five, pentas
Of five, quinarius
Five (times), quinquiès; (as much), quintuplus; (years), quinquennium; (years old), quinquennis
Fivefold, quincuplex
Five hundred, quingenti
Of five hundred, quingenarius

[46]

FLA   FLO   FLY

Five hundredth, quingentesimus
Five hundred times, quingenties
To fix (fasten), firmo, figo; (a day), diem constituere
Flabby, flaccidus, lentus
A flag, vexillum, insigne; (of a ship), aplustre; (rush), juncus   [esseo
To flag, flaccesco, langueo, marceo
A flageolet, fistula minor
Flagging, languens, lentus
Flagitious, scelestus, nefarius
A flagon, lagena
Flagrant, apparens, insignis
A flail, flagellum
A flake, fragmen; (of fire), scintilla; (of ice), frustum; (of snow), floccus
To flake, in lamellas abire
A flam, prætextus, nugæ
To flam, deludo, ludificor
A flambeau, fax, funale
A flame, flamma
To flame, flammo, flagro
To be in a flame, incendor
To set on a flame, incendo
Flaming, flagrans, splendidus
Flamingly, flagranter, splendidè
The flank, ilia; (of an army), cohortes alares
Flanked, à latere protectus
Flannel, lanula
A flap, pars pendula; (of the ear), auris lobus; (slap), alapa; (of the throat), epiglottis; (a flyflap), muscarium
To flap (strike), alapam impingere; (hang down), dependeo; (let down), demitto
A flapping, percussio
To flare, liquando scintillare; (in one's eyes), oculos præstringere
A flash (of light), fulgor; (of fire), coruscatio; (sudden impulse), impetus; (boasting fellow), thraso, jactator; (of wit), ingenii æstus   [assilio
To flash, fulguro, emico; (as water),
Flashy, mollis, fatuus, levis, evanidus, subitaneus
A flask, lagena; (bottle), ampulla vinum cooperta; (for powder), capsa
A flasket, cophinus
Flat (smooth), planus; (and plain), manifestus, apertus; (dull), frigidus; (drink), vappa; (in taste), insipidus; (along), pronus; (note), sonus gravis
To flat, exæquo, sterno
The flat part, planum; (or level), planities
A flat (shelf), syrtis; (flats in the seas), brevia, vadum
Flat, or Flatly (in sound), graviter; (plainly in speech), perspicuè; (absolutely), præcisè
Flatness, planities, æquor; (of a discourse), jejunitas sermonis; (in taste), insulsitas
To flatten, complano; (grow flat), insulsus esse
To flatter, adulor, parasitor
Flattered, permulsus, delinitus
A flatterer, adulator, parasitus
Flattering, blandiens
A flattering, or Flattery, adulatio
Flatteringly, adulatoriè, blandè
Of flattery, adulatorius
Flatulency, ventris inflatio
Flatulent, inflans, flatuosus
To flaunt, cinciané vestiri
Flavour, gustus, odor
A flaw (chink), rimula; (defect), vitium, defectus
[47]

Flawy, vitiosus
To flaw, dehisco
Flax, linum
Made of fine flax, carbaseus
A flax-dresser, linarius
Of flax, lineus
Flaxen, flavus
To flay, pellem detrahere
Flayed, pelle exutus
A flaying, pellis detractio
A flea, pulex
Full of fleas, pulicosus
Flea-bites, pulicum vestigia
Flea-bitten, maculis variis distinctus
A fleam, scalpellum equinum
Fled, profugus, elapsus
Fledged, pennatus, pinnatus
To be fledged, pumesco
To flee, fugio. See Fly
A fleece, vellus
To fleece (shear), tondeo; (strip), emungere aliquem
Fleeced, tonsus, detonsus, emunctus
Fleecy, laneus
To fleer, derideo, irrideo
A fleerer, derisor
A fleet, classis
The fleet-prison, fleta
Fleet (swift), velox, celer
Fleeting, fugax, fluxus
Flesh, caro
Living on flesh, carnivorus
Fleshiness, corpulentia
Fleshiness, carnalitas
Fleshly, libidinosus, pravus
Fleshy, corpulentus, carnosus
A fletcher, sagittarum faber
A flew, tragula
Flexibility, flexibilitas
Flexible, flexibilis, flexilis; (easy to be intreated), exorabilis
Flexibleness, placabilitas
Flexure, curvatura
To flicker, alas motitare
A flier, libramentum
A flight (escape), effugium, fuga; (of birds), volatus, grex avium; (of the brain), impetus animi
To put to flight, fugo, in fugam dare, or vertere
To take flight, aufugio, fugam capessere
Flimsy, flaccidus, lentus
To flinch (give out), desisto; (desert), desero; (quit), tergiversor; (start), absilio; (give ground), retrocedo
A flinching, tergiversatio
To fling, mitto, jacio; (away), abjicio; (out), ejicio; (down), dejicio; (in), injicio; (up a place), depono
A fling, jactus, deceptio
A flinger, jaculator
A flint, silex
Of flint, siliceus
Flinty, siliceus, saxis asper
Flippant, loquax
To flit, volito, migro
A flitch of bacon, succidia
A float of timber, schedia
To float, fluctuo; (a meadow), rivum in pratum deducere
Floating, fluctuans
A flock, grex, cœtus, turba; (of wool), floccus
To flock together, convenio, coëo
Of a flock, gregalis
In flocks, gregatim, confertim
A flock-bed, culcita lanea
A flocking together, congregatio
A flood, diluvium, inundatio
The flood (tide), fluxus maris

A land flood, torrens
A flood-gate, emissarium
To flood, inundo, exundo
The flook, pars anchoræ adunca
A floor (of a house), tabulatum; (paved), pavimentum; (of a barn), area
To floor, consterno, asso
A flooring, contabulatio
A florentine, torta
Florid, floridus, nitidus
Floridness, concinnitas
A florist, florilegus
A flounce, fimbria
A flounder, passer niger
Flour of meal, farina
To flour, farinâ conspergere
To flourish, floreo, vigeo; (weapons), arma vibrare; (brag), glorior
A flourish, inanis, jactatio, prælusio, ornamentum
Flourishing, vegetus
A flout, scomma, dicterium
To flout, irrideo, derideo
Floating, dicax
A flouting, cavillatio, derisio
To flow, fluo, labor; (about), circumfluo; (abound), affluo; (abroad), diffluo; (back), refluo; (before a place), præfluo; (between), interfluo; (by), præterfluo; (continually), fluito; (down), defluo; (in), influo; (out), effluo; (over), exundo; (as the sea), æstuo; (together), confluo; (under), subfluo; (unto), accedo, affluo
To flower, floreo, germino; (as beer), scintillo, spumo
A flower, flos
A flower de lis, iris
Flower of age, adolescentia
A flower of a family, gloria
Made of flowers, floreus
The flowers, menses
Flowery, floridus
Flowing, fluidus, fluens; (about), circumfluus; (over), redundans; (and ebbing), reciprocus; (in speech), volubilis
A flowing, fluxus
Flowingly, volubiliter
To fluctuate, fluctuo, dubito
A fluctuation, fluctuatio
Fluent, fluidus, eloquens
Fluency, volubilitas linguæ
Fluid, fluidus, liquidus
Fluidity, fluor
A fluke, dens anchoræ
Flung, jactus, abjectus, deceptus
Flush (abundance), copia, vis; (abounding), abundans; (of money), nummatus
Flushed with success, elatus
A flushing, sanguineus fluxus
Flustered (in drink), semiebrius
A flute, fistula, tibia
Fluted, laqueatus
Flutings, canaliculi
To flutter (fly), volito; (be doubtful), dubito; (to and fro), curaito; (in speech), balbutio
A fluttering, volitatio, hæsitatio
A flux (looseness), profluvium; (of humours), humorum fluxus; (of blood), hæmorrhagia
A fly, musca; (Spanish), cantharis
Fly-blows, muscarum ova
Fly-blown, corruptus, infectus
To fly (as a bird), volo; (about), circumvolo; (against), involo; (as news), publicor; (at), peto, impeto; (in pieces), dissilio; (away), avolo, aufugio; (back),

refugio; (before), prævolo; (beyond), prætervolo; (down), devolo; (far), profugio; (from place to place), transfugio; (into a passion), iracundiâ ardere; (out, or squander), prodigo; (for refuge), asylum petere; (or run away), fugio
To let fly (shoot), displodo
A flying, volatus; (away), effugium
Flying, expeditus, vagus, aversus
A foal, pullus equinus; (of an ass), asellus
To foal, fœtum edere
To foam, spumo, frendo
Foam, spuma
A foaming, spumatus
Foamy, spumeus, spumatus
To fob, eludo, frando
A fob, loculus minor
Fob, commentitius, fictitius
The focus, apex
Fodder, pabulum, fœnum; (of lead), vehes; (of straw), pabulum stramineum
Of fodder, pabularis
To fodder, fœno pascere
A foddering, pabulatio
A foe, inimicus, inimica
A fog, nebula
Fogginess, aëris crassitudo
Foggy, nebulosus
A foible, imbecilitas
A foil (for fencing), rudis; (for a diamond), substratum; (repulse), repulsa
To foil (beat), sterno, repello
To foist in, obtrudere furtim, adultero
Foisted in, subditus
A fold, plica, sinus
To fold, plico, complico; (in), implico; (about, or up), complico; (sheep), stabulo
Fold for sheep, ovile, crates
Folded (plaited), plicatus; (up), involutus; (as cattle), stabulatus
A folding, plicatura; (of sheep), stabulatio
Foliage, folia
In folio, in folio
Folk (people), vulgus, plebs
To follow, sequor (after), assequor, insector; (close), insto; (succeed), succedo; (a trade), exerceo; (in course), alterno; (diligently), assector; (close at the heels), in terga hærere
Followed, comitatus, deductus
May be followed, imitandus
A follower, comes, discipulus
Following, sequens
A following (attending upon), deductio; (consequence), consequentia
Folly, stultitia, ineptia
Fome, apuma
To fome, spumo, fremo; (at the mouth), spumas ore agere
To foment, foveo, alo
A fomentation, fomentum
A fomenter, conciator
A fomenting, fomentatio
Foming, spumans
A foming, spumatio
Fond, ineptus, futilis, vanus, cupidus; (overkind), indulgens
To be fond of, indulgeo
To fondle, foveo, indulgeo
A fondling, delicatus puer
Fondly, blandè, cupidè, ineptè
Fondness, indulgentia, ineptia
A font, baptisterium
[48]

Food, cibus, victus, pabulum
Fit for food, esculentus
A fool, stultus; (jester), morio; (in a play), sannio
To fool, ludifacor, irrideo
To play the fool, ineptio
To be fooled, derideor, deludor
To fool away (money), pecuniam incautè erogare; (time), tempus terere inutilitèr
Fooled, derisus, illusus
Foolery, deridiculum, nugæ
Foolhardiness, temeritas
Foolhardy, temerarius, audax
Foolish, ineptus, fatuus, insulsus
To make foolish, infatuo
Foolish tricks, ineptiæ
Foolishly, stultè, insulsè
Foolishness, stultitia
A foot, pes; (of a table), fulcrum; (of a hill), radix; (of a pillar), basis
Belonging to a foot, pedalis
On foot, pedester, pedes
To foot (away), cito pedo ambulare; (stockings), concinno
A footman (soldier), pedes; (servant), assecla
The foot (soldiers), peditatus
A footstep, vestigium
A footstool, scabellum
Of half a foot, semipedalis
Of two foot, bipedalis
On the same foot, æquali gradu
Two-footed, bipes
Three-footed, tripes
Four-footed, quadripes
Many-footed, multipes
Brazen-footed, æripes
Broad-footed, planipes
A sure footing, stabilitas
A fop (beau), bellus homo; (impertinent), nugator
To play the fop, nugor
Foppery, nugæ, tricæ
Foppish, nugax, nimis nitidus
Foppishly, ineptè, stolidè
Foppishness, ineptia
For, conj. nam, enim, etenim, quippe; prep. à, ad, de, ex, in, ob, per, præ, pro, propter, secundum
For (for the sake of), causâ, ergo, gratiâ, per, pro, propter
Forage, pabulum
To forage, pabulor
A forager, pabulator
A foraging, pabulatio
To forbear (let alone), abstineo; (leave off), desisto; (spare), parco; (suffer), patior
Forbearance, indulgentia
To forbid, veto, prohibeo; (strictly), interdico
Forbidden, interdictus, prohibitus
Forborn, omissus, lenitèr tractatus
Force (endeavour), conatus; (importance), momentum; (necessity), necessitas; (violence), vis, impetus; (strength), robur
To force, cogo, compello, adigo, impello; (back), repello; (down), detrudo, demergo; (in), defigo; (out), depello; (a woman), stupro; (a trench), aggerem exscindere; (or take by force), vi capere
To be of force, valeo
Of great force, valens, potens
Of small force, levis
Of more force, valentior
By main force, vi et armis
By open force, aperto marte

Forces, copiæ
Forcible (clear, or strong), clarus, potens, efficax; (violent), violent
Forcibly, vehementèr [lent
A forcing, compulsio, vis
A ford, vadum
To ford, vado transire
Fordable, quod transiri potest
Fore, anterior
To forearm, præmunio
To forebode, præsagio, ominor
A foreboder, hariolus
A foreboding, præsagium
Forecast, providentia
To forecast, provideo
A forecasting, provisus
The forecastle, prora
To foredoom, prædestino
The fore-door, antica
Forefathers, proavi
Fore-feet, pedes anteriores; (finger), index; (head), frons
To forego (quit), abdico; (not meddle with), abstineo; (a claim), de jure suo recedere
Foregoing, præcedens
Having two foreheads, bifrons
Foreign, externus, alienus
A foreigner, advena
To forejudge, præjudico
To foreknow, præscio
A foreknowing, prænotio
Foreknowledge, præscientia
Foreknown, præcognitus
A foreland, promontorium
A foreman, præses, præjurator
The foremast, malus anterior
Foremost, primus, præcipuus
First and foremost, imprimis
The forenoon, tempus antemeridianum
To fore-ordain, prædestino
Fore-part of the head, sinciput
A forerunner, præcursor
To foresee, prævideo, prospicio
A foreseeing, prævisio
Foresight, prospicientia
The foreskin, præputium
To forespeak, prædico, fascino
A forest, saltus, nemus, sylva
Forest-like, sylvestris
To forestal, anticipio, præmercor
Forestalled, interceptus
A forestaller, annonæ flagellator; (of a market), præemptor
A forestalling, interceptio
A forester, viridarius
A forestaste, anticipatio
To foretel, prædico
A foreteller, vates, fatidicus
A foretelling, prædictio
A forethought, præmeditatio
A foretoken, præsagium, omen
A foretop, antiæ
To forewarn, præmoneo
A forewarning, præmonitus
A forfeit, mulcta, pœna
To forfeit, mulctâ damnari; (one's credit), existimationem perdere; (one's favour), gratiâ excidere; (a recognisance), vadimonium deserere; (one's word), fidem violare
Forfeited, confiscatus, perditus
A forfeiture, confiscatio, damnum
To forge (as smiths do), cudo, fabricor; (devise), fingo; (counterfeit), ementior, subjicio; (melt), conflo, liquefacio
A forge, furnus fabrilis
Forged, fabricatus, fictus, adulteratus, confictus, ementitus
A forger, fabricator; (of writings), falsarius; (of tales), delator

A forgery, figmentum, fraus
A forging (of lies), calumnia; (of tales), fictio
To forget, obliviscor; (neglect), negligo, prætereo
Forgetful, obliviosus
Forgetfulness, oblivio
A forgetting, prætermissio
To forgive, condono, ignosco, remitto
Forgiven, condonatus, remissus; (not to be forgiven), inexpiabilis
Forgiveness, condonatio, venia
A forgiving, remissio
Forgotten, oblivioni traditus
To be forgotten, obruor, exolesco
A fork, furca; (for dung), bidens; (for flesh), creagra
Forlorn, derelictus, solus, perditus
A form (figure), figura; (manner), modus; (bench), scamnum; (in printing), unum latus schedæ; (of words), certa verba; (class), classis
A set form, formula, exemplar
To form, formo, reformo
Formal, formalis, affectatus
Formalities (robes), magistratûs vestitus
Formality, solemnis formula
Formally, formalitèr, ex formulâ
A formation, formatio
Former, prior, superior, priscus
Formerly, prius, antehàc
Formidable, formidabilis
A forming, formatio, creatio
Formless, informis, rudis
Fornication, fornicatio
A fornicator, scortator
To forsake, desero, abdico, deficio, renuncio
A forsaking, derelictio, desertio; (of the faith), apostasia
Forsooth, sane, scilicèt
To forswear, pejero, perjuro
A forswearer, pejerator
A forswearing, perjurium
Forsworn, perjurus
A fort, præsidium, castellum
Forth, foras, extrà
Forth-coming, præstò, in promptu
Forth of, extra; (forthwith), confestim, continuò, protinùs, mox
A fortification, munimentum; (before a wall), antemurale
To fortify, firmo, circumvallo, munio, præmunio
Fortitude, fortitudo, virtus
A fortnight, dies quatuordecim
A fortress, arx, præsidium
Fortuitous, fortuitus, casu accidens
Fortunate, fortunatus, faustus
Fortunately, faustè, auspicatò
Fortune, fortuna, sors; (estate), facultates, opes
Ill-fortune, infortunium
A fortune-teller, fatidicus, astrologus
Forty, quadraginta; (of forty), quadragenarius; (times), quadragiès
Forward (bold), audax; (inclined), proclivis, propensus; (made a progress), provectus, progressus; (soon ripe), præcox; (ready), promptus, alacer
Forward, prorsùm
To forward, promoveo, urgeo
Time forward, deincèps, posthàc
Forwarding, promovens, conducens

[49]

Forwardness, promptitudo, progressus, progressio
A fosse, fossa; (way), via fossa
Fossile, fossilia
To foster, nutrio, alo
A foster-father, nutritius; (mother), nutrix; (child), alumnus
Fought, pugnatus; (against), oppugnatus, impugnatus
Foul, fœdus, squalidus, impurus, lutulentus; (unfair), dolosus, turpis; (ill-favoured), deformis; (vicious), obscœnus; (stormy), turbidus; (weather), tempestas
To foul, fœdo, inquino
To be foul, sordeo, squaleo
Foulness, turpitudo, squalor; (of a crime), atrocitas; (in appearance), deformitas
Found, inventus, repertus; (out), inventus, investigatus
To found, fundo, construo
A foundation, fundamentum
From the foundation, funditùs
To founder (as a horse), titubo; (as a ship), dissolvor
A founder, fundator, conditor
Foundered, claudus, mancus, dissolutus
A founding (of a house), fundatio; (of metal), fusio
A foundling, infans expositus
Of a fountain, fontanus
A fountain, fons
Four, quatuor; (at cards, &c.), quaternio; (cornered), quadrangulus; (square), quadratus; (day's space), quatriduum; (year's space), quatriennium; (times), quatèr; (times as much), quadruplò; (fold), quadruplex; (ways, or parts), quadrifariàm; (footed), quadrupes; (hundred) quadringenti; (hundred times), quadringentiès; (hundredth), quadringentesimus; (teen), quatuordecim; (teen times), quatuordeciès
The fourth, quartus
Fourthly, quartò
A fowl, volucris, avis
To fowl, aucupor
A fowler, auceps
A fowling, aucupatio; (piece), tormentum aucupatorium
A fox, vulpes
Belonging to a fox, vulpinus
An old fox (knave), veterator
To play the fox, vulpinor
A fraction, fractio, infractio
Fractious, litigiosus, rixosus
A fracture, fractura
To fracture, frango, confringo
Fragile, fragilis, caducus
Fragility, fragilitas
A fragment, fragmentum, rustum
Fragments, reliquiæ
Fragrance, fragrantia
Fragrant, fragrans, suaveolens
Fragrantly, suavè
Frail, fragilis, fluxus, caducus
A frail, fiscella, fiscina
Frailty, fragilitas, imbecillitas
To frame (fashion), formo; (contrive), molior; (build), fabricor, condo; (join together), compingo, contabulo; (a story), fingo, comminiscor
The frame (of a building), compages ædificii; (of the world), compages mundi; (of a table), fulcrum; (of a picture), tabella; (for work), modulus

A framer, fabricator, faber
A framing, formatio
To franchise, manumitto
Franciscan, Franciscanus
Frank, liberalis, ingenuus, liber
To frank letters, gratis signare
Frankincense, thus
Of frankincense, thureus
Frankly, ingenuè, liber
Frankness, liberalitas, sinceritas
Frantic, mente captus, insanus
To be frantic, insanio, furo
Franticness, dementia
Fraternal, fraternus
A fraternity, fraternitas, societas
A fratricide, fratricida
Fraud, fraus, dolus
Fraudulence, fraudulentia
Fraudulent, dolosus
Fraudulently, fraudulentèr, vafrè
Fraught, oneratus, plenus
A fray, rixa, jurgium, lis
To fray (as cloth), dehisco; (fright), terrefacio
A freak, subitum impetus animi, petulantia, deliramentum
Freakish, petulans
Freakishness, petulantia, dementia
A freckle, lentigo, nævus
Free, immunis, liber; (citizen), civis natus; (in giving), liberalis; (from business), otiosus; (in conversation), sincerus, candidus; (common), communis; (gift), munus gratuitum
To free, emancipo, libero
To make free, civitate donare
Freeborn, ingenuus, liberalis
A freehold, possessio libera
A freeholder, fundi liberi possessor
A freeman, liber, civis
Freed, liberatus, laxatus
Freedom, immunitas, facilitas; (from), vacuitas
A freeing, liberatio, manumissio
Freely, liberè, liberalitèr, apertè, spontè, gratis
Freeness, benignitas
Freestone, saxum vivum
Free-will, liberum arbitrium
To freeze, gelo, congelo
To freight, navem onerare
To pay freight, naulum solvere
Freight, naulum, onus
French, Gallicus, Gallicanus
In French, Gallicè
A Frenchman, Gallus
A frenzy, dementia, insania
Frequency, frequentia
Frequent, frequens, creber
To frequent, frequento, celebro
A frequenting, frequentatio
Frequently, frequentèr, sæpè, crebrò
A fresco, aura refrigerans
Fresh (cool), frigidulus; (new), recens novus; (lusty), vigens; (unsalted), insulsus; (not tired), integer, recens; (and fasting), jejunus
To be fresh and lively, vigeo
A fresh colour, color floridus; (man), tyro, novitius
Afresh, or again, de integro
Freshness, novitas, color vegetus
To fret (vex), crucio, crucior; (or eat away), corrodo; (as wine), acesco; " (rub), frico; (grieve), doleo
To put in a fret, irrito
A fret, ira
Fret-work, striatura

D

FRO

Fretful, morosus
Fretfulness, morositas
Fretted, cruciatus, attritus
A fretting, angor animi; (rubbing), attritus
A friar, frater religiosus, monachus
Friction, frictio
Friday, dies Veneris
Good Friday, Parasceve magna
Fried, frixus; (meat), caro frixa
A friend, amicus, amica
Friendless, inops, desertus
Friendliness, benevolentia
Friendly, benevolus, humanus
Friendly, amicè, benevolè
Friends (kindred), propinqui
Friendship, amicitia
A frigate, liburna, celox
A fright, terror, formido
To frighten, terreo, perterreo
Frightful, terribilis, horridus
Frightfully, horridè
Frightfulness, terror, horror
A frightening, consternatio
Frigid, frigidus, gelidus
Frigidity, frigiditas, frigus
Frigidly, frigidè
A fringe, lacinia, fimbria
To fringe, fimbriam consuere
Fringed, fimbriatus
To frisk, tripudio, lascivio, exulto
Frisky, lætus, hilaris
To frisle, crispo, torqueo
Frisled, calamistratus, cirratus
A frisling-iron, calamistrum
A frith, æstuarium, fretum
A fritter, artolaganus
Frivolous, vanus, inanis, levis
Frivolously, nugatoriè
Friese, pannus villosus
To frizzle, crispo
To and fro, ultrò citròque
A frock, sagum, palla
A frog, rana
To be frolic, hilaresco, exulto
A frolic (whim), repentinus animi impetus
Frolicsome, jocosus, hilaris
From, à, ab, de, è, ex, per; (above), desupèr; (abroad), peregrè; (beneath), infernè; (house to house), domesticatim; (door to door), ostiatim; (hence), hinc; (street to street), vicatim; (thenceforth), exindè; (time to time), continuò; (whence), undè; (without), ab extra
The front, frons
A front, audacia; (of an army), prima acies
A frontier, confinium, limes
A frontispiece, frontispicium
A frontlet, frontale
A frost, gelu, pruina
Frosty, pruinosus
Froth, spuma
To froth, spumo, bullio
Frothy, spumeus, spumosus; (trifling), ineptus, futilis, nugax
Frothing, spumans
A frothing, spumatus
Frouzy, olidus, putidus
Froward, protervus, morosus
Frowardly, protervè, morosè
Frowardness, protervitas
A frown, ruga; (of fortune), casus adversus
To frown, frontem contrahere; (upon), iniquis oculis intueri
Frowning, torvus, nubilus
A frowning, frontis corrugatio; (countenance), frons caperata
Frowningly, diro vultu

[50]

FUR

Fructiferous, fructifer, frugifer
To fructify, fœcundo
Frugal, frugi abstinens
Frugality, frugalitas
Frugally, frugalitèr, parcè
Fruit, fructus; (profit), lucrum; (of the womb), fœtus
Bearing fruit, fructifer
A fruiterer, pomarius
Fruit-time, autumnus
Fruitful, fertilis, ferax, fœcundus
To be fruitful, abundo
To make fruitful, fœcundo
Fruitfully, fertilitèr
Fruitfulness, fertilitas
Fruition, fruitio, possessio
Fruitless (barren), sterilis; (disappointed), frustratus; (unprofitable), inutilis
First-fruits, primitiæ
To frustrate, frustror, fallo
Frustrating, fallens
To fry, frigo, æstuo, sudo
Fryed, frictus, frixus
A frying, frixura
A frying-pan, sartago
To fuddle, inebrio, inebrior
Fuddled, potu obrutus
A fuddling-bout, compotatio
Fuel, fomes
A fugitive, fugitivus, profugus
To fulfil, impleo, perago
Fulfilled, expletus, impletus
A fulfilling, peractio, perfectio
Fulgency, splendor, nitor
Fulgent, fulgidus, splendidus
Full, plenus, expletus, refertus; (quite), omninò, prorsùs, ad plenum; (speed), citatus; (very), valdè, vehementèr; (perfect), perfectus, integer; (plentiful), affluens, exundans; (of words), loquax
To be full, abundo, satior
Half-full, semiplenus
Full age, adultus, puber
To full cloth, pannos densare
Fulled, à fullone densatus
A fuller, fullo
Fuller, adj. plenior
Of a fuller, fullonius
Fuller's earth, terra Cretosa
Fully, plenè
To fulminate, fulmino
Fulmination, fulminatio
Fulminating, fulminens
Fulness, plenitudo, satietas
Fulsome, nauseosus, ingratus
Fulsomeness, nausea
To fumble, inscitè aggredi
A fumbler, qui ineptè tractat
A fumbling, inepta administratio
Fumblingly, ineptè, infabrè
A fume, vapor, exhalatio
To fume, exhalo, irascor
In a fume, iratus
Fumed, exhalatus
To fumigate, fumigo, suffio
A fumigation, suffitus
Fun, ludus, jocus
A function, functio, munus
A fund, ingens vis, cumulus
The fundament, anus, culus
Fundamental, fundamentalis
Fundamentals, fundamenta
A funeral, funus, exequiæ
Of a funeral, funebris, funereus
Funeral rites, inferiæ, justa
Fungous, spongiosus
A funk, vapor suffocans
A funnel, infundibulum; (of a chimney), nares camini
To furbish, polio, recudo

GAI

A furbisher, politor
A furbishing, interpolatio
The furies, Furiæ
Furious, furiosus, rabidus
To be furious, furio, insanio
Furiously, furiosè, furentèr
Furiousness, rabies
To furl, complico, contraho
A furling, complicatio
A furlong, stadium
A furlough, commeatus
A furnace, fornax; (for brewing), caldarium; (for a potter), fignina
To furnish, suppedito, instruo
A furnisher, instructor
A furnishing, suppeditatio
Furniture, apparatus, supellex
Fur, pellis, villus
To fur, pellibus consuere
A furrier, pello
A furrow, sulcus; (of a pulley), lacuna
To furrow, sulco
Farther, adv. ultrà, ulteriùs, longiùs; adj. ulterior
To further, proveho, promoveo
A furtherance, adjumentum
A furtherer, adjutor
Furthermore, porrò, insupèr
Furthest, extremus, ultimus
At the furthest, ad summum
Fury, furor, rabies
Full of fury, furiosus, rabiosus
Like a fury, furialis
Furse, genista spinosa
A fusee, scloppetum
Fuss, tumultus, strepitus
Fustian, gossipinus, xylinum
Of fustian, gossipinus, xylinus
Fustian (bombast), turgida verba, sermo inflatus, ampullæ
Fustiness, putor
Fusty, putidus, mucidus
To be, or smell fusty, puteo
Futility, futilitas
Future, futurus
For the future, in futurum
Futurity, tempus futurum
Fy! phy! vah!

G.

To gabble, garrio
A gabbler, garrulus
A gabbling, garrulitas
A gabion, corbis terrà oppletus
To gable, domûs fastigium anterius
A gad, massa; (bee), œstrum
A gadder, vagus, erro
Gadding, errabundus
A gadding, vagatio
A gag, epistomium
To gag, os obstruere
A gage (pledge), pignus
To gage (pawn), oppignero (casks), vasa metiri
To gaggle, giocito
Gaiety, splendor, nitor
Gaily, nitidè, splendidè
Gain, lucrum, quæstus
To gain, lucrifacio, lucror; (approbation), movere approbationem; (credit), fidem impetrare; (increase), augeo; (ground, or end), voto potiri
Gainful, lucrosus, quæstuosus
Gainsaid, negatus
To gainsay, contradico

GAR — GEN — GIB

Gainsaying, repugnax
Garish, lautus, splendidus
A gait, incessus, passus
A gale, flatus, flamen, aura
The gall, fel
Like gall, felleus
A gall (nut), galla
To gall, uro, attero, destringo
Gallant, nitidus, lautus
A gallant, homo scitus; (to a woman), mœchus, adulter
Gallantly, nitidè, egregiè
Gallantness, nitor, magnificentia; (of spirit), magnanimitas
Gallantry, magnificentia
A gallery, ambulacrum, porticus
An open gallery, procestrium
A galley, navis actuaria, or longa
A galliard (dance), saltatio festiva
A gallipot, narthecium
A gallon, congius
Galloon-lace, lacinia
To gallop, cursu concitato ferri
A gallop, cursus effusus
A galloper, eques rapidus
A galloway, mannus
A gallows, patibulum, furca
A gambol, saltus, ludus
Game, lusus, ludus
Game, præda
To game, lusibus studere, ludo
Game, *adj.* pugnax, audax
Gamesome, procax, ludibundus
Gamesomeness, petulantia
A gamester, lusibus addictus; (gambler), aleator dolosus
Gaming, alea, lusio
For gaming, aleatorius
A gammon of bacon, perna
The gamut, scala musica
A gander, anser mas
A gang, grex, sodalitium
A gangrene, gangræna
A gantlet, manica militaris
A gap, apertura, fissura
A stopgap, impedimentum
To gape (with the mouth), oscito, hio; (after, *or* covet), appeto, inhio; (chink, as the ground), dehisco; (for breath), respiro, anhelo; (at one), aspecto, intueor
Gaping, hians, impudens
A gaping (opening), hiatus; (yawning), oscitatio
A garb, habitus, gestus
Garbage, viscera; (refuse), quisquiliæ, sordes
To garble, pergo, excerno; (cull out), excerpo
A garbler, purgator
A garbling, purgatio
Garboil, tumultus
A garden, hortus; (of flowers), floretum; (nursery), seminarium; (of pleasure), viridarium; (for pot-herbs), olitorium; (for salad), acetarium; (of roses), rosetum
Of a garden, hortensis
A gardener, hortulanus, olitor
A gargle, gargarismus
To gargle, gargarizo
A gargling, gargarisatio
A garland, sertum, corona; (of bays), laurea
Garlick, allium
A garment, vestis; (an under garment), tunica; (an upper garment), pallium
Of garments, vestiarius
A garner, horreum
To garnish, orno, adorno
A garnishing, ornamentum, exornatio

[51]

A garret, contignatio superior
To garrison, præsidio munire
A garrison, præsidium
To be in garrison, præsidium agitare
Of a garrison, præsidiarius
Garrisoned, præsidio firmatus
Garrulity, garrulitas
A garter, genuale, persicellis
To garter, subligo
Garter (the officer), garterius
A gasconnade, jactatio
A gash, vulnus, cæsura
To gash, vulnero, scindo
A gasp, hiatus
To gasp, respiro, anhelo
A gate, janua, ostium; (in going), incessus, passus
A gate-way, semita, callis
A gate-keeper, janitor
To gather, colligo, decerpo; (from arguments), concludo; (as a crowd), circumfundor; (guess), conjector; (as a hen her chickens), foveo; (again), recolligo; (corn), frumentor; (curd), coagulo; (flowers), flores carpere; (grapes), vindemio; (out), excerpo; (strength), reviresco; (on heaps), congero, accumulo; (persons together), congrego; (up), colligo; (wealth), opes conquirere; (alms), stipem colligere
Gathers, plicæ
A gatherer, collector; (of fruit), strictor; (of grapes), vindemiator; (of toll), publicanus; (of olives, &c.), legulus
A gathering, collectio; (together), congregatio; (of fruits), carptura; (of grapes), vindemiatio; (round), conglobatio; (of matter in a sore), suppuratio
Gaudily, lautè, splendidè
Gaudiness, lautitia
Gaudy, lautus, splendidus
A gauger, doliorum mensor
Gauging, doliorum mensura
A gauntlet, manica ferrea
Gauze, nebula linea
Gay, comptus, lautus
To be gay, niteo, splendeo; (in temper), exhilaro
To make gay, exorno
Gay (brisk), hilaris, alacer
Gaiety, lautitia, hilaritas
To Gaze, avidè spectare
A gazer, spectator
A gazette, statæ literæ rerum novarum nuncies
Gehenna, gehenna
To geld, castro, emasculo
Gelt, castratus, eviratus
A gelding, castratio
A gelding (nag), cantherium
Gelly, jus gelatum
A gem, gemma
A gender, genero, procreo
A genealogy, genealogia
Genealogical, genealogus
A genealogist, genealogus
General, generalis, universus; (frequent), frequens, communis
A general (of an army), imperator; (of an order), generalis
The generality, plerique omnes
Generally (universally), generatim; (commonly), generaliter, plerumque; (in general), in universum
To generate, genero, procreo
A generation, generatio; (lineage), genus, prosapia; (age), seculum, ætas
Generative, genialis
Generic, secundum genus
Generosity, generositas, liberalitas
[liberalis
Generous, generosus, magnificus,
Generously, liberalitèr
Genesis, Genesis
Genial, genialis, hilaris
The genitals, genitalia, pudenda
A geniting, pomum præcox
Genitive, genitivus
A genius, genius, indoles, ingenium, captus
Genteel, honestus, generosus
Genteelly, venustè, pulchrè
Genteelness, venustas, liberalitas
A Gentile, ethnicus, gentilis
Gentilism, superstitio ethnica
Gentility, nobilitas, venustas
Gentle (mild), mitis, lenis; (courteous), comis, affabilis; (tame), cicur
To grow gentle, mitesco
To make gentle, domo
Gentle and simple, nobiles et ignobiles
A gentleman, generosus; (of the royal bedchamber), regis cubicularius   [nestus
Like a gentleman, ingenuus, ho-
Gentleness, clementia, lenitas
A gentlewoman, generosa
Gently, pacatè, lenitèr; (slowly), lentè, placidè
Gentry, nobilitas   [flexio
Genuflection (kneeling), genu-
Genuine, genuinus, purus
A geographer, geographus
Geographical, geographicus
Geography, geographia
Geometrical, geometricus
A geometrician, geometra
Geometry, geometria
Georgics, georgica
Germane, germanus, genuinus
To germinate, germino, pullulo
A germination, germinatio
Gerund, gerundium
A gerund, gerundium
Gesticulation, gesticulatio
A gesture, gestus, status
Full of gestures, gestuosus
To get, acquiro, adipiscor; (gone), abeo, secedo; (acquainted), familiaritatem inire; (above), supero, vinco; (abroad, *or* be told), emano; (before), anticipo; (beget), gigno, procreo, genero; (with child), gravido; (gain), lucror, prætereo; (by labour), demereo; (cold), frigus contrahere; (by heart), memoriæ mandare; (to land), arenâ potiri; (on a horse), equum ascendere; (on a garment), vestem induere; (or gather together), colligo; (or come together), convenio; (by force), extorqueo; (the victory), victoriam consequi; (up, *or* rise), surgo; (up upon), conscendo; (or lift up), elevo
A getting, acquisitio
Gewgaws, nugæ, tricæ
Ghastliness, horror, pallor
Ghastly, horrificus, pallidus
A ghost, spiritus, anima
The Holy Ghost, Spiritus Sanctus, paracletus
Ghosts, manes, umbræ, spectra
A giant, gigas
Giant-like, giganteus
Gibberish, striblgo   D 2

GLA • GNA • GOL

A gibbet, patibulum
To gibbet, suspendo
Gibbous, gibbus, gibbosus
A gibe, sanna, scomma
To gibe, illudo, subsanno
Giblets, anseris trunculi
Giddiness, vertigo
Giddily, negligentèr
Giddy (foolish), ineptus; (fickle), inconstans; (headed), vertigine correptus, inconstans
A gift, donum, munus
A gig, turbo
Gigantic, giganteus
To giggle, effusè ridere
A giggling, risus effusus
To gild, inauro, deauro
A gilder, inaurator
A gilding, auratura
A gill, hemina
A gilliflower, caryophyllum
Gills of fishes, branchiæ
Gilt, *adj.* inauratus
Gilt, *subst.* pecunia
A gimlet, terebra
A gin, laqueus, pedica
Ginger, zinziber; (bread), panis zinzibere conditus
Gingerly, levi pede, cautè
To gingle, tinnio, crepito; (in words), sermonem affectare
A gingle (of words), verba inania; (gingling), tinnitus
A gipsy, mulier fatidica
To gird, cingo; (about), circumcingo; (under), succingo; (unto), accingo
A girder, trabs, tignum
A girding, cinctus, cinctura
A girdle, cingulum, cingula; (marriage-girdle), cestus
A girl, puella, virgo
Girlish, puellaris
Girlishly, puellaritèr
Girt, cinctus, præcinctus
A girth, cinctorium
To girth, cingulo substringere
To give, do, dono, largior; (or hand a thing), cedo; (advice), consulo; (alms), stipem erogare
A giver, dator, largitor
Gives (fetters), compedes
A giving, donatio, largitio; (into), concessio; (over), discessio; (up), cessio, deditio
The gizzard, avium ingluvies
Glad, lætus, hilaris
To be glad, gaudeo, lætor [fico
To make glad, *or* Gladden, lætiA gladiator, gladiator
Gladly, lætè, lubens
Gladness, lætitia, gaudium
A glade, interstitium silvaticum
A glance, contuitus, intuitus
To glance, raptim obtueri; (upon, or hint), innuo; (*or* slide by), præterlabor
A gland, glandula; (of the throat), tonsillæ
Full of glands, glandulosus
To glare, oculos perstringere
Glaring crimes, atrocia flagitia
Glass, vitrum; (for drinking), calix vitreus; (or draught of liquor) haustus; (over a glass), inter pocula
Of glass, vitreus
A looking-glass, speculum
A glass-house, vitreorum officina
A glass-maker, vitri conflator
Glass-making, vitri conflatio
Glass ware, vitrea
A perspective-glass, tubus opticus
Glassy, *or* like glass, vitreus

[59]

To glase (*or* polish), polio; (windows), vitro instruere; (earthenware), incrusto
A glazier, vitrarius
A gleam, jubar, lumen
Gleaming, coruscans
To glean (corn), legere spicas; (grapes), racemor
A gleaning, spicilegium, racematio; (gleanings), reliquiæ
A glebe, gleba; (land), prædium sacerdotale
Glee, hilaritas, lætitia
A gleet, sanies, tabum, ichor
Glib, lubricus, lævis
Glibly, lubricè, volubilitèr
Glibness, volubilitas
To glide, labor, prolabor
A gliding, lapsus
To glimmer, subluceo
Glimmering, sublustris, creperus
A glimmering, lux dubia
A glimpse, coruscatio, aspectus obscurus
To glister, *or* Glitter, corusco, fulgeo
Glittering, nitens, coruscans
A glittering, coruscatio, fulgor
Glitteringly, splendidè, nitidè
A globe, globus, sphæra
Globe-like, in formâ sphæræ
Globular, sphæricus
A globule, globulus
Gloomily, obscurè, torvè
Gloominess, obscuritas, caligo
Gloomy, obscurus, nubilus
Glorification, glorificatio
To glorify, laudo, celebro
A glorifying, celebratio
Glorious, gloriosus, illustris
Gloriously, amplitèr, eximiè
Glory, gloria, decus
To glory, glorior, superbio
A glorying, gloriatio
Glorying, gestiens, superbus
To gloss (expound), commentor (polish), lævigo, polio, nitorem rei inducere
A gloss (exposition), commentarius, interpretatio; (lustre), fulgor, nitor
A glossary, glossarium
A glossing, lævigatio
Glossy, nitidus, expolitus
A glove, chirotheca, manica
A glover, chirothecarius
To glout, frontem contrahere
To glow, candeo, caleo
Glowing, candens, ardens
To glose, blandior, adulor
Glue, gluten
To glue, glutino, agglutino
A glue-house, glutinarium
Gluiness, viscositas
A gluing together, conglutinatio
Gluey, glutinosus
A glut, satias, satietas
To glut, satio, saturo
Glutinous, glutinosus
A glutton, gulosus, helluo [viens
Gluttonous, gulosus, gulæ serGluttonously, gulosè, avidè
Gluttony, gula, ingluvies
A glyster, clyster
To gnash, dentibus frendere
A gnashing, dentium stridor
A gnat, culex
To gnaw, rodo, corrodo, mordeo, arrodo, circumrodo, derodo, perrodo; (be vexed), stomachor
A gnawing, rosio; (pain), verminatio; (of the guts), tormina; (of the conscience), stimulus

To go, vado, incedo, gradior, proficiscor; (about), circumeo, perambulo; (about business), aggredior, conor; (after), sequor; (against), adversor; (with), comitor; (aside), discedo; (astray), vagor; (away), discedo, abeo; (away with), aufero; (awry),obliquo;(back), recedo; (before), præcedo; (between), intervenio; (beyond), transeo; (beyond, *or* excel), ancello, præsto; (beyond, *or* overreach), circumvenio; (by), prætereo; (down), descendo; (down, as the sun) occido; (for, *or* fetch), peto; (forth), exeo; (forward), pergo; (forward, *or* profit), proficio; (from), discedo; (a journey), proficiscor; (near), accedo, appropinquo; (off, as a gun), displodor; (often unto), frequento; (on), pergo; (over), transeo; (over a river), trajicio; (out, as fire), extinguor; (out of the way), locum dare, a viâ excedere; (quickly), festino; (to), adeo; (together), comitor; (by the ears), pugnam inire; (through), pervado, penetro; (under), subeo; (up), ascendo; (up and down), cursito; (without, *or* want), careo
Go to, age
A goad, stimulus, pertica
To goad, stimulo, exstimulo
A goal, meta, terminus
A goar of a garment, assumentum
A goat (he), caper, hircus, hœdus; (she), capra
Of a goat, caprinus, hircinus
Goatish, hircosus, libidinosus, salax
The gob, os
A gobbet, offa, frustum
To gobble up, diglutio, devoro
A gobbler, vorax
A goblet, crater, patera
Goblins, larvæ, lemures
God, deus
A goddess, dea, diva
God be with you, vale
God forbid, absit, prohibeat Deus; (God grant), faxit Deus
The Godhead, deitas, divinitas
Of God, divinus
Household-gods, lares, penates
A godfather, pater lustricus; (mother), mater lustrica; (son), filius lustricus; (daughter), filia lustrica
Godliness, sanctitas, pietas
Godly, *or* godlily, *adj.* pius, religiosus; *adv.* piè, religiosè
Agog, avidè concupiscens
Goggle, volubilis; (eyed), strabo
Going, incedens, inclinans
A going (down), declinatio, descensus; (walking), incessus, gressus; (about), ambitus, ambages; (away), discessio; (out of the way), aberratio; (back), reditus; (before), præcessio; (aside), digressio; (down of the sun), occasus; (forth), exitus; (forward), progressio; (from), digressio; (out of a place), egressus; (out, as a fire, &c.), extinctio; (to), aditus, accessus; (from place to place), commigratio
Gold, aurum; (mine), aurifodina; (ore), aurum crudum;

(leaf), aurum foliaceum; (dust), balus; (coin), aurum signatum, nummus aureus; (wire), aurum ductile
Of gold, aureus
A goldbeater, auri foliacei ductor; (finer), auri purgandi artifex; (finder), foricarum redemptor
A goldsmith, auri faber
Golden, aureus
A gondola, navicula Veneta
Gone, elapsus; (about), peragratus; (back), regressus; (before), praegressus; (out), egressus; (forth), profectus; (with child), praegnans, gravida; (in drink), temulentus; (in years), aetate provectus
Good, bonus; (at), peritus; (deal), magnus; (many), benè multi; (for something), utilis; (for nothing), inutilis; (honest), probus, integer
Good (profit, advantage), lucrum, commodum; (to do), benefacio; (to make), compenso
To do good (as physic), prosum
Good cheer, epulæ
A good (fellow), combibo, congerro; (mate), fama
In good (health), valeo; (earnest), profectò, bonâ fide
Goods, bona, res, facultates, fortunæ, opes; (own), peculium; (immoveable), res solidæ; (by inheritance), bona hæreditaria
Goodly, egregius, eximius
Goodliness, species, decor
Good-liking, comprobatio
Goodness, bonitas, probitas
Good-will, benevolentia
A goose, anser
Of a goose, anserinus
A gooseberry, grossulæ acinus; (bush), grossularia
A gore, sinus, plica
Gore (blood), tabum, sanies
To gore, cornu ferire, perforo
A gorge, jugulum, ingluvies
To gorge, exsaturo, voro
Gorgeous, nitidus, splendidus
To be gorgeous, resplendeo
Gorgeously, magnificè, lautè; (clad), splendidè vestitus
Gorgeousness, splendor
A gorget, mamillare, colli armatura; (of mail), lorica
To gormandize, voro, helluor
A gormandizer, helluo
A gormandizing, ingluvies, gula
A goslin, anserculus
The gospel, evangelium
Of the gospel, evangelicus
A gossip (in drinking), compotrix; (in walking), ambulatrix; (in tattling), mulier loquax
A gossip, susceptor, or susceptrix initialis
To gossip, tempus conterere
To govern, guberno, moderor; (a family), administrare rem familiarem; (guide), duco; (one's self), se gerere; (the state), regno præesse; (a province), provinciam procurare; (a ship), navem gubernare; (as a king), regno
Governable, tractabilis
Governance, gubernatio, administratio. See Government
A governante, gubernatrix
A governess, gubernatrix
Governing, gubernans, imperans
A governing, gubernatio

A government, regnum, imperium, provincia, respublica; (arbitrary), dominatio; (of a family), œconomia, rei familiaris administratio; (of the tongue), moderatio; (of a state), politia; (in grammar), regimen, consecutio
A governor, gubernator; (in chief), princeps, præses; (of a country), præfectus, procurator
Governors, magistratus
A gourd, cucurbita, pepo
The gout, podagra, arthritis
Gouty, arthriticus
A gown, toga, stola
Grace, gratia; (in speech, &c.), decor, venustas, dignitas; (at meals), benedictio; (favour), favor, beneficium; (pardon), venia
A grace (privilege), privilegium; (in speaking), lepor, eloquentia
Ill-grace, invenustas
To grace, exorno, orno
Graceful, venustus, elegans, decorus, concinnus, decens
Gracefully, decorè, venustè
Gracefulness, venustas
Graceless, perditus, dissolutus
The graces, gratiæ
Gracious, gratiosus, benignus; (most), serenissimus
Graciously, humanitèr, benignè
Graciousness, benignitas, comitas, benevolentia
A gradation, gradatio
Gradual, per gradus, constans
Gradually, gradatim, pedentim
A graduate, graduatus
To graff, or graft, insero, inoculo; (between), internero
A graft, insitum
A grafter, insitor
A grafting, inoculatio
Grain (corn), frumentum; (of salt, &c.), mica
A grain (in weight), granum
Grain (to dye with), coccus
The grain (of wood), stamen; (of leather), corii rugæ
Grains (of paradise), grana paradisi; (of metal), semina metalli; (in a brewery), brasii excocti reliquiæ; (of allowance), excusatio, condonatio
In grain, coccineus
Against the grain, invitè
Grainy, granatus, granosus
A grammar, grammatica
Of grammar, grammaticus, grammaticalis
A grammarian, grammaticus
Grammatical, grammaticus
Grammatically, grammaticè
A granary, horreum
Grand, grandis, ingens
A grandson, nepos; (daughter), neptis; (father), avus; (mother), avia; (inquest), inquisitio major
A grandee, optimus
Grandeur, dignitas, amplitudo
A grange, prædium, villa
A grant, permissio; (thing granted), concessum
To grant, concedo, sino; (acknowledge), fateor
A granter, donator
A granting, concessio
A grape, uva, staphyle
A grape-gatherer, vindemiator
A grape-gathering, vindemiatio
A grape-stone, acinus
Bearing grapes, uvifer

Graphical, graphicus, accuratus
Graphically, graphicè, accuratè
A grapple, harpago
To grapple, corripio; (a ship), unco apprehendere; (with), obluctor, confligo
To grase, pasco, depasco; (as a bullet), strictim attingere
A grasier, pecuarius
A grasp, pugillum
To grasp, pugno constringere; (at), capto, aucupor
Grasping, avidus, avarus
Grass, gramen, herba
Bearing grass, herbifer
Of grass, gramineus
Grassy, graminosus, herbosus
A grasshopper, locusta
A grass-plot, viridarium
A grate (for fire), craticula; (to look through), clathrus
To grate, rado; (the ears), perstringo; (the teeth), dentibus frendere; (vex), dictis mordere
Grateful, gratus, acceptus, jucundus, suavis
To be grateful, gratum se præbere
Gratefully, gratè, jucundè
Gratefulness, jucunditas, gratitudo, suavitas
A grater, radula
To gratify (oblige), obsequor; (indulge), indulgeo; (requite), munero, compenso
A gratification, gratificatio
Grating, mordax
A grating, rasura
Gratis, gratis, gratuitò [tus
Gratitude, gratitudo, animus gratus
Gratuitous, gratuitus
A gratuity, præmium, munus, merces
Gratulatory, gratulabundus
Grave (serious), gravis, severus, constans, modestus; (sad), tristis, mœstus; (in speech), graviloquus; (ancient), senior
A grave, sepulchrum, tumulus; (digger), tumulorum fossor
Of a grave, sepulchralis
To grave, insculpo, sculpo
Gravel, sabulum; (in the reins), calculus
To gravel, sabulo insternere; (perplex), scrupulum injicere
To have the gravel, calculo laborare
Gravelling, difficilis
Gravely, gravitèr, seriò
Gravelly, sabulosus
Graven, sculptus, sculptilis
A graver, sculptor
A graver (tool), cælum
To gravitate, pondero
Gravitation, ponderatio
Gravity (in person), severitas, gravitas; (in weight), pondus, gravitas
Gravy, succus, cremor
Full of gravy, succi plenus
Gray (with age), canus; (in colour), cinereus; (eyed), cæsius
To grow gray, canesco
A grayhound, canis Gallicus
To graze, pasco, perstringo
Grease, adeps; (dripping), liquamen; (for wheels), axungia
To grease, inungo, ungo
Greased, linitus
Greasy, pinguis; (nasty), squalidus
Greasily, sordidè, squalidè
Greasiness, pinguedo, illuvies
A greasing, inunctio
Great, vastus, grandis, magnus; (exceeding), ingens, immensus;

GRI   GRO   GUN

(remarkable), insignis; (violent), vehemens; (grievous), gravis, durus; (with one), familiaris, intimus; (many), plures; (men), optimates; (with child), gravida; (very), prægrandis
Greater, major
Greatest, maximus; (chiefest), supremus, summus
Greatly, valdè, maximè
Greatness, magnitudo; (of honour), dignitas; (with), familiaritas; (immensity), vastitas, immensitas
Greaves, ocreæ
A Grecian, Græcus, Graius
A Grecian, Græcissans
Greedy, avidus, vorax; (of honour), ambitiosus; (hungry), jejunus
A greedy-gut, helluo, comedo
To be greedy, avidè concupiscere
Greedily, avidè, cupidè
To eat greedily, voro
Greediness, avaritia; (in eating), voracitas, aviditas
To speak Greek, Græcè loqui
Green (in colour), viridis; (as grass), gramineus; (fresh), recens, mustens; (not ripe), immaturus
A green (plat), viretum; (for bowls), sphæristerium
To be green, vireo, viresco
Greenish, subviridis
Greenness, viriditas, viror
To greet, saluto
A greeting, salutatio
To send greeting, salutem alicui dicere, or impertire
A gridiron, craticula
Grief, dolor, mœror, solicitudo, tristitia, molestia
Full of grief, tristis, mœstus
A grievance, offensio, injuria
To grieve (trouble), vexo, crucio, molesto; (be grieved), doleo, mœreo
Grieving, dolens, mœrens
Grievous, infestus, gravis, durus, immanis, atrox
Grievously, ægrè, molestè
Grievousness, atrocitas
A griffin, gryps, gryphus
A grig, anguilla; (merry grig), congerro festivus
Grim, torvus, acerbus, trux
To look grim, torvum intueri
A grimace, oris depravatio
With grimace, fictè, simulatè
To grime, denigro
Grimly, torvè, torritèr
Grimness, torvitas
A grin, oris distortio; (forced laugh), risus sardonicus
To grin, subrideo
To grind (corn), frumentum molere; (to powder), in pulverem reducere; (on a stone), exacuo; (in a mortar), contundo; (the teeth), dentibus frendere; (with the teeth), mando
A grinder, molitor, tritor
The grinders, dentes molares
A grinding, molitura; (on a stone), exacutio
A grindstone, cos versatilis
A gripe (handful), manipulus; (of the belly), tormina
To gripe (take hold), constringo; (as pain doth), pervello; (as a ship), in ventos nimiùm discurrere; (as a miser), pertinax esse pecuniæ
[54]

Grisly, asper, incultus; (hideous), horribilis, horrendus
Grisly, adv. asperè, horridè
Grist, farina molenda
A gristle, cartilago
Gristly, cartilageus
Grit, arena, scobs
Gritty, arenosus
A groan, gemitus
To groan, gemo, ingemo
Groats, farina crassior
A groat, drachma
A grocer, aromatopola; (-'s shop), aromatopolium
Grocery, aromata
The groin, inguen
A groom, agaso; (of a chamber), cubicularius; (of the stable), stabularius; (of the stole), primarius à regio cubiculo; (porter), janitor regius, or primarius
A groove (in wood), stria
To groove, strio
To grope, palpor, expalpo, prætento
A groper, palpator
A groping, palpatio; (for), prætentatio
Gross (thick), crassus, corpulentus; (fat), obesus, pinguis; (very great), ingens, immensus; (manifest), manifestus
In the gross, in toto
Grossly, crassè, inconcinnè
Grossness, crassitudo, atrocitas
Grotesque, miscellaneus, promiscuus
A grotto, crypta, antrum
A grove, nemus, lucus
To grovel, humi serpere [uus
Grovelling, humi prostratus, proThe ground, terra, humus, solum, tellus; (of a thing), causa, fundamentum
Aground, in vado hærens
On the ground, humi
To ground (teach), instruo, doceo; (upon, or trust to), innitor, fundo; (establish), sancio; (a ship), subduco
Ground-work, fundamentum
Under-ground, subterraneus
Ground (of grind), molitus, contritus; (on a stone), exacutus
Ground-ivy, hedera terrestris
The ground of a floor, contignatio
Of the ground, terrestris
Groundless, sine causâ
The groundsil, inferum limen
A group, turba, corona
To group, constipo, commisceo
Grout, agriomelum
To grow, cresco; (spring up), exorior; (again), regermino; (become), evado, fio; (among), innascor; (bigger), adaugesco; (cheap), laxo, vilesco; (dear), carior fieri; (fat), pinguesco; (heavy), ingravesco; (in grace), virtute adolescere; (lean), maresco; (old), senesco; (out of fashion), desuesco; (out of use), exolesco; (poor), ad paupertatem redigi; (proud), superbio; (rich), ditesco; (strong), convalesco; (tame), mansuesco; (together), concresco; (up in stature), adolesco; (weary), fatigor
To growl, ringor, irascor
To be grown (increased), augeor; (become), fio
Full-grown, adultus
Growth, incrementum, fructus

A grouse, tetrao
A grub, lumbricus
To grub up, eradico, effodio
Grubbed up, averruncatus
A grudge, simultas, odium
To grudge, murmuro, invideo
Bearing a grudge, invidus
A grudging, livor, invidia
Grudgingly, avarè, gravatìm, ægrè
Gruel, pulmentum
Gruff, tetricus, torvus
Gruffly, torvè, truculentèr
To grumble, murmuro, massito
A grumbler, murmurator
A grumbling, murmuratio
To grunt, grunnio, perfremo
A grunting, grunnitus
A guarantee, fide jussor, sponsor
To guarantee, in se recipere
A guard, custodia; (of soldiers), satellitium, præsidium
Life-guards, regii satellites
Advanced guards, excubitores
Guards, satellites
The guard of a sword, capulus
To be upon the guard, excubo
To guard (against), caveo; (protect), defendo, munio; (secure), custodio
A guardian, tutor
A guarding, stipatio, defensio; (against), cautio
A guardianship, tutela
A gudgeon, gobio
A guerdon, merces, præmium
A guess, conjectura, augurium
To guess, conjicio, conjecto
By guess, ex conjecturâ, conjecturâ
Guessed, conjecturâ notus
A guesser, conjector
A guest, hospes; (at a feast), conviva; (chamber), cœnaculum
Guidance, ductus, curatio administratio
A guide, dux, ductor
To guide, duco, adduco, dirigo
A guider, ductor, moderator
A guiding, auspicium
A guild, sodalitium, societas
Guildhall, curia municipalis
Guile, fallacis, dolus
Guileful, fraudulentus, vafer
Guilt, culpa
Guiltless, innocens, insons
Guilty, nocens, sons, noxius, conscius
A guinea-pig, porcellus Indicus; (hen), gallina Iudica
A guise, mos, modus
A guitar, cithara
A gulf, gurges; (bay), sinus; (abyss), abyssus
A gull (bird), larus; (person cheated), stultus
To gull, fallo, fraudo
The gullet, gula, gurgulio
A gulling, illusio, fraudatio
A gulley-hole, cloacæ craticula
Gulosity, luxuria
A gulp, haustus avidus
To gulp, avidè haurire
Gum, gummi
To gum, gummi sublinere
Gummy, gummosus
The gum of the eyes, gramia
The gums, gingiva
A gun, sclopptus; (great), tormentum murale
A gunner, tormentarius
Gunshot, teli jactus
A gunsmith, sclopporum faber
Gunnery, ars tormenta bellica dirigendi

Gunpowder, pulvis nitratus
To gush out, effluo, profluo
A gushing out, eruptio
A gusset, interserta particula
A gust (taste), gustus, gus'atus; (of wind), flatus subitaneus
A gut, intestinum; (great gut), colon
Guts, intestina, exta; (small), ilia, lactes
To gut (a fowl), exentero, eviscero; (fish), purgo; (a house), praedam è tecto egerere
A gutter, canalis, lacuna; (between two houses), compluvium; (into which eaves drop), colliquiæ; (in pillars), stria; (tile), imbrex
To gutter, lacuno, strio
To guttle, helluor
A guttler, helluo
A guttling, helluatio
Guttural, gutturalis
To guzzle, poto, pergræcor
A guzzler, potator
Guzzling, potans, pergræcans
A guzzling, potatio
Gymnastic, gymnasticus
Gyves (fetters), compedes

H.

A haberdasher (of hats), pilio; (of small wares), dardanarius
Habiliment, apparatus, vestitua
A habit (custom), mos, consuetudo; (of apparel), vestitus; (of body), temperamentum, crasis
Habitable, habitabilis; (not), inhabitabilis
A habitation, domus
Habited (clothed), vestitus
Habitual, usu contractus
To habituate, assuefacio
Habituated, assuefactus, consuetus
To hack, concido, cædo
Hacked, concisus, cæsus
A hacking, cæsio
A hackney (horse), conductitius equus; (coach), currus mercenarius; (writer), scriba conductitius
To hackney, loco, eloco
A haddock, asinus marinus
A haft, manubrium, capulus
To haft, manubrio instruere
A bag, furia, venefica; (nightmare), incubus
Haggard, macer, ferus
A haggis, tomaculum
To haggle, licitor
A haggler, licitator verbosus
A haggling, licitatio verbosa
Hail, *adj.* sanus, saluber
Hail, *subst.* grando
Hail, *verb.* salve, ave
To hail, compello, saluto
The hair, crinis, capillus, cæsaries, coma, capillitium; (of a beast), villus; (of the forehead), antiæ; (of the eyelids), palpebræ
Of hair, capillaceus
Having long hair, comatus; (bushy hair), cæsariatus; (curled hair), cirratus; (much hair), criniger
To a hair's breadth, ad amussim
Haircloth, cilicium
Haired, crinitus; (red), rufus;

(shag), villosus; (rough), hispidus; (thin), raripilus
Hairy, pilosus, hirsutus
Hairiness, hirsuta
Hairless, depilis, calvus
A halberd, bipennis militaris
The halcyon, halcyon
Halcyon, serenus, tranquillus
To hale, traho; (in), substringo
A hailing, tractus
Half, dimidium, medietas. (In composition it is rendered by *semi;* as, *semi-vivus*, half-alive, *semi-hora*, half an hour.)
Half a dozen, sex
A halfpenny, obolus
By half, dimidio
A hall, atrium, aula; (town), forum municipale
Hallelujah, hallelujah
The halliards, antennarum pedes
To halloo (dogs), canes incitare; (shout), vociferor, inclamo
An hallooing, vociferatio
To hallow (consecrate), sacro, consecro
A hallowing, consecratio
A halo (meteor), corona, halo
A halser, helsium
A halt, gradus suppressus
To halt, sisto; (be lame), claudico; (be doubtful), fluctuo, dubito
A halter (for a house), capistrum; (for the neck), laqueus; (cripple), claudus
A halter, restis, laqueus
To halter, capistro
Halting, claudicans, claudus sistens
Halting, claudicatio
To halve, bipartior
By halves, imperfectè
A ham, armus porci
The ham, poples
A hamlet, villa, vicus
To hamstring, supperno
A hammer, malleus, tudes
To hammer, cudo; (in speech), balbutio, hæsito; (out), ægrè proferre; (into the head), sæpè inculcando docere
A hammering, malleatio; (doubting), dubitatio
A hammock, lectus pensilis
A hamper, corbis, fiscina; (of osiers), cista vitilis
To hamper, impedio, illaqueo
A hampering, impeditio
A hanaper, fiscus
The hanaper-office, hanaperium
A hand, manus; (right), dextra; (left), sinistra; (writing), scriptura; (of pork), humerus porcinus; (of a dial, &c.), index, gnomon; (clinched), pugnus; (open), palma
One-handed, uninanus
Hundred-handed, centimanus
On the right hand, ad dextram; (on the left hand), ad sinistram; (on the other hand), alterā parte
Out of hand, confestim, illicò
Hand to hand, cominùs, comfertim
Hand over head, inconsultò
Hand-in-hand, junctis manibus
At hand, propè, præstò
A hand at cards, sors
Of the hand, manualis
A handbreadth, palmus
A handful, manipulus
A handkerchief, sudarium
A handmaid, ancilla

Underhand, occultè, clam; (dealing), dolus, fraus
To hand (a thing), per manus tradere; (down to posterity), transmittere memoriæ
With cap in hand, submissè
To give the upper hand, loco cedere
To have a hand in, particeps esse
Even hands, æquo marte
Upper hand, locus superior
A handicraftsman, opifex
Handiwork, opus manufactum
Handily, solertèr, callidè, peritè
Handiness, solertia, peritia
To handle, tracto; (a subject), disserere de; (briefly), attingo; (gently), demulceo; (often), pertracto; (one roughly), acerbius tractare
A handle (of a tool), manubrium; (of a target), umbo; (of a cup), ansula; (occasion), occasio
Having a handle, ansatus
A handling, tractatio; (rudely), tractatio indigna
Handsome (beautiful), venustus, pulcher, formosus; (fine, or genteel), liberalis, honestus, ingenuus; (fittings), æquus, justus; (worthy of notice), præclarus, illustris, laudabilis; (artful), lepidus
To make handsome, decoro, polio
Handsomely, venustè, concinnè
Handsomeness, elegantia, venustas
Handy, solers, peritus [tas
Handicraft, mechanica
Hang it! apage!
To hang (up), suspendo; (or be hanging), pendeo; (down before), præpendeo; (back), tergiversor; (by a line, &c.), appenso; (a place with paper), locum aulæis ornare; (loose), dedino; (one's ears), auriculas demittere; (together), cohæreo; (over), emineo, promineo; (upon one), parasitor
A hanger-on, parasitus
A hanger, sica, harpe, ensa
Hanging, pendens, pendulus; (down), demissus; (loosely), fluidus, laxus; (over), impendens, prominens; (together), cohærens
A hanging, suspensio; (together), cohærentia
Hangings, aulæa
A hangman, carnifex, tortor
A hank (of thread), glomus
To hanker after, anxiè appetere
A hankering, appetentia, desiderium
The Hanse-towns, civitates sociæ
A hansel, primus rei usus, strena
To hansel, or handsel, primus uti
Hap, casus, sors
By hap, fortè, fortuitò
Hap-hazard, prorsùs incertum
To hap, or happen, contingo, accido, evenio, procedo
Happened lately, recens, nuperus
Happening, contingens, accidens
A happening, exitus, eventus
Haply, fortè, fortassè
Happily, felicitèr, beatè
Happiness, felicitas, beatitudo
Happy, felix, beatus, faustus
To make happy, felicito, beo
A hapse (catch), sera
An harangue, oratio, concio
To harangue, verba facere, concionor

D 4

HAR HAU HEA

To harass, vexo, fatigo; (a country), vasto, depopulor
A harassing, fatigatio, vexatio
A harbinger, prodromus
A harbour (for ships), portus; (refuge), receptaculum
To harbour (entertain), hospitor; (take up lodgings), diversor; (an opinion), sentire de
A harbourer, hospes, receptator
A harbouring, receptio
Hard (not soft), durus; (difficult), arduus; (stingy), parcus, tenax; (to get), rarus; (hearted), crudelis, terreus; (by), vicinus, proximus; (to learn), indocilis; (to be understood), obscurus; (to be pleased), morosus, protervus; (of belief), incredulus; (skinned), duricorius; (times), tempora calamitosa
To make hard, induro, obduro
To be hard, obduresco; (as brawn), calleo
To be hard put to it, premi angustiis
To stand hard (faggle), licitor
To be too hard for, supero
Hardily, fortitèr, strenuè
Hardiness (boldness), audacia, fortitudo; (of constitution), corpus benè constitutum
Hardish, paulò durior
Hardly, difficultèr, ægrè, vix; (sharply), rigidè, austerè, severè; (stoutly), strenuè
Hardness, durities; (cruelty), sævitia; (difficulty), difficultas; (stiffness), rigor; (of skin), callus; (of heart), duritia; (sparingness), parsimonia; (stinginess), tenacitas; (of body, or mind), corporis, or animi robur
Hardships, difficultates
Hardy (valiant), intrepidus; (that can endure), laboris patiens
To be hardy, audeo, fortis esse
A hare, lepus
Of a hare, leporinus
To hare (terrify), perterrefacio
Hare-brained, temerarius
Hark! heus! heo!
A harlequin, sannio, mimus
A harlot, meretrix, scortum
Of a harlot, meretricius
Harm, damnum, malum, clades, calamitas
To harm, noceo, lædo; (be harmed), damno affici
Harmless, innoxius, insons; (to bear harmless), indemnem præstare
Harmlessly, innocentèr, innocuè
Harmonious, modulatus, musicus
Harmoniously, modulatè; (with one consent), unâ mente
To harmonise, modulor, consentio
Harmony, harmonia, symphonia
Harness, habena, armatura; (for drawing), helcium; (trappings), phaleræ; (for the breast), thorax; (for the thighs), cruralia; (complete), panoplia
To harness, instruo, induo, phaleras induere
A harness-maker, armorum faber
A harnessing, loricatio
A harp, cithara, lyra
To harp, eandem incudem tundere
Of a harp, citharoedicus
A harper, citharista, citharistria, fidicen
Harping-irons, harpagones

A harpsichord, sambucha
A harpy, harpia
A harrow, occa
To harrow, occo
A harrower, occator
A harrowing, occatio
Harsh (severe), asper, morosus; (in taste), acer; (in sound), discors, ingratus, stridulus
Harshly, tetrè, asperè, malè
Harshness, severitas, asperitas; (in taste), acerbitas
A barelet, exta porcina
A hart, cervus
Of a hart, cervinus
Hart's-horn, cornu cervinum
Harvest, messis; (time), autumnus
Harvest, adj. autumnalis
Of harvest, messorius
Hay-harvest, fœnisecium
A barvest-man, messor
A hazel-tree, corylus; (grove), coryletum
A hash of meat, minutal
To hash, minutim concidere
A hasp, crena ferrea
To hasp, obsero, oppessulo
A hasping, oppessulatio
A hassock, scirpiculum
Haste, festinatio, celeritas
In haste, festinantèr, festinè
To hasten, festino, propero; (one's pace), gradum accelerare
A hastening, festinatio
Hastily, properè, festinè, festinantèr; (passionately), iracundè
Over-hastily, præproperè, præmaturè
Hastiness, præcipitatio, velocitas; (testiness), iracundia
Hasty, concitatus, præceps; (hot), fervens; (sudden), subitus; (testy), iracundus, morosus
To be hasty, ardeo, ferocio
A hat, galerus, pileus; (band), vpira; (maker), pileo
To hatch (chickens), pullos excludere; (mischief, lies), dolos procudere
A hatch (of chickens), pullities
The hatches, tabulatum
Under the hatches, in egestate; (in the power of), sub potestate
A hatchet, securis, ascia
A hatchet-face, vultus informis
A hatching of chickens, fœtura
Hate, invidia, odium
Full of hate, invidus, malignus
To hate, odisse, detestor; (each other), mutuis odiis flagrare; (with disdain), fastidio
To be hated, odio haberi
Hateful, odiosus, invidiosus
A hater, osor; (of women), misogynos; (of men), misanthropos; (of marriage), misogamos
Hating, perosus, exosus
A hating, aversatio
Hatred, odium, simultas
To have, habeo, teneo, potior; (a thing cried), præconi aliquid subjicere; (away), abduco
A haven (harbour), portus
Haughtily, superbè, elatè
Haughtiness, fastus, arrogantia
Haughty, superbus, fastuosus
Having, habens, gaudens
A haunch (hanch), coxa
A haunt, consuetudo, recessus
To haunt, frequento, infesto
Haunted by spirits, umbris inquietatus
A haunter, frequentator; (of

stews), ganeo; (of taverns), popino; (of men's tables), parasitus
A haunting, frequentatio
Havock, clades, strages
To make havock, vasto, spolio
A hautboy, tibia soni acutioris
A haw, morum sentis
A haw-thorn, spina alba
To hawk (spit), screo, exscreo; (cry things), res venales clamitare; (go a hawking), aucupor
A hawk, accipiter
Hawk-nosed, naso aquilino præditus
A hawker (pedlar), mercator circumforaneus
A hawking (of things), venditio circumforanea; (spitting), screatus
A hawser, helcium
Hay, fœnum
Made of hay, fœneus
A haymaker, fœnifex
Hay-harvest, fœnisecium
A hay-cock, fœni meta; (loft), fœnile; (stack), fœni meta major
Hazard, periculum
A hazard (at billiards), fundula; (at tennis), caverna
To hazard, periclitor, experior
Hazardous, anceps, periculosus
A haze, nebula
Hazel, corylus
Hazy, nebulosus
He, ille, ipse, iste, is, hic
A head, caput; (heads, or chiefs), proceres, primates; (of a college), præses; (of hair), coma; (of an arrow), spiculum; (point), cuspis; (of land), promontorium
Of one's own head, spontè
To make head, resisto
Head, adj. primarius; (strong), tenax, temerarius, contumax
Forepart of the head, sinciput; (hinder part), occiput
Having two heads, biceps; (three heads), triceps; (a hundred heads), centiceps
A head-piece (ability), sagacitas, sapientia, judicium; (stall of a bridle), frontale; (of a lute, or viol), citharæ jugum; (helmet), cassis; (of a spring), fontis origo
To head (a cask), dolio fundum immittere; (a spear), ferrum hastæ præfigere; (an army), exercitum ducere
Hand over head, inconsultè
Brought to a head, suppuratus
Headed, capitatus; (as an army), ductus
A headborough, decurio
Headiness, contumacia [max
Heady, potens, inebrians, contu-
Headless, sine capite
Headlong, pronus, præceps
Headship, principatus
Headstrong, indomitus, ferox
To heal, medior, sano; (a wound), vulnus conglutinare; (divisions), concilio; (be healed), sanor, convalesco
That may be healed, medicabilis; (not to be healed), immedicabilis
Healing, salutaris, pacificus
A healing, sanatio
Health, salus, valetudo
To be in health, valeo, vigeo
Healthful, salubèr, salutaris
Healthfulness, salubritas, sanitas

HEA   HEP   HIE

Healthy, sanus, validus
A heap, strues, acervus, cumulus, congeries
To heap (up), cumulo, accumulo, congero; (upon), superingero
A heaping, cumulatio
By heaps, cumalatim, acervatim
To hear, audio, exaudio, subaudio; (be informed), certior fieri, rescisco; (a cause), causam cognoscere
A hearer, auditor
A hearing, auditus, auditio
Hard of hearing, surdaster
Within hearing, præstò esse
To hearken, ausculto, subausculto
Hearsay, fama, rumor
The heart, cor; (middle), medium; (of a tree), medulla
Full of heart, animosus
To have a heart, audeo
Out of heart, exanimis; (as ground), sterilis, infœcundus
In heart, animosus; (as land), fertilis, optimus
To be in heart, vigeo, valeo; (out of heart), animum despondere
Heart of oak, robur
Next to one's heart, carissimus
By heart, memoriter
To lay it to heart, ægrè ferre
Sick at heart, graviter ægrotans
A sweetheart, amica, amicus, procus
Heartbreaking, acerbissimus
Heartburning, cardialgia; (grudge), simultas
Hardhearted, immisericors, durus
Hardheartedness, inhumanitas
Lighthearted, hilaris, lætus
The heart-strings, præcordia
To hearten, animo, incito
A heartening, animatio
A hearth, focus, foculus
Belonging to a hearth, focarius
Heartily, sincerè, fortitèr, avidè, ex animo, acri appetitu, effusè, valdè, toto pectore
Heartiness, sinceritas
Heartless, despondens, excors
Hearty (sincere), sincerus, integer; (not sick), sanus, validus
Heat, calor, fervor, calliditas; (passion), ira
A heat in races, cursus
To heat (make hot), calefacio; (be in a heat), candeo, æstuo; (an oven), furnum igne calefacere
With great heat, ardentèr
An iron-heater, ferrum ad lintea polienda aptum
A heating, calefactio
Heath, erica; (common land), ager compascuus
A heathen, paganus, infidelis
Heathenism, gentilismus
Heathenish, ethnicus
To heave, allevo, allevo; (swell), tumeo; (up), attollo, elevo
Heaven, cœlum, olympus
Heavenly, cœlestis; (beings), cœlites; (minded), rebus cœlestibus intentus; (mindedness), rerum cœlestium cura; (things), cœlestia, divina
Heavily, gravitèr, ægrè; (slowly), lentè, torpidè
Heaviness (weight), gravitas; (drowsiness), sopor, torpor; (dulness), stupiditas; (sorrowfulness), tristitia, mœror
Heavy (sad), tristis, tardus, mœstus; (drowsy), torpidus; (dull), segnis, iners; (in weight), ponderosus, gravis; (requiring much labour), laboriosus; (dirty), lutosus

To make heavy, or sad, contristo; (in weight), ingravo
A Hebraism, Hebraismus
Hebrew, Hebraicus, Hebræus
In Hebrew, Hebraicè
A hecatomb, hecatombe
Hectic, hecticus
A hector, sicarius, gladiator
To hector, insulto, minor
A hedge, sepes, septum
To hedge, sepio; (before), præsepio; (about), circumsepio
A hedge-hog, echinus
A hedge-priest, sacerdos tressis; (marriage), nuptiæ clandestinæ
A hedging, septio
Heed, cura, cautela
To take heed, caveo, attendo
Heedless, oscitans, incautus
Heedlessly, negligentèr, incautè
Heedlessness, negligentia
The heel, calx
To heel, inclino, supplanto
To be at the heels, insto
A heifer, juvenca, buculâ
Height, altitudo; (of a distemper), crisis; (top), culmen; (tallness), proceritas
Height, summus, maximus
To heighten, erigo; (encourage), excito, animo
A heightening, exaggeratio
Heinous, detestabilis, atrox
To make heinous, exaggero
Heinously, ægrè, facinorosè, infensè, iratè
Heinousness, immanitas
An heir, or heiress, hæres; (at law), hæres lege; (apparent), hæres præsumptus; (joint), cohæres
Heirship, hæreditas
Hell, tartarus, infernum
A hellhound, improbus, perditus
Hellish, infernalis, infernus
A helm, gubernaculum, clavus
A helmet, cassis, galea
With a helmet, galeatus
Help, auxilium, subsidium, adminiculum, suppetiæ; (remedy), remedium
To help, opitulor, juvo, subsidio alicujus venire, promoveo, suppedito, libero, extrico; (up), sublevo, sustineo; (avoid), evito, vito, effugio
By God's help, Deo juvante
A helper, auxiliator, adjutor
Helpful, auxiliaris
Helping, adjuvans, opem ferens
Helpless, inops, opis desertus
Helter-skelter, confusè, temerè
Hem! hem!
A hem, fimbria limbus
To hem, fimbria ornare; (in), obsidio, circumsideo
A hemisphere, hemisphærium
Hemlock, cicuta
A hemming, prætextura, screatus
Hemp, cannabis, linum
Hempen (of hemp), cannabinus, linens
A hen, gallina
Of a hen, gallinaceus
A henroost, pertica gallinaria
Henhearted, timidus, ignavus
Hence, or from hence, ex hoc; (begone!) apage te! (from hence), adhinc; (forth), dehinc, deinceps, porro, posthâc
Hepatic, hepaticus
A heptarchy, heptarchia

Her, ejus, illius, ipsius; (herself), illa ipsa, seipsam
By herself, sola
Her own, sua
A herald, fecialis
Heraldry, jus feciale
An herb, herba; (for the pot), olus
Herbage (pasture), pascuum; (tithe of herbs), decimæ pro herbis; (tithe of grazing), jus de pascuis
An herbal, botanologia
An herbalist, botanicus
Full of herbs, herbosus
An herb-market, forum olitorium
Herb-seller, olitor, olitrix
A herd, armentum
To herd together, convenio
A herdsman, armentarius
Here, hic; (behold!) ecce! en! (hither), huc; (and there), hic illîc, passim, sparsim; (after), posthâc; (about), in his partibus; (at), hinc, indè, ex hoc; (by), ex hac, per hoc, hac re, hinc; (in), in hac re; (of), hujus, de hac re; (tofore), anteà, antehâc, olim; (upon), hinc; (unto), ad hoc, adhuc; (with), hoc
Hereditable (hereditary), hæreditarius
Heresy, hæresis
An heretic, hæreticus
Heretical, hæreticus
Heretically, hæreticè
An heritage, hæreditas
An hermaphrodite, hermaphroditus
Hermetical, chemicus
Hermetically, hermeticè
An hermit, eremita
An hermitage, eremitæ cella
A hero, heros
Heroical, Heroicus
Heroically, fortitèr
A heroine, herois
Heroism, fortitudo
A heron, ardea
A herring, halec; (pickled), halec conditanea; (red), halec salita et fumo durata
Hers, ejus, illius, ipsius
A herse, feretrum
To hesitate, hæsito, dubito
Hesitation, hæsitatio, mora
Heterodox, heterodoxus
Heterogeneous, heterogeneus
To hew, cædo, disseco; (asunder), discindo; (down), succido; (in pieces), consido; (with an axe), dedolo, dolo
A hewing of wood, lignatio
A hexagon, hexagonus
Heyday! ohe!
Hiccough, or hiccup, singultus
To hiccup, singultio
Hid, hidden, abditus, arcanus
A hide, pellis, corium; (of land), hida terræ
To hide, abscondo, occulto; (again), recondo; (before), prætego; (cover), operio; (from), celo; (in the ground), defodio; (together), cooperio, lateo, deliteo, latito, delitesco
A hider, occultator
Hideous, perhorridus, horridus
Hideously, torvè, tetrè, horridè
Hideousness, horror
A hiding, occultatio; (place), latebra, latibulum
Hierarchical, hierarchicus
An hierarchy, hierarchia
Hieroglyphical, hieroglyphicus

HIT — HOL — HON

Hieroglyphics, hieroglyphica
A higgler, dardanarius
High, altus, excelsus, supremus, sublimis, præaltus; (in stature), procerus; (prized), pretiosus
On high, in sublime, sursùm; (above us), supernus, superus
Highborn, illustri genere natus
Highmettled, fortis, acer, ferox
Highminded, animo elatus, superbus, fastidiosus
The high-priest, pontifex maximus
The highway, via regia
A highwayman, viatoris insidiator
To be higher (excel), supereminoe
Highest, summus, supremus
Highly, altè, excelsè
Highness, celsitudo, altitudo
Hilarity, hilaritas
A hill, mons, collis
A hillock, colliculus
Hilly, montanus, montosus
A hilt, capulum
Of him, illius, ejus, hujus, de illo; (self), sui, per se
He himself, ille ipse
A hind, cerva, hinnulus, rusticus
Hinder, posterior; (feet), pedes posteriores; (part of the head), occiput; (part of the neck), cervix
To hinder, impedio, obsto, inhibeo, prohibeo; (interrupt), interpello, interturbo
A hindrance, (impediment), impedimentum, mora; (loss, or prejudice), damnum, incommodum
To be hindered, impedior
A hinderer, interpellator, lucri oppugnator
A hindering, retardatio
Hindmost, postremus
A hinge, cardo
A hint, indicium, monitio
To hint, innuo, suggero
A hinting, monitio
Hip! heus! heo!
The hip, coxendix, coxa
The hip-gout, sciatica
Hippish (hypochondriac), atrâ bile percitus
Hipshot, delumbatus
Hire, merces, stipendium
To hire, conduco
To let to hire, eloco
The hire of, locarium
A day's hire, diarium
Belonging to hire, stipendiarius
A hireling, mercenarius
A hirer, conductor [tio
A hiring, conductio; (out), locaHis, ejus, illius, ipsius, hujus; (own), suus, proprius
A hiss, or hissing, sibilum
To hiss, sibilo; (like a goose), gingrio; (off the stage), explodo
An historian, historicus
Historical, historicus
Historically, historicè
A history, historia
To hit (strike), ferio, percutio; (happen, or succeed), contingo, accido, succedo; (on a thing), in rem incidere; (against) collido, allido; (or beat down), disjicio
A hit, ictus, percussio; (chance), sors, casus
Hit, ictus, percussus
A hitting against, collisio
[58]

Hit or miss, jacta est alea
To hitch, fune arripere; (move farther), paulùm movere
An hithe, portus, sinus
Hither, huc, horsùm; (and thither), huc illùc, ultro citròque
Hither, or nearer, citerior
Hithermost, citimus
Hitherto, adhùc, hactenùs, usquè, adhùc, hucusquè
Hitherward, horsùm
A hive, alveare
A place for hives, apiarium
Hoar-frost, pruina
To hoard, coacervo. See Hord
Hoariness, canities
Hoarse, raucus, fuscus
To be hoarse, rauceo; (to grow hoarse), irraucesco
Hoarsely, raucè, raucùm
Hoarseness, raucitas; (of speech), ravis
Hoary, canus, albescens; (as frost), pruinosus; (mouldy), mucidus
To be hoary, caneo, incanesco, impactus
Hoary hairs, cani
To hobble, claudico; (do carelessly), negligentèr, or levitèr agere [asper
Hobbling, inconcinnus; (rough), Hobblingly, malè, inconcinnè
A bobby, mannus
A hobby-horse, arundo longa
A hobgoblin, larva, spectrum
A hock of bacon, perna porcina
Old hock, vinum Rhenense vetustum
A hocus-pocus, præstigiator
A hod, trulla
Hoddy, lætus, sanus
A bodge-podge, miscellanea, farrago
A hoe, rastrum, pastinum
To hoe, pastino
A hog, sus, porcus; (little), porcus; (sty-fed), porcus altilis
Like a hog, porcinus, suillus
A hoggrel, ovis bidens
A hogherd, subulcus
Hog's hanslet, exta porcina
A hogsty, suile, hara
A hogshead, dolium, cadus
Hoggish (clownish), rusticus; (surly), morosus; (niggardly), sordidus [rosè
Hoggishly, rusticè, sordidè, moHoggishness, rusticitas, morositas
To hoist, levo, erigo
A hold (cave), latibulum; (thing to hold by), adminiculum; (of a ship), penetrale; (of wild beasts), ferarum cubile; (strong), præsidium
To hold, retineo, teneo, obtineo; (on, or continue a debate), duro; (affirm), assero, vindico; (think), puto; (a candle), facem alicui prælucere; (contain), capio, contineo; (last), duro, resto; (back), detineo, retineo; (close together), comprimo; (one's breath), spiritum comprimere; (in), cohibeo; (in the reins), habenas premere; (off, or refrain), abstineo; (out, or persevere), persevero; (one's peace), taceo, sileo; (out), perduro; (up), attollo
In hold, in custodiâ
A holdfast, uncus ferreus
Holding, tenens; (one's purpose), consilii, or propositi tenax

A holding (back), retentio; (down), suppressio
Holding fast, tenax, pertinax
A holding (in), cohibitio; (up), sustentatio; (one's peace), silentium, taciturnitas
A hole, foramen; (to lurk in), latebra; (or cave in the earth), spelunca; (in a prison), tullianum; (chink), rima
To make a hole through, transfodio, penetro, terebro
A breathing-hole, spiramentum
Full of holes, foraminosus
Holily, sanctè, piè
Holiness, sanctitas, pietas
Hollow, cavus, cavernosus
A hollow, concavum
To hollow, excavo, cavo; (whoop), vociferor, inclamo
To be hollow like a spunge, fistulo
The hollow of the feet, subtal
Hollow (as a pipe), tubulatus; (voice), vox fusca; (hearted), fallax; (eyed), pætus; (as a reed), fistulosus
A hollowing, excavatio
Hollowness, cavitas; (under ground), caverna; (of the eyes), conchus
Holy, sacer, sanctus
Holy things, sacra
Holy writ, scriptura sacra [rum
Holy of holies, sanctum sanctoTo make holy, consecro, sacro
A holy-day, dies festus, feriæ
Holy Ghost, Spiritus Sanctus
Holy Thursday, dies ascensionis
Homage, clientela, obsequium
Home, domus; (at home), domi, in domo; (from home), domo
Home (in argument), clarus, certus; (blow), validus, fortis; (domestic), domesticus; (onset), violentus; (accusation), acris; (spun), crassus, agrestis
Home (freely), adv. liberè, audactèr
Short of home, in viâ deficere
Homeliness, rusticitas
Homely, rudis, impolitus, rusticus, inconcinnus, deformis, invenustus
Homeward, dómum versus
A homicide (that doth murder), homicida; (the act), homicidium
A homily, homilia, concio
Homogeneous, homogeneus
Homologous, congener
A hone, cos
Honest, honestus, probus, integer, castus, pudicus, verecundus
An honest fellow, homo frugi
Honestly, honestè, probè, castè
Honesty, honestum, rectum, probitas, integritas, pudicitia
Honey, mel
Making honey, mellificus
Of honey, melleus
A honey-comb, favus
Honey-moon, Veneris festa
Honour, honor, honos; (reputation), fama, existimatio; (chastity), pudicitia
To honour, honoro, colo
Your honour, dominatio vestra
Full of honour, honoratus, venerabilis
Bringing honour, honorificus
Of honour, illustris, nobilis
Honourary, honorarius [rus
Honourable, honorabilis, præclaEight honourable, illustrissimus, amplissimus, ornatissimus

HOR — HOU — HUM

Honourableness, nobilitas
Honourably, magnificè, amplissi-
An honouring, cultus, reverentia
A hood (veil), velum; (for the head), cucullus, capitium; (for a priest, or woman), redimiculum; (to ride in), pallium femineum; (for a graduate, &c.), epomis
To hoodwink, caput obvolvere
A hoof, unguis; (of a horse), ungula
Hoofed, ungulas habens
A hook, hamus, uncus; (sheephook), pedum; (flesh-hook), fuscina; (of a clasp), ansula; (for a boat), hamus; (to wed with), runcina; (to cut with), falx; (for a garment), fibula; (great iron hooks), harpago; (hooks of a door), cardines
To hook (grapple), inunco; (together), confibulo, necto; (in), allicio, capio
Hookedness, aduncitas
A hoop, vimen, circulus
To hoop, vieo; (hollow), vociferor, exclamo
The hooping-cough, tussis ferina
To hoot, exclamo, inclamo
A hop, or hops, lupulus
A hop, or jump, saltus
To hop, saltito, subsulto; (to hop beer), cerevisiam lupulis condire
Hope, spes, fiducia; (a hope), dorsum montis, specula
To hope, spero, expecto
Past hope, desperatus, insperatus
The forlorn hope, antecursores
Hopeful, de quo benè speratur
Hopeless, exspes, desperatus
Hoping, sperans
A hopper, saltator; (of a mill), infundibulum
A hord, acervus
To hord, accumulo, colligo
A horder up, accumulator
Horehound, marubium
The horizon, horizon
Horizontal, horizontalis
A horn, cornu
A bugle-horn, cornu venatorium
Horn-work (fortification), munimentum angulare
Of horn, corneus
Hard as horn, corneolus
Having one horn, unicornis; (two horns), bicornis
A horner, cornuum opifex
A hornet, crabro
Horny, corneus
A horoscope, horoscopus
Horrible (terrible), horribilis, horridus; (heinous), dirus, infandus; (excessive), immoderatus
Horrid, tremendus, dirus
Horrific, horrificus
Horror, horror, terror
Full of horror, horrore perfusus
A horse, equus; (little horse), mannus, equulus; (ambling horse), equus tolutarius; (sorry), caballus; (cart-horse), jumentum; (coach-horses), bijuges; (to dry clothes on), cantherius; (hackney), equus conductitius; (hobby-horse), arundo longa; (hunting), equus venator
Horse (cavalry), equitatus
To horse, in equum mittere
Of a horse, equinus
A horse-courser, equorum mango

[59]

Horse-coursing, equorum permutatio
Horse-guards, satellites equestres
A horsekeeper, agaso
A horseleech, hirudo
A horse-load, sagma
A horseman, eques
Light-horsemen, velites
Of a horseman, equester
A horse-race, hippodromus
Horsemanship, ars equestris
Horse-radish, rapharius agrestis
Horse-shoe, equi calceus
Hortative, hortativus
Wearing hose, caligatus
Of hose, caligarius
A hosier, caligarius
Hospitable, hospitalis, benevolus
Hospitably, hospitalitèr
A hospital, xenodochium, nosoconium; (for old people), gerontocomium; (for orphans), orphanotrophium
Hospitality, hospitalitas
A host (army), exercitus, copiæ; (innkeeper), hospes, caupo; (wafer in the mass), hostia
A hostage, obses, vas
A hostel, or hotel, diversorium
A hostess, hospita, hospes
Hostile, hostilis, hosticus, infestus
Hostility, hostilitas
An hostler, stabularius
An hostry, stabulum
Hot, calidus, ardens; (upon the tongue), acris, mordicans; (headed), temerarius
To be hot, caleo, æstuo; (scalding), inferveo; (within), incaleo
To grow hot, calesco, excandesco
To make hot, calefacio
Hotly, fervidè, calidè; (furiously), acritèr, vehementèr
Hotness, calor
A botch-potch, farrago
A hovel, casa, tugurium
To hover (as a hawk), circumvolo; (float), fluctuo, fluito; (over), immineo; (soar), pennas librare
Hovering, imminens, propinquus
A hound, canis venaticus; (bloodhound), canis sagax, investigarius; (greyhound), canis Gallicus
To hound a dog, canem animare
An hour, hora; (in a bad hour), haud auspicatò; (in a good hour), auspicatò, opportunè
Half an hour, semihora; (an hour and half), sesquihora
An hour-glass, clepsydra
Hourly, horis singulis, in horas
A house, domus, ædes; (country), villa, suburbanum; (of lords), domus parium; (of commons), domus communium; (of correction), ergastulum; (of office), latrina
Of the same house, familiaris
A house, or family, familia, genus, prosapia
Of a house, domesticus
House by house, domesticatim
To house (cattle), ad stabulum deducere; (one's self), tectum subire; (corn), frumentum horreis condere
To keep a good house, elegantèr vivere; (an open house), exposità uti hospitalitate
House-breaking, latrocinium
House-rent, pensum pro domo
Housing, stragulum

A household, familia
Of the household, familiaris
Household (bread), panis secundarius; (affairs), res familiares; (fare), victus quotidianus; (government), imperium œconomicum; (stuff), supellex
A householder, paterfamilias
A housekeeper, fœmina cui domûs cura committitur [tratio
Housekeeping, familiæ administ-
Houseleek, sedum
House-room, locus in domo
A housewife, materfamilias
How, quàm; (far), quatenùs, quantò; (great), quantus quàm magnus; (greatly), quàm valdè; (long), quàm diù, quàm pridèm, quoad, quousquè; (many), quot, quoteni, quàm multi; (often), quoties [nihilominùs
Howbeit, at, tamen, attamen,
However (at least), saltèm, certè; (or howsoever), ut ut, utcunquè, quomodò, quomodocunquè
How great soever, quantuscunque; (little), quantuluscunque; (many), quotcunque, quotquot; (often), quotiescunque; (long), quamvis diù; (much), quantumcunque, quantumvis
To howl (cry), ululo
A howl (or howling), ululatus, ejulatus
A hubbub, turba, tumultus
The huckle-bone, talus
Huck-backed, gibbosus
A huckster, propola; (-'s trade), cauponaria
A huddle, confusio
To huddle, confundo agere; (together), confundo, misceo
In a huddle, confusè
A hue (colour), color
Hue and cry, sontis insecutio
A huff, or huffer, thraso
To huff (look big, or boast), glorior; (insult), insulto; (make a noise), verbis intonare; (threaten), minitor
To be in a huff, ægrè ferre
A huffing fellow, miles gloriosus
A huffing (boasting), jactatio; (threatening), minatio; (clamouring), vociferatio
Huffish, arrogans, ferox, insolens
Huffishly, arrogantèr, superbè
Huffishness, arrogantia, insolentia
A hug, amplexus
To hug, amplector; (himself), sibi placere, or plaudere
Huge, vastus, immanis, ingens
Hugeness, vastitas, immanitas
A hugging, amplexus
A hulk, navis oneraria
A hull (of beans, &c.), siliqua; (of a ship), corpus navis sine malo
To hull (as a ship), vacillo; (beans, &c.), decortico
A hum, admurmuratio, fallacia, bombus
To hum and haw, hæsito
To hum (as bees), bombilo; (a tune), vocem modulari; (deceive), fallo
Human, humanus [nus
Humane, comis, affabilis, benig-
Humanely, humanitèr
Humanity, humanitas, comitas
To humanise, erudio
Humble, humilis, supplex
To humble, or make humble, reprimo; (one's self), se humiliare
Humbleness, humilitas

D 6

HUS   IGN   IMM

A humbling (of others), coërcitio; (of one's self), submissio
Humbly, humilitèr, submissè
A humdrum, fatuus, ineptus
Humid, humidus, uvidus
Humidity, humiditas, humor
Humiliation, humiliatio, submissio
Humility, humilitas
A hummer (deceiver), deceptor
A humming, deceptio; (of bees), apum bombus
Humour, humor; (fancy), arbitrium; (pleasant), facetia; (in the body), corporei temperamenti affectus; (inclination), indoles, mores; (good), festivitas
Good-humoured, facetus, lepidus
Ill-humoured, austerus, morosus
To humour, morigeror
A humourist, inconstans, levis
Humourous (or humoursome), pervicax, morosus; (pleasant), lepidus, facetus
Humourously, lepidè, facetè
To hunch, tundo, trudo
Hunchbacked, gibbus, gibbosus
A hundred, centum, centenus
Of a hundred, centenarius
By hundreds, centuriatim
A hundred (of soldiers), centuria; (part of a shire), hundredum
A hundred times, centiès
The hundredth, centesimus
Two hundred, ducenti, duceni
Hunger, fames, esuries; (extreme), inedia
To hunger, esurio
Hungered, Hungry, Hungry, esuriens, rabidus
Hungrily, rabidè, jejunè
To hunt, venor, venatum ire; (after), aucupor, investigo; (after riches), opes consectari; (out), exploro, perquiro; (up and down), exagito
A hunter, venator
A hunting, venatio, venatus; (or seeking out), indagatio
For hunting, venatorius, venaticus
A hunting-match, venatio præfixa
A hurdle, crates
A hurl, jactus
To hurl, jacio, projicio
Hurled, emissus, jactus, conjectus
A hurler, jaculator
A hurling, jaculatio
A hurly-burly, tumultus
A hurricane, turbo
A hurry (haste), festinatio; (confusion), tumultus
To hurry, festino, urgeo
Hurried, festinatus, acceleratus
A hurrying, festinatio
A hurt (damage), damnum, injuria; (wound), vulnus, plaga
To hurt, lædo, noceo, corrumpo
Hurtful, nocens, nocivus, damnosus, perniciosus, exitiosus
A hurting, nocumentum
Hurtless, innocuus, illæsus
A husband, vir, maritus
A husband's brother, levir; (sister), glos
To husband, cautè dispensare; (or till ground), agrum colere
A husbandman, agricola
Husbandry, agricultura; (good), frugalitas, œconomia
To practise husbandry, rusticor
Hush! desine! tace!
To be hush, taceo

[60]

To hush (calm), placo; (keep secret), rem celare
A husk (hull), siliqua
Husk of corn, acus, gluma
Husky, acerosus; (in voice), raucus
A hussy, mulier nequam
Hustings, hustinga
A hut, casa, tugurium
A hutch, mactra
To huzz, obstrepo
Huzza, lætus clamor, acclamatio
To huzza, vociferor
A hyacinth, hyacinthus
An hydrographer, hydrographus
Hydrography, hydrographia
Hydropical, hydropicus
To hye, festino, propero
Hyemal, hyemalis
A hyena, hyæna
Hymen, Hymen
A hymn, hymnus, ode
An hyperbole, hyperbole
Hyperbolical, hyperbolicus
Hyperbolically, hyperbolicè
Hyphen (a), hyphen
Hypochondriac, hypochondriacus
Hypocrisy, hypocrysia
A hypocrite, hypocrita
To play the hypocrite, simulo
Hypocritical, simulatus, falsus
Hypocritically, simulatè
Hypothesis, positio, hypothesis
Hypothetical, hypotheticus
Hypothetically, hypoteticè
Hyssop, hysopus
Hysterical, hystericus
A hyth, sinus, portus

I.

I, ego; (myself), egomet, ipse ego
Iambic, Iambicus
Ice, glacies, gelu
An icicle, stillicidium, stiria
Icy, glacialis
An idea, idea, conceptio
Identity, identitas
The idea, idus
An idiom, idioma
An idiot, idiota, stultus
An idiotism, idiotismus; (foolishness), stultitia, fatuitas
Idle, otiosus, negligens, ignavus, nugatorius, futilis; (fellow), cessator; (trick), ineptia; (story), fabula; (discourse), sermo absonus, or alienus
Very idle, desidiosus
To be idle, cesso, torpesco
Idleness, ignavia, inertia
Idly, ignavè, otiosè, ineptè
An idol, idolum, imago
An idolater, idolatra
Idolatrous, idolis inserviens
Idolatry, idololatria
To idolise, hominem devenerari
Idyl, idyllium
If, si; (not), si minùs, si nou, ni, nisi; (as if), quasi, tanquam, perindè ac si; (but if), sin, quòd si; (but if not), sin alitèr, siu minùs, sin sectùs; (whether) num, an, utrùm, si
Ignoble, ignobilis, obscurus
Ignobly, obscurè, abjectè
Ignominious, infamis
Ignominiously, cum dedecore
Ignominy, dedecus, infamia
An ignoramus, ignavus, fatuus
Ignorance, inscientia, imperitia

Ignorant, ignarus, inscius, rudis
To be ignorant, ignoro, nescio
Ignorantly, inscientèr, inscitè
Ill, infortunium, malum; adj. pravus, nequam, malus; adv. perperàm, malè
To be ill, ægroto, malè se habere
Ill-conditioned, morosus; (disposed), pravus; (favoured), deformis; (bred), asper, agrestis
Ill-will, invidia, livor
Illegal, illicitus
Illegally, contra fas
Illegality, injustitia
Illegitimacy, ortûs infamia
Illegitimate, spurius, adulterinus
Illiberal, illiberalis
Illiberality, illiberalitas
Illiberally, illiberalitèr
Illicit, illicitus
Illiterate, indoctus, rudis
Illness, morbus, ægrotatio
Ill-natured, perversus
To illude, illudo, eludo
To illuminate, illumino
An illuminating, illuminatio
An illusion, phantasma, error
Illusory, Illusive, fallax
To illustrate, illustro, explico
An illustrating, illustratio [rus
Illustrious, illustris, eximius, clarus
To be illustrious, clareo
Illustriously, eximiè, clarè
Illustriousness, claritudo
Imaginable, quod fingi potest
An image, imago, statua
Image-worship, cultus simulacrorum
Imaginary, imaginarius, fictus
Imagination, imaginatio, cogitatio, machinatio, opinio
Full of imagination, cogitabundus
To imagine (think), existimo, suppono; (invent), imaginor
Not to be imagined, incomprehensibilis
To imbank, munio, sepio
To imbattle, aciem instruere
Imbattled (as an army), instructus; (as a wall), pinnatus
Imbecility, debilitas
To imbellish, polio, decoro. See *Embellish*
To imbezzle (waste), peculor, dilapido; (purloin), surripio
An imbezzler, peculator
An imbezzlement, dissipatio
To imbibe (suck in), imbibo
To imbitter (exasperate), exaspero
To imbolden, animo, incito
To imboss, cælo
Imbossed-work, toreuma
An imbosser, cælator
An imbossing, cælatura
Art of imbossing, toreutice
To imbroil, confundo, turbo; (a state), res novas moliri; (sow discord), dissidium concitare
To imbrue, imbuo, contamino
To imbue, imbuo
To imburse, nummos reponere
To imitate, imitor; (a thing), delineo; (with ambition), æmulor
Imitable, imitabilis
An imitating, or imitation, imitatio, delineatio
An imitator, imitator, æmulator
Immaculate, immaculatus, purus
Immanent, inhærens
Immanity, crudelitas
Immaterial (void of matter), materiæ expers; (of no moment), res levis

Immature, immaturus, crudus
Immaturity, cruditas
Immaturely, immaturè
Immeasurable, immensus [mus
Immediate, immediatus, proxi-
Immediately, immediatè, illicò, statim
Immedicable, immedicabilis
Immemorable, immemorabilis
Immemorial, immemoratus
Immense, immensus, infinitus
Immensity, immensitas
Immensely great, ingens
To immerge, immergo
Immersion, immersio [fusus
Immethodical, indigestus, con-
Immethodically, sine methodo
Imminent, imminens, impendens
To be imminent, immineo
Immoderate, immoderatus, profusus
Immoderately, immoderatè, immodicè
Immodest, impudicus
Immodestly, immodestè, inverecundè
Immodesty, immodestia
To immolate, immolo
Immoral, improbus, pravus
Immorality, improbitas morum
Immorally, improbè, impiè
Immortal, immortalis, æternus
Immortality, immortalitas
Immortally, æternùm
To immortalize, æterno
Immoveable, immotus, constans
An immunity, privilegium
To immure, intra muros includere
Immutability, immutabilitas
Immutable, immutabilis, constans
Immutably, constantèr, firmè
An imp, parvus dæmon
To impair, diminuo, imminuo
Impairing, diminuens
An impairing, diminutio
To impale (fence in), septo munire; (a punishment), stipitem per medium hominem adigere
To impannel, eligo, designo
Imparity, inæqualitas
To impark, consepio
Imparlance, interlocutio
To impart, impertio, impertior
Impartial, æquus, justus
Impartiality, æquitas, justitia
Impartially, æquè, justè
An imparting, communicatio
Impassable, invius, avius
Impassible, impassibilis
Impatience, impatientia
Impatient, impatiens; (hasty in temper), iracundus
Impatiently, iracundè, ægrè
To impeach, accuso, anquiro
Impeaching, accusans
Impeachment, accusatio, dica
Impeccability, impeccabilitas
Impeccable, impeccabilis, peccare nescius
To impede, impedio
An impediment, impedimentum; (in speech), hæsitatio
To impel, impello
To impend, immineo, insto
Impending, impendens, imminens
Impenetrable, impenetrabilis
Impenetrability, impenetrabilitas
Impenitence, impœnitentia
Impenitent, impœnitens
Imperative, imperativus
Imperceptible, incompertus
Imperfect, imperfectus, mancus

Imperfectly, non perfectè
Imperfection, defectus
Imperial, imperatorius, augustus
Imperious, imperiosus, arrogans
Imperiously, superbè, arrogantèr
Imperiousness, arrogantia
Impersonal, impersonalis
Impersonally, impersonalitèr
Impertinence, ineptiæ
Impertinent, petulans; (not pertinent), absurdus, ineptus
Impertinently, petulantèr, insulsè
Impervious, impervius
Impetuous, violentus, vehemens
Impetuosity, vehementia
Impetuously, vehementèr, oppidò
Impiety, impietas, scelus
Impious, impius, scelestus
Impiously, impiè, scelestè
Implacable, inexorabilis
Implacability, implacabilitas
Implacably, implacabilitèr
To implant, insero
Implements (tools), instrumenta; (goods), supellex
To implicate, implico
Implication, implicatio
Implicit, implicitus
Implicitly, implicitè
To implore, imploro, obsecro
An imploring, imploratio
To imply (comprehend), comprehendo; (denote), significo; (infer), infero, concludo
Impolite, inurbanus, rudis
Impolitic, incautus, imprudens
Impoliticly, inconsideratè, incautè
To import (by ships), importo, inveho; (concern), intersum; (signify), significo
Import (use), utilitas; (meaning), significatio; (and export), invectio et exportatio
Of importance, magni momenti
Of little importance, levis
Importance, vis, sensus
Important, momentosus, gravis
Importation, invectio
Importunate, importunus, instans
Importunately, importunè
To importune, efflagito, solicito
Importunity, importunitas
To impose (enjoin), injungo, impono; (cheat), fraudo
An imposition (cheat), fraus; (command), mandatum; (tax), vectigal, tributum
Impossibility, impossibilitas
Impossible, impossibilis
An impost, vectigal; (in architecture), incumba
An imposthume, abscessus; (about the ear), parotis; (in the lungs), tabes
Imposthumated, ulceratus
An impostor, impostor, planus
Imposture, fraus, impostura
Impotence, debilitas
Impotent, impotens, debilis
Impotently, impotentèr, infirmè
To impoverish, depaupero
An impoverishment, compilatio
To impound, includo
An impounding, inclusio
To impower, potestate instruere
Impracticable, quod fieri non potest
To imprecate, imprecor
An imprecation, execratio
Impregnable, inexpugnabilis
To impregnate, gravidam facere
To impress (men), milites invitos conscribere
Impressed (marked), signatus

An impression, impressio; (on the mind), mentis sensus; (of a book), editio
Imprest money, auctoramentum
To imprint, imprimo, excudo
To imprison, incarcero
Imprisonment, incarceratio
Improbability, quod vix credi potest
Improbable, improbabilis
Improbably, haud probabilitèr
Improbity, improbitas
Improper, improprius; (unseasonable), intempestivus
Improperly, impropriè, abusivè, absurdè
An impropriation, sacerdotium gentilitium and avitura
An impropriator, laïcus donator beneficii ecclesiastici
Impropriety, improprietas
Improvable, quod utilius evadere potest
To improve (grow better), proficio; (arts, &c.), artes colere; (a victory), uti victoriâ
An improvement, fructus, cultura, questus
An improver, amplificator
An improving, amplificatio
Improvident, improvidus, incautus
Improvidently, incautè, temerè
Imprudence, imprudentia
Imprudent, imprudens, incautus
Imprudently, imprudentèr, insanè
Impudence, impudentia, audacia
Impudent, impudens, effrons
Impudently, impudentèr, probè
To impugn, impugno
An impulse, impulsus
Impulsive, impellens
Impunity, impunitas
Impure, impurus, pollutus
Impurely, impurè, immundè
Impurity, immundities, sordes
An imputation, vituperatio
To impute, imputo, tribuo
An imputer, imputator
In, ad, apud, de, ex, in, inter, intra, per, præ, pro, secundum, sub, and tenus
In, adv. intrò
In all, omninò; (in as much as), quando, quoniam; (in brief), ad summum; (in deed), reverà; (in comparison of), præ; (in a manner), ferè, fermè; (in the mean time), interea, interim
In (inward), internus, insitus
Inability, impotentia
Inaccessible, inaccessus
Inaccurate, minimè exactus
Inactive, ignavus, iners
Inactivity, inertia, socordia
Inadequate, non aptè quadrans
Inadvertence, incogitantia
Inadvertent, incogitans, imprudens
Inadvertently, imprudentèr
Inanimate, inanimatus
Inanity, inanitas [quit
Inapplicable, quod applicari nequit
Inarticulate, indistinctus, confusus
Inarticulately, confusè
Inattention, negligentia
Inattentive, negligens, socors
To inaugurate, inauguro
An inauguration, inauguratio
Inauspicious, inauspicatus, infaustus
Inbred, insitus, innatus
To incamp, castra ponere
Incantation, incantamentum

Incapable, incapax, inhabilis
Incapacity, imperitia
To incarnate, incarno [Dei
The incarnation, incarnatio Filii
An incendiary, incendiarius
Incense, thus, suffitus
An incenser, irritator
An incensing, irritatio
An incensory, thuribulum
An incentive, incitamentum
Inceptive, inceptivus
Incertitude, dubitatio
Incessant, constans, assiduus
Incessantly, constantèr, assiduè
Incest, incestus, incestum
Incestuous, incestus, incestuosus
An inch, uncia, pollex
To inchant, incanto [tator
An inchanter, veneficus, incan-
An inchanting, incantatio
Inchantingly, magicè, blandis-
simè
An inchantment, incantamentum
An inchantress, venefica
To inchase, cælo
Inchoative, inchoativus
Incident, incidens, contingens
An incident (circumstance), cas-
us accessio; (event), eventus
Incidentally, obitèr
To incircle, circumdo
An incircling, circumscriptio
An incision, incisio, incisus
To incite, incito, stimulo
An inciter, incitator
An inciting, incitatio
Incivility, rusticitas
Inclemency, inclementia
Inclement, inclemens
Inclinable, propensus, pronus
An inclination, proclivitas, pro-
pensio; (one's own), sponte suâ
To incline, inclino, vergo
To be inclined, propendeo
Inclining, proclivis, declivis; (as
the day), inclinatus
To inclose, includo, præcingo,
circumsepio
An inclosing, inclusio
An inclosure, sepimentum
To include, includo, comprehendo
Inclusive, comprehendens
Inclusively, inclusivè
Incognito, clam, incognitus
Incoherence, incongruentia
Incoherent, disjunctus, absurdus
Incoherently, disjunctè, absurdè
An income, reditus
To incommode, incommodo
Incommodious, incommodus, mo-
lestus [lestè
Incommodiously, incommodè, mo-
Incommodity, incommodum
Incommunicable, incommunica-
bilis [positus
Incompact, inconcinnus, incom-
Incomparable, incomparabilis
Incomparably, longè, multò
To incompass, circumdo, cingo
An incompassing, ambitus
Incompassionate, immitis, inhu-
manus
Incompatibility, repugnantia
Incompatible, insociabilis, re-
pugnans [fectus
Incompetency, jurisdictionis de-
Incompetent, non legitimus, non
conveniens
Incomplete, imperfectus
Incomprehensible, incomprehen-
sibilis [cipi
Inconceivable, quod nequit con-
Incongruity, incongruitas
Incongruous, non congruens
Inconsiderable, vilis, nihili
[62]

Inconsiderateness, incogitantia
Inconsiderate, præceps, temera-
rius [merè
Inconsiderately, inconsultè, te-
Inconsistency, repugnantia
Inconsistent,repugnans, absurdus
Inconsistently, absurdè
Inconsolable, inconsolabilis
Inconstancy, inconstantia, levitas
Inconstant, inconstans, levis
Inconstantly, inconstantèr, levitèr
Incontestable, non contendendus
Incontinence, incontinentia
Incontinent, incontinens, libidi-
nosus [mox
Incontinently, continuò, illicò,
Incontrovertibly, sine controversiâ
An inconvenience, incommodum
Inconvenient, incommodus, in-
tempestivus [tempestivè
Inconveniently, incommodè, in-
Inconvertible, insociabilis
Inconvertible, non convertendus
To incorporate, incorporo
An incorporating, coagmentatio,
cooptatio
Inecorporeal, incorporeus
Incorrect, mendis scatens, vitiosus
Incorrectly, mendosè, vitiosè
Inecorrectness, accurationis expers
Incorrigible, incorrigibilis
Incorrigibleness, emendationis
desperatio [ger
Incorrupt, purus, sincerus, inte-
Incorruptible, corruptionis expers
Increase, incrementum
To increase (add to), augeo, accu-
mulo, cresco, augeor
An increasing, auctus
Increasing, augens, crescens
Incredible, incredibilis, fide major
Incredibility, incredibilitas
Incredulity, incredulitas
Incredulous, incredulus
To incroach, invado, intrudo
An incroacher, qui res alienas in-
vadit
An incroachment, alieni invasio,
impetus in res alienas factus
Incrustation, incrustatio
Incubation, incubatio
To inculcate, inculco, itero
An inculcating, inculcatio
Inculpable, insons, culpæ expers
Incumbent, incumbens
An incumbent, beneficii possessor
To incumber, impedio
Incumbered, impeditus, obrutus
An incumbering, oneratio
An incumbrance, impeditio, mora
Incurable, insanabilis
To incur, incurro, mereor
An incursion, incursio
Indecency, indecorum
Indecent, indecens, indecorus
Indecently, indecentèr, indecorè
Indeed, reverà, profectò, itanè?
itanè verò?
Indefatigable, indefessus
Indefatigably, summâ diligentiâ
Indefeasible, inviolabilis, irrevo-
cabilis
Indefinite, indefinitus
Indefinitely, indefinitè
Indelible, indelibilis
Indeliberate, non præmeditatus
Indelicacy, indecorum
To indemnify, illæsum præstare
Indemnity, indemnitas
An act of indemnity, amnestia
To indent, paciscor, incido
An indenture, syngrapha denticu-
lata
Independence, summa potestas
Independent, nemini subjectus

Independently, cum summâ liber-
tate
Indeterminate, indefinitus
Indeterminately, indeterminatè
Indevoutly, irreligiosè
An index, index, syllabus
An Indian, Indus
Indian, Indicus
To indicate, indico
Indication, indicatio
Indicative, indicativus [cere
To indict, diem dicere, reum fa-
Indictable, accusationi obnoxius
An indicter, accusator
An indicting, accusatio [torius
An indictment, libellus accusa-
Indifference, æquabilitas; (un-
concernedness), animus in nul-
lam partem propendens
With indifference, frigidè, jejunè
Indifferent, indifferens, medius,
æqualis; (ordinary), mediocris,
ferendus [esse
To be indifferent, æquo animo
Indifferently (without partiality),
indifferentèr, indiscriminatim;
(coolly), jejunè, frigidè
Indigence, indigentia, egestas
Indigent, egenus, pauper
Indigenous, indigena
Indigestible, concocta difficilis
Indigestion, stomachi cruditas
Indignant, indignans, iratus
Indignation, indignatio
To have indignation, stomachor
Indignity, indignitas, contumelia
Indigo, lapis cæruleus
Indirect, indirectus, obliquus
Indirectly, indirectè, obliquè
Indiscreet, imprudens, inconsul-
tus
Indiscreetly, imprudentèr, temerè
Indiscretion, imprudentia
Indiscriminately, sine discrimine
Indispensable, inevitabilis
Indispensably, necessariò
Indispensableness, rei necessitas
Indisposed, æger, alienus
Indisposition, mala habitudo
Indisputable, indubitabilis
Indissoluble, indissolubilis
Indistinct, indistinctus, impromis-
cuus
Indistinctly, promiscuè [tus
Indistinguishable, indiscrimina-
To indite (dictate), dicto; (ac-
cuse, or indict), in judicio pos-
tulare [singuli
Individual, individuus; (every),
Individually, singulatim
Indivisible, individuus
Indocile, indocilis, tardus
Indolence, indolentia
Indolent, lentus, ignavus
To indorse, à tergo scribere
An indorser, à tergo scribens
An indorsement, in aversâ parte
nominis inscriptio
Indubitable, indubitabilis, certus
Indubitably, sine dubio
To induce (prevail with), exoro;
(allure), allicio; (persuade),
persuadeo
An inducer, suasor
An inducement, incitamentum
To induct, induco
An induction, inductio
To indue, imbuo, dono
To indulge, indulgeo, parco
Indulgence, indulgentia
Indulgent, blandus, obsequiosus
Indulgently, indulgentèr
Indurable, tolerabilis
To indurate, obduro, duro
Industrious, diligens, assiduus

INF — INI — INS

Industriously, sedulò, diligentèr
Industry, industria, diligentia
To inebriate, inebrio
Ineffable, ineffabilis
Ineffably, more ineffabili
Ineffectual, inefficax, inanis
Ineffectually, sine effectu
Inelegant, inelegans
Inequality, inæqualitas
Inert, iners, segnis
Inertly, segnitèr, ægrè
Inestimable, inæstimabilis
Inevitable, inevitabilis
Inexcusable, inexcusabilis
Inexorable, inexorabilis
Inexpedient, parùm conducens
Inexperience, imperitia
Inexperienced, inexpertus
Inexpert, imperitus
Inexpiable, inexpiabilis
Inexplicable, inexplicabilis
Inexpressible, ineffabilis
Inexpugnable, inexpugnabilis
Inextinguishable, inextinctus
Inextricable, inextricabilis
Infallibility, infallibilitas, errovis vacuitas [pers
Infallible, certissimus, erroris ex-
Infallibly, certissimè, sine dubio
Infamous, infamis, famosus
Infamously, turpitèr, famosè
Infamy, infamia, dedecus
Infancy, infantia
An infant, infans
Infantine, infantilis
Infantry, peditatus
To infatuate, infatuo, demento
Infatuation, stupiditas
To infect, inficio, imbuo
To be infected, corrumpor
An infection, contagium
Infectious, contagiosus, pestiferus
To infeeble, debilito
Infelicity, infelicitas
To infer, infero, colligo
An inference, consequens
Inferior, inferior, minor
Inferiority, inferioritas
Infernal, infernus, inferus
To infest, infesto, vexo
An infesting, molestia, vexatio
An infidel, infidelis, infidus
Infidels, infideles
Infidelity, infidelitas
Infinite, infinitus, immensus
Infinitely, infinitè, ad infinitum
Infinitive, infinitivus
Infinity, infinitas
To infinity, ad infinitum
Infirm, infirmus, languidus
An infirmary, valetudinarium
An infirmity, infirmitas
Infirmities, peccata leviora
To inflame, inflammo, accendo
To be inflamed, excandesco
An inflammation, inflammatio; (of the lungs), peripneumonia; (of the body), phlegmona
Inflammatory, ardens
To inflate, inflo
An inflation, inflatio
To inflect, inflecto
Inflexibility, pertinacia [bilis
Inflexible, inflexibilis, inexora-
Inflexion, inflexio
To inflict, infligo, punio
Inflictive, puniens
An influence, impulsus, auctoritas
To influence, moveo, impello
Influencing, movens, impellens
Influx, illapsus, infusus
To infold, implico
To inforce, compello, cogo; (argument), suadeo, (by necessity), adigo, subigo, cogo
[63]

An inforcing, impulsio
To inform (teach), instruo; institio; (give information), monstro, certiores facere; (against), defero; (himself), disco
An information, informatio, accusatio, delatio
To be informed, certior fieri
An informer, delator
An informing, admonitio
Infortunate, infortunatus, infelix
Infraction, infractio
To infringe, infringo, violo
An infringement, violatio
An infringer, violator
To infuse (pour in), infundo; (opinions), animum imbuere; (herbs), herbæ succum elicere; macero
An infusion, infusio
Ingathering, frugum perceptio
To ingender, genero, gigno
Ingendered, generatus, genitus
An ingendering, generatio
Ingenious, ingeniosus, subtilis, solers [gutè
Ingeniously, acutè, solertèr, ar-
Ingeniousness, ingenuitas
Ingenuous, ingenuus, liberalis
Ingenuously, ingenuè, liberalitèr
Ingenuity, ingenuitas
Inglorious, inglorius, ignobilis
Ingloriously, turpitèr, fœdè
To ingorge, devoro, deglutio
An ingorger, helluo, vorax
An ingorging, devoratio
An ingot, auri massa
To ingraff, insero
Ingraffed, insitus
An ingraffment, insitio
To ingratiate, insinuo
Ingratitude, ingratitudo
To ingrave, cælo, sculpo
Ingraving, cælatura
An ingredient, pars compositionis
Ingress and egress, ingrediendi et egrediendi permissio
To ingross (deeds), pulchrè perscribere; (goods), merces flagellare [flagellator
An ingrosser of goods, mercium
To ingulf, ingurgito
To inhabit, inhabito, incolo, colo
Inhabitable, inhabitabilis
An inhabitant, incola
Inhabitants (without), desertus
Inhabiting, habitans, incolens
To inhale, inhalo
To inhere, hæreo
Inherent, inhærens
To inherit, aliquid jure hæreditatis possidere; (as heir at law), ab intestato succedere
An inheritance, hæreditas
An inheritor, hæres
To inhibit, inhibeo, veto
An inhibition, prohibitio
Inhospitable, inhospitalis
Inhuman, inhumanus, crudelis, sævus, inurbanus
Inhumanity, inhumanitas, crudelitas
Inhumanly, inhumanè, crudelitèr
To inhume, sepelio
To inject, injicio
An injection, injectio
Inimical, inimicus, hostilis
Inimitable, inimitabilis
Inimitably, modo inimitabili
Iniquitous, iniquus, injustus
Iniquity, iniquitas, nefas
Initial, initialis
To initiate, initio
Initiating, initians

An initiation, initiatio
Injudicious, inconsideratus, inconsultus [acitè
Injudiciously, inconsideratè, in-
An injunction, injunctio, mandatum
To injure, noceo, lædo
Injurious, injurius, noxius
Injuriously, noxiè, injustè
An injury, injuria, damnum
Injustice, injustitia
Ink, atramentum
An inkhorn, atramentarium
To ink, atramento inquinare
Inky, atramento inquinatus
Inkle, tænia, vitta
An inkling, rumusculus; (given), obscura significatio; (to get), subsentio
Inlaid, tessellatus
Inland, mediterraneus
To inlay, tessello, vario
An inlet, aditus [light'en
To inlighten, illumino. See En-
To inlist, milites conscribere; (one's self), nomen militiæ dare
An inlisting, militum conscriptio
An inmate, inquilinus
Inmost, intimus
An inn, diversorium
To inn, diversor; (corn), messes domum vehere [sultorum
Inns of court, hospitia jurscon-
An innholder, caupo, stabularius
Innate, innatus [bilis
Innavigable, innavigabilis, inna-
Inner, interior
An inner chamber, penetrale
Innermost, intimus
Innocence, innocentia
Innocent, innocens, insons
Innocently, innocentèr, innocuè; (without thought), impruden-
To innovate, innovo, novo [tèr
Innovation, innovatio, immutatio, novæ res
An innovator, novator
Innoxious, innoxius, innocuus
An innuendo, monitio [tus
Innumerable, innumerus, indini-
To inoculate, inoculo, insero
Inoculation, inoculatio
Inoffensive, innocuus, innoxius
Inoffensively, innocuè, innocentèr
Inoffensiveness, innocentia
Inordinate, inordinatus, incompositus
Inordinately, inordinatè
Inordinateness, immoderatio
Inorganical, aptis instrumentis destitutus
An inquest, inquisitio; (grand inquest), criminum quæsitores
Inquietude, inquietudo
To inquire, inquiro, quæro; (or search diligently), investigo, exploro; (after), quærito
An inquirer, quæsitor, explorator
An inquiry, inquisitio
Inquisition, examen, inquisitio
The inquisition, inquisitio
Inquisitive, curiosus
Inquisitively, curiosè, studiosè
An inquisitor, inquisitor
An inroad, incursio, irruptio
Inrobed, prætextatus
To inrol, conscribo
Inrolled, conscriptus
An inrolling, in tabulas relatio
Insane, insanus [bilis
Insatiable, insatiabilis, inexple-
Insatiableness, insatiabilitas
Insatiably, insatiabilitèr
Insatiate, inexplebilis
To inscribe, inscribo

INS

An inscription, inscriptio
Inscrutable, non vestigabilis
Insects, insecta
Insecure, partim securus
Insensate, sensûs expers
Insensible, insensibilis, insensilis
Insensibility, habetudo
Insensibly, sensim, paulatim
Inseparable, inseparabilis, individuus
Inseparably, indivisè
To insert, insero, interpono
An insertion, insertio
The inside, pars interior
Insidious, insidiosus, fallax
Insidiously, insidiosè
An insight, intuitus inspectio
Insight (skill), peritia
To have an insight, perspicio
Having an insight, perspicax
Insignificancy, inutilitas
Insignificant, inutilis
Insignificantly, inutilitèr
Insincere, insincerus, fallax
Insincerity, dissimulatio
To insinuate, in·inuo; (flatter), assentor, adulor
An insinuation, insinuatio
Insipid (without taste), insulsus; (dull), hebes, tardus
Insipidity, insulsè
Insipidness, insulsitas
To insist, insto, urgeo
To inslave, in servitutem redigere
To insnare, irritio, allaqueo
Insnaring, insidias struens
An insnaring, illaqueatio
Insociable, insociabilis
Insolence, arrogantia
Insolent, insolens, arrogans
Insolently, arrogantèr, superbè
Insoluble, insolubilis
Insolvent, solvendo impar
Insomuch, adeò ut, usque adeò
To inspect, inspicio
Inspection, inspectio
An inspector, inspector
Inspersion, aspersio
To inspire, inspiro, injicio
Inspiration, afflatus divinus; (by divine inspiration), divinitùs
Instability, instabilitas
To instal, constituo, inauguro
Installation, instalment, or installing, inauguratio, installatio
An instance, exemplum ; (request), impulsus, flagitatio
To instance, exemplum dare
For instance, exempli gratiâ
Instant (earnest), importunus ; (present), præsens, instans
An instant, momentum ; (in an instant), dicto citiùs, confestim
Instantly, instantèr, vehementèr
Instantaneously, extemplò
Instauration, instauratio
Instead of, loco, vice
The instep, tarsus; (of a shoe), calcei convexum
To instigate, stimulo, excito
Instigation, instigatio, incitatio
An instigator, instigator
To instil, instillo, infundo
Instinct, instinctus
Instinctively, instinctu
To institute, instituo
Institutes, instituta
Institution, institutio
To instruct, imbuo, erudio, doceo, instituo
An instructor, præceptor
An instructing, institutio
Instruction, documentum ; (instructions to ambassadors), mandata

INT

Instructive, ad docendum aptus
An instrument, instrumeutum; (servant), minister; (of war), machina bellica; (in writing), formula; (instruments, or tools), arma [tus
Instrumental (useful), utilis, ap-
Instrumentally, eo ministro
To insue, æquor, consequor
Insufferable, intolerabilis
Insufficiency (unskilfulness), imperitia ; (impotency), impotentia
Insufficient, insufficiens, impar
An insult, insultatio
To insult, insulto
Insuperable, insuperabilis
Insupportable, intolerabilis
Insurmountable, inexuperabilis
An insurrection, insurrectio, seditio
An intail (or entail), jus hæreditarium
To intail, hæredi addicere
An intailing, hæredi addictio
To intangle, illaqueo, irretio
An intangling, implicatio
An integer, numerus integralis
Integrity, integritas, sinceritas
An integument, integumentum
The intellect, intellectus
Intellectual, intellectualis
Intelligence, intelligentia, notitia
Intelligent, intelligens
Intelligible, intelligibilis
Intelligibleness, perspicuitas
Intelligibly, clarè, planè
Intemperance, intemperantia
Intemperate, intemperatus, immodicus
Intemperately, intemperatè
Intemperateness, intemperantia; (of weather), intemperies
To intend, intendo, statuo
An intendment (purpose), propositum ; (meaning), significatio
Intense, intensus
Intensely, valdè, magnoperè
Intenseness, intensio
Intent, intensus, attentus
An intent, propositum, institutum; (meaning), significatio; (to all intents and purposes), omninò, prorsus
An intention, intentio, consilium
Intentionally, de industriâ
Intentive, intentus, attentus
Intently, animo attento
Intercalary, intercalaris
Intercalation, intercalatio
To intercede, intercedo, deprecor
Interceding, deprecans
To intercept, intercipio
An intercepting, interceptio
An intercession, intercessio
An intercessor, deprecator
To interchange, alterno, commuto
An interchange, commutatio
Intercourse, commercium
To interdict, interdico, prohibeo
An interdict, or interdiction, interdictio, interdictum
To interest one's self in an affair, se alicui negotio immiscere
Interested in, particeps
An interest in, participatio
Interest (advantage), emolumentum ; (for money), fœnus
To have interest with one, gratia apud aliquem valere
Interest (right), jus; (to make interest for), munus aliquod ambire

INT

To interfere (interpose), interpono; (clash), discrepo
An interfering, dissidium
An interjection, interjectio
In the interim, intereâ temporis
Interior, interior
To interlace, intersero
To interlard, intersero
To interleave, folia interserere
To interline, lineas interponere
Interlineation, intersertio linearum
Interlocution, interlocutio
Interlocutory, interlocutorius
To interlope, anticipo
An interloper, anticipator
An interlude, drama, exodium
To intermeddle, immisceo
Intermediate, medius
Interment, humatio
To intermingle, commisceo
Intermission, intermissio ; (by intermission), intermissu ; (without intermission), assiduè, perpetuò
To intermit, remitto
Intermittent, intermittens
To intermix, intermisceo
Internal, internus, intimus
Internally, internè, intimè
Interpellation, interpellatio
To interpolate, interpolo
Interpolation, interpolatio
An interpolator, interpolator
To interpose, interpono
Interposition, interpositio
To interpret, explico, expono
Interpretation, interpretatio
An interpreter interpres
To inter, inhumo, sepelio
An interreign, interregnum
An interring, humatio
An interrogate, interrogo
An interrogating, interrogatio
An interrogation, interrogatio
Interrogative, interrogativus
Interrogatively, interrogativè
An interrogator, interrogator
An interrogatory, interrogatio
To interrupt, interrumpo; (in a tale), intercipio; (an affair), rem dirimere
An interrupter, interpellator
Interruption, interruptio
Without interruption, continentèr
To intersect, interseco
An intersection, intersectio
To intersperse, interspergo
An interstice, interstitium
An interval, intercapedo
To intervene, intervenio
Intervening, interveniens
An interview, congressus
To interweave, intertexo
Intestate, intestatus
Intestine, intestinus, civilis
The intestines, intestina
To inthral, mancipo
Inthralment, mancipatio
To inthrone, in solio collocare
Intimacy, necessitudo, familiaritas
Intimate, intimus, familiaris
To intimate, indico, innuo
Intimately, intimè, familiaritèr
Intimation, indicatio
To intimidate, timidum reddere
Intirely, integrè, sincerè
Intitle, appello, inscribo
Intitled, appellatus, inscriptus
Into (prep. with accus.), in
Intolerable, intolerandus
Intolerably, intolerabilitèr
To intomb, sepelio, tumulo
To intoxicate, demento; (with drink), inebrio

[64]

INV — IRR — JAV

Intoxicating, inebrians
Intractable, intractabilis
Intransitive, intransitivus
To intrap, decipio, capio
An intrapping, deceptio
To intreat, obsecro, supplico; (speak of), tracto, dissero
Not to be intreated, inexorabilis
To intrench, vallo et fossâ munire; (a camp), castra vallo cingere
An intrenchment, vallum
Intrepid, intrepidus, interritus
Intrepidity, animi fortitudo
Intrepidly, intrepidè, fortitèr
Intricacy, perplexitas
Intricate, implicatus, perplexus
Intricately, implicitè, dubiè
An intrigue, vaframentum
To intrigue, vafrè agere
Intriguingly, clandestinò
Intrinsical, Intrinsic, internus
Intrinsically, intrinsecùs
To introduce, introduco
An introduction, introductio; (to a discourse), exordium
Introductory, introducens
To intrude, intrudo; (into an estate), hæreditatem injustè capessere; (upon patience), patientia abuti
An intruder, invasor
Intrusion, usurpatio
To intrust, fidei committere
Intrusting, fidei committens
Intuition, intuitus, inspectio
Intuitive, ad intuitum pertinens
To invade, invado, adorior
An invader, invasor
Invalid, invalidus, irritus
An invalid, miles emeritus
To invalidate, invalidum reddere; (a will), testamentum rescindere [mans
Invalidating, rescindens, infirInvaluable, inestimabilis
Invariable, immutabilis, constans
Invariableness, immutabilitas
Invariably, immutabilitèr, sempèr
An invasion, impressio, incursio
An invective, oratio objurgatoria
To inveigh, maledictis insectari
To inveigle, seduco, pellicio
An inveigler, deceptor
An inveigling, blanditiæ verborum
To invelop, involvo, obvelo
Inveloped, coopertus
To invent (devise), invenio, fingo; (find out), excogito, exudo; (craftily), machinor; (deceit), dolos nectere; (words), verba cudere
Inventing, excogitans, moliens
An inventing, inventio
An invention, inventio; (device), dolus, artificium
An inventor, inventor, auctor; (crafty), machinator
An inventory, bonorum index
An inversion, inversio
To invert, inverto
To invest (one with an estate), possessionem alicui dare; (in an office), inauguro, coopto; (besiege), obsidione urbem cingere
To investigate, investigo, indago
Investigation, investigatio
Investiture, inauguratio
Inveterate, inveteratus
To grow inveterate, inveterasco
Invidious, invidus, malignus
Invidiously, invidiosè, malignè
Invidiousness, invidia
To invigorate, extimulo
[65]

Invincible, invictus, indomitus
Inviolable, inviolatus, sacer
Inviolably, inviolatè
Inviolate, inviolatus, sanctus
To invirou, cingo, ambio
Invironing, cingens, ambiens
Invisible, invisibilis
Invitation, invitatio, vocatio
To invite, invito, voco
An inviter, invitator
Inviting (attracting), alliciens
An inundation, inundatio
To invocate, invoco, imploro
Invocation, invocatio, imploratio
An invoice, bonorum recognitio
To invoke, invoco, imploro
To involve, involvo, implico
An involving, involucrum
Involuntarily, invitè
Involuntary, invitus
Involution, involutio
To inure, assuefacio, assuesco
Inutility, inutilitas
Invulnerable, invulnerabilis
Inward, *adj*. internus, intestinus; *adv*. intùs, intrinsecùs, introrsùm
The inwards (intestines), intestina
To inwrap, involvo, implico
Ionic, Ionian, Ionicus
Irascible, irascibilis, iracundus
Ire, ira, iracundia
Ireful, iracundus
Irish, Hibernicus
Irksome (tedious), molestus; (disagreeable), gravis, acerbus
Irksomeness, tædium
Iron, ferrum
Of iron, ferreus
Done with iron, ferratus
Iron-coloured, ferrugineus
An iron, massa ferrea
Tipped with iron, præpilatus
Iron-work, ferramentum
An ironmonger, mercator ferrarius
To iron (clothes), lævigo
Ironical, ironicus
Ironically, ironicè
Irony, ironia, simulatio
To irradiate, irradio
Irradiation, radiatio
Irrational, rationis expers, iniquus
Irreconcileable, inexorabilis
Irrecoverable, irreparabilis
Irrecoverably, penitùs, omninò
Irrefragable, certissimus
Irrefragably, sine dubio
Irregular, irregularis, abnormis
Irregularity, irregularitas
Irregularly, irregularitèr
Irreligious, irreligiosus, scelestus
Irreligiously, impiè, scelestè
Irremediable, immedicabilis
Irremissible, veniâ indignus
Irreparable, irreparabilis
Irreparably, funditùs, penitùs
Irreprehensible, inculpatus
Irreprehensibly, innocuè
Irreproachable, irreprehensus
Irresistible, inevitabilis
Irresolute, anceps, inconstans
Irresolutely, levitèr, inconstantèr
Irresolution, inconstantia
Irretrievable, irreparabilis
Irretrievably, funditùs, penitùs
Irreverence, irreverentia
Irreverent, parùm reverens
Irreverently, parùm reverentèr
Irreversible, immutabilis
Irrevocable, irrevocabilis
To irrigate, irrigo
Irriguous, irriguus
To irritate, exaspero, lacesso

An irritation, irritatio
An irruption, irruptio
Isinglass, icthyocolla
An island, *or* isle, insula
An islander, insulæ habitator
Isles, *or* aisles in a church, semitæ
An Israelite, Israelita
Israelitish, Israeliticus
An issue (going forth), exitus; (end), eventus; (offspring), proles, progenies; (sore), ulcus; (of blood), fluxus sanguinis; (spring), scaturigo; (in the arm, &c.), fons, fontanella; (profit), reditus
To issue, *or* sally out, erumpo, (a proclamation), edictum publicare; (forth), emano, elabor, emico, prorumpo
Issuing, emanans, erumpens
An Issuing, emanatio, fluxio
An isthmus, isthmus
It, is, ea, id
The itch, scabies
To itch, prurio
Itchy, scabiosus
An itching, pruritus
An itching desire, cupiditas
An item, cautio; (in an account), ratiuncula
To give an item, innuo
To iterate, itero, repeto
An iteration, iteratio, repetitio
Itinerant, itinerans
An itinerary, itinerarium
Itself, sui, ipse
Ivory, ebur
Of ivory, eburneus, eburnus
Ivy, hedera
Of ivy, hederaceus
Full of ivy, hederosus

J.

To jabber, garrio, blatero
A jabberer, garrulus
A jabbering, garritus
A jack (of a ship), vexillum; (in a kitchen), veruversorium; (to saw wood on), cantherius
A jackdaw, monedula
A jackpudding, mimus
A jackel, lupas aureus
A jackanapes, simia
A jacket, sagitium, sagum
A little jacket, tunicula
A jade, equus ignavus; (woman), mulier improba, *or* nequam
To jade (tire), defatigo
A jag, lacinia
To jag, laciniosè incidere
Jagged, dentatus
A jail, carcer
A jailer, ergastularius
A jakes, forica, latrina
Jalap, jalapium
The jambs of a door, antæ
To jangle, altercor, litigo
A jangler, litigator
A jangling, argutatio
Jangling, argutus
January, Januarius
To japan, more Japonum linire
Jargon, sermo inconditus
A jar (vessel), testa, urceus; (disagreeing), rixa, contentio; (half open), semiapertus
To jar, discrepo, altercor
Jarring, discrepans, dissonus
A jarring, altercatio
Jasper-stone, Iaspis
A javelin, hasta, lancea

The jaundice, morbus regius, icterus
Sick of the jaundice, ictericus
To jaunt, vagor, discurso
A jaunt, vagatio, discursus
The jaw, *or* jaw-bone, maxilla
Of the jaw, maxillaris
The jaws, fauces, rictus
Jealous, suspiciosus; (person), suspicax, zelotes
To be jealous, suspicor
Jealously, suspiciosè
Jealousy, zelotypia, suspicio
A jeer, dicterium, sanna
To jeer, derideo, illudo
A jeerer, derisor, irrisor
A jeering, irrisio
Jeeringly, jocosè
Jehovah, Jehovah
Jejune, jejunus
Jejunely, jejunè
Jejuneness, tenuitas, penuria
Jelly (of meats), jus gelatum ; (of quinces). cydonia gelata
Jeopardy, periculum
To be in jeopardy, periclitor
With jeopardy, periculosè
Jeopardous, periculosus
To jerk, cædo, verbero, calcitro
A jerk, verber, ictus ; (start), impetus
A jerkin (coat), vestis curta
Jessamine, jessamynum; (yellow), polemonium
A jest, jocus, facetia, sales
In jest, jocosè, joco; (spoken in jest), jocularia, joculatorius
Full of jests, jocosus, facetus
To jest, jocor, ludo ; (upon), irrideo
A jester, joculator, scurra
Jesting, jocosus, salsus
A jesting, jocatio, derisio
A Jesuit, unus è societate Jesu
Jesuit's bark, cortex Peruviana
Jet, gagates
To jet out, promineo
A Jew, Judæus
Jewish, Judaicus
Jew's trump (harp), crembalum
A jewel, gemma; (my jewel!) meum corculum !
A jeweller, gemmarius
A jig, tripudium
To jig, tripudio
A jill (measure), hemina
A jilt, femina fallax
To jilt, amantem ludificari
To jingle, tinnio
A jingling, tinnitus
A job, negotiolum; (good), res lucrosa ; (blow), ictus
A jockey, equiso
Jocose, jocosus, facetus
Jocosely, jocosè, facetè
Jocoseness, facetiæ
Jocular, jocularis, facetus
Jocund, lætus, alacer, hilaris
To be jocund, lætor, gestio
A jog, concussio, quassatio
To jog, concutio, quatio ; (with the elbow), cubito submovere ; (as a coach), subsulto; (shake), contremisco ; (on), procedo
To be jogging, abeo, discedo
To join (unto), adjungo; (or be joined unto), accedo, adjungor; (forces), conjungo; (together), connecto; (or be joined together), cohæreo ; (or cleave to), adhæreo ; (in battle), confligo; (as a joiner), conglutino; (fellowship), consocio, socio; (under), subnecto
Joining (adjoining), contiguus
[66]

A joining, junctio, conjunctio; (of boards), tabulatio ; (of words), constructio
A joint, articulus, junctura; (in stalks), geniculum ; (of the body), artus; (of meat), membrum
To joint, deartuo
To put out of joint, disloco
Out of joint, luxatus
A joint heir, cohæres
Joint tenants, simûl tenentes
Joint, *adj.* mutuus
Joint by joint, articulatim
Of the joints, articularis
Full of joints, articulosus
Jointly, junctim, conjunctim
A jointure, dos
A joist, tignum, trabs
To lay joists, tigna aptare
A joke, jocus
To joke, jocor, alicui illudere
A jole, caput ; (cheek by jole), æquâ fronte
Jolly, hilaris, festivus
To be jolly, lætor, gestio
Jollily, hilarè, lætè, festivè
Jolliness, Jollity, festivitas
A jolt, concussio, subsultus
To jolt, quatio, subsulto
A jot, hilum, punctum
Jovial, alacer, lætus; (fellow), congerro lepidus
Jovially, alacritèr, jucundè, lætè
A journal, diarium
A journalist, diarii scriptor
A journey, iter, peregrinatio
To journey, itineror
A journeyman, opifex diurnâ mercede conductus; (journey-work), opus diurnâ mercede locatum
Joy, gaudium, lætitia
To joy (congratulate), congratulor; (rejoice), gaudeo ; (make glad), exhilaro, lætifico [tus
Joyful, *or* joyous, alacris, perlæ-
To be joyful, lætor, jucundor
Joyfully, lætè, hilarè
Joyfulness, hilaritas, gaudium
The jubilee, annus jubilæus
A jubilee, Jubilum
Judaical, Judaicus
Judaism, Judaismus
A judge, judex, æstimator
A judge's assistant, assessor
A judge's seat, tribunal
To judge, judico, adjudico ; (think), opinor, existimo ; (before), præjudico ; (between), dijudico
A judging, judicatio
Judgment (ability), judicium ; (opinion), opinio; (sentence), judicium, sententia
A judgment-place, tribunal
Judicial, judicialis
Judicially, more judiciali
Judiciary, judiciarius
Judicious, sagax, sapiens,cordatus
Judiciously, sagacitèr, sapienter
Judiciousness, sagacitas
A jug, cantharus
To juggle, præstigiis decipere
A juggler, præstigiator
A juggling-trick, præstigiæ
Jugular, jugularis
Juice, succus
Juiceless, exsuccus
Juiciness, succi abundantia
Juicy, succulentus, succidus
A julep, julepus
July, Julius
A jumble, strepitus, confusus, confusio

To jumble together, confundo, collido; (shake), concutio
A jumbling together, confusio
A jump, saltus, subsultus
To jump, salto, subsulto; (in judgment), idem sentire; (first), præsulto ; (over), transulto ; (upon), assulto; (down), dissilio
A jumper, saltator
A jumping, saltatio
A juncture, junctura ; (of time), articulus temporis ; (of affairs), rerum status
June, Junius
Junior, junior, minor natu
A junto, concilium clandestinum
Juridical, juridicus
Jurisdiction, jurisdictio
A juror, *or* juryman, jurator
Just, justus, æquus, rectus
With just cause, meritò
Just so many, totidem omninò ; (just now), modo, jam primûm; (just as, just so), haud aliter, haud secùs
Justice, justitia ; (punishment for a crime), supplicium; (of the peace), justitiarius
To justify (acquit), innocentem pronunciare; (prove), probo, evinco ; (one's self), se purgare
A justifying, *or* justification, justificatio ; (clearing from blame), culpæ liberatio; (proving), probatio; (by witnesses), testimonium, attestatio
A justle, *or* justling, conflictus
To justle, confligo, trudo; (with the elbow), cubito pellere
Justly, justè, jurè, merito
Justness, æquitas, justitia
To jut, promineo, propendeo
Jutting out, prominens
Juvenile, juvenilis
Juvenility, ardor juvenilis

K.

A kalendar, calendarium
The kalends, calendæ
To kaw, cornicor
To keck, screo, exscreo
A kecking, screatus
A kecks, cremium
A keel, carina
To keelhale, sub carinum trahere
Keen, acutus, subtilis, acer, mordax, acerbus
Keenly, acutè, acritèr
Keenness (of appetite), cupiditas edendi ; (of expression), asperitas
To keep (preserve), servo, reservo ; (detain), custodio ; (last), maneo, duro ; (restrain), teneo ; (the assizes), forum agere; (back), sisto, detineo; (one's bed), lecto affigi; (close, *or* conceal), premo, occulto, celo; (close, *or* lie hid), lateo; (one company), comitor; (defend), tueor, defendo; (down), deprimo; (off, *or* at bay), depello
A keeper, custos, conservator
Keeping, tenax
A keeping, custodia, conservatio; (back), depulsio; (down), suppressio; (in *or* under), cohibitio, coercitio
A keg, testa

KIN   KNO   LAC

To ken, agnosco, prospicio
Within ken, in conspectu
A kennel, canalis ; (for a dog), latibulum caninum; (of hounds), canum grex
A kerchief, rica, calantica
A kernel (of a nut), nucleus; (in meat), glandula; (of corn), granum ; (of grapes, &c.), acinus; (in the throat), tonsillæ, strumæ
To kernel, enucleo
Kernels taken out, enucleatus
Kernelly, granosus
Kersey, pannus rasus
A ketch, navicula
A kettle, ahenum, lebes; (great), caldarium ; (little), cacabus
A key, clavis; (of a river), portus manu factus; (keys of organs), manubria
Keyage, portorium
A kick, ictus calce factus
To kick, calco, calcitro; (out), abigo; (down), calce depellere; (the door with his heels), fores calcibus insultare
A kicker, calcator
A kicking, calcitratus
A kid, hœdus
Of a kid, hœdinus
To kid, hœdum parere
A kidnapper, plagiarius
To kidnap, abducere plagio
A kidney, ren; (disposition), indoles, ingenium ; (bean), phaseolus
Of the kidneys, renales
A kilderkin, doliolum
To kill, occido, interficio, interimo, trucido, neco; (himself), mortem sibi consciscere; (outright), eneco ; (a sacrifice), macto
A killer, necator, occisor; (of a brother), fratricida; (of one's equal), parricida; (of a man), homicida; (of a parent), parricida
A killing, occisio, trucidatio, cædes ; (of parents), parricidium ; (for sacrifice), mactatio; (in battle), internecio, occidio
Killing (deadly), lethalis, lethifer
A kiln, clibanus, fornax
A kiln-cloth, cilicium
Kin, cognatio ; (by blood), consanguinitas ; (by marriage), affinitas; (next of kin), consanguinitate proximus ; (near of kin), affinis
A kind (sort), genus, species; (sex), sexus; (of what kind), qualis, cujusmodi ; (of this), hujusmodi ; (of all), omnigenus; (of the same), homogeneus; (of another), heterogeneus; (another kind of), alius
Kind (charitable, &c.), humanus, benignus; (grateful), gratus
Kindly, comiter, benignè, humaniter, gratè, blandissimè
Kindness, benignitas, beneficium, gratitudo, affabilitas
To kindle, accendo, suscito ; (anger), irrito, incito ; (bring forth), pario
A kindling, accensio
Kindred, consanguineus. See Kin
Kine, pecus   (rex armorum
A king, rex; (at arms), fecialis,
The King's Bench, bancus regius ; (prison), banci regis carcer ; (fisher), halcyon; (evil), strumæ, morbus regius

[97]

King-like, Kingly, regalis, reginæ
Kingly, regiâ, regalitèr
A kingdom, regnum
Kinsfolk, necessarii
A kinsman, propinquus, cognatus
A kinswoman, cognata
A kiss, osculum, basium
To kiss, osculor, basio; (the cup), labiis gustare, or libare
A kisser, osculator, basiator
A kissing, osculatio, basiatio
A kit (for water, &c.), sinus, mulctra; (fiddle), fidicula
A kitchen, coquina, culina ; (boy), lixa
Of a kitchen, culinarius
Kitchen-stuff, unguina
A kite, milvus
To kitten, feles parere
A kitten, catulus felis
A knack, dexteritas, peritia
A knacking, crepitus
Knaggy, nodosus, ramosus
The knap of a hill, cacumen
To knap (off), abrumpo ; (asunder), frango, diffringo
A knapping off, avulsio
Knappy, verrucosus
A knapsack, pera viatoria
A knave, nebulo ; (at cards), miles, eques; (base), verbero ; (crafty), veterator; (beggarly), vappa ; (saucy), improbus
Knavery, fraus, dolus
Knavish, celestus, improbus ; (fellow), nequam, nefarius ; (construction), militiosa interpretatio
Knavishly, nefariè, veteratoriè
Knavishness, nequitia
To knead, subigo, depso
A kneading, subactio; (trough), mactra
A knee, genu, poples; (of a ship), navis costæ
The knee-pan, genu, patella
Knee-strings, genualia
To kneel, in genua procumbere
Kneeling, genibus nitens
A knell for the dead, pulsus campanæ
To kniek (cheat), decipio
Knicknacks, nugæ
A knife, culter, cultellus ; (cleaver), clunaculum ; (for sacrifices), secespita ; (for pens), scalpellum
Made like a knife, cultratus ; (edged like a knife), cultellatus
A knight, eques, eques auratus ; (banneret), eques vexillifer ; (of the bath), eques balnei ; (of the garter), eques auratæ periscelidis; (of the shire), comitatûs eques parliamentarius
To knight, equitem creare   (tare
Knight's service, servitium militare
Of a knight, Knightly, equester
Knighthood, ordo equestris
To knit, necto, nexo ; (tie), nodo, stringo, ligo ; (the brow), frontem corrugare ; (in), innecto; (under), subnecto; (unto), annecto ; (together), connecto
A knitting, nexus
A knitting together, connexio
A knob, tuber, nodus ; (of a buckler), umbo   (latus
Knobbed, Knobby, asper, bullatus
A knock, alapa, verber
To knock, pulso, tundo; (strike), ferio, percutio ; (against), allido ; (down), prosterno; (in), impello; (often), pulsito; (off, or out), excutio; (together),

collido ; (the breast), pectus cædere, plango
A knocker of a door, cornix
A knocking, pulsatio
A knocking together, collisio
To knoll (bells), pulso
A knoll (little hill), colliculus
A knot, nodus, nexus ; (for the head), vitta, tænia ; (difficulty), scrupulus; (in wood), tuber; (or joint), articulus
To knot (bud), germino ; (as young trees), nodos emittere; (as hair), nodo, implicor
Without knots, enodis
Full of knots, nodosus
Knotty, nodosus, difficilis
Knottiness, nodositas, asperitas, difficultas   (latio
The knotting of a tree, geniculatio
To know, scio, cognosco, rescisco, agnosco, dignosco, præcognosco, comperio
To let know, certiorem facere; (to make one know), commonefacio, ostendo
To know well, calleo, intelligo
Knowing, sciens, gnarus ; (not knowing), ignarus, inscius
A knowing, cognitio
Knowingly, scientèr
Knowledge (skill), peritia; (understanding), intellectus; (in law), jurisprudentia ; (learning), eruditio
To be known, enotesco, innotesco ; (abroad), emano; (make known), publico, manifesto
It is well known, liquet, constat
The knuckles, condyli; (on the back of a hook), bulla
To knuckle down, succumbo

L.

A label, lemniscus, appendix
A laboratory, officina chemica
Laborious, sedulus, impiger, difficilis, arduus, operosus
Laboriously, sedulò, impigrè, difficultèr, molestè
Laboriousness, labor
Labour, labor, industria ; (of women), puerperium, partus
To labour (as a ship in the waves), colluctari cum ventis et fluctibus ; (take pains), laboro ; (endeavour), enitor; (against), renitor; (earnestly), summâ ope uti; (with child), parturio ; (for), ambio; (in vain), operam ludere ; (a point), summa diligentiâ elaborare; (under great difficulties), summis angustiis premi; (for hire), operam mercede locare
Not laboured, illaboratus
A labourer, opifex, operarius; (fellow-labourer), socius operum
Labouring, laborans, enitens
A labouring to do, conamen, nisus
A labyrinth, labyrinthus
Lace, lacinia, fimbria ; (for stays), funiculus
To lace (edge with lace), pretexo ; (fasten with a lace), astringo ; (beat), cædo, verbero
A laceman, limbolarius
To lacerate, lacero, dilacero

LAN   LAS   LAW

A lacing (beating), verberatio; (binding together), colligatio
Lack, inopia, penuria, indigentia, egestas; (of parents), orbitas; (of custom), desuetudo; (of provisions), inedia; (defect), defectus
To lack, careo, indigeo, egeo
Lacker (varnish), lacca
To lacker, laceâ ornare
Lacking, orbus, egenus, inops
To be lacking, desum, deficio
Laconic, laconicus
Laconically, laonicè, brevitèr
A lacquey, pedissequus
Lacrymal, lacrymas generans
Lacteal, lacteus
A lad, adolescens
A ladder, scalæ; (ship-ladder), pons
To lade, onero
Sore-laden, oppressus
Lading, onerans
A lading, onus
A ladle, spatha, ligula; (ladles of a water-mill), pinnæ
A lady, domina, heroina
Lag, postremus, extremus
To lag, tardo, tergiversor
A lagging, tergiversatio
Laic, or laical, laicus
Lain, positus; (down), decumbens; (in wait), insidiis petitus
Lair (of a deer), cervi latebra; (at stool-ball), clava pilaris
The laity, laici
A lake (a colour), lacca
A lake, lacus, palus, stagnum
A lamb, agnus, agna
Of a lamb, agninus
Lamb (meat), caro agnina; (grass-lamb), graminæ pasta; (house-lamb), stabulo nutrita
Lambent, lambens
A lambkin, agnellus
Lame, claudus, mancus; (comparison), iniqua comparatio; (with age), decrepitus; (imperfect), imperfectus
To walk lame, claudico
To make lame, mutilo, debilito
Lamed, claudicans
Lamely, imperitè, inconcinnè
Lameness, claudicatio
To lament, deploro, lugeo; (together), commiseror; (for), ingemo
Lamentable, flebilis, plorabilis
Lamentably, lugubrè, lugubritèr
A lamentation, lamentatio; (at funerals), threnodia, planctus
Full of lamentation, gemebundus
Not lamented, indeploratus
A lamenter, plorator
Lamenting, luctuosus, luctificus
A lamenting, deploratio
Lammas, calendæ sextiles
To lamm, cædo, fustigo
A lamp, lampas, lucerna
A lampoon, satyra
To lampoon, dicto mordaci aliquem insectari
A lampooner, scurra
A lamprey, muræna
A lance, lancea, hasta; (lancet), scalpellum chirurgicum
To lance, scarifico
To lanch (a ship), navem deducere; (into the sea), oceano navem committere; (into eternity), terram relinquere
A lanching, deductio
Land (with a house upon it), prædium, fundus; (country),

[58]

terra, regio, tractus; (ground), tellus, terra, solum
To land (put ashore), in terram exponere; (in a vessel), appello; (get to land), arenâ potiri
Land, *adj.* terrestris
Of land, agrarius
A landgrave, provinciæ præfectus
A landlord (victualler), hospes; (of a house, &c.), dominus domûs, &c.; (lady), hospita
A landmark, limes, terminus
A landing, appulsus; (place), portus
A landscape, tabula chorographica
A lane (street), angiportus; (in the country), via publica, diverticulum
Language (speech), lingua, sermo; (style), stilus; (smooth), blandiloquentia; (rude), convicium; (its propriety), idioma
Languid, languidus, debilis
To languish, langueo, tabeo, languesco, tabesco, marcesco
To cause to languish, tabefacio
Languishing, languens, languescens
A languishing, languor
Languishingly, languidè
Lank (limber), mollis, flaccidus; (slender), tenuis
Lankness, mollities, gracilitas
A lantern, laterna
The lap, gremium, sinus
A lap (fold), plica; (of the ear), lobus; (dog), catullus Melitæus
To lap (lick), lambo, lingo; (wrap up), complico
A lapidary, lapidarius
Lapidation, lapidatio
Lapped, *or* lapt, involutus
A lapper, lambens
A lappet, lacinia, sinus
A lapping (licking), linctus; (folding), involutio
A lapse, lapsus
To lapse, labor, prætereo
The larboard, latus sinistrum
Larceny, latrocinium
Lard, lardum
To lard, lardo suffigere; (a discourse), sermonem miscere
Larded, lardo suffixus
A larder, promptuarium
A lathe, tornus
Large, spatiosus, latus; (at large), liber; (to discourse at large), copiosè disputare
Very large, perampius
Largely, amplè, abundè; (so largely), eò usquè
Largeness, amplitudo, magnitudo
A largess, donativum
A lark, alauda
Lascivious, lascivus, petulans
Lasciviously, impudicè, procacitèr
Lasciviousness, libido, incontinentia
A lash (stripe), plaga, verber; (mark), vibex; (thong), lorum
To lash (whip), flagello, cædo; (tie unto), alligo
A lashing, verberatio
A lash, ventris profluvium; (stopped), venter suppressus
A lashing wind, venti quadrans
A lass, puella, virgo
Lassitude, lassitudo
Last, *or* latest, ultimus, extremus, novissimus, supremus, postremus

Last, *adv.* proximè, postremûm, novissimè; (at last), deniquè, postremò, demûm, tandèm
The last (save one), penultimus; (but two), antepenultimus
A last, calcei modulus; (lastage), onus, saburra
To last, duro, perduro
Lasted (continued), duratus
A lasting, duratio, continuatio
Lasting, stabilis, diû manens; (all day), perdius; (all night), pernox; (for ever), sempiternus
Lastly, ultimò, deniquè
A latch, obex
To latch, obice claudere
The latchet of a shoe, corrigia
Late, *adj.* serus, tardus, nuperus
Late, *adv.* serò, tardè
It is late, vesperat
It grows late, vesperascit
Lately, modò, nupèr; (very), nuperrimè
Latent, latens, latitans
Later, recentior, tardior
Lateral, lateralis, à latere
Latest, postremus, ultimus
A lath, assula
To lathe, assulis substernere
A lathe, tornus
A lather, aquæ saponatæ spuma; (to make), sapone bullas excitare
Latin, *adj.* Latinus
Latin, *subst.* Latinitas
In Latin, Latinè
A Latinist, Latinè doctus
Latish, tardiusculus, tardior
Latitude (breadth), latitudo; (liberty), licentia
Latter, posterior
The latter math, *or* crop, fœnum
Latten, *or* lattin, orichalcum
A lattice, clathrus
To lattice, cancello, clathro
Like a lattice, *or* latticed, reticulatus, cancellatus, clathratus
Lattices, cancelli
Laud, laus, gloria
To laud, laudo, celebro
Laudable, laudabilis, laudandus
Laudably, laudabilitèr
Laudanum, laudanum
To lave, capulo, exhaurio
Lavender, nardus
A laver, labrum
To laugh, rideo; (at), irrideo; (aloud), cachinnor; (together), corrideo; (from the teeth outward), sardonicum ridere
Laughable, risum movens
To be laughed at, rideor
Laughed at, ludibrio habitus, risu dignus, ridiculus [irrisor
A laugher, risor; (at), derisor,
A laughing, cachinnatio
Given to laughing, ridibundus
A laughing, risus; (at), irrisus; (stock), ludibrium; (immoderate), cachinnus
Laughter, risus
Lavish, prodigus, profusus
To lavish away, prodigo, profundo
A lavisher, nepos, prodigus
Lavishing, prodigens, profundens
Lavishly, prodigè, effusè
Lavishness, prodigalitas, profusio
To launch. See *Lanch*
A laundress, lotrix
A laundry, lavatrina
Laureate, laureatus
Laurel, laurus, laurocerasus
Of laurel, laureus
Crowned with laurel, laureatus
Law, lex; (right), jus; (canon-

law), jus canonicum; (civil), jus civile; (statute), jus municipale; (law of arms), jus militare; (of merchants), lex mercatorum; (of nature), jus naturale; (of nations), jus gentium; (of the senate), senatusconsultum; (made by the people), plebiscitum
Ever at law, litigiosus
Learned in the law, juris peritus
Of the law, juridicialis, legalis
Law-days, dies juridici
A lawgiver, legislator
Lawful, justus, æquus, licitus
Not lawful, illegitimus, injustus
It is lawful, licet, æquum est
Lawfully, legitimè, licitè
Lawfulness, jus, fas
Lawless, exlex, illex
Lawn, sindon, carbasus; (in a park), saltus
Of lawn, carbaseus
A lawyer, causidicus, jurisconsultus
Lax, laxus, segnis, socors
A lax, diarrhœa
Laxative, alvum subducens
Lay, *adj.* laïcus
A lay, cantelina; (course, rank, &c.), series; (man), laïcus
To lay, pono; (about), circumpono; (abroad), expando; (against), objicio; (along), prosterno; (an ambush), insidior; (apart), sepono; (aside), supersedeo, loco movere; (a bait), inescor; (before, *or* represent), repræsento; (between), interjicio; (blame upon), vitupero; (by), sepono, repono, rejicio, omitto; (claim to), vendico; (commands upon), in mandatis dare; (a complaint before), querelam deferre; (to one's charge), imputo; (the cloth), mensam sternere; (corn), sternere segetes; (down), depono, demitto
A layer (graff), propago; (oysterbed), ostrearium; (of a deer), lustrum
Laying asleep, soporifer; (laying as a hen), parturiens
A laying (on), impositio; (on heaps), accumulatio, coacervatio; (aside), remotio, rejectio; (out), erogatio, impensa; (to), applicatio; (to one's charge), imputatio, accusatio; (unto), adjectio
Past laying, effœta
Lays (in music), moduli
A lazar, leprosus
Lazily, ignavè, pigrè, segniter
Laziness, segnitia, pigritia
Lazy, ignavus, piger, iners
To grow lazy, torpesco [eus
Leacherous, libidinosus, impudicus
Leacherously, libidinosè, obscœnè
Leachery, libido, salacitas
Lead, plumbum; (black), stibium; (red), minium; (white), cerussa
To lead, plumbo obducere
Of lead, Leaden, plumbeus, plumbosus
Lead-coloured, ferrugineus
Lead-ore, plumbago
Leaded, plumbo obductus
A leading, plumbo obductio
The leads, tectum plumbo obductum
To lead, duco; (about), circumduco; (about often), ductito;

(against), contra ducere; (along), per viam ducere; (an army), exercitui præesse; (aside), diverto; (aside, *or* seduce), seduco; (away), abduco; (back), reduco; (before), præduco; (by force), perduco; (in), induco, introduco; (forth), produco; (off), abduco; (one's life), vitam degere; (on, *or* entice), illicio; (over), transduco; (out), educo; (through), perduco; (unto), adduco; (up and down), deduco; (the way), præeo
A leader, ductor; (commander, *or* general), dux, imperator; (of a dance), præsultor; (of the way), dux viæ
Leading, ducens
A leading, ductus; (about), circumductio; (aside), seductio; (in), inductio; (back), reductio
A leading man, vir primarius; (people), princeps populus
A leaf, folium; (of a vine), pampinus; (of a book), duæ paginæ; (of gold), lamina bractea, auri folium; (of herbs), coma; (of fat), unctum; (of tin), stanni folium
A league (three miles), leuca; (confederacy), fœdus, pactum, pactio
In league, fœderatus
A leaguer, obsidio, obsidium
A leak, rima
To leak, rimas agere
Leaky, rimosus, rutilis [sus
Lean, macer, macilentus, strigoTo be lean, maceo, emacesco
To make lean, emacio
Made lean, emaciatus
To lean (upon), nitor, innitor, recumbo; (forward), acclino; (back), reclino; (over), promineo; (to), propendeo; (in opinion), sententiæ favere; (towards), inclino
Leaning, nixus, innixus, reclinis, acclinis, incumbens
A leaning-stock, fulcrum
A leaning downwards, declivitas
Leanness, macies, macritudo
A leap, saltus
To leap, salto, salio; (against), assilio; (away), absilio; (a little), subsilio, subsulto; (back), resilio; (down), desilio; (in), insilio; (forward), prosilio; (for joy), exulto, gestio; (off), desilio; (often), saltito; (on, *or* upon), insilio; (over), transilio; (*or* jump up), emico
A leap for fish, nassa
Leap by leap, saltim, exultim
A leaper, saltator, saltatrix
Leaping, saltans
A leaping, saltatio, saltatus; (for joy), exultatio; (on), insultatio
To learn, disco; (be informed of), certior fieri; (an art), artem percipere; (before), prædisco; (by experience), discere experiendo; (by heart), memoriæ mandare; (together), condisco; (teach), doceo
The learned, docti, eruditi
Learnedly, doctè, eruditè
A learner, discipulus
Learning, doctrina, eruditio
Belonging to learning, literarius
A lease, fundi elocandi instrumentum, formula locationis

To lease out, eloco
To lease (lie), mentior; (corn), spicas legere
A leash (thong), lorum; (of hounds), canum ternio
A leasing, locatio, spicilegium
A leassee, cui locatur
A leassor, locator
Least, *adj.* minimus; *adv.* minimè; (at least), ad minimum, certè
Leather, corium, aluta
A leather-dresser, alutarius, coriarius; (seller), pellio
Leather-dressing, corii subactio
Leathern, ex corio confectus
A leather bottle, uter; (jerkin), tunica scortea; (thong), lorum terginum
Covered with leather, pellitus
Leave, venia, copia, licentia, libertas, potestas; (to enter), admissio
Without leave, injussu, injussus
To leave, omitto, relinquo, prætereo; (forsake), desero, destituo; (off), desino, desisto, absisto; (out), prætermitto, omitto; (by will), testamento legare; (quit), decedo; (unto), committo; (utterly), penitùs derelinquere
Leaven, fermentatum
To leaven, fermento
A leavening, fermentatio
A leaver, vectis
Leaves, frondes, folia
Full of leaves, frondosus, frondeus
A leaving (off), cessatio; (out), omissio, prætermissio
Leavings, reliquiæ
Lecherous, impudicus
Lechery, libido, salacitas
A lecture, lectio, prælectio
To lecture, prælego, objurgo
A lecturer, lector; (afternoon preacher), concionator pomeridianus
To be led, trahor, ducor
A led horse, equus desultorius
A ledge, projectura
A ledger, actorum codex; (ambassador), legatus ordinarius
The lee, navis inclinatio; (shore), littus vento immune
To come off by the lee, pessimè abire, malè mulctari
A leech, hirudo, sanguisuga
A leek, porrum
Leek-green, prasinus
Of leeks, porraceus
A leer, *or* Leering-look, obliquus contuitus, *or* oculorum conjectus
To leer, limis intueri
Leering, limis obtutus, limus
Leeringly, limis oculis
Lees, fæx
Leet (court), curia
The leetch of a sail, laxa pars veli
Leeward, navis inclinatio
Left, (remaining), reliquus; (alone), solus, solitarius, desolatus; (destitute), orbus, orbatus; (off for a time), intermissus; (out), prætermissus; (hand), manus sinistra
On the left hand, à sinistris, ad sinistram
Lefthanded, scævus
A leg, tibia, crus; (of mutton), coxa ovina; (of a table), pes
To make a leg, genu flectere
Belonging to a leg, tibialis, cruralis

LET   LIB   LIF

A legacy, legatum
Legal, legalis, legitimus
Legality, legibus consentaneum
Legally, juxta leges
A legate, legatus, orator
A legatee, legatarius
Bow-legged, valgus; (wry-legged), loripes
A legend, legenda; (of a coin), inscriptio
Legerdemain, ars præstigiatoria; (tricks), præstigiæ
Legible, lectu facilis
A legion, legio
Belonging to a legion, legionarius
Legislation, actus ferendi leges
Legislative, legislativus
A legislator, legislator
The legislature, qui habent potestatem leges ferendi
Legitimate, legitimus
Leisure, otium, quies
At leisure, *adj.* otiosus, vacuus; *adv.* otiosè, per otium
Leisurely, otiosè, pedetentim
To be at leisure, vaco, otio frui
A lemon, malum citreum
To lend, mutuum dare, commodo; (an ear), aurem præbere; (at interest), fœnero
A lender, creditor, fœnerator
Lending, commodans
A lending, commodatio, fœneratio
Length, longitudo; (of a way), viæ spatium; (of time), diuturnitas
At length, tandem, demùm, denique; (in length), in longum; (at one's length), extento corpore
To run all lengths, in omnibus inservire
To lengthen, protraho, extendo
A lengthening, productio
Lenitive, leniens, anodynus
A lenitive, anodynum
Lenity, lenitas, clementia
Lent (of lend), commodatus
Lent, quadragesima
Of lent, quadragesimalis
A lentil, lens
Leonine, leoninus
A leopard, leopardus
A leper, leprosus
The leprosy, lepra
Leprous, leprâ laborans
Less, *adj.* minor; *adv.* minùs
For less, minoris
Much less, nedum, ne quidem
To lessen (make less), diminuo, minuo, extenuo; (grow less), decresco, minuor; (depreciate), depretio
A lessening, diminutio
Lesser, *or* less, minor
A lessee, cui locatur
A lesson, lectio, prælectio; (instruction), monitum
To give a lesson (teach), doceo; (chide), objurgo
A lessor, locator
Lest, *or* lest that, ne; (any one), nequis; (any thing), nequid; (at any time), nequando; (by any means), nequâ; (in any place), necubi
A let, *or* hindrance, impedimentum, mora; (disturbance), interpellatio
To let (hinder), obsto, impedio; (interrupt), interpello; (alone), omitto; (blood), sanguinem detrahere; (down), demitto; (fly *or* shoot at), jaculor; (go), dimitto; (loose), emitto, educo;

[70]

(in), admitto, intromitto; (into secrets), secreta impertire; (off), displodo, exonero; (out), emitto; (out to hire), eloco; (pass), omitto, prætereo; (suffer), sino, permitto
A leecher, scortator
Lethargic, lethargicus, veternosus
The lethargy, lethargus
Letted (hindered), impeditus
A letter (hinderer), morator; (out to hire), locator; (of blood), phlebotomus
A letter (of the alphabet), litera, elementum, character; (epistle), literæ, tabellæ, epistola; (carrier), tabellio, tabellarius
Letters (patent), literæ patentes; (of appeal), literæ dimissoriæ; (of commendation), literæ commendatitiæ; (of exchange), tesseræ nummariæ; (of marque), represalia; (used in printing), typi
Of letters, literarius
A man of letters, homo doctus, veliteris clarus
To letter, titulum inscribere
Lettuce, lactuca
A letting, mora; (of blood), phlebotomia; (down), demissio; (go), dimissio; (out for rent), locatio; (pass), emissio; (permission), permissio
The Levant, oriens
A levee, salutantium comitatus
Level, æquus, planus
A level, planities; (used by carpenters), libella, perpendiculum; (of a gun), bombardæ scopus
To level, æquo, complano, coæquo; (at), ad scopum collineare
To be upon a level, par esse
A leveller, complanator
A levelling, æquatio, petitio
A lever, vectis
A leveret, lepusculus
A leviathan, draco aquaticus
To levigate, lævigo, polio
A Levite, levita
Levitical, leviticus
Levity, levitas, inconstantia
A levy, census
To levy (money), vectigal exigere; (soldiers), milites conscribere [actio
A levying of money, pecuniæ exigendæ
Lewd, improbus, sceleratus, nequam, obscænus, turpis
Lewdly, flagitiosè, turpitèr
Lewdness, scelus, nequitia
A lexicographer, lexicographus
A lexicon, lexicon
Liable, obnoxius, expositus
Liar, mendax
Libation, libatio
A libel (in the civil law), libellus accusatorius; (satirical reflection), libellus famosus
To libel (accuse), accuso; (defame in writing), scriptis infamare
A libeller, scriptor famosorum carminum
A libelling, sugillatio scriptis mandata
Libellous, famosus, probrosus
Liberal, liberalis, munificus; (giver), largitor beneficus; (giving), largitio, erogatio
Liberality, liberalitas, benignitas
Liberally, liberalitèr, largè
A libertine, homo dissolutus
Libertinism, morum licentia

Liberty, libertas, licentia, potestas, copia; (of will), liberum arbitrium
At liberty, liber, era, erum
To be at liberty, sui juris esse
To set at liberty, libero
Libidinous, libidinosus, salax
A library, bibliotheca
A librarian, bibliothecæ custos
Libration, libratio
Lice, pediculi
Licence (leave), licentia, venia, copia, potestas, facultas; (privilege), privilegium
To license, privilegio munire
A licensing, privilegii donatio
A licentiate, licentiatus; (in law), lyta
Licentious, licentiosus, improbus
Licentiously, licentèr, improbè
Licentiousness, nequitia, improbitas
A lick, lincitus; (stroke), ictus
To lick, lingo, lambo; (strike), aliquem cædere; (about), circumlambo; (off, *or* away), delingo; (daintily), ligurio; (dishes), catillo; (all over), delambo
Licking, lingens, lambens
Licorice, glycyrrhiza
Licorish, delicatulus, gulosus; (fellow), liguritor, catillo; (dainties), cupediæ
Licorishness, gula, liguritio
A lid, operculum
Lie to wash with, lixivium
Of, *or* belonging to lie, lixivius
To lie (in a posture), jaceo; (about), circumjaceo; (in disorder), confusim jacere; (against), objaceo; (along), recumbo, recubo; (before), præjaceo; (between), interjaceo; (by), accubo, accumbo; (down), decumbo; (in), ob puerperium cubare; (down to sleep), decumbo; (in the dirt), in luto hærere; (flat), prosterno; (near), adjaceo, juxta cumbere; (at a banquet), discumbo
A lie, mendacium
Liege, fidelis, deditus
A liege, dominus supremus
A liege-man, cliens [ator
A lier, mendax; (in wait), insidiator
Full of lies, fabulosus, mendosus
In lieu of, loco, vice [fectus
A lieutenant, locum tenens, præfectus provinciæ
The lord lieutenant of a county, præfectus
The lieutenant of the tower, arcis præfectus
Lientenantship, præfectura
Life, vita, spiritus, anima; (sprightliness), vigor
To give life, animo, vivifico
Life-giving, vivificus
A giving of life, animatio
Long life, longævitas
To the life, ad vivum [tam
All one's life time, per totam vitam
To come again to life, revivisco
To be tried for one's life, causam capitis dicere
To venture one's life, capitis periculum adire [supremum
To depart this life, diem obire
Having life, vivus, animatus
Full of life, vividus, vivax
Lifeless, exanimis, inanimatus
A life-guard, cohors prætoria
A lift (assistance), auxilium
To lift, levo, tollo, eveho; (up again), relevo; (up himself), se efferre; (up on high), in

LIM LIS LOA

sublime tollere; (one's voice), vocem attollere; (upright), erigo
Lifting up, elevana, attollens
A lifting up, elevatio
A ligament, ligamentum
A ligature, ligatura, ligamen
To light (as a bird), sido, desido, insido; (from a horse), descendo; (fall upon, or against), incido, incurro; (upon, or find), reperio, offendo
Light (in weight), levis, perlevis; (bright), fulgens, lucidus, splendidus; (nimble), agilis, expeditus; (inconstant), instabilis; (merry), hilaria, lætus; (trifling), facilis, nugax, ineptus; (fingered), furax; (hearted), hilaris, alacris, lætus; (horse),equites expediti;(horseman), levis armaturæ eques; (of no value), futilis
Light (as day), lux; (brightness), lumen; (knowledge), cognitio, intelligentia; (candle, or lamp), lucerna, candela, lampas
To set lightly by, contemno
To light (set on fire), accendo; (one), præluceo
To be light, luceo, lucesco
To cast, or give light, illumino
Lightheaded, delirans, insaniens
To lighten (in the sky), fulguro; (ease), exonero, levo, allevo
To be made lighter, allevor
Lightly, leviter, leniter; (easily), facilè; (nimbly), velociter, agiliter; (carelessly), negligenter, perfunctoriè
Lightness (tickleness), inconstantia; (nimbleness), agilitas; (wantonness), lascivia, petulantia
Lightning, fulgor
Of lightning, fulgurans
A lightning (in the sky), fulguratio; (easing), lenamen; (kindling), incensio
A lighter, cymba oneraria
A lighterman, naviculator
A lighting (down), descensus; (kindling), incensio
The lights, pulmones
Lightsome (bright), fulgidus; (cheerful), hilaris, lætus
Like (unto), similis, consimilis; (equal), par, æquus; (likely), probabilis, verisimilis
Like, or like unto, adv. tanquàm, velùt, instar; (as), sicùt, perindè ac, quemadmodùm; (a friend), amicè; (a gentleman), ingenuè, liberalitèr; (a man), fortitèr, viriliter; (in like manner), pariter, itidem, similiter
To like (approve), probo, approbo, comprobo, gaudeo; (of, or please), placeo
Such-like, hujusmodi
Likely, adj. probabilis, credibilis, venustus
Likely, adv. probabilitèr
Likelihood, verisimilitudo
To liken, comparo, confero
Likeness, similitudo
A likening, comparatio [tèr
Likewise, itidem, paritèr, similiLiking, favens, approbans
A liking, favor, approbatio
In good liking, valens, validus
To one's liking, acceptus, gratus
A lily, lilium
Of a lily, liliaceus
Limb from limb, membratim
[71]

A limb (edge), ora, margo; (member), artus, membrum; (of the law), leguleius
Limber, flexilis, laxus
To grow limber, lentesco
Limberness, lentor
Limbo, limbus
Lime, calx
Of lime, calcarius
Limy, viscosus, glutinosus
A limit, limes, terminus
To limit, termino, præfinio
Limitation, limitatio
Limiting, terminans, præfiniens
A limiting, determinatio
Limits, fines, limites
To limn, delineo, depingo
Limned, ad vivum expressus
A limner, humani oris pictor
A limning, pictura
Limp, or limber, flaccidus, lentus
To limp, claudico
A limper, claudus, claudicans
Limpid, limpidus, clarus
Limping, claudicans, mutilus
A limping, claudicatio
Limpingly, mutilè
Limpness (limberness), lentor
Linch pin, embolium
A line (lineage), stirps, progenies, prosapia, propago, genus, proles; (small cord), funiculus; (order), series, ordo; (for fishing), linum, seta; (drawn), linea
Lines of the hand, incisuræ
To line, munio; (as a dog), meo; (a garment), intùs assuere
Line (flax), linum
Linseed, lini semen
Lineal, or linear, linearis
Lineally, rectà lineà
A lineament, lineamentum
Linen, linteum
Fine linen, sindon
Of linen, linteus, lineus
A linen-draper, linteo
To linger, ægrotesco, diù ægrotare; (loiter), cunctor, cesso
Lingering, cunctans; (with illness), lentà tabe consumens
A lingering, cunctatio
A linger, metalli massa
A linguist, linguarum peritus
A liniment, emplastrum
The lining of a garment, pannus interior, or subditius
A link, lynchus; (boy), lychnuchus; (of a chain), annulus
To link, connecto, conjungo
A linking, connexio, conjunctio
A linnet, linaria
Lint, linamentum
The lintel, superliminare
A lion, leo
Lion-coloured, fulvus
A lioness, leæna, lea
Like a lion, leoninus
A lip, labium, labrum; (barelip), labellum fissile; (of a beast), rictus; (of a wound), os
To liquify (melt), liquefacio
Liquid, liquidus, liquens
To be liquid, liqueo
To grow liquid, liquesco
To liquidate, liquefacio
Liquids, liquida
Liquor, liquor, succus, potus
Full of liquor, ebrius
To liquor, macero, iuungo
To lisp, balbutio, blæsè loqui
A lisper, balbus, blæsus
A lisping, balbuties
A list (catalogue), catalogus; (of cloth), limbus panni; (de-

sire), libido, cupido; (will), voluntas; (to fight in), arena
To list (soldiers), conscribo; (for a soldier), nomen inter milites dare; (will, or desire), volo
To listen, ausculto, attendo
A listener, auscultator
A listening, auscultatio
Listening, auscultans, attendens
Listless, torpidus, segnis
To be listless, torpeo, stupeo
Listlessly, segnitèr, oscitantèr
Listlessness, torpor
The litany, litania
Literal, literalis
Literally, sensu proprio
Literature, literatura, eruditio
Of literature, doctus, eruditus
Litharge, lithargyros, scoria
Lithotomy, lithotomia
To litigate, litigo, contendo
Litigation, litigatio, lis
Litigious, litigiosus, rixosus
Litigiousness, litium amor
A litter, foetura, partus
Litter, substramentum
A horse-litter, lectica
To litter, res turbare, pario
Little, parvus, tenuis, exiguus
Little, adv. parùm, paululùm, aliquantò, nonnihil, aliquantum
A little one, infantulus; (while), paulispèr, parumpèr; (and pretty), scitus [sim
By little and little, paulatim, senVery little, minimus [que
How little soever, quantuluscunEver so little, paulum modò
Littleness, parvitas, exiguitas
The liturgy, liturgia
To live, vivo; (again), revivisco; (a country life), rusticor; (in exile), exulo, (well), lautè vivere; (in gluttony), helluor; (from hand to mouth), in diem vivere, (together), convivo; (in a city), urbem incolere
Likely to live, vividus
Long lived, longævus
Short lived, caducus, fragilis
Lively, ducens, vividus, virus
To be lively, vigeo, vigesco
Livelihood (maintenance), victus et vestitus; (trade, or business), ars
Liveliness, vigor
A good liver, homo pius
A bad liver, scelestus, nequam
The liver, jecur, hepar
Of the liver, hepaticus
Liver-coloured, fuscus
White-livered, pallidus, socors
A livery, vestis servilis; (stable), stabulum conductitium
Livid, lividus
Living, vivus, vivens, spirans
A living (maintenance), victus; (benefice), beneficium; (together), convictus, cohabitatio
A lizard, lacerta
Lo! en! ecce!
A load, sarcina, onus; (on the spirits), tristitia
To load, onero, gravo; (heavily), opprimo
A loadstone, magnes
Of a loadstone, magneticus
Loading, onerans, aggravans
A loaf, panis; (of sugar), sacchari meta
Loam, lutum [tuum
A loan, aliquid mutuatum, muTo loath, nauseo, fastidio
A loathing, nausea, fastidium
Loathing, nauseans, fastidiens

Loathsome, odiosus, squalidus, foedus
A lobby, porticus, pergula
A lobe, lobus
A lobster, astacus
Local, localis
Locally, juxta locum
Locality, existentia localis
A lock, sera; (of wool), floccus; (of hail), cinnus, cirrus
To lock (a door), sero, obsero; (a wheel), rotas stringere; (in one's arms), complector; (out), excludo; (up), includo
A locker, loculamentum
A locket, collare
A locust, locusta
A lodge, casa silvestris; (of free masons), capella latomorum liberorum; (porter's lodge), gurgustium
To lodge (in a place), habito; (all night), pernocto; (with), diversor; (stick fast), inhaereo
To be lodged, collocor
A lodger, hospes
A lodging, commoratio; (room), cubiculum; (place), diversorium
A lodgement, munimentum
Lodgings, ædium pars conducta
A loft, tabulatum, repositorium
Lofty (high), sublimis, excelsus, celsus; (haughty), fastuosus, arrogans, superbus, elatus; (stile), oratio turgida
To grow lofty, tumeo, insolesco
Loftily, superbè, elatè
Loftiness (in height), sublimitas, excelsitas; (in behaviour), fastus, superbia
A log, truncus, stipes
A logarithm, logarithmus
A loggerhead, hebes, somnolentus
Logic, dialectica, logica
Logical, logicus
A logician, dialecticus
A loin, lumbus
To loiter, moror, cesso
A loiterer, cunctator
A loitering, cessatio, mora
To loll, innitor; (the tongue), exerere linguam; (in bed), lecto indulgere
A lolling, nixus cubito
Loneliness, solitudo
Lonely, lonesome, solus, solitarius
Long, longus, prolixus
A long time, diù, longùm; (ago), olim, jamdudùm; (after), multò pòst; (before), multò antè; (enough), satis diù; (of), causâ, culpâ
Long continuance, diuturnitas
A long (in music), respiratio longa
Long (in speech), productus; (winded), prolixus
Long-suffering, patiens
Long-suffering, patientia
To long after, appeto, exopto
Longevity, longevitas
A longing, desiderium, votum
Longitude, longitudo
A look, obtutus
The look, aspectus, vultus
To look, video; (about), circumspicio; (seem), videor; (after, or care for), curo; (at), intueor; (back), respicio; (before), prospicio; (down), despicio; (or seek for), quæro, requiro; (for, or expect), spero, exspecto; (in), inspicio; (into or examine), perscrutor; (on), in-
[72]

tueor; (out, or choose), deligo, seligo; (up), suspicio; (upon), aspicio, inspicio, inspecto; (upon, or esteem), duco, æstimo, habeo
Look (behold)! ecce! en!
A looker on, spectator
Looking, aspiciens; (about), circumspiciens, lustrans
A looking-glass, speculum
A loom, textoris jugum
A loop, amentum; (hole), transenna; (for ordnance), fenestella
Loose, laxus; (dissolute), dissolutus; (bad), pravus; (careless), remissus, negligens; (in body), lientericus
To loose, solvo, laxo
To loosen, laxo, solvo
Loosely, laxè, dissolutè, remissè
A looseness, laxitas; (of the belly), alvi proluvies
To lop, tondeo, decacumino, cædo
A lopping, putatio
Loppings, sarmenta
Loquacious, loquax, garrulus
Loquacity, loquacitas, garrulitas
A lord, dominus, dynasta
To lord it, dominor
The lords of the realm, proceres
Lordliness, fastidium
Lordly, adj. fastuosus, imperiosus; adv. elatè, imperiosè
Lordship, dominatus; (manor), manerium
To lose, perdo, amitto; (colour), decoloror; (credit), fidem labefactare; (one's labour), operam perdere; (ground, or go back), retrocedo; (be worsted), superor, vincor; (one's hopes), despero; (one's life), mortem oppetere; (one's way), aberro, deerro; (time), tempus terere frustrà; (use of the limbs), membris capi; (utterly), disperdo
A losing, amissio, perditio
Loss, damnum, jactura; (of life), vitæ privatio
Causing loss, damnosus, exitiosus
To be lost, perdor, pereo
A lot (part), pars, portio; (by lot), sortitò, sorte, casu; (chance), sors, casus
To lot, distribuo; (to cast lots), sortior; (to draw lots), sortes trahere
Gotten by lot, sortitus
Loth, aversus, invitus
A lotion, lotio, lavatio
A lottery, tesserarum sortitio
Loud, sonorus, clarus; (in voice), vocalis, concitatus
Loudly, sonorè, clarè
Loudness, claritas
Love, amor, benevolentia, charitas; (self), amor sui; (of God, or parents), pietas
To love, amo, diligo; (to make love), solicito, ambio; (ardently, or dearly), ardeo, depereo, deamo, flagro
Love (desire), desiderium; (sort of silk), nebula
A love, corculum; (fit), impetus amoris; (potion), philtrum
In love, amans
Belonging to love, amatorius
Worthy to be loved, amabilis
Lovely, decorus, venustus
Loveliness, decor, venustas
A lover, amator; (suitor), procus; (of wine), vinosus

To be lovesick, depereo
A lough, lacus [gens
Loving, amans, benignus, indulLovingly, amanter, amicè
To lounge, otior
A lounger, cessator
A louse, pediculus
Lousy, pediculosus
Low, humilis; (humble), depressus, afflictus; (in the world), inops, pauper; (mean), abjectus, sordidus; (shallow), brevis; (in stature), brevis, humilis; (in price), vili pretio, vilis
To be low in circumstances, egeo
To bring low, humilio, enervo
To low (as an ox), mugio, boo
Lower, inferior
To lower, reprimo, comprimo; (make lower), deprimo; (let down), demitto; (the price), pretium imminuere
To lower, or lour (frown), frontem corrugare; (as the sky), nubibus obduci
Lowering, Louring, torvus, tristis; (weather), cælum nubilum
A lowering, torvitas
Loweringly, torvè, tetricè [mus
Lowest, Lowermost, imus, infiA lowing, mugitus, boatus
Lowly, humilis, demissus
Lowliness, humilitas, modestia
Loyal, fidelis, fidus
Loyally, fideliter, fidè
Loyalty, fidelitas, fides
A lozenge, rhombus
A lubber, segnis, ignavus
Lubberly, adj. socors, piger; adv. segniter, pigrè
To Lubricate, lubrico
Lubricity, lubricitas, lubricum
Lubricous, lubricus
Lucid, lucidus, clarus
Lucifer, lucifer
Luck, fortuna, successus
Bad luck, infortunium
Luckless, infelix, infaustus
Lucky, felix, faustus, prosper
Luckily, auspicatò, faustè
Lucrative, lucrativus, lucrosus
Lucre, lucrum, quæstus
Lucubration, lucubratio
Luculent, luculentus, clarus
Ludicrous, ludicer, jocularis
Ludicrously, jocosè
To lug (hale, pull), traho, vello
The lug, auris lobus
Luggage, onus, sarcina
Lugubrious, lugubris, luctuosus
Lukewarm, tepidus, remissus
To be lukewarm, tepeo, tepesco
Lukewarmly, tepidè
Lukewarmness, tepor
To lull, demulceo, sopio
Lumber, instrumenta domestica ponderosiora
A luminary, luminare
Luminous, luminosus
A lump, massa, frustum; (of earth), gleba; (heap), acervus
The lump, or whole, solidum
Lumpish, hebes, tardus
To grow lumpish, hebesco
Lumpishness, stupor, tarditas
Lunacy, insania
Lunar, lunaris
Lunatic, phreneticus
A lunch, or luncheon, frustum; (in the afternoon), merenda
The lungs, pulmones; (a person of good lungs), stentor
A lurch, duplex palma
To lurch, subduco, deglutio

MAD — MAI — MAN

To leave in the lurch, in angustiis deserere
A lurcher (glutton), lurco, nepos; (lier in wait), insidiator; (dog), canis indagator
A lure, illecebra
To lure, delinio, demulceo
To lurk, lateo, latito
A lurker (loiterer), cessator; (in corners), tenebrio
A lurking, latitatio
A lurking-hole, latebra
Luscious, suavis, prædulcis
Lusciously, suavitèr, dulcè
Lusciousness, dulcedo
Lusory, lusorius
Lust, cupido, appetitus
To lust, prurio, concupisco
Lustful, libidinosus, salax
Lustfully, libidinosè, lascivè
Lustfulness, lascivia
Lustily, fortitèr, validè
Lustiness, corporis robur
Lustral, lustralis
Lustration, lustratio
Lustre, splendor, nitor
Lusty, validus, robustus, vegetus
To be lusty, vigeo
A lute, cithara
Lutestring, serici genus nitidissimus
Luteous, lutosus
Lutulent, lutulentus, cœnosus
Luxation, luxatio
Luxuriance, luxuries, luxuria
Luxuriant, Luxurious, luxuriosus
Luxuriously, luxuriosè
Luxuriousness, luxus
Luxury, luxuria, luxus
A lye, mendacium, fabula
To lye, mentior, fingo
Lying (along), decumbens, prostratus; (between), interjacens; (by), adjacens; (down), reclinis; (flat), pronus; (hid), latens; (near to), contiguus, conterminus; (open), patens; (in wait), insidians; (telling lies), mentiens
A lying (at ease), recubitus; (in wait), insidiæ; (in of women), puerperium
Lymphatic, lymphaticus
A lynx, lynx
A lyre, lyra
Lyric, lyricus
A lyrist, lyrista

M.

A mace, sceptrum
A serjeant's mace, fasces
Mace, macis
A mace-bearer, lictor
To macerate, macero; (make lean), emacio
To machinate, machinor
A machination, machinatio
A machine, machina
A mackerel, scombrus
Mad, insanus, demens, vesanus
To be mad, insanio, furo
To mad, furio, demento
Madam, domina mea
A madcap, vesanus, furiosus
A madhouse, hospitium insanorum
Raving mad, furiosus, furibundus
Madly, dementèr, insanè
Madness, dementia, insania; (of a dog), rabies
To be made, fio

To madefy, madefacio
Madid, madidus, udus
A madrigal, cantilena sylvestris
A magazine, apotheca; (of arms), armamentarium; (of powder), cella; (for corn), horreum
A maggot, termes; (in the pate), impetus animi [dosus
To be maggotty (whimsical), lenMagic, magice, magia
Magic, or belonging to magic, magicus
A magician, magus, veneficus
Magisterial, imperiosus
Magisterially, imperiosè, dogmaticè
Magistracy, magistratus
A magistrate, magistratus
Magnanimity, magnanimitas
Magnanimous, magnanimus, fortis
Magnanimously, strenuè, fortitèr
A magnet, magnes
Magnetical, magneticus
Magnetism, vis magnetica
Magnificence, magnificentia
Magnificent, magnificus, augustus [didè
Magnificently, sumptuosè, splenTo magnify (praise), exalto, laudo, extollo; (aggravate), exaggero; (an object), amplifico, augeo
Magnifying, amplificans, augens
A magnifying, amplificatio
Magnitude, magnitudo
A magpie, pica
Mahometans, mahometani
Mahometanism, mahometanismus
A maid, or maiden, virgo, puella; (old), virgo grandis; (ready for a husband), virgo matura, or nubilis; (servant), ancilla, famula; (cook), coqua; (chamber), ornatrix; (nursery), ancilla infantes curans; (waiting), ministra, pedissequa
A maid (fish), raia minor
Of a maid, virgineus, puellaris
Majestic, augustus, regius
Majesty, majestas, jubar regale
Majestically, augustè, regalitèr
A mail (budget), bulga, saccus; (bundle of letters), fasciculus epistolarum
A maim, vulnus, plaga
To maim, mutilo, vulnero
Maimed, mancus, mutilus, vulneratus
A maiming, mutilatio
Main, primus, præcipuus
Main force, vis, violentia
The main (land), continens; (sea), oceanus, altum mare; (body), summa; (chance), sors, rerum summa; (mast), malus navis præcipuus; (yard), antenna præcipua; (of a horse), juba equina
Mainly, valdè, maximè
Mainprise, vadimonium
To maintain (affirm), assevero, affirmo; (defend), vindico, tueor, sustineo, defendo; (keep), nutrio, ulo, sustento
Maintainable, quod defendi potest
A maintainer, vindex, assertor
A maintaining (affirming), affirmatio; (defending), vindicatio; (keeping), victûs suppeditatio
Maintenance (support), defensio, tutamen; (allowing necessaries), ad victum sumptus

A major (of a troop), legatus; (general), exercitûs instructor
Major (greater), major, melior
Majority, pars major, plures
Maize, frumentum Indicum
A make, or form, forma, figura
To make, facio, compono, conficio; (acquainted), significo, certiorem facere; (afraid), terreo; (an appointment), diem et locum constituere; (ashamed), pudefacio; (away, or go off), aufugio; (away with one's self), sibi mortem consciscere; (away an estate), bona prodigere; (a bed), lectum sternere; (blind), excæco; (words about), litigo, discepto
A maker, fabricator, formator
A making, formatio; (free), manumissio; (good), restitutio, compensatio; (much of), indulgentia; (ready), paratus
A malady, morbus, ægritudo
Malapert, procax, petulans
Malapertness, procacitas
The male (creature), mas
Of the male kind, masculinus
Malcontent, ægrè ferens
Malediction, maledictio
A malefactor, reus, maleficus, sons
Malevolence, malevolentia
Malevolent, malevolens, malignus
Malice, malitia, invidia, simultas; (prepense), ultionis studium
Malicious, malignus, invidus
Maliciously, malignè, invidè
Maliciousness, livor, invidia
To malign (detract), invideo
Malignancy, malignitas, malitia
Malignant, malignus, gravis
Malignity, malignitas; (of a distemper), acerbitas
A mall, or mallet, malleus
To mall, batuo, tundo
A mallard, anas palustris mas
Malleable, ductilis
Mallows, malva
Marshmallows, althea
Of mallows, malvaceus
Malt, brasium, byne
To make malt, byuem parare
A maltster, brasiator
Malting, or malt-making, byneficium
Mamma, mamma, mater
Mammocks, offulæ
A man, homo, vir, mas; (any man), aliquis, quivis
The man of the house, paterfamilias
A man-servant, famulus, servus
Every man, omnis quisque
No man, nemo, nullus
Man by man, viritim
Like a man, virilitèr
To man, hominibus complere, or instruere
To act the man, virum agere
An old man, senex
A poor man, pauper
A rich man, dives
A wise man, sapiens
A young man, juvenis, adolescens
A man of war, navis bellica
Manslaughter, homicidium
Belonging to man, humanus
Manacles, manicae ferreæ
To manacle, manicis constringere
To manage, administro, tracto; (an estate well), rem tueri; (a war), bellum obire; (the temper of the people), plebis animos permulcere; (youth)

[73]

MAP

ætati juvenum temperare ; (a horse), subigere equum
A manager, curator, conductor
A managing, or management, administratio ; (of public money), dispensatio ; (of the voice), moderatio
Mancipation, mancipatio
A manciple, mancipatrix
A mandamus, diploma regium
Mandatory, mandans, imperans
A mandate, mandatum, jussum
A mandrake, mandragoras
Manducation, manducatio
The mane of a horse, juba equina
Manful, virilis, strenuus, fortis
Manfully, viriliter, strenuè
Manfulness, fortitudo, virtus
The mange, scabies canina
A manger, præsepe
Manginess, porrigo
Mangy, scabiosus
To mangle, lacero, lanio
A mangler, mutilator
A mangling, laceratio
Manhood (courage), fortitudo ; (man's estate), ætas virilis
A maniac, insanus, demens
Manifest, manifestus, clarus
To manifest, manifesto
To be made manifest, innotesco ; (it is manifest), patet, constat, liquet
Manifestation, manifestatio
Manifestly, manifestè, clarè
Manifestness, evidentia, claritas
Manifold, multiplex
Mankind, genus humanum
Manliness, fortitudo, virtus
Manly, virilis, strenuus, fortis
Manly, viriliter, fortiter
A manly woman, virago
Manna, manna
Manned, viris instructus
A manner, mos, modus, consuetudo ; (quality), qualitas
In a manner, quodammodo
All manner, omnimodus
Of divers manners, multimodus
In like manner, similiter
In such a manner, ita
Manners (conditions), mores ; (good manners), urbanitas ; (ill manners), inurbanitas
A mannerly person, civilis, comis
A manor, manerium
Of a manor, prædiatorius
A man-servant, famulus, servus
A mansion, sedes, domus
A manteau, palla muliebris
A manteau-maker, sartrix
To mantle, spumesco, pennas dispandere
A mantle, penula
A manual, liber manualis
Manuduction, manuductio
Manufacture, opificium
To manufacture, manu facere
A manufacturer, opifex
Manumission, manumissio
Manure, stercus, fimus
To manure, stercoro, fœcundo
A manurer, ruricola
A manuring, cultus   [tus
A manuscript, liber manu scriptus
Many, multi, plures, complures, perplures ; (how many), quot ? (as many as), quot, tot quot ; (a good many), aliquam multi ; (many times), sæpe, multotiès ; (as many times as), totiès quotiès ; (how many times), quoties ? (so many), tot ; (many ways), multifariam
A map, charta geographica ; (of
[74]

MAR

the world), tabula cosmographica
A maple, acer
To mar (spoil), vitio, depravo
Marble, marmor   [variare
To marble, in marmoris modum
Of marble, marmoreus, è marmore
March (month), Martius
A march, iter
To march, incedo, gradior, proficiscor ; (in), ingredior ; (on), progredior ; (out), egredior ; (an army to), exercitum ducere ad ; (off), recedo
The marches, fines, limites
A marching, progressus
A marchioness, marchionissa
A mare, equa
A margin, margo
Marginal, in margine scriptus
A margrave, marchio
A marigold, caltha
Marine, marinus
A marine, classicarius miles
A mariner, nauta
Belonging to a mariner, nauticus
Marjoram, amaracus
Marital, maritalis
Maritime, maritimus
A mark, signum, nota ; (of money), marca ; (brand), stigma ; (for sheep), character ; (impression), vestigium ; (to shoot at), meta, scopus ; (of a stripe), vibex ; (of a wound), cicatrax ; (set to a writing), signatura
To mark, signo, noto ; (observe), animadverto ; (out), designo
Fit to be marked, notabilis
A marker, annotator ; (observer), observator ; (of bounds), metator
A market, forum, emporium
A market-man, nundinator ; (place), forum ; (town), emporium
Marketable, venalis
A marketing, emptio ; (thing bought), res empta
A marking, notatio, observatio
A marking-iron, cauterium
A marksman, qui rectè collineat
Marl, marga, tasconium
Marmalade, cydonites
Marmorium, marmoreus
A marquess, or marquis, marchio
A marquisate, marchionatus
To marr, corrumpo, vitio ; (the form, or fashion), deformo
A marriage, nuptiæ, conjugium
Of marriage, nuptialis, conjugalis
A marriage-song, epithalamium
Marriageable, nubilis
A married man, maritus ; (woman), uxor
Twice married, bigamus
A marring, corruptio, depravatio
Marrow, medulla
To the very marrow, medullitùs
Full of marrow, medullosus
To marry (as the priest), connubio jungere ; (as the man), uxorem ducere ; (as the woman), viro nubere ; (give in marriage), nuptum dare
A marrying, nuptiæ
Mars, Mars   [licosus
Belonging to Mars, Martius, bellicosus
A marsh, palus
Marsh-ground, pratum palustre ; (a salt-marsh), æstuarium
Marshy, paludosus, palustris
A marshal, mareschallus

MAT

To marshal, ordino
A marshalling, ordinatio
A marshalsea, mareschalsia
A mart, emporium
Martial, militaris, bellicosus
Martial-law, lex belli ; (court), curia martialis ; (affairs), res bellicæ ; (man), bellator
A martin, hirundo agrestis
Martinmass, festum sancti Martini
A martyr, martyr
To martyr, discrucio
Martyrdom, martyrium
A martyrology, martyrologium
A marvel, mirum, res mira
To marvel, miror, admiror
A marvelling, admiratio
Marvellous, mirabilis, mirus ; (thing), mirandum, mirum
Marvellously, mirè, mirabiliter
Marvellousness, mirabilitas
Masculine, masculinus, masculus
A mash (mixture), mixtura ; (for cattle), potio medica
To mash, commisceo
A mask, larva ; (dance), mimus ; (pretence), prætextus
A mason, latomus
A mason's rule, amussis
Masonry, opus cæmentitium
A masquerade, personatorum hominum saltatio ; (habit), habitus personatus ; (person), homo personatus
A mass, massa, moles
The mass, missa ; (book), missale ; (dress), habitus sacerdotalis
A massacre, cædes, occisio
To massacre, cædo, trucido
A massacring, occisio, trucidatio
Massive, Massy, solidus
Massiveness, soliditas
A mast of a ship, malus ; (foremast), malus anticus ; (mainmast), malus præcipuus ; (mizen-mast), malus puppis
Mast for swine, balanus, glans
Belonging to mast, glandarius
A master, dominus, herus ; (one's own master), sui juris ; (master of arts), artium magister ; (of the ceremonies), magister admissionum
Of a master, dominicus, herilis
A masterpiece, opus præcipuum
To master, supero, vinco ; (a city), urbe potiri ; (one's self), seipsum continere ; (one's boldness), audaciam frangere
Masterless, contumax, pertinax
Masterly, imperiosus ; (like an artist), graphicè, peritissimè
Mastery, dominatus
To get the mastery, supero
Mastic, mastiche
Mastication, masticatio
A mastiff, molussus
A mat, matta, teges
To match (compare), comparo, confero ; (be suitable), quadro ; (be of the same colour), ejusdem esse coloris ; (in marriage), nuptum dare   [ciliator
A matchmaker, connubiorum conciliator
A matching, comparatio
Matchless, incomparabilis
A mate, socius, collega
Material, corporeus ; (important), magni momenti, necessarius
Materially, materialiter
Materials, res necessariæ
Maternal, maternus
Mathematical, mathematicus

Mathematically, mathematicè
A mathematician, mathematicus
The mathematics, mathematica
Matins, preces matutinæ
The matrice, matrix, uterus
Of the matrice, uterinus
A matricide, matricida
Matricide, matricidium
To matriculate, nomen in tabulas referre
Matrimonial, conubialis
Matrimony, matrimonium, conubium
A matron, matrona
A matt, matta, scirpea
Matter (corruption), sanies, tabum; (substance), materia, substantia; (business, or thing), res, negotium, opus
Full of matter, purulentus
A matter of (or about), quasi, circiter
A mattock, marra
A mattress, culcita lanea, gvabatus
Mature (ripe), maturus; (accurate), accuratus, exatus
Maturely, maturè, consultà, cautè
Maturity, maturitas, ætas matura
Maugre, invitè
To maul, pugnis, &c. contundere
A maulkin (for an oven), peniculus furnaceus; (scarecrow), larva
To maunder, murmuro
A maundering, marmuratio
The maw, ventriculus
Mawkish, nauseam pariens
A mawks, puella insulsa
Maxillary, maxillaris
A maxim, axioma, præceptum
I may (am able to do), possum, queo
May (the month), Maius
A maygame, ludibrium
A mayor, prætor urbanus
Mayoralty, prætoris urbani munus, or dignitas
To be in a maze, stupeo
A maze, labyrinthus; (astonishment), stupor, consternatio
Me, me; accus. of Ego
Mead (drink), mulsum; (meadow), pratum
Of a meadow, pratensis
Meagre, macilentus, macer
Meagreness, macies, macritas
Meal, farina, pollen; (of meat), cibus
Of meal, farinarius, pollinarius
Mealy (full of meal), farraceus; (mouthed), pudens, verecundus
A mealman, farinarius
A mean, or means, modus, ratio, opera, causa; (by fair means), sponte, blandè; (by foul means), invitè, per vim; (by some means), quocunque modo; (by all means), prorsùs, quàm maximè
Mean, mediocris, abjectus, humilis, tenuis, vulgaris, ignobilis
The mean, medium; (in the mean time), intereà, interim
To mean, volo, intelligo
A meander, labyrinthus
Means (wealth), opes, divitiæ, facultates
Meanest, infimus, imus
A meaning, sensus, animus
Well-meaning, probus, justus
Meanly, mediocrittèr, malè, abjectè
Meanness (indifference), mediocritas; (poverty), tenuitas; (of birth), obscuritas, humilitas, ignobilitas; (of spirit, or timi-
[76]

dity), timiditas; (of spirit, or niggardliness), sordes
Meant, propositus, significatus
A measle, rotis macula
The measles, rubiolæ; (in a hog), lepra, porrigo; (in a tree), patella
Measurable, mensurabilis
A measure, mensura; (of wine), modus; (mean), modus
Beyond measure, immodicè, præter modum
In some measure, aliquatenùs
Out of measure, immodicè, extra modum
Within measure, intra modum
To measure, metior; (out), admetior
A measurer, mensor, metator
Measures (purposes), consilia, proposita, rationes
A measuring, metatio, dimensio
Meat, cibus, esca; (flesh), caro; (and drink), victus; (dainty), dapes, cupediæ, lautitiæ
Mechanic, Mechanical, mechanicus
A mechanic, opifex, faber
Mechanics, mechanalia scientia
Mechanically, mechanicè
Mechanism, mechanismus
A medal, numisma solenne
To meddle (with), tracto, curo, attingo; (in an affair), se immiscere rei; (no more), desisto, abstineo
A meddler, or meddlesome person, ardelio, musca
A meddling with, tractatio
To mediate, intercedo
A mediation, intercessio
A mediator, intercessor, conciliator, arbiter
Mediatorial, intercedens [oris
Mediatorship, munus intercessoris
A mediatrix, conciliatrix
Medicable, medicabilis
Medical, medicus, medicinalis
A medicament, medicamentum
Medicinal, medicinalis, medicatus
Medicine (the science), medicina, medendi scientia; (physical potion), medicamentum, medicamen
Mediocrity, mediocritas, modus
To meditate, meditor, præmeditor
A meditation, meditatio
Mediterranean, Mediterraneus
A medlar, mespilum
A medley, Farrago
Medley, adj. mixtus
To make a medley, turbo, misceo
Medullar, medullaris
A meed, præmium
Meek, mitis, lenis, placidus
To grow meek, mitesco
Meekly, mansuetè, leniter
Meekness, mansuetudo, lenitas
Meer, or mere, adj. merus
A meer (lake), palus; (limit), terminus, limes, meta
Meet, aptus, idoneus
To be meet, conducit
To meet, obvenio, occurro, obviam ire, convenio, occurso
Meeting, obvius, congressus
A meeting (together), occursus, congressio; (assembly), conventus; (congregation), congregatio; (of people), frequentia; (of two streams), confluens
A meeting-house, conventiculum
Meetly, aptè, convenientèr
Meetness, convenientia

The megrim, vertigo
Melancholy, tristia, mœstus
Melancholy, melancholia, atrabilis, tristitia, mœstitia
Melancholic, melancholicus, hypochondriacus
To be melancholy, tristitiâ affici
Melilot (herb), melilotos
To meliorate, meliorem reddere
Mellifluous, mellifluus
Mellow (ripe), maturus, mitis; (with liquor), temulentus
To mellow, mitesco; (with liquor), potu calescere; (as wine), languesco
Not mellow, crudus, acidus; (very mellow), permitis, valdè maturus
Mellowness, maturitas
Melodious, harmonicus, canorus
Melodiously, suavitèr, modulatè
Melodiousness, harmoniæ suavitas
Melody, harmonia, modulatio
A melon, melo, pepo
To melt (metals), liquo, liquefacio; (as snow), regelo; (into tears), in lacrymas solvi; (to be melted), liquor, liquesco
That may be melted, fusilis
A melter, fusor, conflator
A melting, liquefactio; (of metal), fusio, fusura; (discourse), sermo aptus
A melting-house, astrina
A member, membrum; (the privy members), pudenda; (of parliament), senator; (of a society), socius; (of an university), alumnus, academicus
By members, membratim
A membrane, membrana, tunica
Full of membranes, membranaceus
Memoirs, commentarius
Memorable, memorabilis
A memorandum-book, libellus memorialis [numentum
A memorial, narratio scripta, monumentum
The memory, memoria
Of blessed memory, sacer apud posteros
Out of memory, oblitus
Of the memory, memorialis
To call to memory, recordor
Men, homines
To menace, comminor, minor
Menacing, minans, minax
A menacing, minatio
To mend (correct), emendo, castigo, corrigo; (grow better), melioresco; (repair), reficio, reparo, restauro
A mender, emendator, corrector, castigator; (of old things), veteramentarius
Mendicant, mendicans, mendicus
A mendicant friar, frater ex ordine mendicantium
A mending, emendatio, castigatio; (of old things), interpolatio
On the mending hand, meliusculè se habens
Menial, domesticus, servilis
A menial servant, famulus
Menstrual, Menstruous, menstruus
Mensurable, mensurabilis
Mensuration, metatio [uus
Mental, mentis conceptus, intermus
Mention, mentio, commemoratio
To mention, memoro, commemoro
Not to mention, silentio præterire
Mercantile, ad commercium pertinens

E 2

MET

Mercenary, mercenarius, venalis
A mercer, sericarum textarum mercator, propola
Merchandise, merx, mercatura
To merchandise, mercor, negotior
A merchant, mercator
Merchantable, mercabilis
Merchant-like, mercatorius
A merchantman, navis mercatoria
Merciful, misericors, clemens
Mercifully, clementèr
Mercifulness, misericordia
Merciless, immisericors, inhumanus
Mercilessness, inhumanitas
Mercurial, vividus, levis, acer
Mercurials, mercurialia
Mercury (the god), Mercurius; (quicksilver), hydrargyrum; (sprightliness), vigor
Mercy, misericordia, commiseratio, clementia
Mercy-seat, propitiatorium
To have mercy, misereor
To be at mercy, in potestate esse
Mere (only), merus, purus
Merely, merè, tantùm
Meretricious, meretricius
The meridian, circulus meridianus
Meridional, meridianus, australis
Meridionally, ad austrum
Merit, meritum
To merit, mereo, promereo
Of merit, præclarus, illustris
Meritorious, merens, meritus
Meritoriously, meritò, justè, jure
Meritoriousness, meritum
A mermaid, siren
Merrily, festivè, lætè, facetè
Merriment, hilaritas, lætitia
Merry, hilaris, festivus, lætus, jocosus, lepidus, jucundus
To make one merry, exhilaro; (to make merry, or be merry), lætor, gaudeo
Made merry, exhilaratus
The merry thought, claviculæ
Mersion, mersio
A mesh, retis macula
A mesh-vat, dolium, cadus
Meslin, farrago
Meslin, miscellaneus
A mess (of meat), cibus; (of pottage), jusculi catillus; (or share of meat), cibi portio
To mess with, unà cum aliis cibum capere
A message, mandatum
To tell a message, mandata ferre; (to send a message), lego, mitto
A messenger, nuncius; (special), certus homo; (ambassador), legatus; (officer of justice), lictor, stator; (letter-carrier), tabellarius; (postboy), cursor, veredarius
The Messias, Messias, Christus
A messuage, domus, fundus
Metal, metallum
Metallic, or of metal, metallicus
To metamorphose, transformo
A metamorphosis, metamorphosis
A metaphor, metaphora
Metaphorical, metaphoricus
Metaphorically, metaphoricè
Metaphysical, metaphysicus
Metaphysics, metaphysica
To mete, metior, dimetior
Meteors, meteora
A meter, mensor
Metheglin, mulsum

[76]

MIL

A method, methodus, ratio, via
Methodical, methodicus
Methodically, methodicè
Methodists, qui puriorem religionem profitentur [rere
To methodize, in ordinem digeMetonymical, translatus
A metonymy, translatio
Metre (rhyme), rhythmus
Metrical, ad carmen pertinens
A metropolis, metropolis
A metropolitan, metropolitanus
Mettle (sprightliness), vigor, agilitas; (courage), virtus, magnanimitas
Mettlesome, ardens, vehemens, acer
To mew (as a cat), myauliso; (as a stag), cornua mutare
Mice, mures
Michaelmas, festum sancti Michaëlis
Microcosm, microcosmus
A microscope, microscopium
Mid-day, meridies
Middle, medius, intermedius
The middle, medium
Middlemost, in medio positus
Middling, modicus, mediocris
Midland, mediterraneus
Midnight, media nox
The midriff, diaphragma
Midsummer, solstitium æstivum; (day), natalis dies Sancti Joannis Baptistæ
The midst, medium
Midway, via media
A midwife, obstetrix
Midwifery, obstetricium
The mien, vultus
Might, vis, potentia, potestas
Mighty, potens, valens, validus; (adv.), valdè, vehementèr
To be mighty, valeo, polleo
To grow mighty, valesco
Mightily, validè, potentèr
Mightiness, potentia, potestas
A migration, migratio, commigratio
A milch-cow, vacca lactaria
Mild (gentle), mitis, lenis, mansuetus, placidus; (indulgent), indulgens, obsequiosus, blandus
To make mild, sedo, placo
To grow mild, mitesco, mansuesco
Mildew, rubigo, ros melleus
Mildly, leniter, mansuetè
Mildness, lenitas
A mile, milliare, mille passus
A mile-mark, lapis
Of a mile, milliarius
Militant, militans
Military, militaris, bellicosus
The militia, militia
Milk, lac; (new), recens lac
Of milk, lacteus
A milk-house, lactarium; (a milk-maid), lactaria; (a milk-man), lactarius; (a milk-pail), mulctrale
To milk, mulgeo, emulgeo
Milkiness, mollitia, lenitas
Milky, lacteus
The milky-way, galaxia
A mill (for corn), pistrinum; (hand-mill), mola trusatilis; (fulling-mill), mola fullonia; (paper), mola chartaria
A mill-dam, stagnum molare
A mill-stone, lapis molaris; (the upper), catillus; (the nether), meta
Of a mill, molarius, molaris
To mill, molâ densare

MIN

A miller, molitor
Millet, milium
A million, deciès centena millia
The milt, lien; (of fish), lactes
Mimical, mimicus
A mimic, mimus, pantomimus
To mimic, imitari jocularitèr
A mimicking, imitatio jocularis
To mince, concido, comminuo; (a matter), rem verbis extenuare; (pass slightly over), rem levitèr tangere; (in walking), levi pede incedere
Minced meat, minutal; (pie), artocreas ex intritâ carne confectum
A mincing (gait), incessus, affectatus; (of meat), concisura carnis; (of a matter), extenuatio
The mind, animus, mens; (opinion), opinio, sententia; (desire), desiderium, studium, votum, cupiditas, cupido
To mind (look after), curo, observo; (regard), respicio, curo; (consider), animadverto, perpendo, attendo, consulo, video, considero, specto; (put in mind), moneo, admoneo
To have a mind, exopto, concupisco
Out of mind, oblitus
Of the mind, internus [ditèr
Of one mind, unanimus, concorMinded (regarded), observatus, notatus; (inclined), affectus, animatus; (high), elatus, superbus; (ill), malevolus
Mindful, memor, attentus, diligens
Minding, curans, incumbens
Mine, or mine own, meus
A mine, fodina; (of silver), argenti fodina; (of gold), auri fodina; (of lead), stannarium; (used in a siege), cuniculus
Full of mines, cuniculosus
A miner (of metals), metallicus; (in a siege), cuniculorum fossor
Mineral, fossilis, metallicus; (water), aqua per venas metalli fluens [silis
Minerals, cognata metallia fosTo mingle (mix), misceo
A mingling, mistura
Miniature, pictura minuta
A minion, deliciæ, corculum
To minish. See to Diminish
A minister, minister; (of state), rerum publicarum administer; (of God's word), prædicator; (of a parish), ecclesiæ pastor, parochus; (of justice), justitiæ curator; (preacher), prædicator
To minister, ministro [nens
Ministerial, ad ministrum pertiMinisterially, ope ministri
Ministration, ministerium
A ministring, suppeditatio
The ministry, reipublicæ curatores
Ministry, evangelii prædicatio
A minikin (pin), spinula minor
A minor (in age), minor ætate; (of a syllogism), assumptio minor
Minority (in number), pars minor
A minster, templum, monasterium
A minstrel, fidicen, fidicina
Minstrelsy, harmonia
Mint, mentha
A mint (for coining), officina nummum cudendum

MIS

Minute, minutus, exiguus
A minute, sexagesima pars horæ; (instant), momentum
To minute, scripto consignare
Minutely, sigillatim
Minuteness, parvitas
Minutes, exemplaria prima, capita rei alicujus
A minx, puella fastidiosa
A miracle, miraculum
Miraculous, mirificus, mirus
Miraculously, mirificè, mirè
Mire, cœnum, lutum
Miry, cœnosus, lutosus; (daubed with mire), lutulentus
A mirror (glass), speculum; (pattern), exemplar
Mirth, gaudium, lætitia
Full of mirth, hilaris, lætus
Of mirth, jocosus, ludicer
Misacceptation, comprehensio absurda
A misadventure, infortunium; (in law), homicidium fortuitum
To misadvise, perperàm consulere
Misapplication, applicatio prava
To misapply, perperàm applicare, or adhibere
To misapprehend, malè intelligere
Misapprehension, sinistra interpretatio
Misbecoming, indecorus
To misbehave, malè se gerere
Misbehaviour, morum pravitas
Misbelief, fides prava
To miscalculate, malè computare
To miscal, falso, or ficto nomine appellare, ignominioso nomine dehonestare, conviciis insectari
To miscarry (in business), malè succedere; (of a child), aborto
A miscarriage (in business), malus successus; (in manners), delictum; (of females), abortio, abortus [tus
Miscellaneous, miscellaneus, mistus
Miscellanies, miscellanea
A miscellany, farrago
A mischance, infortunium
A mischief, malum, exitium
Mischievous, nocens, malignus
A mischievous deed, facinus, flagitium, scelus
Mischievously, improbè, malè
Mischievousness, malitia
To misconceive, hallucinor, malè intelligere
Misconception, sinistra interpretatio
To misconstrue, malè explicare
A misconstruction, depravatio
To miscount, malè numerare
A miscreant, infidus, nocens
A misdeed, culpa, delictum
To misdemean, malè se gerere
A misdemeanor, delictum, culpa
A misdoer, nocens, noxius
Misdoing, delinquens, peccans
Misdoubt, suspicio
To misdoubt, suspicor
To misemploy, malè collocare; (time), ineptiis vacare
A miser, avarus, miser
Miserable (afflicted), afflictus, calamitosus; (niggardly), avarus
Miserableness, avaritia
Miserably, miserè, avarè
Misery, miseria, ærumna
Misfortune, infortunium, clades
To misgive, præsagio
To misguide, seduco, fallo
A mishap, infortunium
Misinformed, malè doctus
Misinformation, falsus rumor

[77]

MIT

To misinterpret, perperàm exponere [pretatio
A misinterpretation, mala interpretatio
To mislay, extra locum ponere
To mislead, seduco, fallo
A misleader, seductor
A misleading, seductio
To misle, irroro, stillo
Misletoe, viscus
To mislike, improbo, aversor
Misling, irrorans, tenuis
To mismanage, malè administrare
Mismanagement, mala administratio
To mismatch, malè sociare
Mismatched, malè sociatus
To misname, agnomino
Misnamed, falsò appellatus
A misnomer, transnominatio
To mispend, prodigo, profundo
A mispending, profusio
To misplace, perperàm locare
Misprision, neglectus
A misquotation, falsa quotatio
To misquote, falsò citare
To misreckon, falsè numerare
A misreckoning, falsa computatio
To misrelate, falsò narrare
To misrepresent, falsò exprimere
A misrepresentation, falsa descriptio
Misrepresented, falsò descriptus
Misrule, dominatio iniqua
A miss, adolescentula; (mistress), amica; (wrong), damnum
To miss (leave out), intermitto, omitto, prætermitto; (one's mark), scopum non attingere; (or be disappointed), de spe decidere; (in duty), pecco, erro, labor; (fire), ignem non concipere; (or be out in judgment), erro, hallucinor, fallo
A missal, missale
Missed, Mist, desideratus
Misshapen, deformis, deformatus
To be missing, desideror
A mission, missio
A missionary, emissarius
Missive, Missile, missilis
To misspell, malè literas connectere
A mist, nebula, caligo
To be in a mist, perturbor
Misty, nebulosus
To mistake, erro, fallo
A mistake, error, erratum
A mistaking, erratio
To mistate, falsò proponere
To misteach, perperàm docere
To misterm, falsò appellare
To mistime, tempore malè dividere
A mistress, domina, hera, amica
A mistrust, diffidentia
To mistrust, diffido, suspicor
Mistrustful, suspicax, auspiciosus
Mistrustfully, curculio; (coin), nummulus
A mistrusting, diffidentia
To misunderstand, malè intelligere
A misunderstanding, sinistra interpretatio; (among friends), dissidium, discordia
Misusage, abusus; (ill treatment), injuria, inhumanitas
To misuse, abutor, lædo; (with the tongue), convicior
A mite (insect), acarus; (weevil), curculio; (coin), nummulus
A miter (in joinery), coadunatio semiquadra; (of a bishop), mitra

MOL

Mithridate, antidotum Mithridaticum
To mitigate, mitigo, lenio
A mitigation, mitigatio, lenimen
A mitre, mitra
Mitred, infulatus
Mittens, chirothecæ dimidiatæ
To mix, misceo, commisceo; (be mixed), misceor; (adulterate), vitio, adultero, corrumpo; (with water), diluo
A mixture, mistura farrago
To mizzle (misle), irroro
Moan, luctus, planctus
To moan, lugeo, doleo, deploro, condoleo
Moanful, flebilis, lugubris
Moanfully, lugubrè
A moaning, fletus, lamentatio
A moat (ditch), fossa
A mob, turba confusa
The mob, plebecula
A woman's mob, caliendrum
To mob, plebeculam in aliquem concitare, conviciis insectari
Mobility, inconstantia
A mock, dicterium, sanna
To mock, ludo, deludo, ludificor
A mocker, derisor, sannio; (deceiver), planus
Mockery, irrisus
Mocking, deridens, deludens
A mocking, ludificatio, irrisus
A mocking-stock, ludibrium
A mode (manner), modus, ratio; (fashion), consuetudo, usus
A model, modulus, forma, exemplar, exemplum
To model, delineo, formo
A modeller, formator
Moderate, moderatus, mediocris
To moderate (govern), moderor, guberno; (suppress), coërceo, diminuo; (decide), decido, dirimo
Moderately, temperatè, leniter
Moderateness, temperantia
Moderation, moderatio; (in expense), frugalitas
A moderator, moderator
Modern, recens, hodiernus
The moderns, recentiores
To modernize, ad hodiernum usum redigere
Modest, modestus, pudicus, æquus
Modestly, modestè, pudicè, castè
Modesty, modestia, pudicitia
A modicum, modicum
To modify, modum adhibere
A modification, modificatio
Modish, scitus, concinnus
Modishly, scitè, concinnè
Modishness, concinnatus hodierna
To modulate, modulor
Modulation, modulatio
The moiety, dimidium
To moil and toil, impigrè laborare
Moist, humidus, udus, succidus
To be moist, madeo, humeo
To grow moist, humesco
To moisten, humecto
To be made moist, madefio
A moistening, humectatio
Moistness, humiditas
Moisture, humor, vapor; (of the earth), uligo
Without moisture, exsuccus
A mole, talpa; (in the body), macus, nævus; (fence toward the sea), agger
A mole-hill, grumus
To molest, infesto, vexo

E 3

A molester, vexator
A molesting, or molestation, molestia, vexatio, infestatio
Mollient, molliens, deliniens
To mollify, mollio, mitigo
A mollifier, pacator
A mollifying, pacatio, levatio
Molosses, sacchari spuma
To molt (as birds), plumare, defluvio laborare
Molten, fusus, conflatus, fusilis
A molting, plumarum defluvium
A moment, momentum, temporis punctum
Of great moment, gravis
Of little moment, leviculus
Momentary, unius momenti
Momentous, gravis
A monarch, monarcha
A monarchy, monarchia
A monastery, monasterium
Monastical, monasticus
Monday, feria secunda
Money, moneta, pecunia, nummus, numisma ; (current), nummus receptus ; (clipped), pecunia accisa ; (borrowed), æs alienum ; (present), pecunia numerata
Of money, nummarius
Full of money, pecuniosus
Money expended, impensa; (lent), æs fœneratum
A moneyed man, locuples, benè nummatus
A moneyer (coiner), monetarius
Moneyless, sine pecuniâ
A mongrel, bigener, hybrida
A monitor, monitor
Monitory, ad monitionem pertinens
A monk, monachus
Monkish, monasticus
A monkey, simia caudata
Monkey-tricks, gesticulationes
To monopolize, monopolium exercere
A monopoliser, monopola
A monopoly, monopolium
A monosyllable, monosyllaba
Monotony, unius modi sonus
A monster, monstrum, portentum
Monstrous, monstrosus
Monstrously, monstruosè, valdè
Montanous, montanus
A month, mensis
Of a month, menstruus
Monthly (for a month), per mensem ; (month by month), singulis mensibus
Of two months, bimestris ; (of three months), trimestris ; (of four months), quadrimestris
A monument, monumentum ; (tomb), mausoleum, tumba
Monumental, ad monumentum pertinens
Mood (humour), animi affectus; (of a verb), modus
In good mood, alacer; (ill mood), mœstus, tristis
The moon, luna; (new), novilunium ; (half), luna falcata ; (half moon in fortification), opus lunatum; (moon's first quarter), cornua prima lunæ ; (full moon), plenilunium ; (-'s increase), luna crescens; (decrease), luna decrescens
A moon (month), mensis
Like the moon, lunatus
Of the moon, lunaris
By moonlight, per lunam
Moon-eyed, lusciosus
Moonshine, lunaris lampas
[78]

A Moor, Æthiops, Maurus ; (marsh), palus
Of a moor, palustris
Moorish, palustris ; (or tawny), Mauritanicus
To moor, retineo ; (a ship), navem anchoris in fundo idoneo statuere
A mop, peniculus
To mop, peniculo purgare
A mope, stupidus
Mope-eyed, luscus
To mope, obstupeo
A moppet, pusio
Moral, moralis, ethicus
The moral, epimythium
Morality, moralitas
To moralise, mythologizo
A moraliser, mythologus
A moralizing, mythologia
Morally (in a moral sense), sensu morali ; (speaking), ex communi sensu
Morals, mores, instituta
A morass, palus
Morbid, morbidus, morbosus
Morbific, morbificus
Mordacity, mordacitas
More, adj. plus, major; adv. magis, plus, quàm, amplius ; or else it is the sign of the comparative degree
More and more, impensius ; (more or less), plùs minùs ; (more than enough), plùs satis
To be more than enough, supersum, redundo
More than usual, ultra solitum
Moreover, insupèr, præterea
The morn, or morning, mane, aurora, tempus matutinum
In the morning, manè (betimes), diluculò
Of the morning, matutinus
The morning-star, phosphorus
Next morning, postridiè, manè
Morose, perversus, austerus
Moroseness, protervitas
Morosely, morosè, perversè
To-morrow, cras, crastinò
Of to-morrow, crastinus
To-morrow morning, cras manè
To-morrow night, crastinâ nocte
Day after to-morrow, perendiè
A morsel, frustum, buccea
To a morsel, ad summam inopiam
Mortal (deadly), lethalis, capitalis, lethifer, mortifer ; (subject to death), mortalis ; (implacable), implacabilis, acerbissimus; (destructive), internecinus
Mortality (destruction), clades ; (frailty), mortalitas ; (death), mors
A mortality, pestis, pestilentia
Mortally, lethalitèr, vehementèr
Mortals, mortales homines
A mortar, mortarium
Mortar, cæmentum
Of mortar, cæmentitius
Daubed with mortar, gypsatus
A mortgage, hypotheca, pignus
To mortgage, pignori opponere
A mortgagee, cui oppigneratur
Mortification (in the body), gangræna; (self-denial), mortificatio, coërcitio; (grief), dolor
A mortise, cavus
To mortise, cavo inserere
Mortmain, mortua manus
A mortuary, mortuarium
Mosaic, mosaïcus
A mosque, templum Turcicum
Moss, muscus
Covered with moss, muscosus

Mossy, muscosus, lanuginosus
Most, adj. plerique ; adv. maximè, plurimùm, præcipuè
Most of all, quàm maximè
Mostly, ferè, plerumquè
For the most part, magnâ ex parte ; (generally), plurimùm, ut plurimùm ; (most frequently), sæpissimè
To make the most of, parcè uti
A mote, atomus
A moth, tinea, teredo
Full of moths, tineosus
Moth-eaten, a tineis erosus
A mother, mater, genitrix ; (in law), noverca ; (grand), avia
Mother (native), vernaculus ; (chief), primarius, præcipuus
Of a mother, maternus
Motherly, maternus ; (prudent), prudens
Motherless, matre orbatus
Mothery, fæculentus
A motion, motio ; (of the mind), perturbatio ; (for a bill), rogatio ; (in chancery, &c.), rogatus
To make a motion, sententiam dicere
At one's own motion, ultrò; (at another's motion), alio instigante
Motions of an army, itinera
To motion, propono, rogo
Motionless, immobilis, fixus
A motive, incitamentum, causa
Motive, movens
Motley, variè distinctus
A motto, symbolum
To move (stir), moveo, agito; (disturb), turbo, perturbo; (persuade), excito, hortor (propose), propono, rogo; (one's dwelling), commigro ; (one to pity), ad misericordiam inducere ; (shake), concutio; (or stir up), extimulo, incito; (to), admoveo ; (to anger), irrito, excandefacio ; (to laughter), risum commovere ; (to sedition), seditionem conflare; (or affect the mind of the hearers), animos movere ; (violently), impello; (up and down), vacillo
Moveable, mobilis
Moveables, supellex
Not to be moved, immobilis
Easily moved, agitabilis
A movement, motus
A mover, motor, suasor, instigator, stimulator, concitator
Moving, movens, commovens
A moving, motus, suasio, instigatio ; (or shaking), concussio
Mould (earth), solum, terra ; (to cast in), matrix, forma ; (of the head), sutura
To mould (cast), formo ; (bread), panem subigere;(grow mouldy), mucesco
A moulder, formator
To moulder away, dissipor
Mouldiness, mucor
A moulding, formatio ; (of bread), subactio
Mouldings, toreumata
Mouldy, mucidus, rancidus
To moult, plumas exuere
Moulting, plumas exuens
A moulting, pennarum defluvium
A mound, sepimentum
To mound, sepio, sepe munire
A mount, mons, collis

MUD — MUR — NAI

To mount (up), ascendo; (a cannon), tormentum rotis imponere; (guard), excubo; (a horse), conscendo
A mountain, mons
Of a mountain, montanus
A mountaineer, monticola
Mountainous, montosus
A mountebank, circulator
A mounting up, ascensus
To mourn, lugeo, defleo; (bewail), deploro, lamentor; (together), condoleo
A mourner, plorator, pullatus
Mournful, lugubris, mœstus
Mournfully, lugubritèr, mœstè
A mourning, luctus, mœstitia; (of the door), gemitus
Mourning, tristis, lugubris, ater
Mourning, vestis lugubris
In mourning, atratus, pullatus
A mouse, mus
A dormouse, glis
Of a mouse, murinus
A mousetrap, muscipula
A mouth, os, rictus; (of a beast), faux; (of a bird), rostrum; (of a bottle), lura; (of a haven, or river), ostium; (of an oven, or stove), præfurnium; (of the stomach), œsophagus
To mouth, conviciis proscindere
To make mouths, os distorquere
Foulmouthed, maledicus
Hardmouthed, oris contumacis
A mouthful, bolus [rixosus
A mouthing fellow, clamosus,
To mow (cut down), meto
A mow, cumulus; (of hay), fœnile
A mower, messor, falcator; (of hay), fœniseca
A mowing, messio, messis
Time for mowing, fœnisecium
Mown, messus, attonsus
Much, adj. multus, plurimus; adv. longè, multùm, admodùm, vehementèr, valdè, magnoperè; (ado), vix, ægrè, difficultèr; (in value), magni, permagni
Overmuch, nimietas; adv. nimis, nimiùm, pernimis; adj. nimius; (as much), quantum; (as much again), alterum tantum; (as much as may be), quantum maximum; (very much), abundè; (just so much), tantundem; (a little too much), paulò nimis
For how much? quanti?
For so much, tanti
Much like, assimilis
Much less, multò minùs; (much the same), idem ferè
Thus much, hactenus
To make much of, indulgeo, magni facere
To run much upon, hæreo
To think much of, invitè agere
Made much of, indultus
Mucid, mucidus, rancidus
Mucilage, mucus
Mucilaginous, mucosus
Muck, stercus, simus
A muckworm (miser), avarus
Mucous, mucosus
Mud, lutum, limus
To mud, limo polluere; (water), aquam turbare
Mudded (troubled), turbatus; (daubed with mud), limo conspersus
To muddle (with drink), inebrio
Muddy, cœnosus, limosus; (in looks), nubilus, tortuosus, tetricus; (wine), vinum fæculentum
A muff, manica villosa
To muffle up, obvolvo, cooperio
Muffling up, obvolvens
A mug, poculum
Mugwort, artemesia
Muggish, or muggy, mucidus, calidus
A mulatto, hybrida [rus
A mulberry, morum; (tree), mo-
A mulct, mulcta
To mulct, mulcto
A mule, mulus, mala; (young), hinnulus
Of a mule, mularis
A muleteer, mulio [quere
To mull, vinum aromatibus co-
Mulled wine, vinum adustum
A mulier, lapis molaris
A mullet, mugil
Multifarious, multifarius
Multiform, multiformis
Multiparous, plures uno partu edens
Multiplicable, multiplicabilis
A multiplicand, numerus multiplicandus
Multiplication, multiplicatio
A multiplicator, multiplicator
Multiplicity, magna copia
To multiply, multiplico; (to be multiplied), multiplicor
A multiplier, multiplicator
Multiplying, multiplicans, augens
A multitude, multitudo
The multitude, vulgus, plebs
Mum! tace! au!
To mumble, mussito; (in eating), ægrè manducare; (beat), pugnis tundere
A mumbler, mussitator
A mumbling, murmuratio
A mummer, larvatus
A mummy, cadaver conditum
To beat to a mummy, valdè contundere
To momp, mendico; (a dinner), parasitor, epulis insidiari
A mumper, mendicus, parasitus
Mumping, mendicans
To be in the mumps, animo angi
To munch, manduco
A muncher, comedo
Mundane, mundanus
A mungrel, hybrida
Municipal, municipalis; (town), municipium
Munificence, munificentia
Munificent, munificus, liberalis
Munition, arma; (defence), præsidium, tutela
Mural, muralis
Murder, homicidium, cædes
To murder, trucido, cædo
A murderer, homicida, sicarius, interfector
Murdering, ferus, truculentus
A murdering, trucidatio; (squandering away), profusio, dissipatio
Murk, caligo
Murky, tenebrosus
A murmur (complaint), querela; (speaking low), fremitus, murmur, susurrus
To murmur, murmuro, fremo; (again), remurmuro; (much), perfremo; (against), obmurmuro; (at), adfremo
A murmurer, murmurator
A murmuring, murmuratio
A little murmuring, susurrus
The murrain, scabies, lues
A muscle, musculus
Muscular, ad musculos pertinens
A muse, musa; (the muses), Pierides, Camœnæ
To muse, meditor, contemplor; (beforehand), præmeditor
Musing, meditans, cogitans
A mushroom, fungus
Music, cantus, musice, musica
Musical, musicus, harmonicus
Musically, musicè, modulatè
A musician, musicus
A music-school, ludus fidicinius
Musk, moschus
A musk-melon, melo odoratus
Musky, moschatus
A musket, sclopetum
A musqueteer, sclopetarius
Mnalia, nebula linea
Must (new wine), mustum
To must, mucesco
I must, debeo, oportet me
The mustaches, barba alata
Mustard, sinapis
A muster, copiarum lustratio
A muster-master, militum censor
To muster, exercitum lustrare
To pass muster, approbor
Mustered, conscriptus, census
A mustering, lustratio, census
Mustily, mucidè
Mustiness, mucor
Musty, mucidus, rancidus
To be musty, muceo, mucesco
Mutable, mutabilis, mobilis
To be mutable, muto, vario
Mutability, mutabilitas
A mutation, muratio
Mute (dumb), mutus
To be mute, obmutesco
To mute (as a hawk), alvum egerere
Mutely, tacitè
To mutilate, mutilo
Mutilation, mutilatio
A mutineer, homo turbulentus
Mutinous, turbulentus, seditiosus [tiosè
Mutinously, turbulentèr, sedi-
A mutiny, motus seditio
To mutiny, tumultuor
A mutinying, seditio, tumultus
To mutter, musso, mussito
A muttering, murmuratio
Mutton, caro ovina, or vervecina
Mutual, metuus, reciprocus
Mutually, mutuò, invicèm
A muzzle, capistrum
The muzzle of a gun, sclopetti os
To muzzle, capistro constringere
A muzzling, capistro colligatio
My, or mine, meus
A myriad, myrias
Myrrh, myrrha
Of myrrh, myrrheus, myrrhinus
A myrtle, myrtus
Of myrtle, myrteus, myrtinus
Like myrtle, myrtuosus
Mixed with myrtle, myrtatus
A mystery, mysterium, arcanum
Mysterious, Mystical, mysticus
Mystically, mysticè
Mythological, mythologicus
A mythologist, mythologus
Mythology, mythologia

N.

To nab, prehendo
A nag, mannus, equuleus, veredus, asturco
A nail, clavus; (of the foot, or

NAV   NEE   NEW

hand), unguis; (in measure), digiti duo cum quadranti; (tenter-hook), uncus
To nail, clavum pangere, suffigo; (up cannon), obstruo; (to a cross), crucifigo; (down), defigo; (up), suffigo
A nailer, faber clavorum
Naked, nudus; (half), seminudus; (stark), nudior ovo; (as a sword), strictus; (truth), veritas non simulata
To strip naked, nudo, denudo
Nakedly, apertè, perspicuè
Nakedness, nuditas; (to uncover), pudicitiam violare
A name, nomen; (first), prænomen; (surname), cognomen; (nick), ficta appellatio; (renown, or reputation), fama, existimatio, celebritas
A namesake, cognominis
To name, nomino, nuncupo, voco, appello; (mention), mentionem facere, memini
By name, nominatim
Nameless, anonymus
Namely, nominatim, videlicèt, scilicèt
A naming, nominatio
A nap, somnus brevis; (of cloth), villus
To take a nap, obdormisco; (at noon), meridior
The nape, ima colli vertebra
Napery, lintea
A napkin, linteolum, mappa
Napping, dormitans, dormiens
Nappy, villosus; (ale), cerevisia generosa
Narcotic, narcoticus
Nard (the shrub), nardum; (ointment), nardus
To narrate, affero, narro
A narration, narratio
A narrative, enarratio
Narrow, arctus, angustus, exiguus; (covetous), parcus, avidus
To narrow, arcto, coarcto
Narrowly, angustè, arctè; (with difficulty), ægrè, difficultèr
Narrowness, angustia
Nastily, fœdè, naturalitèr
Nastiness, sordes, spurcities
Nasty, fœdus, squalidus, sordidus
Natal, natalis
A nation, natio, gens
Of a nation, gentilis, è gente
National, ad nationem pertinens
Native, nativus, innatus
A native, indigena
Nativity, nativitas, partus
Of a nativity, natalitius
Natural, naturalis, nativus, radicalis; (foolish), stultus, insipiens; (spurious), spurius, nothus; (on its own accord), sponte nascens
Natural disposition, indoles
A naturalist, rerum naturalium investigator [donare
To naturalise, civitate aliquem
Naturalization, civitatis donatio
Naturally, natura, naturalitèr; (of its own accord), ultrò, sponte
Nature, natura; (disposition), ingenium, indoles; (sort), genus
By nature, secundum naturam
Good-natured, affabilis, mitis
Ill-natured, morosus, difficilis
Naval, navalis, nauticus
A nave (of a wheel), modiolus; (of a church), ampla pars

The navel, umbilicus
Like a navel, umbilicatus
Naught, malus, scelestus, nequam
To set at naught, vilipendo
Naughtily, malè, pravè
Naughtiness, malitia, malignitas
Naughty, malus, scelestus
Navigable, navigabilis
To navigate, navigo
Navigation, navigatio
A navigator, navigator
To nauseate, nauseo, fastidio
Nauseous, fastidiosus, putidus
Nauseously, cum nauseâ
Nauseousness, nausea, fastidium
Nautic, nauticus
A navy, vis maritima, classis
Of the navy, classicus, classiarius
The navy-office, curia navalis
Nay, minimè, imò
A saying nay, negatio, repulsa
Neap, decrescens
Near (to a place), vicinus; (in blood), proximus; (in expenses), parcus
Near, adv. proptèr, proximè, penè, ferè, propè
Near, prep. juxta, secundum
Far and near, longè latèque
Near at hand, in promptu
Near now, modò, jam nunc
To be near at hand, adsto, insto
Nearer, propior; adv. propius
Nearest, proximus
Nearly, propè, cautè, parcè
Nearness, proximitas; (of kin), cognatio, affinitas; (niggardliness), parsimonia
Neat, nitidus, scitus, lepidus, accuratus, concinnus, elegans
Very neat, elegantissimus
To be neat, niteo
Neat (black cattle), boves
Neat's tongue, lingua bubula; (feet), pedes bubuli
A neatherd, bubulcus
Neatly, nitidè, elegantèr
Neatness, nitor, concinnitas
Nebulous, nebulosus
Necessary, necessarius
Necessaries of life, necessitates
It is necessary, opus est
A necessary-house, forica
Necessarily, necessariò
To necessitate, cogo, adigo
Necessitous, indigus, egenus, inops
Necessity, necessitas, inopia; (to make a virtue of necessity), errorem in consilium vertere
The neck, collum, cervix; (of an instrument), jugum
A neck of land, isthmus
Neck or nothing, furiosè, inconsultè
A neckcloth, collare
A necklace, monile
A necromancer, veneficus, magus
Necromancy, necromantia
Nectar, nectar
Of nectar, nectareus
A nectarine, nucipersica
Need (want), egestas, inedia, penuria; (necessity), opus, usus, necessitas
To need, egeo, indigeo
I must needs, oportet me
Needful, opus opportunus
It is needful, expedit, convenit
Needfulness, necessitas
Neediness, inopia, indigentia
A needle, acus
Needlework, opus Phrygium, or acupictum; (case), acuum theca

Needless, supervacuus, inutilis
Needs, necesse; (or necessaries), res necessariæ; (to do), alvum levare
Needy, egens, inops, indigens
Nefarious, impius, scelestus
A negation, negatio
A negative, repulsa, negatio
Negatively, negando
Neglect, neglectus, negligentia
To neglect, negligo, omitto
Neglectfully, negligentèr
A neglecting, neglectus
Negligence, negligentia
Negligent, or neglectful, negligens; (person), ignavus, oscitans [mio
To be negligent, negligo, indor-
Negligently, negligentèr
To negotiate, negotior, gero
A negotiation, negotiatio, administratio, transactio
A negotiator, curator
A negro, maurus, æthiops
To neigh, hinnio; (after), adhinnio
A neighing, hinnitus
A neighbour, vicinus, accola, proximus
To be a neighbour, in viciniâ habitare
Neighbourhood, vicinitas, vicinia
Neighbourly, familiaris, benignus
Neighbourly, adv. benignè
Neither, adj. neuter; conj. nec, neque, neu, neve
Neither way, neutrò
Nemoral, nemoralis
Neoteric, neotericus
A nephew, fratris, or sororia filius.
Nephritic, renum morbo laborans
Neptune, Neptunus
A nerve, nervus
Nervous, nervosus, fortis
A ness, promontorium
A nest, nidus; (of boxes, or drawers), nidi; (of thieves), grex furum; (of wasps), vesparum nidulus
To nestle, nidulor; (about), in omnes partes versari
A net, rete, plagæ; (cabbage), excipulus caulium; (drag, or fishing), verriculum, tragum, sagena; (work), opus reticulatum
Like a net, reticulatus, retiformis; adv. reticulatim
To take in a net, irretio
The net produce, reditus purus; (weight), simplex pondus
Nether, inferior
Nethermost, infimus
Netting, opus reticulatum
A nettle, urtica, lanium
Full of nettles, urticosus
To nettle, or vex, stimulo, pungo
A nettling, stimulatio
Nettling, stimulans, mordax
Never (no or not), nullus, ne unus; (at no time), nunquàm; non unquàm; (never the), nihilò
Nevertheless, nihilominùs
Never a whit, nihil quicquam
Never before, nunc primùm
Never after, nunquàm dehinc
Never so great, ut ut maximus
Never so often, usquè
Neuter, neuter, media
To stand neuter, neutri parti se adjungere
Neutrality, neutram in partem propensio, or inclinatio
New, novus, integer, recens
New things, nova

[80]

NIN — NON — NOT

New year's day, festum circumcisionis Dominicæ
A new year's gift, strena
To make new, innovo, instauro
To grow new, integrasco
New-coined, novatus, fictus
Anew (over again), denuò, ab integro
Newly, nupèr, nuperrimè
Newness, novitas
News, novitas, novellæ, fama, rumor, res novæ
A newsmonger, rerum novarum studiosus, ardelio
A newspaper, novellæ scriptæ
Next, *adj.* proximus, vicinus; *adv.* deindè, deincèps ; (after, *or* to), juxta, secundum
The next day, postridiè
A uib (of a bird), rostrum ; (of a pen), cuspis, crena calami
To nibble, rodo, carpo
Nibbling, rodens, morsicans
Nice (dainty), delicatus ; (exact), accuratus ; (dangerous, *or* ticklish), periculosus ; (difficult), difficilis ; (hard to be pleased), morosus ; (effeminate), mollis
Nicely, delicatè, bellè, accuratè
Niceness, mollities, accuratio
Niceties, cupediæ
Nicety, mollitia, mollities ; (in work), elegantia ; (in style), concinnatus
A niche, statuæ loculamentum
A nick, crena, incisura
In the nick of time, opportunè
To nick, incido
A nickname, nomen probrosum
To nickname, contumelioso nomine appellare
Nidorous, nidorem reddens
A niece, fratris, *or* sororis filia
A niggard, avarus, parcus
Niggardliness, avaritia, sordes
Niggardly, avarus, parcus, sordidus
Niggardly, avarè, parcè
Nigh, *adj.* vicinus, propinquus; *adv.* propè, juxtà, proptèr, secundum
To be nigh, adsum
To draw nigh, insto, appropinquo
Nigher, propior
Nighest, proximus
Nighness, proximitas
A night, nox
All night, per totam noctem
By night, nocte, noctu ; (and day), nocte diuque
This night, hâc nocte
Of the night, nocturnus
A nightwalker, noctivagus
Two nights, binoctium
A nightcap, pileus nocturnus
A nightgown, toga cubicularis
A nightingale, luscinia, philomela
Nightly, singulis noctibus
Nimble, agilis, velox, celer
Nimbleness, agilitas
Nimbly, agilitèr, expeditè
Nine, novem, noveni
Of nine, novenarius
Nine times, noviès
Nine at cards, ennœas
Nine days, novendium
Nineteen, novendecim, undeviginti ; (nine and twentieth), undetrigesimus ; (and thirty), undequadraginta ; (and forty), undequinquaginta ; (and fifty), undesexaginta ; (ninety-nine), undecentum
The ninth, nonus, novenarius ; (nineteenth), undevigesimus.
[81]

decimus nonus ; (forty-ninth), undequinquagesimus
Thirty-nine times, undequadragiès
Ninety times, nonagiès
Ninety, nonaginta
Of ninety, nonagenarius
Ninetieth, nonagesimus
Nine hundred, noningenti
Nine hundred times, noningentiès
A ninny, vacerra
A nip, vellicatio
To nip, vello, vellico, digitis stringere ; (off), seco, deseco ; (cruelly), fodico ; (as cold), uro ; (with the teeth), dentibus stringere ; (or taunt), mordeo, uro
Nippers, forceps
A nipping, vellicatus, morsus
Nipping, mordax ; (jest), dicterium
The nipple, papilla
A nit, lens
Nitre, nitrum
Nitrous, nitrosus, nitratus
Nitid, nitidus
Nitty, scatens lendibus
A nizy, *or* nizzy, stultus
No, *adj.* nullus ; *adv.* non, minimè, haud
Nobody, nemo ; (but I), ego verò solus
By no means, nequaquàm, minimè
No more, nihil amplius
To no purpose, frustrà [nusquam
No where, *or* whither, nullibi,
To nobilitate, nobilito
Nobility, nobilitas
The nobility, nobiles, proceres
Noble (illustrious), nobilis, illustris, insignis, clarus, splendidus ; (generous, *or* free), liberalis, generosus, munificus ; (stately), magnificus ; (brave), heroïcus
A nobleman, vir amplissimus ; (woman), fœmina primaria
Noblemen, optimates
A noble (money), tertia pars libræ
Nobleness, claritas, splendor ; (of soul), magnanimitas ; (rosè)
Nobly, præclarè, magnificè, generosè
Nocturnal, nocturnus
A nod, nutus ; (in sleeping), somnus brevis, *or* levis
To nod, nuto, nuo ; (or sleep), dormito ; (to), annuo
A nodding, nutatio, nutus
Nodding, nutans, dormitans
A noddy, fatuus, stultus
A noggin, cotyla, lagena
A noise, sonitus, clamor, strepitus ; (report), rumor ; (of thunder), fragor
To make a noise, obstrepo
To noise abroad, promulgo
Without noise, tacitus, silens
Making a noise, obstrepens ; (on high), altisonus ; (like waves), undisonus
It is noised about, rumor est
Noisiness, clamor
Noisome, nocens, noxius, gravis
Noisomeness, spurcities, fœtor
Noisy, clamosus, rixosus
The nombles, exta cervina
A nomenclator, nomenclator
A nomenclature, nomenclatura
Nominal, nominalis
Nominally, nomine, disertè
To nominate, nomino, designo
A nominating, *or* nomination, nominatio, designatio
Nominative, nominativus, rectus
Nonage, infantia

A nonconformist, dissentiens
None, nullus, non ullus
Nonpayment, solutio non præstita
Nonperformance, inopia præstationis
The nones, nonæ
A nonplus, incita [religere
To nonplus (puzzle), ad incitas
Nonresidence, absentia
Nonresident, non residens, absens
Non-resistance, non repugnantia
Nonsense, absurdà dictum
Nonsensical, absurdus, ineptus
Nonsensically, absurdè, ridiculè
Nonsensicalness, ineptiæ
A nonsuit, litis desertio ; (to suffer), formulâ cadere
A noodle, hebes, stultus
A nook, angulus, latebra
Noon, meridies
Of noon, meridianus
Afternoon, pomeridianus
The afternoon, tempus pomeridianum
Before noon, antemeridianus
A noose, laqueus nexilis
To noose, irretio, illaqueo
Nor, nec, neque
The north, septentrio
Of the north, septentrionalis, arcticus, boreus, borealis
The north-star, stella polaris
The north-wind, boreas, aquilo
North-east-wind, cæcias
North-west, caurus
North-westerly, caurinus
Northerly, borealis . [regula
A nose, nasus ; (of wax), Lesbia
With a great nose, nasutus
A nosegay, florum fasciculus
Flat-nosed, simus
Hawk-nosed, camurus, aquilinus
The nostrils, nares
Not, non, ne, haud, minùs, nec, neque
Not at all, nullo modo, nequaquàm, ne minimè ; (not yet), nondùm, vixdùm ; (not so), minimè, neutiquàm, nequaquàm ; (not any), nullus
Notable (considerable), illustris, insignis, eximius, spectabilis
Notable (very), valdè, vehementèr
To be notable, eniteo, clareo
Notableness, claritas, dexteritas
Notably, eximiè, egregiè, benè
A notary, notarius
Done by a notary, in publicas tabulas illatus
Notation, notatio
A notch, incisura
To notch, incido, denticulo
A notching, incisio
A note (mark), signum, nota ; (bill), syngrapha ; (observation), annotatio, observatio ; (in music), tonus, modus
Of note, notabilis, illustris, clarus, egregius, eximius
Of little note, obscurus, ignotus
To note (mark), noto, assigno ; (observe), observo, animadverto ; (set down), scripto mandare [gratis
Nothing, nihil ; (for nothing), Good for nothing, inutilis, nihili, abjectus, vilis, infimus, nullius momenti, contempti habitus
To make nothing of (do with ease), aliquid facilè facere ; (slight), sperno, contemno ; (not to understand), minimè intelligere ; (not to succeed), nihil promovere
Notice (knowledge), notitia, sci-

E 5

NUM — OBE — OBS

entia, cognitio; (advice), admonitio, monitum
To give notice, notum facere
To receive notice, certior fieri
To take notice, noto, observo; (of a person), saluto
To take no notice of (a person), insalutatum praeterire; (dissemble), dissimulo; (neglect), negligo
A notification, notificatio
To notify, significo, denuncio
A noting, notatio, observatio
Notion (knowledge, or understanding), notio, cognitio, notitia, peritia, scientia; (idea), idea; (opinion), opinio, sententia [mosus
Notorious, manifestus, notus, famous
Notoriously, apertè, manifestò
Notoriousness, Notoriety, evidentia, notitia pervulgata
Notwithstanding, tamen, attamen, nihilominùs, etiamsi, quamvis, licèt, nihilo seciùs
Novel, novus, recens; (unusual), inusitatus
A novel, historia novella
A novelist, fabularum scriptor
Novelty, res nove, novitas
November, November
Nought, nihil; (to nought), ad nihilum; (at nought), nihilo, pro nihilo; (a nought in arithmetic), ciphra
A novice, novitius, tiro
A noun, nomen; (without cases), aptoton; (of one case), monoptoton; (of two cases), diptoton; (of three cases), triptoton
To nourish, nutrio, alo, foveo, nutrico; (or bring up), educo, sustento
Nourishing, nutriens, fovens
Nourishment, alimentum, cibus
Of nourishment, alimentarius
Now, nunc, jam; (a-days), nunc dierum, hodiè, his temporibus; (and then), nonnunquam, identidèm, subindè
Just now, modò, jam jam
Noxious, noxius, nocens, nocivus
Nubilous, nubibus obductus
Nude, nudus, simplex
The nuel, scapus, truncus
Nugatory, nugatorius, ineptus
A nuisance, nocumentum, offensa
Null, irritus, cassus
To null, abrogo, irritum reddere
A nullifidian, nullius fidei homo
A nulling, abrogatio
A nullity, nullitas, nihilum
To numb, stupefacio
To be numbed, torpesco
A number, numerus; (of men), multitudo; (of things), copia
To number, numero, computo
In great number, frequentes
Without number, innumerabilis
Of what number? quotus?
More in number, numerosior
By number, numero
Of number, numeralis
May be numbered, numerabilis, computabilis
A numberer, numerator
A numbering, numeratio; (of names), nomenclatio; (of people), census
Numberless, innumerus
Numbers (book of), Numeri
Numbness, stupor, torpor
Numerable, numerabilis
Numeration, numeratio
Numerical, Numeral, numeralis
[83]

Numerically the same, idem ad numerum
The numerator, numerator
Numerous, numerosus
Numerously, numerosè
A nun, nonna, monialis
A nuncio, legatus papalis
Nuncupative, nuncupativus
A nunnery, domus monialium
Nuptial, nuptialis, conjugalis
Nuptials, nuptiæ
A nurse, nutrix, alumna
A nurse-child, alumnus
A wet nurse, nutrix lactans
A dry nurse, nutrix mercenaria
aine lacte [cillari
Nurse-keeping, ægrotantibus anTo nurse, nutrio, foveo, curo, ancillor
A nursery (for children), cubiculum nutrici appropriatum; (child at nurse), alumnus; (of learning), seminarium doctrinæ, academia; (of plants), seminarium, plantarium
A nursing, nutricatio; (of the sick), nutricium, curatio; (father), nutritius
A nursling, delicatus puer
Nurture, educatio, alimentum, disciplina
To nurture, educo, instituo
To nustle, indulgeo, foveo
A nut, nux; (of a screw), theca; (cracker), nucifrangibulum; (kernel), nucleus; (shell), putamen; (of a musical instrument), magas; (of a crossbow), astragalus; (of a leg of mutton), glans coxæ ovinæ
A nutmeg, nux moschata
Nutriment, nutrimentum
Nutrition, nutritio
Nutritive, nutrimentum præbens
To nuzzle in bed, lecto indulgere
A nymph, nympha

O.

O, adv. O
O, inter. O! Oh! utinam!
An oaf, stultus, hebes
Oafish, insulsus, fatuus
An oak, quercus, robur
Oaken, quernus, querceus, roboreus
An oak-grove, quercetum
An oar, remus, tonsa
A pair of oars, scapha biremis
Oatmeal, avenacea farina
An oatmeal man, avenarius
Of oatmeal, Oaten, avenaceus
An oath, juramentum, jusjurandum; (military), sacramentum; (solemn), dejurium
To take the oath of allegiance, in regis verba jurare; (to keep the laws), in leges jurare
A false oath, perjurium
With an oath, jurejurando, persancta, juratò
Oats, avena
Wild oats, bromus sterilis
Obambulation, obambulatio
Obduracy, obstinatio
Obdurate, induratus, pertinax
To be obdurate, obduresco
Obdurately, pertinacitèr
Obdurateness, obstinatio, rigor
Obedience, obedientia, obsequium
Under obedience, sub potestate
Obedient, obediens, obsequens

Obediently, obedientèr, obsequentèr
Obeisance, salutatio
To make an obeisance, capite inclinato, or poplite flexo, aliquem salutare
An obelisk, obeliscus
Obesity, obesitas
To obey, obedio, obsequor, pareo
An object, objectum, res oblata; (of sense), quod sentitur; (of sight), quod oculis percipitur; (of love), dignus amore; (of one's wishes), optabile; (pleasant), res venusta
To object, objicio, oppono
Objecting, objiciens, culpans, carpens
An objection, objectio
Objective, quod objici potest; (pertaining to an object), ad rem objectam spectans
An obit, feralia
To objurgate (chide), objurgo
An oblation, oblatio
An oblectation, oblectamentum
To obligate, obligo, devincio
An obligation, obligatio, meritum, vadimonium
Obligatory, obligatorius
To oblige (compel), cogo, impello; (one by kindness), benè de aliquo mereri
An obliger, qui tradit syngrapham
Obliging (courteous), comis, blandus, affabilis; (kind, or liberal), liberalis, beneficus; (forcing), cogens
Obligingly, benignè, comitèr
Obligingness, comitas, affabilitas
Oblique, obliquus
Obliquely, obliquè
Obliqueness, Obliquity, obliquitas
To obliterate, deleo, expungo
Oblivion, oblivio, oblivium; (an act of oblivion), amnestia
Oblong, oblongus
Obloquy, contumelia, infamia
Obnoxious, obnoxius, expositus
Obscene, obscœnus, impurus
Obscenely, obscœnè, impurè
Obsceneness, Obscenity, obscœnitas
Obscure (dark), tenebrosus, caliginosus; (difficult), obscurus, difficilis; (in person), ignotus, ignobilis; (style), intortus
To make obscure, obscuro
Obscurely, obscurè, occultè
Obscurity, obscuritas; (to be in obscurity), abditus esse [bius
Full of obscurity, ambiguus, duAn obsecration, obsecratio
Obsequies, exequiæ [rus
Obsequious, obsequens, morigeTo be obsequious, obsequor
Obsequiously, obsequentèr
Obsequiousness, obsequium
Observable, insignis, notabilis
Observance, observantia
Observant, observans, obediens
An observation, observatio
An observatory, specula ex quâ sidera observantur
To observe, observo, noto; (dutifully), obedio, colo; (laws), legibus parere, or obedire
An observer, observator
Observing, observans, notans
Obsolete, obsoletus, antiquatus
To grow obsolete, obsolesco
An obstacle, impedimentum
Obstinacy, contumacia, pertinacia
Obstinate, pertinax, obstinatus; (in opinion), tenax

To be obstinate, animum obfirmare
Obstinately, obstinatè, mordicùs
Obstreperous, obstrepens
To be obstreperous, vociferor
To obstruct (hinder), impedio, obsto; (stop up), obstruo
Obstructing, Obstruction, obstructio
Obstructive, impediens
To obtain, obtineo, potior; (by chance), sortior; (by request), impetro, exoro; (favour), gratiam inire; (as a custom), inveterasco; (or get ground), supero, vinco; (by flattery), blandior
Obtainable, impetrabilis
Having obtained liberty, libertatis compos; (his wish), voti compos
An obtaining, adeptio, impetratio
To obtrude, obtrudo, impono
An obtruder, qui sese aliis obtrudit
Obtuse, obtusus, hebes
Obtusely, obtusè
Obtuseness, hebetudo
Obventions, obventiones
To obviate, præverto, præripio
An obviating, anteoccupatio
Obvious, obvius
To obumbrate, obumbro
Occasion (opportunity), occasio, opportunitas; (cause, or reason), causa, materia, ansa; (need, or want), opus, usus
To occasion (make), facio; (procure), paro, concito, excito; (grief, joy, &c.), alicui causa doloris, gaudii, &c. esse; (vomiting), vomitum movere
Occasions (business), negotia
Occasional, ansam præbens, accommodans
Occasionally, pro re natâ
Occidental, occidentalis
Occult, occultus, abditus
Occupancy, occupatio
An occupation, occupatio, negotium, ars, artificium, res
Occupation (tenure), possessio
Occupied, occupatus, cultus
An occupier, possessor, cultor
To occupy, occupo, colo; (in business), in arte, or negotio se occupare; (the place of another), alterius locum supplere, or vice fungi
An occupying, occupatio, cultus
To occur, occurro, obvenio
An occurrence, occasio, casus
Occurring, obvius
The ocean, oceanus
Octangular, octo habens angulos
An octave (eight days), ogdoas; (in music), diapason
October, October
Ocular, ocularius
An oculist, medicus ocularius
Odd (not even), impar; (fantastical), levis; (uncommon), inusitatus
Oddly, insolitè, insolentèr
Oddness, raritas, insolentia
Odds, lites, discordia, dissensio, inimicitiæ; (difference), discrimen
An ode, ode, cantilena
Odious, odiosus, invisus
Odiously, odiosè, invidiosè
Odiousness, qualitas rei odiosæ
An odium, odium
Odoriferous, odoratus, odorifer
To make odoriferous, odoro

[83]

Odorous, odorus
An odour, odor
Œconomical, domesticus
An œconomist, œconomus
Œconomy, œconomia
Œcumenical, generalis
O'er (over), super, supra
Of, à, ab, de, è, ex
Off, hinc, abhinc; (off and on), utcunquè, mediocritèr
Far off, procul
From off, de
To be off, muto
Off hand, continuò, confestim
Offals, reliquiæ
An offence (displeasure), offensio; (fault), offensa, culpa, flagitium; (affront), injuria, contumelia
To be an offence to one, offensione alicui esse
To offend, erro, pecco, delinquo, offendo, displiceo, lædo, læcsso; (the laws), violo
An offender, delinquens, reus
Offending, nocens, lædens
Offensive (weapons), arma lædentia; (in words), ingratus, molestus; (to the stomach), stomacho ingratus
Offensively, injuriosè, molestè
Offensiveness, qualitas noxia
An offer (attempt), conatus; (thing offered), res oblata, conditio
To offer, offero, præbeo; (or bid money), licitor; (propose), propono; (dedicate), dedico, dico; (attempt), conor; (up a request), supplico; (itself), occurro; (in sacrifice), sacrifico, immolo
An offering, oblatio, donum; (of a sacrifice), immolatio
An offertory, offertorium
An office (good turn), officium, beneficium; (public charge), munus, magistratus; (place of business), officina; (workhouse), taberna operaria; (house of office), latrina, forica
An officer (or magistrate), magistratus; (in the army), dux, præfectus; (of state), maximis reipublicæ muneribus præpositus; (serjeant, or bailiff), lictor; (of excise), publicanus; (chief officers), magnates
An official, surrogatus
To officiate (in business), officium præstare, munus implere; (as a clergyman), rem divinam facere; (for another), alterius vice fungi
Officinal, ad officinam pertinens
Officious, officiosus, obsequiosus
Not officious, inofficiosus
Officiously, officiosè
Officiousness, officium, obsequium
The offing, mare apertum
An offset, surculus
Offscouring, purgamentum
An offspring, proles, progenies, propago, soboles
Offward, versus mare
Often, adj. frequens
Often, adv. sæpe, crebrò, frequentèr, sæpenumerò; (very often), sæpissimè; (how often), quoties; (how often soever), quotiescunquè; (as often as), toties quoties; (so often), totiès; (not often), rarò; (too often), sæpius, nimis, sæpè
Oftentimes, multotiès, sæpè

Oh! oh! ah!
Oil, oleum
Of oil, olearis, olearius
An oilman, olearius
An oil-stone (for painters), abacus pigmentarius triturœ
To oil, inungo, oleo unguere
Mixed with oil, oleatus
An oilet-hole, ocellus
Oiliness, oleacitas
An oiling, inunctio
Oily, oleosus
Ointment, unguentum
Of ointment, unguentarius
An oister, ostrea; (pit), ostrearium; (shell), testa; (man), ostrearius; (woman), ostrearia
Abounding with oisters, ostreosus
Oker, ochra; (red), rubrica
Old, antiquus, priscus, pristinus, vetus; (in age), annosus, ætate provectus, senex; (out of use), obsoletus; (worn), exesus, tritus
An old man, senex; grandævus; (woman), anicula, vecula, anus
Like an old woman, anilis; adv. anilitèr
Old age, senectus, senecta
Of old age, senilis
Somewhat old, grandior, senior
Very old, senio confectus
Of old, olim, jampridèm, priscâ, antiquitùs, apud veteres
To grow old (by continuance), inveterasco; (as a man), senesco; (out of use), exolesco
Oldness, antiquitas, vetustas
Oleaginous, oleagineus
An oligarchy, oligarchia
An olitory, hortus olitorius
An olive, oliva; (tree), olea; (grove), olivetum; (yard), olivina
An olympiad, olympias
Olympic, olympicus
An omen, omen
Ominous, ominosus, portentosus
Ominously, ominosè
An omission, omissio
To omit, omitto, prætermitto, intermitto, negligo
An omitting, prætermissio
Omnipotence, omnipotentia
Omnipotent, omnipotens
Omnipresent, ubiquè existens
Omniscient, omnisciens, omniscius
On, à, ab, ad, cum, de, è, ex, in, secundum, sub, super
On (go on), age, eja, progredere
Once, semel; (on a time), olim, quondam
One, unus; (any), aliquis; (every), singulus
One another, mutuò; (after another), adj. alternus; adv. invicèm; (with another), adj. promiscuus; adv. promiscuè; (or the other), alteruter
One thing, unum
One by one, singulatim
On one side, hinc, ex hâc parte
One while, modò, nunc
Only, adj. unicus, solus; adv. solùm, duntaxat, tantùm
An onion, cepa, cepe
An onion-bed, cepetum
An onset, impetus
Onwards, prorsùm, deinceps
An onyx-stone, onyx
Oosy, palustris, paludosus
Opacity, opacitas
Opake, opacus

E 6

OR   ORG   OVE

Open, patens, apertus, patulus; (evident), evidens, manifestus, clarus; (candid, sincere), ingenuus, candidus, simplex
To open, aperio, resero; (a letter), resigno; (a discourse), ordior; (a campaign), in expeditionem educere; (the pores), recludo.
To be open, pateo, patefio
Open-handed, liberalis; (hearted), sincerus
Open-heartedness, liberalitas
In the open air, sub dio
Opening, aperiens, reserans
An opening, apertio; (in the earth), hiatus; (of dogs), latratus; (of a root), ablaqueatio; (or expounding), explicatio
Openly, apertè, palàm; (in sight), coràm; (plainly), perspicuè; (sincerely), sincerè, candidà
Openness (sincerity), candor; (of the weather), cœli temperies humida et calida
To operate, operor, ago
An operation, operatio; (of a campaign), belli actiones
Operative, operans
An operator, opifex
Operose, arduus, difficilis
Ophthalmic, ophthalmicus
An opiate, potio, soporifera
An opinion (sentiment), opinio, sententia, mens, animus; (esteem), existimatio
To hold an opinion, judico, censeo; (to be of another's opinion), assentio, consentio; (to be of a contrary opinion), dissentio
Opinionated, pertinax, pervicax
Opinionative, pertinax
Opinionatively, pertinaciter
Opinionativeness, pertinacia
Opium, opium
An opponent, opponens
Opportune, opportunus, tempestivus
Opportunely, opportunè
Opportunity, opportunitas, occasio; (leisure), otium
To oppose (object to), oppono, objicio; (resist), repugno, resisto, adversor
An opposer, oppugnator
Opposite (contrary to), oppositus, objectus, adversus; (over against), è regione, ex adverso
An opposing, or opposition, oppositio, oppositus; (obstacle), impedimentum, mora
In opposition to nature, repugnante naturà
To oppress, opprimo, premo
An oppression, oppressio
Oppressive, opprimens   [tor
An oppressor, oppressor, spoliaOpprobrious, probrosus; (speech), opprobrium, contumelia
Opprobriously, contumeliosè
Opprobriousness, contumelia
To oppugn, oppono, adversor
Optative, optativus
Optic, optical, opticus
An optic glass, telescopium
Optics (science of), optice
An optician, opticees peritus
Option (choice), optio
Opulence, opulentia, opes
Opulent, opulentus, dives
Opulently, opulenter, opiparè
Or, an, vel, seu, sive, ne
Or else (either), aut, vel; (whether), sive, an; (otherwise), aliàs, aliter

[84]

Or ever, cum nondùm, antequàm
An oracle, oraculum; (of wisdom), sapientiæ antistes
Oracular, sapientissimus
Oral, verbo traditus
An orange, malum aureum
An orange-tree, malus aurea; (colour), color aureus
An oration, oratio, concio
To make an oration, concionor, verba facere, divulgo
An orator, orator
Like an orator, eloquenter, disertè
Oratory, rhetorice
An oratory, sacellum
An orb, orbis
Orbicular, orbiculatus
Orbicularly, orbiculatim
An orbit, orbita
An orchard, pomarium; (of cherries), cerasetum
To ordain, ordino, instituo; (order), jubeo, impero; (a law), sancire legem; (as a bishop), sacris initiare
An ordainer, ordinator
An ordaining, ordinatio, institutio, latio
Ordeal, ordalium; (fire), ignis sententia
Order (disposition), ordo, dispositio; (custom), mos, ritus, consuetudo; (decree), decretum, mandatum, præceptum, præscriptum; (rank), series; (of words), consecutio verborum; (of authority), edictum
By my order, me jubente; (in order to), ut; (in order, or from), ex ordine, ordinatè; (in order, adj.) aptus, maturus
Out of order, turbatus, confusus
To order (or put in order), ordino, dispono; (give order), impero, jubeo, constituo; (affairs), provideo; (as a judge), pronuncio; (govern), moderor, rego, tempero
Out of order, without order, incompositè, confusè; (sick), ægrotus; (without command), injussu
An ordering, dispositio, digestio, curatio, administratio
Orderly (set in order), compositus, digestus; (obedient), obediens; (sober, quiet), modestus, temperatus
Orderly (adv.), aptè, idoneè
Orders, instituta, regulationes; (holy), sacri ordines
To take orders, sacris initiari
Ordinal, ordinalis, ritualis
An ordinance, edictum
Ordinarily, usitatè, ferè
Ordinary (customary), consuetus, usitatus; (common), vulgaris, obvius, tritus, quotidianus; (indifferent), mediocris; (not handsome), invenustus, partim decorus
An ordinary (of a diocese), episcopus; (eating-house), popina, caupona
An ordination, ordinatio sacra
Ordnance, bombardæ
Ordure, simus, stercus
Ore, metallum crudum
An organ (instrument), instrumentum, organum; (musical), organa musica
Organic, organicus
Organs of the body, instrumenta corporis organica
An organist, organicus

To organize, effingo, formo
Orient, oriens; (bright or beautiful), splendens, nitidus, rutilus, venustus, egregius
Oriental, orientalis
An orifice, os, orificium
An origin (source, or beginning), origo, fons, initium, primordium, principium, ortus, exordium; (cause), causa; (motive), occasio, ansa; (subject-matter), materia, argumentum
An original (to copy from), exemplar; (first draught), prototypon; (writing), autographum
Original, autographus, archetypus; (born with one), avitus, congenitus, innatus, nativus, ingenitus
Original (descent, or birth), genus, stirps, prosapia; (etymology), notatio, etymon; (text), textus
Originally, primitùs, ab origine
Orisons, preces, orationes
An ornament, ornamentum, ornatus, decus; (for the neck), monilia; (for gates, porches, &c.), antepagmenta
To be an ornament to, decori esse
Without ornament, inornatus
Ornamental, decorus, speciosus
An orphan, pupillus, pupilla
Orthodox, orthodoxus
Orthodoxly, orthodoxè
Orthodoxy, recta fides   [los
Orthogonal, rectos habens anguOrthographical, orthographicus
Orthography, orthographia
Oscillation, oscillatio
Oscitancy, oscitatio, incuria
An osier, vitex, salix
Of osiers, vimineus
Ostentation, ostentatio
Ostentatious, ambitiosus, magnificus   [ficè
Ostentatiously, ambitiosè, magniOsteology, osteologia
An ostler, stabularius
Ostracism, ostracismus
Ostrich, Struthi camelus
Other, alius; (any other), alius quispiam
The other, alter
Some or other, nonnulli
The other day, nudiustertiùs
Otherwhere, alibi
Otherwise, aliàs, aliter
Otherwise (adj.), aliusmodi
Every other, alternus
Some time or other, aliquandò
An otter, lutra
Oval, ovatus; (figure), figura ovata, or ad formam ovi
Ovation, ovatio
An oven, furnus, clibanus
An oven-tender, furnarius
Of an oven, furnaceus
Over (prep.), super, supra, per, trans, in; (adv.), nimis, nimiùm, plùs, ex nimio; (and above), præterea, insuper; (and over again), iterùm ac sæpius; (much, adj.) nimius; adv. nimis, nimiò, nimiùm
Over against, ex adverso
Over-night, præcedente nocte
To be over, defervesco, desino, mitigor; (or rule), præsum; (left), supersum
All over, per totum
Over or under, plùs minùs
To overact, plùs quàm satis est facere

OVE — OUT — OZI

To overawe, metu coërcere
Overbig, prægrandis
Overboard, è nave
Overbold, temerarius
Overborne, superatus, victus
Overcast, obnubilus, tristis
An overcasting, obductio
To overcharge, plus æquo onerare; (the stomach), stomachum crapulâ opprimere
An overcharging, onus injustum; (of the stomach), crapula
Over-clouded, obnubilus, tristis
To overcome, vinco, supero
Not to be overcome, invictus, inexpugnabilis
Over-curious, nimis curiosus
To overeat, satio
To overflow, inundo, exundo, redundo
An overflowing, inundatio
Overfond, nimis cupidus
To overgo, prætereo, transeo
An overgoing, transitus
To overgrow, supercresco
Overgrown (with weeds), noxiis herbis obductus; (with age), ætate gravis, prægrandis
To overhale, examino
Overhappy, nimis fortunatus
To overhasten, præcipito
Overhastiness, præcipitatio
Overhasty, præproperus, præceps
Overhastily, præproperè
To overhear, subausculto
An overhearing, subauscultatio
To overheat, excalefacio
Overjoyed, nimio gaudio perfusus
To overlay, incubando suffocare
To overlive, supersum
To overload, nimis onerare
Overlong, prælongus
To overlook (inspect), inspicio, intueor; (take care of), curo, accuro, provideo; (neglect), prætermitto, negligo; (pardon), condono; (scorn), contemno, despicio; (be higher), supereminco
An overlooking (inspection), inspectio; (taking care of), curatio; (neglecting), prætermissio; (pardoning), condonatio
To overmatch, viribus superare
An overmatch, iniquum certamen
Overmeasure, auctarium
Overmuch, nimis, nimius
Overnight, nocte præteritâ
Overofficious, nimis officiosus
To overpass, transgredior; (excel), supero
Overpast, præteritus
An overplus, additamentum, auctarium; (of weight), superpondium
To be overplus, resto, supersum
To overpoise, præpondero
To overpower, viribus vincere, opprimo
To over-rate, nimiùm æstimare
An over-rating, iniqua æstimatio
To over-reach, circumvenio; (hurt one's self in reaching), se nimis extendendo lædere
An over-reacher, fraudator
An over-reaching, fraudatio
Over-ripe, præmaturus
To over-rule, vinco, guberno
To over-run (outrun), cursu præterire; (cover all over), coöperio; (destroy), vasto, depopulor
Over-righteous, superstitiosus
Over-sea, transmarinus
To oversee, curo
Overseen (mistaken), deceptus
[85]

To be overseen, erro
An overseer, inspector, curator; (of the poor), pauperum procurator
To overset, everto, opprimo
To overshadow, obumbro
An overshadowing, obumbratio
To overshoot, transgredi metam; (one's self), consilio labi
An oversight, error, incuria
The oversight, inspectio, curatio
To overspread, obduco, operior
An overspreading, obductio
Overstocked, redundans
To overstrain, or overstretch, nimis extendere
Overt (open), apertus, manifestus
Overtly (slightly), perfunctoriè
To overtake, assequor
An overtaking, clades, strages
To overthrow (demolish), subverto, diruo; (defeat), prosterno, devinco, supero; (a kingdom), regnum evertere
An overthrower, eversor, victor
An overthrowing, eversio
Overthwart, transversus, obliquus
Overtly, apertâ, manifestè
To overtop (in height), emineo, superemineo; (in excellence), antecello, præsto
An overture, propositio
To overturn, everto, subverto
An overturning, subversio
To overvalue, pluris justo æstimare
Overweening, arrogans, superbus
To overweigh, præpondero
Overweight, auctarium
To overwhelm, obruo; (with earth), terrâ infodere; (with water), aquâ immergere
Ought (any thing), res, quicquam; (or good for ought), frugi
Oviparous, oviparus
An ounce, uncia; (beast), lynx
Of an ounce, uncialis
Half an ounce, semuncia; (an ounce and half), sescuncia; (two ounces troy weight), sextans; (three ounces), triens; (four ounces), quadrans; (five ounces), quincunx
The fourth part of an ounce, sicilicium; (the sixth part), sextula; (eight part), drachma; (twenty-fourth part), scriptulum
By ounces, unciatim
Our, or ours, noster
Of our country, nostras
To oust, ejicio, rescindo
Out of, â, ab, de, è, ex, extra, præ
Out of doubt, proculdubiò; (out of doors), foris; (out of hand), properè, citò
Out, get out, apage!
The time is out, tempus elapsum est
Out of patience, impatiens
Out of place (disordered), confusus; (of office), officio privatus; (of pocket), damnum ex impensis; (of sight), oculis subductus; (of sorts), ineptus ad agendum
Out of use, desuetus
Out of time, intempestivus
Out of the way, devius
Out of one's wits, demens
Out of breath, anhelus
To be out of the way (absent), absum; (stray), aberro; (deceived), hallucinor; (out of memory), è memoriâ elabi;

(out of hope), despero; (out of humour), irascor; (out of one's wits), insanio
To outbid, pluris licitari
To outbrave, territo, insulto
Outbraved, metu absterritus
An outbraving, insultatio
To outbrazen, audaciâ vincere
An outcast, ejectus
An outcry, quiritatio, exclamatio; (public sale), auctio
To outdo, supero, excello
Outer, exterus, externus
To outface, pertinaciissimè adversari
To outgo, præcedo, præverto
An outgoing, prægressio
Outjutting, projectilis
Outlandish, peregrinus, externus
Outlandish person, alienigena
To outlast, diutius durare
To outlaw, proscribo
An outlaw, exul
An outlawry, proscriptio
An outlet, exitus
An outline, linea exterior
To outlive, supersum
An outliver, superstes
The utmost, extremus, extimus
To outnumber, numero superare
An outrage, atrox injuria
Outrageous, ferox, furiosus
To be outrageous, furo
Outrageously, furiosè, atrociter
Outrageousness, furor
To outreach (cheat), fallo, circumvenio
To outride, equitando superare
Outright, prorsùs, omninò
To outrun, cursu vincere
The outside, superficies; (of price), pretium maximum
On the outside, extrinsecùs
To outstrip, præcurro, anteeo
To outwalk, ambulando superare
Outward, exterus, externus
Outward show, prætextus
Outwardly, exteriùs
To outweigh, præpondero
To outwit, circumvenio
Outwitted, astutiâ victus
Outworks, antemurale
To owe, debeo
Owed, or owing, debitus
An owing, debitio
An owl, bubo, noctua; (screechowl), strix
An owler (smuggler), qui merces illicitè invehit, er exportat
One's own, proprius, suus
One's own estate, peculium; (one's own right), propriâ personâ
Of one's own accord, ultro, sponte
To own, fateor, confiteor, agnosco; (claim), vendico, assero; (possess), possideo
An owner, dominus
An owning, agnitio
An ox, bos
Of place (disordered), con-Out of place (disordered), con-
An ox-stall, bovile
Oxen, boves
Oxymel, oxymel
A commission of oyer and terminer, commissio ad causas criminosas audiendas et terminandas
O yes! audite!
An oyster. See Oister
An ozier, salix, vimen; (ground), salictum

PAI   PAN   PAR

P.

A pace (in going), gradus, gressus, incessus; (herd of asses), caterva; (in measuring, five feet), passus
Apace, celeritèr
To pace (as a horse), tolutim incedere
A pacer, equus tolutaris
Pacing, tolutaris, tolutarius
Pacific, pacificus, pacificatorius
A pacification, pacificatio
A pacificator, pacificator
To pacify, paco, pacifico, sedo, mulceo, mitigo, lenio; (again), remulceo; (a tumult), tumultuantes compescere
That may be pacified, placabilis
No pacified, implacatus
Not to be pacified, implacabilis
A pacifier, pacificator
Pacifying, pacificatorius
A pacifying, placatio, sedatio
A pack (bundle), fascis; (burden), onus; (crew), conventus, turba; (of cards), fasciculus; (of hounds), grex canum; (of knaves), grex flagitiosorum; (of wool), lanæ fascia; (horse), jumentum sarcinarium; (thread), filum sarcinarium; (saddle), clitellæ
Of a pack, sarcinarius
To pack (make up), consarcino; (or go away), fugio; (or drive away), amoveo, fugo; (cards), chartas pictas componere; (up one's awls), vasa colligere
A packer, suffarcinator
A packet (little pack), fasciculus, sarcinula; (boat), navis actuaria ad literas comportandas; (of letters), literarum fasiculus
A packing, mercium in fasces colligatio
To send packing, abigo
A paction, or pact, pactum, pactio, couventum
A pad, pannus suffarcinatus; (for a horse), ephippium; (of straw), culcita stramentitia; (nag), mannus; (lock), sera pensilis
To pad (stuff), suffarcino; (rob), prædor, latrocinor
A pad (on the highway), latro
A paddle, agito
A paddle, remus curtus
A paddling, agitatio
A paddock (park), septum
A pagan, paganus, ethnicus
Paganism, Paganismus
A page (attendant), assecla; (soldier's), calo, lixa; (of honour), ephebus honorarius; (of a book), pagina, pagella
To page a book, paginas notare
A pageant, spectaculum, ludus; (carried in triumph), ferculum
Pageantry, ostentatio, pompa
A pail, situla; (for milk), mulctra, mulctrale
Pain (punishment), pœna, supplicium; (of the mind), cura, dolor, anxietas
To be in pain, doleo; (for one's safety), de alicujus incolumitate dubitare; (be full of pain), summo dolore affici; (put to pain), crucio; (give pain), dolorem alicui inurere
Painful, crucians, dolorem afferens; (difficult), arduus, difficilis; (laborious), laboriosus, sedulus
Painfully, ægrè, impigrè
Pains, labor, industria; (punishment), pœna, supplicium
To take pains, laboro, molior
A painstaker, laboriosus, industrius
With great pains, ægrè, difficultèr
Paint, pigmentum, cerussa
To paint, depingo, pingo; (or beautify), orno, exorno
A painter, pictor
Painting, depingens, pingens
A painting, res picta; (art), ars pingendi coloribus
A pair (couple), par; (of bellows), follis; (of breeches), femoralia; (of scales), scalæ
A loving pair, conjuges venusti
To pair (match), accommodo, apto; (couple), copulo, conjungo
A pairing (matching), accommodatio; (coupling), conjunctio
A palace, palatium, regia
Of a palace, palatinus
Palatable, grati soporis, gratus
To palate, gusto, degusto
The palate, palatum
Palatine, palatinus
A palatinate, palatinatus
A pale, palus, sudes
To pale, sudibus obsepire
Paled, sudibus munitus
Pale (in colour), pallidus, pallens
To be pale, palleo, expalleo
To grow pale, pallesco
Palefaced, oris luridi
Paleness, pallor
A palfrey, caballus
A palisade, palorum ordo
Palish, subpallidus
A pall (robe), pallium, palla; (for a coffin), loculi operimentum, pannus feretrum tegens
To pall (die), vappesco; (upon the stomach), nauseam creare
A pallet (bed), grabatus; (used by painters), assula
To palliate, dissimulo, celo, elevo, extenuo   [atio
A palliating, dissimulatio, extenuatio
Palliative, imperfectus
Pallid, pallidus
The palm (tree), palma; (fruit), dactylus; (of the hand), palma, vola
A palm (measure), palmus
To palm (handle), manu contrectare; (a die), aleam subdolè subducere; (upon), fraudo
Of the palm, palmeus
Full of palm-trees, palmosus
Palm-Sunday, Dominica palmarum
Of a palm (measure), palmaris
Palmistry, chiromantia
Palpable, palpandus, (manifest), clarus, manifestus, evidens
Palpableness, perspicuitas
Palpably, tactu, apertè, clarè
To palpitate, palpito
A palpitation, palpitatio
The palsy, paralysis; (dead), sideratio paralytica
To palter, prævaricor, prodigo
Paltry, vilis, sordidus, tressis
A paltry knave, balatro; (quean), scortum truobolare
To pamper, indulgeo, curo
A pampering, saginatio
A pamphlet, libellus
A pamphleteer, libellio
A pan, discus, catinus; (for a stool), lasanum, scaphium; (of a gun), scloppeti conceptaculum; (for frying), sartago; (for stewing), authepsa; (warming-pan), thalpolectrum; (the brain-pan), cranium; (knee-pan), genu patella; (brass-pan), ahenum
Panacea, panacea
A pancake, laganum
Pandects, pandectæ
A pander, leno
To play the pander, lenocinor
Playing the pander, lenocinium
A pane, quadra, plaga
A panegyric, oratio panegyrica
A panegyrist, panegyrista
The panel of a jury, panellum
A pang, dolor, angor
Panic (fear), panicum
A pannel (of a horse), dorsuale; (of wainscot), quadra, plaga
A pannier, corbis, cista
Panoply, armatura corpus totum tegens, panoplia
To pant, palpito, subsulto; (for fear), trepido; (for breath), anhelo; (after), valdè expetere
A panther, panthera, pardus
Of a panther, pantherinus
A panting, palpitatio; (for breath), anhelatio; (for fear), trepidatio, tremor
Panting, anhelus, trepidans
A pantofle, crepida, solea
A pantomime, pantomimus
A pantry, panarium
A pap (dug), uber; (of apples), pomorum pulpa; (made for infants), alimentum infantibus paratum
The papacy, papatus
Papal, papalis, pontificius
Papaverous, papavereus
Paper, charta, papyrus; (royal), regia; (fine), augusta; (blotting), bibula; (writing), scriptoria
Made of paper, chartaceus
Belonging to paper, chartarius
Paper, adj. chartarius; (slight), levis, infirmus; (weak in understanding), inconsideratus
To paper, chartâ ornare
A papist, papista
To be on a par, par esse
A parable, parabola
Parabolical, parabolicus
The Paraclete, Paracletus
Parade (pomp), pompa; (ostentation), ostentatio; (place of exercise), locus exercendi
Paradise, paradisus, beatorum sedes
A paradox, paradoxon
Paradoxical, paradoxicus
A paragon, exemplum perfectum, incomparabilis, non æquandus
A paragraph, paragrapha
The parallax, parallaxis
Parallel, parallelus
A parallel (comparison), comparatio, collatio
To parallel, exæquo, confero
Not to be paralleled, incomparabilis
Paralytic, paralyticus
Paramount, supremus
A paramour, procus, amasia, amiculus, amicula
A parapet, lorica
A paraphrase, paraphrasis
To paraphrase, illustro, explano
A paraphrast, paraphrastes
Paraphrastic, paraphrasticus
A parasite, parasitus

[86]

PAR   PAS   PAT

To act the parasite, parasitor
To parboil, levitèr coquere
Parboiled, semicoctus
A parcel (or bundle), fasciculus; (little quantity), particula
By parcels, particulatim
To parcel out, partior [butus
Parcelled out, minutatim distri-
To parch, arefacio, aduro, torreo
Parched, arefactus, adustus
To be parched, areo, aresco
Parching, torridus
A parching, adustio
Parchment, pergamena
Made of parchment, membraneus
Of parchment, membranaceus
Pardon, venia; (general), amnestia, lex oblivionis
To pardon, ignosco, condono, absolvo, remitto [tendus
Pardonable, condonandus, remit-
Not pardonable, veniâ indignus
To be pardoned, condonor
A pardoning, condonatio
To pare, praecido, recido; (about), amputo; (away), abrado; (nails), ungues resecare; (or chip off), destringo
A parent, parens
Parentage, genus, prosapia
A parenthesis, parenthesis
A pargetting, dealbatio
A paring (of nails), praesegmen; (off), resectio; (shovel), pala; (knife), culter sutorius
A parish, parochia
A parish-church, ecclesia parochialis
Of a parish, parochialis
A parishioner, parochus
Parity, paritas, aequalitas
By parity of reason, pari ratione
A park, vivarium
A park-keeper, vivarii custos
A parley, colloquium
To parley, in colloquium venire, colloquor
A parliament, senatus
A parliament-house, senaculum
A parliament-man, senator
Parliamentary, ad senatum pertinens
A parlour, coenaculum, triclinium
Parochial, parochialis
Parole, verbum, fides
Parole, adj. nuncupativus
A paroxysm, paroxysmus
A parricide, parricida; (the crime), parricidium
A parrot, psittacus
To parry, averto
To parse, flecto
Parsimonious, parcus, frugalis
Parsimoniously, parcè, frugalitèr
Parsimoniousness, Parsimony, parsimonia, frugalitas
A parsing, examinatio, or flexio partium orationis
Parsley, apium
A parsnip, pastinaca, siser
A parson of a parish, pastor
A parsonage, parœcia
A part, pars, portio; (duty), munus, officium
A little part, particula
In part, partim, ex parte; (on the other part), ex alterâ parte; (for the most part), maximâ ex parte
To part (divide), divido, partior, dispertio, in partes distribuere; (asunder), separo; (a fray), litem componere; (in two), bipartior; (asunder of itself), dissilio; (depart), digredior, de-
[87]

cedo; (distribute), distribuo; (with), dimitto; (from, or leave), abscedo, abeo
To take part with, participo
To take one's part, à parte stare
Parts (natural), ingenium, indoles
Of good parts, acris judicii
In two parts, adj. bipartitus; adv. bipartitò [què
On all parts, circumquaquè, undi-
To partake of, participo
A partaker, particeps
Partaking, participans
That may be parted, dividuus
Partial (unjust), iniquus; (biassed), partium studio abreptus
Partiality, iniquitas, studium partium
Partially, iniquè, injustè
Particle, dividuus
To participate, participo
Participation, participatio
A participant, particeps
Participial, participialis
Participially, participialitèr
A participle, participium
A particle, particula
Particular, particularis, singularis, proprius, specialis, peculiaris; (person), quidam, quaedam
Particularity, qualitas particularis
To particularise, speciatim recitare
Particularly, particulatim, speciatim, seorsim, singulatim, sigillatim
Parties, factiones
In parties, partibus, per partes
A parting, divisio; (separation), discessio; (from), discessus; (in the middle), bisectio
A partisan (favourer), adjutor, fautor; (weapon), sarissa; (commander's staff), vitis
Partition, partitio; (inclosure), sepimentum; (wall), paries intergerinus
Partly, partim, aliquatenus
A partner, particeps, socius, consors
Partnership, consociatio, societas
A partridge, perdix
Parturition, parturiendi status
A party (person), quidam, quaedam; (faction), factio secta, partes; (detachment), manus
Partycoloured, discolor
A partyman, factiosus
Party-rage, studia partium
The paschal lamb, agnus paschalis
Pasquinade, famosum scriptum publicè propositum
A pass (condition), conditio, status; (passage), angustia, fauces; (passport), commeatus; (in fencing), ictus
To make a pass at, peto
To pass (over), transeo; (an account), rationes exaequare; (a compliment), adblandior; (one's word for), pro aliquo spondere; (sentence), sententiam dicere; (go by), praetereo; (time in a place), degere vitam in
To come to pass, evenio
To let pass, dimitto
To be well to pass, opibus affluere
Passable (indifferent), mediocris, tolerabilis; (in the way), pervius
A passage, transitus; (of a book), sententia, locus
The passage of the throat, gula

A passenger (by land), viator; (by water), vector, portitor
Passibility, passibilitas
Passible, passibilis
Passing, transiens, praeteriens; (away), transitorius, caducus; (lightly over), perfunctorie agens; (beyond), transgrediens
A passing (along), progressus; (beyond), praetervectio; (over), transitus; (from place to place), migratio, demigratio
Passing (excellent), praestans; (fair), satis venustus; (well), perbenè
Passing (very), valdè, egregiè
A passing-bell, nola funebris
Passion (anger), ira, iracundia; (affection, or inclination), animi affectus, motus, impetus, concitatio; (love), amor; (suffering), dolorum perpessio, supplicium, cruciatus
Passion-week, sabbatum magnum
Passionate, iracundus, morosus, irritabilis, stomachosus; (lover), amator ardens
Passionately (angrily), iracundè; (with great desire), ardentèr
Passions, cupiditates, motus
Passive, passivus
Passively, passivè
The Passover, pascha
A passport, commeatus
Past, post; (in times past), olim, quondam; (last past), ultimò praeteritus
Paste (dough), farina aquâ subacta; (for sticking), gluten ex farinâ
To paste, agglutino, conglutino
The pastern, suffrago
A pastil, pastillus
Pastime, ludus, facetiae
To take pastime, se recreare
For pastime, animi causâ
A pastor (keeper of cattle), pastor, gregis custos; (shepherd), opilio; (minister of a church), ecclesiae minister
Pastoral, pastoralis
A pastoral, carmen bucolicum
A pastry, pistrinum, pistrina
A pastrycook, pistor dulciarius
Pasturable, pascuus
Pasturage, pabulatio, pastus
A pasture, pascuum
Of a pasture, pascuus [caus
Common pasture, ager compas-
To pasture, pasco; (together), compesco
A pasturing, pabulum
A pasty, artocreas
Pat (fit), aptus, congruus, idoneus
A pat, ictus levior
To pat, levitèr percutere
A patch (piece of cloth), assumentum; (to cover a wound), splenium; (for the face), macula serica; (of ground), agellus
A cross-patch, homo morosus
To patch, pannum assuere; (the face), maculis vultum ornare; (or mend clothes), resarcio, reconcinno; (up), coagmento
Patched (ragged), pannosus; (mended), refectus, reconcinnatus
Patched garments, &c., scruta
A patcher, interpolator
A patching, interpolatio
Patchwork, opus versicolor
The pate, caput

PAY

Shallow-pated, stultus, rudis
Patent, patens, apertus
A patent, diploma
A patentee, qui regio diplomate donatur
Paternal, paternus, patrius
The paternoster, oratio dominica
A path, semita, callis; (beaten), via trita; (cross), trames
Pathetic, patheticus
Pathetically, patheticè, vehementèr
Pathless, sine semitâ
Pathos, vehementia in dicendo
Patience, patientia; (long), longanimitas
To be out of patience; indignor
Out of patience, impatiens
Patient, patiens, mitis, placidus
A patient, æger, ægrotus
Patiently, patientèr, sedatè, æquo animo
A patriarch, patriarcha
Patriarchal, patriarchalis
A patriarchate, patriarchatus
A patrician, patricius; (his dignity), patriciatus
Like a patrician, patriciè
Patrimonial, patrimonialis
A patrimony, patrimonium
A patriot, civis boni publici studiosus, poplicola
Patriotism, amor patriæ
Patrol, vigiles nocte ambulantes
To patrol, excubias agere
A patron, patronus
Patronage, patrocinium; (right of presentation), jus patronatûs
A patroness, patrona
To patronize, patrocinor, tueor
Patronymic, patronymicus
A patten, sculponea; (of a pillar), basis
To patter down, cado, decido
A pattern (model), exemplar, specimen, modulus
To be a pattern, exemplum præbere
Paucity, paucitas
To pave, pavio, sterno
A pavement, pavimentum; (beater), pavicula, fistuca
A paver, or pavier, pavitor
A pavilion, conopeum
A paving, stratura
A paunch, abdomen; (of an ox), echinus; (belly), lurco
To paunch, eviscero, exentero
A pause (stop), pausa, mora; (in music), intermissio
To pause, quiesco, meditor
Pausing, cogitabundus, meditabundus
A pausing, intermissio, meditatio
A paw, ungula, unguis
To paw, unguibus tractare; (or fawn upon), unguibus blandiri
A pawn, pignus; (at chess), pedes
To pawn, oppignero
A pawnbroker, pignerator
A pawning, pigneratio
Pay, stipendium
To have in pay, stipendio alere
Payday, dies solutionis
To pay, solvo, persolvo; (again), remunero; (all), exsolvo; (back), reddo, rependo; (upon the nail), præsentem pecuniam solvere; (beforehand), pecuniam repræsentare; (beat), cædo; (debts), æs alienum solvere
Not able to pay, solvendo impar
Payable, solvendus, numerandus

[88]

PEE

Not payed, insolutus [vit
A pay-master, qui pecuniam solA paying, or payment, solutio; (of rent), pensio; (of wages), stipendium
A pea, pisum
Peace, pax, quies, requies, otium; (of mind), pax, or tranquillitas animi [mus
In a profound peace, pacatissiTo make peace (with), pacem inire
To be in peace, quiesco, requiesco
A peacemaker, pacis conciliator
A making of peace, pacificatio
To hold one's peace, sileo, taceo
Peace! tace! tacete!
A peace-officer, curator publicæ pacis; (a constable of the night), irenarcha; (a justice), justiciarius pacis
Holding his peace, silens
Belonging to peace, pacificus
Bringing peace, pacifer
Peaceable, tranquillus, sedatus, placidus
Peaceableness, tranquillitas
Peaceably, tranquillè, sedatè
A peach, malum Persicum; (tree), malus Persica; (colour), color Persicus
A peacock, pavo, pavus
Of a peacock, pavoninus
A peahen, pava [Peek
A peak, cacumen, tumulus. See
A peal of bells, modulatus, or concentus campanarum
To peal, tundo
A pear, pyrum; (tree), pyrus
A pearl, margarita, bacca; (in the eye), albugo
Decked with pearls, baccatus
Pearly, gemmis abundans, gemmæ similis
A peasant, villicus, rusticus
The peasantry, plebs rustica
Pease, pisum; (pottage), jusculum ex piso confectum; (cod), siliqua pisi; (straw), pisi culmus
A pebble, calculus
Pebbly, calculis abundans
A peccadillo, error levis
Peccant, peccans, vitiosus, noxius
A peck, quarta pars modii; (of troubles), ilias malorum
To peck, excudo
Pectoral, pectoralis
Peculation, peculatus
Peculiar, peculiaris, proprius
Peculiarly, præcipuè, propriè
Peculiarity, qualitas peculiaris
Pecuniary, pecuniarius
A pedagogue, pædagogus
A pedant, grammatista
Pedantic, literaturæ ostentator, linutius
Pedantically, ineptè, insulsè
Pedantry, eruditio insulsa
A pedestal, columnæ basis
A pedicle, pediculus
Pedicular, pedicularis
A pedigree, stemma, prosapia
A pedlar, mercator circumforaneus
Pedling, circumforaneus
A peek (point), apex, fastigium; (grudge), odium, simultas
To peek, obtueor
A peel (for an oven), infurnibulum; (or paring), cortex; (of an onion), tunica
To peel off, decortico
The peep of day, diluculum
To peep, aspicio; (in), introspi-

PEN

cio, per rimam speculari; (as birds), pipio
A peeper, speculator officiosus
A peeping into, inspectio
A peeping-hole, conspicillum
A peer (equal), par; (of the realm), satrapa, patricius; in. pl. proceres, optimates, primates
Peerage, dignitas optimatum
Peerless, incomparabilis
Peevish, morosus, iracundus, asper [ribus
To be peevish, asperis esse moPeevishly, morosè, acerbò
Peevishness, morositas
A peg, paxillus, impages
To peg, paxillo figere
A pegasus, Pegasus, equus alatus
Pegged, paxillo fixus
Pelf, lucellum, pecunia
A pelican, pelicanus
A pellet, pilula
A pellicle, pellicula
Pell-mell, uno agmine, confusè
Pellucid, pellucidus
A pelt, corium, tergus, pellis
A peltmonger, coriarius
To pelt, lapidibus petere
A pen (to write with), penna, calamus, stylus; (or coop), cors; (for sheep), ovile
Of a pen, calamarius
A penknife, scalpellum
A penman, scriba
A pencase, theca calamaria
To pen (write), scribo; (up), in exiguum concludere; (up sheep), oves stabulo includere
Penal, pœnalis
A penalty, pœna, muleta
Penance, supplicium, pœna
To do penance, culpam pœnâ luere
Pence, denarii
A pencil, penicillum
To pencil, penicillo delineare
A pendant (streamer), lemniscus; (in a ship), aplustre; (for the ear), inauris
Pendent, Pending, pendens
Pendulous, pendulus
A pendulum, pensile libramentum
Penetrable, penetrabilis
To penetrate, penetro
May be penetrated, penetrabilis
A penetration, penetratio
Of penetration, sagax, perspicax
Penetrative, penetrans
A peninsula, peninsula
Penitence, pœnitentia
Penitent, pœnitens
To be penitent, resipisco
Penitential, pœnitentialis
A penitentiary (priest), piacularis sacerdos; (place), expiationum sacrarium
Penitently, pœnitentèr
A pennant, aplustrum
Penniless, omnium rerum egenus
A penny, denarius
Pensile, pensilis
A pension, pensio
A pensioner, mercenarius
Gentlemen-pensioners, satellites regis honorarii
Pensive, meditabundus, mœstus, tristis
To be pensive, cogitatione defigi, mœreo, doleo
Pensively, mœstè, solicitè
Pensiveness, tristitia, solicitudo, mœstitia, anxietas
A penthouse, compluvium
Pentagonal, pentagonus

Pentameter, pentameter
The pentateuch, pentateuchum
Pentecost, pentecoste
Penurious, avarus, parcus, sordidus, indigus, egenus, egens, pauper
Penuriously, avarè, parcè
Penuriousness, avaritia, sordes
Penury, penuria, egestas
People, populus ; (common), plebs, plebecula, vulgus
Of the people, popularis ; (common people), vulgaris, plebeius
To people, coloniam deducere
Full of people, populo frequens
Pepper, piper
To pepper, pipere condire ; (with a disease), morbo inficere ; (with ill words), conviciis vehementèr lacessere
Peppered, piperatus
A peppering, piperis conditura
Peptic (easy of digestion), pepticus
Peradventure, forsàn, fortassè
Peregration, peregratio
To perambulate, perambulo, obeo
Perambulation, perambulatio
Perceivable, perceptibilis
Not perceivable, imperceptus
To perceive, percipio, sentio ; (well), persentio ; (or have some feeling), persentisco ; (beforehand), præsentio
A perceiving, perceptio
Perceptible, percipiendus
Perceptibly, ità ut percipiatur
Perceptive, percipiens
A perch, pertica ; (fish), perca
To perch, arbori insidere (eidens
Perched (as a bird), illapsus, in-
Perchance, forsàn, forsitan
Percussion, percussio
Perdition, perditio, exitium
Peregrination, peregrinatio
Peregrine, peregrinus, externus
Peremptorily, præcisè, definitè
Peremptoriness, pertinacia
Peremptory, peremptorius ; (in opinion), tenax, pertinax
Perennial, perennis
Perennity, perennitas
Perfect (complete), perfectus, absolutus, consummatus, exactus ; (skilful), peritus
To perfect (complete), perficio, absolvo ; (one in a thing), perfectè docere
A perfecting, consummatio
Perfection, perfectio
To bring to perfection, consummo
In perfection, optimè, eximè
Perfective, perficiens
Perfectly, perfectè, exactè ; (by heart), memoritèr, ad unguem ; (thoroughly), penitùs
Perfectness, perfectio ; (skill), peritia
Perfidious, perfidus, perfidiosus
Perfidiously, perfidè, infidè
Perfidiousness, Perfidy, perfidia
To perforate, perforo
Perforation, perforatio
Perforce, vi et armis, violentèr
To perform, perficio ; (accomplish), perago ; (bring to pass), efficio ; (one's word), promissum præstare ; (a journey), iter conficere
A performer, effector
A performing, peractio
A performance (work), opus
Perfume, odor, suffitus
To perfume, fumigo, suffumigo, odoribus imbuere
[89]

A perfumer, myropola
Perfuming, suffiens, aromaticus
A perfuming, suffitio
A perfuming pan, thuribulum
Perfunctorily, perfunctoriè, levitèr
Perfunctory, negligens, levis
Perhaps, forsàn, forsitan
The pericardium, pericardium
The pericranium, pericranium
Peril, periculum, discrimen
To be in peril, periclitor
Perilous, periculosus
Perilously, periculosè
A period, periodus ; (conclusion), finis, exitus
Periodical, periodicus
Periodically, periodicè
Peripatetic, peripateticus
To perish, pereo, intereo ; (as fruit), putresco [fluxus
Perishable, fragilis, caducus,
A perishing, interitus
Periphrasis, circumlocutio
To perjure one's self, perjuro
A perjured person, perjurus
Perjury, perjurium
A periwig, capillamentum
A periwinkle, cochlea marina
To perk up, erigo, attollo
Permanence, duratio
Permanent, permanens, stabilis
Permanently, diù, diutinè
Permission, permissio, venia
A permit, schedula mercatoria testans vectigal esse persolutum
To permit, permitto, sino
A permitting, permissio, licentia
A permutation, permutatio
Pernicious, perniciosus, nocens
Perniciously, perniciosè
Perniciousness, pernicies, exitium
A peroration, peroratio
A perpendicular, perpendiculum
To perpetrate, perpetro, patro
A perpetration, perpetratio
Perpetual, perpetuus, perennis
Perpetually, perpetuò, sempèr
To perpetuate, perpetuo
A perpetuation, in perpetuum sanctio
Perpetuity, perpetuitas
To perplex (confound), turbo ; (mix), permisceo ; (vex), vexo, affligo, ango ; (make doubtful), incertum reddere
Perplexedly, perplexè, turbatè
Perplexity, perturbatio ; (of mind), solicitudo, anxietas
A perquisite, additamentum
To persecute, exagito, insector
Persecution, persecutio
A persecutor, exagitator
Perseverance, perseverantia
To persevere, persevero, perstò
Persevered in, constantèr servatus
Persevering, perseverans, perstaus
A persevering, perseverantia
Perseveringly, constantèr
To persist, persisto, permaneo
A persisting, perseverantia, contumacia, pervicacia
Persisting, persistens, obstinatus
A person, homo, persona ; (certain man), quidam ; (certain woman), quædam ; (of either sex), non nemo
Any person, quivis, quilibet
Personable, venustas
A great personage, vir clarus
Personal, personalis
Personality, personalitas

Personally, personalitèr, per se
To personate, personam inducre
Perspicacious, perspicax, sagax
Perspicacity, perspicacitas
Perspicuity, perspicuitas
Perspicuous, perspicuus, clarus
Perspicuously, perspicuè, planè
Perspiration, perspiratio
To perspire, perspiro
Persuadable, persuasibilis
To persuade, persuadeo, suadeo
A persuader, suasor, impulsor
Persuasible, exorabilis
A persuading, or persuasion, persuasio ; (opinion), opinio
Persuasive, suasorius, efficax
Pert (brisk), vividus, agilis ; (saucy), audax, procax ; (talkative), loquax ; (smart), astutus, argutus
To pertain, pertineo, specto
Pertaining, pertinens, attinens
Pertinacious, pertinax, obstinatus
Pertinaciously, obstinatè
Pertinaciousness, pertinacia
Pertinence, aptitudo, convenientia
Pertinent, aptus, idoneus
Pertinently, aptè, appositè
Pertly, argutè, audacitèr
Pertness, alacritas, audacia, sagacitas, loquacitas
Perturbation, perturbatio
To pervade, pervado
Perverse, perversus, protervus
Perversion, pravitas ; (of words), prava verborum interpretatio
Perversity, Perverseness, pravitas
Perversely, perversè, obstinatè
To pervert, perverto, depravo ; (one's meaning), pravè, or malè interpretari
A perverter, corruptor
A perverting, depravatio
Pervicacious, pervicax, pertinax
Pervicacity, pertinacia
Pervious, pervius
A peruke, capillamentum ; (maker), capillamentorum opifex
To peruse, perlego, percurro
A perusal, or perusing, perlectio
A pest, pestis, lues
To pester, vexo, infesto
A pestering, vexatio
Pestiferous, pestiferus
A pestilence, pestilentia, pestis
Pestilent, Pestilential, pestilens
A pestle, pistillum
A pet, offensa, offensio
To be in a pet, irascor, indignor
Petit (small), parvus, levis
A petition, petitio
To petition, supplico, peto
A petitioner, supplex
A petitioning, petitio
Petitory, petitorius
To petrify, in lapidem convertere
To be petrified, lapidesco
A petticoat, subucula, induaium muliebre [gator
A pettifogger, lugulcius, vitilitiPettish, iracundus, morosus
Pettishness, morositas
Petty, parvus, exiguus
Petulance, petulantia, procacitas
Petulant, petulans, procax
Petulantly, petulantèr, procacitèr
A pever, fusi extremitas
A pew, subsellium septum
Pewter, stannum
Of pewter, stanneus
A pewterer, stannarius
A phantasm, phantasma

Phantastic, inconstans, levis
Pharisaical, pharisaicus
A pharisee, pharisæus
Pharmaceutical, pharmaceuticus
Pharmacy, ars medica
A pharos, pharos
The phases, phases
A pheasant, avis phasiana
A phenix, phœnix
A phenomenon, phænomenon
A phial, phiala
Philanthropy, humanitas
A philologer, philologus
Philological, philologus
Philology, philologia
Philomel, philomela
A philosopher, philosophus
Philosophical, philosophicus
Philosophically, philosophicè
To philosophize, philosophor
Philosophy, philosophia
Philtres, philtra
Phlebotomy, phlæbotomia
Phlegm, pituita
Phlegmatic, pituitosus
A phrase, phrasis, locutio
Phraseology, ratio scribendi, or loquendi
Phrenetic, amens, demens
A phrensy, dementia, insania
The phthisic, phthisis
Phthisical, phthisi laborans
A phylactery, phylacterium
Physic (the science), medicina, ars medicinalis; (medicine), medicamen; (dose), potio medica
To physic, medicamentum præscribere; (take physic), medicamentum sumere
Physical, medicinalis, medicus; (natural), physicus
Physically, physicè
A physician, medicus
Physics, physica
Physiognomy, physiognomia
Physiology, physiologia
The phyz, vultus, facies
Piacular, piacularis
A piazza, porticus
A pickaxe, bipennis
To pick (choose), eligo, lego; (gather), decerpo; (a pocket), crumenam furtim secare; (a quarrel), rixæ causam quærere
A picklock, instrumentum quo sera furtim aperitur
A pickpocket, manticularius
A picker of quarrels, vitilitigator
A picking (out), delectus, selectio; (up), collectio
Pickle (brine), salsugo, muria; (condition), conditio
To pickle, muriâ condire
Pickled, salitus, conditivus
A pickled rogue, veterator; (a pickled herring), halec conditanea
A pickling, conditura salsa
Pictorial, ad pictorem spectans
A picture, pictura, effigies
To picture, pingo, delineo
To piddle (trifle), ineptio; (in eating), liguric
A piddler, nugator, nugax
A pie, artocrea; (sea), larus
Pie (amongst printers), indigesta typorum strues
A pie (bird), pica
Piebald, maculatus
A piece (part), portio, pars, frustum; (patch), assumentum
All of a piece, sibi constans; (or of one colour), unicolor
A piece of antiquity, monumen-
[90]

tum antiquitatis; (a broken piece), fragmentum, fragmen
Piecemeal, frustatim
Apiece (each), singuli
To piece, resarcio, conjungo
Pied, maculatus, versicolor
A pier, pila, agger
To pierce, penetro, terebro; (through), transfigo; (with a weapon), perfodio; (set a broach), dolium retinere; (as cold), uro
That may be pierced, penetrandus
A piercer (person), penetrator; (instrument), terebra, terebellum
Piercing, penetrans, urens
A piercing, penetratio; (with a gimblet), terebratio
Piercingly, acritèr, vehementèr
Piety, pietas, religio
A pig, porcellus; (barrow), verres; (sow), scrofula; (sucking), porcus lactens; (of lead), massa plumbi oblonga
To pig, porcellos parere
Of a pig, suillus, porcinus
A pigsty, suile, hara
A pigeon, columbus, columba; (wood), palumbes
Of a pigeon, columbinus
A pigeon-hole, loculamentum; (house), columbarium; (pie), columbæ crusto incoctæ
Pigment, pigmentum
A pike, lancea, hasta; (fish), lucius; (sea), lupus piscis
A pilaster, columella
A pilchard, halecula; (made of flannel), fascia
A pile (heap), moles, cumulus, acervus; (post), sublica; (of wood), strues; (of building), structura; (in heraldry), pila; (on coin), aversa facies nummi
The piles, hæmorrhois, ficus
To pile up, acervo, accumulo
To pilfer, surripio, suffuror
A pilferer, suffurator, fur
Pilfering, furax, rapax
A pilfering, surreptio
Pilferingly, furacitèr
A pilgrim, peregrinus
A pilgrimage, peregrinatio
A piling up, acervatio, extructio
A pill, pilula
To pill, decortico, stringo
Pillage, præda, spolium; (the action of), direptio, vastatio
To pillage, vasto, diripio; (a kingdom), depeculor
To be pillaged, expilor, vastor
A pillager, spoliator
A pillaging, spoliatio
A pillar, columna; (its shaft), scapus; (foot), stylobata
Pillars (buttresses), anterides
A pilled-garlic, timidus, ignavus
A pillion, sella equestris fœminea
A pillory, columbar
To pillory, numellâ collum includere
A pillow, pulvinar, cervical
A pillowbear, pulvini, or cervicalis integumentum
A pilot, navis gubernator, or rector   [mium
Pilotage, rectoris navigii præ-
A pimp, leno
To pimp, lenocinor
Pimping (small), parvus, tenuis; (pitiful), spernendus
A pimple, pustula; (red), lentigo, lenticula rubra
Full of pimples, pustulatus

A pin, acicula; (of a window), clavus ferreus; (crisping), calamistrum; (rolling), cylindrus; (peg), paxillus
Not to care a pin, flocci pendere
A pinmaker, spinularius
A pinfold, septum
Pindust, ramentum
To pin (with a pin), spinulâ figere; (with wood), paxillo configere; (by articles), cautione obligare; (compel), injungo; (on another's faith), alterius sententiâ niti; (one's self upon one), parasitor; (up in a fold), septo includere
Pincers, forceps
A pinch, vellicatio, morsus; (of snuff), frustum sternutamenti; (necessity), necessitas, summæ angustiæ
At a pinch, necessariò, subitò
To a pinch, ad extremum
To pinch, vellico, premo; (grieve), crucio, molesto; (in biting), mordeo; (as cold), uro, aduro; (one of his wages, &c.), defraudo; (hurt), lædo; (off), avello
Pinching, digitis comprimens
A pinch-penny, perparcus
A pindaric, carmen pindaricum
A pine-tree, pinus; (wild), pinaster; (apple), nux pinea
Of pine, pineus
To pine (grieve), doleo, mœreo; (languish), languco, tabesco; (to death), dolore mori
A pining away, languor, tabes
A pinion, ala; (of a watch), rota minor
Pinions (fetters), compedes, manicæ
To pinion, manicis constringere
A pink (flower), caryophyllum; (small ship), navicula
Pink-eyed, pætus
A pinking, terebratio
A pinnace, phaselus, paro
A pinnacle, pinnæ fastigium; (or height of honour), summus gradus honorum
A pinner, capital muliebre
A pint, sextarius, pinta
A pioneer, cuniculariús
Pious, pius, religiosus
Piously, piè, religiosè
The pip, pituita
A pip, macula, nota
A pipe, fistula, tibia; (bag), fistula utricularis; (conduit), canalis; (clyster), sipho; (for tobacco), tubus; (of wine), cadus, dolium
To pipe, fistulâ canere
A piper, tibicen; (bag), utricularius
A piping, cantio fistularis
Piping-hot, calidissimus
A pipkin, ollula
A pippin, malum petisium
Piquant, pungens, acer
A pique, animosus, odium, rixa, jurgium
To pique, offendo, perstringo
To have a pique, alicui irasci
Piracy, piratica, prædatio
A pirate, pirata, prædo maritimus
Piratical, prædatorius
Piscatory, piscatoriús
Pish, phy! vah!
A pismire, formica
Full of pismires, formicosus
A pistol, scloppus minor
A pistole, septemdecim solidi

PLA

A pit, fossa, puteus; (dent), impressio, vestigium digiti
A pitfal, fovea
The pit of the stomach, ventriculus stomachi; (of a theatre), orchestra
Pit-coal, carbo fossilis, fossitia [nigra
A clay-pit, argilletum; (coal), fodina carbonaria; (gravel), sabuletum; (sand), fodina arenaria; (bottomless), abyssus
Of a pit, putealis
To go pit-a-pit, celeritèr palpitare
Pitch, pix
To pitch, pico, pice illinere; (throw), jacio, projicio; (put down), depono; (fix), figo; (pave), pavio; (tents), castrametor; (or fall down), præceps ruere; (choose), deligo; (upon a time), tempus constituere; (a net), rete tendere; (alight), descendo
A pitch (measure), modus; (extreme), extremitas
The pitch of a hill, clivus
A pitched battle, pugna stataria; (camp), stativa castra
A pitcher, lagena, amphora, urceus, hydria
A pitchfork, merga
Pitchy, piceus
Like pitch, picinus
Piteous, misericors; (miserable), miserabilis, miser
Piteously, miserabilitèr, miserè
Pith, medulla; (of trees, &c.), alburnum; (-less), siccus
Pithily, nervosè
Pithiness, robur
Pithy (full of marrow), medulla abundans; (nervous), nervosus
Pitiable, miserationis dignus
Pitiful, miserabilis, miser, misericors, lacrimosus, tristis
Pitifully, miserè
Pitifulness, misericordia; (meanness), exiguitas
Pitiless, immitis, crudelis, durus
A pittance, modicum
Pituitous, pituitosus
Pity, misericordia, miseratio
To pity, misereor, miseresco
A pix, pyxis
Placable, placabilis, exorabilis
A placart, edictum
A place, locus; (office), munus magistratus; (passage in a book), locus; (degree), ordo
In place of, vice, pro; (another place), alibi; (any place), alicubi, usquàm; (every place), ubiquè; (that place), illuc, ibi; (the same place), ibidèm; (this place), hic; (no place), nusquàm; (what place soever), ubicunquè, ubivis
By some place, aliqua; (this place), hac; (that place), illac; (what place), quà
From this place, hinc; (that place), illinc; (the same place), ab eodem loco; (some place), alicundè; (what place), undè? (what place soever), undecunquè; (place to place), huc illuc, ultrò citròque
To some place, aliquò; (another place), aliò; (the same place), eodem; (this place), huc; (that place), illuc; (what place?), quò?
Towards what place? quorsùm? (this place), horsùm; (some other place), aliorsùm

[91]

PLA

To place, loco, colloco; (again), repono; (before), præpono; (behind), postpone; (titly), apto; (out), eloco
A giving place, cessio
Placid, placidus
A placing, locatio; (between), interpositio
A plagiary, plagiarius
The plague, pestis, pestilentia; (sore calamity), lues
To plague, crucio, vexo; (one's self), se afflictare, or macerare
Having the plague, peste infectus
Plaguily, molestè, valdè
Plaguy, pestilens, pestifer
A plaice, psetta
Plain (even), planus, æquus; (manifest), manifestus, evidens; (honest), sincerus; (open), apertus; (without ornament), inornatus; (simple), simplex, non dissimulatus
Plain, adj. distinctè
To make plain, explano, expono, complano
To be plain, pateo
It is plain, patet, constat
A plain, plana, superficies
Plainly, planè, manifestè, evidentèr, distinctè; (simply), simplicitèr; (openly), apertè, palàm
Plainness, perspicuitas; (simpleness), simplicitas; (smoothness), planities, lævitas
A plaint, querela, questus
A plaintiff, accusator
A plaister, emplastrum
To plaister (a sore), emplastrum imponere; (with lime), gypso
A plaisterer, cæmentarius
A plait, plica, sinus
To plait, plico, complico
A plaiter, plicator
A plaiting, plicatura
Full of plaits, sinuosus, rugosus
A plan, exemplar
To plan, delineo, formo
A plane-tree, platanus
Of a plane-tree, platanius
A plane (tool), runcina
To plane, lævigo, dedolo
A planet, planeta
Planetary, sideralis
Planetstruck, sideratus
A planing, dedolatio
A plank, tabula, assis
To plank, contabulo, coasso
A planking, contabulatio
A planisphere, planisphærium
A plant, planta, virgultum
To plant, planto, sero; (again), resero; (a cannon), tormentum disponere; (a colony), coloniam constituere; (a vineyard), vineam instituere
Plantain, plantago
A plantation, colonia; (of trees), plantarium; (of vines), vitium propagatio
That may be planted, sativus
Newly planted, neophytus
A planter, plantator, sator
A planting, plantatio, satio
A planting-stick, pastinum
A plash, lacuna
To plash (trees), tondeo; (with water), aspergo
A plashing, aspersio
Plashy, stagnis frequens
Plastic, plasticus
A plat of ground, agellus
A platform, agger
To plat, implico, intexo

PLA

Plate (gold and silver vessels), aurea et argentea vasa; (enchased), toreuma
A plate (of metal), lamina, lamella; (trencher), scutella
To plate, obducere laminâ
The platen, torcularis tabula
Platonic, Platonicus; (love), amor seraphicus
A platoon, manipulus
In platoons, manipulatim
Platted, plexus, implexus
A plaister, discus, catinus
A platting, implicatio
Plausible, plausibilis, speciosus
Plausibility, Plausibleness, venustas
Plausibly, venustè, decorè
A play, ludus, lusus; (public), spectaculum; (stage), fabula, comœdia; (house), theatrum; (fellow), collusor; (things), crepundia
Belonging to play, lusorius
Full of play, ludibundus
To play, ludo; (at bowls), globum mittere; (away money), pecuniam lusu perdere; (before), prælindo; (at ball), pilâ ludere; (the child), pueriliter se gerere; (the boy), adolescenturio; (at cards), chartis ludere; (the coward), tergum dare; (an engine), machinam exercere; (at odd or even), par impar ludere; (soft and loose), prævaricor; (on the harp), citharam pulsare; (on a fiddle), fidibus canere; (at hazard), aleâ ludere; (the hypocrite), simulare pietatem; (the knave), fallo, defraudo
To keep in play, moror
Plays, mimi, ludi scenici
A player, lusor; (on a harp), citharista; (of tricks), prestigiator; (on the stage), histrio; (with swords), gladiator, lanista; (puppet), gesticulator
Of a stage player, histricus
Playful, Playsome, ludibundus
Playing, ludens
Belonging to playing, lusorius
A playing-place, lusorium
A plea, placitum; (excuse), excusatio, color
To plead, causas agere; (for one), aliquem defendere; (against), contra aliquem causam dicere; (guilty), crimen fateri; (not guilty), crimen negare
A pleader, advocatus, orator
A pleading, causæ dictio, or defensio, litigatio
Pleasant, amœnus, gratus
To grow pleasant, hilaresco
To make pleasant, exhilaro
Pleasant sayings, facetiæ; (meats), deliciæ, dapes, cupediæ
Very pleasant, amœnissimus
Pleasantly, amœnè, jucundè, lepidè
Pleasantness, amœnitas, jucunditas; (in speech), lepor; (in manners), comitas, urbanitas
Pleasantry, jocosa dicacitas
To please, placeo, complaceo; (delight), oblecto; (one's self), voluptatem capere; (or humour one), alicui obsequi; (by sacrifice), placo, propitio
Easy to be pleased, placabilis
Hard to be pleased, morosus, asper
Not to be pleased, implacabilis

4

PLO — POE — POL

Very well pleased, perlubens
Pleasing, gratus, jucundus
A pleasing, gratificatio
Pleasingness, amoenitas
Pleasurable, gratus, jucundus
Pleasure (delight), voluptas, delectatio, oblectamentum ; (will), arbitrium ; (service), beneficium, gratia
Of pleasure, voluptarius
A pleasure-boat, thalamegos
To pleasure (do a favour), gratificor ; (humour), morigeror, obsequor ; (accommodate), accommodo ; (or take pleasure in), delector, oblector
Doing a pleasure, benignus
Plebeian, plebeius
A pledge (pawn), pignus, depositum, arrhabo ; (proof), testimonium ; (surety), præs, vas
To pledge (pawn), pignero ; (in drinking), propinanti vices reddere
A pledget, peniculus
A pledging, pigneratio
Plenarily, plenè, perfectè
Plenary, plenus, perfectus
A plenipotentiary, legatus plenâ potestate instructus
Plenitude, plenitudo
Plenteous, abundans, copiosus
To be plenteous, abundo
Plenteously, abundantèr, copiosè
Plenteousness, copia
Plentiful, affluens, copiosus ; (shower), largus imber
Plentifully, ubertìm, copiosè, abundantèr
Plentifulness, Plenty, copia, abundantia, affluentia
Plenty (of corn), magnus frumenti numerus ; (of honey), vis maxima mellis ; (of words), orationis flumen, copia verborum ; (of leaves), foliorum luxuria ; (of furniture), multa supellex
Plethoric, plethoricus
A plethory, plethora
A pleurisy, pleuritis
Pleuritic, pleuriticus
Pliable, Pliant, flexilis, flexibilis, tractabilis, facilis, mansuetus
Pliableness (of temper), facilitas ; (bending), flexibilitas
To be pliant, obsequor
To grow pliant, lentesco
To make pliant, emollio
Pliantly, obedientèr, facilè
Pliantness, flexibilitas
A plight, status, conditio ; (of body), habitudo, habitus
To plight, spondeo
In good plight, benè curatus
A plinth, plinthus
To plod, sedulò operam navare, incumbo
A plodder, sedulus, diligens
A plot (conspiracy), conspiratio ; (design), consilium, ratio ; (of a building), ichnographia ; (of the front of a building), orthographia ; (of ground), agellus, area ; (of a play), consilium præcipuum
To plot (consult), consulto ; (conspire), conspiro, conjuro ; (contrive), excogito, machinor
A plotter, conjuratus
A plotting, conspiratio
To be plotting, machinor
A plough, aratrum ; (joiner's tool), planula ad oras asserum atriandas ; (man), arator, agricola ; (share), vomer ; (handle), stiva, bura ; (staff), rulla ; (land), arvum
Plough-oxen, triones
To plough, aro, sulco ; (again), renovo
Ploughed, aratus, cultus
A ploughing, aratio
A pluck, exta, viscera
A pluck (pull), vellicatio
To pluck, vello, vellico ; (asunder), divello ; (down), diruo ; (from), abstraho ; (flowers), flores carpere ; (off), decerpo
A plucking (away), avulsio ; (out), evulsio ; (up by the roots), extirpatio, eradicatio
A plug, clavus ligneus, cuneolus
A plum, prunum
A plum-tree, prunus
Plumage, sertum plumatile
A plumb-line, amussis, libella
To plumb, opus ad libellam exigere
Plumbean, plumbeus [meus
A plume of feathers, apex plumeus
To plume (adorn), decoro, orno
A plummer, plumbarius
A plummet (used by builders), bulla ad libellam pensilis
Plump, nitidus, obesus, pinguis
To plump up, tumeo, info
Plumpness, nitor, venustas
Plunder, præda, spolium
To plunder, prædor, peculor, spolio, vasto, depopulor
A plunderer, prædator, vastator
A plundering, spoliatio, vastatio
A plunge, immersio ; (trouble), difficultas, angustia
To plunge, immergo, mergo, ad incitas redigi ; (often), merso, (dive), urino
Plunging, immergens, mergens
A plunging, immersio, submersio
Plural, pluralis
Plurality, numerus major, turba
Pluralities, plura beneficia ecclesiastica ab uno viro occupata
Plurally, pluralitèr
Plush, pannus villosus ex pilis confectus, holosericum
To ply (bend), flecto ; (give way), cedo ; (to business), operam navare, incumbo ; (urge), urgeo
Plyers, forceps minor
Plying, flexilis, sequax
A plying, flexio, applicatio
Pneumatic, pneumaticus
Pneumatics, pneumatica
To poach, coctilio ; (kill game illegally), illicitâ venatione uti
A poached egg, ovum sorbile
A poacher, qui illicitâ venatione utitur
A poaching, venatio illicita
A pock, pustula, papula
Pock-holes, variolarum vestigia
A pocket, sacculus, loculus ; (of wool), dimidius saccus
To pocket, in loculis condere ; (hide), celo ; (an affront), contumeliam dissimulare
Poculent, poculentus
A pod, siliqua, valvulus
A poem, poema, carmen
Poesy, Poetry, poesis, poetica
A poet, poeta, vates ; (paltry), poetaster
Like a poet, poeticè
A poetess, poetria
Poetic, Poetical, poeticus
Poetically, poeticè
To poetize, versifico, versus facere
Poignancy, mordacitas
Poignant, pungens, aculeatus
A point, punctum ; (case), causa, status, caput, locus ; (chief matter), caput ; (in law), casus ; (of land), promontorium ; (or subject in hand), argumentum, res, consilium ; (in the tables), punctum
The point (of a rock), vertex, cacumen ; (of a weapon), cuspis, mucro, acies ; (ot a clock, &c.), gnomon ; (of the compass), ventorum diversi tractus ; (of the matter), cardo rei
At the point, jam jamque
Point-blank, præcisè, prorsùs
A nice point, scrupulus
To point (sharpen), acuo ; (at), monstro, digitis designare ; (or distinguish by points), interpungo ; (a cannon), tormentum dirigere, or obvertere
Pointedly, acritèr, acutè
A pointer (dog), canis subsidens
A pointing, interpunctio ; (at), indicatio
Pointless, hebes, obtusus
At all points, omnibus rebus
To poise, pondero, pendo
A poise, pondus ; (equal), æquipondium
Poison, venenum, virus
To poison, veneno tollere ; (corrupt), depravo, vitio ; (things without life), veneno inficere
A poisoner, veneficus
A poisoning, veneficium
Poisonous, venenosus, virulentus
A poitrel, pectorale
A poke, saccus, marsupium
To poke, digito, &c. explorare
A poker, ferrum ad ignem excitandum
Polar, polaris
A pole, pertica ; (in the heavens), polus, mundi cardo ; (waterman's), trudes, contus ; (hunting), venabulum ; (ax), bipennis, securis ; (star), cynosura
A polecat, putorius
Polemic, Polemical, polemicus
Policy (art of governing), politia ; (counsel), consilium ; (craft), calliditas, astutia ; (stratagem), stratagema
A policy of assurance, syngrapha quâ cavetur
A polish, politura
To polish, polio, limo, excolo
A polisher, polio
A polishing, politura
Polite, politus, elegans, excultus, concinnus, ornatus, urbanus
Politely, politè, urbanè
Politeness, urbanitas, civilitas
Politic, astutus, callidus
Politics, politica
Political, politicus
A politician, politicorum peritus
Politicly, astutè, calidè
Polity, politia
The poll (head), caput ; (list of votes), suffragantium catalogus
A poll, electio viritìm facta
Poll-money, capitatio
To poll (shear), tondeo, reseco ; (for magistrates, &c.), suffragia viritìm dare
A pollard (tree), arbor cædua
Polled (clipped), tonsus
A polling, tonsura
To pollute, polluo, corrumpo, contamino

A polluting, or pollution, pollutio
A polt (blow), ictus
A poltron, ignavus, timidus
Polygamy, polygamia
A polygon, polygonia
A polypus, polypus
A pomegranate, malum granatum
To pommel, pugno demulcere
The pommel, ensis manubrii, or ephippii orbiculus
Pomp, pompa, splendor
Pompous, splendidus, magnificus
Pompously, splendidè, magnificè
Pompousness, pompa
A pond, stagnum, lacus; (for fish), piscina
Of a fishpond, piscinalis
To ponder, perpendo, pensito
Pondering, meditans, contemplans
A pondering, meditatio, contemplatio
Ponderous, ponderosus, gravis
Ponderously, graviter
Ponderousness, gravitas
A poniard, pugio
Pontic, Ponticus
A pontiff, pontifex
Pontifical, pontificalis
A pontifical (book), ritualis pontificum
The pontificate, pontificatus
A pontoon, ponto
A pony, equulus
A pool, palus
The poop, puppis
Poor (in circumstances), pauper, inops, egens, humilis, tenuis; (barren), aridis, jejunus, frigidus; (mean), vilis, sordidus, miser; (lean), macer, macilentus, macie confectus; (trifling), malus, tergiversans
To be poor, egeo
To make poor, depaupero; (to be made poor), ad inopiam redigi
Poorly, miserè, tenuiter, malè
Poorness, paupertas, egestas; (of ground), sterilitas
To pop into the mouth, ori indere; (off a gun), sclopphum displodere; (out), subitò egredi; (out a word), temerè verbum effutire; (into a place), subitò ingredi
A popgun, sclopphus
The pope, papa
The popedom, papatus
Popery, papismus
Popish, papalis, pontificius
A poplar-tree, populus
Of poplar, populeus
A poppet, pupa
Poppy, papaver
Of poppy, papaverus
Poppy-coloured, papaveratus
Poppy-juice, meconium
The populace, plebs, vulgus
Popular (vulgar), vulgaris, plebeius; (pleasing), popularis, vulgo acceptus
Popularity, popularitas
Popularly, popularitèr
Populous, populo frequens
Populousness, populi frequentia
Porcelain, vasa murrina
A porch, porticus; (of a church), vestibulum, atrium
A porcupine, hystrix
A pore, porus, meatus
To pore, attentius considerare
Pork, caro suilla, or porcina
A porker, porcellus, nefrendis
Porous, poris abundans
Porosity, or porousness, qualitas rei poris abundantis
[93]

Porphyry, porphyrites
A porpoise, or porpus, tursio
Porrection, porrectio
Porridge, jusculum
A porridge-pot, olla, cacabus
A porringer, scutella
A port, portus
Port, gustus, vitæ
Port-wine, vinum rubrum
Having many ports, portuosus
Portable, portabilis
A portal, porticus
A portcullis, porta clausa
To portend, præsagio
A portent (omen), portentum, omen
A porter (at a gate), janitor, ostiarius; (carrying burthens), bajulus
Porterage, bajulorum merces
Portholes, fenestellæ
A portico, porticus
A portion (share), portio, sors, pars; (in marriage), dos; (to live upon), peculium
Having a portion, dotata
To portion, doto; (divide), partior, distribuo
Portliness, corporis dignitas
Portly, corporis dignitate præditus
A portmanteau, hippopera
A portrait, pictura, imago
A posey, florum fasciculus; (of a ring), annuli symbolum
A position (placing), locatio, positio, situs; (thesis), thesis
Positive, positivus, certus; (man), tenax, confidens
Positively, præcisè, confidentèr
Positiveness, pervicacia
To possess, possideo, teneo, occupo; (before), præoccupo
Possession, possessio; (by prescription), usucaptio;(in trust), possessio fiduciaria
To take possession of, occupo, adeo, ineo
A taking possession of, occupatio
In possession of, penes
Possessive, possessivus
A possessor, possessor, dominus
A posset, lac vino coagulatum
Possibility, possibilitas
Possible, possibilis
Possibly, fortè, fortassis
A post (stake), postis; (office, or place), munus; (station), statio, sedes stativa; (letter-carrier), tabellarius; (horse), veredus; (house), veredorum statio
An advanced post, accessus propior
Posthaste, festinus [tus
A postmaster, veredorum præfectus
To post, locum occupare; (make haste), festino; (one for a coward), timiditatis notam alicui palam inurere; (a book), in librum transcribere; (up in public places), publicè proponere
Posterior, posterior
The posteriors, partes posteriores
Posterity, posteritas, posteri, minores
A postern, janua postica
Posthumous, posthumus
A postillion, equorum præductor
A postscript, scripti additamentum
To postpone, postpono, posthabeo
A postulate, postulatum
A posture, corporis positio; (of mind), status; (of affairs), conditio, status
A pot, poculum, olla; (for water), situlus aquarius
Of a pot, ollaris, ollarius
To pot, butyro condire
Potashes, cineres ad saponem conficiendum
A pot-companion, combibo; (gun), sipbunculus; (herbs), olera; (hooks), ansæ ollares; (ladle), rudicula; (lid), operculum; (sherd), testa
Potable, potabilis, potulentus
Potatoes, battata
Potency, potentia
Potent, potens, valens
A potentate, princeps
Potential, potentialis
Potently, potentèr, validè
A pother, turba
A potion, potio, philtrum
Pottage, jus, jusculum; (of barley), ptisana; (thick), pulmentarium
Of pottage, pulmentaris
A potter, figulus [fictilis
Belonging to a potter, figulinus,
A pottle, quatuor libræ liquidorum
Potulent, potulentus
A pouch, pera, marsupium
One pouch-mouthed, labeo
To pouch the lips, labia demittere
Poverty, paupertas, inopia
To be in poverty, egeo, indigeo
A poulterer, pullarius
A poultice, cataplasma
To poultice, cataplasma adhibere
Poultry, pullities
A keeper of poultry, gallinarius
Where poultry is kept, gallinarium
Of poultry, gallinaceus
A pounce, unguis
To pounce (as a hawk), unguibus comprehendere; (paper), pulvere chartam ad scribendi usum aptam reddere
A pound (weight), libra, pondo, as; (in money), viginti solidi, libramina; (for cattle), septum
Half a pound, selibra
A pound and a half, sesquilibra
Two pounds, dipondium
Of two pounds, bilibris; (three pounds), trilibris; (four pounds), quadrilibris; (five pounds), quinquelibralis
Ten pounds, decussis
Twenty pounds, vicessis
Thirty pounds, tricessis
A hundred weight, centipondium
To pound (bruise), contero, contundo; (cattle), pecora septo inclusa detinere
Poundage, vectigal ex singulis minis solutum
A pounding, contusio; (of cattle), pecoris in septo inclusio
To pour, fundo; (about), circumfundo; (back), refundo; (down), defundo; (in), infundo; (often), fundito; (out), effundo; (out of one into another), elutrio, transfundo; (upon), infundo, perfundo
That may be poured, fusilis
A pourer, fusor
A pouring in, infusio; (by drops), instillatio; (all over), perfusio; (out), effusio, transfusio
To pourtray, delineo, depingo
Pourtrayed, depictus
A pourtrait, or pourtraiture, pictura, imago, effigies
To pout, stomachor, labia exerere

PRE   PRE   PRE

Pouting, morosus, stomachosus
Poutingly, labiis exertis
Powder, pulvis; (gun), nitratus, or pyrius pulvis
To powder, pulvere conspergere; (with salt), sale condire; (the hair), pulvisculo crinem aspergere; (reduce to powder), in pulverem redigere
Powdering, pulvere inspergens; (a seasoning), salitura
Power, potentia, potestas, virtus, facultas; (authority), auctoritas; (force, or strength), vis; (great number), copia
The powers of the mind, dotes animi
To be in, or have power, valeo, polleo, auctoritate muniri
Powerful (having power), potens, validus; (efficacious), efficax
Not powerful, impotens; (ineffectual), inefficax
Powerfully, potentèr, efficacitèr
Powerfulness, vis, potentia
Practie, Practical, practicus
Practicable, quod fieri potest
Practice, exercitatio, usus, experientia; (custom), consuetudo; (secret), molimen, molitio
To practise, exerceo, experior; (law), legum nodos solvere; (physic), medicinam exercere
To put in practice, exequor
A practiser, exercitator; (in law), causarum actor; (in physic), medicinæ professor
A practising, exercitatio
A practitioner, exercitator
Pragmatical, pragmaticus, ineptus
Pragmatically, ineptè, insulsè
Pragmaticalness, insulsitas
Praise, laus, præconium
With praise, laudabilitèr
Praiseworthy, laudabilis
Not praised, illaudatus
To praise (commend), laudo, extollo; (prize), æstimo
A praiser, laudator; (prizer), æstimator
A praising, laudatio; (prizing), æstimatio
To prance, subsulto
Prancing, subsultans
A prank, ludus; (wicked), scelus, flagitium
To prate, garrio, blatero; (foolishly), ineptio, nugor; (pertly), argutor; (as a nurse), lallo
A prater, garrulus, loquax
Prating, loquax, dicax
A prating, dicacitas, loquacitas
Hold your prating, tace, tacete
Prattle, garritus, dicacitas
Pravity, pravitas, nequitia
A prawn, caris
To pray, oro, rogo, precor; (earnestly), enixè petere; (against), deprecor; (for), intercedo; (together), comprecor
A prayer, oratio, deprecatio, obtestatio
Prayers, preces; (morning), matutinæ preces; (evening), vespertinæ preces
By prayer, prece
A praying, obsecratio, rogatio
To preach, prædico, concionor; (a sermon), sacram orationem habere; (up an opinion), opinionem inculcare; (over one's cups), verbis mucida vina facere
A preacher, præcor, prædicator
A preaching, prædicatio
A ——amble, procœmium
[94]

To make a long preamble, longâ circuitione uti
A prebend, præbenda
A prebendary, præbendarius
Precarious, precarius
Precariously, precariò [cariæ
Precariousness, conditio rei præ-
A precaution, cautio, provisio
To use precaution, præcaveo
To precede (go before), præcedo; (excel), præsto, supero
Precedence, or precedency, jus præcedendi antè alios, principatus
Precedent, præcedens, antecedens
A precedent, exemplum
Precedently, antè, priusquàm
A precentor, præcentor
A precept, præceptum, mandatum
Preceptive, præceptivus
A precinct, ditio
Precious, pretiosus, carus
Preciously, pretiosè, carè
Preciousness, rei caritas
A precipice (steep place), præcipitium; (danger), discrimen, periculum
Precipitancy, temeritas
A precipitant, temerarius, præproperus
Precipitantly, præproperè
To precipitate (cast headlong), præcipito; (hurry), præproperè agere
Precipitate, præceps, temerarius; (subst.) mercurius præcipitatus rubèr
Precipitately, præproperè
Precipitation, præcipitatio
Precise (certain), certus, definitus; (finical), affectatus; (scrupulous), scrupulosus, nimis religiosus; (exact), exactus
Precisely (exactly), accuratè; (finically), mollitèr, affectatè; (scrupulously), scrupulosè
Preciseness, affectatio, accuratio
To preclude, præcludo
Precognition, præcentia
To preconceive, præsentio
A precontract, pactio antecedens
A precursor, præcursor
Predatory, prædatorius
A predecessor, antecessor
Our predecessors, majores
To predestinate, prædestino
Predestination, prædestinatio
Predetermination, prædeterminatio
To predetermine, antè terminare
Predial, prædiatorius
Predicable, predicabilis
The predicables, decem elementa logicæ
A predicament, prædicamentum; (state, or condition), status
To predicate, prædico
The predicate, prædicatum
Predication, prædicatio
To predict, prædico
A prediction, prædictio, vaticinium
To predispose, antè disponere
Predisposition, propensio
Predominance, prævalentia
Predominant, prævalens
To predominate, prævaleo
Pre-elected, antè electus
Pre-election, prælectio
Pre-eminence, præeminentia; (excellence), præstantia; (supreme rule), primatus, principatus
Pre-emption, præemptio
To pre-engage, antè obligare

A pre-engagement, obligatio antecedens
To pre-exist, antè existere
Pre-existence, præexistentia
Pre-existent, antè existens
A preface, præfatio, procœmium
Without preface, abruptè
To preface, præfari, procœmior
Prefatory, introducens
A prefect, præfectus, præses
A prefecture, præfectura
To prefer, præfero, præpono; (advance), eveho, effero; (exhibit), exhibeo; (propose), propono
Preferable, præferendus
Preference, partes priores
To give preference, antepono
Preferment, honor, dignitas
Preferring, anteferens, præponens
Prefigured, præfiguratus
To prefix, præfigo, antè statuere
A prefixing, præfixio
Pregnancy, graviditas
Pregnant, prægnans, gravidus
Pregnànt wit, ingenium subtile
To prejudge, præjudico
Prejudicate, præjudicatus
Prejudice (damage), damnum, detrimentum; (rash judging), præjudicium
Without prejudice, salvo jure
To prejudice, incommodo
To be prejudiced, præjudicio abripi
Prejudicial, noxius, incommodus
Prelacy, præsulis dignitas, or munus
A prelate, præsul
Prelection, prælectio
Prelibation, prælibatio
Preliminary, procœmium
Preliminary article, proludium
A prelude, præludium
Premature, præmaturus, præcox
Maturely, maturè
To premeditate, præmeditor
A premeditation, præmeditatio
To premise, præfari
The premises (spoken of before), præmissa; (lands, houses, or what belongs thereto), fundi, prædia
A premium, præmium
To premonish, præmoneo
A premonition, præmonitio
Premonitory, præmonens
A premunire, bonorum confiscatio; (danger); periculum
A prentice (apprentice), tyro
To preoccupy, præoccupo
To preordain, antè designare
A preparation, præparatio; (for a journey), viaticum, apparatus
With preparation, præparatè
A preparative, præparatio
Preparatory, præparatorius; (discourse), sermo paratus ad rem
To prepare, præparo, paro; (a feast), convivium ornare; (for fight), ad pugnam instruere; (for death), de animæ salute cogitare; (victuals), opsonor; (a way), viam parare, or munire; (or be prepared for), ad agendum accingi
Prepense, præmeditatus
To preponderate, præpondero
A preposition, præpositio
Prepositive, præpositivus
To preposess, præoccupo
Prepossession, præoccupatio
Preposterous, perversus, monstrosus
Preposterously, perversè, monstrosè

PRE

Preposterousness, qualitas præpostera
The prepuce, præputium
Prerequisite, antè necessarius
A prerogative, prerogativa
Prerogative, prærogativus
A presage, omen, præsagium
To presage, portendo, ominor
Presaging, præsagus, portendens
A presbyter, presbyter
Presbytery, presbyterium
A presbyterian, presbyterianus
Prescience, præscientia
Prescient, Prescious, præscius
To prescribe, præscribo; (bounds), termino, metas ponere
A prescribing, præscriptio
A prescript, præscriptum
Prescription, præscriptio
Presence, præsentia; (mien), oris, *or* formæ species; (look), aspectus, vultus
In presence, coram, in conspectu
Present, præsens; (at hand), præstò
For the present, nunc, jam, impræsentiarùm, in præsenti
By these presents, per has præsentes literas
Present money, pecunia numerata
To be present, adsum
A present, donum, munus
To present, dono; (to a living), beneficium offerre, donare, *or* comparco, se coram aliquo sistere; (the naked breast), nudum pectus præstare; (for a fault), apud curiam de aliquo queri; (a gun), bombardâ aliquem petere
A presentation, præsentatio; (by a patron), vocatio ad beneficium
A presentment, citatio
A presenting, collatio
Presently, statim, illicò, mox
Preservation, conservatio
A preservative, antidotus
A preserve, confectio
To reserve, tueor, conservo; (from), eripio, libero; (fruits), saccharo condire; (in health), sospito [defensor
A preserver, conservator, custos,
A preserving, *or* preservation, conservatio, tutela
To preside, præsum, præsideo
A president, præses
A press, torcular, prelum; (for clothes), armarium; (for books), pluteus
A press-room, torcularium
A press of people, turba
To press, premo, deprimo, exprimo, comprimo; (urge), urgeo, insto; (forward), annitor, contendo; (upon), insto; (soldiers), invitos conscribere
Press-money, auctoramentum
A pressing, pressura, pressus; (down), depressio; (together), compressio
A pressman, vectiarius
A pressure, pressura; (of mind), angor, ærumna
Prest (ready), paratus
To presume (be presumptuous), præfido, arrogo; (hope), spero; (suppose), conjicio, reor
Having presumed, ausus
Presumption, arrogantia, audacia; (conjecture), suspicio
Presumptive, præsumens, proximus
Presumptuous arrogans, audax
[95]

PRI

Presumptuously, arrogantèr, insolentèr
Presumptuousness, audacia
To presuppose, præsuppono
A pretence, prætextus, color
To pretend, simulo, obtendo, confingo, præ se ferre
A pretender (dissembler), simulator; (candidate), competitor
Pretending, simulans, causatus
Pretendingly, sub pretextu
A pretension (claim), vendicatio, postulatio; (design), consilium; (hope), spes; (promise), promissum
The preterperfect, præteritum
The preterimperfect, præteritum imperfectum
Preternatural, præter naturam accidens
Preternaturally, præter naturam
Preterpluperfect, plusquàm perfectum
A pretext, species, color
A pretor, prætor
Pretorian, prætorianus
Pretty, bellus, scitus; (merry), lepidus, facetus
A pretty while, aliquandiû
Very pretty, perelegans
Prettily, scitè, benè, venustè; (very), pereleganter
Prettiness, elegantia, venustas
To prevail, valeo, prævaleo, polleo; (by intreaty), impetro, exoro; (over), supero, vinco
Prevailed upon, eventus; (by intreaties), exoratus, precibus flexus
Prevailing, efficax; (opinion), opinio recepta, *or* popularis
Prevalence, Prevalency, efficacia, vis
Prevalent, valens, prævalens
Prevalently, efficacitèr, vulgò
To prevaricate, prævaricor
A prevarication, *or* prevarication, prævaricatio, collusio
A prevaricating (person), homo vafer, *or* subdolus; (speech), sermo simulatus, *or* fictus
A prevaricator, prævaricator
To prevent, prævenio, præverto
A preventer, impeditor
A preventing, *or* prevention, anticipatio, præoccupatio; (hindering), impeditio, tarditio
Preventive, anticipans, præoccupans
A preventive, alexipharmacum
Previous, prævius
Previously, primùm
A prey, præda, spolium
To prey upon, prædor
Of prey, prædatorius, rapax
A preying upon, prædatio
A price, pretium; (a reasonable), optima ratio
Of so great price, tanti; (of no price), nihili
At that price, tantidem; (at so little a price), tantulo; (at a great price), magno, carè; (at what price), quanti
For a little price, minimo
A prick (point), punctum, punctus; (goad), aculeus; (or pricking), punctura; (with a pin, &c.), punctiuncula; (of conscience), stimulus, morsus
To prick, pungo, repungo, pungito, stimulo, concito; (up the ears), aures arrigere; (notes in music), notas depingere
Pricking, pungens, stimulans

PRI

A pricking, punctio; (forward), incitatio, concitatio
A prickle, spina, sentis
Prickly, aculeatus, spinosus
Pride, superbia, fastus; (glory), prima gloria
To pride one's self, glorior, jacto
A priest, sacerdos, pontifex
Priesthood, sacerdotium
Priestly, sacerdotalis
A prig, nimiæ elegantiæ studiosus
Prim (formal), affectatus
A primacy, primatus
Primage, mercea nautica pro oneranda nave
Primarily, primitùs, primùm
Primary, primarius, primus
A primate, primas, princeps
Prime, primus, præcipuus; (or chief men), primores
In one's prime, juvenis, ætate florente
To prime (a gun), pulverem conceptaculo immittere; (in painting), primum colorem inducere
Primely, præcipuè, potissimùm
A primer, liber elementarius
Primeval, primævus, primitivus
Primitive, primitivus
Primitively, primitùs, primò
Primogeniture, primogenitura
Primordial, primordialis
A primrose, veris primula
A prince, princeps [regalia
Prince-like, Princely, principalis,
Princely, principalitèr, regiè
A princess, princeps
Principal, principalis, præcipuus
A principal (of a society), præses; (of a college), præfectus; (actor), auctor, caput, dux
The principal, summa, caput
Principality, principatus
Principally, potissimùm, maximè
A principal (original), principium, origo; (in philosophy), axioma; (opinion), sensus, opinio, sententia
Principles (of art), rudimenta; (of action), incitamentum, mores
To prink, exorno, orno
A print (impression), nota, impressio; (picture), imago, sculptura; (of a foot), vestigium
In print, litteris impressis; (nicely), affabrè, graphicè
The prints (newspapers), nuncii publici
To print, imprimo, excudo; (deep), infigo, inculpo
A printer, typographus
Printing, typographia
A printing-house, typographeum
A printing, impressio
A prior (before), prior, anterior
Prior (before), prior, anterior
A prioress, antistita
Priority, primatus, primum
A priory, cœnobium
A prism, prisma
A prison, carcer, ergastulum
To be in prison (imprisoned), in vinculis esse
A prisoner, vinctus; (of war), captivus, bello captus
Pristine, pristinus, antiquus
Prittle-prattle, gerræ, fabulæ
To prittle-prattle, blatero
Privacy (place), recessus; (in counsel), taciturnitas
Private, privatus, secretus, arcanus; (person), homo priva'

PRO

Privately, privatim, secretò, clam
A privateer, navis prædatoria
Privation, privatio
Privative, privativus
A privilege, privilegium, immunitas [tas
To privilege, eximo, immunitatem habere, *or* dare
A privileged place, refugium
Privily, occultè, secretò, clàm
Privy, privatus, arcanus, secretus; (to a thing), conscius, particeps, testis; (chamber), penetrale, conclave interius; (parts), pudenda, naturalia
A privy, latrina, forica
To prize (value), æstimo, pondo; (much), magni æstimare
A prize (plunder), spolium, præda; (trial of skill), certamen
Probable, probabilis, verisimilis
Probability, probabilitas
Probably, probabilitèr
A probate, probatio
A probation, probatio; (of a learner), examinatio
Probationary, ad probationem pertinens
A probationer, novitius, tyro
Probationership, tyrocinium
A probe, instrumentum argenteum ad vulnera exploranda
To probe, exploro, tento
Probity, probitas, honestas
A problem, problema
Problematical, problematicus
Problematically, problematicè
A procedure, *or* proceeding, ordo, forma, series, continuatio
The proceed, proventus, reditus
To proceed (go on), pergo, progredior, procedo; (in learning), proficio; (or spring from), enascor, exorior; (in a degree), gradum capessere; (at law), lite persequi
Proceeded (sprung from), exortus
A proceeding, processus; (transaction), res gesta; (at law), controversia judiciaria
A process, processus; (in law), formula, actio, lis [gressu
In process of time, temporis proTo serve in a process, comprehendo, in jus trahere
A procession, processio, agmen instructo ordine procedens; (in rogation-week), solennis limitum lustratio
To proclaim, proclamo, denuncio, edico; (war), indico; (peace), promulgo
A proclaimer, proclamator
A proclamation, proclamatio, edictum
Proclivity, proclivitas
A proconsul, proconsul
Proconsular, proconsularis
A proconsulship, proconsulatus
To procrastinate, differo
Procrastination, procrastinatio, dilatio
To procreate, procreo, gigno
A procreating, *or* procreation, procreatio, generatio
A proctor, procurator
Proctorship, munus procuratoria
Procurable, procurandus
A procuration, procuratio
To procure (get), acquiro, paro; (stir up), excito, moveo
A procurer, conciliator; (male bawd), leno
A procuring, *or* procurement, comparatio, conciliatio
[96]

PRO

Prodigal, prodigus, profusus, effusus
A prodigal, nepos
Prodigally, prodigè, effusè
Prodigality, effusio, dissipatio
Prodigious (monstrous), prodigiosus, mirus; (great), ingens, profundus
Prodigiously, prodigiosè, valdè
A prodigy, prodigium, ostentum, portentum
Prodition (treason), proditio
Produce (product), fructus
To produce (bring forth), produco, procreo, edo, pario, fero; (cause), gigno; (propose), in medium afferre; (show), exhibeo, profero
To be produced, provenio
A producing, productio
Product (of the earth), fructus; (of industry), commodum, emolumentum; (*or* amount of money), summa; (of the brain), fœtus ingenii
Production, productio; (of animals), procreatio, generatio; (of plants), germinatio; (of sprigs), fruticatio
Productive, generans, efficiens
A proem, prœmium, prologus
Profanation, rei sacræ violatio
Profane, profanus, nefastus
To profane, profano, violo
Profanely, profanè, impiè
A profaner, violator
Profaneness, impietas
To profess (own), profiteor, confiteor; (practise), exerceo; (protest), contestando, denunciare
A professed enemy, hostis apertus
Professedly, ex professo
Professing, profitens, exercens
A profession (acknowledgment), professio; (calling, *or* trade), ars, quæstus; (way of living), genus vitæ; (protestation), contestata denunciatio
A professor, professor [nus
A professorship, professoris muProfest (professed), professus
A proffer (attempt), conatus; (thing proposed), conditio ablata, *or* proposita
To proffer (attempt), conor, tento; (propose), propono, offero
Proffering, proponens, offerens
Proficiency, progressus
To make a proficiency, proficio
A proficient, progressus, faciens
A profile, catagraphum
Profit, commodum, lucrum, fructus, quæstus
Of profit, quæstuosus
Profits of lands, reditus, fructus
To profit, proficio, prosum; (in learning), progressus in studiis facere; (get advantage), lucror
Profitable, lucrosus, commodus
Very profitable, perutilis
It is profitable, conducit, confert
Profitableness, utilitas
Profitably, commodè, utilitèr
Profited, progressus, profectus
Profiting, proficiens, promovens
A profligate, profligatus, nequam perditus
Profligateness, scelus
Profound, profundus, altus; (a profound scholar), doctissimus
Profoundly, profundè, altè

PRO

Profoundness, Profundity, profunditas, altitudo [gus
Profuse, profusus, effusus, prodiProfusely, profusè, effusè
Profuseness, Profusion, profusio, prodigentia
To prog, obsonor, furor
A progenitor, major, avus
A progeny, progenies, proles, soboles, genus
Progging (catering), obsonans; (raking together), corradens, spolians
A prognostic, præsagium
To prognosticate, hariolor, prædico
A prognostication, prædictio
A prognosticator, hariolus, augur
A progress, *or* progression, progressus [cuitus
A progress (journey), iter, cirProgressive, proficiens
Progressively, gradibus, gradatim
To prohibit, prohibeo, veto
Prohibited, prohibitus, vetitus
A prohibitor, inhibitor
A prohibiting, *or* prohibiting, prohibitio, interdictum
Prohibitory, prohibitorius
A project, conatus, molimen
To project, designo, molior; (jut out), promineo
Projectile, impulsus
A projector, designator
A projection, designatio
A projecture, *or* projecting, projectura, prominentia
To prole, venor, aucupor
Prolepsis, prolepsis
Proleptic, prolepticus
Prolific, Prolifical, fœcundus
Prolix, prolixus, longus
Prolixly, prolixè
Prolixity, prolixitas
A prolocutor, prolocutor
A prologue, prologus
To prolong, protraho, extendo, duco; (life), vitam prolatare
A prolonger, dilator
A prolongation, *or* prolonging, prolatio, dilatio
A prominence, prominentia
Prominent, prominens, extans
Promiscuous, promiscuus
Promiscuously, promiscuè
A promise, promissum; (to pay money), stipulatio nummaria
To promise, polliceor, promitto; (in marriage), despondeo; (often), pollicitor; (*or* assure one's self), sibi promondere, spero; (openly), profiteor; (for another), expromitto; (conditionally), stipulor; (mutually), compromitto; (again), repromitto
A promiser, promissor
A promising, promissio
A promissory note, cautio chirographi
A promontory, promontorium
To promote, promoveo, offero; (a design), consilio favere; (one to honour), ad honores promovere; (learning), rem literariam juvare
A promoter, qui promovet; (of strife), fax seditionis
Promotion (honour), honor, dignitas, amplitudo
Prompt, promptus, paratus; (payment), pecunia numerata
To prompt, suggero, subjicio, concito, hortor
A prompter, monitor, hortator

PRO — PRO — PRU

A prompting, solicitatio, hortatio, suggestio
Promptitude, alacritas
Promptly, promptè, paratè, expeditè
Promptness, facilitas, alacritas
A promptuary, penus
To promulge, *or* promulgate, promulgo, publico
Promulgation, promulgatio
Pronus, pronus, propensus
Proneness, propensio, proclivitas
A prong, furca, bidens
A pronoun, pronomen
To pronounce, enuncio, recito, pronuncio, profero
A pronouncing, pronunciatio, recitatio
Pronunciation, *or* speaking in public, elocutio, recitatio publica
A proof, documentum; (argument), argumentum, probatio; (evidence), testimonium ; (in printing), specimen, exemplum
Proof (against ball), impenetrabilis; (against vice), inconcussus vitiis
A prop, fulcrum; (for a vine), adminiculum
To prop, fulcio, adminiculor
To propagate, propago; (to posterity), diffundo
A propagator, propagator
A propagating, *or* propagation, propagatio
To propel, propello [pronus
Propense, propensus, proclivis,
Propensity, propensio
Proper (fit), aptus, idoneus, commodus; (peculiar), peculiaris, proprius; (tall), procerus; (to be done), opportunus, tempestivus; (sufficient), competens
Properly, propriè, aptè, idoneè, tempestivè, ad vivum, affabrè, graphicè
Properness (propriety), proprietas; (tallness), proceritas
Property, proprium, proprietas; (disposition), natura, indoles, ingenium [tio
A prophecy, vaticinium, prædictio
Prophesied of, prædictus
A prophesier, vaticinator
To prophesy, vaticinor, divino
A prophesying, vaticinatio
Prophesying, præsagus, præsagiens
A prophet, propheta, vates; (false), pseudopropheta
A prophetess, mulier vaticinans
Prophetic, Prophetical, fatidicus
Propinquity, propinquitas
To propitiate, propitio, placo
Propitiation, propitiatio
Propitiatory, propitiatorius
A propitiatory, propitiatorium
A propitiator, reconciliator
Propitious, propitius, benignus
Propitiously, benignè
Propitiousness, benignitas
Proportion, proportio, ratio, comparatio, analogia
To proportion, rectè distribuere, uti normâ proportionis
In proportion, pro ratione
Proportionable, Proportional, analogus
Proportionably, analogicè
A proportioning, accommodatio
A proposal, propositio
To propose, propono, destino ; (resolve), statuo, constituo
A proposer, qui proponit
[97]

A proposition, propositio
To propound, propono
A thing propounded, quæstio
A propounder, propositor
A propounding, propositio
Propping, fulciens
A proprietary, proprietor, dominus proprius
A propriety (property), proprietas; (of speech), locutio propria
Propulsion, propulsatio
The prore, prora
To prorogue, prorogo, differo
A proroguing, *or* prorogation, prorogatio, dilatio
To proscribe, proscribo, relego
A proscript, exul relegatus
A proscription, *or* proscribing, proscriptio, relegatio ; (open sale), venditio, sub hastâ
Prosaic, prosaicus
Prose, prosa, oratio soluta
To prosecute, prosequor; (a criminal), sontium persequi; (a design), in consilio pergere; (a matter), de re aliquâ disserere
A prosecuting, *or* prosecution, lis, actio
A prosecutor, prosecutor, actor
To be prosecuted, in jus dici
A proselyte, proselytus
Prosody, prosodia
Prospect (distant view), prospectus; (viewing), inspectio; (design, hope, *or* view), consilium, spes
Prospective, prospiciens, providus
To prosper, floreo, valeo; (make to prosper), prospero, secundo
Prosperity, prosperitas, felicitas, res secundæ [felix
Prosperous, prosperus, secundus,
Prosperously, prosperè, felicitèr
A prostitute, scortum, meretrix
To prostitute, prostituo
A prostituting, *or* prostitution, prostitutio
Prostrate, prostratus
To prostrate (lay flat), prosterno; (fall down before), procido, procumbo, abjicio
A prostration, prostratio
To protect, defendo, tueor, tego
Protecting, protegens
A protection, tutela, tutamen
A protector, patronus, defensor
Protervity, protervitas
A protest, denunciatio contestata
To protest, testor, obtestor; (against), intercedo; (solemnly), solemnitèr affirmare
A protestant, protestans, religionis reformatæ professor
A protestation, affirmatio solennis; (against), intercessio
A protester, qui contestando aliquid denunciat
A protomartyr, protomartyr
A prototype, prototypon
To protract, protraho, differo
A protracting, productio, dilatio
A protractor, dilator
To protrude, protrudo
A protuberance, tumor, inflatus
Protuberant, prominens
Proud, elatus, superbus, fastosus
To be proud, tumeo, superbio; (of a thing), aliquid ostentare
To grow proud, insolesco
Proud words, ampullæ ; (bitch), canis salax, *or* catulliens; (flesh), caro putris
Proudly, superbè, arrogantèr, insolentèr

Proudness, fastus, superbia
To prove (make good), probo, confirmo, evinco ; (a thing false), refello; (try), experior, periclitor; (happen), accido; (become), fio
Proveable, probabilis
Provender, pabulum ; (providing of), pabulatio
Of provender, pabularis
A proverb, proverbium, adagium
Proverbial, proverbialis, adagio similis
To provide (procure), paro, præparo; (for hereafter), in futurum consulere; (beforehand), præcaveo ; (for), provideo, prospicio; (or furnish with), suppedito
Provided (yet), tamen, nihilominus
Providence, providentia
Provident, providus, cautus; (person), frugalis, frugi
Providential, favente Deo
Providentially, divinâ providentiâ
Providently, providè, cautè
A provider, provisor; (of corn), frumentarius; (of wood), lignator; (of victuals), obsonator; (of fodder), pabulator
Providing, parans, præparans
A providing, præparatio, procuratio; (of fodder), pabulatio
A province, provincia; (office, *or* station), munus, negotium
Of a province, provincialis
The United Provinces, provinciæ fœderatæ
A provincial, præpositus provinciæ
Proving, probans, comprobans; (essaying), periculum faciens
Provision (necessaries), alimentum, victus, penus, cibus, annona; (preparation), præparatio ; (for a day), diarium; (for a journey), viaticum; (for war), in rem bellicam apparatus ; (caution), provisio, cautio
To make provision, prospicio, apparo
Provisional, cautionalis
Provisionally, sub conditione
A proviso, exceptio, cautio
A provocation, provocatio
Provocative, provocatorius
Provocatives, ad libidinem stimulantia
To provoke, provoco, stimulo ; (allure), allicio, pellicio; (appetite), stomachum acuere ; (a stool), alvum ciere ; (urine), urinam citare; (sweat), sudorem elicere
A provoker, irritator
Provoking, provocans, irritans, ciens
A provost, præfectus urbis
A provostship, præfectura
The prow, prora
Prowess, fortitudo, virtus
To prowl, prædor
A prowler, prædator
Proximity, proximitas
A proxy, vicarius
A prude, fœmina modestiam falso affectans
Prudence, prudentia, sapientia
Prudent, prudens, sapiens
Prudential, ad prudentiam pertinens
Prudentially, Prudently, prudentèr, sapientèr, rectè, providè
A prune, prunum
To prune, amputo, tondeo

PUL — PUR

A pruner, putator, fondator
A pruning, putatio, frondatio
A pruning-knife, falx
Prurient, pruriens
To pry into, observo, investigo, perscrutor
A pryer, speculator
Prying, investigans, emissitius
A prying, intuitus propior
A psalm, psalmus, ode
A psalmist, psalmista, psaltes
Psalmody, psalmodia
A psalm-book, psalterium
Puberty, pubertas
Public, publicus, communis; (known), pervulgatus, notus
A public-house, popina
Public-spirited, publicæ salutis studiosus
At public charge, publicis sumptibus
Public good, commune bonum
Public weal, reipublicæ salus
A publican, publicanus
A publication, publicatio
Publicly, publicè, apertè, palàm
To publish abroad, publico, evulgo, divulgo, promulgo; (a book), librum edere
A publisher, vulgator, editor
A publishing, promulgatio
Pucelage, virginitas
To pucker, corrugo
In a pucker, confusus
A pudder, strepitus, tumultus
A pudding, fartum; (black), botulus; (plumb), fartum uvis refertum; (suet), fartum sabo refertum
In pudding time, oppidò, opportunè
A puddle, fossula, lacuna
To puddle, se inquinare
Pudicity, pudicitia
Puerile, puerilis
Puerility, puerilitas
A puff (of wind), flatus; (paste), crustulata; (want of breath), anhelitus; (barber's), instrumentum ad pulverem aspergendum; (deception), deceptio
To puff, flo; (and blow), anhelo; (the fire), ignem sufflare; (at), sperno, flocci facere; (extol), extollo; (deceive), decipio, fraudo; (up), tumefacio, inflo
To be puffed up, intumesco
A puffing, mergus
Puffing, anhelans, anhelus
A puffing, sufflatio, anhelitus; (at an auction), falsa representatio; (extolling), laudatio
Puffy, tumens, inflatus
Pugh! vah! apage!
Puissance, potentia, potestas, vis, virtus
Puissant, potens, validus
To be puissant, polleo, valeo
Puissantly, potentèr, validè
A puke, vomitus
To puke, vomo, vomito
A pull, nisus, vellicatio
To pull, vello, vellico; (again), revello; (at), pervello; (away), avello, divello; (back), retraho; (back, or hinder), impedio; (down), diruo, subruo, demolior; (down pride), superbiam comprimere; (by force), rapio; (away by force), eripio; (fruit), carpo, decerpo; (in), retraho, contraho; (in his horns), retraho; (in the reins), habenas premere; (off), exuo, detraho; (off bark), decortico

A puller up, avulsor
A pullet, gallinula, pullastra
A pulley, trochlea
A pulling, nisus, vellicatio; (off, or away), avulsio; (over), evulsio; (together), convulsio; (up by the roots), eradicatio, extirpatio
To pullulate, pullulo, pullulasco
Pulmonary, pulmonarius
The pulp, pulpa
A pulpit, pulpitum, rostrum
Pulpous, pulpâ abundans, mollis
Pulsation, pulsatio
Pulse, legumen, puls; (of the body), pulsus
To feel the pulse, venam tentare
To pulverise, in pulverem redigere
A pulverizing, pulveratio
A pumice-stone, pumex
A pump, antlia; (of a ship), sentina
To pump, exantlo, sentino; (a thing out of one), consilium callidè expiscari
A pumpion, or pumpkin, pepo
Pumps, calcei nitidi
A pun, lusus verborum
To pun (quibble), verborum sono ludere
A punch (person), pumilio obesus; (used by shoemakers), terebra cavata
To punch (thrust), propello; (bore), terebro
A puncheon, vas vinarium octoginta congios continens
A punctilio, res nihili, or levis
Punctilious, officiosus, comis
Punctual, accuratus
Punctuality, accurata observatio
Punctually, accuratè
Punctuation, interpunctio
A puncture, punctura
Pungency, acrimonia
Pungent, pungens
To punish, punio, castigo; (with death), morte mulctare
Punishable, puniendus, poenâ dignus
A punisher, punitor, ultor
A punishing, punitio, castigatio
Punishment, supplicium, poena; (in purse), mulctatio
Without punishment, impunè
Puny (little), parvus, exiguus; (lesser), inferior; (sickly), infirmus
To pup, catulos edere, or parere
A pupil, pupillus, discipulus; (of the eye), pupilla
Papillary, pupillaris
A puppet, pupa
A puppy, catulus; (silly fellow), ineptus, stultus
Purblind, luscus, myops
To purchase (buy), emo; (get), acquiro, paro
A purchaser, emptor
A purchasing, Purchase, emptio
Pure (clean), purus, mundus; (clear), clarus; (chaste), castus; (fine), tersus; (uncorrupt), incorruptus, immaculatus; (unmixt), merus
Pure good, optimus
To make pure, purifico, lustro
Made pure, purificatus
A making pure, purificatio
Purely, purè, integrè, castè, incorruptè, sincerè
Pureness, puritas, sinceritas
To purfle, aureo filo intexere
Purgation, purgatio, lustratio

Purgative, purgans, catharticus, purgatorius
Purgatory, purgatorium
A purge, catharticum
To purge, purgo, expurgo; (the body), alvum ciere; (liquid things), eliquo; (humours), humores evacuare; (by sacrifice), expio, lustro; (one's self of a fault), crimen diluere
Purging, purgans
A purging, purgatio; (by sacrifice), expiatio; (of the sea), maris ejectamentum
Purification, purificatio
A purifier, purgator
To purify, purifico, purgo, expio; (metals), metalla purgare; (from dregs), defæco
Purifying, purificans, purgans
A purifying, purificatio
A puritan, catharus
Purity, puritas, munditia, castitas; (of language), purus sermo; (of the Latin tongue), incorrupta Latini sermonis integritas
A purl, limbus
Purl, potus absynthio mixtus
To purl, lenitèr fluere
Purling, lenitèr fluens
To purloin, surripio, suffuror
A purloiner, fur privatus
A purloining, compilatio privata
Purple, purpura
Of purple, purpureus
Purple odour, murex, ostrum
To make purple, purpuro
In purple, purpuratus
To become purple, purpurasco
The purples, febris purpurea
A purport, sensus, significatio
To purport, propono, designo
A purpose, propositum, consilium
Of set purpose, consultò
To the purpose, appositus; (not to the purpose), nihil ad rem, absurdus
To the purpose, appositè, aptè
To good purpose, bono consilio
Fit for the purpose, idoneus
To another purpose, aliorsum, aliò; (to what purpose), quò; quorsum; (to that purpose), eò, ideò; (to the same purpose), in eandem sententiam; (to no purpose), frustrà, incassùm, nequicquàm [tino
To purpose, propono, statuo, destinopurposely
Purposely, cogitatò, eò, ideò
A purposing, designatio
To purr, felis sonitum edere
A purse, crumena, marsupium
To purse, contraho, corrugo
Purse-bearer, marsupii argentarius
Purse-proud, præ divitiis elatus
A purser, bursarius
Purseness, obesitas
Purslain, portulaca
In pursuance of, persequendo
Pursuant to, secundum, juxta
To pursue, prosequor; (diligently), insequor; (close, or hard), vestigiis adhærere; (a design), in proposito persistere
A pursuer, consectator [satio
A pursuing, or pursuit, consecA pursuivant, apparitor; (at arms), fecialis assecla
Pursy (fat), obesus; (shortwinded), anhelans, asthmaticus
A purtenance, appendix
To purvey, abs'condor; (for wood), lignor

QUA

A purveying, annonae emptio
A purveyor, annonae curator
Purulency, puris abundantia
Purulent, purulentus
A push (wheal), pustula; (thrust), impetus, ictus
To push, pello, impello; (at, or attempt), molior, tento; (on in battle), acriùs instare; (back), repello; (on, or encourage), instigo, stimulo; (forward, or make haste), festino, accelero; (forward in a design), consilio progredi
A pusher forward, impulsor
A pushing (back), repulsus; (on), impulsio, instigatio
Pusillanimity, timiditas
Pusillanimous, timidus, ignavus
A puss, felis
A pustule, pustula
Pustulous, pustulosus
A put off, mora, impedimentum
To put, pono, colloco, statuo; (again), repono; (against), oppono; (aside), sepono; (in array), instruo; (away), amoveo; (away a wife), uxorem repudiare; (or send away), ablego; (back), depello; (before), antepono; (between), interpono, interjicio; (to death), morte mulctare; (an end to), finem dare; (forth), exero, emitto; (forth the hand), manum porrigere; (forth strength), vires exserere; (forth a book), librum edere; (forth leaves), frondeo, frondesco
Putative, existimatus, habitus
Putid, putidus
A putter away, depulsor
A putting, positio; (away), amotio, rejectio; (between), interpositio; (between of days), intercalatio; (into), immissio; (off), dilatio; (forward), impulsio; (or blotting out), deletio; (out of fire), extinctio; (to), appositio; (together), compositio; (under), subjectio
Putrefaction, putredo
Putrefactive, septicus
To putrefy, putrefacio; (be putrefied), putreo, putresco
A putrefying, putredo
Putrefying, ulcerosus, ulceratus
Putty, creta oleo mixta
A puzzle (hard question), quaestio obstrusa, or obscura
To puzzle, confundo
Pygmean, pygmaeus
A pygmy, nanus, pumilio
A pyramid, pyramis
Pyramidal, pyramidatus
Pyrrhonism, pyrrhonismus
Pythagoric (Pythagorean), pythagoraeus
A pythoness, pythonissa
A pyx, pyxis

Q.

A quack, medicus circumforaneus, empiricus
Quackery, empirice
To quack, empiricen exercere; (as a duck), tetrinnio
Quadragesimal, quadragesimalis
A quadrangle, area quadrata
Quadrangular, quadrangulus
A quadrant, quadrans
[99]

QUA

Quadrate, quadratus
To quadrate, quadro, convenio
Quadratic, quadraticus
Quadrature, quadratura
Quadrilateral, quadrilaterus
Quadripartite, quadripartitus
A quadruped, quadrupes
The quadruple, quadruplum
Quadruple, *adj.* quadruplex
To quaff, perpoto; (all out), ebibo, exsorbeo
A quaffer, ebriosus, bibax
A quaffing, compotatio; (about), circumpotatio
A quaffing-cup, poculum
A quag, or quagmire, vorago
Quaggy, paludosus
A quail, coturnix
To quail, divuo
Quaint (polite), elegans, bellus, acitus; (odd, strange), rarus
Quaintly, comptè, nitidè
Quaintness, elegantia, nitor
To quake, tremo, trepide; (extremely), horreo, inhorreo
To make to quake, tremefacio
A quaker, tremulus fanaticus
Quakerism, tremulorum superstitio
A quaking, horror, tremor
A qualification (endowment), dos, indoles; (condition), status, conditio
To qualify (make fit), idoneum facere; (appease), paco; (moderate), moderor, tempero
A qualifying (appeasing), sedatio
A quality, qualitas, dos; (degree), gradus, ordo
The quality (nobles), nobiles
Quality (nobility), nobilitas
Qualities, mores
A qualm, levis stomachi aegritudo
Qualmish, crudus
A quandary, dilemma, confusio
A quantity, quantitas, vis
A quarantine, mora quadragenaria in statione propter pestem
A quarrel, jurgium, rixa; (of glass), vitri rhombus; (of a cross-bow), speculum quadratum
To quarrel, litigor, rixor, jurgor, altercor, litem serere
A quarrelling, altercator
A quarrelling, contentio, lis
Quarrelling, Quarrelsome, litigiosus
Quarrelsomeness, litigatio
A quarry, lapidum fodina
A quarryman, lapicida
A quart, sextarius
Quartan, quartanus
A quarter, quarta pars; (coast), regio; (of corn), octo medii
Quarters (lodgings), hospitium; (for soldiers), contubernia stativa; (of the moon), lunae phases; (winter), hiberna
Into all quarters, in omnes partes; (from all quarters), undiquè
A quarter-staff, batulus
Quarter (in fighting), salus, vita
Quarter-sessions, trimestria pacis curatorum, comitia
To quarter (into four pieces), in quatuor partes dissecare; (or lodge with), diversor; (receive into a house), hospitium praebere; (or cut up meat), dearticulo, lanio
Quarterage, pensio trimestris
A quartering (in pieces), dissec-

QUI

tio; (lodging), hospitalis receptio
A quarter-master, castrorum metator
Quarterly, quolibet spatio trimestri; *adj.* trimestris
A quartern, sextarii quarta pars
Quartilis, quartilis
A quash, pepo
To quash, quasso, opprimo, extinguo, discutio
A quashing, quassatio
A quaternion, quaternio
To quaver, cantillo, modulor
Quavering, modulans, vibrans
A quavering, modulatio
A quean, scortum, meretrix
Queasiness, fastidium
Queasy, fastidiosus, dissolutus
A queen, regina; (consort), regina uxor; (dowager), regina vidua
Queer, ineptus, insulsus; (in health), delicatulus
Queerly, ineptè, insulsè
To quell, domo, debello, subigo
A queller, domitor, victor
A quelling, domitus
To quench, extinguo; (thirst), sitim sedare, or compescere
Quenchable, extinguibilis
A quenching, extinctio, restinctio
Querimonious, queribundus
A quern, mola trusatilis
A query, quaestio
To query, dubito, quaestionem proponere
Querulous, querulus
Querulousness, querela
A quest, inquisitio; (man), quaesitor
To quest, latro, nicto
To go in quest of, ad investigandum ire
A question, quaestio, interrogatio; (doubt), dubitatio
In question, in dubium
To question (doubt of), dubito; (with), interrogo; (examine), ad examen, or in jus vocare, examino, scrutor
Questionable, dubius, incertus
A questioning, dubitatio, inquisitio, disquisitio
Questionless, sine dubio, certè
A questor, quaestor
A quibble, cavillum, sophisma
To quibble, verbis ludere
A quibble, cavillator, sophista
A quibbling, captio, cavillatio
Quibbling, cavillans, captiosus
Quick (nimble), agilis, celer; (alive), vivus; (hasty), festinus; (diligent), diligens; (in scent), sagax; (in sight), perspicax; (of wit), solers; (with child), foetu vivo gravida
Quick, quick! festina!
To the quick, ad vivum
To be quick (or lively), vigeo; (with child), foetum vivum utero gestare
A quickeand, syrtis
Quickseta, plantaria viva; (hedge), sepes viva
Quicksilver, argentum vivum
Quick, or quickly, citò; (subtlely), acutè
To quicken (enliven), animo, vivifico; (hasten), instigo; (make haste), deproperò; (wine), vinum resuscitare; (as a woman with child), foetum vivum in utero sentire
A quickener, animator

RAC   RAI   RAN

Quickening, animans, stimulans
A quickening, animatio
Quickness (nimbleness), agilitas; (liveliness), vivacitas; (of sight), perspicuitas; (of wit), sagacitas, acumen
A quiddity, captiosa quæstio
Quiescence, quiescentia
Quiescent, quiescens
Quiet, quies, otium
Quiet, quietus, tranquillus, placidus; (silent), tacitus
To be quiet (silent), sileo, taceo; (live at ease), otior; (to be at quiet), quiesco, requiesco
To quiet, paco, sedo, placo
Not to be quieted, implacabilis
A quieter, pacator
A quieting, pacatio, sedatio [cidè
Quietly, quietè, tranquillè, plaQuietness, requies, serenitas, otium, pax
A quill, penna, calamus; (of a barrel), sipho; (for a musical instrument), plectrum
To quilt, pannum, &c., bombyce fartum consuere
A quilt, culcita
Quinquennial, quinquennis
A quinsy, angina
A quintal, centumpondium
A quintessence, medulla
A quire, papyri scapus; (of singers), see *Choir*; (of a church), locus ubi chorus canit
A quirk, cavillatio, captio
Full of quirks, versutus, subdolus
Quit, absolutus, impunitus
To quit (leave), relinquo, desero; (yield), cedo; (let go), libero, relaxo; (one's post), provinciam, or stationem tradere
Quit, *adv.* impunè
Quite, omninò, penitùs, longè
A quittance (receipt), acceptilatio
Quitting horses, equis dimissis
A quitting (leaving), desertio; (freeing), liberatio
A quiver, pharetra
With a quiver, pharetratus
To quiver, contremisco; (with cold), præ frigore horrere; (for fear), expavesco
Quivering, tremulus, horridus
A quivering, tremor, horror
A quoil of cable, rudentis in circulum convolutio
To quoil, in circulum convolvere; (as a serpent), nodis aggestis plicare
A quoit, discus
A quota, pars, proportio
A quotation, citatio, prolatio
To quote, cito, laudo, adduco
Quoth he, inquit ille
Quotidian, quotidianus
A quoting, citatio, laudatio

R.

A rabbi, *or* rabbin, rabbinus
Rabbinical, rabbinicus
A rabbit, cuniculus
Rabid, rabidus, rabiosus
A rabble, turba, fæx populi
A race, cursus, curriculum, stadium; (stock), stirps, progenies, genus; (or root of ginger), radix zinziberis; (of mankind), genus humanum; (of life), spatium
[100]

Of an illustrious race, honesto loco natus
A racehorse, equus cursor
A rack (for beasts), falisca; (for torture), equuleus; (for a spit), cratenta; (for bacon), crates porcina; (for bottles), crates utricularis; (for cheese), crates casearia; (for a crossbow), harpago; (of mutton), cervix vervecina; (for hay), præsepe, crates   (otiosus
At rack and manger, satur et
Rack (arrack), potus Indicus
To rack (*or* put upon a rack), crati suspendere; (torment), torqueo, excrucio; (off beer, &c.), defæco; (one's self), macero, afflictor
To be racked in pain, excrucior
Racked (with pains), excruciatus; (as liquor), defæcatus
A racker, tortor, extortor
A racket, reticulum; (stir), strepitus, turba, tumultus
To make a racket, tumultuor
A racking, tortura
A racking of liquors, defæcatio
Racking pains, cruciamenta
Racy, saporis gratissimi
Radiance, nitor, splendor [tens
Radiant, radians, coruscans, niTo radiate, niteo, splendeo
Radiation, radiatio
Radical, radicalis, vitalis
Radically, radicitùs
To radicate, radico, infigo
A radish, raphanus
Of a radish, raphaninus
The raff (refuse), rejectanea
To raffle, aleâ ludere
A raffle, *or* raffling, alea
A raft, ratis
A rafter, tignum, cantherius
To rafter, contigno
A raftering, contignatio
Of rafters, tignarius
Rafty, sentibus obductus
A rag, panniculus, linteolum
Full of rags, pannosus
To tear to rags, lacero
A ragamuffin, mendicabulum
Rage, rabies, furor, ira; (of the sea), æstus, fremitus
In a rage, furibundus; *adv.* rabidè, rabiosè
To rage, furo, insanio, sævio; (a wound), recrudesco; (as the sea), æstuo; (in drink), debacchor
Raging, furiosus, furens
A raging, rabies, furor
Ragingly, furiosè, rabidè
Ragged, pannosus; (jagged), laciniatus, dentatus
Raggedness, pannositas
A ragoo, *or* ragout, cupediæ
A rail, palus, repagulum
To rail, malè sepire; (at), maledico, convicior, malè loqui
Railed (at), conviciis insectatus; (with rails), palis septus
A railer, insectator
Railing, convicians
Railingly, contumeliosè
Raillery, convicium, facetia
Raiment, vestis, vestitus
Rain, pluvia, imber
Of rain, pluvius, pluvialis
In the rain, per imbrem
To rain, pluo; (downright), depluo; (in, *or* upon), impluo; (through), perpluo
A rainbow, iris
Rainy, pluvialis, imbrifer

To raise, elevo, attollo; (up one's self), surgo; (prefer), promoveo; (anger), commoveo; (a wall), extruo; (a battery), dispono
A raiser, concitator, excitator
A raisin, uva passa; (of the sun), uva sole siccata
A raising, concitatio, excitatio; (of a bank), aggestio; (of money), exactio; (of soldiers), delectus; (of a siege), discessus ab obsidione
A rake (tool), rastrum; (for an oven), rutabulum; (amongst), fodins; (to pull up weeds), irpex; (spendthrift), prodigus, homo dissolutus, *or* infamis, nepos
To rake, sarculo, sarrio; (scrape), rado; (again), resarcio; (together, *or* up), corrado; (up fire), ignem cineribus condere
A raker, sarritor
A raking, sarculatio, sarritio
Rakish, dissolutus, infamis
To rally, aciem instaurare; (return to the charge), ex fugâ convenire; (joke), jocor, irrideo
A rallying, instauratio pugnæ
A ram, aries
To ram, fistuco; (stuff), infercio; (in gunpowder), pulverem nitratum virgâ adigere
A rambler, vagator, excitator
To ramble, vagor, erro, circumcurro; (in discourse), à proposito aberrare
A rambling person, *or* rambler, erro; (house), sparsa domus; (discourse), oratio aberrans
A rammer, fistuca, pavicula; (of a gun), virga sclopetaria
A ramming, fistucatio   [dus
Rammish, rancidus, hircosus, oliRammishly, rancidè
To smell rammishly, hircum olere
Rammishness, rancor, fœtor
A ramp, virago procax
To ramp, procacitèr se gerere
Rampant, procax; (in heraldry), insaliens; (as a lion), erectus
A rampart, vallum, agger
A ramping, exultatio
Ran (run), cucurri
Rancid (rank), rancidus
Rancor, invidia, odium
Rancorous, malignus, invidus
Rancorously, malignè, invidiosè
A rand, margo, ora
At random, temerè, inconsultò
Random-shot, sine scopo emissus
It rang, sonuit
A range (of a coach), temo; (order), series, ordo; (ramble), vagatio
To range (set in order), dispono, instruo; (stand in order), rectâ serie disponi; (up and down), evagor, erro; (meal), farinam cernere
A ranger (setter in order), digestor; (searcher), explorator
A ranging (in order), digestio; (inspecting), lustratio
Rank (too much), præfertilis, nimis luxurians; (in smell), rancidus
A rank rogue, nebulo; (poison), acre venenum   [nitas
A rank, ordo, series, locus, digOf rank, illustris
To rank, ordino, dispono
To be rank, luxurio, muceo

A ranker, ordinator
To rankle, suppuro, putreo
A rankling, suppuratio
Rankly (offensively), rancidè; (luxuriantly), luxuriosè
Rankness, rancor, fœtor; (in growth), luxuries, luxuria
To ransack, diripio
A ransacker, spoliator
A ransacking, direptio, vastatio
A ransom, redemptio
To ransom, redimo
A ransomer, redemptor
A ransoming, redemptio
Rant, vaniloquentia
To rant, superbè loqui, debacchor
A ranter, nepos ineptus, demens
A ranting, bacchatio
Rantingly, ineptè, insulsè, gloriosè
A rap, ictus, alapa; (over the fingers), talitrum
To rap (strike), percutio, ferio, pulso; (swop), commuto; (swear), juramentum temerè profero
A rattle, crepitaculum
Rapacious, rapax
Rapaciously, avidè
Rapacity, Rapaciousness, rapacitas, rapina
A rape, raptus, per vim stuprum; (of a county), portio; (wild turnip), rapum
To commit a rape, stupro
Rapid, rapidus, velox
Rapidness, Rapidity, rapiditas, velocitas
Rapidly, rapidè, velociter
A rapier, verutum, ensis
Rapine, rapina
A rapper, pulsator; (knocker),
A rapping, pulsatio
Rapt, or rapped up with joy, effusâ lætitiâ exultans
A rapture, animi impetus; (of joy), effusa lætitia
Rapturous, mirabilis
Rare (uncommon), rarus, infrequens; (excellent), eximius, egregius; (thin), rarus, subtilis, tenuis
Rarefaction, rarefactio
To rarefy, rarefacio
To be rarefied, raresco, tenuor
A rarefying, tenuatio
Rarely, rarò
Rareness, Rarity, raritas, paucitas
A rarity, res eximia
A rascal, balatro; (vile), furcifer, homo nihili, flagitiosus, bipedum nequissimus
Rascally, flagitiosus, scelestus
A rase (blot), litura; (small wound), leve vulnus
To rase (scratch), stringo; (out), erado, deleo, expungo; (pull down), everto, solo æquare
Rash, inconsideratus, temerarius, præceps, inconsultus
A rash, eruptio cutanea
A rasher of bacon, offella lardi
Rashly, temerè, inconsultè
Rashness, præcipitatio, temeritas
A raising, rasura; (demolishing), subversio, demolitio; (blotting out), deletio
A rasor, novacula
A rasp, radula
To rasp, rado, limo
Raspberry, rubi Idæi fructus
A rasping, rasura
A rasure, rasura
A rat, sorex
Of a rat, soricinus
Ratsbane, arsenicum
To smell a rat (mistrust), suboleo
[101]

A rat-catcher, muricidus
A rat-trap, decipula
Ratably, pro ratâ
A rate, pretium; (proportion), proportio; (tax), census; (manner), modus; (size), magnitudo
To rate (tax), taxo, tributum impono; (esteem), æstimo, pendo; (chide), objurgo, increpo
Rateable, censualis
A rater, censor, æstimator
Rather, potius, magis; (I had rather), malo
A ratification, or ratifying, confirmatio, ratificatio, sanctio
To ratify, confirmo, ratum facere
A rating, census; (chiding), objurgatio, reprehensio
Ratiocination, ratiocinatio
Rational, rationis particeps; (reasonable), rationi consentaneus
Rationality, facultas ratiocinandi
Rationally, è ratione, æquè, justè
To rattle (make a noise), crepito, strepitum edere; (chide), increpo; (talk idly), ineptè garrire
Rattleheaded, loquax, insulsus
Rattled off, graviter increpitus
Rattles for children, crepundia
A rattling (shaking), concussio, quassatio; (fellow), garrulus, ineptus; (chiding), objurgatio
Rattlings, scalarum nauticarum gradus
Ravage, direptio, vastatio
To ravage, diripio, vasto, populor
A ravager, spoliator
A ravaging, direptio, vastatio, populatio
To rave, deliro, insanio
To ravel, retexo, involvo
Ravelled, retextus, involutus
A raven, corvus, corax
Of a raven-colour, coracinus
To raven, or ravin, voro
A ravener, raptor, helluo [dus
Ravening, Ravenous, vorax, avidus
A ravening, raptio, rapacitas
Ravenously, avidè, voraciter
Ravenousness, voracitas
A raver, delirus
A raving, delirium, deliratio
To ravish, constupro, vitio; (charm), delecto, voluptate magnâ afficere; (from), vi abripere
A ravisher, raptor, stuprator
A ravishing, or ravishment (committing a rape), raptus, stupratio; (of the mind), ecstasis
Ravishing (to the eye), eximius, egregius; (to the ear), suavissimus, admirabilis, jucundissimus
Raw, crudus; (not sodden), incoctus; (unwove), nondùm textus; (unskilful), rudis, imperitus
A raw scholar, novitius
To grow raw, crudesco
Raw weather, tempestas frigida et nubila
Rawboned, strigosus
Rawly (crudely), crudùm; (unskilfully), imperitè
Rawness, cruditas
A ray, radius; (fish), raia
To rase, rado; (foundations), fundamenta evertere. See Rase
A rasor, novacula
To reach (come up to), assequor; (one's meaning), intelligo; (out), extendo; (neut. to reach), extendo, porrigor; (or arrive

at), pertingo; (vomit), vomo, evomo
A reach, ambitus, tractus; (fetch), dolus; (capacity, ability), captus; (power), potestas; (of thought), sagacitas; (by water), intervallum
Reached (given), allatus, datus; (extended), extentus, porrectus
A reaching, extensio, porrectio; (vomiting), vomitio
Reaction, reactio
To read, lego; (over again), relego; (often), lectito; (over), evolvo, periego; (out), publicè recitare; (unto), prælego
Read, lectus; (openly), publicè recitatus; (over), perlectus
Well read, doctissimus
A reader, lector; (in schools), professor; (to scholars), prælector; (curate), vicarius
A great reader, helluo librorum
A reading, lectio; (openly), prælectio; (over), evolutio
To readmit, iterùm admittere
Ready, paratus, promptus, pronus, propensus, expeditus, accinctus; (to please), affabilis, comis, mitis; (willing), volens, lubens; (to lie in), instat partus; (furnished), hospitium supellectili instructum
Ready, Readily, jam, jamdudùm
Of ready wit, sagax, perspicax
Ready money, argentum præsentaneum, pecunia numerata
To be ready at hand, adsum, præstò esse
To get, or make ready, paro, expedio; (hastily), accelero; (forward), apparo
Readily, expeditè, paratè; (without book), memoriter; (willingly), libenter, comiter
Readiness, promptitudo, alacritas; (to please), obsequium, comitas
In readiness, in promptu, præstò
To get in readiness, paro
Real, realis, verus
A real estate, patrimonium
Reality, veritas
In reality, reverâ
To realize, ad amussim exprimere
Really (in earnest), reverâ, sinicerè, canè; (surely), profectò, certè, sanè
A realm, regnum, imperium [pyri
A ream of paper, scapus major patio
To reanimate, denuò animare
To reannex, denuò adjungere
To reap, meto, demeto
Fit to reap, maturus
A reaper, messor
A reaping, messio; (hook), falx
Reaping-time, messis
In reaping-time, per messes
Of reaping, messorius
The rear, extremum; (of an army), agmen extremum
To rear (up), tollo, erigo; (up a building), extruo, ædifico; (up children), infantes alere
A rearing, erectio, educatio
To reascend, denuò ascendere
Reason (the faculty of), ratio; (cause, or motive), ratio, causa, argumentum; (understanding), consilium; (moderation), modus; (right), æquum, jus
Against reason, absurdus, ineptus
By reason of, ob, propter, præ, propriereà; (by reason), quùm, quandò, propterea quod
F 3

To reason, argumentor, ratiocinor, discepto; (against), oppono, oppugno
Reasonable (rational), rationalis; (just), æquus, justus; (in measure), mediocris, modicus
Reasonableness, æquitas
Reasonably, justè; (moderately), mediocriter, modicè; (well), sic satis
Having reasoned, ratiocinatus
That may be reasoned, disputabilis
A reasoner, ratiocinator
A reasoning, ratiocinatio
To reassemble (call together again), iterùm convocare; (meet again), rarsùm convenire
To reassign, iterùm assignare
A reassignment, assignatio iterata
To reassume, reassumo, revoco
To reattempt, retento
To rebate (check), reprimo; (blunt), hebeto; (in accounts), subduco; (or make a rebate), strio
Rebating, reprimens, refrenans
A rebating, Rebatement, repressio; (in heraldry), diminutio
A rebel, rebellis, perduellis
To rebel, rebello, deficio
A rebeller, rebellator
A rebelling, or rebellion, rebellio
Rebellious, rebellis, factiosus; (disobedient), perversus, obstinatus, contumax
A rebound, resultus
To rebound, resilio
A rebounding, repercussio
A rebuff, repulsa
To rebuild, ræedifico
A rebuilding, ræedificatio
A rebuke, reprehensio
To rebuke, increpo, castigo; (with a sneer), sugillo; (sharply), increpito; (despitefully), exprobro
Rebukeful, objurgatorius
A rebuker, objurgator
A rebuking, objurgatio
A rebus, symbolum
To rebut, re retrahere
To recall, revoco; (one's words), verba reprendere
A recalling, revocatio
To recant, recanto; (an opinion), sententiam mutare
A recanting, or recantation, recantatio, palinodia
To recapitulate, breviter repetere, summatim colligere
A recapitulation, summarium
To recede, recedo, discedo
A receipt (receiving), receptio; (discharge), acceptilatio, syngrapha; (by a physician), præscriptum
To receive, recipio, accipio; (visits), salutantes admittere; (a wound), vulnero; (drink in), imbibo; (into company), admitto, coopto
A receiver, receptor, acceptor; (of taxes), publicanus; (chymical vessel), vas recipiens; (of the king's demeane), regis procurator
Receivers-general, tribuni ærarii
A receiving, receptio, acceptio, admissio; (before), anticipatio
Recent, recens, nuperus
Recently, recentèr, nupèr, modò
A receptacle, receptaculum
[102]

A reception, receptio; (entertainment), acceptio
Receptive, capax
A recess, recessus, latebra
A recipe, præscriptum
Reciprocal, reciprocus, mutuus
Reciprocally, mutuò, alternatim
To reciprocate, alterno
Reciprocation, reciprocatio
Recision, recisio
A recital, recitatio, enumeratio
To recite, recito, enumero
A reciter, recitator
A reciting, recitatio
To reck, solicitus esse, curo
Reckless, remissus, negligens
To reckon (count), numero, computo; (up), enumero; (judge), arbitror; (esteem), existimo, duco, habeo; (design), statuo, constituo; (or, depend upon), confido; (little of), parvi pendere; (with), rationes conferre, or componere
That may be reckoned, computabilis
Not to be reckoned, innumerabilis
A reckoner, computator
A reckoning, numeratio; (of one with child), tempus prægnationis; (shot), symbola, collecta; (account to be given), ratio
To reclaim, corrigo
A reclaiming, emendatio
To recline, reclino
Reclining, reclinis
A recluse, monachus
Recluse, seclusus, solitarius
A recognisance, obligatio, vadimonium
To recognise, agnosco
A recognizing, or recognition, agnitio
To recoil, resilio, recedo
Not to recoil, subsisto
A recoiling, Recoil, recessio
Recoiling, resiliens
To recoin, iterùm cudere
To recollect, recolligo, recordor, in mentem revocare
A recollecting, Recollection, recordatio, recognitio
To recommence, renovo, instauro
A recommencing, instauratio
To recommend, commendo; (send compliments to), saluto
Recommendable, commendatio
A recommendation, commendatio
Recommendatory, commendatitius
A recommender, commendator
A recompence, præmium, merces; (requital), retributio
Without recompence, gratuitò, gratis
To recompense, remunero, compenso, rependo; (requite like for like), par pari referre
That may be recompensed, revocabilis
Not to be recompensed, irreparabilis
A recompenser, remunerator
A recompensing, or recompensation, compensatio, retributio
Recompensing, compensans
To recompose, denuò componere
To reconcile, reconcilio, in gratiam restituere
Reconcileable, exorabilis
Not to be reconciled, inexorabilis
A reconciler, reconciliator
A reconciliation, or reconcilement, reconciliatio, conciliatio
Recondite, occultus, abditus

To reconduct, reconduco
A reconducting, deductio iterata
To reconnoitre, exploro, indago
A record (of time), annales; (before a court), testimonium; (books of), tabulæ publicæ
To record, in acta referre; (a law), legem in tabulas referre; (in the mind), in memoriâ figere
To bear record, testor
A recorder, proprætor urbanus
A recording, in fastos relatio
The office of records, tabularium
To recover (get again), recupero, recipio, reconcilio, reperio, invenio; (from a fright), ad se redire; (health), revalesco, convalesco; (one's wits), resipisco, ad se redire; (from death), revivisco
Recoverable, recuperabilis
A recoverer, recuperator
A recovering, or recovery, recuperatio; (in law), evictio; (remedy), remedium
To recount, enumero, memoro
A recounting, enumeratio
A recourse, refugium
To have recourse, refugio, recurro
Recreant, iguavus, falsus
To recreate, oblecto, reficio
Recreation, oblectatio; (of children), lusus
For recreation, animi causâ
Recreative, amœnus, gratus
Recrement, recrementum
To recriminate, crimen in accusatorem rejicere
A recrimination, criminis in accusatorem rejectio
A recruit, supplementum
To recruit, suppleo; (one's self), se reficere; (health), convalesco; (soldiers), supplementum scribere
A recruiting one's self, refectio
A recruiting, figura quatuor rectos angulos habens
Rectangular, rectos angulos habens
Rectifiable, quod corrigi potest
To rectify, corrigo, emendo; (in chemistry), puriores partes extrahere
A rectifying, or rectification, rectificatio, correctio
Rectilineal, Rectilinear, rectilineus
Rectitude, rectum, rectitudo
A rector, rector [munus
A rectorship, or rectory, rectoris
Recumbent, recumbens
To recur, recurro
Recurrent, recurrens
A recusant, recusans, schismaticus
Red, ruber, rubeus; (dark-red), puniceus; (sea-red), rufus; (red hot), candens; (bloodred), sanguineus
To be red, rubeo; (hot), candeo; (grow-red), rubesco
Marked red, rubricatus
The red-gum, scrophulus
Red-haired, rufus
Reddish, rubicundulus
To redden, rubefacio
Reddition, redditio
Redditive, redditivus
To redeem, redimo; (a pawn), repignero
Redeemable, redimendus
A redeemer, redemptor
A redeeming, redemptio

To redemand, reposco, repeto
Redemption, redemptio
To redintegrate, Renew, renovo
Redintegration, renovatio
Redness, rubor; (of the eyes), lippitudo
Redolent, redolens, fragrans
Redolence, fragrantia
To be redolent, redoleo
To redouble, ingemino
A redoubling, duplicatio
A redoubt, munimentum minus
Redoubtable, formidandus
To redound, redundo
Redress, emendatio, restitutio
To redress, emendo, corrigo, reformo, restituo ; (one's self), jus suum vindicare
Not to be redressed, irreparabilia
A redresser, emendator; (of manners), censor
A redressing, correctio
To reduce, reduco, redigo; (to dust), in pulverem vertere; (expenses), sumptus contrahere
Reducible, quod reduci potest
A reducing, Reduction, reductio
A redundance, redundantia
Redundant, redundans, superfluus
Redundantly, redundantèr
To reduplicate, duplico
To re-echo, resono
A reed, arundo, canna, calamus
Of reed, arundineus, canneus
Full of reeds, arundinosus
Like a reed, arundinaceus
Bearing reeds, arundifer
To re-edify, reædifico
A reek (smoke), fumus; (vapour), exhalatio, vapor
To reek, fumo, exhalo
Reeking, fumosus, fumidus
A reeking, exhalatio, vapor
A reel, rhombus
To reel (like a drunken man), titubo, vacillo; (thread), filum glomerare
A reeling (staggering), vacillatio; (of yarn), glomeratio
Reem, pruina
Covered with reem, pruinosus
To re-embark, navim rursùs conscendere
To re-enforce, reparo, adurgeo, suppleo
A re-enforcement, supplementum
To re-enter, rursùs intrare
A re-entry, introitus iteratus
To re-establish, restituo
Re-established, restitutus
A re-establisher, instaurator
A re-establishing, or re-establishment, instauratio, renovatio
A reeve, villicus, procurator
To re-examine, ad examen revocare
A refection, refectio
A refectory, cœnaculum
To refel, refello, refuto
To refer, refero, remitto, relego; (to an author), auctorem citare; (to arbitration), rem arbitrorum judicio permittere
A reference, arbiter
A reference, arbitrium
Reference (regard), respectus
A reference in a book, nota referens
In reference to, quantum attinet
Having reference, relativus
Referrible, ad quod referri potest
To refine, purgo, elimo, excoquo; (upon), accuratiùs tractare
A refiner, purgator
A refining, purgatio
[103]

To refit, reficio
A refitting, refectio
To reflect, reverbero; (in the mind), considero, revolvo ; (upon a person), aliquem carptim perstringere, reprehendo
Reflecting, reflectens; (as light), irradians; (in the mind), considerans; (blaming), reprehendens, sugillans
A reflection, repercussio; (of the mind), consideratio; (blame), reprehensio
Without reflection, incogitans
Reflexive, considerationis capax
To reflow, refluo
Refluent, refluens, refluus
A reflux, refluxus, recessus
To reform, reformo, emendo, corrigo, castigo, ad frugem redigere; (troops), militum partem exauctorare
A reformation, or reforming, reformatio, correctio, emendatio
A reformer, reformator, corrector, emendator
To refract, irradio, refringo
Refraction, refractio, declinatio
Refractory, refractarius, contumax, pervicax
Refractorily, contumacitèr
Refractoriness, pervicacia
To refrain (forbear), abstineo ; (curb), refreno, compesco, cohibeo, comprimo
A refraining, temperantia
Refrangible, quod refringi potest
To refresh, recreo, relaxo; (vamp up), resarcio; (the mind), animum oblectare ; (the body), membra fovere ; (the memory), memoriam renovare ; (take refreshment), cibum capere
A refreshing, Refreshment, recreatio
Refreshing (cooling), refrigerans
To refrigerate, refrigero
Refrigerative, refrigeratorius
A refuge, refugium, asylum
Refulgence, nitor, splendor
Refulgent, refulgens, nitens
Refulgently, nitidè, splendidè
To refund, refundo, rependo
A refusal, repulsa, optio
The refuse (of things), purgamentum, recrementum, quisquiliæ ; (of corn), excretum ; (of metals), scoria
To refuse, recuso, renno, respuo; (absolutely), pernego
A refusing, recusatio
To refute, refuto, refello
A refuting, Refutation, confutatio
To regain, redipiscor, recupero
Regained, recuperatus
A regaining, recuperatio
Regal, regalis, regius
To regale, convivio excipere
A regale, epulæ, convivium
Regalia, insignia regum
A regaling, epulatio opipara
Regality, regia dignitas
Regally, regalitèr, regiè
Regard, respectus, ratio, cura
To regard, respicio, curo; (mind), attendo ; (observe), observo, intueor, aspicio ; (concern), specto; (esteem, or value), æstimo, pendo ; (much), magni facere
Not to regard, negligo, sperno
In regard to, quod attinet ad
Regardable, considerations dignus
Not regarded, neglectus

To be not regarded, sordeo
A regarder, observator
Regardful, attentus, observans
A regarding, respectus
Regarding, attinens, pertinens
Regardless, negligens, remissus
Regardlessly, remissè, improvidè
Regardlessness, incuria
Regency (government), regimen ; (of a kingdom), administratio regni
To regenerate, regenero [ratus
Regenerate, Regenerated, regeneRegeneration, regeneratio
A regeat (in studies), moderator, præfectus, rector; (of a realm), regni procurator ; (viceroy), protex; (queen), regni procuratrix
To regerminate, regermino
A regicide, regis interfector
Regimen (government), regimen, moderamen, rerum administratio; (in diet), diæta; (in physic), medicinæ regimen præscriptum
A regiment, legio
Regimental, legionarius
A region, regio, tractus
A register (book of records), acta, archivum ; (of names), nomenclatura; (officer), registrarius
To register, in tabulas referre
A registering, in tabulas relatio
A registry (office for registers), locus ubi acta publica conservantur
To regorge, vomo, revomo
To regrant, iterùm donare
To regrate, præmercor
A regrater, mango, propola
A regress, regressus
Regret, indignatio, dolor
To regret, ægrè ferre; (bemoan), defleo, lugeo
Regular (according to art), ad normam exactus; (usual), usitatus; (methodical), methodicus, ordine progrediens ; (moderate), moderatus, temperatus; (under a rule), regulâ astrictus
Regularity, regularitas
Regularly, ex ordine, certò
To regulate, dispono, ordino, moderor, præscribo
A regulating, or regulation, moderatio, temperatio
A regulator, moderator, ordinator
To reheat, denuò aurire
A rehearing, auditio iterata
To rehearse, recito, repeto
A rehearsal, recitatio
A rehearsing, enumeratio
To reject, rejicio, repudio, abdico, respuo
To be rejected, respuendus
A rejecting, Rejection, rejectio
A reign, regnum
To reign, regno ; (prevail), vigeo, ingravesco; (be in vogue), obtineo, floreo
Reigning, regnans; (distemper), morbus ingravescens [scendere
To reimbark, navem rursùs conA reimbarking, Reimbarkment, or reimbarkation, in navem iterata conscensio
To reimburse, pecuniâ rependere
A reimbursement, restitutio
The rein, habena, lorum
Reins (of government), imperium; (or kidneys), renes
To reinforce, instauro, reparo; F 4

(an army), exercitum supplere; (an argument), adurgeo
A reinforcement, supplementum
To reingage (in fight), iterùm confligere; (in business), iterùm negotio se implicare
To reinstal, instauro
To reinstate, restituo
A reinstating, restitutio
To rejoice (be glad), lætor, gaudeo; (make glad), exhilaro, lætifico; (with), gratulor
A rejoicing, lætitia, gaudium; (day), dies exultationis
To rejoin (reply), iterùm respondere
A rejoinder, responsio iterata
To reiterate, itero, repeto
A reiteration, repetitio
To rekindle, iterùm accendere
To reland, in terram denuò exponere
A relapse, novus, or iteratus lapsus
To relapse, relabor, recido
To relate, narro, enarro, expono
A relater, narrator
A relating, Relation, narratio
Relation (kindred), consanguinitas, affinitas
A relation (by blood), consanguineus; (by marriage), affinis
In relation to, quod attinet ad
Relative, relativus
A relative, relativum
Relatively, pro ratione
To relax, relaxo, remitto
A relaxation, or relaxing, relaxatio, remissio
A relay, statio
To relay (station), colloco
To release (set at liberty), dimitto; (a prisoner), libero; (from a contract), stipulationi non insistere
A release, absolutio, liberatio
A releasing, Releasement, relaxatio, remissio, liberatio
To relent (grow gentle), mollesco, mitesco; (be moved with compassion), misericordiâ moveri; (be troubled for), solicitudine affici; (yield), cedo
A relenting, remissio, molestia
Relentless, inflexibilis
Reliance, fiducia
A relict (widow), vidua
Relief (comfort), consolatio, solatium, solamen; (help, succour), suppetiæ, subsidium, auxilium
To relieve (comfort), consolor; (help), succurro; (a town), oppidanis suppetias ferre
A reliever (helper), opitulator
A relieving, auxilium
Religion, religio, pietas
Religious, religiosus, pius; (in appearance only), hypocrita; (exact, punctual), qui religiosè se gerit
Religiously, religiosè, piè
To relinquish, relinquo, derelinquo
A relinquishing, derelictio
Reliques, reliquiæ
A relish, gustus, sapor
Of no relish, in-ipidus
To relish, gusto, sapio; (be pleased with), delector, placeo
High-relished food, acres acutique cibi
Relishable, gustui jucundus
Reluctance, Reluctancy, aversatio
With reluctance, invitè, ægrè
Reluctant, abhorrens, aversans
To rely upon, confido, innitor
[104]

Relying upon, fretus
To remain (or tarry), maneo, remaneo, permaneo; (behind), resto; (be over), supersum; (as he was), antiquum obtinere
A remainder, residuum
Remaining, residuus, reliquus
Remains, reliquiæ
To remand (send for back), revoco; (send back), remitto
A remanding, revocatio; (dismission), dimissio
A remark, observatio, notatio
To remark, noto, animadverto
Remarkable, notabilis, insignis
Remarkably, notabiliter, insigniter
A remarking, observatio
A remedy (medicine), remedium, medicamentum, medicina; (for all distempers), panacea
To remedy, medicor, medeor
Remediless, immedicabilis
A remedying, curatio, sanatio
To remember, reminiscor, recordor, memini; (put in mind), moneo, commoneo, suggero
To be remembered, memorabilis
A rememberer, monitor
A remembrance, reminiscentia, recordatio, memoria
To put in remembrance, commoneo, commonefacio
A remembrancer, monitor
To remind, admoneo, moneo
A reminding, admonitio
Reminiscence, recordatio
Remiss (slack), remissus, negligens; (slothful), socors, piger
To grow remiss, pigritiæ se addicere
Remisly, negligentèr, supinè
Remissness, negligentia, dilatio
Remission (pardon), venia, remissio
A remission, relaxatio
To remit (send back), remitto; (grow less), diminuor, imminuor; (refer unto), refero; (forgive), absolvo, condono; (money), transmitto [nandus
Remittable, Remissible, condoA remittance, remissio; (of money), pecuniæ pro alio præfinita numeratio
A remitting, remissio
A remnant, residuum, reliquum
A remonstrance, declaratio
To remonstrate, declaro, ostendo
A remora (obstacle), impedimentum, mora
Remorse, angor, stimulus, dolor
Remorseless, immitis
Remote, remotus, longinquus
Remotely, remotè, longè
Remoteness, distantia
Removeable, mobilis
Not removeable, immobilis
Removal (of persons), migratio; (of goods), exportatio
To remove, moveo, amoveo, submoveo, removeo, demoveo; (goods), aliò exporture; (with difficulty), amolior; (from place to place), transmoveo; (a dwelling), migro;.(send away), amando; (kill), interficio
A remove, or removing, remotio, amotio; (or one remove), gradus
Remove, stir! aufer te hinc !
Not removed, immotus, fixus
A removing, remotio, amotio; (one's dwelling), migratio
To remount, rursùs conscendere
To remunerate, compenso
Remuneration, compensatio

To renconter, occurro
A renconnter, occursus
To rend (tear), lacero, discerpo
To render (restore, or give), reddo, do, restituo; (translate), verto, latinè, &c., reddere; (yield up), trado, dedo; (like for like), pari referre; (a reason), rationem reddere; (thanks), gratias agere
A rendering, redditio; (translating), interpretatio; (up), deditio (præscriptus
A rendezvous, conventus, locus
To rendezvous, convenio
A renegado, apostata
To renew, renovo; (a battle), redintegro
A renewal, renovatio, integratio
To be renewed, integrasco
A renewer, novator
A renewing, renovatio
Rennet, coagulum
To renovate, renovo, redintegro
To renounce, renuncio, abdico; (the faith), fidem abjurare; (a covenant), fœdus ejurare
Renown, fama, gloria
Of renown, insignis, celebris
Without renown, inglorius
Renowned, inclytus, clarus, insignis, celebris
To be renowned, eniteo
Rent (torn), laceratus, discerptus
A rent (tear), scissura, fissura
Rent (income), reditus, vectigal; (charge), vectigal annuum
To rent (let), loco, eloco; (hire), conduco
To rent (rend), lacero, dilanio
A rental, catalogus redituum
A renter (hirer), conductor
A renting (hiring), conductio
Renunciation, renunciatio
Repaid, iterùm solutus
To repair, reparo, reficio;(clothes), resarcio; (unto), frequento
Repairable, reparabilis
Irrepairable, irreparabilis
A repairer, reparator [ratio.
A reparation, or repairing, reparaTo make reparation, damnum sarcire
A repartee, argutiæ, acuta responsio, salsum dictum
To repartee, argutè respondere
To repass, iterùm transire
A repast, refectus, cibus
To repay, reddo, iterùm solvere
A repaying, solutio iterata
A repeal, abrogatio
To repeal, abrogo, rescindo
To repeat, repeto, itero
Repeatedly, iterùm atque iterùm
A repeater, repetitor
Repeating, repetens, iterans
A repeating, repetitio, iteratio
To repel, repello, depello
A repeller, depulsor
A repelling, depulsio
To repent, resipisco, pœniteo
Repentance, pœnitentia
Repenting, pœnitens
To repeople, populum inducere
A repercussion, repercussio
Repercussive, retundens
A repertory, repertorium
A repetition, repetitio
To repine, doleo, queror, murmuro
A repiner, querens
A repining, questus, querela; (envying), invidentia
Repining, querens, murmurans
To replace, suppleo, substituo
A replacing, supplementum

To replenish, repleo, impleo, compleo, expleo
A replenishing, expletio
Replete, repletus, abundans
A repletion (of blood), plethora; (of humours), humorum copia
To replevy, replegiamentum
To replevy, replegio
A replevying, replegiatio
A replication, or reply, replicatio, responsio, responsum
To reply, respondeo, replico
A replying, responsio
A report, rumor, fama; (in law), narratio, relatio; (of a gun), sonitus; (a good), elogium; (a bad), infamia
To report, nuncio, narro; (ill of), diffamo, calumnior
By report, famâ
A reporter, nunciator; (accuser), accusator
A reporting, rumoris propagatio
Repose, quies, somnus
To repose, otior, quiesco; (trust), confido; (place), repono, pono, colloco
A repository, repositorium
To repossess, iterum possidere
To reprehend, objurgo, arguo
A reprehender, correptor
A reprehending, reprehensio
Reprehensible, reprehendendus
Reprehensive, objurgatorius
Reprehension, objurgatio
To represent, repræsento, exhibeo; (shew), declaro, ostendo, demonstro; (a person), alicujus personam gerere; (the form of a thing), imitor, adumbro, assimilo; (to the life), veram similitudinem delineare; (to one's self), animo cernere
A representation, declaratio; (likeness), similitudo
A representative, vicem cujuspiam gerens
A representing, adumbratio
To repress, reprimo, refreno, comprimo, coërceo, cohibeo, domo, frango, compesco; (wickedness), improbitatem restinguere
A represser, frænator, domitor
Repression, repressio
A reprieve, supplicii prorogatio
To reprieve, supplicium prorogare
A reprimand, objurgatio
To reprimand, objurgo, increpo
To reprint, denuò imprimere
Reprisals, clarigatio   [objecto
To reproach, exprobro, convicior, opprobrium, vituperatio, exprobratio, contumelia   [cens
Without reproach, integer, innoReproachable, convicio dignus
Reproached, exprobratus
Reproachful, probrosus, contumeliosus
Reproachfully, contumeliosè
A reproaching, exprobratio
A reprobate, improbus, perditus
To reprobate, rejicio, damno
Reprobation, improbatio
A reproof, reprehensio
To reprove, redarguo, objurgo
Reproveable, culpandus
A reprover, reprehensor
A reproving, reprehensio
A reptile, animal repens
A republic, respublica
A republican, libertatis fautor
To repudiate, repudio, dimitto
To repugn, repugno, oppugno
Repugnance, repugnantia

Repugnant, repugnans, aversans
Repugnantly, repugnantèr, invitè
A repulse, repulsa
To repulse, repello, propello
Reputation, existimatio, nomen
Reputable, bonæ famæ, honestus
Reputably, cum honore
Repute, fama, nomen
To repute, habeo, existimo
A request, petitio, supplicatio
To request, rogo, supplico; (earnestly), obsecro; (demand), postulo, posco, afflagito
A requester, rogator
Requesting, rogans, postulans
A requesting, rogatio, petitio
To requicken, resuscito
A requiem, oratio pro mortuis
Requirable, exigendus
To require, exigo, postulo, reposco, repeto, flagito
A requiring, postulatio
Requisite, necessarius
Requisitely, necessariò
A requital, retributio
To requite, retribuo, compenso
Having requited, remuneratus
A requiting, compensatio
The rere-ward, ultima acies
Resaluted, resalutatus
To rescind, rescindo, abrogo
Rescinded, rescissus, abrogatus
A rescission, abolitio
A rescript, rescriptum
A rescue, recuperatio
To rescue, recupero, libero, ex custodiâ vi eripere; (from ruin), ab interitu vindicare
A research, inquisitio, disquisitio
Resemblance, similitudo
To resemble, refero; (compare to), comparo
Resembling, assimilis
A resembling, assimilatio
To resent, indignè ferre
Resented, dolore affectus
Resenting, indignans, molestè ferens
A resentment, indignatio
A reservation, conservatio; (mental), exceptio in animo
With reservation, dissimulantèr
To reserve, reservo, repono, recondo, seponero
A reserve (exception), exceptio, conditio interposita; (of soldiers), subsidium
Without reserve, sine exceptione
Reservedly, parcè
Reservedness (in speech), taciturnitas; (in behaviour), fastus
To resettle, denuò stabilire
To reside, habito, commoror
A residence, habitatio, sedes
Resident, residens, manens
A resident, legatus inferior
A residentiary, residentiarius
The residue, residuum
To resign (quit), resigno, cedo, concedo, trado; (to another's will), se ad alterius voluntatem accommodare
Resignation, cessio, concessio; (of a benefice), à beneficio ecclesiastico abdicatio
A resigner, qui cedit
A resigning, abdicatio
Resilient, resultans, resiliens
Resinous, resinaceus
To resist, resisto, obnitor, repugno, renitor

Resistance, repugnantia
A resister, oppugnator
Resistible, resistendus
Resisting, repugnans, obsistens
Resistless, inexpugnabilis
A resolve, statutum, propositum
To resolve (purpose), statuo, constituo, decerno; (explain), explano, explico, enodo; (or reduce into), reduco, resolvo, redigo; (discuss), discutio; (be resolved), resolvor, redigor, reducor
Resolvent, discutiens
A resolving (or dissolving), resolutio; (of a question), explicatio, enodatio
Resolute (bold), audax; (firm), constans, firmus
Resolutely, audactèr, obstinatè
A resolution (design), consilium, propositum; (courage), animus, fortitudo; (of mind), constantia; (of an assembly), decretum; (of a question), solutio
Resolutive, resolvens, discutiens
Resonant, resonans, resonus
Resort, frequentia, congressus; (refuge), refugium; (in law), jurisdictio
To resort (unto), frequento; (together), convenio, confluo
Resorted unto, frequentatus, celebratus
A resorting, congressus, frequentia; (unto), frequentatio
To resound, resono; (one's praise), laudo, extollo
Resounding, resonans, resonus
A resounding, resonantia
A resource, fons, origo
Respect (regard), respectus, ratio; (reverence), reverentia, veneratio, honor
In respect of, præ, propter
Worthy of respect, venerabilis
To respect (consider, or regard), respicio; (relate to), ad aliquid pertinere; (esteem, or honour), revereor, veneror; (love), diligo, amo
A respecter, cultor, amator
Respectful, officiosus, reverens
Respectfully, officiosè, reverentèr
Respectfulness, reverentia
Respective, reciprocus, mutuus
Respectively, singulatim, mutuò
Respiration, respiratio
To respire, spiro
Respite, mora, relaxatio, cessatio, intermissio
Without respite, sine intermissione
To respite, differo, profero, traho. See to Reprieve
A respiting, dilatio, prorogatio
Resplendency, nitor, splendor
Resplendent, resplendens, rutilus
Resplendently, clarè, nitidè
A response, responsum
Responsible (able to pay), pecuniosus; (for damages), obnoxius
Rest, quies, requies, otium, cessatio; (peace), pax, tranquillitas
The rest, reliquus, residuus; (the others), cæteri, reliqui
The rest (subst.), residuum
A rest (in music), pausa; (prop), fulcrum
To rest (take rest), quiesco; (compose to sleep), requiesco; (or lean upon), innitor, eclino,

ROL — ROT — ROW

A roamer, erro, homo vagus
Roaming, vagans, errans
A roaming, vagatio, erratio
Roan, fulvus, subalbidus
To roar, rugio, clamo, vociferor; (as the sea), fremo; (again), rebo; (for grief), ploro, ejulo
A roarer, clamator
Roaring, vociferans, clamosus
A roaring, rugitus, clamatio
To roast, asso; (deride), derideo, verbis cædere
A roasting, adustio
To rob, prædor, spolio, furor, latrocinor, deprædor; (the public), depeculor; (privily), surripio
A robber, latro, fur; (of a church), sacrilegus; (at sea), pirata; (of the public), peculator; (of a house by night), prædo nocturnus
Robbery, latrocinium, rapina
A robbing, spoliatio; (of the public), peculatio, peculatus; (of churches), sacrilegium
Of robbing, prædatorius
A robe, palla, vestis, vestimentum; (of honour), stola; (purple), purpura; (loose), pallium, lacerna
A master of the robes, vestiarius
A robbin red-breast, rubecula
Robust, robustus, validus
Robustness, robur
A rochet, rochetum
A rock, rupes, petra, cautes
Of a rock, saxeus, petrosus, saxatilis, scopulosus, præruptus
To rock (or reel), vacillo; (a cradle), cunas agitare
A rocker, cunas agitans
A sky-rocket, ignes missilia
Rockiness, saxis abundans
A rocking, cunarum agitatio
Rocky, saxeus, scopulosus
A rocky place, saxetum
A rod, virga; (twig), vimen; (whip), flagrum, flagellum; (to measure with), pertica
Made of rods, vimineus
A rodomontade, gloriatio inepta
A roe, caprea; (buck), capreolus; (of a fish), piscis ova; (soft), lactes
A rogue (wicked person), scelestus; (in grain), ab ingenio improbus
To play the rogue, lascivio
Roguery (knavery), scelus, flagitium, nequitia, fraus; (banter), jocatio, cavillatio
Roguing about, vagans, oberrans
Roguish (knavish), improbus, nequam; (wanton), lasciviens, lascivus
Roguishly, scelestè, lascivè
Roguishness (knavishness), nequitia, improbitas; (wantonness), lascivia
To roist (boast), jacto
A roll (catalogue), catalogus, album; (of any thing), volumen; (of cloth), pannus in se convolutus
A court-roll, volumen curiale
The rolls, scriniorum sacrorum repositorium, archivum
Master of the rolls, magister scriniorum sacrorum
To roll, volvo, plico; (or wind about), circumvolvo, circumroto; (again, or back), revolvo; (along), pervolvo; (down), devolvo; (the eyes), oculos volvere; (in money), pecuniâ abundare; (towards), advolvo; (from, or out), evolvo; (under), subvolvo; (up), involvo
That may be rolled, volubilis
A roller (for heavy bodies), cylindrus; (for a wound), napeus
Rolling, volubilis, versatilis; (tempestuous), procellosus, turbidus
A rolling, volubilitas, volutatio; (pin), cylindrus, magis; (stone), cylindrus, saxum volubile
Rollingly, volubilitèr
Roman, Romanus
A romance, narratio ficta; (falsity), mendacium [tior
To romance, fabulas fingere, mendacior, vaniloquus
A Romanist, papista, pontificius
Romantic, fabulosus, fictitius, fictus
A rood, pertica; (of land), quarta pars jugeri; (cross), crux; (loft), statuarium
A roof, tectum, solarium; (vaulted), laquear; (of the mouth), palatum
A rook, cornix; (at chess), elephantus; (cheat), planus, fraudator
To rook, defraudo, fallo
A rooking, fraudatio
Room, locus, spatium; (chamber), conclave; (dining), triclinium, cœnaculum; (withdrawing), penetrale
To make room, submoveo, decedo
Roomy, spatiosus, amplus
A roost, gallinarium
To roost, quiesco, dormio
A root, radix, stirps
To root (take root), radicor, radicesco; (as a hog), ruspo; (up), eradico, extirpo, evello
Up by the roots, radicitùs
Of the root, radicalis
That may be rooted out, extirpandus [bilis
Not to be rooted out, inextirpabilis
A rooting, radicatio; (up), eradicatio, extirpatio
Full of roots, radicosus
A rope, funis, restis; (of onions), caparum series
To be ropy, viscor
A roper, or ropemaker, restio
A ropedancer, funambulus
Rope-yarn, funis retexti fila
Ropy, viscidus, glutinosus
A rosary, rosarium
A rose, rosa; (bud), alabastrus; (cake), rosarum caput mortuum
Rosey, or rosy, roseus, rosaceus
A rose noble, aureus nummus rosâ signatus
A rose-tree, rosa frutex
Rosemary, rosmarinus; (tree), rosmaris
Rosewood, lignum Rhodium
Rosin, resina
Of rosin, resinaceus
Full of rosin, resinosus
The rot, morbus mortiferus, lues
To rot, putrefacio; neut. putrefio; (in jail), in carcere mori; (inwardly), tabesco; (be crumbled into earth), in terram resolvi
A rotation, rotatio; (of government), vicissitudo imperitandi
By rote, memoritèr
Rotten, corruptus, putris, putridus; (as a sore), purulentus; (ripe), fracidus; (wood), lignum cariosum
To be rotten, putrefio
To grow rotten, patresco
To make rotten, putrefacio
That maketh rotten, tabificus
Rottenness, putror, putredo, putrefactio; (in bones, &c.), caries
Rotting inwardly, tabidus
Rotundity, rotunditas
To rove, vagor, erro
A rover, erro
Rouge, ruber, rubens
Rough, asper, horridus; (hairy), hirsutus; (grim), austerus; (homely), rusticus; (prickly), spinosus; (in temper), asper, durus, severus, morosus; (proud), fastuosus, insolens; (in taste), gustu austerior; (bad way), salebrosus; (tempestuous), procellosus
A rough place, salebræ; (if full of bushes), aspertum; (if untilled), tesqua
To be rough, horreo, fremo
To grow rough, inhorreo; (or nasty), squaleo
To make rough, aspero
To roughcast, incrusto
Roughcast, crustatus
A rough draught, inconcinna delineatio [lineatus
Rough-drawn, incompositè, delineatus
Rough-hewn, rudis, agrestis
Roughly, asperè, acerbè, torvè
Roughness, asperitas; (of hair), hirsutia; (of the sea), fremitus maris
Roving, vagans, errabundus; (pillaging), prædatorius
A roving, vagatio, erratio; (pillaging), prædatio
The rounce, manubrium preli
Round, rotundus, globosus; (as a circle), circularis; (and long), teres; (like a top), terbinatus
Round about, circà, undiquè
A round (or circle), circulus; (or whole sum), summa solida
A half round, semicirculus
In a round, in orbem
The round of a ladder, climacter
To round, rotundo; (by clipping), attondeo
Made round, orbiculatus
A round-house, ergastulum
A round-root, Rolinus
A roundelay, cantilena silvestris
Roundish, ferè, rotundus
Roundly (in form), rotundè, orbiculatim; (in pace), curaìm; (in speaking), volubilitèr, ore rotundo; (freely), audactèr, liberè; (honestly), ingenuè, sincerè
Roundness, rotunditas
The rounds, excubiæ
A roundle, circulus
To rouse, excito, animo; (a deer), excutere feram cubili
A rousing up, excitatio
A rout, cœtus; (overthrow), clades, strages; (unlawful assembly), concursus illicitus; (noise), rixa, turba
To rout, vinco, supero; (out), depello; (grunt), grunnio; (snore), sterto; (as swine), ruspor
To make a rout, turbo, perturbo
A routing, dissipatio
A row, series, ordo, versus

A row-barge, ponto
To row, remigo, remis agere
A rowel (of a spur), stimulus
A rower, remex
A master-rower, pausarius
A rowing, remigium, remigratio
Royal, regalis, regius
A royalist, regiarum partium assertor
Royally, regaliter, regiè
Royalty, regia dignitas
A rub, mora; (banter), joculare cavillum
To rub (chafe), frico, affrico; (against, or upon), attero;(with a clout), distringo; (gently), demulceo, delinio; (all over), perfrico; (off the dirt), abstergeo, detergeo
A rubber, qui, or quæ fricat; (whetstone), cos
Rubbers, gemina victoria
A rubbing, fricatio, frictio; (brush), peniculus setis asper; (brush for the body), strigil
Rubbish, rudus; (sorry stuff), quisquiliæ
Rubble, rudus
To lay rubble, rudero
To cast out rubble, erudero
Rubicund (red), rubicundus, rubens
A rubric, præcepta literis miniatis scripta, or impressa
A ruby, rubinus; (carbuncle), carbunculus
Ructation, ructatio
The rudder, clavus, gubernaculum
Raddle, rubrica
Marked with ruddle, rubricatus
Full of raddle, rubricosus
Ruddiness, rubor, rubedo
Ruddy, ruber, rubens, rubeus, rufus
To be ruddy, ore rubere
To grow ruddy, rubesco
Rude (clownish), rudis, rusticus; (impudent), impudens, procax; (immodest), impudicus; (unhandsome), impolitus; (unskilful), imperitus, inexpertus, rudis
Rudely (unskilfully), rudi minervà; (clownishly), rusticè, inurbanè
Rudeness, inurbanitas, immodestia, impudentia
A rudiment, rudimentum, elementum, principium
Rue, ruta
Of rue, rutaceus
Made of rue, rutatus
To rue, doleo, lugeo
Rueful, luctuosus, tristis
Ruefully, tristè, mœstè
The ruel-bone, patella
A ruff (of a garment), plica, or sinus vestis
A ruffian, sicarius
Ruffian, furens, violentus
To ruffle (disorder), turbo, inquieto; (wrinkle), corrugo
A ruffling, turbatio, inquietatio; (wrinkling), corrugatio
A rug, gausape
Rugged, asper, inæqualis; (in temper), rigidus, durus, difficilis
Ruggedly, asperè, duritèr
Ruggedness, asperitas, diritas
Ruin, ruina, exitium; (slaughter), strages, clades; (of a state), interitus; (ruins), vestigia
To ruin (a house), demolior, deturbo, deleo, diruo; (one's self),
[109]

fortunas dissipare; (walls, &c.), dejicio, everto; (in reputation), famam lædere; (one in his morals), mores corrumpere; (destroy), perdo, pessundo
To be ruined (as a building), deturbor, evertor; (in one's goods), bonis exui; (in one's fortune), fortuniâ everti
Ready to be ruined, periclitans
A ruiner (demolisher), demolitor
A ruining, demolitio
Ruinous, ruinosus, ruiturus;(dangerous), periculosus; (destructive), perniciosus, exitiosus
To be ruinous, collabefio
Rule (government), dominatio, gubernatio, imperium; (precept to be governed by), regula, norma, præscriptum; (of court), præscriptum; (custom), mos, consuetudo; (example), modulus, exemplar; (order, or constitution), lex, constitutio, institutum; (law), præceptum; (to live by), vivendi disciplina, norma, lex
Under rule, regularis
According to rule, regularitèr
Out of rule, irregularis, abnormis
To rule, rego, impero, guberno, moderor, administro; (one's self by example), imitor; (a line), lineam ducere
By rule, ad amussim
To be ruled, regor
Well ruled, benè constitutus
A ruler, dominus, gubernator; (of a province), præfectus, rector
Rulers, primates, proceres
Ruling, dominans, imperans
Rumb, cursus navis
To rumble, crepo, crepito
Rumbling, crepitans, fragosus
A rumbling, fremitus, fragor; (of the guts), tormina
To ruminate, rumino; (think), secum reputare, revolvo
A ruminating, ruminatio
Rumination, meditatio
To rummage, scrutor, perscrutor
A rummaging, investigatio
A rummer, calix amplior
A rumor, rumor, fama
To rumor, rumorem serere, or spargere
To rumple, rugo, corrugo
A rumple, ruga, plica
A rumpling, corrugatio
The run (of a ship), cursus; (at cards), fortuna; (in trade), facilis venditio
To run, curro; (make haste), propero, festino; (drop), stillo, distillo; (flow), mano, fluo; (at the eyes), lippio; (at the nose), muco stillare; (as a sore), suppuro; (about), vagor; (about, as water), diffluo; (abroad), vagor; (ahead), præcurro; (after), sequor, subeo, insector, persequor
A runagate, fugitivus, transfuga
A rundle, circulus
A rundlet, quadrantal
A runner, cursor, excursor; (rope), funis ductarius
Runnet, coagulum
Running, currens; (at random), vagus, erraticus; (water), aqua viva, fontana, or profluens
A running, cursus; (against), cecursus; (away), fuga; (back), recursus; (to and fro), discur-

sus; (forth), procursio; (out), excursio, excursus; (over), transcursus; (over, or superfluity), redundantia, superfluitas; (place), stadium, curriculum; (sore), ulcus; (together), concursus
Running before, præcursorius
A running title, titulus singulis paginis appositus
A rupture (or falling out), discordia, simultas, dissidium; (breach of peace), violatio pacis; (in the groin), hernia
Having a rupture, ramicosus
Rural, ruralis, rusticus
A rush, juncus, scirpus; (light), candela ex junco facta
Rushy, juncosus
Of rushes, junceus, scirpeus
To rush, ruo; (forward), propello, impello; (in, or upon), irruo, irrumpo; (out), proruo; (through), perrumpo
A rushing in, irruptio
Russet, subrufus, ravus
Rust, rubigo; (of copper), ærugo; (of iron), ferrugo
To rust, rubiginem contrahere
Rust-coloured, ferrugineus
Rustic, rusticus, agrestis, inurbanus [amandare
To rusticate, rusticor, in rus
Rusticity, rusticitas
Rustiness, situs, rancor
To rustle, strepo, crepo
A rustling, strepitus, crepitus; (of armour), clangor
Rusty, rubiginosus, ferrugineus
Rusty (as bacon), rancidus; (as cloth), squalidus, tritus
To rut, ad venerem prurire
The rut (of deer), coïtûs desiderium; (of a wheel), rotæ vestigium
Full of ruts, orbitis sectus
Ruthful, misericors
Ruthfulness, misericordia
Ruthfulness, immisericors, crudelis
Rye, secale
Of rye, secalicus

S.

A Sabbatarian, Sabbatarius
The Sabbath, Sabbatum
Of the Sabbath, Sabbaticus
Sable, pullus, ater, niger
A sable, mus Ponticus
A sabre, acinaces
Sacerdotal, sacerdotalis
Sack, vinum Canarium
A sack, saccus
A sackbut, sambuca
Sackcloth, cilicium
Of sackcloth, cilicinus
To sack (plunder), diripio, vasto; (put into a sack) sacco inserere
Sacked, spoliatus, vastatus
A sacker, spoliator, vastator
A sacking, spoliatio, vastatio
A sacrament, sacramentum
The sacrament eucharistia
Sacramental, sacramentalis
Sacred, sacer, sanctus
To make sacred, consecro, dedico, dico
Sacredly, sacrè, sanctè
Sacredness, sanctitas
A sacrifice, sacrificium, sacrum; (for sin), piaculum; (for vic-

SAI · SAN · SAT

tory), victima, hostia; (to the infernal gods), inferiæ
Of sacrifice, sacrificalis
To sacrifice, sacrifico, immolo, macto, libo; (ruin), diruo; (devote), consecro, devoveo, morti exponere; (kill), occido, interficio, interimo, trucido; (quit, or abandon), relinquo, desero
A sacrificer, sacrificus
A sacrificing, immolatio
Sacrilege, sacrilegium
Sacrilegious, sacrilegus
Sacrilegiously, more sacrilegii
A sacrist, æditunus
A sacristy, sacrarium
Sad (sorrowful), tristis, mœstus; (grievous), acerbus, molestus, gravis; (foul, nasty, horrible), fœdus, immundus, spurcus, sordidus; (shameful), turpis, indignus, infamis; (wicked), improbus, malus, pravus; (fellow), homo perditus
To be sad, mœreo, contristor
To make sad, contristo
Making sad, tristificus
A saddle, ephippium
Saddle-backed, pandus
A saddle-cloth, instratum equestre
A saddle-horse, equus vectarius
To saddle, ephippium imponere
A saddler, ephippiorum opifex
The Sadducees, Sadducæi
Sadly (sorrowfully), mœstè; (grievously), gravitèr, acerbè
Sadness, tristitia, mœstitia, gravitas, sobrietas
Safe, tutus, sospes, incolumis; (and sound), integer, solidus
A safe (pantry), cella penaria
A safeguard, præsidium, tutela, clientela
Safely, tutò, securè
Safety, salus, incolumitas
A place of safety, asylum
Saffron, crocus
Of saffron, croceus
Coloured with saffron, crocatus
To sag, onero
Sagacious, sagax, subtilis
Sagaciously, sagacitèr, subtilitèr
Sagacity, sagacitas, solertia
Sage, salvia ; (of virtue), salvia minor; (of Jerusalem), pulmonaria
Sage (wise), sapiens, prudens
Sagely, sapientèr, prudentèr
Sageness, sapientia, prudentia
Sagittary, sagittarius
A sail, carbasus, velum ; (main), artemon ; (up), thoracium ; (sprit), dolon ; (mizen), epidromus; (of ships), plures naves simul navigantes ; (yard), antenna
To sail, navigo; (about), circumnavigo; (backwards), renavigo; (before), prænavigo; (forward), nave provehi; (over), nave tra\jicere; (by), præternavigo; (out of), enavigo ; (through), pernavigo ; (unto), adnavigo; (with a fair wind), vento secundo vehi
Of a sail, velaris
That may be sailed on, navigabilis
A sailor, or seaman, nauta
A sailing, navigatio
Sailing, navigans
A saint, sanctus
Saints in heaven, cœlites
To saint (canonize), aliquem in divos referre
intlike, sanctum referens
[110]

Sake, causa, gratia
For God's sake, per Deum oro ; (my sake), meâ causâ ; (his sake), illius gratiâ
Salacious, libidinosus
A salad, acetaria
A salamander, salamandra
A salary, stipendium, merces
A sale, venditio ; (by inch of candle), venditio per præfinitam mensuram candelæ facta
Open sale, auctio
Set to sale, venalis
To set to sale, auctionem facere, proscribo, vendo
To be set to sale, venalis prostare
Saleable, venalis, vendibilis
Saleably, venalitèr
A salesman, venditor, vestiarius
Salient, saliens, prominens
Salient, salsus
Salique, Salicus
Salival, salivarius
To salivate, salivo
Salivation, salivatio
A sallet, olus, acetaria
Sallow, pallidus, luridus
A sallow colour, pallo
To grow sallow, pallesco
Sallowness, pallor
A sally, eruptio, impetus
To sally out, procurro, erumpo
A salmon, salmo
Salt, sal; (sea), sal marinus
Salt-fish, salsamenta
Saltpetre, nitrum
Mixed with saltpetre, nitratus
Full of saltpetre, nitrosus
A saltcellar, salinum; (box), cista salem continens
A salter, salarius
Of salt, salarius [pergere
To salt, salio, sale condire, or assalt meats, salsamenta
A salt-pit, salina ; (marshes), æstuaria
Salt, adj. salsus
Saltish, subsalsus
A salting, salitura
A salting-tub, vas salsamentarium
Saltless, insulsus
Saltness, salsugo
Salvation, salus, salvatio
Bringing salvation, salutifer
Salubrious, saluber
A salve, unguentum, medicamentum ; (eye), collyrium
To salve, ungo; (preserve), servo, conservo ; (extenuate), extenuo
A salver, vas ad calices manus sustineendum
A salving, unctio, extenuatio
A salvo, cautio, exceptio
Salutary, salutaris, salubris
To salute, saluto; (kiss), osculor; (at parting), valedico ; (again), resaluto
A saluter, salutator
Salutiferous, salutaris, salubris
Of saluting, salutatorius
A saluting, or salutation, salutatio ; (again), resalutatio
The same, ipse, idem
The very same, ipsissimus
Sameness, identitas
At the same time, eodem tempore, simul et semel
A sample, exemplar ; (pattern), specimen
To sample, comparo
Sanative, medicinalis
Sanctification, sanctificatio, consecratio, dedicatio; (a making holy), sanctitatis infusio
To sanctify (set apart for holy

uses), sacro, consecro, dedico; « (make holy), sanctum facere; (celebrate), celebro
A sanctifier, sanctificator
A sanctifying, sanctificatio, celebratio, cultus
Sanctimony, sanctitas
A sanction, sanctio ; (decree), decretum
Sanctity, sanctitas, sanctimonia
A sanctuary, sanctuarium, asylum, refugium, ara
Sand, arena, sabulum ; (beds), arenariæ
Of sand, arenaceus, sabulosus
To load with sand, saburro
The sands, arenæ littoris
Quick sands, syrtes
Sandblind, luscus
Sandy, arenaceus ; (mixed with sand), arenatus ; (full of large sand), sabulosus; (full of small sand), arenosus
Sanguinary, sanguinarius
Sanguine, sanguineus, sanguinolentus ; (cheerful), alacer, hilaris
The sanhedrim, synedrium
Sanity, sanitas
Sap, succus
Without sap, exsuccus
To sap (undermine), suffodio
Sapidity, Sapidness, sapor
Sapient, sapiens
Sapless, exsuccus, stolidus
A sappling, virgultum
Sapphic, Sapphicus
The sapping, suffossio
Sappiness, humiditas ; (folly), stultitia
Sappy (full of sap), succosus ; (foolish), stultus, stolidus, hebes
A sapphire, sapphirus
The Saracens, Saraceni
A sarcasm, sarcasmus
Sarcastical, satyricus, amarus
Sarcastically, satyricè
A sarce, cribrum
To sarce, cribro, excerno
A sash, cingulum; (window), fenestra ex lignea compage confecta
Satan, Satanas
Satanical, satanicus, diabolicus
A satchel, sacculus, pera
To sate, or satiate, satio, expleo
A satellite, satelles
Satiety, satietas, saturitas
Satin, pannus sericus densior ac nitens
A satire, satyra, carmen mordax
Satirical, satyricus, acerbus
Satirically, satyricè, mordacitèr
A satyrist, poëta satyricus
Satisfaction, satisfactio, compensatio, restitutio ; (contentment), oblectatio animi
To make satisfaction, satisfacio, compenso; (for damage), damnum sarcire
To give satisfaction, voluptate perfundere
Satisfactory, satisfaciens, acceptus, gratus, jucundus
Not to be satisfied, insatiabilis
To satisfy (please), satisfacio ; (one's humour), animo morem gerere ; (ambition), ambitionem explere ; (for injuries), de injuriis satisfacere; (one's request); petenti satisfacere ; (creditors), æs alienum dissolvere
Satisfying, satisfaciens

SCA — SCA — SCO

A satisfying, satisfactio
To saturate, satio, expleo
Saturday, dies Saturni
Saturity, saturitas, satietas
Saturn, Saturnus
Feasts of Saturn, Saturnalia
Saturnine, saturninus
A satyr, satyrus
Savage, ferus, immanis, crudelis; (uncultivated), incultus, horridus
A savage beast, fera
To make savage, effero
Savagely, crudelitèr, barbarè
Savageness, feritas, crudelitas
Sauce, condimentum; (of gravy), eliquamen
The same sauce, par pari
A saucer, acetabulum
A sauce-box, homo impudens
Saucy, petulans, insolens
A saucy fellow, effrons
To grow saucy, insolesco
Saucily, petulantèr, procacitèr
Sauciness, petulantia
Save (except), præter, nisi, extra, præterquam
To save (preserve), servo, conservo, salvum præstare; (or deliver from danger), libero, eripere aliquem periculo; (harmless), incolumem servare; (till another time), in aliud tempus reservare
Saving (frugal), parcus, frugalis
A saving (preserving), conservatio; (exception), exceptio, cautio
Saving, præter, præterquàm, extra; (that), nisi quòd
Savingly, frugalitèr, parcè
Savingly, frugalitas
A saviour, servator; (of mankind), humanæ salutis instaurator, salvator
To saunter, erro, vagor
A savor, sapor, gustus
Ill-savor, fœtor
To savor (smell of), oleo; (taste of), sapio
Savorily, gustui jucundè
Savory, gustui jucundus
Savoys, brassica Sabaudica
A sausage, isicium, lucanica
A little sausage, botellus
A sausage-maker, botalarius
A saw, serra, serrula
Like a saw, serratus
Sawdust, scobs
To saw, serro
A sawyer, serrarius
A sawing, serratura
To say, dico, aio; (again), repeto; (against), contradico; (beforehand), prædico; (nay), nego; (yes), affirmo; (by heart), memoritèr pronunciare; (nothing), sileo, taceo; (one's prayers), Deum precari
That is to say, scilicet
Say on, perge, age
A saying, dictum; (again), repetitio; (old), proverbium; (witty), facetiæ
A scab, scabies; (a dry), impetigo; (of sheep, &c.), porrigo
A scabbard, vagina; (scaleboard amongst printers), assula lignea inter lineas interserenda
Scabbed, Scabby, scabiosus, morbidus
Scabbiness, scabies
Scabrous, scaber, asper
A scaffold, tabulatum; (for beheading), locus supplicii editior
[111]

Scaffolding, tabulati constructio
A scalado, ascensus in murum
By scalado, scalis admotis
To scald (a thing), ferventè liquore aliquid macerare; (a pig), porcellum calidâ aquâ perfundere; (scorch), uro, subura
Scald-pated, scabiosa capite
Scalding-hot, fervidus, fervens
A scale (of a fish), squama; (of a balance), lanx; (of miles), scala milliarium; (of music), scala musica; (of a sore), crusta; (in measurement), scala
Like a scale, squamatim
Having scales, squamosus
To scale (a fish), desquamo, purgo; (as a wound), crustâ excidere; (a bone), ossis scabritiem deradere; (walls), per scalas muros ascendere
A scaling (of fish), desquamatio; (of walls), per scalas conscensio ad muros
A scaling-ladder, scalæ
A scall, impetigo
A scallion, ascalonia
A scallap. See Scollop
The scalp, pericranium
To scalp, caput exuere, plagis luculentis aliquem deformare
Scaly, squameus, squamosus
A scamble, or scambling, dissipatio; (scramble), raptio, promiscua
Scamblingly, raptim, promiscuè
To scamper away, fugio, aufugio
To scan (examine), examino, perpendo; (a verse), versum metiri
A scandal (offence), offensa; (disgrace), dedecus, ignominia
To be a scandal to one, aliquem dedecorare
To scandalise (give offence), malo exemplo offendere; (disgrace one), convicior, calumnior
Scandalous, infamis, turpis; (libel), libellus famosus
A scandalous action, flagitium
Scandalously, malo exemplo, turpitèr
Scandalousness, dedecus
Scant, exiguus, minor justo
Scantiness, defectus, brevitas
Scantly, parcè, vix, ægrè
A scantling, proportio; (little piece), frustulum
Scanty, brevior, contractior
A scape, effugium
To scape (escape), evado
Scapular, scapularis
A scar, cicatrix
To scar, cicatricem inducere
Full of scars, cicatricosus
Scarce (rare), rarus, carus
To grow scarce, raresco
Scarcely, vix, ægrè, difficultèr; (scantily), exiguè, parcè
Scarceness, Scarcity, caritas, difficultas, inopia
To scare (frighten), terreo, territo
A scarecrow, terriculum
A scarf, mitella, fascia
The scarfskin, cuticula exterior
A scarifying, scarificatio
To scarify, scarifico
Scaring, territans
Scarlet (the grain), coccum; (color), coccineus, coccinus; (in grain), dibaphus, cocco intinctus; (cloth), coccus coccinum

Of scarlet, coccineus, coccinus
Clothed in scarlet, coccinatus
A scarp (in fortification), ima muri declivitas; (in heraldry), fascia minor
Scarred, cicatricibus obductus
A scate (fish), squatina
Scathful, damnosus, noxiosus
To scatter, spargo, dispergo
That may be scattered, dissipabilis
A scattering, sparsio, dispersio
Scatteringly, sparsim, pasaim
Scavage, scavagium
A scavenger, vicorum purgator, scabinus
A scene, scena; (of affairs), series, ordo, or status rerum
Belonging to scenes, scenicus
A scent, odor
Ill-scented, fœtidus
Sweet-scented, odoriferus
To scent (smell out), olfacio, suboleo; (give a smell), odorem diffundere
A scepter, sceptrum
Bearing a scepter, or sceptered, sceptriger
A sceptic, scepticus; (in religion), dubitans, or hæsitans de fide
Sceptical, scepticus, dubitans
Scepticism, sceptica
A schedule, schedula
A scheme, schema, forma, ratio, methodus
Schism, schisma
A schismatic, schismaticus
Schismatical, schismaticus
Schismatically, schismaticè
A scholar (at school), discipulus, scholasticus; (man of learning), homo literatus, or eruditus
Scholar-like, doctè, eruditè
Scholarship, doctrina, eruditio; (exhibition), exhibitio in scholasticum alendum [ticus
Scholastic, Scholastical, scholasticus
Scholastically, scholasticè
A scholium, scholium
A school, schola, gymnasium
A schoolboy, discipulus; (fellow), condiscipulus; (master), ludimagister, præceptor; (mistress), ludimagistra; (man), scholasticus
To school, increpo, objurgo
The sciatica, sciatica
Science, scientia, eruditio
Scientific, scientificus
A scimeter, acinaces
Scintillation, scintillatio
A sciolist, semidoctus
A scion, insitum, surculus
Scissars, or scissors, forfex
Scission, scissio
A scissure, scissura, fissura
A scoff, dicterium, scomma, sarcasmus
To scoff, irrideo, derideo
A scoffer, scurra, derisor
Scoffing, scurra
A scoffing, irrisio, irrisus
Of scoffing, scurrilis
Scoffingly, scurrilitèr
A scold, mulier rixosa
To scold, rixor, objurgo; (at), inclamo, convicior, increpo
Scolded at, conviciis lacessitus
Given to scolding, rixosus
A scolding, rixa, jurgium
A scollop (fish), pecten; (shell), pectunculi testa
Scolloped, denticulatus

SCR

A sconce (fort), propugnaculum; (for a candle), lychnuchus; (fine), mulcta pecuniaria
A sconcing, mulctatio
A scoop, haustrum
To scoop (make hollow), excavo
A scope (design), scopus
Scope (room), spatium
Free scope, licentia, copia
Scorbutic, scorbuticus
To scorch, torreo, aduro
Scorched, torridus, adustus
Scorching, torrens, torridus
A scorching, adustio, æstus
A score (account), ratio, nomen, merces; (in number), numerus vicenarius, viginti
To score (up), noto, signo; (upon), imputo; (make a line under), lineam sub verba ducere
A scorning, notatio
Scorn, contemptus
To scorn, contemno, dedignor
Scorned, contemptus, irrisus
A scorner, irrisor, derisor
Scornful, fastidiosus, fastosus
Scornfully, contemptim, fastosè
A scorning, dedignatio
A scorpion, scorpio, prester
Of a scorpion, scorpionius
A scot (share), symbola, proportio; (and lot), tributum, census parochiales
Scotfree, immunis, impunis
Scotfree, adv. impunè
To scoul (scowl), frontem corrugare
Scouling, torvus
Scoulingly, torvè, vultuosè
A scoundrel, nequam, trifurcifer
To scour, detergo, purgo; (vessels), vasa mundare; (a ditch), fossam tergere; (or run away), fugio
A scourer, purgator
A scouring (cleansing), expurgatio; (danger), periculum, malum; (purging), alvi fluxus
To scourge, verbero, castigo, flagello, verberibus cædere
A scourge, fagellum, flagrum; (of leather), scutica
A scourger, flagellator
A scourging, verberatio
A scout, explorator, speculator
Scouts, excubitores
To scout (lurk), latito; (up and down), exploro, speculor
To scowl. See Scoul
To scrabble, unguibus lacerare
A scrag, corpus strigosum; (end of a neck), cervicis pars sanguinea
Scragginess, macies
Scraggy, macilentus, strigosus
To scramble, raptim colligere
A scramble, direptio
To scramble up, manibus pedibusque ascendere
A scrambling up, conscensio
To scranch, mordeo, admordeo
A scrap, fragmentum
A scrape, difficultas, periculum
To scrape, rado, scalpo, scabo; (away), abrado; (before), præ-rado; (off), derado; (of dirt), detergeo; (out), erado, deleo; (round about), circumrado; (together), corrado
A scraper (person), rasor; (instrument), radula; (fiddler), fidicen
Scraping (badly tuned), parùm modulatè sonans

[113]

SCU

A scraping, rasura; (of or out), deletio; (together), accumulatio; (iron), scalprum
Scraps, fragmenta
A scratch, levis incisura
To scratch, scalpo, scabo; (out), excalpo, expungo
A scratcher, scalptor
A scratching, scalptura
To scrawl, malè scribere
A scrawler, scriba malus
A scrawling, scriptio mala
To screak, strideo, strido
Screaking, stridens
A screaking, stridor
To scream, vociferor, exclamo
A screaming, vociferatio
To screech, ululo
A screen, umbraculum
A screw, cochlea
To screw, torquendo perforare; (fasten with screws), torquendo firmare cochleam; (or oppress one), opprimo; (into favour), insinuo
Scribble, scriptio mala
To scribble, scriptito
A scribbler, malus scriba
A scribbling, scriptio mala
A scribe, scriba, notarius
A scrip, pera, culeolus
The scripture, scriptura sacra
A scrivener, scriba, trapezita
A scrivener's shop, trapeza
Scrofulous, scrofulâ laborans
A scroll, schedula
A scrub (person), homo vilis; (poet), poetaster; (horse), equus strigosus
To scrub, frico, scalpo
Scrubbing, scalpens, defricans
A scrubbing, fricatio vehementior; (brush), scopula ex firmioribus setis confecta
Scrubby, sordibus squalidus, vilis
Scruff, ejectamentum
A scruple (doubt), scrupulus; (of conscience), stimulus animi; (in weight), scrupulum
To scruple (doubt), dubito, hæsito, cunctor
Scupulous, scrupulosus, dubitans
Scrupalously, scrupulosè
A scrutineer, scrutator
Serutinous, argutus, scrutans
A scrutiny, scrutatio
To scrutiny, or scrutinize, scrutor, exploro, investigo
A scud of rain, imber subitus
To scud, or scuddle away, aufugio
A scuffle, jurgium, pugna
To scuffle, certo, decerto; (with), concerto, configo
A scuffling, conflictio
To sculk (hide), lateo, latito; (about), conspectum fugere
Sculking, latens, latitans
A sculking hole, latibulum, latebra
The scull, cranium, calva
A scull-cap, pileolus
A scull, or sculler; (boat), cymbula unius remigis; (man), remex singularis
A scullery, lavatrina
A scullion, lixa; (wench), servula coquinaria
A sculptor, sculptor
Sculpture, sculptura
Of sculpture, sculptilis
Scum, spuma, spumatus; (of metals), scoria; (of the people), fæx populi
Full of scum, spumosus

SEA

Of scum, spumeus
To scum, despumo
A scummer, spatha
A scumming, despamatio
A scupper-hole, latrina navalis
Scurf of the head, &c.), porrigo; (of a sore), crusta ulceris
Scurfy, furfurosus
Scurfiness, psora
Scurrility, scurrilitas
Scurrilous, scurrilis, probrosus
Scurrilously, scurriliter
Scurvily, pravè, improbè
Scurviness, pravitas, improbitas
Scurvy, pravus, improbus
The scurvy, scorbutus
Of the scurvy, scorbuticus
Scurvygrass, cochlearia
A cut (tail), cauda
A scutcheon, scutum
A scuttle (basket), sportula, corbis; (of a ship), navis valvæ; (of a mast), carchesium
The sea, pelagus, mare, æquor; (narrow), fretum; (main), altum, oceanus; (coast), ora maritima; (shore), littus
Of the sea, marinus
At, or by main sea, mari
Sea, adj. maritimus, marinus
Beyond sea, transmarinus
A sea-calf, phoca; (coal), carbo fossilis
On the sea-coast, maritimus
A seaman, nauta, nauticus
A seaport, oppidum maritimum
Seasick, nauseabundus
To be seasick, nauseâ marinâ laborare
Of the sea-shore, littoralis
Seaweed, alga
A seal, signum, sigillum; (fish), phocæna
To seal, sigillo consignare; (a letter), epistolam signare
To set a seal to, subsigno
Of a seal, sigillaris
A seal-ring, annulus signatorius
A sealer, obsignator, signator
A sealing, signatio; (signature), signatura
A seam, sutura; (of corn), frumenti mensura octo modios continens; (fat of hogs), adeps porcina; (of glass), vitri quantitas 120 libras ponderans
To seam, assuo, consuo
Full of seams, abundans suturis
Seamless, non consutus
A seamstress, sutrix; ('s shop), sutrina
A sean (net), sagena
To sear, uro, ustulo, inuro
A searcloth, ceratum
Seared, adustus, inustus
A searing, ustio; (iron), cauterium
A search, inquisitio, indagatio, investigatio
To search, inquiro, exploro; (after), quæro; (out) exquiro; (examine), scrutor; (or fish out), expiscor; (as a customhouse officer), perscrutor; (penetrate), penetro, insinuo; (or trace out), investigo, vestigo
Having searched, scrutatus
A searcher, explorator, scrutator
A searching, scrutatio, indagatio
In season, tempestivè, opportunè
In season, adj. tempestivus
A fit season, occasio, opportunitas
Out of season, intempestivus

SEC — SEL — SEN

To season, condio; (accustom), assuefacio; (instruct), imbuo
Seasonable, tempestivus, opportunus
Seasonableness, tempestivitas, opportunitas
Seasonably, tempestivè, opportunè
A seasoning, conditio, condimentum
Of seasoning, conditivus
A seat, sedes, sella; (of justice), tribunal; (mercy-seat), propitiatorium; (of state), solium; thronus; (or mansion-house), domus rustica, villa; (bench), scamnum; (or form in a school), classis; (of war), sedes; (place), locus; (of commerce), emporium; (in a boat), transtrum; (situation), situs, statio
To seat, sede locare; (sit down), sedeo, consideo
A secant, recta linea secans
Secession, secessus
To seclude, secludo, excludo
Second, secundus
Every second, alternus
Of second sort, secundarius
Second-hand, usu nonnihil tritus
A second (or another), alter; (or assistant), adjutor
Second (thoughts), maturus
A second (of time), momentum, punctum
To second, juvo, adjuvo
Second time, secundò, iterùm
Secondary, secundarius
The secondine, secundæ
Secondly, secundò
Secrecy (silence), silentium; (retirement), recessus
Secret, secretus, arcanus, occultus; (clandestine), clandestinus; (not common), haud vulgaris; (that keeps close), tacitus
In secret, clàm, arcanò
A secret, arcanum, secretum; (chamber), penetrale, conclave, (place), claustrum, secessus, abditum, latebra; (accuser), delator; (accusation), delatio
To keep secret, celo, supprimo
A secretary, scriba, amanuensis; (of state), scriba regius publicis rebus præpositus
To secrete, occulto, celo
A secreting, occultatio furtiva
Secretly, occultè, clàm, furtim
Secretness, silentium
A sect, secta, schola
Of our sect, nostras
Of your sect, vestras
A sectary, sectator
A section, sectio
Secular (worldly), mundanus, profanus; (priest), sacerdos secularis; (affairs), negotia civilia; (arm, or power), magistratuum potestas; (belonging to an age, or 100 years), secularis
A secundary, subpræfectus
Secure, securus, tutus, salvus; (careless), negligens, remissus
To secure, salvum præstare; (from danger), à periculo defendere, servare, or eripere; (from enemies), ab inimicis protegere
Securely, securè, tutè; (carelessly), remissè, negligentèr
A securing, in tutum collocatio
Security, securitas, tranquillitas, otium; (bail), vadimonium; (bail in criminal matters), vas; (bail for debt), præs, sponsor; (engagement), sponsio
To give security, satisdo
To take security, satis accipere
A sedan, sella portatitia
Sedate, sedatus, pacatus, placidus, serenus
Sedentary, sedentarius
Sedge, ulva, carex
Sedgy, ulvis obductus
Sediment, sedimentum, fæx
Sedition, seditio
Seditious, seditiosus, factiosus
Seditiously, seditiosè, factiosè
To seduce (deceive), seduco, decipio; (debauch), corrumpo, depravo
A seducement, irritamentum
A seducer, deceptor, corruptor
A seduction, seductio, deceptio
Sedulity, diligentia
Sedulous, assiduus, diligens
Sedulously, sedulò, strenuè
A see (diocese), sedes episcopalis
See! en! ecce!
To see, video, cerno, conspicio; (take care), caveo, curo, provideo; (afar off), prospicio; (clearly), perspicio; (or look into), introspicio; (one's intention), penetro, intelligo; (into, or examine), examino, inquiro, investigo, perscrutor
Seed, semen; (time), tempus sationis, sementis
Of seed, seminalis
A seed-plot, seminarium
Produced by seed, seminatus
A seedsman, seminum venditor
To seed, semento, semen ferre
Seeding, sementaturus
Seedy, seminosus
A seeing, visio
Seeing clearly, oculatus, perspicax
Seeing that, quandò, quandoquidèm, quoniàm, cùm, siquidèm
To seek, quæro, conquiro; (for aid), imploro; (diligently), quærito, perscrutor, investigo; (endeavour, or contrive), conor, machinor, molior
A seeker, indagator, quæsitor
A seeking, indagatio
Seeming (likely), verisimilis
Seeming (dissembled), simulatus
Seemingly, simulatè, externè
Seemliness, decorum, decor
Seemly, decorus, decens
Seemly, adv. decorè, decentèr
Not seemly, indecorus, indecens
It is seemly, decet
It is not seemly, non decet, dedecet
That may be seen, visibilis
A seer, vates, propheta
A seesaw, motus reciprocus
To seesaw, vacillo
To seethe, coquo, elixo, ferveo, exæstuo; (or boil over), ebullio, exundo
A seething, coctio, ebullitio
A segment, segmentum
To segregate, segrego, separo
A seignior, dominus; (grand), Turcorum imperator
A seigniory, ditio, dominium
Seisin, possessio
To seize (take possession), occupo, possessionem capere; (apprehend), capio, prehendo, corripio
A seizure, occupatio, captio
Seldom, rarus, insolitus, infrequens
Seldom, adv. rarò
Very seldom, perrarus, rarissimus
Very seldom, adv. rarissimè
To select, seligo, eligo, sepono
Select, or selected, selectus, sepositus
A selection, selectio
A selector, elector
Self, or selfsame, ipse, idem
I myself, egomet, ego ipse
By one's self, solus
Self-conceit, arrogantia
Self-conceited, arrogans
To be self-conceited, altum sapere
Self-denial, sui ipsius abnegatio
Self-evident, manifestus
Selfish, nimis se amans
Selfishness, amor sui
Self-murder, suicidium
Self-will, contumacia
Self-willed, obstinatus, contumax
To sell, or expose to sale, vendo, venundo; (be exposed to sale), veneo; (by auction), auctionor; (in the market), nundinor; (often), vendito
A seller, venditor, venditrix; (of old things), scrutarius; (of toys), nugivendus
A selling, venditio
A selvage, fimbria, limbus
Selves, ipsi, ipsæ
Semblable, similis
A semblance, similitudo, species
A semibrief, nota semibrevis
A semicircle, semicirculus
Semicircular, semicircularis
A semicolon, semicolon
A semidiameter, circuli radius
Seminal, seminalis
A seminary, seminarium
Sempiternal, perpetuus
Sena, or senna, sena
Senary, senarius
A senate, senatus
A senate-house, senaculum
Act of senate, senatus consultum
A senator, senator
Senatorian, senatorius, patricius
Senators, patres conscripti
To send, mitto; (about), circummitto; (away), ablego, amando; (back), remitto; (before), præmitto; (for), accerso, evoco; (forth), emitto; (forth breath), exhalo, spiro, halo; (into exile), relego; (a letter), literas dare; (on an errand), mitto, lego; (out of the way), amoveo, ablego; (over), transmitto; (word), nuncio; (word back), renuncio, rescribo
A sending, missio; (away), dimissio, relegatio; (back), remissio; (for), accitus; (over), transmissio; (out), emissio; (forth), dimissio
A seneschal, seneschallus
A senior, major natu
Seniority, ætatis prærogativa
Sensation, facultas sentiendi
A sense (the faculty), sensus; (understanding), mens, judicium, intelligentia; (wit, sharpness), ingenium, solertia, sagacitas; (prudence, wisdom), prudentia, sapientia, consilium; (opinion), opinio, sententia, significatio
Of good sense, sapiens, prudens
Without sense, absurdè, ineptè
Senseless (without feeling), nihil sentiens; (foolish), absurdus,

[113]

SER — SET — SHA

ineptus ; (stupid), stupidus, plumbeus ; (void of reason), expers rationis, mentis inops
Senselessly, absurdè, ineptè
Senselessness, vecordia
Sensibility, sensibilitas
Sensible, sensilis ; (of good sense), sapiens ; (affecting the senses), sensum movens, or afficiens
Sensibly (feelingly), cum sensu ; (wisely), sapientèr, prudentèr
Sensitive, sensitivus, sensu præditus
Sensual, voluptuosus, mollis
Sensuality, voluptas corporea
Sensually, jucundè, voluptariè
A sentence, sententia ; (by a judge), judicium ; (period), periodus
To sentence, judicium ferre, or pronunciare, addico, damno
Sententious, sententiosus
Sententiously, sententiosè
Sentient, sentiens, percipiens
A sentiment (opinion), sensus, sententia, opinio
A sentry, excubiæ ; (box), specula ; (or sentinel), excubitor, speculator
To stand sentry, excubo, excubias, or vigilias agere
Separable, separabilis
Separate, separatus, disjunctus
To separate, separo, sejungo ; (or retire from), discedo ; (from others), segrego, secerno ; (or break company), dissocio
Separately, separatim, divisim
A separating, or separation, separatio, disjunctio, secretio ; (divorce), divortium, repudium
September, September
Septenary, septenarius
Septennial, septennis
Septentrional, septentrionalis
Septic, or septical, septicus
The septuagint, septuaginta interpretes
Septuple, septuplus, septuplex
Sepulchral, sepulchralis
A sepulchre, sepulchrum, mausoleum
Sepulture, sepultura
A sequel, or sequence, consequentia ; (or series), series ; (or upshot), eventus, exitus
Sequent, sequens
To sequester, sequestro, proscribo, confisco
A sequestering, or sequestration, sequestratio, confiscatio
A sequestrator, sequestrator
A seraglio, gynæceum
Seraphical, Seraphic, seraphicus
A seraphim, seraphim
A serenade, cantiuncula nocturna
To serenade, occentare ostium
Serene, serenus, tranquillus, placidus
To make serene, sereno
Serenely, serenè, placidè
Sereneness, Serenity, tranquillitas
Serge, panni rudi genus
A sergeant, or serjeant, lictor, apparitor ; (at arms), ad arma serviens ; (at law), ad legem serviens
A sergeantship, apparitura
Of a sergeant, lictorius
Sergeantry, servitium
A series, series, ordo
Serious, serius, gravis, sobrius
Seriously, seriò, gravitèr
Seriousness, gravitas
A sermon, concio, oratio sacra

Serosity, serum
Serous, serosus
A serpent, serpens ; (with two heads), amphisbæna ; (horned), cerastes ; (burning), dipsas ; (water), hydrus ; (.'s skin), exuviæ
Serpentine, serpentinus, sinuosus
Like a serpent, flexuosus, sinuosus
To serr, or serry, compingo
A servant, servus, famulus, minister ; (woman), ancilla, famula, pedissequa
An humble servant, procus
Of a servant, famularis
To serve (as a servant), alicui servire ; (up dinner), cibos apponere ; (with drink), pocula administrare ; (or supply with), suppedito, præbeo ; (or be useful for), prosum
Service, or servitude, servitium, famulatus ; (done to a master), opera, ministerium ; (respect), obsequium, officium ; (labour), labor ; (worship), cultus
A service at table, ferculum ; (the first service, &c.), prima mensa
To do service, prosum
Serviceable (useful), utilis, commodus ; (officious), obsequens, officiosus ; (fit for service), servitio aptus
Serviceableness, utilitas
Serviceably, utilitèr, officiosè
Servile, servilis
Servilely, servilitèr, vernilitèr
Servileness, Servility, vernilitas
Serving (as a servant), serviens, ministrans ; (a purpose), aptus, utilis
A servitor, servus, famulus
Servitude, servitus, servitudo
A session, sessio
A session of parliament, parliamenti sessio, senatûs habitus
A sessor, censor
A sesterce, sestertius, sestertium
A set battle, pugna stataria
Well set, compacto corpore
Set for rain, pluviosus
Set on mischief, proclivis
On set purpose, dedità operà
A set (of things), apparatus, instrumentum
To set (put, or place), pono, colloco ; (appoint), statuo, constituo
A setter (planter), sator ; (to hire), locator ; (forth), editor ; (on), ductor
A setting, positio ; (apart), sepositio, separatio ; (off), distinctio ; (forward), progressus ; (stick), pastinum ; (up), erectio ; (upon, or an assault), impetus ; (of the sun), solis occasus ; (dog), canis cubitor
Setaceous, ex setis aptus
A settle, sedile, sella ; (bed), lectus sellæ formam habens
To settle, statuo, constituo, firmo, confirmo ; (in a place), sedem figere ; (a thing by arguments), argumentis confirmare ; (accounts), rationes conferre ; (an estate upon one), aliquem hæredem suum facere ; (affairs), res disponere ; (expenses), sumptus moderari ; (on the lungs), incumbo ; (an habitation), sedem figere
Settledness, stabilitas

A settlement, or settling, constitutio ; (agreement), pactum, fœdus, stipulatio ; (fixed place of abode), sedes, habitaculum ; (of liquor), fæx, sedimentum
Seven, septem ; (at cards), heptas ; (times), septiès ; (years old), septennis ; (years), septennium
The seven stars, Pleiades
Sevenfold, septuplex, septemplex
Seven foot, septempedalis
A sevennight (se'nnight), septimana
Seventeen, septemdecim
The seventeenth, decimus septimus
The seventh, septimus
Seventhly, septimùm
Seventy, septuaginta
Of seventy, septuagenarius
Seventy times, septuagiès
The seventieth, septuagesimus
Seven hundred, septingenti
The seven-hundredth, septingentesimus
Seven hundred times, septingentiès
To sever, separo, secerno, segrego, divido
Several (more than one), plures, nonnulli ; (distinct), distinctus, separatus, diversus, varius
Severally, separatim, singulatim
Severance, separatio, divisio
Severe (hard, rigorous), severus, durus, asper, austerus, morosus ; (very cold), frigidissimus ; (grave, sober), gravis, sobrius
Severed, separatus, sejunctus
Severely, severè, asperè
A severing, separatio
Severity, severitas, asperitas
To sew, suo ; (before), præsuo (behind), desuo ; (in), insuo ; (to), assuo ; (together), consuo
That may be sewed, sutilis
A sewer, sutor ; (common shore), cloaca
Sewet, sebum, sevum ; (melted), liquamen
Of sewet, sevosus, sebaceus
Mixed with sewet, omentatus
A sewing, sutura ; (together), consutura
A sex, sexus
Sexennial, sexennalis
Sextile, sextilis
A sexton, edituus, sacrista
Shabbily, malè
Shabbiness, malus vestitus
Shabby, malus, sordidus, pannosus
A shabby fellow, homo tressis
A shackle, manica, compes
To shackle, compedibus vincire
Shad (a fish), clupea
A shade, umbra ; (worn by women), nimbus
To shade, umbro, tego
To be shaded, umbror
Shades (ghosts), umbræ, manes
Shadiness, opacitas
A shadow, umbra
Of a shade, or shadow, umbratilis
A mere shadow, valdè macilentus
To shadow, or cast a shadow, umbro, obumbro, opaco, obscuro
To shadow out, adumbro
Shadow (favour, protection), tutamen, tutela ; (pretence, or appearance), prætextus, species ; (sign, trace, or footstep),

SHA

vestigium ; (type, *or* figure), typus
A shadowing, adumbratio
Shady, umbrosus, opacus
A shady place, umbraculum
A shaft, telum, sagitta ; (spire), pyramis ; (of a pillar), scapus ; (in a mine), scapteusula
Shag, pannus villosus
Shagged, Shaggy, villosus, hirsutus
Shagreen, *subst.* mœror, solicitudo ; *adj.* mœstus, solicitus
Shagreen-leather, squali corium
To shagreen, mœrorum creare
A shake, *or* shaking, motus, concussio ; (in music), modulatio
To shake, quatio, concutio, vibro, exagito ; (hands), manus conjungere ; (the head), nuto ; (for fear), tremo, contremisco, horreo ; (off), excutio ; (often), agito, quasso ; (with cold), frigore tremere ; (in trotting), succutio ; (up and down), jacto ; (in singing), modulor
To be shaken, nuto, titubo
That may be shaken, agitabilis
A shaker, concussor ; (with trotting), succussator
Shaking (for fear), trepidus ; (with cold), frigore horrens ; (up and down), tremulus, mobilis
A shaking (*in an active sense*), quassatio, concussio ; (*in a passive sense*), tremor ; (with cold), horror ; (up and down), agitatio ; (*or* jolting), succussus
A shallop, scapha, lembus
Shallow (not deep), brevis, minime profundus ; (in wit), ineptus, hebes ; (dull, insipid), insulsus
A shallow place, vadum
A shallow river, fluvius tenui fluens aquâ
Shallowly, insulse, inepte
Shallowness (of water), minima aquæ profunditas ; (in understanding), imperitia, tarditas
Shallows, brevia
A shalot, allium Lusitanicum
A sham, fallacia, dolus
Sham, fictus, fictitius, commentitius
To sham, fingo, simulo
The shambles, macellum, laniena
Of shambles, macellarius
Shame (bashfulness), pudor, modestia ; (disgrace), dedecus, infamia, opprobrium, ignominia
To shame (make ashamed), pudefacio ; (disgrace), infamiam afferre
Shamed, perfusus rubore ; (disgraced), dedecoratus
Shamefaced, verecundus   [tèr
Shamefacedly, verecundè, pudenShamefacedness, verecundia
Shameful, fœdus, turpis, probrosus, inhonestus, ignominiosus
Shamefully, turpitèr, impudentèr
Shamefulness, turpitudo, probrum
Shameless, impudens, inverecundus
Shamelessly, inverecundè
Shamelessness, impudentia
Shamois, pellis rupicapræ
The shank (of the leg), tibia, crus ; (bone), parastata ; (of a chimney), fumarium ; (of a candlestick), scapus candelabri ; (of a plant), plantæ caulis
[115]

SHE

A shanker, ulcus
A shape, forma, figura
To shape, formo, figuro
Shapeless, informis
Ill-shapen, deformis
Well-shapen, venustus
Of two shapes, biformis
Of many shapes, multiformis
A shaping, formatio
A shard, *or* sherd, testa fracta
Of a shard, testaceus
A shard (gap), sepis ruina ; (fish), trutta minor
A share, pars, portio
The share-bone, os sacrum
To share (divide), divido, partior, distribuo ; (give a share), impertio ; (take a share), participo ; (have a share), partem ferre
Having shared, sortitus
A sharer, partitor ; (*or* partaker of), particeps, consors
A sharing by lot, sortitio
To shark (cheat), aliquem emungere
A shark (fish), canis, carcharias
Sharp (in action), acer ; (in taste), acidus, subacidus ; (in wit), acutus, astutus, sagax ; (in words), mordax ; (fight), pugna atrox ; (cruel), severus, rigidus, ferus, crudelis ; (cold), frigus durum ; (rough), asper ; (set), - famelicus, esuriens ; (sour), acerbus, austerus ; (sighted), oculatus, perspicax ; (of edge), acutus
To be sharp, aceo
To grow sharp, acesco
To sharpen, acuo, exacuo, acumino ; (at the end), cuspido, spiculo ; (at the top), cacumino
A sharpening, exacutio
Sharper, acutior, acrior
A sharper, astutus, versutus ; (cheat), fraudator, veterator
Sharply, acutè, acritèr ; (by way of reproach), contumeliosè ; (roughly), asperè, acerbè ; (wittily), acutè, argutè, sagacitèr, salsè
Sharpness (of edge), acies, acumen ; (severity), rigor, severitas ; (smartness), acrimonia ; (of words), mordacitas ; (sourness), acerbitas ; (of wit), sagacitas, solertia
A shash, cingulum ; (turban), tiara
To shatter, quasso, comminuo
A shatterpate, futilis, ineptus
To shave, tondeo, rado ; (about), circumrado ; (off, *or* away), abrado ; (close), attondeo
A shaver, tonsor
A shaving, rasura, tonsura
Of shaving, tonsorius
Shavings, ramenta
She, ea, illa, ipsa, ista, hæc
A sheaf, fascis, manipulus ; (of arrows), pharetra
To shear, tondeo, detondeo ; (*or* reap corn), meto ; (run as a ship), labo ; (round about), circumtondeo
A shearer, tonsor
A shearing, tonsura
A shearman, panni tonsor
Shears, forfex
A sheat (rope), funiculus quo velum transfertur ; (anchor), anchora maxima ; (cable), funis anchorarius ; (pig), porcellus, verres ; (fish), silurus

SHI

A sheath, theca, vagina
To sheath, in vaginam recondere ; (a ship), assulas ad imam navim affigere ; (in one's body), defigo
A sheath-maker, vaginarius
A shed (*or* cottage), casula ; (adjoining to a house), appendix ædificii
To shed (liquor), fundo, effundo ; (about), circumfundo
A shedding, fusio, effusio
Sheds, allegiæ, septa
Sheen, *or* sheeny, nitidus
A sheep, ovis ; (fold), ovile ; (hook), pedum ; (walk), pascuum
Of sheep, ovillus, ovinus
Sheepish, insulsus, insipiens
Sheepishness, insulsitas, insipientia
Sheer (pure), purus, merus
To sheer off, clancultm discedere
A sheet (for a bed), lodix ; (of paper), folium ; (of lead), lamina
Sheeted, lodicibus stratus [mina
Sheeting, pannus ex quo lodices conficiuntur
A shekel, siclus
A shelf, pluteus, abacus ; (of sand), brevia, syrtes
A shell, testa ; (of nuts, &c.), putamen ; (of a fish), concha ; (of a snail), cochlea
To shell, decortico, deglubo
Shelly, testaceus
Like a shell, conchatus
A shelter, refugium
To shelter, protego, defendo, tueor
Sheltering, protegens, defendens
Shelving, declivis
A shepherd, pastor, opilio
A shepherd's crook, pedum
Of a shepherd, pastoralis
A shepherdess, femina oves custodiens
A sheriff successor
A sheriffalty, vicecomitis munus
The sheriffdom, vicecomitatus
A -heriffwick, vicecomitis jurisdictio
Sherry, vinum Andalusianum
A shew (outward appearance), species, simulatio, prætextus ; (sight), pompa, spectaculum
Shew-bread, panis propositicius
To shew, monstro, demonstro, ostendo, indico, declaro ; (beforehand), prædico ; (expose to view), propono, exhibeo ; (cause), rationes afferre
To make a shew of, simulo
To shew kindness, diligo ; (mercy), misereor ; (fear), timeo ; (respect), revereor, veneror
A shewing, indicatio
Shewy, speciosus
A shield, clypeus, scutum ; (used by Amazons), pelta ; (used by Moors), cetra
Armed with a shield, clypeatus, cetratus, parmatus
A shield-bearer, scutigerulus ; (maker), scutarius
To shield, defendo, protego
A shielding, protectio
A shift (expedient), ratio, modus ; (remedy), remedium ; (device), dolus, effugium, stropha, techna, vaframentum ; (a woman's shirt), subucula feminea
To shift (escape), evado, effugio ; (change), permuto, muto ; (as

SHO — SHO — SHU

the wind), verto ; (off), detrecto ; (remove), amoveo, removeo ; (from place to place), migro, denigro
To make a shift, egrè facere
A shifter, veterator
A shifting, mutatio, migratio ; (trick), fallacia, dolus
A shilling, solidus
The shin, tibia
To shine, fulgeo, mico, niteo, luceo, splendeo ; (about), circumfulgeo ; (bright), inniteo, effulgeo ; (before), præfulgeo ; (like gold), rutilo ; (a little), subluceo ; (out), eniteo, enitesco ; (through), perluceo, transpareo ; (together), colluceo ; (upon), alluceo, affulgeo, illustro
To begin to shine, splendesco
A shingle (lath), asser
The shingles, herpes
Shining, part. nitens, fulgens, splendens, rutilans ; adj. rutilus, coruscus, nitidus, splendidus, fulgidus ; (through), pellucidus
A shining, fulgor, nitor
Shiningly, splendidè, nitidè
A ship, navis, navigium ; (with a flat bottom), navis planâ carinâ ; (of war), navis bellica
Master of a ship, nauclerus
Of a ship, navalis
Ship-money, tributum pro navibus construendis
A ship-boat, scapha ; (boy), puer nauticus ; (man), nauta ; (timber), materia navalis
Shipwreck, naufragium
Shipwrecked, naufragus
A ship-carpenter, naupegus
A ship's fare, naulum
To ship off, in naves imponere
To govern a ship, naviculor
A shipping, in navem conscensio ; (a putting on board), in navem impositio
Shipping, plures naves
A shire, provincia, comitatus
To shirk about, parasitor
A shirt, indusium
A shittlecock, suber pennatum ; (silly fellow), levis, inconstans
To shiver, frango, comminuo, conscindo ; (with cold), præ frigore horrere ; (or be shivered in pieces), comminuor, frangor
Shivered to pieces, comminutus
Shivering (to pieces), comminuens ; (quaking), tremulus, horrens
A shivering (to pieces), dissecatio ; (or quaking), horror
In shivers, assulatim
A shoal (of fishes, &c.), grex, agmen, caterva ; (of sand), brevia
A shock (of corn), acervus ; (in battle), certamen, conflictus ; (upon the spirits), impetus, horror
To shock, confligo, congredior, terreo, permoveo
To be shocked, permoveor
Not shod, discalceatus
A shoe, calceus, solea
A high shoe, pero
To shoe (or put on shoes), calceo, calceos induere ; (a horse), ferreas soleas aptare
To put off shoes, excalceo
A shoemaker, sutor
Belonging to shoemakers, sutorius
A shoemaker's shop, sutrina ; (a trade), ars sutrina
A shoe-latchet, corrigia
A shoe-sole, solea ; (upper-leather), obstragulum
A shoeing, or fitting with shoes, calceatus ; (horn), cornu calceatorium
I shook, concussi
A shoot, germen, surculus ; (young pig), porcellus ; (from a bow, &c.), ictus, jactus
Full of shoots, surculosus
Of shoots, surcularius
To shoot (as trees), germino ; (an arrow, &c.), jaculor, emitto ; (as an ear of corn), spico ; (as lightning), emico, corusco ; (or jet out), promineo, exto ; (or run upon one), irruo, insilio ; (pain), doleo, uro ; (or grow up), cresco ; (at a mark), telum collineare, ad metam dirigere ; (at one), sagittis petere
A shooter of darts, jaculator ; (of a lock), sera obex
The shooting of a star, trajectio
A shooting, jaculatio ; (of trees, &c.), germinatio
To go a shooting, aucupor
A shooting-star, sidus volans
A shop, taberna, officina ; (barber's), tonstrina ; (bookseller's), bibliopolium
A shopkeeper, tabernarius
Belonging to a shop, tabernarius
A shore, littus, arena, ripa, terra ; (prop), fulcrum ; (common sewer), cloaca
To shore up, suffulcio, fulcio
A shoring up, suffulsio
Not shorn, intonsus
Short, brevis, curtus, concisus, compendiosus, succinctus
To be short, breviter
In a short time, brevi
Very short, perbrevis
In a short manner, summatim
To stop short, repentè consistere
Short of a place, cis, citra
To be short, deficio
To take up short, increpo
To cut short, præcido
To grew short, decresco
Shorter days, dies contractiores
Shortlived, caducus
Shortsighted, luscinus
Shortwinded, anhelus
Short hand, notæ breviores
A short cut, via compendiaria
To shorten, decurto, contraho, in compendium redigere ; (one's commons), cibum deducere
A shortening, contractio
Shortly (in words), breviter, summatim, ad summam ; (in time), brevi ; (after), paulò pòst, mox
Shortness, brevitas ; (of breath), asthma, spirandi difficultas
Shot (small), pilulæ plumbeæ minores ; (large), glandes terreæ ; (at a club), symbola, collecta
Shotten, effœtus, coagulatus
A shove (thrust), impulsus
To shove, impello, trudo ; (back), depello ; (on), propello ; (away), submoveo
A shovel, ligo ; (fire), batillum ; (paring), pala
To shovel, ligone anferre
A shovel-board, mensa longa lusoria
A shoulder (of a man), humerus ; (of a beast), armus
With great shoulders, humerosus
The shoulder-blade, scapula ; (piece), humerale
Over left shoulder, parûm succedens
To shoulder, humeris tollere ; (up), suffulcio ; (a pike), hastam in humero attollere
A shout, acclamatio, clamor
To shout, acclamo, clamo, exclamo
Shouting, clamosus
A show, pompa. See Shew
A shower, imber, pluvia ; (great), nimbus
To shower down, depluo
Causing showers, imbrifer
Showery, nimbosus, pluvius, pluvialis
A shred, segmentum panni
To shred, concido, præseco
Shred small, minutim concisus
In small shreds, minutè, minutim
A shredding, concisura
A shrew, mulier rixosa ; (mouse), mus araneus
Shrewd (sharp, cunning), vafer, subdolus, astutus, argutus ; (ticklish, dangerous), difficilis, periculosus ; (unhappy), malus, improbus, pravus
A shrewd turn, maleficium
Shrewdly, astutè, pravè, subdolè
Shrewdness, astutia, sagacitas
Shrewish, perversus, clamosus
To shriek, ejulo, exclamo
A shriek, or shrieking, ejulatus
Shrift, confessio auricularis
Shrill, argutus, sonorus, clarus
Shrilly, argutè, sonorè
Shrillness, sonus argutus
A shrimp, squilla parva ; (dwarf), nanus, pumilio
A shrine, conditorium
To shink (or contract itself), se contrahere ; (grow less), decresco ; (from one's word), tergiversor ; (in courage), labasco
A shrinking, contractio ; (from one's word), retractio ; (of sinews), spasmus, nervorum convulsio
Shrivalty, vicecomitis munus
To shrive, sacerdoti confiteri
To shrivel, rugo, corrugo
To be shrivelled, corrugor
A shriver, confessor
Shrovetide, bacchanalia
A shroud (shelter), tectum, tutela, præsidium ; (for the dead), amiculum ferale
To shroud (a dead body), amiculum ferale imponere ; (cover), tego, operio, velo
The shrouds, rudentes majores
A shrub (little tree), frutex, arbuscula ; (dwarf), nanus, pumilio ; (liquor), potus ex vino adusto, malis aureis, et zacharo commistis, confectus
Shrubby, fruticosus
To grow shrubby, frutico
A shrubbery, fruticetum
Shruff, scoria, recrementum
To shrug, tremo ; (up the shoulders), scapulas attollere
To shudder, horreo, tremo
Shuddering, horrens, tremens
A shuddering, horror, tremor
To shuffle, misceo ; (and out), tergiversor, callidè cunctari ; (along), acceleratè et tremulo gradu incedere ; (off a fault), culpam transferre ; (off a troublesome business), extricare se
A shuffling, mistura ; (or boggling), cavillatio, tergiversati ;
Shufflingly, dolosè, fraudulenter

[116]

SID   SIL   SIN

To shun, devito, fugio, declino
That may be shunned, evitabilis
That cannot be shunned, inevitabilis
Shunning, devitans, fugiens
A shunning, devitatio, evitatio
To shut, claudo; (or bar fast), occludo, obsero; (in), includo; (out), excludo; (up), intercludo, concludo
To get shut (of business), ab aliquo negotio se expedire; (of a person), aliquem amovere
To shut up shop, tabernam occludere; (or leave off trade), foro cedere
A shutter, claustrum
A shutting (out), exclusio; (up), conclusio
The shutting in of the day, crepusculum vespertinum
A shuttle, radius textorius
Shy (wary), cautus; (disdainful), fastosus, supercilious; (apt to start), pavidus; (not friendly), vultus minimè fraternus
Shy, adv. frigidè, indifferentèr
Shyness, fastus, cautela
A sibyl, sibylla
The sice-point, senio
Sick, ægrotus, æger; (at stomach), stomachicus
To be sick, ægroto; (in bed), lecto æger affigi; (dangerously), gravitèr ægrotare; (of a fever), febricito; (of a thing), ægrè ferre
To fall sick, languesco
Sickish, malè se habens
A sickle, falx messoria
Sickliness, ægrotatio, valetudo
Sickly, infirmus, valecudinarius
A sickly time, quo plurimi ægrotant
Sickness, morbus, ægrotatio; (green), chlorosis; (contagious), contagium; (falling), epilepsia; (plague), pestilentia, pestis
A side, latus, &c.; (of a cup, &c.), pars; (or party), pars, causa; (of a country), ora, regio; (of a leaf), pagina; (of a river), ripa; (or brim), margo; (or the shore), littus; (of a bed), sponda; (of a hill), clivus
Belonging to a side, lateralis
A sideboard, abacus; (of plate), abacus vasis argenteis refertus
A side-blow, ictus obliquus
A side-face, facies obliquè depicta
A sidesman, adjutor, quæsitor; (of a fowl), portio oblonga è lumbis dissecta
A side-wind, ventus obliquus
Sideways, obliquus, transversus; adv. obliquè, transversè
Sideling, corpore inclinato
By the side of, juxta, prope
the same side, collateralis
on all sides, quaquaversùs, undiquè
on both sides, utrinquè; (either side), alterutrinquè; (every side), undiquè, ex omni parte; (the inside), intùs; (one side and the other), ultrò citròque; (the outside), extrinsecùs; (neither side), neutrò
To side with (or favour), faveo, partes sequi, cum aliquo stare
A siding with, partium studium
To side along, corpore inclinato incedere
[117]

To change sides, fidem mutare
Sideral, sideralis
A siege, obsidio, obsidium, obsessio, circumcessio
To lay siege, obsideo
Belonging to a siege, obsidionalis
A sieve, cribrum
Belonging to a sieve, cribrarius
To sift, cerno, cribro; (out a matter), exquiro, pervestigo, scrutor
Sifted (out), patefactus, retectus; (as meal), cribratus
A sifting (of meal), cribratio; (or searching), scrutatio
Siftings, recrementum
A sigh, suspirium, gemitus
To sigh, suspiro, gemo
A sighing, suspiratio
A sight (shew), spectaculum
The sight, visus, aspectus, conspectus, obtutus; (or faculty of seeing), facultas videndi; (in a cross-bow), scutula; (of the eye), oculi acies
At first sight, primâ facie
To come in sight, appareo
Dimness of sight, caligatio
Dim sighted, luscus, caliganus
Quick-sighted, benè oculatus
Sharp-sighted, perspicax, sagax
Sightless, cæcus, lumine captus
Sightly, spectabilis, speciosus
A sign (token), insigne, signum, nota, indicium; (footstep), vestigium; (presage), præsagium, (manual), chirographum; (at a house), signum, insigne
To sign, signo, obsigno
Signal, notabilis, clarus, insignis
A signal, signum, symbolum
To signalize, insignio, re gestâ clarum reddere
Signally, insignitèr, eximiè
A signature, signatura; (in printing), literæ schedæ index
Signed, signatus, consignatus
A signer, signator
A signet, sigillum
Signification (meaning), sensus, significatus, vis or weight), vis, momentum, pondus
Significant (denoting), significans, denotans, exprimens; (of great force), magni momenti
Significantly, clarè, planè
A signification (or shewing), significatio; (or sense of a word), sensus, vis, potestas, notio
Significative, significativus
To signify (mean), valeo, significo; (declare), denuncio, declaro, notifico, denoto; (presage), prædico, portendo
A signifying, significatio, significatus, prædictio
Signifying, significans, declarans
A signing, signatio, obsignatio
Silence, silentium, taciturnitas; (secrecy), reticentia
To silence, os obturare
To break silence, profari
To keep silence, sileo, taceo
Silenced, cui os obstruitur
A silencing, oris obstructio
Silent, silens, tacitus, taciturnus
To become silent, obticeo, conticeo
Silently, tacitè, silentèr
Silk, sericum, bombyx
Silk, sericus, bombycinus (throughout), holosericus
Of silk, sericus
Covered with silk, sericatus
A silkman, sericarius; (shop),

bombycini operis officina; (weaver), sericæ textor; (worm), bombyx
Silky, mollis, flexilis
A sill, limen
A sillabub, oxygala
Sillily, ineptè, insulsè, absurdè
Silliness, ineptia, insulsitas
Silly, vecors, ineptus; (fellow), asinus; (action), ineptè factum
Silvan, silvosus
Silver, argentum; (quick), argentum vivum
Of silver, argenteus
Full of silver, argentosus
To silver, argento obducere
A silversmith, faber argentarius
Similar, similis, similaris
A simile, collatio, similitudo; (example), exemplum
A similitude (parable), parabola; (likeness), similitudo
Simoniacal, simoniacus
Simony, simonia
A simper, risus levis
To simper, subrideo, arrideo
Simple (unmixed), simplex, merus, purus; (single, alone), unicus, solus; (harmless), innoxius, innocens, innocuus; (plain without ornament), simplex, inornatus; (sincere, honest), simplex, integer, probus, sincerus; (silly), ineptus, insipiens, fatuus, insulsus; (fellow), homo crassi ingenii; (trifling), frivolus, vilis, levis
Simpleness, or simplicity, simplicitas, sinceritas; (in understanding), insipientia, stultitia
A simpler, or simplist, artis botanices peritus
A simpleton, fatuus
Simply, simplicitèr, sincerè; (without ornament), nullo ornatu; (in wit), ineptè, insipientèr
Simulation, simulatio
Sin, peccatum, delictum, flare
A sin-offering, sacrificium piaculare
To sin, pecco, delinquo
Since (seeing that), cùm, quùm, quandò, quia, quandoquidèm, siquidèm, quoniàm; (from that time), postquam, cùm, quòd; (before that time), antè, abhinc
Ever since, jam indè [dèm
Long since, jamdudùm, jampriNot long since, nupèr, non pridèm
How long since? quàm pridèm?
Sincere, sincerus, integer
Sincerely, sincerè, simplicitèr
Sincerity, sinceritas
A sinew, nervus
Sinewy, nervosus
Sinful, impius, flagitiosus
Sinfully, impiè, flagitiosè
Sinfulness, impietas, scelus
To sing, cano, psallo, canto, decanto, modulor; (ballads), in triviis diaperdere carmen; (before), præcino; (between), intercino; (as a nurse), lallo; (treble), medio sono modulari; (often), cantito; (in parts), concino; (to a harp), succino
To singe, ustulo, amburo
A singer, cantor, cantator
A singing, cantio, harmonia; (together), concentus; (place), odeum; (school), scola musica; (boys), pueri symphoniaci; (man), cantator, cantor; (wo-

SIX

man), cantatrix; (master), musices professor
Single, singularis, unicus; (hearted), integer, probus
A single life, cœlibatus; (person), cœlebs
To single out, seligo, excerpo
Singleness, simplicitas, integritas
Singly, singulatim, singillatim
Singular (belonging to one only), unicus, simplex, singularis; (particular), peculiaris; (rare, excellent), clarus, egregius, eximius, præstans; (odd, or affecting singularity), à communi usu alienus
Singularity, singularitas, affectatio, insolentia
Singularly, singulariter, unicè
Sinister (unlucky), sinister, mali ominis; (unlawful, unjust), malevolus, iniquus, injustus
To sink, sido, desido, consido, subsido, labo; (in courage), animo labare; (one's spirits), detrecto; (a ship), navem demergere; (under its own weight), mole suâ ruere; (credit), fidem imminuere; (a well), puteum fodere; (principal money), sortem alienare; (or waste by sickness), contabesco; (or penetrate into), penetro
A sink, sentina, latrina, cloaca; (hole), ostium cloacale
Sinking (down), subsidens, residens; (in), imbibens
Sinking paper, charta bibula
A sinking in fortune, fortuna inclinata, opes penè exhaustæ
The sinking of ground, labes agri
Sinless, innocens, sceleris purus
A sinner, peccator, peccatrix
A sip, or sipping, sorbitio
To sip, sorbillo, gusto
A sippet, panis quadra
Sir, domine; (signifying a knight), eques, miles
A sire, pater, genitor
A siren, siren
A sirname, nomen paternum
A sister, soror, germana
Of a sister, sororius
A sisterhood, feminarum sodalitium
To sit, sedeo; (at table), accumbo; (by), accubo, assideo; (crosslegged), coxim sedere; (down), decumbo, consideo; (down before a town), obsideo; (or cleave fast), adhæreo; (close to work), operi diligenter incumbere; (as a hen), ovis incubare; (in the sun), apricor; (still), quiesco, nihil agere; (round), circumsideo; (together), considéo; (up), erigo; (up, or watch), vigilo; (upon), insideo
A site (situation), situs
Sitting, sedens, accumbens; (as a garment), aptatus
A sitting, sessio; (at table), accubatio; (as a hen), incubatio; (by), assessio; (as a commissioner), consessio
Belonging to sitting, sessilis
Situate, situatus, situs, positus
To be situate near, adjaceo
A situation, situs, positio
Six, sex, seni
Six at cards, or dice, senio
Six times, sexiès
Of six, senarius
Sixfold, sextuplus
Six years, sexennium
[118]

SKR

The sixth, sextus
The sixth time, sextùm
A sixth part, sextans [deciès
Sixteen, sexdecim; (times), sex-
The sixteenth, decimus sextus
Sixty, sexaginta, sexageni
Of sixty, sexaginarius
Sixty times, sexagiès
The sixtieth, sexagesimus
Six hundred, sexcenti; (times), sexcentiès
The six hundredth, sexcentesimus
Size, moles, modus, mensura, magnitudo; (used by plaisterers), gluten è corio factum; (to gild with), chrysocolla
To size (measure), metior, admetior
Sizeable, justæ molis
A sizer (servitor), batalarius
Sizy, glutinosus
A skain, glomus fili
A skate (scate), squatina
A skeleton, sceletos; (one very lean, or thin), admodùm macilentus
A sketch, lineatio, adumbratio
To sketch out, delineo, adumbro
To skewer, festucis colligere
A skiff, scapha
Skill, peritia, ars, scientia
Skilful, Skilled, peritus, expertus; (in the law), juris peritus
To be skilful, calleo, intelligo
Skilfully, peritè, eruditè, callidè
To skim, despumo; (milk), cremorem eximere; (or pass over lightly), leviter perstringere
A skin, pellis, cutis; (little), cuticula; (of a beast), corium, tergus; (of parchment), scheda pergamena; (husk), siliqua
Between the skin and flesh, intercus
Having a thick skin, callosus
Of the skin, cuticularis
To skin (or take the skin off), deglubo, pellem exuere
A skinker, à poculis, pincerna
A skinner, pellio; (-'s trade), ars pellionis
Skinny, macilentus
A skip (or jump), saltus; (jack), ardelio, homunculus
To skip, salio, salio; (back), resilio; (before), præsulto; (often), saltito; (over), transilio; (over, or omit), prætermitto, omitto, prætereo; (out), prosilio
A skipper (jumper), saltator; (Dutch ship), navis Hollandica; (master of a ship), nauclerus
Skipping, saltans, saltabundus
A skipping, saltatus, saltatio
By skips, per saltus
Of skipping, saltatorius
A skirmish, velitatio
To skirmish, velitor
Of a skirmish, velitaris
A skirmisher, veles, excursor
A skirmishing, velitatio
A skirt, fimbria, ora, limbus; (of a country), confinium, limes
Skittish (humoursome, wanton), petulans, protervus, levis, inconstans, procax, lascivieus; (horse), equus pavidus
A skittish humour, protervitas
Skittishly, exultìm
Skittishness, protervitas, levitas
A skreaking of a saw, stridor
To skream out, exclamo
A skreaming out, exclamatio

SLA

A skreen, umbraculum; (used by bricklayers, &c.), cribrum
To skreen, tego, cribro
The sky, æther, æthra, cælum
Of the sky, æthereus
Skycoloured, cæruleus
A slab (puddle), lacuna; (of timber), asser externus; (marble hearth), marmor focarium
To slabber, madefacio; (drivel), salivâ manare
Slabbered, madefactus
A slabbering bib, pectorale linteum
Slabby, madidus, cœnosus
To slack, or slacken, laxo, remitto; (one's pace), gradum minuere; (be slackened), laxor, remittor; (flag), langueo, tardesco
Slack, laxus, remissus, lentus; (careless), remissus, negligens; (slow), segnis, tardus
A slackening, laxatio
Slackly, remissè, perfunctoriè
Slackness, tarditas, mora
Slain, cæsus, occisus
To slake (quench), extinguo, sedo; (lime), calcem aquâ macerare; (hunger), famem explere, or satiare; (thirst), sitim sedare
Slaked (as lime), aquâ maceratus
Slander, calumnia
To slander, calumnior, detrecto
Slandered, infamatus
A slanderer, calumniator
A slandering, calumniatio
Slanderous, maledicus, calumniosus; (words), convicia
Slanderously, maledicè, calumniosè
Slank, gracilis, gracilentus
Slant, obliquus
Slantly, obliquè, transversè
A slap (blow), colaphus, ictus, plaga; (on the face), alapa
To slap, verbero, percutio, cædo; (up, or devour), devoro; (or catch up greedily), capto; (slop), madefacio
Slapt, Slapped, ictus, percussus
A slash (cut), cæsura; (blow), ictus; (wound), vulnus
To slash, cædo, concido; (or beat with a whip), flagro
Slashed, percussus, cæsus, vulneratus
A slashing, percussio, vulneratio
A slate, tegula; (for cyphering), palimpsæston
To slate, tegulis obtegere
Slated, tegulis constratus
A slater, scandularius
A slattern, mulier improvida
A slave, verna, servus
To be a slave, mancipor; (to passion), cupiditatibus servire
To make one a slave, in servitutem dare [laboro
To slave, laborando se fatigare
Slaver (drivel), saliva
To slaver, salivam emittere
A slavering, salivæ emissio
Slavering, ineptus, insulsus
Slavery, servitium, servitus; (hard labour), labor gravis
Slavish, vernilis, servilis; (laborious), fatigans, cruciars
Slavishly, serviliter, abjectè
Slavishness (bondage), servitus; (laboriousness), laboris assiduitas
Slaughter, cædes, clades, strages, occisio; (general), internecio; (man), homicidium; (house), laniena

SLI — SLO — SMA

To slaughter (slay), macto
A slay (for weavers), pecten
To slay, macto, neco, trucido, occido, interficio, interimo
A slayer, interfector, interemptor
A man-slayer, homicida
Slaying, mactans, trucidans
A slaying, cædes, interemptio
A sledge, traha; (hammer), malleus ferreus major
Sleek, politus, lævis, planus; (stone), lapis lævigatorius
To sleek, lævigo, polio
Sleeked, lævigatus, politus
A sleeking, lævigatio
Sleekly, lævè, politè
Sleep, somnus, quies
To sleep, dormio
To fall asleep, obdormisco
To go to sleep, dormitum se conferre
To be half asleep, dormito; (in a sound sleep), altùm dormire
To sleep (in a whole skin), periculum evitare
To sleep (away cares), somno curas pellere; (one's self sober), crapulam edormire; (upon), indormio
Causing sleep, soporifer
Laid to sleep, sopitus
A sleeper, dormitor
Sleepily, somniculosè
Sleepiness, somnolentia
After sleeping, à somno
A sleeping-place, dormitorium
Sleepless, exsomnis, vigil
To be sleepy, dormito
Sleepy, somnolentus, soporus, somniculosus, veternosus
A sleepy disease, lethargus
Sleet, nix tenuis
A sleeve, manica
Sleeved, manicatus
Sleeveless (insignificant), futilis, ineptus; adv. frustrà
A sleight (or knack), dexteritas, artificium; (of hand), præstigia
Slender, gracilis, tenuis, exilis
To make slender, attenuo
Made slender, attenuatus
To grow slender, gracilesco
Slender and tall, junceus
Slenderly, tenuitèr, exilitèr
Slenderness, gracilitas
A slice (of bread, &c.), offula; (of any thing), assula, fragmentum; (to take meat up), spatha
In slices, assulatim
To slice, concido, seco
A slicing, concisura
Slick, lævis, lævigatus
To slide, labor; (along), perlabor; (away), elabor; (back), relabor; (by), præterlabor; (or fall down), delabor; (in, or into), illabor; (over), translabor; (to, or near), allabor; (on), perlabor
Sliding, labens, lapsans
A sliding, lapsus; (place), glacies pedibus lævigata
Slight (thin), levis, levidensis; (small, of no moment), futilis, nugatorius
To slight, temno, contemno, despicio, parvi facere; (or slumber over), perfunctoriè agere
To be slighted, contemnor
A slighter, contemptor
A slighting, contemptus
Slighting, contemnens, negligens
Slightingly, Slightly, levitèr, perfunctoriè, negligentèr, contemptim

Slightly, astutè, callidè
Slightness, tenuitas, levitas
Slighty, levidensis
Slim, gracilis. See *Slender*
Slime, humor viscidus
Sliminess, viscositas
Slimy, viscidus, limosus
To be slimy, lenteaco
Sliness, astutia, vafrities
A sling, funda, catapulta, balista ▸ (string), scutale; (staff), fundibulum; (for an arm), fascia, mitella
To sling, è fundâ jaculari
A slinger, funditor; (of stones), fundibalator
A slinging, jaculatio è fundâ
Slink, abortivus
To slink (away), clanculùm sese subtrahere; (home), domi redire clanculùm; (back), sese clam retrahere
Slinking away, sese subducens
A slip (with the foot), lapsus; (of the tongue), lapsus; (mistake), lapsus, error levis; (of yarn), glomus; (or small piece), particula, fragmentum, frustum; (or sprig of a plant), surculus
Slipshod, crepidatus
Slipslop, cinnus
Full of slips, surculosus
To slip, labor, lapso; (or let slip), omitto, dimitto, prætermitto; (aside), elabor; (away, as time), elabor, transeo, abeo, effluo; (down), cado, concido, decido; (into privately), subrepo, irrepo; (into, put, or thrust), immitto, insero; (or put off), exuo
A slipper, crepida, solea
Slipperily, lubricè
Slipperiness, lubricitas, lubricum
Slippery, lubricus, incertus; (deceitful), subdolus, versutus, vafer; (difficult), difficilis, periculosus; (tongue), loquax, futilis
A slippery trick, dolus, fraus
To make slippery, lubrico
Slipping, labens, lapsans; (away), elabens; (down), cadens, decidens; (in), irrepens; (over), omittens, prætermittens; (out), excidens, effluens
A slipping, lapsus, lapsio; (off of leaves), frondatio
Slipt (slipped), elapsus
A slit, fissura, crena
To slit, findo, diffindo
That may be slit, fissilis
A slitter, fissor
Slitting, findens, diffindens
A slitting, fissio, fissura
A slive, or sliver, segmen
To slive, findo
To slobber (slabber), madefacio
A sloe, prunum sylvestre
A sloop, lembus
To slop, madefacio
A slop (trowser), subligar
Slope, obliquus, transversus
To slope, obliquo
Slopeness, obliquitas
Sloping, obliquus
Made sloping, obliquatus
A sloping, obliquatio
Slopingly, obliquè, transversè
To slot, claudo
Sloth, desidia, ignavia
Slothful, desidiosus, piger, segnis
To be slothful, desideo, torpeo
Slothfully, desidiosè, pigrè
Slothfulness, segnities, torpor

A slouch, homo inurbanus
A sloven, homo sordidus, squalidus, insicetus, spurcus, or turpis
Slovenliness, sordes, squalor
Slovenly, sordidè, squalidè
A slough, lacuna lutosa; (of a snake), anguis exuviæ; (of bears), ursarum turma
Slow, piger, tardus, lentus; (dull), hebes; (footed), tardigradus
To be slow, pigreo, cunctor; (in one's motions), lentè agere
To grow slow, pigresco
Slowly, tardè, lentè, pigrè
Slowness, tarditas
A slug (snail), limax; (slow ship), navis tarda; (bullet), glans plumbea oblonga
A sluggard, dormicator, piger
Sluggish, piger, segnis, ignavus
To grow sluggish, segnesco
Sluggishly, ignavè, pigrè, segnitèr
Sluggishness, ignavia, desidia
A sluice, objectaculum
Sluicy, effusus
A slumber, somnus levis, quies
To slumber, dormio, obdormisco; (over business), alicui rei indormire
A slumbering, dormitatio
Slumbering, somniculosus
A slur, labes, dedecus
To slur, maculo, inquino, lædo
A slurring, maculatio
A slut, mulier squalida
Sluttish, sordidus, squalidus
To be sluttish, sordeo, sordesco
Sluttishly, sordidè, squalidè
Sluttishness, immunditia
Sly, vafer, astutus, subdolus
Slyly, vafrè, astutè, subdolè
Slyness, calliditas, astutia
A smack (relish), sapor; (of a whip), flagelli sonus; (kiss), basium; (small ship), lembus, navigiolum. See *Smatch*
To smack (taste), gusto, degusto; (or savour of), sapio; (or savour a little of), subsipio; (or kiss), suavium premere; (one's lips), labiis strepitum edere; (a whip), insonare flagello
A small number, paucitas
Small, parvus, exiguus, minutus; (slender), gracilis, exilis; (in esteem), vilis, nullius momenti
To be of small account, vilesco
To make small, attenuo, diminuo
A making small, attenuatio
Made small, attenuatus, diminutus
A small time, parumpèr
So small, tantulus; (how small), quantulus; (how small soever), quantuluscunque
Small arms, sclopeti
Small craft, navicula
Small of the back, leg, &c., pars gracilior dorsi, &c.
Smaller, minor
Smallest, minimus
Smallness, exiguitas; (slenderness), gracilitas
Smally, tenuitèr
Smart, dolor, cruciatus
Smart (sharp), asper, acer; (in discourse), argutus, acutus, acer; (words), verba mordacia; (fight), acre certamen; (pain), dolor vehemens, or gravis; (pleader), vehemens orator; (repartee), falsum dictum

[119]

SMU · SNO · SOF

To smart, doleo
To make to smart, crucio, ango, mordeo, uro, pungo
Causing pain, cruciana, pungens
Smarting, plenus dolore, asper
A smarting, cruciatus, dolor
Smartly, argutè, acerbè
Smartness (liveliness), vigor, vis, agilitas ; (sourness), acritudo, acrimonia; (wittiness), argutiæ, sagacitas, acumen ingenii ; (of pain), doloris vehementia
A smatch (taste), sapor, gustus ; (small remains), reliquiæ
A smatterer, sciolus, semidoctus; (in grammar), grammatista ; (in poetry), poëtaster ; (in physic), empiricus
A smattering, levis scientia
A smear, unguen, denigratio
To smear, illino, oblino, conspurco, inquino ; (over), superlino ; (under), subterlino
A smearer, unctor
A smearing, unctio, litura
To smell, oleo, redoleo, suboleo; (or smell to), odoror, olfacio ; (or cast a smell), oleo
A smell, odor ; (sweet), fragrantia ; (ill), fœtor ; (of meat, or provisions), nitor
Sweet smelling, odoriferus, odoratus, odorus, jucundè olens
A smelling, odoratio
The act of smelling, odoratus
Smelling rank, olidus, rancidus, fœtidus ; (out), odorans
Smelt (or smelled out), odoratus
To smelt ore, metalla cruda liquefacere
A smelt (fish), apua, violacea
To smerk, arrideo
Smerking, arridens
A smile, risus lenus
To smile, subrideo ; (at), arrideo
To smite, ferio, percutio
A smiter, percussor
A smiting, percussio
A smith, faber ferrarius
A smithy, ferramentorum fabrica
Smiting, feriens, percutiens
A smock, subucula feminarum
Smoke, fumus, vapor
To smoke (or send forth smoke), fumo, fumum emittere
Causing smoke, fumificus
Smoking, fumans
A smoking, fumigatio
A smoking under, suffitus
Smoky, fumosus, fumidus, fumeus, fumo infestatus
Smooth, lævis, æquus ; (table), mensa accuratè lævigata ; (road), via plana ; (without hair), glaber, depilis ; (style), oratio dulcis ; (tongued), blandiloquus ; (faced), comis, dulcis
To smooth, lævigo, complano, polio ; (the forehead), explico ; (coax), blandior, demulceo
A smoother, lævigator
A smoothing, lævigatio
Smoothly, planè, dulcè
Smoothness, lævitas ; (of behaviour), urbanitas, comitas
To smother (stifle), suffoco ; (suppress), sedo, extinguo ; (conceal), celo, reticeo
A smothering, suffocatio
Smouldering, fumosus, suffocans
Snug, concinnus, nitidus
To smug one's self, se concinne ornare
To smuggle, merces sine portorii solutione invehere
[120]

Smugly, elegantèr, nitidè
Smugness, elegantia
Smut, fuligo; (obscenity), obscœnitas
To smut, fuligine inquinare
Smutted, fuligine inquinatus
A smutting, denigratio
Smutty (obscene), obscœnus, fœdus
A snack, pars, portio
To go snacks, particeps esse
A snaffle, fræni lupus
Snaffled, lupatus
A snag, nodus ; (tooth), dens ultra cæteros prominens
Snagged, Snaggy, nodosus
A snail, testudo, cochlea
Of a snail, testudineus
A snake, anguis, coluber ; (water), hydrus
Of a snake, anguineus
A snap (noise), crepitus; (morsel), frustulum ; (sack), pera militaris
To snap, crepitum edere ; (break), frango, rumpo ; (or be broken), frangor, rumpor, diffringor ; (or catch hold of), rapio, corripio; (snub), iratè corripere
Snapping, frangens, rumpens
Snappish, captiosus, mordax
Snappishly, morosè, iracundè
Snappishness, mordacitas
A snare, laqueus, insidiæ
To snare, illaqueo, irretio
A snaring, illaqueatio
To snarl (as a dog), ringo ; (at), obloquor ; (thread, or silk), involvo, impedio
A snarler, homo morosus
A snarling, rictus
Snarling, ringens ; (at), morosus
A snatch, moriuncula ; (and away), præpropere
To snatch, rapio, corripio ; (away), abripio, surripio ; (at), capto
A snatcher, raptor, captator
Snatching, rapax, rapidus
A snatching, raptio, rapacitas
To sneak (creep), repo, serpo, repto ; (be ashamed), verecundor ; (cringe to), serviliter devenerari ; (or lurk about), lateo, latito ; (away), clanculum se subducere
Sneaking (creeping), repens ; (niggardly), parcus ; (pitiful), abjectus, sordidus; (fire), ignis malignus
Sneakingly (niggardly), parcè ; (meanly), abjectè, sordidè
Sneakingness (niggardliness), parsimonia ; (meanness), tenuitas
To sneer, irrideo, derideo
Sneering, irridens, deridens
A sneerer, irrisor
To sneeze, sternuo ; (often), sternuto
A sneezing, sternutamentum
To sniff up, resorbeo, retraho
A snip (or part), segmen ; (natural mark), macula ; (snap), crotalum
To snip, amputo ; (off), præcido, decerpo
Snipping off, præcidens, decerpens
Snippings, præsegmina
Snivel, mucus, stiria
Snively, full of snivel, mucosus
To snore, or snort, sterto
A snoring, rhoncus
Snorting (fearful), meticulosus

A snout, rostrum, nasus ; (of an elephant), proboscis
Snouted, rostratus
Snow, nix ; (ball), globus nivalis
To snow, ningo
Snowy, niveus, nivalis
Full of snow, nivosus
To snub (chide), increpo, corripio ; (curb), fræno, reprimo
Snubbed, correptus, frænatus
Snubbing, increpans, frænans
The snuff (or wick), myxa ; (for the nostrils), sternutamentum, pulvis sternutatorius
To snuff (a candle), candelam emungere ; (with disdain), rhoncisco ; (up the nose), naribus haurire ; (at), irascor ; (at, or despise), contemno
A snuffer, emunctor
Snuffers, emunctorium
A snuffing, emunctio
To snuffle, vocem è naribus proferre
Snug (close, secret), secretus, arcanus ; (compact), nitidus, concinnus
Snug, Snugly, adv. secretò
So, ità, sic, ad hunc modum, hoc pacto ; (so much), adeò, ità, perindè, tantoperè ; (so that), dum, dummodò, modò, ità, si, si tantum ; (so then), quamobrèm, quapropter, quarè, quocircà ; (far), eò, eatenus, quòd ; (far from), adeò non, ut—ita non, ut—tantum absit, ut—non modò, ne—nedum ; (far as), quod, quoàd, quantùm ; (far off), tam procul, tam longè ; (great), tantus, tam magnus ; (little), tantulus, tantillus, tam parvus ; (long), tamdiù, tandiù ; (long as), dum, donec, usque dum, tamdiù dum, tamdiù quam, diù, quoàd ; (much), tantum ; (much, adv.), tam ; (many), tot ; (often), toties ; (so), mediocriter ; (so, in health), meliusculè
Just so many, totidèm
Why so ? quamobrèm
And so forth, et sic de cæteris
To soak, macero ; (in or up), imbibo ; (through), permano
Soap, sapo
To soar, volo
To sob, singultio
A sob, or sobbing, singultus
Sober, sobrius, temperatus ; (of sober conversation), probis moribus
To sober, sobrium reddere
Soberly, sobriè, moderatè
Soberness, Sobriety, sobrietas
Soccage, soccagium
Sociable, Social, socialis, sociabilis ; (not), insociabilis
Sociableness, socialitas
Sociably, socialitèr
Society, societas, communitas, sodalitas, consociatio
A sock, pedale, udo ; (used by comedians), soccus
Wearing socks, soccatus
The socket of a candlestick, scapus ; (of a tooth), loculamentum
Sod, Sodden, lixatus, coctus
Half-sodden, semicoctus
A sod, cespes
Soder, ferrumen
A Sodomite, pædicator
Sodomy, pæderastia
Soft, mollis, tener, lentus ; (silly),

SOL — SOR — SOU

ineptus, stupidus ; (footed), molipes ; (pace), gradus, lentus, or suspensus; (voice), vox submissa
Softish, molliusculus
To make soft, or soften, emollio; (mitigate), mitigo
To grow soft, mollesco
To be soft, mollior
Softish, ineptus, stupidus
Softly (gently), lenitèr; (effeminately), muliebritèr, lascivè ; (leisurely), lentè ; (not too loud), submissè, submissâ voce
Softness, mollitia, mollities, lenitas, teneritas
A soil, solum, fundus; (native), patria; (filth), sordes; (compost), stercus, lætamen
To soil, inquino, conspergo
A soiling, inquinatio, sordes
To sojourn, diversor, commoror
A sojourner, hospes, peregrinus, incola
A sojourning, peregrinatio
To soke, macero; (up), imbibo, absorbeo; (through), permano
Soking, macerans, madefaciens
Solace, consolatio, solatium, levamen, solamen
To solace, consolor ; (one's self), oblectare sese ; (in the sun), apricor
Solar, solaris
A solar, solarium
To be sold, veneo, vendor
Solder, ferrumen
To solder, ferrumino, conglutino
A soldering, conglutinatio; (iron), glans ferraminatrix
A soldier, miles; (fellow), commiles, commilito ; (old), miles veteranus ; (common), miles gregarius ; (discharged for age), miles emeritus
A soldier's boy, lixa, calo
Of a soldier, militaris
Like a soldier, bellicosè, fortitèr
The soldiery, militia, copiæ militares
Sole (alone), solus, solitarius
The sole (of the foot), planta pedis ; (of a shoe), solea, assumentum
To sole, calceo assumentum inducere
A sole (fish), solea
A solecism, solœcismus
Solely, solùm, solummodò
Solely and wholly, ex asse
Solemn, solemnis, festis ; (authentic), ratus, comprobatus ; (sacred), sacer
Solemnity, solemnitas, ritus solennis
To solemnize, celebro
A solemnizing, celebratio
Solemnly, solemnitèr, sanctè
To solicit, solicito, instigo; (supplies), flagitare subsidia
A soliciting, solicitatio
Solicitation, solicitatio, impulsus
A solicitor, solicitator; (in law), advocatus
Solicitous, solicitus, anxius
Solicitude, solicitudo, anxietas
Solid, solidus, stabilis, firmus, gravis
To make solid, solido
Solidity, soliditas, firmitas
Solidly, solidè, firmè
A soliloquy, soliloquium
Solitary, solitarius, solus, secretus; (melancholy), tristis, mœstus

Solitarily, privatim, secretò
Solitariness, Solitude, solitudo
The solstice, solstitium
Of the solstice, solstitialis
Solvable, par solvendo
Soluble, dissolubilis
To solve, solvo, enodo, explico
A solution, or solving, solutio; (of a question), enodatio
Some, quidam, aliquis, nonnullus ; (body), aliquis, aliquisquam ; (one), unusquisquam
Somewhat, aliquantò, aliquantulùm, nonnihil ; (sometimes), aliquandò, quandòque, interdum ; (somewhile), aliquandiù ; (somewhere, or whither), alicubi, uspiàm ; (at some other time, or in some other manner), aliàs ; (in some sort), quodammodò
Someiferous, somnificus
A son, filius, natus ; (in law), gener ; (step-son), privignus
Sonship, filiatio
A song, cantilena, canticum, cantio, carmen
For a song (cheap), vili
A songster, cantor, cantator
A songstress, cantatrix
A sonnet, ode, cantiuncula
Sonorous, sonorus, canorus
Soon, citò, statim, illicò
Soon after, paulò pòst
Very soon, extemplò
Too soon, præmature
As soon as, quamprimùm, simul ac, simul atque; (as soon as ever), cum primum
Sooner, citius, maturius
At soonest, quàm citissimè
Soot, fuligo
Belonging to soot, fuligineus
Soot-coloured, leucophus
Sooty, fuliginosus, fumosus
In sooth, verè, certò ; (forsooth), sanè, profectò
To sooth, blandior, adulor, permulceo
A soother, assentator
Soothing, blandiens, permulcens
A soothing, assentatio
A soothsayer, augur, aruspex
To soothsay, auguror, ominor
A soothsaying, augurium
A sop, offa, offula
To sop, intingo
Sope, sapo, smegma ; (boiler), saponis confector
Of sope, smegmaticus
To sope, sapone oblinere
Soped, smegmate oblitus
A sophism, sophisma
A sophist, sophista
Sophistical, sophisticus, fallax, captiosus
To sophisticate, adultero, commisceo ; (waste), consumo
Sophisticated, adulteratus, disperditus
A sophisticating or sophistication, rerum diversarum mixtura
Sophistry, cavillatio captiosa
Soporiferous, soporus
Sopped, Sopt, intinctus
A sorcerer, veneficus
A sorceress, venefica, saga
Sorcery, veneficium
Sordid (covetous), sordidus, avarus ; (in apparel), sordidatus, pannosus ; (base), infamis, fœdus, turpis, famosus
Sordidness, sordes, avaritia
Sore, asper, gravis, durus, moles-

tus, vehemens; (as flesh), tener ; (grievous), atrox
A sore, ulcus
To make sore, exulcero
Made sore, exulceratus
Sore, Sorely, gravitèr, vehementèr
Soreness, exulceratio
Sorrel, oxalis
Sorrel-coloured, helvinus
Sorrily, malè, miserè
Sorrow, dolor, mœror, tristitia
To sorrow, doleo, mœreo
Sorrowful, tristis, mœstus, luctuosus
Sorrowfully, ægrè, mœstè
Sorry (sorrowful), tristis, mœstus, lugubris, luctuosus; (paltry, vile), vilis, nihili; (fellow), homuncio
To make sorry, contristo
To be sorry, doleo, mœreo
A sort (manner), mos, modus ; (kind), genus
Common sort of people, plebs ; (better sort of), honesti, ingenui
After a sort, quodammodò ; (a new sort), novo modo ; (this sort), hujusmodi; (that sort), ejusmodi ; (the same sort), itidem ; (what sort ?) quomodo? quo pacto ?
In like sort, paritèr, eodem modo ; (such sort), usquè adeò
Of all sorts, omnium generum, omnigenus; (the first sort), primarius ; (the second sort), secundarius; (what sort ?), cujusmodi ? qualis ? (what sort soever), qualiscunque ; (this sort), hujusmodi; (that sort), ejusmodi
To sort, distribuo, aptè digerere ; (or be suitable to), accommodor ; (or come together), congregor
A sorting, apta collocatio
A sot, ebriosus ; (fool), stultus
To sot, sese inebriare
Sottish, ebriosus, fatuus
Sottishly, ebriosè, stultè
Sottishness, ebrietas, stultitia
Souce (pickle), salsugo
To souce (pickle), muriâ condire ; (plunge), immergo ; (box), colaphum impingere
Souced, muriâ maceratus ; (with rain), pluviâ obrutus
Sovereign, supremus, maximus ; (most efficacious), efficacissimus
A sovereign, dominus supremus
Sovereignly, supremo jure
Sovereignty, principatus, suprema potestas, or dominatio
The soul, anima, animus ; (person), homo
Souls, manes, umbræ
A sound, sonus, sonitus ; (noise), strepitus, crepitus, fragor ; (of a trumpet), clangor
Sound (entire), integer, sincerus ; (healthy), validus, sanus, robustus ; (valid), firmus, rarus; (in judgment), sagax ; (in faith), orthodoxus ; (in principles), probus; (and safe), incolumis ; (of mind), mentis compos
To sound (or yield a sound), sono, strepo; (or blow as an instrument), buccinam inflare; (an alarm), classicum canere ; (a bell), tintinnabulum pulsare ; (a march), vasa conclamare ; (a

[121]

SPA — SPE — SPI

retreat), recepturi canere ; (a word), pronuncio ; (the depth), profunditatem explorare ; (one's intention), animum perscrutari
The sound-board, pinax ; (hole of a viol), chelyos rima
To make sound, consolido
To grow sound, solidesco, convalesco
To be sound, valeo, vigeo
Sounded (as an instrument), inflatus ; (forth, or praised), laudatus
Sounding, sonans, resonans ; (ill), dissonus ; (shrill), sonorus, argutus
A sounding-lead, bolis
Soundly, solidè, firmitèr, sanè, acritèr, vehementèr, validè
Soundness, soliditas, firmitas ; (of body), sanitas, vigor
Soup, decoctum, sorbillum
A source, origo, fons
Sour, acerbus, acidus, asper, austerus, immitis ; (in looks), torvus, tetricus ; (in temper), morosus
Sourness, acor, acerbitas, asperitas ; (of look), torvitas, tetricitas   [perb
Sourly, torvè, morosè, acerbè, asTo become sour, acesco
To sour (vex), exaspero, exacerbo
Soured (vexed), exasperatus
Souse, salsugo
The south, auster, meridies ; (wind), auster, notus ; (east wind), euronotus; (west wind), libs
Southern, australis, meridionalis
Southward, meridiem versus
A southing, meridiatio
A sow, sus
Sow, of a sow, suillus
To sow (seed), sero, semino, consero ; (between), intersero ; (up and down), spargo, disssemino ; (round), circumsero
A sower, sator, seminator
A sowing, satio, seminatio
Of sowing, seminalis
Sowing-time, sementis
A space, spatium ; (of time, or place), intercapedo, intervallum, interstitium ; (or term of life), vitæ curriculum ; (or tract of land), tractus ; (between pillars), intercolumnium
Spacious, spatiosus, amplus, diffusus, patens
Spaciously, spatiosè, amplè
Spaciousness, amplitudo
A spade (tool), ligo ; (in cards), vomerculus
A span, palmus, spithama
Of a span, palmaris
To spane (wean), ablacto
A spangle, bractea, bracteola
A spaniel, canis Hispanicus
The Spanish fly, cantharis
Spanking, magnus, robustus
Spar, lapis selenites
A spar (or bar), obex, vectis ; (of a gate), assula spicata
To spar, obdo
A sparkle, clavulus
Spare (lean, thin), macer, gracilis, macilentus ; (horse), equus desultorius ; (money), pecunia residua ; (time), horæ subsecivæ
To spare, parco, comparco ; (an hour), detrahere horam ; (a word), auscultare paucis; (for-

give), condono, remitto ; (favour), faveo, indulgeo
Spare, or sparing, subst. parsimonia, frugalitas ; adj. parcus, tenax   [ratio
A sparing (laying up), conserTo be sparing, parco
Sparingly, parcè, restrictè
Sparingness, parsimonia
A spark (of fire), scintilla ; (lover), procus, amasius ; (beau), homo bellus
Sparkish, nitidè vestitus
To sparkle, scintillo ; (glitter), fulgeo, niteo, corusco ; (as wine), subsilio
A sparkling, scintillatio ; (or glittering), coruscatio, nitor, fulgor
Sparkling, scintillans, coruscus
A sparrow, passer
A sparrow-hawk, frigillarius
A spasm, spasmus
To spatter, conspergo, inquino ; (defame), calumnior
Spatterdashes, perones
A spattle, spathula
Having the spavin, suffraginosus
To spawl, spuo, sputo
A spawler, sputator
Spawn, ova, semina
To spawn, genero, procreo
A spawning, generatio
To speak, loquor, dico ; (aloud), eloquor ; (against), obloquor, contradico; (at random), garrio, effatio ; (before), proloquor ; (big), jactantia verba proferre ; (briefly), perstringo ; (evil of), maledico, calumnior ; (well off), collaudo; (face to face), in os dicere ; (for), interecedo ; (merrily), jocor ; (of), tracto, memoro ; (often), dictito ; (out), eloquor ; (to a person), alloquor, aliquem affari; (together), colloquor
A speaker, prolocutor, locutor ; (of parliament), senatûs præses
Speaking, loquens, loquax
A speaking, locutio, dictio ; (of), mentio, commemoratio ; (out), pronunciatio ; (to), alloquium ; (with), colloquium ; (of evil), maledictum, convicium, calumnia
A spear, hasta, lancea ; (a boar), venabulum ; (an eel), fuscina, tridens ; (man), hastatus ; (staff), hastile
Special (chief, particular), præcipuus, peculiaris, specialis ; (excellent), excellens, eximius, eminens, præclarus, egregius
Specially, specialitèr ; (excellently), excellentèr, optimè
Specialty, proprietas ; (bond,) syngraphus
A species, species, soboles
Specific, Specifical, specialis, singularis, specificus
Specifically, specialitèr, specificè
Specification, designatio specialis
Specified, notatus, enumeratus
A specifying, singularium notatio
To specify (mention), denoto, enumero, describo, designo
A specimen, specimen, exemplar
Specious, speciosus, plausibilis
A speck, macula, labes ; (pimple), varus; (natural blemish), nævus
To speckle, maculis variare
A speckling, maculis notatio
A spectacle, spectaculum
A pair of spectacles, conspicillum

A spectator, spectator
A spectre, spectrum, visum
To speculate, speculor
Speculation, contemplatio
Speculative, contemplativus
A speculator, speculator
The speech, sermo, vox
A speech, oratio, concio
To make a speech, concionor, concionem habere, verba facere
Fair speeches, blanditiæ
Lofty speeches, superbiloquentia
Speechless, mutus, elinguis
Speed, festinatio, expeditio; (success), successus
Great speed, celeritas
With all speed, citatim
To make speed, festino, propero, accelero, maturo
To speed, fortuno, prospero, succedo, procedo
Done with speed, acceleratus, festinatus
Speedily, celeritèr, festinè
Speediness, celeritas
Speedy, citus, expeditus, properus
A spell, incantamentum
To spell, syllabas connectere
Spelling (art of), orthographia
To spend, consumo, expendo, impendo, insumo ; (a day), diem producere ; (one's life), ætatem conterere; (labour in vain), operam perdere
A spendthrift, nepos, prodigus
Spending, consumens, impendens
A spending, consumptio ; (lavishly), prodigalitas, profusio, effusio
Sperm, sperma, semen
Spermatic, ad sperma pertinens
To spew, vomo. See Spue
A sphere, sphæra, globus
Spherical, sphæricus, globosus
Like a sphere, sphæroides
Spherically, globi instar
A sphinx, sphinx
Spice, Spicery, aroma
To spice, aromata inspergere
Spiced, aromatibus conditus
Tasting of spice, Spicy, aromaticus
A spider, aranea ; ('s web), araneum, aranea
Full of spiders, araneosus
A spigot, epistomium
A spike, clavus ferreus major ; (pointed iron, or wood), ferri, or ligni pars cuspidata
To spike, or sharpen the end, cuspido, spico ; (or nail up), clavis adactis obstruere
Spikenard, nardus
Oil of spike, nardum
To spill, fundo, effundo
A spilling, fusio, effusio
To spin, neo ; (as a top), in gyrum versari ; (out, or prolong), protraho, produco, traho ; (or issue out), effluo, prosilio
Spinage, spinacea
Spinal, spinalis
A spindle, fusus ; (of a wheel, or press), rotæ axis ; (newel), scapus
Spindle-shanks, crura exilia
The spine, spina
A spinning, netio ; (wheel), gyrgillus
A spinster, lanifica ; (in law), femina innupta
Spiny, spinosus
Spiral, ad spiram pertinens
A spiral line, linea in spiram ducta

[122]

A spire, pyramis; (of grass), spica
To spire (as corn), spico
A spirit, spiritus, genius; (goblin), larva, spectrum
The spirit, mens, anima; (courage), animus, virtus; (wit), indoles, ingenium; (briskness), vigor, alacritas; (of contradiction, discontent, or sedition), cacoëthes
With spirit, solertèr, ingeniosè
To spirit up (encourage), animo, instigo, hortor, stimulo; (away children), infantes furtim abducere
High-spirited, animosus, superbus
Low-spirited, animo fractus
Mean-spirited, abjectus, sordidus
Public-spirited, publicæ salutis studiosa
Spiritual, spiritualis; (incorporeal), incorporalis; (devout), pius, religiosus, sanctus; (belonging to the church), ecclesiasticus [cus
Spiritualities, reditus ecclesiastiSpiritually, spiritualitèr, piè, sanctè
Spirituous, spirituosus, ardens
A spirt, impetus brevis
To spirt out, exilio, ejicio
Spiss, spissus, densus
Spissitude, spissitudo
A spit, veru, obelus
To spit (meat), veru transfigere; (or spawl), spuo; (blood), sanguinem exscreare; (down), despuo; (often), sputo; (out), expuo, exscreo; (at), inspuo, consputo; (with retching), sereo, exscreo
To be spit upon, inspuor
Spite, spitefulness, malitia, malevolentia
To spite, invideo
Spited, invisus
Spiteful, invidus, malitiosus, malignus
Spitefully, malitiosè, malignè
A spitter, sputator
A spitting, sputatio, expuitio
Spittle, saliva, sputum
Full of spittle, salivosus
A spittle, nosocomium
A splash, luti aspersio, or macula
To splash, conspurco, inquino
Splashed, luto aspersus
A splashing, luti aspersio
Splashy, humidus, aquosus
Splay, distortus; (footed), valgus
To splay, luxo, frango
Splaying, luxatio, infractio
The spleen, splen, lien; (grudge), odium, livor, simultas
Of the spleen, splenicus
Spleenful, iracundus, morosus
Splendent, splendens, nitens
Splendid (bright), splendidus, rutilus, nitidus; (magnificent), splendidus, illustris, magnificus, lautus, opiparus
Splendidly, splendidè, lautè
Splendor (brightness), fulgor, nitor; (magnificence), splendor, lautitia, magnificentia
Splenetic, spleneticus
To splice, partes inter se texere
A splinter, fragmentum, assula
To splinter (cut into pieces), in assulas secare, diffindo
To be splintered, diffindor
To split (asunder), diffindo; (upon a rock), in scopulum impingere; (sides with laughing), risu ferè emori
[123]

Splitting, diffindens
Spoil, spolium, præda, rapina; (of war), manubiæ, exuviæ
To spoil (mar), vitio, corrumpo, depravo; (plunder), compilo, spolio, devasto, depopulor, diripio, (disturb), conturbor; (interrupt), intertucbo
A spoiler, corruptor, corruptrix, vitiator; (plunderer), prædo, populator, prædator, spoliator, direptor
A spoiling (marring), corruptio, depravatio, vitiatio; (of children), inepta lenitas; (or plundering), vastatio, spoliatio, direptio
A spoke (of a wheel), radius; (delay), scrupulus, mora
Not to be spoken, tarpe dictu
Having spoken, locutus, fatus
That may be spoken, effabilis
A spokesman, orator; (a good spokesman), facilis ad dicendum
A spondee, spondæus
A spondyl, spondylus
A sponsor, or surety, sponsor; (in baptism), pater lustricus
Spontaneity, voluntas spontanea
Spontaneous, spontaneus
Spontaneously, spontè, ultrò
A spool, fusus
To spoom, spumam excitare
A spoon, or spoonful, cochlear
Spoon-meat, cibaria liquida
Sport (pastime), ludus, jocus, oblectamentum, delectamentum, oblectatio; (public shew), spectaculum, ludus
To sport, ludo, jocor, joculor; (with others), colludo; (trifle), nugor
In sport, jocosè, per jocum
Having sported, jocatus
A sporter, ludio
Sportful, Sporting, Sportive, ludibundus, jocularis, joculatorius
Sporting (wantonly), lasciviens; (with religion), ludens cum sacris
Sportingly, jocularitèr, facetè
A sporting, jocatio
A sportsman, venator
A spot, macula, labes; (natural blemish), nævus; (of ground), agellus
To spot (stain), maculo, inquino; (speckle), maculis notare
Spotless, immaculatus, innocens
Spotted, maculatus; (spotted fever), febris purpurea
Spotty, maculosus
Spousal, connubialis, maritalis
Spousals, sponsalia
A spouse (husband), maritus, sponsus; (wife), sponsa, uxor
A spout, tubulus, sipho; (torrent), torrens, cataracta
Spouts (drains, gutters), colliquiæ, colliciæ
To spout, or flow out, effluo, emano; (or pour out), effundo; (or pour down), defundo; (or pour up), in sublime effundere
Spouting out, prosiliens
A spouting (or issuing out), eruptio; (or pouring out), effusio
A sprain, luxatio
To sprain, membrum luxare
A sprat, sardina
To sprawl, humi prostratus jacere, or repere
To lay sprawling, prosterno

A spray, cremium
To spread (extend), pando, dispando, expando, extendo; (run abroad), emano, vagor, discurro, serpo; (scatter), dispergo, spargo; (a rumour), rumorem serere; (a table), mensam insternere
A spreading, distentio; (of a distemper), contagio, contagium
Spreading, serpens, diffundens
A sprig, ramulus, surculus
Full of sprigs, surculosus
A spright, larva, spectrum
Sprightly, agilis, alacer, vividus
Sprightliness, agilitas, alacritas
A spring (of water), scaturigo, fons; (or beginning), origo, ortus; (of a machine), momentum; (of action), motûs principium; (tide), eluvies
Full of springs, scaturiginosus
Of a spring, fontanus
The spring-season, ver, tempus vernum
In the spring, vere, verno tempore
Early in the spring, primo vere
Of the spring, vernus
To spring (from a person, or thing), orior, enascor, gignor; (out, as liquors), effluo, scateo; (or bud out), germino, pullulo, gemmasco; (again), revivesco, repullulasco; (leap), salio, prosilio; (or suddenly upon), irruere in aliquem; (or leap into a place), in locum insilire; (a leak), rimas agere [tio
The springing of trees, germinaSpringiness, vis resiliendi
Springy, vi resiliendi præditus
A sprinkle, aspergillum
To sprinkle, spargo, baptizo; (abroad), dispergo; (at, upon, or with), aspergo, conspergo, inspergo
A sprinkling, sparsio; (upon, or with), aspersio, inspersio
To sprout, pullulo, germino
A sprout (young twig), surculus
Sprouts, caules prototomi
Sprouting, germinans
A sprouting, germinatio
Spruce, comptus, bellus; (fellow), homo concinnus, or elegans
To be spruce, elegantèr ornari
Sprucely, nitidè, bellè
Spruceness, concinnatus
Sprung, ortus, enatus, editus
A spud, cultellus
To spue, vomo, evomo
A spuer, vomitor
Spuing, vomitio, vomitus
Of spuing, vomitorius
Spume (scum), spuma
Spumy, spumeus, spumosus
Spun, netus
Homespun (plain), inurbanus, rusticus, incultus; (cloth), pannus domi netus
A spunge, spongia
To spunge, spongiâ extergere; (in company), alieno sumptu edere, or potare
A spunger, assecla
Spunging (upon), alieno sumptu vivens; (houses), caupone debitoribus comprehensis accommodate [novæ
A spunging (cancelling), tabulæ
Spunginess, spongiosa qualitas
Spungy, spongiosus
A spur, calcar, stimulus; (enticement), illecebra, irritamen-
G 2

SQU — STA — STA

tum; (of a ship), rostrum navis
To spur (on), incito, stimulo; (gall), calcaribus sauciare
Spurious, spurius, adulterinus
To spurn, calcitro, aspernor
A spurner, calcitro
A spurning, calcitratus
A spurrer, stimulator
A spurring, stimulatio
A spurt, impetus præceps; (of wines), status subitaneus
To spurt, *or* cast out, ejicio, expuo; (out, as liquids), exilio, prosilio, erumpo, emico
Sputation, sputandi actus
A sputter, tumultus, turba
To sputter, sputo
A spy, explorator, speculator
To spy (watch, *or* observe), exploro, speculor, observo; (see, *or* perceive), video, conspicio, cerno, percipio, intelligo, adverto, animadverto
A spying (beholding), conspectus, intuitus; (afar off), prospectus
A squab (couch), grabatus; (pigeon), pipio
Squab, *adj.* obesus, pumilus
To squabble, litigo
A squabble, turba, altercatio
Squabbling, rixosus
A squadron, turma; (of ships), classis
In, *or* into squadrons, turmatim
Squalid, squalidus, spurcus
To squall, clamo, vocifero; (as a child), vagio, vagito
Squalling, clamans, vagitans
A squalling, vociferatio, exclamatio, vagitus
Squamous, squamosus, squameus
To squander away, profundo, effundo, prodigo, dissipo
A squanderer, nepos, homo profusus, luxuriosus, *or* prodigus
A squandering, profusio, effusio, prodigentia
Square, quadratus; (honest), honestus, probus, integer
A square, quadra; (tool), norma; (in checks), tessella; (*or* cube), cubus; (of glass), quadra vitrea
Four-square, quadrarius
To square, quadro; (rule, *or* govern), rego, dirigo; (*or* agree with), congruo, convenio
Upon the square, æquâ conditione
Out of square, enormis, abnormis
A squaring, quadratura
To squash (dash against), illido; (put an end to), finem imponere, comprimo
A squashing, illisus, compressio
Squat, brevis et compactus
To squat, succumbo, recumbo
Squatting down, succumbens
To squawl, exclamo, vociferor; (as an infant), vagito
Squawling, vagiens, vagitans
To squeak, *or* squeal, argutè vociferari, *or* stridere; (like a mouse), dintrio
Squeaking, argutus, stridulus
A squeaking, stridor
Squeakingly, argutè stridens
Squeamish, nauseans, fastidiosus
To be squeamish, nauseo, fastidio
Squeamishly, fastidiosè
Squeamishness, nausea, fastidium
To squeeze, premo, comprimo; (out), exprimo, elicio; (hard), perstringo, presso; (together), comprimo, collido
A squeezing, pressio, pressura
A squelch, casus, lapsus
A squib, pyrobolus
A squill (sea-onion), squilla
The squinsy, angina
Squint-eyed, strabus; (look), aspectus distortus, *or* obliquus
To squint, limis spectare, *or* intueri
A squinting, oculorum distortio
A squire, armiger
A squirrel, sciurus
A squirt (syringe), syrinx; (looseness), alvi proluvies; (mean person), homo nihili
To squirt out, ejicio, exilio
A stab, vulnus gladio, &c. factum
To stab, confodio, punctim petere
A stabber, sicarius
Stabiliment, stabilimentum
Stability, stabilitas, firmitas
Stable, stabilis, firmus, constans
A stable, stabulum, equile
To stable, stabulo claudere
Stableness (stability), stabilitas
Stabling, stabulandi locus
To stablish, stabilio, sancio
A stack (of hay, &c.), acervus, cumulus, congeries, strues, meta; (of chimneys), series caminorum
A staff, baculus, bacillum; (an augur's staff), lituus; (a ploughstaff), rulla; (of a spear), hastile; (to walk with), scipio
A stag, cervus
A stage, scena, theatrum; (for pageants), pegma; (play), fabula histrionalis; (of a journey), statio; (of life), gradus vitæ
A clear stage, liber campus
A stage-player, histrio, actor
Stage-playing, histrionia
Of the stage, scenicus, histrionalis, histrionicus
An old stager, homo diû versatus
To stagger (reel), titubo, vacillo; (doubt), dubito, fluctuo, hæsito, hæreo; (make one doubt), scrupulum injicere
Staggering (reeling), titubans, vacillans; (wavering), fluctuans, dubitans, hæsitans; (affected), percussus
Staggeringly, dubiè, incertè
The staggers, vertigo
Having the staggers, vertigine correptus
Stagnant, stagnans, stans
To stagnate, stagno, sto
Stagnation, motûs cessatio
A stain, macula, labes; (in reputation), dedecus, infamia, nota
To stain (spot, *or* sully), maculo, contamino, inquino, polluo; (discolour), decoloro; (violate), violo, lædo; (dye), tingo, inficio
A stainer, infector, tinctor
A paper-stainer, coloribus pingens
A staining (dying), tinctura, tinctus; (discolouring), decoloratio
Stainless, purus, immaculatus
A stair, gradus; (pair of stairs), scalæ
The one pair of stairs (*or* story), tabulatum primum
A stake (post), sudes, postis, palus; (to tie cattle to), vacerra; (at play), depositum, pignus
To lie at stake, periclitor
To stake (lay stakes), depono, oppigneio
Stale, vetus, vetustus, tritus;
(bread), panis diû coctus; (maid), virgo annosa; (antiquated), obsoletus, antiquatus
Stale, urina, lotium [lesco
To grow stale, inveterasco, obsoGrown stale, obsoletus
To stale (as a horse), mingo
Staleness, vetustas
A stalk (of a plant), caulis, scapus; (of fruit), petiolus; (of onions, &c.), thallus; (of corn), stipula, culmus
To stalk, pedetentim ire, baccher
A stall (for cattle), stabulum; (for horses), equile; (for oxen), bovile, bubile; (little shop), catasta, taberna minor; (seat in a choir), sella
A head-stall, capistrum
To stall, stabulo, sagino
Stallage, locarium
A stalling, stabulatio
A stallion, equus admissarius; (gallant), admissarius
Stammelling, robustus et agrestis
To stammer, balbutio, hæsito
A stammerer, balbus, blæsus
Stammering, balbutiens, hæsitans
A stammering, balbuties; (at), hæsitantia, hæsitatio
Stammeringly, hæsitanter
A stamp (mark), nota, signum; (made with the foot), vestigium; (to mark with), typus; (impression made), impressio; (cut, *or* print), tabula, figura, imago
To stamp (kick), pedibus ferire; (walk heavily), pedem supplodere; (mark), noto, signo; (coin), nummum cudere; (pound, *or* bruise), contundo; (under foot), conculco, proculco
A stamping (with the feet), calcatura, calcatus; (upon), conculcatio; (marking), signatio
Stanch, bonus, firmus, constans
To stanch (stop), sisto, supprimo
Stanched, suppressus, restinctus
A stanching, suppressio
A stanchion, fulcrum
Stanchness, bonitas, firmitas
A stand (stop), mora, intervallum; (station), septum, statio; (doubt, suspense), dubitatio, hæsitatio; (prop), fulcrum, adminiculum
To stand, sto; (still), sto, consisto, subsisto; (in one place), moror, commoror; (about), circumsto; (against), resisto, obnitor, oppugno; (aside), recedo, secedo; (asunder), disto; (by), asto, assisto; (by, *or* assist), defendo, tueor
To be at a stand (doubt), hæreo, hæsito, dubito; (as work), pendeo [redigere
To put to a stand, ad angustias
To make a stand, gradum sistere, obviam ire
A standard, vexillum; (bearer), vexillarius, signifer; (in weight and measures), norma publica; (pattern), exemplar, modulus
A stander by, satans
Standers, arbores inceduæ
A standing-place, statio
Standing out, extans, prominens; (resolute), pertinax, obstinatus
A standing (time), tempus, ætas; (situation), positio; (of a short standing), nuper natus, *or* ortus

[124]

A standish, atramentarium
A stanza, series, ordo
A staple (mart), emporium
Staple commodities, merces primariæ; (staple of a lock), cavum
A star, stella, sidus, astrum; (the day, or morning-star), venus, phosphorus; (blazing-star), cometa, stella crinita; (dog-star), sirius, canicula; (the seven stars), vergiliæ, pleïades; (in writing), asteriscus
Full of stars, stellatus
The star-chamber, camera stellata
The starboard, dextra pars
A stargazer, astrologus
Starless, sine stellis, tenebrosus
Starlight, sublustris
Starlike, illustris, splendidus
Starch, amylum; (ready made), amylum aquâ dilutum
To starch, amylo imbuere
Starched, amylo imbutus; (affected), putidus, homo affectatis moribus, affectatus; (spruce), mundulus, nitidiusculus
To stare, obtutu hærere; (or look wildly), efferato aspectu intueri; (about), oculos volvere; (as hair), horreo, inhorresco, arrigor
Staring (rough), hirtus, horridus; (wildly), efferatus, efferus; (hair), arrectæ comæ
Staringly, ferociter
Stark, penitùs, omninò; (blind), talpâ cæcior
Starry, stellatus, sidereus
A start, saltus, impetus, motus
To start (or give a start), trepido, subsilio, expavesco ; (back), resilio; (a hare), leporem excitare; (a question), quæstionem proponere; (a point in law), quæstionem de jure facere; (or mention first), infero; (an opinion), opinionem inferre; (a difficulty), scrupulum injicere; (or deviate from), à proposito aberrare
Starting, or startish, meticulosus
A starting-place, meta, repagula, career
To startle, trepido, expavesco; (or make one to startle), territo, nec opinantem opprimere
Startling, trepidans; (making afraid), territans, pavorem injiciens
To starve (with hunger), fame enecare; (a town), oppidum fame premere; (with cold), præ frigore horrere; (a cause), causam fraudare
Starving with hunger, famelicus
A state (condition), conditio, status, fortuna; (manner), ratio, institutum; (degree, or rank), ordo; (charge, or office), munus, dignitas; (government), regnum, imperium, respublica; (affairs), res politicæ; (show, magnificence), splendor, apparatus, pompa, magnificentia
A state-room, camera magnifica; (bed), lectus ad pompam ornatus; (house), basilica
States (nobility), proceres
The states-general, ordines provinciarum fœderatarum
To state (regulate), ordino, moderor, tempero, dispono, definio; (an account), rationes inter se conferre; (a question), quæstionem proponere
[125]

To live in state, magnificè vivere
Stateliness, magnificentia
Stately, magnificus, splendidus, elatus, superbus; adv. magnificè, splendidè, elatè
A statesman, politicæ scientiæ peritus
States, statice
Stating, ordinans, disponens
A station, statio, locus; (post, or office), munus
To station, in statione ponere
Stationers (company of), stationarii
A stationer, chartopola
Stationary, stationarius, fixus
A statuary, statuarius
Statuary (art of), sculptura
A statue (image), statua, simulacrum, signum; (of brass), signum æneum; (of wax), imago cerea
A stature (size), statura
Statutable, legibus consentaneus
Statutably, juxta leges
A statute, statutum, decretum, præscriptum, lex, sanctio; (of parliament), senatûs consultum
To stave (off), depello, propello, proteio; (or break in pieces), frango, diffringo
Staves, see Staff; (of a barrel), asculæ doliares
A stay (delay), impedimentum, mora; (tarrying in a place), mansio; (prop), fulcrum; (band), retinaculum
To stay (abide), maneo, remoror, commoror, moror; (or stop one), detineo, sisto; (or curb), cohibeo, coërceo; (or appease), mollio, placo; (the stomach), famem depellere; (or prop), fulcio; (for), præstolor, opperior; (or loiter), cunctor, moror; (away), absum
Stayedly, serio, graviter
Stayedness, gravitas, severitas
A stayer (stopper), stator
Staying, manens, consistens; (for), expectans, præstolans, opperiens; (upon), nixus, innixus
A staying up, sustentatio
A pair of stays, thorax nexilis
Stead, or place, locus
Steadfast, stabilis, firmus, constans
Steadfastly, constantèr, attentè
Steadfastness, constantia
Steadily, firmiter, constanter
Steadiness, stabilitas, firmitas
Steady, firmus, stabilis, fixus
A steak, offula, ofella
To steal (rob), furor, latrocinor; (privily), subripio; (away), secedo, clanculùm sese subducere; (a marriage), nuptias clandestinas celebrare; (into), irrepo; (or insinuate into), insinuo
A stealer, fur, latro
A stealing, direptio, spoliatio
Given to stealing, furax
By stealth, furtim, clanculùm
Pertaining to stealth, furtivus
A steam, vapor, halitus
To steam, exhalo, vaporo
Stedfast, firmus
A steed, equus, sonipes
Steel, chalybs
Of steel, chalybeïus
A steel (to strike fire), ignisrium; (for a butcher), instrumentum ex chalybe fungens vice cotis

A steelyard, statera
To steel, chalybe temperare; (one's face), os induere
Steep, præceps, præruptus; (ascending), acclivis; (descending), declivis
A steep place, præcipitium
To steep, macero, mollio
A steeping, maceratio
A steeple, templi pyramis
Steeply, præruptè
Steepness (of ascent), acclivitas; (of descent), declivitas
A steer, juvencus
To steer (govern), guberno, impero, rego, rerum habenas agitare; (one's course), proficiscor, pergo, vado, iter facere, cursum dirigere
Steerage, or steering, gubernatio
The steerage, nauclerî statio
A steersman, gubernator, nauclerus
Stellar, stellaris
The stem (of a plant, or herb), caulis, scapus; (or stock of a tree), truncus; (of corn), culmus, stipula; (race, or parentage), stirps, progenies, prosapia, familia, genus, stemma; (of a ship), rostrum
To stem (or stop), retardo, reprimo, coërceo, cohibeo, sisto
To grow to a stem, caulesco
A stench, fœtor; (of a thing burnt, &c.), nidor; (of a foul breath), halitus graveolentia
A stentorean voice, vox stentorea
A step, passus, gradus, gressus
A step, or footstep, vestigium
Step of a ladder, climacter; (before a door), podium
The step of a door, limen
Step by step, gradatim
A step-father, vitricus; (mother), noverca; (son), privignus; (daughter), privigna
To step, gradior, incedo; (or go to a place), pergo, proficiscor; (after), sequor; (along with), comitor; (ashore), in terram egredi; (aside), secedo; (it away), gradum accelerare
Made with steps, gradatus
A stepping, gradatio; (aside), secessus; (in), ingressus; (in unlooked for), adventus inopinatus
Sterile, sterilis, infœcundus
Sterility, sterilitas
Sterling, bona et legalis moneta, sterlingus
A pound sterling, viginti solidi
Stern, torvus, severus, tetricus, durus
The stern, navis clavus, puppis; (tail), canda
Sternly, torvè, austerè, tetrè
Sternness, torvitas, austeritas
Sternutation (sneezing), sternutatio
A stew (fishpond), piscina; (pan), anthepsa; (bawdy-house), lupanar
A haunter of stews, ganeo
To stew (meat), carnem lento igne coquere; (put into a fret), irrito
A steward, procurator, curator, dispensator
A house-steward, curator domesticus
Lord-steward of the king's household, dominus seneschallus hospitii domini regis

G 3

STI — STO

A stewardship, munus procuratoria, dispensatio, curatio, administratio
A stick, baculus, baculum, bacillum, scipio
To stick, hæreo; (fix), figo, affigo; (up before), præfigo; (or cleave to), adhæreo, adhæresco; (into), defigo; (stab), confodio; (at, or doubt), hæsito, dubito; (or put between), intersero; (by, or support), sustineo, sustento; (in), infigo; (in the mud), in luto hærere; (in the ground), defigo; (fast, or be fixed in), insideo; (or jut out), promineo, exsto; (out, or refuse), recuso, renuo
A sticking unto, adhæsio
To stickle, laboro, multum agere; (for a person), ab aliquo stare; (for a party), parti studere; (for liberty), libertatem vindicare
A stickler, studiosus
A stickling, studium
Sticky, viscosus, viscidus
A stie for hogs, hara
Stiff (not pliable), rigens, rigidus; (benumbed), torpens, torpidus; (inexorable), inexorabilis; (obstinate, resolute), pertinax, pervicax, contumax; (rigid, severe), asper, acerbus, rigidus, durus, severus; (strong), validus; (necked), pertinax, contumax
To be stiff, rigeo, torpeo
To stiffen, induro, duro; (with gum, &c.), gummi sublinere
Stiffly, rigidè, obstinatè
Stiffness, rigor; (numbness), torpor; (obstinacy), pertinacia, pervicacia
To stifle, suffoco; (a report), famam comprimere; (conceal), celo, tego
A stifling, suffocatio
To stigmatize (mark with a hot iron), stigmate inurere; (brand with infamy), famam alicujus lædere
A stile, climax, septum
A turnstile, septum versatile
A stile (in writing), stilus
To stile, denomino, voco
A stiletto, sica, pugio
A stiling, appellatio
Still (yet, continually), adhùc, etiamnùm, assiduè
Still (calm, quiet), tranquillus, placidus, sedatus, quietus, serenus, lenis
To be still, sileo
Still-born, abortivus
A still, alembicum
To still (calm, or pacify), placo, sedo, mulceo, lenio
To still (distil), distillo, exprimo
Stillicidious, stillans
Stilly, sedatè, tranquillè
Stillages, quies, serenitas
A stillstand, cessatio
Stilts, grallæ
A walker on stilts, grallator
To stimulate, stimulo, incito
A stimulating, Stimulation, stimulatio
A sting, stimulus, aculeus, spiculum, incitamentum; (of conscience), angor, or morsus conscientiæ
To sting, pungo; (to be stung in conscience), mentis malè sibi consciæ angoribus confici
[126]

Having a sting, aculeatus
Stinging, stimulans, stimuleus
A stinging, punctura, compunctio
Stingingly, punctim, severè
Stinginess, nimia parsimonia
Stingily, perparcè, sordidè
Stingy, deparcus, sordidus
A stink, fœtor, fœditas
To stink, fœteo, puteo; (very much), peroleo
Stinking, fœtidus, putidus, olidus
Stinkingly, fœtidè, rancidè
A stint, limitatio, modus
To stint (limit), finio, modum adhibere; (curb), fræno, moderor, coërceo
Stinted, finitus, repressus
A stipend, stipendium
A stipendiary, stipendiarius
Stiptic, stypticus, astringens
To stipulate, stipulor, paciscor
A stipulation, stipulatio, pactio
A stipulator, stipulator
To stir (move), se movere; (up, or provoke), provoco, irrito, urgeo, lacesso; (up to anger), excandefacio; (up sedition), seditionem commovere, or conflare; (in business), sursum studio aliquid agere; (or circulate), abundo, circulor; (out of doors), foràs prodire, or exire; (up), suscito; (the fire), focum excitare
To make a stir, tumultuor
With much stir (or tumult), tumultuosè; (or difficulty), ægrè, vix
That may be stirred, agitabilis
A stirrer, concitator
To be stirring, è lecto surgere
A. stirring, concitatio; (moving), motio; (provoking), instigatio; (about), agitatio
Stirring (or bustling), diligens
A stirrop, or stirrup, stapes
A stitch (in sewing), sutura; (in the side), pleuritis, lateris dolor
To stitch, suo, consuo; (round), circumsuo
Stitched, Stitcht, sutus, consutus
A stitching, sutura
A stithy, incus
To stive with heat, suffoco
A stiving-heat, æstus
Stiving hot, calidissimus
A stock (stump), truncus, stipes, caudex; (family), prosapia, familia, genus, stemma; (estate), res, bona, census; (of goods), copia, varietas; (of cattle), pecuariæ; (of sheep), oviaria; (or fund of money), nummorum vis [bulis
Of the same stock, gentilis, triA stockdove, palumbes
A stockfish, salpa
A stock (gilliflower), lucoton
Stocks (for building ships), lignea compages in quâ naves construi solent; (for punishment), cippus, numella; (public funds), sortes pecuniariæ
To stock (or furnish), instruo, suppedito; (job), sortibus pecuniariis negotiari; (root out), eradico
A stockjobber, sortibus pecuniariis negotians
A stocking (furnishing), suppeditatio; (or hose), tibiale, caliga
A stoic, stoicus

Stoically, stoicè
Stoicism, stoicismus
A stole, stola, palla
Having stolen, furatus
Stolidity, stoliditas
The stomach, stomachus; (appetite), appetitus, fames; (anger), ira; (courage), animus, virtus [laborans
Sick at the stomach, stomacho
To have a stomach, esurio
To get a stomach, stomachum acuere [mere
To stay the stomach, famem exiTo stomach, indignor, irascor.
A stomacher, pectorale
Stomachful, animosus, ferox
Stomachic, stomacho gratus
A stone, lapis; (flint), silex; (rock), saxum, petra; (load), magnes; (pebble), calculus; (precious), gemma; (pumice), pumex; (whet), cos
To become stone, or hard as stone, lapidesco
To stone (throw stones), lapido, lapidibus obruere
A stone (of wool), quatuordecim libra; (of meat), octo libræ
The stone (disease), calculus
Having the stone, calculosus, calculo laborans
The stones, testiculi
Of stone, lapideus, saxeus
A stonecutter, lapicida
Stone-dead, penitùs emortuus
A stone-quarry, lapicidina
A stone-mason, latomus
A stoner, lapidator
Stoniness, qualitas lapidosa
Stony, lapidosus, petrosus
A stoning, lapidatio
A stool, sella, sedes; (three-footed), tripus
A footstool, scabellum
A closestool, lasanum
A stool, or going to stool, alvus
To go to stool, alvum exonerare; (to cause to go), alvum ciere
To stoop, inclino, proclino; (cringe), serviliter flectere, or submittere
Stooping, inclinis, pronus
A stooping, inclinatio
A stop (hinderance), mora, impedimentum; (pause), pausa, respiratio; (point), punctum; (full), periodus
To be at a stop, consisto
To stop, prohibeo, coërceo, impedio; (a journey), iter intercludere; (a looseness), sistere alvum; (the breath), spiritum intercludere; (stand still), continere gradum; (the ears), aures claudere; (the mouth), os obstruere; (chinks), obstipo; (or cease from), desisto; (blood), sanguinem reprimere; (a cough), tussim reprimere; (up), obstruo, oppilo; (up, fill, or stuff), impleo, repleo; (up a way), viam intercludere; (or tarry), moror, cunctor; (or assuage), paco, sedo; (with points), punctis distinguere
A stoppage, obstructio; (of money, &c.), retentio
A stopper, or stopple, obtumentum
Stopping, impediens, retardans
A stopping of the breath, suffocatio; (or holding of the breath), retentio halitûs, or animæ

Store (plenty), abundantia, copia; (provision), penus, commeatus; (military), belli instrumentum et apparatus
To store, suppedito, instruo
To have store, abundo, affluo
To lay up in store, repono
A storehouse, armarium; (for victuals), promptuarium; (for armour), armamentarium; (keeper), condus
Stories, fabulæ
A stork, ciconia
A storm, procella, tempestas; (of rain), nimbus; (of wind), turbo; (tumult), tumultus, seditio; (violent assault), vehemens aggressio
To take by storm, expugno
To storm (rail), debacchor, furo; (a town), totis viribus oppidum oppugnare
Stormy, procellosus, nimbosus
A story, historia, narratio, fabula; (lie), mendacium
A strange story, res mira dictu
To tell stories, fabulor
A story (in building), tabulatum
A stove (hothouse), vaporarium; (fire-grate), craticula ignis
Stout (courageous), strenuus, fortis, intrepidus; (fierce, proud), ferox, fastidiosus; (strong, vigorous), validus, robustus, acer
Stout (beer), cerevisia generosa
Stouthearted, magnanimus
Stoutly (courageously), strenuè, fortiter, intrepidè; (proudly), fastidiosè; (strongly), validè, acriter
Stoutness (courage), fortitudo, virtus; (haughtiness), arrogantia, superbia; (strength), robur, vires
To stow, loco, colloco
Stowage-room, repositorii capacitas; (money), locarium
To straddle, varico, divarico
Straddling, varicus, divaricatus
To straggle, vagor, erro
A straggler, erro, vagus
Straggling, palans, vagans, errans
Straight (not crooked), rectus, directus; (upright), erectus; (tall), procerus; (by line), ad amussim; (directly, adv.), rectà, rectè, directè
Straight against, è regione; (up), sursum versus; (down), deorsùm versus; (on), rectà
To straighten, rectum facere
Straightness (tallness), proceritas
Straightway, mox, statim, illicò
A strain (stretching), contentio; (in speaking, or writing), stylus; (of the sinews), nervorum intentio; (in music), suavis modulus
To strain (stretch), contendo; (hurt), lædo; (bind hard), comprimo, coarcto, constringo; (or press out), exprimo; (compel), cogo, compello; (or stretch a point), plus justo torquere; (liquids), percolo; (or labour hard), enitor; (a joint), luxo; (a sinew), nervum intendere
A strainer, colum, saccus
Straining, contendens, constringens
A straining, or stretching, contentio; (or pressing out), expressio
Strait (narrow), angustus, arctus; (handed), deparcus, tenax; (laced), nimis scrupulosus
A strait (difficulty), difficultas
Straits (want), inopia, paupertas; (difficulties), angustiæ, incitæ; (narrow seas, &c.), fretum, angustiæ; (of Gibraltar), fretum Gaditanum, or Herculeum
To straiten, arcto, coarcto
To be straitened, indigeo, premor
Straitening, arctans, coarctans
A straitening, coarctatio
Straitly, arctè, angustè
Straitness, angustia
The strake of a wheel, canthus
A strand (shore), ripa, littus; (of a rope), filum, plica
To strand, vadis impingere
Strange (foreign), peregrinus, alienus; (far fetched), longinquus; (odd, uncommon), rarus, inusitatus; (shy, disdainful), fastosus, superciliosus; (wonderful), mirus, mirabilis, mirificus
A strange thing, miraculum, portentum; (man), homo mirus
Strange (coolly), frigidè
O strange! papæ!
Strangely, mirificè, miris modis
Strangeness, raritas, novitas; (shyness), fastus; (in pronunciation), peregrinitas
A stranger, advena, peregrinus, hospes; (metaph.), ignotus, ignarus, rudis, imperitus, alienus
To strangle, strangulo, suffoco; (to death), laqueo interimere
A strangling, suffocatio
The strangury, stranguria
A strap, strupas, lorum
To strap, strupis alligare; (a person) loris cædere
The strappado, equuleus
A strapper (lass), virago
A stratagem, stratagema, dolus
Full of stratagems, dolosus, versutus
Straw, stramen, palea; (for thatch), culmus, stipula; (or fescue), festuca
Of straw, stramineus
Made of straw, stramentitius
Not worth a straw, nihili, fatilis
A straw-colour, color melinus
A strawberry, fragum; (tree), arbutus
Of a strawberry-tree, arbuteus
Strawy, stramineus
A stray, bestia errans
To stray, erro, vagor
Straying, vagans, erraticus
A straying, erratio, vagatio
A streak, radius, linea; (of a wheel), canthus
To streak, vario colore distinguere
A stream, fluentum, flumen
A small stream, rivulus
To stream, or flow (along), fluito, fluo, profluo, labor, curro; (out), effluo, emano
A streamer, vexillum, signum; (in a ship), aplustre
Streaming, fluens, fluitans, effluens
Streamingly, fluenter, prosperè
A street, vicus, platea
Street by street, vicatim, plateatim
Strength, robur, vires, firmitas, sanitas, vigor, fortitudo; (force), vis, virtus; (power), potentia, potestas; (of a place),
munimentum, præsidium; (of an argument), vis, pondus
Full of strength, nervosus
Of great strength, efficax, valens
To recover strength, convalesco
To strengthen, roboro, confirmo; (a place), munio; (the sight), visum acuere
A strengthening, confirmatio
Strenuous, strenuus, fortis, acer
Strenuously, validè, fortitèr
Strenuousness, fortitudo, vis
A stress (chief point), cardo, summa, caput; (of weather), tempestas, procella
To lay a stress, nitor, confido
A stretch, or stretching, distentio
To stretch, tendo, extendo, intendo, porrigo; (abroad), expando, dispando; (enlarge), dilato, profero; (out), distendo, explico; (out, or be extended), protendor; (with yawning), pandiculor
That may be stretched, ductilis
A stretching, distentio; (yawning), pandiculatio
To strew, sterno, insterno, spargo; (sprinkle), aspergo
A strewing, sparsio, aspersio
Striated, striatus
Striature, striatura
A strickle, radius, radula
Strict (close), arctus; (exact, exactus; (accurate), accuratus; (precise, formal), affectatus; (rigid, severe), rigidus, asper, severus
With a strict eye, attentè
With a strict hand, arctè
Strictly, arctè, familiaritèr; (exactly, accurately), accuratè, exquisitè; (precisely, formally), affectatè; (rigidly, severely), rigidè, severè, acerbè
Strictness (of friendship), familiaritas, necessitudo; (exactness), accuratio; (preciseness), affectatio; (rigidness, severity), rigor, asperitas, severitas
A stricture, strictura
A stride, passus, gradus
A long stride, gradus grallatorius
To stride, varico; (across, or over), spatium distentia cruribus metiri
A striding, distentio crurum
Strife, jurgium, rixa, lis
Full of strife, jurgiosus, rixosus
A strig, petiolus
A strike, or bushel, modius
To strike, cædo, ferio; (out of a list), erado; (as a horse), calcitro; (affect), afficio; (or sound as a clock), sono; (a measure), rado, derado; (at one), peto, impeto, adorior; (at, aim, or attempt to do), conor, molior; (or dash against), allido; (down), affligo, dejicio; (at the root), subverto; (back), repello; (blind), cæco, excæco; (fire), ignem elicere; (in pieces), diffringo; (or drive into), indigo; (off), præcido, excindo
A striker, pulsator
A striking, pulsatio, percussio; (back), repercussio
A string, funiculus, ligula
The string of a dart, amentum
Strings (of roots), fibræ; (of musical instruments), fides
To string (an instrument), nervos aptare; (or fasten a dart),

STU   STY   SUB

amento; (pearls), filo conserere gemmas; (things together), res funiculo trajecto connectere
Stringy, fibris abundans
A strip, frustulum, particula
To strip, spolio, denudo; (off clothes), vestem exuere; (off rind), decortico
A stripe, plaga, ictus; (in colour), virga varii coloris
Full of stripes, plagosus
To stripe, lineas varii coloris distinguere
A stripling, adolescens, ephebus
Stripped, Stript, spoliatus, exutus, nudatus
A stripper, spoliator, spoliatrix
A stripping, spoliatio, direptio
To strive, conor, enitor, molior; (against), obnitor, resisto; (hard), obnixè moliri; (together), concertò, confligo
Having striven, nixus
Striven against, impugnatus
A striver with, concertator
A striving, conatus, nixus; (together), concertatio
A stroke, ictus, plaga; (of an oar), pulsus; (on the ear), alapa, colaphus; (with a pen), ductus pennæ
To stroke, palpo, mulceo
A stroking, palpatio   [sum
Strokings, lac ultimâ manu emul-
To stroll, vagor, circumcurso
A stroller, erro, homo vagus
A strolling company, errantium grex
Strong (lusty), firmus, robustus, validus; (limbed), lacertosus; (clear), clarus; (earnest, vehement), solicitus, vehemens, acer; (forcible, efficacious), valens, potens, efficax; (massy), solidus; (mighty, powerful), potens, pollens, valens; (sharp in taste), acer, acidus; (in smell, fœtens; (valiant), fortis, strenuus, intrepidus
Very strong, prævalidus, potentissimus
A strong hand, vis
A strong hold, propugnaculum
To be strong, valeo, polleo
To grow strong, valesco
To make strong, firmo, corroboro; (or massy), consolido
Strongly, firmiter, fortiter, validè
To strow, sterno
Struck, percussus, perculsus
To be struck in a heap, percellor
A structure, ædificium; (construction), structura
A struggle, conatus, luctatio, certatio, contentio
To struggle, conor, luctor, contendo, nitor; (together), congredior, colluctor
A struggler, luctator
A struggling, luctatio, lucta
Strumous, strumosus
A strumpet, scortum, meretrix
Strung, filo instructus
To strut, turgeo, tumeo, superbio; (along), superbè incedere
A strutting, superbus incessus
A stub (of a tree), stipes
A stubnail, clavus detritus
To stub up, eradico, extirpo
Stubble, stipula, culmus
Of stubble, stipularis
Stubborn, contumax, refractarius, pertinax; (saucy), improbus

[128]

To be stubborn, obstinato animo esse, præfractè defendere
Stubbornly, præfractè, obstinatè
Stubbornness, contumacia, obstinatio, pertinacia
Stubby, Stubbed, brevis et robustus
Stuck (run through), perfossus; (adorned), ornatus
A stud, bulla; (of mares), equarum armentum
Studded, bullatus, clavatus, ornatus
A student, studiosus; (great), librorum helluo
Studious, studiosus, amans
Studiously, studiosè, assiduè
Studiousness, studium, cura
Study (application of mind), studium, meditatio
A study, bibliotheca, museum
To study, studeo, meditor, exquiro, investigo, scrutor, exploro
Studying, meditans
A studying, meditatio
Stuff (materials), materia; (cloth), pannus; (baggage), sarcinæ; (household), supellex; (kitchen), unguina
To stuff (cram), farcio; (one's belly), cibis se ingurgitare; (with flocks, &c.), flocco infercire; (or choke), suffoco; (or stop up), obstruo, oppilo
A stuffing, fartura, sagina
The stuffing of a quilt, tomentum; (for veal, &c.), fartum, farcimen
To stumble, titubo, offenso; (against), impingo, incurro; (at, or scruple), hæsito, dubito; (upon), incido
A stumble, offensa, offensio
Stumbling, titubans, offensans
A stumbling-block, offendiculum
A stump, caudex, stipes, truncus; (stumps), pedes, crura; (broken limb), membrum mutilatum
To stump, trunco; (boast), glorior, jacto, ostento   [tus
Stumpy, stipitum plenus, robus-
To stun (astonish), stupefacio, perturbo, perterreo; (with noise), aures obtundere
To be stunned, stupefio, stupeo
Stung, punctus
To stunt, incrementum impedire
To stupe, foveo
Stupefaction, stupor, torpedo
Stupefactive, narcoticus
To stupefy (astonish), terreo, perturbo; (dull, or benumb), hebeto, tundo, obtundo
To be stupified, stupeo
Stupendious, Stupendous, mirus, mirabilis
Stupid (blockish), stupidus, fatuus, ineptus; (without feeling), stupedus, torpens, torpidus
Stupidity, stupiditas, stupor
Stupidly, stupidè, insulsè
Stupration, stupratio
Sturdily, pertinaciter, fortiter
Sturdiness, contumacia, fortitudo; (strength), robur
Sturdy, obstinatus, ferox, robustus
A sturgeon, stario, acipenser
To stut, or stutter, balbutio
A stutterer, bambalio
Stuttering, balbutiens
A sty, suile; (pimple), tumor palpebræ

A style (in writing), stylus, dicendi genus; (or form), formula; (of a dial), gnomon; (in the account of time), stylus
To style, appello
A styling, appellatio
Styptic, stypticus, restringens
Suasory, suasorius, hortativus
Suavity, suavitas, dulcedo
Subaction, subactio
A subaltern, legatus
A subchanter, succentor
A subdeacon, subdiaconus
To subdelegate, substituo
Subdititious, subditivus
To subdivide, iterum dividere
A subdivision, divisio iterata
Subduable, domabilis, superabilis
To subduct, subduco, detraho
To subdue, domo, supero, debello, expungo, subigo, vinco; (passions), frango, domo
To be subdued, cedo, succumbo
A subduer, debellator
A subduing, expugnatio
Subject, subjectus, subditus; (obliged to), obligatus, obstrictus; (liable to), obnoxius, expositus
A subject (person), civis, subditus, subjectus; (argument of discourse), argumentum, materia, thesis; (in logic), subjectum
To be subject to, pareo, obedio; (the subject of discourse), sermonem subire
To subject, subjicio, subigo
Subjection, servitus, jugum
A subjecting, subjectio
To subjoin, subjungo, annecto
Subitaneous, subitaneus, repentinus
To subjugate, supero, domo
Subjunctive, subjunctivus
To sublimate, sublimo
Sublimate, pulvis rodens ex argento vivo, nitro, &c., confectus
Sublime, sublimis, excelsus; (most excellent), præstantissimus
Sublimely, excellenter, summè
Sublimeness, Sublimity, sublimitas, celsitudo, altitudo
Sublunary, sub lunâ positus
Submersion, submersio
To subminister, subministro
Submission, obsequium
Submissive, submissus, humilis
Submissively, submissè, humiliter
To submit, submitto, cedo; (to another's judgment), permitto
A submitting, submissio
Subordinate, inferior, substitutus
Subordination, conditio inferior
To suborn, suborno
A suborning, subornatio
A subpœna, citatio
To subpœna, citare in curiam
To subscribe, subscribo, assentior
A subscriber, subscriptor
A subscribing, subscriptio
A subscription, subscriptio
Subsecutive, Subsequent, subsequens, consequens
Subsequently, per modum consecutionis   [datio
Subservience, gratia, accommo-
Subservient, subserviens
To be subservient, subservio
To subside, subsideo, subsido
Subsidiary, subsidiarius, auxiliaris

| SUC | SUI | SUP |

Subsidy (aid), subsidium, auxilium ; (tax), vectigal, tributum, census
To subsign, subsigno
To subsist, subsisto ; (maintain), sustento ; (continue), existo
A subsistence, victûs suppeditatio, existentia
Subsistent, existens
Substance (matter), substantia, res, materia, summa, caput ; (estate), fortunæ, divitiæ, opes, peculium, hæreditas
Of substance, opulentus, dives
Of the same substance, consubstantiali
Substantial, solidus, firmus, validus, gravis, certissimus ; (wealthy), locuples, opulentus, dives, pecuniosus
Substantially, solidè, firmè
A substantive, substantivum
Substantively, substantivè
A substitute, vicarius
To substitute, substituo, suppono
A substitution, substitutio
To substract, or subtract, subtraho, detraho, subduco, deduco
A substracting, or substraction, subtractio, deductio
To subtend, subtendo
A subtense, subtensa
Subterfluent, subterfluens
A subterfuge, effugium, dolus
Subterraneous, subterraneus
Subtile, subtilis, tenuis ; (cunning), subtilis, acutus, astutus, sagax
Subtlety, subtilitas, astutia
Subtle. See Subtile
Subtilely, subtilitèr, acutè
A subversion, subversio, excidium
To subvert, subverto, everto
Subverted, subversus, dirutus
A subverter, subversor
Suburbs, suburbana
Of the suburbs, suburbanus
Succedaneous, succedaneus
To succeed, succedo, sequor, excipio, evenio, cedo
Succeeding, succedens, excipiens
Succeeding generations, minores
A succeeding, successio
Success, successus, exitus
Successful, prosperus, faustus, felix
Successfully, prosperè, faustè
Succession, successio ; (entail), hæreditas ; (continuation), consecutio, series
Successive, succedens, sequens
Successively, continuatâ serie
A successor, successor ; (our successors), posteri nostri
Succinct, brevis, succinctus
Succinctly, brevitèr, concisè
Succinctness, brevitas
Succory, cichorium
Succour, auxilium.
To succour (comfort), consolor; (aid), succurro, subvenio ; (a place besieged), auxilia et commeatus suppeditare
Succoured, adjutus
A succourer, solator, opitulator
Succouring, consolans, auxilians
Succourless, destitutus, desertus, miser
Succulency, succi abundantia
Succulent, succulentus, succosus
To succumb, succumbo, cedo
Such, adj. talis, ejusmodi, istiusmodi ; adv. adeò, tam
Such as, qualis, istiusmodi

In such manner, tali modo, paritèr
To suck, sugo ; (in), imbibo, absorbeo, sorbeo ; (out), exsugo ; (up), sorbeo
To give suck, lacto, nutrico
Sucked in, or up, absorptus
A sucker of trees, stolo
The sucker of a pump, antlia canrheter
A sucking, suctus
Sucking up, absorbens, imbibens
Sucking the breast, lactens
To suckle, lacto, nutricio
Suckled, mammis admotus
A suckling, animal lactens
Suction, suctus
Sudatory, sudatorius
Sudden, subitus, improvisus, repentinus
On a sudden, repentinò
Suddenly, repentè, inopinatò
Suddenness, eventus subitaneus
Sudorific, diaphoreticus
Suds, spuma saponis; (to be in the suds), ad incitas redigi
To sue (at law), litigo, in jus vocare ; (entreat), deprecor, supplico ; (for peace), solicitare pacem ; (for a place), munus ambire
Suet (sewet), sevum, liquamen
To suffer (bear with), patior, fero, tolero, suffero ; (be punished), poenas dare, luere, or solvere; (disgrace), in offensam incurrere ; (some hurt), aliquo incommodo affici ; (shipwreck), naufragium facere; (permit), patior, sino, permitto
Sufferable, tolerabilis
Sufferance (toleration), tolerantia ; (of evils), malorum perpessio ; (permission), permissio, venia
On sufferance, permissu
Long sufferance, longanimitas
Having suffered, passus
A sufferer, damno affectus
Suffering, patiens, permittens
Long-suffering, ad iram tardus
A suffering, passio, perpessio
To suffice, sufficio
Sufficiency, sufficientia ; (capacity), captus, peritia, habilitas, facultas, prudentia ; (self), arrogantia, superbia
Sufficient (able), sufficiens, capax, aptus, idoneus, habilis
Not sufficient, impar, ineptus
Sufficiently, sat, satis, affatim, abundè
To suffocate, suffoco
A suffocating, suffocatio
Suffocation, præfocatio
A suffragan, suffraganeus
A suffrage, suffragium
To give suffrage, suffragor
Of suffrages, suffragatorius
Suffumigation, suffumigatio
To suffuse, suffundo
A suffusion, suffusio
Sugar, saccharum ; (candy), sacchari cremor; (loaf), sacchari meta; (cane), canna mellifera
To sugar, saccharo condire
To suggest, suggero, moneo, insuo
A suggester, monitor [surro
A suggesting, or suggestion, admonitio, monitus, suggestio
To sigillate, sugillo
Suicide, suicidium
Suing, litigans, litem intendens
A suit (request), petitio, rogatio ; (at law), actio, causa ; (of apparel), vestitus, vestimentum ; (complete), omnis apparatus ; (at cards), genus
To suit (match), adapto, accommodo ; (with), congruo
Suitable, aptus, congruus, idoneus
Suitably, aptè, congruitèr
Suited, aptatus, accommodatus
A suitor (petitioner), supplex ; (in chancery), orator ; (for an office), candidatus ; (wooer), procus, amator
A suiting, accommodatio
Sullen, contumax, morosus
Sullenly, protervè, torvè, morosè
Sullenness, tetricitas, torvitas
To sully, maculo, inquino ; (a character), famam aspergere
A sullying, macula
Sulphur, sulphur
With sulphur, sulphuratus
Sulphureous, sulphury, or of sulphur, sulphureus, sulphurosus
The sultan, Turcorum imperator
A sultaness, regina Turcica
Sultriness, vis æstûs
Sultry, torridus, fervidus, candens
A sum (of money), summa pecuniæ ; (in cyphering), summa ; (total), summa totalis ; (of a matter), summa, argumentum, caput ; (brief rehearsal), summarium
To sum up, computo, supputo ; (a discourse), res brevitèr repetere ; (all), deniquè, brevitèr
Summarily, brevitèr, summatim
A summary, summarium, compendium
Summed up, computatus, repetitus
Summer, æstas ; (or country house), suburbanum ; (great beam), transtrum
Of summer, æstivus
To summer, æstivo
A summering, æstiva commoratio
A summing up, computatio
The summit, vertex, cacumen
To summon (cite), cito, arcesso ; (command), impero ; (up courage), animum recipere
A summoner, apparitor
A summoning, or summons, citatio
Sumpter, oneratus viatico
Sumptuary, sumptuarius
Sumptuous, sumptuosus, magnificus, splendidus, lautus, opiparus
Sumptuously, sumptuosè
Sumptuousness, splendor, luxus
The sun, sol
Of the sun, solaris
Sunburnt, exustus sole
A sundial, solarium
Sunshine, apricitas
Sun-rising, solis ortus ; (set, or setting), solis occasus
At sunset, cum sole occidente
To sun, soli exponere
Set in the sun, soli expositus
Sunday, dies Dominica
To sunder, separo, sejungo
Sundry, diversus, varius
Sundry ways, diversè, variè
To be sunk with age, esse inutilis annis ; (deep in debt), ære alieno demersus
A sunning, apricatio
To sit in the sun, apricor
Sunny, apricus, soli expositus
A sup, haustus, sorbitio

SUP . SUR . SUS

To sup, sorbeo; (a little), sorbillo; (again), resorbeo; (up), absorbeo; (eat supper), cœno
Superable, superabilis
To superabound, redundo
A superabounding, or superabundance, redundantia
Superabundant, superfluens, redundans
Superabundantly, redundantèr
To superadd, superaddo
Superannuated, annosus, senior
Superb, magnificus, illustris, ingens
A supercargo, navium oneris curator [perbus
Supercilious, superciliosus, superbus
Superciliously, superbè
Superciliousness, superbia, fastus
Supereminence, eminentia
Supereminent, præcellens [tèr
Supereminently, eximiè, insignitèr
To supererogate, supererogo
Supererogation, supererogatio
Superexcellent, supereminens
Superficial, superficiarius, levis, levitèr eruditus
Superficially, perfunctoriè, levitèr
The superficies, superficies
Superfine, tenuissimus
Superfluity, Superfluousness, superfluitas, redundantia
Superfluous, superfluus, supervacaneus, supervacuus, redundans
Superfluous spending, profusio
To be superfluous, redundo
Superfluously, redundantèr
To superinduce, superinduco
Superinduction, superinductio
To superintend, curo, inspicio
Superintendence, curatio, inspectio, primatus
A superintendent, curator, inspector, præfectus
Superior, superior
A superior, superior, præfectus
Superiority, magisterium
Superlative (excellent), eximius, eminens, excellens, egregius, præstans, præclarus, præcellens; (degree), superlativus gradus
Superlatively, excellentèr, eximiè
Supernal, supernus
Supernally, supernè
Supernatural, naturam superans
Supernaturally, super naturæ vires [dens
Supernumerary, numerum excedens
To superscribe, inscribo
A superscription, inscriptio
To supersede, supersedeo
A supersedeas, exauctoramentum
Superstition, superstitio
Superstitious, superstitiosus
Superstitiously, superstitiosè
To superstruct, superstruo
A superstructure, structura
To supervene, supervenio
To supervise, inspicio, curo
Supervised, inspectus, curatus
A supervisor, inspector
Supervising, inspiciens, curans
Supine (face upwards), supinus; (careless, negligent), improvidus, inconsideratus, oscitans, socors, negligens
A supine, supinum
Supinely, supinè, negligentèr
Having supped, cœnatus
A supper, cœna; (Lord's), cœna dominica
Of supper, cœnatorius
To wish for supper, cœnaturio
To be at supper, cœno
[139]

Supperless, incœnatus
Supper-time, tempus cœnandi
Supping, cœnans; (room), cœnaculum, cœnatio
A supping (sipping), sorbitio
To supplant, supplanto, per dolum dejicere
A supplanter, fraudator, parasitus
Supplanting, per dolum dejiciens
Supple (limber), flexilis, lentus, tener
To supple, mollio, macero
To grow supple, lentesco
Supplely, lentè, laxè
A supplement, supplementum, appendix, complementum
Suppleness, lentor, mollities
A suppling, maceratio
A supplicant, or suppliant, supplex
Like a supplicant, supplicitèr
To supplicate, supplico, obsecro, rogo
A supplication, supplicatio
Supply, subsidium, suppetiæ, supplementum, auxilium, suppeditatio
To supply, suppleo; (furnish), suppedito; (relieve), levo, succurro, subvenio
A supplying, suppeditatio
A support (prop), fulcrum, columen; (favour), gratia, tutamen, subsidium
To support (bear up), sustento, fulcio; (bear up under), tolero, patior; (defend), defendo, vindico, tueor; (assist), juvo, auxilior, succurro
Supportable, tolerandus
A supporter (patron), patronus; (in a building), telamo; (supporters in heraldry), animantia scuta sustinentia [uixus
Supporting one's self, nixus, innixus
A supporting, defensio, sustentatio, auxilium
Supposable, opinabilis
To suppose, suppono; (imagine), opinor, reor, credo; (or allow a thing), admitto, concedo
Supposing, opinans, suspicatus
A supposing, or suspicion, opinio
Suppositious, suppositius
To suppress, supprimo, aboleo
Suppressing, supprimens, reprimens
A suppressing, or suppression, suppressio, coërcitio
To suppurate, suppuro
Suppuration, suppuratio
Suppurative, suppuratorius
A supputation, supputatio
Supremacy, primatus
Supreme, supremus, summus
A surcease, cessatio, omissio
To surcease, supersedeo, cesso
A surcharge, onus novum, or injustum, crapula
To surcharge (overload), onus injustum imponere, nimis onerare
A surcingle, cingulum equinum
A surcoat, tunica exterior
Surd, surdus
Surdity (deafness), surditas
Sure (certain), certus, manifestus; (faithful), fidelis, fidus; (safe), tutus, securus, incolumis; (stable), stabilis, firmus; (footed), pes minimè labens
To be sure, certò scire
Surely (certainly), certè, profectò, certò, equidèm, sanè; (faithfully), bonâ fide; (safely), tutò, securè; (stedfastly), firmè, constantèr

Sureness, fidelitas, incolumitas, stabilitas
Suretyship, or a putting in sureties, satisdatio, sponsio
Surety, vadimonium
A surety, vas; (for debt), præs, sponsor
To be surety, spondeo
To put in surety, vador
The surface (outside), superficies (or being surfeited with), satietas [tuor
To surfeit one's self, saturo, helluor
Surfeiting, crapulam, fastidium, or nauseam afferens
A surge (wave), fluctus ingens
A surgeon, chirurgus
Surgery (art of), ars chirurgica
A surgery, officina chirurgica
Of surgery, chirurgicus
Surging, fluctuans
A surging, undarum tumultus
Surly, fluctuosus, undosus
Surlily, morosè, ferocitèr
Surliness, morositas
Surly, morosus, ferox
To be surly, ferocio, superbio
A surmise, suspicio
To surmise, suspicor, imaginor
To surmount, exsupero, vinco
A surmounting, superatio
A surmounting, superatio
A surname, cognomen
To surname, cognomino
To surpass, præcello, præsto, vinco
Surpassable, superabilis
Surpassing, superans, vincens
A surpassing, præstantia
Surpassingly, optimè, præclarè
A surplice, linteum amiculum sacerdotale
A surplus, auctarium
A surprise, Surprisal, superventus; (astonishment), consternatio, animi stupor, pavor, or torpor
To surprise (or come suddenly), de improviso supervenire; (astonish), percello; (fright), terreo, exterreo, perturbo; (a town), improvisò capere
Surprising (new, unexpected), novus, improvisus, inopinatus; (astonishing, marvellous), mirus, mirabilis, admirabilis, mentem perturbans
Surprisingly, mirè, mirabilitèr
A surrender, deditio
To surrender (restore), reddo, restituo, resigno; (as a prisoner), dedo
A surrendering, deditio, abdicatio
Surreptitious, surreptitius
Surreptitiously, furtim, clàm
A surrogate, surrogatus, delegatus
To surround, circumsto, circumdo
Surrounding, circundans
A surrounding, circuitio, circuitus
A survey (viewing), inspectio; (measuring), metatio
To survey (view), lustro, inspecto; (measure), metior; (oversee), curo, procuro
A surveyor, inspector, metator, procurator, curator; (architect), architectus [toris
A surveyorship, munus procuratoris
Survival, Surviving, superstitis status
To survive, supervivo, supersum
A survivor, superstes
A surviorship, munus superstitis
Susceptible, facile suscipiens
To suscitate, suscito, excito

SWA

To suspect, suspicor, suspecto, suspicio
Suspecting, suspicatus, suspiciosus
A suspecting, suspicio
Suspense, dubium
In suspense, dubius, incertus, suspensus, scrupulosus
To be in suspense, dubito, hæsito
To suspend (or defer), suspendo, differo; (an assent), assensum sustinere; (remove for a time), ad tempus removere, or interdicere
Suspending, suspendens
A suspension (suspense), suspensio, hæsitatio; (from an office), muneris interdictio; (of arms), induciæ
A suspicion, suspicio
Suspicious (distrustful), suspiciosus, suspicax; (suspected), suspectus
Suspiciously, suspiciosè
Suspiration (sighing), suspiratio
To sustain (prop, defend), sustento, sustineo, fulcio, defendo, tueor; (bear, or suffer), sustineo, fero, tolero, patior; (a loss), detrimentum accipere
Sustainable, sustinendus
A sustaining (supporting), sustentatio
Sustenance, alimentum, victus
A suttler, caupo castrensis
A suture, sutura
A swabber, nauta inferior
A swaddle, fascia
To swaddle, fascio; (cudgel), verbero, verberibus cædere
A swaddling, fasciis involutio
To swag down, præpondero; (the arms), brachia jactare
Swag-bellied, ventricosus
To swage, mitigo, sedo
To swagger, jacto, glorior
A swaggerer, thraso, jactator
A swaggering, ostentatio
Swagging down, propendens
A swain, agrestis, colonus
A swallow, hirundo
To swallow, sorbeo, absorbeo, haurio, exhaurio; (greedily), voro, ingurgito, devoro; (one's words), dicta retractare
A swallowing down, haustus
A swamp, locus paludosus
Swampy, paludosus, nebulosus
A swan, cygnus, olor
Of a swan, cygneus, olorinus
To swap (swop), commuto
The sward (of bacon), cutis lardi; (of earth), superficies agri graminosi
A swarm (great number), multitudo; (of bees), examen, grex; (of people), turba, magnus concursus
To swarm (as bees), examino; (or come together in numbers), magno numero concurrere; (or climb up), adrepo
Swarming with people, incolis, or populo frequens
By swarms, tumatim
Swarthiness, nigredo, nigror
Swarthy, fuscus, nigellus
To grow swarthy, nigresco
A swash of water, impetus aquæ
To swash, allido
A swasher, jactator, thraso
A swath, fascia, tænia; (of grass), striga fœni demessi
To swathe, fasciis involvere
Sway (government, rule), impe-

[131]

SWE

rium, dominium, dominatio, potestas, dominatus, principatus, rerum administratio
To sway (rule, govern), guberno, impero, rego, res administrare; (with one), valeo
To be swayed, gubernor, regor
A swaying, gubernatio
To sweal (melt away), inæqualitèr eliquescere
To swear, juro; (against), abjuro, ejuro; (allegiance), fidei sacramentum dicere; (falsely), perjuro; (one), juramentum exigere
A swearer, jurator
A false swearer, perjurus
A profane swearer, temerè dejerans
A swearing (taking an oath), jurisjurandi interpositio; (solemn swearing), dejurium
Sweat, sudor
To sweat, sudo, exsudo; (all over), perfundi sudore, consudo; (blood), sanguine sudare
To cause sweat, sudorem ciere
Sweated out, exsudatus
A sweater, sudator, sudatrix
A sweating, sudatio; (place), sudatorium
Of sweating, sudatorius
Causing sweat, sudorificus
Sweaty, sudans, laboriosus
To sweep, verro, everro, purgo; (away, or carry off), aufero, absumo, converro; (before), præverro
A sweeper, scoparius; (of chimneys), caminorum mundator
A sweeping, purgatio scopis
Sweepings, purgamenta, quisquiliæ
Sweet (pleasant to taste, or smell), dulcis, jucundus, suavis, gratus; (breath), halitus suavitèr olens; (look), aspectus lætus, frons hilaris
The sweetbread, pancreas
A sweet-ball, pastillus
Sweet-cane, acorus
Sweet-william, armeria
A sweetheart, procus, amator; (female), amica
Sweetmeats, bellaria
Sweetscented, odoriferus
To grow sweet, dulcesco, mitesco
To sweeten, edulco; (with sugar, &c.), saccharo condire; (pacify), paco, pacifico, mitigo, muleeo, lenio
To be sweet upon, adulor, assentor, palpo
A sweetener (sycophant), assentator
A sweetening, conditura; (pacifying), pacificatio, sedatio
Sweetish, subdulcis
Sweetly (pleasantly), dulcè, suavitèr, gratè; (gently, smoothly), lenitèr, mansuetè, placidè, tranquillè
Sweetness, dulcedo; (of smell), suavitas; (of speech), blanditiæ, suaviloquentia; (of temper), affabilitas, mansuetudo, lenitas
To swell (puff up), tumeo, turgeo, intumesco; (or grow in length, or breadth), cresco, accresco, augeor; (out), prominceo, exto
To make swell, tumefacio, inflo
Swelled, turgidus, inflatus, tumidus
A swelling, tumor, inflatio; (in

SYL

the neck, &c.), struma; (of the sea), æquoris asperitas
To swelter, penè suffocari
Sweltering, penè suffocatus
To swerve (go from), erro, aberro
Swerving from, devius, declinans
A swerving from, deflexus
Swift, celer, velox; (of foot), levipes, alipe
Swiftly, celeritèr, velocitèr
Swiftness, celeritas, velocitas
Swill (hogwash), colluvies
To swill, ingurgito, ebibo; (rinse), lavo, abluo
A swiller, ebriosus, temulentus
Swilling down, ingurgitans, ebibens
A swilling, ebriositas
To swim, nato, no; (against the stream), adverso flumine navigare; (with the stream), secundo flumine vehi; (at the top), supernato; (away), abnato; (back), reno; (before, or by), prænato; (in), innato
A swimmer, natator
Swimming, nans, natans
A swimming, natatio, natatus; (of the head), vertigo
Swimmingly, prosperè, bono successu
A swine, porcus, sus
Of swine, porcillus, suillus
A swine-herd, subulcus, suarius
The swine-pox, boa
Swine-like, more suis
A swing (to swing with), funiculus quo se quis jactat; (full desire), animus, cupiditas; (jerk), impetus
To take his swing, animum explere suum
To swing, agito, jacto, libro; (about), roto, circumverto; (brandish), torqueo, libro
To swinge, verbero, flagello
Swinged about, rotatus, libratus
A swinger, librator
Swinging (hanging), pendulus
Swinging (very large), ingens
A swinging (poising), libratio; (wheeling about), rotatio
To swink, valdè laborare
A swipe, tolleno, grus
A switch (rod), virga, vimen
To switch, flagello
A swivel, verticulum
Swollen, tumidus, turgidus
A swoon, or swooning, deliquium, animi defectus
To swoon, deliquium pati, deficio
To swop, commuto, permuto
Swopped, commutatus
A swopping, permutatio
A sword, gladius, ensis; (naked), gladius strictus
To put to the sword, ad internecionem cædere
A sword-bearer, ensifer; (player), gladiator
Of a sword player, gladiatorius
Sword-playing, gladiatura
A sycamore, sycomorus
A sycophant, sycophanta, delator, adulator, assentator, susurro
To play the sycophant, adulor
Syllabic, Syllabical, syllabicus
A syllable, syllaba
By syllables, syllabatim
Of one syllable, monosyllabus
Of two syllables, bisyllabus; (three syllables), trisyllabus; (four syllables), tetrasyllabus
A syllogism, syllogismus
Syllogistical, syllogisticus

TAC   TAL   TAR

Syllogistically, syllogisticè
To syllogize, ratiocinor, per syllogismos, *or* logicè argumentari
Sylvan, sylvanus, sylvaticus
A symbol, symbolum
Symbolical, symbolicus
Symbolically, symbolicè, opertè
To symbolize (denote), per symbolum indicare; (concur), consentio, convenio, congruo
A symbolizing, symbolica notatio
Symbolizing with, consentiens
Symmetrical, justâ proportione formatus
Symmetry, symmetria
Sympathetical, Sympathetic, sympatheticus
Sympathetically, mutuo affectu
To sympathise, mutuâ miseratione affici, *or* moveri
Sympathizing, sortem alicujus dolens ex animo
Sympathy, mutuus affectus; (natural agreement of things), sympathia
Symphony, symphonia
A symptom, symptoma, indicium, nota
Symptomatic,   Symptomatical, symptomaticus
A synagogue, synagoga
Synchronism, synchronismus
A syncope (swooning), deliquium, animi defectio
A syncope, syncopa, concisio
A syndic, syndicus
A synod, synodus, conventus
Synodal, synodalis, synodicus
A synonym, vox synonyma
Synonymous, similis significationis, synonymus
A synopsis, synopsis
A syntax, syntaxis, verborum structura
A syringe, syrinx, fistula
To syringe, per syringem injicere
Syringed, per syringem injectus
Syrup, syrupus
A system, systema, corpus
Systematical, ad systema pertinens   [tema
Systematically, secundum systema

T.

Tabby, textum sericum undulatum
A tabby-cat, feles *or* felis maculosa
A taber, tympanum minus
A taberer, tympanista
A tabernacle, tabernaculum
Tabid, tabidus, emaciatus
A table, mensa, tabula
Table-beer, cerevisia cibaria; (cloth), mappa; (discourse), fabulæ convivales
Tables, abacus tesserarius
To table (*or* board), in convictum aliquem pacto pretio admittere
To play at tables, talis ludere
A table (in a book), syllabus, index; (for gaming), tabula lusoria; (man), latro
A tabler, convictor quotidianus
A tabling together, convictus
Tabular, tabularis
Tacit, tacitus
Tacitly, tacitè
Taciturnity, silentium
A tack (nail), clavulus; (wind), ventus obliquè flans
To tack (join), conjungo, assuo;

[132]

(up), affigo; (about, as a sailing vessel), cursum obliquare; (about, in opinion, &c.), consilia mutare
Tacking together, assuens
Tackle, *or* tackling, instruments; (for ships), armamenta navium
Tactics, tactica
Tactile, tactilis
A tad-pole, gyrinus
A tag (young sheep), ovicula; (of a lace), bracteola
To tag (a lace), bracteolam inserere; (after), ponè sequi
Tag-rag, fæx populi
A tail, cauda; (of a garment), vestis tractus; (*or* hindermost part), postrema pars; (piece), ornamentum ad finem appositum   [actum
Tailage, tributum veritim exTailed, caudatus
A tailor, vestiarius, sartor
A taint (infection), contagium; (blemish), macula, labes; (crime), accusatio
To taint (*act.*), corrumpo, inficio; (*neut.*), putresco; (accuse), accuso, evinco
Tainted, infectus; (of a crime), accusatus, convictus
Taintless, purus, contagionis expers
To take, capio, accipio, recipio, sumo; (succeed), succedo, prosperè evenire; (understand), intelligo, apprehendo; (by the hand), dextrâ conjungere, manu prehendere; (about), amplector; (a ditch), fossam transire; (after), imitor; (after a father), patrisso; (the air), deambulo, apricor; (air), evulgor, palam enunciari; (alarm), perturbor, excitor; (aside), sevoco; (asunder), separo, sejungo; (away, *or* clear the table), fercula de mensâ tollere; (away by force), spolio, abripio
A taker of advice, deliberator; (away), raptor, direptor, spoliator
A taking, assumptio; (of advice), deliberatio; (away), ademptio, direptio, spoliatio; (back again), resumptio; (before), anticipatio, præoccupatio; (hold of), prehensio; (to), assumptio; (of work by the great), operis redemptio
Taking upon himself, ad se recipiens
A talbot, vertagus
A tale, fabula, narratio; (false), figmentum; (of a tub), anilis fabula, Siculæ gerræ
The tale of money, sheep, &c., recensio, numerus
A tale-bearer, susurro, gerro
A teller of merry tales, congerro
To tell tales, confabulor, fabulas narrare; (lie), mentior
A talent, talentum; (endowment), dos, facultas
Of good talents, magni judicii; (of mean talents), obtusi ingenii
A talisman, imaguncula magica
Talk (mineral), talcum; (discourse), colloquium, confabulatio, sermo
Idle talk, nugæ, gerræ
Foolish talk, stultiloquentia
To talk, confabulor, colloquor;

(at random), figmenta cerebri evomere; (backwards and forwards), perplexè loqui; (of abroad), vulgo, divulgo; (idly), nugas dicere; (softly), susurro, mussito; (to), alloquor; (with), cum aliquo conferre; (to no purpose), incassùm loqui
Talkative, loquax; (fellow), loquaculus, locutuleius
Talkativeness, garrulitas
Having talked, locutus, confabulatus
A great talker, verbosus
An idle talker, gerro
Talking, loquax, garrulus
A talking (together), confabulatio; (much), garrulitas; (to one's self), soliloquium
Tall, procerus, altus, celsus
Tallage, vectigal
Tallness, proceritas
Tallow, sebum; (chandler), candelarum sebacearum venditor
To tallow, sebo, sevo
Of tallow, sebaceus
Tallowish, sebosus
A tally, tessera, talea
To tally (*or* mark on a tally), tesseris numerum notare; (*or* agree with), convenio, quadro
The talmud, liber ritualis Rabbinorum
A talon, unguis
A tamarind, tamarindus
A tamarisk, myrica
Tame, mansuetus, mitis, lenis
To tame, mansuefacio, domo
To grow tame, mansuesco, mitesco
Tameable, domabilis
Tamely, mansuetè, lenitèr
Tameness, mansuetudo
A tamer, domitor, domitrix
A taming, domitus
To tamper, solicitò; (with a disease), imperitè curationem morbi tentare
A tampering with, solicitatio
Tan, cortex ad coria inficienda adhibitus
To tan (leather), corium cortice inficere; (sunburn), sole adurere
A tanpit, fovea ad coria depsenda
Tanned leather, corium depstum; (sunburnt), sole adustus
A tang, sapor ingratus
A tangent, tangens
Tangibility, qualitas tactilis
Tangible, tangibilis, tactilis
To tangle, implico, irretio
A taukard, cantharus, cista
A tanner, coriarius
Tansy, tanacetum
Tantalism, spes vana, *or* decepta
To tantalize, vanâ spe allicere
Tantamount, æquivalens
A tap, sipho, epistomium; (blow), ictus levis
To tap, bolium relinere; (give a tap), leviter percutere; (the belly), humorem epistomio ventri inserto elicere
Tape, vitta ex filo contexta
A taper, cereus
Taper (*adj.*), pyramidatus
Tapestry, tapes, aulæa
Tapestry-maker, phrygio
A tap-house, cerevisiarium
A tapster, caupo cerevisiarius
Tar, pix liquida
To tar, pice liquidâ oblinere
Tardily, tardè, pigrè, lentè
Tardity, tarditas, mora

TAX — TEL — TEN

Tardy (slow), tardus, piger, lentus; (guilty), sons, nocens
To be tardy, pecco, erro
Tare, involucri pondus
Tares, vicia, zizanium
A target, clypeus, scutum; (round), parma; (short), pelta, ancile
To tarnish, infusco; (be tarnished), infuscor, nitorem perdere; (the reputation), famam lædere
A tarpauling, pannus cannabinus pice liquidâ illitus; (sailor), merus nauta
Tarras, cæmentum intritum
Tarried, moratus, cunctatus; (for), expectatus
A tarrier, morator, cessator
To tarry, maneo, moror; (for), expecto, opperior; (all night), pernocto; (behind), tergiversor
To make to tarry, sisto
Tarrying for, expectans, præstolans; (all night), pernox
A tarrying, cunctatio, mora; (for), expectatio; (all night), pernoctatio
Tart (sharp), acidus, acerbus, acer, austerus, acidulus, mordax
To grow tart, acesco
A tart, scriblita; (maker), scriblitarius
Tartly, acritèr, acerbè, austerè
Tartness, acerbitas, acor
Tartar, vini aridi fæx, tartarum
A task, pensum
To task, pensum injungere
A tasking, pensi injunctio
A taskmaster, exactor operis
A tassel, ornamentum pendulum
A taste (or tasting), gustus, gustatus; (in things), sapor
Without taste, insipidus, insulsus
To taste (lightly), libo, delibo, gusto; (beforehand), prægusto, prælibo; (have a taste of), sapio
A taster (cup), gustatorium
A tasting, gustatio
Tasteless, insipidus, insulsus
A tatter, pannus laceratus
Tattle, gerræ, nugæ; (basket), loquax, dicaculus
To tattle, garrio, blatero
A tattler, garrulus, loquax, nugax
A tattling, loquacitas
A tavern, taberna vinaria; (man), tabernarius
Of a tavern, tabernarius
A taunt, dicterium, convicium; (bitter), sarcasmus
To taunt, calumnior, convicior
A taunter, conviciator
Taunting, convicians, mordax
A taunting, exprobratio
Tauntingly, per deridiculum
Tautology, repetitio, iteratio
To taw, depso, macero
Tawdriness, ornatus affectatus
Tawdry, affectatus
Tawdry dress, vestitûs splendor affectatus
Tawny, fuscus, fulvus
A tax, vectigal, census; (upon land), agrorum tributa
To tax, taxo, censeo; (costs), litem æstimare; (blame), culpo, accuso, criminor, reprehendo, redarguo
Taxable, vectigalis
A taxation, or taxing, taxatio

[132]

A taxing (blaming), accusatio
A taxer, taxator
A tax-gatherer, tributi exactor
Tea, thea
To teach, doceo, instituo, erudio; (boys), pueros literis imbuere
Teachable, docilis, aptus
A teacher, doctor, præceptor, magister, præmonstrator
Teaching, docens
A teaching, institutio
A teal, querquedula
A team, rheda
A tear, lachryma; (rent), fissura, scissura
Worthy of tears, deflendus, lugubris
Ready to shed tears, lachrymabundus; (full of tears), lachrymosus
To shed tears, lachrymo, fleo
Shedding tears, lachrymans, flens
A shedding of tears, lachrymatio
To tear (in pieces), lacero, scindo, discindo, dilacero, lanio; (be torn), laceror; (or rant along), debacchor, tumultuor
A tearer, lacerator
A tearing, laceratio, dilaceratio
Tearing, lacerans; (loud, or strong), stentoreus; (or very fine), magnificus, splendidus
To tease (vex), vexo, crucio, torqueo; (wool), lanam carminare
A teasing, sollicitatio assidua
A teaser (&c.), sex denarii
A teat (breast), mamma, uber; (nipple), papilla
To tease. See Toose
Techiness, iracundia, protervitas
Technical, technicus, artificialis; (word), vocabulum arti proprium
Techy, iracundus, morosus
Tedded, ordinibus positus
A tedder, retinaculum
Tedious (lasting, long), diuturnus, longus; (slow), tardus, lentus; (irksome), gravis, molestus
Tediously, diutinè, longè, tardè, lentè, molestè, gravitèr
Tediousness, longitudo, tarditas, tædium, molestia
To teem, abundo, effundo
Teeming, fœcundus, sæpe prægnans
Teeth, dentes; (cheek), maxillares dentes; (eye), dentes canini; (fore), dentes incisores; (gag), dentes exerti
To breed teeth, dentio
Breeding teeth, dentiens
A breeding of teeth, dentitio
Having teeth, dentatus
Breaking the teeth, denti frangibulus
Teeth-powder, dentifricium
A tegument, tegumentum
A teint, or tint, color
A telescope, telescopium
To tell, dico, nuncio, narro, significo; (or blaze abroad), divulgo, publico; (again), recito, repeto; (before), prædico; (or acquaint one with), narro, indico, nuncio; (or admonish of), moneo, admoneo; (or reckon up), numero, computo; (relate), memoro, enarro, refero
A telltale, delator, obtrectator
A teller, narrator; (of stories), fabulator; (of fortunes), fatidicus; (numberer), numerator

A telling, narratio; (reckoning), numeratio, computatio
Temerarious, temerarius
Temerity, temeritas
Temper (constitution of body), constitutio, corporis temperies; (humour, nature), ingenium, animus, indoles; (moderation), moderatio, æquitas
Of an agreeable temper, facetus
Of a genteel temper, liberalis ingenii [cupidus
Of an aspiring temper, imperii
An even temper, animus æquus; (an uneven temper), animus levis
Agreeableness of temper, festivitas; (disagreeableness), morositas
The temper of steel, temperatura
To temper (the passions), animum moderari; (mingle), misceo, commisceo; (iron, &c.), tempero
A temperament (expedient), modus, ratio; (or constitution of body), constitutio, or temperies corporis
Temperance, moderatio, temperantia
With temperance, temperatè
Temperate, temperatus; (calm), serenus, tranquillus
Temperately, temperantèr, moderatè, modicè, sobriè
Temperateness of weather, cœli temperies æqualis
Temperature, temperamentum
A tempering, admixtio
A tempest, tempestas, procella
Tempestuous, procellosus, turbidus
A temple, templum, ædes sacræ
The temples of the head, tempora
Temporal, temporalis; (unhallowed), secularis, profanus
Temporalities, temporalia
Temporally, ad tempus
Temporary, temporarius
To temporize, tempori succumbere
A temporizer, qui scenæ servit
A temporizing, assentatio
To tempt (try), tento, conor, aggredior; (entice), solicito, pellicio, allicio
A temptation (enticement), tentatio, illecebra; (to anger), irritamentum
A tempter, tentator, allector
The tempter, diabolus
A tempting, illecebra
Tempting, alliciens, pellax
Ten, decem, deni
Of ten, denarius
Ten times, decies
Ten years old, decennis
Ten years' space, decennium
The ten at cards, decas
The ten commandments, decalogus
Tenable, tenendus
Tenfold, decuplus, decemplex
Tenacious, tenax, pertinax
Tenaciously, tenacitèr
Tenaciousness, tenacitas, pertinacia
A tenant, inquilinus
Tenanted, mercede conductus
A tench, tinca
To tend (attend), comitor, curo; (to, or aim at), specto, tendo
A tendency (inclination), propen-

TER

sio, inclinatio; (drift, or design), propositum, consilium
Tender (soft), tener, mollis; (nice, dainty), delicatus; (hearted), misericors, benevolus; (scrupulous), scrupulosus, hesitans, dubitans
Tender-heartedness, misericordia
A tender (guard), custos; (offer), conditio oblata; (small ship), lembus, navigiolum; (waiter), assecla
Made tender, emollitus, mollitus
To make tender, emollio, mollio
To grow tender, teneresco
To tender (or offer), porrigo, offero; (regard), indulgeo, curo; (love, or value), amo, diligo
Tender usage, clementia
A tender of money, pecuniæ repræsentatio
A tendering, oblatio
Tenderly, tenerè, mollitèr
Tenderness, teneritas; (love, kindness), benevolentia, caritas, amor; (indulgence), indulgentia; (scrupulousness), scrupulosa dubitatio
Tending to, spectans
A tending, curatio, cura
A tendon, tendo
A tendril, clavicula; (of coleworts, &c.), cyma
Tendrils, cartilagines minores
Tenebrous, tenebrosus
A tenement, domus, ædes
Tenerity, teneritas
A tenet, dogma, placitum
A tennis-ball, pila lusoria
Tennis-play, pilæ ludus
A tenor, impages, cardo
The tenor (or chief course of a matter), tenor, series; (chief intent, or purpose), propositum; (sense, or meaning), sensus, verborum via; (in music), tenor, sonus subgravis
Tense (gram.), tempus
Tension, tensio
A tent, tentorium; (in a fair), velabrum; (for a wound), linamentum; (camp), castra
A tenter, pannitendium
A tenter-hook, uncus hamus
The tenth, decimus
The tenth time, decimùm
Tenthly, decimò
Tenths, decimæ
Tenuity, tenuitas, gracilitas
A tenure, tenura, jus tenendi
Tepid, tepidus, egelidus
Tepidity, tepor
A terce, triens
To terebrate, terebro, perforo
Terebration, terebratio
Tergiversation, tergiversatio
A term (word, or expression), verbum; (bound, or limit), terminus, limes; (limited time), tempus præstitutum; (condition), conditio, lex; (woman's terms), menses, menstrua; (law-terms), termini [justitium
Space between term and term,
To term (name), voco, nuncupo
A termagant, mulier rixosa
Termed, appellatus, vocatus
To terminate (limit), termino, limito; (in), terminor; (a difference), lites componere, controversiam dirimere
A terminating, or termination (bounding), terminatio; (concluding), conclusio, exitus, finis

[184]

THA

Ternary, ternarius
A terrace-walk, terrenus agger
Terraqueous, ex terrâ et aquâ constans
A terrar, terrarium
Terrene, Terreous, terrenus
Terrestrial, terrestris
Terrible, terribilis, horrendus, dirus, atrox; (in looks), torvus, truculentus; (very), perhorridus
Terribleness, terror, horror
Terribly, terribilitèr, atrocitèr
Terrific, terrens, terrificus
To terrify, terreo, territo
To be terrified, horresco, terreor
Terrified, territus, perterritus
Terrifying, terrens, territans
A territory, territorium, ditio
Terror, terror, formido
Terse, tersus, lautus, lævis
Tertian, tertianus
Tesselated, tessellatus
A test (trial), examen; (witness), testis; (oath), sacramentum quo ejuratur auctoritas pontificia
Testaceous, testaceus
A testament, testamentum
Testamentary, testamentarius
A testator, testator
A tester (6d.), sex denarii; (of a bed), lecti umbella
Testicles, testiculi, testes
Testification, testificatio
A testifier, testificator
To testify, testor, testificor
A testifying, testificatio, testatio
Testimonial, testimonialis
A testimonial, literæ testimoniales
A testimony, testimonium; (of a good conscience), conscientia benè actæ vitæ
To bear testimony, testor
In testimony of respect, causâ officii
Testily, morosè, protervè
Testiness, morositas
Testy, morosus, pervicax
A tether, retinaculum
To tether, compedes injicere
A tetrach, tetrarcha
A tetrarchate, tetrarchia
A tetter, impetigo
To tew, conor, nitor
A text, thema; (words of an author), scriptoris verba genuina
Text-letters, literæ unciales
A texture, textura
Than, ac, atque, quam
To thank, gratias agere
Thankful, gratus
Thankfully, gratè, grato animo
Thankfulness, gratitudo
Thankless, ingratus
Thanks, gratiæ, grates
Thanksgiving, gratiarum actio
Thanksworthy, gratiis dignus
That, pron. ille, is, iste; (who, which), qui; conj. ut, ne, quòd, quò
The same that, ac as, idem ac, atque, et, ut
Seeing that, Since that, cùm, quum, quando, quandoquidem, quia, quoniam, siquidem; (insomuch that), adeò ut, usquè adeò ut; (so that), dum, dummodò, modò, adeò, ut, si, si tantùm
Thatch, culmus, stipula
To thatch, culmis tegere
Thatched, culmis tectus
A thaw, glaciei resolutio

THI

To thaw, regelo; (be thawed), gelor, solvor
A theme, thema, argumentum
A theatre, theatrum
Theatrical, theatricus, theatralis
Theft, furtum, latrocinium
Themselves, se, sese, semet, seipsos, semetipsos, seipsas, semetipsas
Of themselves, sui
They themselves, illi ipsi, illæ ipsæ
Then, tum, tunc, ibi, eodem tempore; (after that), tum, indè, posteà, deindè, exindè; (therefore), ergo, igitur, idcirco
Thence, indè, illinc, isthinc
Theological, theologicus
Theologically, theologorum more
Theology, theologia
A theologist, theologus
A theorbo, testudo
A theorem, theorema
Theorematical, theorematicus
Theory, theoretice, contemplatio
Therapeutics, therapeutice
There, ibi, illic, istic
Thereafter, exindè, deindè; (at), de, or, in illâ re; (by), eò, indè; (fore), idcirco, ita, itaque, ergo, igitur, perindè, proindè, proin, proptereà, eâ proptèr, eâ re; (from), indè, exindè, deindè, ab eo, ex eo
A thesis, thesis, positio
They, ii, illi, isti, eæ, illæ, istæ
Thick (not thin), spissus, densus, crassus; (large), amplus, largus, latus, crassus; (fat), obesus; (muddy), lutosus, cœnosus, fæculentus; (skinned), callosus; (skulled), pingue ingenium; (together), densus, frequens, confertus; (of hearing), surdus
Thick and threefold, catervatim
To thicken, spissesco, crebesco; (make thick), condenso, spisso
A thickening, condensatio
Thickest (closest), confertissimus
A thicket, dumetum
Thickly, densè, spissè, craessè
Thickness, densitas; (of hearing), auditûs gravitas; (frequency), frequentia, crebritas
A chief, fur, lavernio
To thieve, furor, surripio
Thievery, furtum
A thieving, direptio, expilatio
Of thieving, furtificus
Thievish, furtivus
Thievishly, furacitèr
Thievishness, furacitas
The thigh, femur, coxa
A thill, temo
A thimble, digitale
Thin (not thick), rarus, tenuis; (easy to be discovered), pellucidus; (few), infrequens; (lean), macer, macilentus; (light), levis
To grow thin, raresco, macesco
To make thin, rarefacio; (or slender), attenuo, tenuo, abrado; (or lean), emacio; (a garden thin), disraro
A making thin, attenuatio
Thine, tuus
A thing, res, negotium
Any thing, quicquam, quidnam
Things (goods), bona; (clothes, &c.), vestitus, apparatus; (of no value), ineptiæ, nugæ
Above all things, imprimis
To think (believe, suppose, imagine), puto, reor, credo, arbi-

tror, opinor, existimo, censeo; (again), recogito; much of a thing), aliquid ægrè ferre; (of, on, or upon), delibero, contemplor, considero; (beforehand), præmeditor; (light of), parvi pendere; (otherwise), dissentio; (well of), probo, comprobo
Thinking, cogitans, meditans
A thinking, cogitatio, reputatio; (upon), meditatio, deliberatio; (beforehand), præmeditatio
Thinly, tenuitèr, exilitèr
Thinness, raritas, raritudo
The third, tertius
A third, triens
Of a third, tertianus
Thirdly, tertiò, tertiùm
To thirl (pierce), penetro, perforo
Thirst, sitis; (of riches, honour, &c.), divitiarum, honorum, &c., sitis
To thirst, sitio
To be thirsted after, sitior
Thirstily, sitientèr
Thirsty, sitiens, aridus
Very thirsty, siti ferè enectus
Blood-thirsty, sanguinarius
Thirteen, tredecim
The thirteenth, decimus tertius
Thirteen times, tredeciès
Thirty, triginta, triceni
Of thirty, tricenarius
Thirty times, triciès, ter deciès
The thirtieth, tricesimus
This, hic, iste
To this place, hucusquè
In this place, hic
From this place, hinc
By this way, hac [pus
A thistle, carduus; (down), pap-
Thistly, carduis obductus
Thither, eò, illò, illuc, istuc
Thitherto, eatenùs
Thitherward, illorsum
A thong, lorum, corrigia
Of thongs, loreus
A thorn, spina; (black), prunus sylvestris; (white), oxyacantha
Bearing thorns, spinifer
Thorny, spinosus, spineus
A place where thorns grow, spinetum
A thornback, raia clavata
Thorough, per
A thoroughfare, via pervia
Thoroughpaced, perfectus
Those, illi, isti
Thou, tu, ipse
Though, ut, etsi, licet, tametsi, etamsi, quanquam, quamvis; (nevertheless), tamen, veruntamen, nihilominus
As though, velut, veluti, perindè quasi, tanquam, tanquàm si
Thought (a thinking upon), cogitatio, meditatio
A thought (thing thought on), cogitatum; (care, or concern), cura, solicitudo, anxietas; (contrivance), inventio, excogitatio; (aim, or design), propositum, conatus, consilium
To take thought for, curo, provideo, consulo; (be concerned at), dolore affici
Thoughtful, solicitus, anxius; (wary, considerate), consideratus, providus, consultus, prudens, circumspectus
To be thoughtful about (consider), contemplor, speculor, considero, perpendo; (for, or troubled about), angor, perturbor, solicitor

Thoughtfully, cautè, consultè, prudentèr; (anxiously), anxiè, solicitè
Thoughtfulness,cautio, solicitudo, circumspectio
Thoughtless, inconsideratus, imprudens, temerarius, præceps
Thoughtlessness, inconsiderantia
A thousand, mille, millia
Two thousand, duo millia, bis mille
Of a thousand, milliarius
A thousand times, milliès
The thousandth, millesimus
Thrall, or thraldom, servitus, servitium
Thread, filum; (in cloth, or silk), licium; (for weaving), linum, stamen
To thread, filum inserere in foramen acûs
Thread by thread, filatim
Threadbare, tritus, detritus
The thread of a discourse, tenor
A threat, minatio, minæ
To threaten, minor, comminor
Threatening, minax, minitans
A threatening, comminatio
Threateningly, minacitèr
Three, tres, trini, terni
The three (at cards, &c.), triss
Of three, trinus, ternarius
Three divers ways, trifariàm
In three parts, tripartitus
Threefold, triplex, triplus
To make threefold, triplico
Three-cornered, triangularis
Three days' space, triduum
Having three colours, tricolor
Three feet long, tripedalis
Three-headed, triceps; (horned), tricornis; (shaped), triformis
Three nights' space, trinoctium
Of three pounds' weight, trilibris
Three-pointed, tricuspis
Having three teeth, tridens
Three years' space, triennium
Three years old, trimus, trimulus
Three-forked, trifurcus
Threescore, sexaginta
Of threescore, sexagenarius
Threescore times, sexagiès
Threescore and ten, septuaginta
Three hundred, trecenti
Three hundred times, trecentiès
To thresh (corn), flagello, tribulo; (beat), cædo
A thresher, triturator
A threshing, tritura; (floor), area trituræ accommodata
A threshold, limen
Thrice, ter
Thrice as much, triplò, triplus
Thrift, frugalitas, parsimonia
Thriftily, frugalitèr, parcè
Thriftiness, parsimonia
Thrifty, frugalis, parcus, frugi; (servant), servus bonæ frugi
To thrill (drill), terebro
To thrive (prosper), vigeo, valeo, floreo, ditesco; (in flesh), pinguesco
A thriving in the world, prosperitas; (in flesh), corporis auctus
Thrivingly, prosperè, felicitèr
The throat, guttur, gula, jugulum
Of the throat, gutturalis
Throat-cut, jugulatus
To throb, palpito, mico, subsilio
A throbbing, palpitatio
A throne, solium, thronus, regia dignitas, summa potestas
To throng (or crowd), premo; (to a place), catervatim confluere

A throng, turba, frequentia
Thronged, pressus, coarctatus
To throttle, strangulo, ango; (to death), laqueo interimere
Throttled, strangulatus, præfocatus
A throttling, strangulatio
Through, a, ex, per, propter
Through and through, penitùs, omninò, prorsùs
Throughout, per totum
A throw (or cast), jactus
To throw (cast, or fling), jacto, jacio, mitto, conjicio
A thrower, jaculator; (down), demolitor
A throwing, jactus, jactatus; (at), petitio; (away), abjectio; (of a dart), jaculatio; (down), dejectio, deturbatio, demolitio, præcipitatio; (from a horse), ab equo excussio; (in), injectio; (off), abjectio; (out), ejectio, repudiatio; (over, or beyond), trajectus
To be thrown out (in an election), rejicior, suffragiis excludi; (or distanced), è stadio excludi
Throws, Throes, labores
To thrum, imperitè pulsare
A thrush (bird), turdus
The thrush (di-ease), aphthæ
A thrust, impetus, ictus
To thrust, impello, trudo; (with a sword), ferro aliquem petere; (against), obdo; (back), repello; (down), detrudo, deturbo; (forward), propello; (forward, or make haste), festino, accelero; (into), ingero, intrudo; (out), expello, excludo, ejicio, abigo, arceo; (through), perfodio, transfigo
A thruster, impulsor
A thrusting back, repulsio; (forward), impulsio; (together), compressio
A thumb, pollex
Of the thumb, pollicaris
A thumbstall, digitale
To thumb, pollice terere
A thump, ictus [pulso
To thump, tundo, obtundo; (at),
A thumper, pulsator
A thumping, pulsatio, pulsus
Thunder, tonitru; (struck), sideratus, attonitus, de cœlo tactus
To thunder, fulmino, tono; (again), retono; (greatly), detono; (down upon), superintono
A thunder-clap, fragor cœli; (bolt), fulmen
Of thunder, fulmineus
A thunderer, fulminator
A thundering, fulminatio
Thundering (from above), altitonans; (voice), vox stentorea
Thursday, dies Jovis
Thus, ità, hoc modo, sic, ad hunc modum; (far), hactenùs, huc usquè; (much), tantùm
A thwack, ictus, verber
To thwack, verbero, fustigo
A thwacking, verberatio
Thwart, transversus, obliquus
To thwart, contradico, adversor
Thwarting, contrarius, repugnans
A thwarting, contradictio
Thy, tuus
Thyme, thymum
Belonging to thyme, thyminus
Full of thyme, thymosus
To tice, allicio
A tick (insect), ricinus; (for a

TIM — TIP — TOL

bed), culcitra; (small pulsation), ictus levis; (trust), fides
A ticket, tessera
To tickle, titillo; (the fancy), adulor
A tickling, titillatio
Ticklish, titillationis impatiens; (captious), captiosus, morosus; (nice), lubricus, difficilis; (dangerous), periculosus
Tid (dainty), delicatulus
Tidbits, dapes opimæ
To tiddle, nimis indulgere
The tide, æstus maris; (ebb of), refluxus maris; (spring), eluvies; (neap), æstus mariæ decrescens
With the tide, secundo flumine
Against tide, adverso flumine
Tide (time), tempus, tempestas
Tidings, nuncius, rumor, fama
To bring tidings, nuncio
A bringer of tidings, nuncius
A bringing of tidings, nunciatio
Tidy, concinnus, solers, habilis
A tie, nexus, vinculum
To tie (or bind), alligo, ligo, obligo, vincio, constringo, obstringo; (about), circumligo, circumvincio; (back), revincio; (before), præligo, prævincio; (together), copulo; (to), astringo; (with a knot), in nodum cogere
To be tied (in bed), constringor; (by the laws), legibus impediri
A tiff (quarrel), contentio, lis, jurgium, rixa; (of drink), modicum
A tiger, tigris; (cruel person), homo crudelis
Of a tiger, tigrinus
A tigress, tigris femina
Tight (neat), nitidus, comptus, belus, concinnus, scitus; (fast), arctus, strictus, constrictus; (safe), tutus, salvus; (sound), sanus, validus
Tightly, nitidè, arctè
A tile, tegula
A gutter-tile, imbrex
Of a tile, tegularis
To tile, tegulis obducere
A tiler, tegularum structor
The tiling, tegulum, tegillum
Till, dum, donec, anteà quàm, ante quam, antea, nisi, quoàd
A till, loculus
To till, colo, subigere agrum
Tillage, agricultura
A tiller (of the ground), agricola; (of a bow), arcûs cornu; (of a boat), cymbæ gubernaculum, or clavus
A tilting, cultus aratio
A tilt, decursio
A tilt-cloth, tentorium
A tilt-yard, decursionis equestris spatium
To tilt a barrel, cadum inclinare
The tilting of a barrel, cadi inclinatio
Timber, materia, lignum; (work), materiatura; (merchant), materiarius; (yard), fabrica materiaria
Of timber, materiarius
To timber, ligno construere
Well-timbered, benè structus
A timbrel, tympanum; (player), tympani pulsator
Time, tempus; (leisure), otium, tempus vacivum
For a time, ad tempus
Leisure-times, horæ subsecivæ
[135]

A long time, diû, jamdudùm
In due time, tempestivus
Out of time, intempestivus
Time out of mind, multis ante seculis
About that time, per id tempus
About this time, in præsenti, jam, nunc; (another time), alias, alio tempore; (that time), eo tempore, tunc; (any time), unquàm; (no time), nunquàm; (what time), quandò; (what time soever), quandocunquè
If at any time, siquandò, sicubi
For that time, ut temporibus illis
From this time, in futurum, dehinc
In due time, tempestivè, temporè
In a short time, brevi tempore, brevì
In a year's time, vertente anno
Of late time, nupèr
In time past, olìm, quondàm; (time to come), deindè, dehinc; (the mean time), interim, intereà; (the day-time), interdiû, de die
After a long time, post diem longum
Before this time, antehàc; (that time), anteà, anteà
Of time, temporalis
Of old time, antiquitùs
From the beginning of time, ab ævo, post homines natos
To that time, eatenûs
To time well, tempestivè agere
Ill-timed, intempestivus
Well-timed, tempestivus
Three times, ter; (four), quater (many), sæpè, sæpenumerò
At all times, semper
How many times soever, quotiescunquè
Timely, opportunus, tempestivus; adv. tempestivè
Time-serving, tempori cedens
Timid, timidus, pavidus
Timidity, timiditas, timor
Timorous, timidus, pavidus
Timorously, timidè, pavidè
Timorousness, timor, metus
Tin, stannum, plumbum album
Of tin, stanneus
A tinman, stanneorum instrumentorum fabricator
Tin piga, bismuthum
To tin, stanno obducere
A tinct, tinctus, color
A tincture, tinctura; (infusion), infusio; (impression on the mind), mentis sensus
To tincture, imbuo, inficio
Tinder, igniarium; (box), pyxidula igniarium continens
To tingle, or tinkle, tinneo, resono
Tinkling, resonans, tinniens, tinnulus
A tinker, sartor circumforaneus vasorum æreorum
A tinning, stanni obductio
Tinsel, pannus metallo aurei coloris contextus; (metaph.), splendor falsus
Tiny (small), perpusillus
A tip (point), apex; (of the nose), nasi extremitas
To tip (with silver), argento circumcludere ab labris; (with iron), ferro præmunire; (or throw down), dejicio, sterno; (one the wink), alicui annuere; (off, or die), morior

A tippet, fascia
To tipple, potito, pergræcor
A tippler, bibax, ebriosus
A tippling house, cauponula
A tippling, comessatio
A tipstaff (officer), lictor, accensus; (instrument), accensi baculus
Tipsy, temulentus, ebrius
A tire (rank), series, ordo
Tires for women, capilli asciti
A tirewoman, ornatrix
To tire, orno, adorno; (weary), fatigo, lasso, delasso; (be tired), fatigor, defatiscor
Tiresome, fatigans, laboriosus
Tiresomeness, fatigatio, labor
A tiring, defatigatio
A tit (little horse), mannus, equulus; (titmouse), parus
Tithe, decimæ
To tithe, decimò
Titheable, decimis obnoxius
Tithed, decimatus
A tither, decimator
A tithing, decimatio; (or hundred), tithinga, decenria; (man), decurio, decennarius
To titillate, titillo
Titillation, titillatio
A title (or inscription), titulus, inscriptio, epigraphe; (name), nomen, appellatio; (of honour), dignitatis titulus; (right), jus, vindicatio; (writings, deeds, &c.), literæ testantes, instrumenta
To title, appello, inscribo
To titter (laugh), cachinno; (totter), vacillo, tremo
A tittle, punctum
Tittletattle, dicacitas, garrulitas
A tittletattle, garrulus
To tittletattle, garrio
Titular, titularis, nomine
To, ad, adversum, apud, cum, de, erga, ex, præ, pro, in
To and fro, huc illuc
To both places, utroque
To no purpose, frustrà, incassùm
To which end, quamobrèm
To wit, nempè, scilicèt
To be, esse
To be short, brevitèr
A toad, bufo, rubeta; (stool), fungus; (fish), rana piscatrix
A toast, tosti panis segmen, vipa
A toast (or health), propinatio
To toast, torreo, propino
Tobacco, tabacum, nicotiana
A tobacconist, tabaci venditor
A tobacco-pipe, ambulus, (box), pyxidula tabaci
A tod, viginti octo libræ
A toe, digitus pedes; (great), pedis pollex; (little), pedis digitus minimus
A toft, toftum; (owner of a toft), toftumannus
Together (at the same time, or place), simùl, unà; (without intermission), continenter, per
Together, adj. continuus
Toil, labor; (toils, or nets), plagæ, indagines
To toil, molior, laboro, sudo
Toiling, Toilsome, laboriosus
A toiling, elaboratio
A token, signum, pignus, omen, argumentum, nota, munus
That may be told (numbered), numerabilis; (may not be told), innumerabilis; (or, not

TOP — TOU — TRA

be expressed), inexplicabilis, inenarrabilis
Tolerable, tolerabilis, mediocris
Tolerably, tolerabiliter, mediocriter
Tolerance, toleratio
To tolerate, tolero, indulgeo, fero
A tolerating, or toleration, toleratio, indulgentia, perpessio
Toll, vectigal, tributum ; (for grinding), emolumentum
To take toll, vectigal exigere
A tollbooth, telonium
A toll-gatherer, exactor
To toll (a bell), leviter pulsare
A tolling, levis pulsatio
A tolsey (toibooth), telonium
A tomb, sepulchrum ; (stone), lapis sepulchralis, cippus
A tome, tomus, volumen
A tone, tonus, sonus
Tongs, forceps
A tongue, lingua; (language), lingua, sermo; (pad), loquax, garrulus
At the tongue's end, in labris natare
To cut out a tongue, elinguo
To hold the tongue, taceo, sileo
Tongue-tied, à loquendo impeditus linguæ vinculo
All tongue, vox et præterea nihil
Tongued, linguâ præditus
One doubled-tongued, veterator
Evil-tongued, maledicus
Smooth-tongued, blandiloquus
Tonnage, ex singulis doliis mercium vectigal
Too (also), etiam, quoque ; (much), nimis, nimiùm, plùs justo, plùs æquo
Too, etiam
I took, cepi, accepi
A tool (instrument), instrumentum; (of iron), ferramentum; (person employed), minister
All sorts of tools, arma
A tooth, dens ; (drawer), qui dentes extrahit ; (ache), dolor, dentium, odontalgia; (powder), dentifricium
Tooth and nail, totis viribus
Toothed, dentatus, denticulatus
Toothless, edentulus
Toothsome, gustui suavis, or gratus
The top (of a thing), apex, culmen, cacumen; (of a house), fastigium tecti; (of a hill), jugum collis; (of a pillar), capitulum
A top, trochus, turbo
To top (lop), obtrunco; (snuff), mungo, emungo; (excel), supero, superemineo
A topaz, topazius
To tope, potito, perpoto
A toper, bibax
Topful, ad summum impletus
Topheavy, prægravis, temulentus
Tophaceous, tophaceus
A toping, perpotatio
A topknot, vitta capitis
The topmast, carchesium
Topped, obtruncatus, emunctus
Sharp-topped, cacuminatus
A topping, obtruncatio; (tuft), crista, apex
Topping, eximius, egregius, dives
A topic, argumentum
Topical, topicus
Topically, topicè
Topics, topica
Topography, topographia
A topsail, thoracium
[137]

Topsy-turvy, inverso ordine
A torch, fax, lampas; (bearer), lychnuchus; (maker), lychnopœus
Torment, tormentum, cruciatus
To torment, crucio, excrucio, vexo, affligo, torqueo
A tormentor, tortor, cruciator, afflictor; (with importunity), vexator
A tormenting, cruciatus
Torpid, torpidus, stupidus
Torpidness, Torpor, torpor
A torrent, torrens, flumen
Torrid, torridus, fervidus
Torsion, torsio
Tort (injury), injuria
Tortile, Tortive, tortilis, tortivus
A tortoise, testudo
Tortuous, tortuosus
Torture (a writhing), tortura ; (rack), tormenta ; (pain), tormentum, cruciamentum, cruciatus
To torture (vex), vexo; (rack), crucio, equuleo torquere
A torturer, tortor, carnifex
A torturing, cruciatus
To toss wool, lanam carpere
A toss, jactus
A tosspot, potator strenuus
To toss, jacto, agito, mitto, jacio, conjicio ; (aside), abjicio ; (back), rejicio; (before), objicio; (down), dejicio; (in), injicio; (over), trajicio; (out), ejicio; (up, as the sea), expuo
A tossing, jactatio, agitatio
Total, totalis, totus, integer
Torally, omnino, penitùs
T'other, alter
To totter, vacillo, titubo; (waver), dubito, hæsito
A tottering, titubatio, dubitatio; (house), ædes ruinosæ
Totteringly, titubanter
Tottery, vacillans, instabilis
A touch (or touching), tactus, contactus, tactio ; (essay, or trial), experimentum, periculum, molimen; (witty expression), dicterium
To touch, tango, contingo, attingo ; (one another), inter se contingere; (upon a subject), leviter tangere; (exactly), acu tangere; (move, or effect), moveo, commoveo, afficio; (to the quick), ad vivum resecare; (at a port), appelli ad portum; (or handle), tracto, attracto
To be touched (in the brain), mente capi
The touchhole, conceptaculum
A touchstone, lapis Lydius
Touchwood, lignum cariosum
Touchable, tangibilis, tactilis
A touching, tactio; (handling), tractatio, tractatus
Touching (another), contiguus ; (affecting), commovens, movens
Touching (concerning), de, quod ad, quod attinet ad
Touchy, morosus, asper, tetricus
Touch (clammy), lentus, tenax ; (hard), durus; (difficult), difficilis, arduus, gravis ; (stout), strenuus, fortis
Toughly, lentè, tenaciter, strenuè, fortiter, animosè
Toughness, lentor, tenacitas ; (hardness), duritia ; (difficulty), difficultas ; (stoutness), fortitudo, magnanimitas

A tour (or going about), circuitus, lustratio
Tournaments, certamina equestria
Tow, stupa, stuppa
Of tow, stupeus, stuppeus
To tow, pertraho, duco
Toward, or towards, à, ad, adversus, contra, ergà, in, obviàm, sub, versus
Towards (some place), aliquoversùm ; (what place), quorsùm, quorsùs, quoquò ; (what place soever), quaquaversum ; (the right hand), dextrorsùm, ad dextram; (the left hand), sinistrorsùm, ad sinistram
Towardly, docilis, dexter, promptus
Towardliness, indoles, docilis
A towel, mantile, mappa
A tower, turris, arx
To tower, altè volare
Like a tower, turritus
Towering, elatus, ambitiosus
A town, oppidum ; (corporate), municipium; (village), pagus, vicus; (house), curia municipalis; ('s man), oppidanus
Of a town-corporate, municipalis
From town to town, oppidatim
A town-talk, fabula, in omni ore
To tows, turbo, perturbo; (wool), lanam carpere
Towzed, turbatus, perturbatus
Towzing, turbans, perturbans
A toy, or toys (silly things), nugæ, ineptiæ; (to play with), crepundia; (little curiosities), minutiæ
A toyman, minutiarium venditor
To toy, nugor, ineptio; (amorously), palpo, blandior
A toyer, nugator
Toying, nugans, ineptiens, lasciviens, blandus
A trace, vestigium
The traces, retinacula
To trace, indago, vestigo
Traced, indagatus
Having traced, vestigia secutus
A tracer, indagator
A tracing, indagatio
A track, vestigium, orbita, nota, semita
To track, vestigiis consequi
Tract (extent), tractus ; (of land), tractus terræ ; (treatise), tractatus, diatriba
In tract of time, progressu temporis
Tractable, mansuetus, mitis, lenis, docilis
To grow tractable, mitesco
To make tractable, domo
Made tractable, domitus
Tractableness, tractabilitas, mansuetudo, docilitas
Tractably, mansuetè, leniter
A tractate, tractatus
Tractile, tractilis, ductilis
Traction, tractus, actus trahendi
A trade, ars, quæstus; (way of life), ratio, via, modus, vitæ institutio
To trade, negotior, mercor ; (in every thing), omnia venalia habere
A trader, or tradesman, negotiator, mercator; (by retail), propola
A trading, commercium, negotiatio
Tradition, traditio
Traditional, ore traditus

Traditionally, ore tenus, memoritèr
To traduce, calumnior, infamo
Traduced, defamatus, sugillatus
A traducer, calumniator
Traducing, calumniana
A traducing, calumnia
Traffic, commercium
To traffic, negotior, mercor
A trafficker, negotiator
A trafficking, negotiatio
A tragedian (actor), tragœdus; (writer), tragicus poëta
A tragedy, tragœdia; (bad end), infelix exitus
Tragical, tragicus
Tragically, tragicè, infelicitèr
A traject, trajectus
To trail, traho, verro; (back), retrò legere; (a pike), pilum trahere
Trailing, trahens, verrens
A train (retinue), comitatus; (of a gown), vestis tractus; (or order of things), series; (baggage of an army), impedimenta
Train-oil, oleum cetaceum
Trainbands, militia
To train, educo, instituo, erudio, instruo; (dispose), dispono, formo
A trainer up, educator, educatrix
A training up, disciplina, educatio
A trait, ductus
A traitor, traditor, proditor
Traitorous, perfidus, infidus
Traitorously, perfidiosè
A trammel, tragula; (for a pot-hanger), cremaster
To trample upon, calco, conculco
A trampling upon, conculcatio
A trampling noise, pedum strepitus
A trance, ecstasis, mentis emotio
To be in a trance, animo percilli
Tranquil, tranquillus, placidus
Tranquillity, tranquillitas; (of mind), animus sedatus, or placidus
To transact (dispatch, or manage), transigo, perago, perficio, expedio; (article, or agree), paciscor, pactionem inire
Transacting, peragens, expediens
A transaction, res, negotium, res gesta; (agreement), pactum, stipulatio, fœdus
A transactor, administrator, curator
To transcend (excel), supero, excello
Transcendency, excellentia
Transcendent, transcendens
Transcendently, excellentèr, præclarè   [bo
To transcribe, transcribo, exscribo
A transcriber, exscriptor
A transcribing, transcriptio
A transcript, exscriptum
A transfer, translatio
To transfer, transfero, traduco
Transferring, transferens
Transfiguration, transfiguratio
To transfigure, transformo
To transfix, transfigo, trajicio
To transform, transformo
A transformation, formæ mutatio
To be transformed, transformor
To transfuse, transfundo
Transfusion, transfusio
To transgress, transgredior; (or trespass against), pecco, delinquo, violo, rumpo
[138]

A transgression, delictum, peccatum, culpa, violatio
A transgressor, legis violator
Transient, Transitory, transitorius; (frail, or lasting a short time), fragilis, perbrevis, fluxus, caducus
Transiently, obitèr, præteriens
A transit, transitus
A transition, transitio, transitus
Transitive, transitivus
To translate, transfero, verto
Translated, translatus, versus
A translation, translatio, versio
A translator, interpres; (cobler) cerdo; (translucid), pellucidus
Transmarine, transmarinus
To transmigrate, transmigro
A transmigration, demigratio; (of souls), metempsychosis
Transmission, transmissio
To transmit (send over), transmitto; (to memory), memoriæ prodere
Transmitting, transmittens
To transmogrify, transformo
Transmutation, transmutatio; (of metals) metallorum conversio
To transmute, immuto, commuto
A transom, transtrum
Transparency, pelluciditas
Transparent, translucens, pellucidus
To be transparent, pelluceo
Transpiration, or a transpiring, transpiratio, spiratio
To transpire, perspiro
To transplant, transfero; (people), coloniam deducere
A transplanter, translator
A transplanting, translatio
A transport (violent passion), effrenati animi motus; (of anger), iracundiæ furens impetus; (of joy), nimia lætitia
Transportation, transportatio
To transport, transporto, exporto, eveho; (malefactors), in servitutem damnatos deportare
To transpose, transpono; (words in printing), verba trajicere
A transposing, or transposition, transpositio, trajectio (tiatio
Transubstantiation, transubstan-
Transverse, transversus, obliquus
Transversely, transversè, obliquè
A trap, laqueus, decipulum
A trap-door, ostium cadens
To trap, illaqueo, irretio
To trape, curaito, discurao
Trappings, phaleræ
Trash, frivola, merces viles
Travail, labor, opera; (in child-bearing), partus, puerperium
To travail with child, parturio
To travel (labour), laboro; (go a journey), iter facere; (on foot), iter pedibus facere; (on horseback), iter equo facere; (in foreign countries), peregrinor
With great travel, laboriosè
A traveller, viator; (abroad), peregrinator
A travelling (with child), partus; (abroad), peregrinatio
Travelling, iter faciens
Of travelling, or travellers, viatorius
Traverse, transversus, obliquus
A traverse (in law), traversa, criminis negatio; (or cross road), iter transversum
To traverse (a place), locum transire; (swim over), transno; (thwart), consiliis alicujus ob-

sistere; (in sailing), cursum obliquare; (ground, as a fencer), componere ad prœliandum gradum
A traversing, peregratio
A tray, trulla, alveus
Treacherous, perfidus, perfidiosus, dolosus
Treacherously, perfidiosè
Treachery, perfidia, dolus
Treacle, theriaca; (Venice), theriaca Andromachi
Of treacle, theriacus
A tread (in walking), incessus
To tread (go along), incedo; (down), conculco, pedibus obterere; (awry), pedem incertum figere; (in another's steps), alicujus vestigiis insistere; (on another's heels), alicujus calces terere, or premere
A treading upon, calcatus
The treadle (of a loom), insile; (of an egg), umbilicus
Treadles, fimus ovinus
Treason, proditio, perduellio; (high), crimen læsæ majestatis; (petty), proditio minor
Treasonable, proditorius, perfidus
Treasonably, proditoriè, perfidè
A treasure, thesaurus, gaza
A prince's treasure, fiscus
To treasure up (wealth), divitias accumulare; (keep in mind), recordor
The treasury, ærarium
A treasurer, quæstor, thesaurarius
The treasurership, quæstura
Of the treasury, quæstorius
A treasuring up, accumulatio
A treat, convivium, epulæ
To treat, convivio aliquem accipere; (or discourse on a subject), de re aliquâ disceptare   [tans
Treating, convivio accipiens, trac-
A treatise, dissertatio, tractatus
Treatment, ratio accipiendi
A treaty, fœdus, pactum, colloquium, conventio
Treble, triplex, triplus
A treble (note), sonus acutus; (string), fidium tenuissima
Treble-forked, trisulcus
To treble, triplico
A trembling, triplicatio
Trebly, tripliciter, tribus modis
A tree, arbor; (little), arbuscula; (dwarf), arbor pumila; (of a crossbow), scapus balistæ; (of a saddle), lignea sellæ formæ
Of a tree, arboreus
Trefoil, trifolium
A trellis, clathrus
To tremble, tremo, tremisco
To make to tremble, tremefacio
Trembling, tremens, tremulus
A trembling, tremor, trepidatio; (for cold), horror
Tremblingly, trepidantèr, trepidè
Tremendous, tremendus, terribilis
A tremor, tremor
Tremulous, tremulus, tremens
A trench, fossa; (in war), vallum, agger
To trench, vallo, fossam facere
A trencher, scutella
Trendle of a mill, molucrum
A trental, triginta missæ
A surgeon's trepan, terebra
To trepan (the scull), calvariam perforatam lamina argenteâ firmare; (decoy), fallo, decipio

TRI — TRO — TRU

A trepanner, dolos struens, veterator
Trepanning, decipiens, fallens
Trepidation, trepidatio
A trespass, culpa, peccatum
To trespass, violo, pecco ; (against), offendere aliquem ; (upon patience), patientiâ abuti [formulâ
Action of trespass, injuriarum
A trespasser, legum violator
A trespassing, peccans, violans
A tress of hair, cirrus
A tressel, fulcrum
Tret, deductio à pondere
The trey-point, ternio
A trial (essay), specimen ; tentamen ; (temptation), tentatio ; (examination), examen ; (beforehand), præludium ; (of skill), certamen ; (before a judge), judicium
A triangle, triangulum
Triangular, triangularis
A tribe (of people), tribus ; (family), progenies, gens, genus, prosapia, familia, stirps
Of the same tribe, contribulis
Of a tribe, tribuarius
By tribes, tributim, per singulas tribus
Tribulation, tribulatio, afflictio
A tribunal, tribunal
A tribune, tribunus
Of a tribune, tribunitius
Tribuneship, tribunatus
Tributary, tributarius, stipendiarius
Not tributary, immunis à tributo
Tribute, tributum, vectigal
A trice, momentum, punctum
In a trice, extemplò, statim
A trick, dolus, techna, fallacia, artificium ; (at cards), vices unæ, duæ, &c., partes potiores ; (foolish), ineptiæ ; (base), facinus indignum ; (full of), dolosus, astutus
To trick (cheat), dolis deludere ; (up, or dress), orno, adorno
A tricker, veterator, planus
A tricking, fraudatio ; (decking), ornatus, cultus
A trickle (drop), gutta
To trickle (down), mano, stillo ; (through), permano
A trickling down, distillatio
A trident, tridens
Triennial, per triennium, triennis
A trier, tentator, probator
A trifallow, tertio
To trifle, nugor, ineptio ; (with one), tergiversor ; (away time), tempus conterere
A trifler, nugator, nugax
Trifles, nugæ, gerræ
Trifling, nugatorius, frivolus, levis, vanus ; (stories), fabulæ
Triflingly, nugatoriè, ineptè
To trig a wheel, sufflamino
A trigger, sufflamen ; (of a gun), instrumentum quo laxatur sclopetum
A triglyph, triglyphus
A trigon, trigonus
Trigonal, trigonalis
Trigonometry, trigonometria
A trill, sonus modulatus
To trill, stillo, vocem vibrare. See Trickle
Trim (neat), comptus, bellus
A trim (dress), vestitus ; (condition), conditio, status
To trim (or adorn), orno, adorno ; (up old things), interpolo, renovo ; (rest), reficio ; (shave), tondeo ; (with lace), vestes fimbriâ ornare ; (be of either party), temporibus servire
Untrimmed, incomptus
A trimmer (dresser), concinnator, ornatrix ; (barber), tonsor ; (temporizer), omnium horarum homo
A trimming, ornatus, cultus
Trimly, bellè, nitidè
Trimness, concinnitas, nitor
Trine, trinus
The Trinity, sacra TRINITAS
Trinkets, nugæ, tricæ
A trip (offence), offensa ; (voyage), cursus ; (stumble), pedis offensio
To trip, offenso, titubo ; (against a thing), in aliquid offendere ; (caper), tripudio ; (up and down), curaito ; (in speech), balbutio, hæsito ; (up), supplanto, dejicio
Tripartite, tripartitus
A tripe, omasum ; (man), allantopola ; (house), allantopolinum
Triple, triplus, triplex
To triple, triplico
A triplet, tres, terni
A triplication, triplicatio
Triplicity, triplicitas
A tripod, tripus
Tripping, offensans, titubans ; (deceiving), hallucinans
A tripping, gressus agilis
Trippingly, agiliter
Tristful, tristis, mœstus
Trisyllabical, trisyllabus
Trite, tritus, vulgaris [rerum
A trivet, ollæ sustentaculum fervilis
Trivial, futilis, levis
A triumph, triumphus, ovatio
To triumph, triumpho, exulto
Triumphal, triumphalis
Triumphant, triumphans
Triumphantly, magnificè
Led in triumph, triumphatus
A triumpher, triumphator
A triumphing, triumphatus
A triumvirate, triumviratus
Of a triumvirate, triumviralis
A trochee, trochæus
A trollop, mulier squalida
Tronage, vectigal pro mercium ponderatione
A troop, turba, caterva ; (of horse), turma ; (of cattle), grex, armentum
Troops, copiæ militares ; (in troopa), catervatim, gregatim
A trooper, eques
A trope, tropus
A trophy, trophæum
The tropics, tropici
Tropical, tropicus
Tropological, tropologicus
To trot, succusso, succutio ; (up and down), cursito
A trot, gradus succussans
A trotter, succussor
Sheep's trotters, crura ovina
Trotting, succussans
A trotting, succussus
Troth, veritas, fides [fectò
By my troth, In troth, sanè, profectò
Trouble (disturbance), turba, molestia ; (of mind), tristitia, anxietas, solicitudo ; (difficulty), difficultas ; (misfortune), afflictio ; (pain, labour), ærumna, labor [bidæ
Troubles (commotions), res turbidæ
To be in trouble, vexor, commoveor
To trouble (or bring into trouble), turbo, inquieto, vexo ; (with care), ango, solicito ; (disturb), obturbo ; (with petitions), petitionibus lacessere
A troubler, vexator, turbator
Troublesome, molestus, importunus ; (fellow), vitilitigator ; (times), tempora calamitosa
A trough, canaliculus, alveus ; (for kneading), mactra ; (for hogs), aqualiculus
To trounce, castigo, punio
A trouncing, castigatio
A trout, truta
A salmon-trout, salar
I trow, ita opinor, or credo
A trowel, trulla
Trowsers, laxæ braccæ
Troy-weight, libra constans ex duodecim unciis
A truant, cessator, emansor
To play truant, cessô, emaneô
A truce, induciæ [lator
A truce-breaker, induciarum violator
Truck, mercium permutatio
To truck, merces permutare
A truckle, trochlea ; (bed), parabystus [cedere
To truckle to, or under, alicui
Truculent, truculentus, ferox
Truculency, sævitas, ferocitas
To trudge, cursito, circumcurso
Trudging, cursitans
True (certain), verus, certus, exploratus ; (genuine, unmixed), simplex, merus, purus, genuinus ; (real, sincere), verus, candidus, sincerus ; (hearted), candidus, ingenuus ; (bred), genuinus
Likely to be true, verisimilis
To be true to, fidem præstare
Trueheartedness, sinceritas
Trueness, sinceritas, fidelitas
A trull, scortillum
Truly, verè, sanè, profectò
A trump (at cards), charta index ; (trumpet), tuba, buccina
To trump up (devise), excogito, effingo, machinor
Trumped up, fictus, machinatus
Trumpery, frivola, scruta
A trumpet, tuba, buccina
To trumpet, buccino ; (divulge), divulgo ; (one's praise), laudo, celebro
Trumpeted, buccinatus
A trumpeter, buccinator
A trumping up, machinatio
A truncheon, scipio, talea
To trundle, volvo, voluto
A trunk, arca, riscus ; (of a tree), truncus, caudex ; (of an elephant), proboscis ; (pipe), tubus
Trunnions, tormenti tubercula
A truss, fasciculus, sarcina ; (of hay), fœni manipulus ; (for a man), fascia
To truss, cingo, succingo, stringo, substringo ; (make up in trusses), in manipulos colligere ; (up the hair), in nodum colligere
A trussel, fulcrum
Trust, fides, fiducia, commissum
To put trust in, fidem habere
To trust with, fidei committere
To trust, confido, spero, credo ; (goods), merces fide vendere ; (unto), innitor, nitor, spem ponere ; (lend), commodo mutuum dare
A trustee, fidei commissarius
Trustily, fideliter, fidè

[139]

TUN   TWE   TYP

Trustiness, fidelitas
Trusting, credens, confidens
Trusty, fidus, fidelis
Truth, veritas, fides
In truth (indeed), sanè, profectò
Speaking truth, verax
To try (attempt), aggredior, experior, probo, tento; (examine), exploro, examino; (purify), defæco, purgo, purifico
A trying, tentatio, periclitatio
A tub, cadus, dolium; (for kneading), alveus pistorius; (for powdering), carnarium
A tube, tubus, tubulus
A tubercle, tuberculum
Tubular, tubulatus
A tuck, ensis caunâ abditus, dolo
To tuck (twitch), vellico; (or gather up), colligo; (in a mill), constipo, denso
Tucked up, colligatus, stipatus
A tucker, mamillare
A tucking (girding), cinctura
Tuesday, feria tertia, dies Martis
A tuft, crista, apex; (of grass), cespes; (of hair), cirrus; (of a tree), apex, vertex; (or nursery of trees), fruticetum
To tuft, in cristæ formam redigere
Tufted, cristatus
Tufty, villosus
A tug, conatus, nixus
To tug, conor, nitor; (along), traho, ducto; (against), renitor, obluctor
A tugging, nisus, conatus
Tuition, tuitio, tutela
Of tuition, tutelaris
A tulip, tulipa, tulpia
To tumble (or be rolled), volvor, volutor; (roll), volvo, voluto; (or throw down), dejicio, everto, diruo; (or fall down), ruo, concido; (together), convolvo; (under), subvolvo; (upon), supervolvo; (rumple), in rugas trahere, corrugo
A tumbler, saltator, saltatrix; (cup), calix
A tumbling, saltatio; (rolling), volutatio
Tumblingly, volutatim [rium
A tumbrel, plaustrum stercorarium
Tumefaction, inflatio, tumor
Tumefied, tumefactus
To tumefy, tumefacio, tumeo
Tumid, tumidus
A tumor, tumor, inflatio
A tump, tumulus
Full of tumps, tumulosus
A tumult, tumultus, turba
To raise a tumult, turbas ciere
Tumultuary, tumultuarius
Tumultuous, tumultuosus, seditiosus
Tumultuously, turbulentèr, temerè
A tun, dolium majus
Of a tun, doliaris
To tun, in alveos infundere
Tunbellied, ventricosus
Tunable, canorus, harmonicus
Tunableness, modulatio
Tunably, modulatè, numerosè
A tune, tonus, numeri
To be in tune, modulatè sonare, or canere; (out of tune), dissono
To tune an instrument, aptè fidiculas contendere
To set a tune, cœtui præcinere
Well-tuned, aptè modulatus
Ill-tuned, malè modulatus, dissonans

[140]

Tuneful, canorus, modulatus
A tuner, modulator
A tunic, tunica
A tuning, modulatio; (beating), verberatio
A tunnel, infundibulum; (of a chimney), camini tubus
A tup (ram), aries
To tup, ineo, coeo
A turban, tiara, cidaris
A turbot, rhombus
Turbulency, animus turbulentus
Turbulent, turbulentus, ferox
Turbulently, qualitas turgida
A turf, cespes, gleba
Turfy, cespititius
Turgescent, turgescens
Turgid, turgidus, tumidus
Turgidity, qualitas turgida
A Turk, Turcus, Turca
Turkish, Turkey, Turcicus
A turkey-cock, gallus Numidicus; (hen), gallina Numidica
Turmeric, turmerica
A turmoil (tumult), turba, seditio
A turn (lathe), tornus; (circuit), circuitus; (in walking), deambulatio; (course), vicissitudo; (good), beneficium, gratia; (ill), injuria
By turns, invicèm, alternè
Done by turns, alternus
At every turn, identidem
To serve a turn, suis rationibus conducere
To take a turn (walk), ambulo
To turn (bend), flecto, verto; (become), fio, evado; (change), muto, converto; (reclaim), revoco, converto, reduco; (about), circumago; (against), oppugno, obverto; (apostate), de fide desciscere; (back), reverto
Of a different turn, diversæ indoles
A turnep, or turnip, rapum
A turner, tornator
Turners' wares, toreumata
That turns, versatilis
Turning, vertens, convertens
A turning, versatio; (away), aversatio; (about), rotatio; (back again), reversio, reditio; (aside), inversio
A crooked turning, anfractus
Full of crooked turnings, tortuosus
A turning-wheel, tornus
A turning (by way), diverticulum
A turn-coat, scenæ serviens; (pike), septam versatile
Turpentine, terebinthina
Of turpentine, terebinthinus
Turpitude, turpitudo
A turret, turris; (of wood), fala
A turtle, turtur, testudo
Tush! vah! phy!
Tushes, or tusks, apri dentes
Tutelage, anni pupillares, tutela
Tutelar, tutelaris
A tutor, tutor, præceptor
To tutor, edoceo
A tutoring, institutio
Tutty, tutia
Twain, duo, bini
A twang (shrill sound), clangor; (ill tone), pravus accentus
With a twang, malè, pravè
To twattle, garrio, blatero
A twattling, garrulitas
A tweag, or tweak, vellicatio, anxietas

To tweag, or tweak, vellico
Tweezers, volsella
The twelfth, duodecimus
Twelfth day, epiphania
Twelve, duodecim, duodeni
Of twelve, duodenarius
Twelve times, duodeciès
Twelve hundred, mille et ducenti
Twelve thousand, duodeciès mille
A twelvemonth, annus
Twenty, viginti, viceni
Of twenty, vicenarius
Twenty years, vicennium
Twenty times, viciès
The twentieth, vicesimus, vigesimus
Twice, bis; (as much), duplo major; (a second time), iterùm
A twig, ramus, sarmentum, virga, vimen
Of twigs, virgeus
Twiggy, sarmentosus
Twilight, crepusculum
Twinborn, eodem partu natus
Twins, gemini, gemelli
Twine, filum retortum
To twine (twist), torqueo; (about), amplector; (thread), filum duplicare
Twined, tortus
A twiner (twister), tortor
A twinge, vellicatio
To twinge, vellico
Twinged, vellicatus
Twining about, amplexans
A twining about, amplexus
To twinkle (as the eye), nicto; (as a star), scintillo
A twinkle, or twinkling, nictatio; (of the stars), scintillatio; (of the eye), nictus
Twinkling, nictans, scintillans
To twirl, circumroto, circumago
Twirling, vertens, circumrotans
Twist, pili camelini contorti
To twist, torqueo, implico
A twister (person), tortor; (instrument), versoria
A twisting, tortus; (of the guts), tormen, vertices dolorum
To twit, exprobro
A twitting, exprobratio
A twitch, or twitching, vellicatio
To twitch, vellico, convello
To twitter (tremble), tremo, (meer), irrideo, derideo
Two, duo, bini, gemini
Two and two, bini
Having two heads, biceps; (two horns), bicornis; (two feet), bipes
One of the two, uter, utervis
Of two colours, bicolor
Twofold, duplex
Twohanded, robustus, ingens
Two days' space, biduum; (nights), binoctium
Of two months, bimestris
Two years old, bimus, bimulus
Two years' space, biennium
Two feet long, bipedalis
In two parts, bipartitus
Every two days, alternis diebus
Two hundred, ducenti
Two hundred times, ducentiès
The two hundredth, ducentesimus
A tyger, tigris
A tying (to), alligatio, annexus; (together), connexio
The tympan, tympanum
The tympany, tympanites
A type, typus, similitudo
Typical, typicus

UNA

Typically, typicè
A typographer, typographus
Typographical, typogiaphicus
Typography, typographia
Tyrannical, tyrannicus
Tyrannically, tyrannicè
Tyrannicide, tyrannicidium
To tyrannize, tyrannidem exercere
Tyranny, tyrannus
A tyrant, tyrannus; (killer), tyrannicida
Tythes, decimæ

U.

Ubiquity, ubiquitas
An udder, uber, mamma
Uglily, deformitèr, fœdè
Ugliness, deformitas, turpitudo
Ugly, deformis, turpis, horridus
An ulcer, ulcus
To ulcerate, ulcero, exulcero
An ulcerating, ulceratio
Ulcerous, ulcerosus
Ultimate, ultimus, postremus
Ultimately, ultimò, postremò
Ultramarine, ultramarinus
Umbilical, umbilicalis
An umbrage (shade), umbra, umbraculum; (offence), offensa, prætextum, prætextus, color; (suspicion), suspicio [dor
To take umbrage, suspicor, offendor
Umbrageous, Umbrose, umbrosus
An umbrella, umbella
Umpirage, arbitrium
An umpire, arbiter
Unabashed, minimè perturbatus
Unable, impotens, infirmus
To make unable, debilito
Made unable, debilitatus
Unabolished, nondùm antiquatus
Unacceptable, ingratus
Unaccompanied, incomitatus, solus
Unaccomplished, infectus
Unaccountable, mirus, mirabilis, inauditus, novus, mirandus
Unaccountably, mirificè, in mirum modum
Unaccustomed, insuetus
Unacknowledged, minimè agnitus
Unacquainted, ignotus, ignarus
Unactive, minimè agilis, ignavus
Unadored, non veneratus
Unadvisable, incommodus
Unadvised, inconsultus, præceps
Unadvisedly, inconsultè, temerè
Unadvisedness, temeritas
Unaffected, simplex, sincerus, candidus, minimè affectus
Unaffectedly, apertè, sincerè
Unaffectedness, sinceritas
Unaided, non adjutus
Unalienable, non alienandus
Unalienated, non alienatus
Unallied, non affinis [dus
Unallowable, minimè concedendus
Unalterable, immutabilis, constans
Unalterably, constantèr
Unaltered, immutatus
Unamased, intrepidus
Unambitious, non ambitiosus
Unanimity, unanimitas, concordia
Unanimous, unanimus, concors
Unanimously, unanimitèr, concorditèr
Unanswerable, irrefragabilis

UNB

Unappalled, intrepidus
Unappeasable, implacabilis
Unappeased, implacatus
Unapprehensive, minimè suspicans [tus
Unapprized, nondùm certior factus
Unapproachable, inaccessus
Unapt, inhabilis, ineptus
Unaptly, incommodè, ineptè
Unaptness, ineptitudo
Unarmed, dearmatus, inermis
Unasked, minimè rogatus
Unassailed, inexpugnatus
Unassayed, inexpertus
Unassisted, minimè adjutus
Unassuaged, implacatus
Unassuming, minimè arrogans
Unassured, incertus
Unatoned, non expiatus
Unattainable, non assequens
Unattempted, minimè tentatus
Unattended, sine comitatu, incomitatus
Unattentive, incautus
Unavailable, nihil conducens
Unavailing, inutilis, inanis
Unavoidable, inevitabilis
Unawares (unwary), incautus, nec opinans; (unlooked for), inopinatus, improvisus
Unawares (*adv*.), improvisò
Unawed, non deterritus
To unbar, pessulum detrahere
Unbarbed, phaleris spoliatus
Unbecoming, indecens, indecorus
Unbecomingly, indecentèr, indecorè
Unbefitting, parùm idoneus
Unbegotten, non genitus
Unbelief, infidelitas, incredulitas
An unbeliever, infidelis, incredulus
To unbend, relaxo, solvo
Unbent, relaxatus, remissus
Unbenign, malignus, malevolus
Unbeseeming, indecorus, indecens
Unbeseemingly, indecorè
Unbewailed, indefletus, indeploratus
To unbewitch, fascino liberare
Unbiassed, in neutram partem proclinans
Unbidden, injussus, invocatus
To unbind, exsolvo, solvo
Unblameable, inculpatus, innocuus [patè
Unblameably, sine culpâ, inculUnblameableness, innocentia
Unblemished, integer, innocuus
Unblessed, execratus
Unbloody, incruentus
Unboiled, incoctus
To unbolt, obicem detrahere
Unborn, nondùm natus
To unbosom, communico
Unbought, inemptus
Unbound, irreligatus
Unbounded, indefinitus, immensus, interminatus, infinitus
Unboundedly, infinitè
To unbowel, exentero, eviscero
Unbowelled, evisceratus
An unbracing, solutio
To unbridle, frænis exsolvere
Unbridled, effrænatus
Unbroken, irruptus, infractus; (not tamed), indomitus
To unbuckle, fibulas solvere
Unbuilt, nondùm ædificatus
To unbung, relino
To unburden, exonero
Unburdened, exoneratus
To unbutton, fibulas solvere
Unbuttoned, fibulis solutus

UNC

Uncalled, invocatus, sponte
Uncancelled, non dele.us
To uncase, capsâ eximere, exuo
Uncased, exuius, nudatus
Uncensured, irreprehensus
Uncertain, incertus, dubius
To be uncertain, dubito, hæsito
Uncertainly, incertè, dubiè
Uncertainty, dubitatio
To unchain, catenâ exsolvere
Unchained, catenâ exsolutus
Unchangeable, immutabilis
Unchangeably, immutabilitèr
Unchangeableness, immutabilitas
Unchanged, immutatus
Uncharitable, inhumanus
Uncharitableness, inhumanitas
Uncharitably, inhumanitèr
Unchaste, impudicus, obscœnus
Unchastely, impudicè, obscœnè
Unchewed, non masticatus
Unchristian, christiano indignus
To unchurch, excommunico
Uncircumcised, uncircumcisus
Uncircumcision, incircumcisio
Uncircumscribed, interminatus
Uncircumspect, incautus, improvidus
Uncircumspectly, incautè, improvidè
Uncivil, incivilis, inurbanus
Uncivilly, incivilitèr, inurbanè
Uncivilised, insociabilis
Unclad, nudus
To unclasp, uncinum laxare
Unclasped, uncino laxato
An unclasping, uncini laxatio
An uncle (by the father), patruus; (by the mother), avunculus
A great uncle, propatruus
Unclean, immundus, sordidus; (in life), impudicus, incontinens
To be unclean, sordeo
To grow unclean, sordesco
To make unclean, inquino, fœdo
Uncleanly, sordidè, fœdè
Uncleanness, immunditia, spurcities; (of life), impudicitia
Uncleft, indivisus
To unclench, recludo
To unclose, disciudo, retego, detego
To unclothe, vestibus exuere
Unclothed, vestibus exutus, *or* spoliatus, non indutus
Unclouded, Uncloudy, serenus
Uncomely, indecens, indecorus; (*adv*.), indecentèr, indecorè
Uncomeliness, deformitas
Uncomfortable, injucundus
Uncomfortableness, injucunditas
Uncomfortably, injucundè
Uncommon, rarus, infrequens
Uncommonly, rarò, infrequentèr
Uncommonness, raritas
Uncompelled, non compulsus
Uncompounded, simplex
Unconceivable, incomprehensibilis
Unconceived, non conceptus
Unconcern, negligentia [tus
Unconcerned, indifferens, immoUnconcernedly, indifferentèr
Unconclusive, quo nil concludi potest
Uncondemned, indemnatus
Unconfined, immunis, liber
Unconfirmed, non confirmatus
Unconquerable, invincibilis
Unconscionable, injustus, iniquus
Unconscionableness, injustitia
Unconscionably, injustè, iniquè

[141]

UND   UND   UNF

Unconscious, non conscius
Unconsecrated, nondum consecratus [actus
Unconstrained, spontaneus, incoUnconsumed, inconsumptus
Uncontaminated, intaminatus, purus
Uncontestable, non disputandus
Uncontested, non litigatus
Uncontrollable, non subjiciendus
Uncontrolled, liber, immunis
Unconvinced, non evictus
Uncorrected, impunitus
Uncorruptly, incorruptè   [tas
Uncorruptness (of mind), integriTo uncover, detego, patefacio
Uncovered, detectus, retectus
An uncovering, patefactio
To uncouple, disjungo, abjungo
Uncourteous, inurbanus, rusticus
Uncourtly, inurbanè, rusticè
Uncouth, rudis, impolitus, insuetus
Uncouthly, invenustè, inurbanè
Uncouthness, rusticitas
Uncreated, increatus
An unction, unctio, inunctio
Unctuous, unctuosus, pinguis
Unctuousness, pinguedo
Uncultivated, incultus, neglectus
Uncurable, insanabilis
To uncurb, lupatum demere
Uncured, incuratus
Uncurious, incuriosus
Uncut, imputatus, intonsus
Undamaged, illæsus
Undaunted, intrepidus, impavidus
Undauntedly, intrepidè, impavidè
Undauntedness, intrepiditas
Undazzled, non præstrictus
Undebauched, incorruptus
Undecayed, non diminutus
To undeceive, errore liberare
Undeceived, ab errore liberatus
Undecided, injudicatus, non decisus
Undecked, inornatus, incomptus
Undeclined, indeclinatus
Undefaced, non eversus
Undefended, indefensus   [tus
Undefiled, impollutus, intaminaUndefrayed, non erogatus
Undelighted, indelectatus
Undemolished, non dirutus
Undeniable, non negandus
Undeplored, indeploratus
Undepraved, incorruptus
Under, sub, subter, infra; (show, colour, or pretence), sub specie, or prætextu
Under, adj. inferior, vicarius
To be under, subsum
To keep under, coërceo, fræno
Under age, ephebus, impubis
To underbid, minoris licitari
To underbind, subligo
Underbound, subligatus
To undergird, subligo, succingo
Undergirt, succinctus
To undergo, subeo, patior, tolero
Underground, subterraneus
Underhand, clam, secretò, clanculùm
Underhand-dealing, prævaricatio
Underived, non derivatus
To underlay, suppono, suffulcio
Underlaid, suppositus, suffultus
An under-leather, solea
An underling, alteri subditus
To undermine, suffodio; (supplant), supplanto, insidias struere
An undermining, suffossio
Undermost, imus, infimus
Underneath, subter, infra
[143]

To underpin, substruo
Underpinned, substructus, subligatus
An underpinning, substructio
To underprop, suffulcio, fulcio
Underpropped, suffultus, fultus
An underpropping, statuminatio
An under-rate, pretium justo minus [mare
To under-rate, justo minori æstiUnder-rated, justo minori æstimatus [vendere
To undersell, minoris quam alii
An under-servant, famulus inferior
To underset, suppono, subjicio
An under-sheriff, subvicecomes
To understand, intelligo, sentio, percipio; (something, not expressed), subintelligo
To give to understand, significo
Given to understand, certior factus
The understanding, intellectus; (agreement), concordia; (knowledge), intelligentia
To undertake, aggredior, tento, suscipio; (work), opus redimere
An undertaker, molitor, inceptor; (of work), operum redemptor; (of funerals), libitinarius
An undertaking, ausum, inceptum
To undervalue, pretio justo minor æstimare, parvi facere, sperno
Undervaluing (slighting), despiciens
An underwood, sylva cædua
To underwork, operam minori pretio locare; (undermine), insidias struere
To underwrite, subscribo
Undeserved, immeritus, indignus
Undeservedly, immeritò, indignè
Undeserving, immerens
Undesirable, minimè expetendus
Undeterminate, Undetermined, non determinatus, indefinitus
Undeterminately, indefinitè
Undevout, irreligiosus
Undevoutly, irreligiosè
Undied, nondum tinctus
Undigested, indigestus, incompositus
Undiminished, imminutus
Undiscernable, imperceptus, incompertus
Undiscerned, minimè perceptus
Undiscerning, minimè percipiens
Undischarged (as a duty), non præstitus; (as a reckoning), non solutus
Undisciplined, indoctus, inexpertus; (troops), copiæ inexercitatæ
Undiscovered, incompertus, non patefactus, or retectus
Undisguised, non celatus, sincerus
Undismayed, imperterritus
Undisposed of, nondum alienatus, or venditus
Undisputable, indubitabilis
Undissembled, non dissimulatus
Undissolvable, indissolubilis
Undistinguished, indistinctus
Undisturbed, pacatus, serenus
Undividable, individuus
Undivided, indivisus, indiscretus
To undo (disannul), abrogo; (slacken), laxo, relaxo; (unravel), extrico, retexo; (untie), solvo, dissolvo; (ruin), perdo, pessundo
Undoing, ruina, interitus
An undoing, abrogatio, relaxatio, dissolutio, perditio
Undone (not done), infectus;

(slackened), relaxatus; (untied), dissolutus; (ruined), perditus
Undoubtable, indubitabilis
Undoubted, indubitatus, certus
Undoubtedly, proculdubiò, certò
To undress, vestes exuere; (another), vestes detrahere alicui
Undried, nondum siccatus
Undue, indebitus, partim justus
To undulate, undo, fluctuo
An undulation, agitatio undatim
Unduly, indebitè, partim justè
Undutiful, inobediens, inobsequens
Undutifully, contumacitèr
Undutifulness, contumacia
Uneasily, ægrè, molestè
Uneasiness, molestia, difficultas; (of mind), anxietas, perturbatio
Uneasy, anxius, æger
Uneaten, haud comestus
Unedified, partim instructus
Unedifying, inutilis
Uneffectual, inefficax   [tus
Uneloquent, infacundus, indisertUnemployed, non occupatus
Unendowed, indotatus
Unenjoyed, minimè perceptus
Unenlightened, non illuminatus
Unenvied, minimè invidendus
Unequal, inæqualis, dispar
Unequally, inæqualitèr
Unequivocal, minimè ambiguus
Unerring, inerrans, infallibilis
Uneven, inæqualis; (places), salebræ, aspreta
Unevenness, inæqualitas
Unexamined, non examinatus
Unexampled, novus, inauditus
Unexceptionable, exceptionibus non obnoxius
Unexecuted, infectus
Unexpected, insperatus, inopinus
Unexpectedly, ex improvisò, insperatò
Unexpert, rudis, imperitus
Unexpired, nondum finitus
Unextended, non extensus
Unexterminable, inextirpabilis
Unfading, non deflorescens
Unfair, injustus, iniquus
Unfairly, injustè, iniquè
Unfairness, injustitia
Unfaithful, infidus, perfidus
Unfaithfully, infidelitèr, perfidè
Unfaithfulness, perfidia
Unfalsified, non adulteratus
Unfashionable, minimè concinnus
Unfashioned, non formatus, informis
To unfasten, refigo, solvo
Unfastened, refixus, solutus
Unfathomable, non explorandus
Unfavourable, minimè benignus
Unfeathered, implumis, deplumis
Unfed, impastus
Unfed, honorario non sanctus
Unfeeling, insensilis, durus
Unfeigned, non fictus, sincerus
Unfeignedly, sincerè, verè
Unfenced, immunitus, inermis
Unfertile, infertilis, infœcundus
Unfertileness, infœcunditas
To unfetter, vincula demere
Unfit, inhabilis, ineptus; (to learn), indocilis; (for labour), debilis
Unfitly, ineptè, improprie
Unfitness, incongruitas
Unfitting, incongruens
To unfix, redigo, labefacio   [mis
Unfledged, non pennatus, deplu-
To unfold, explico, evolvo
That may be unfolded, explicabilis

UNH	UNL	UNN

Unforced, voluntarius, spontaneus
Unforeseen, improvisus
Unforgiving, inexorabilis
Unformed, informis, indigestus
Unfortified, immunitus
Unfortunate, infaustus, infelix; (days), dies nefasti
Unfortunately, infeliciter
Unfrequent, infrequens, inusitatus
Unfrequented, desertus, solitarius
Unfriendly, parùm amicè
Unfruitful, sterilis, instructuosus
Unfruitfulness, infœcunditas
To unfurl, expando, explico
To unfurnish, diepolio, nudo
Unfurnished (deprived of), spoliatus; (not yet finished), imparatus
Ungain, ineptus, inhabilis
Ungainly, ineptè, minùs aptè
Ungarnished, inornatus
Ungathered, nondùm collectus
Ungenerous, degener, illiberalis
Ungenerously, illiberalitèr
Ungenteel, inurbanus, rusticus
Ungenteelly, illiberalitèr, inurbanè
Ungenteelness, illiberalitas
Ungentle, immansuetus, asper
Ungently, asperè, inurbanè
Ungilt, nondùm inauratus
To ungird, recingo, discingo
Ungirded, Ungirt, discinctus
To ungirth, cingulum laxare
To unglue, deglutino
Ungodlily, impiè, scelestè
Ungodliness, impietas, flagitium
Ungodly, impius, irreligiosus; (gut), gula insatiata, venter improbus
Ungorged, nondùm exsaturatus
Ungovernable, immitis, immodicus, indomabilis
Ungovernableness, ingenium intractabile
Ungraceful, indecorus, inconcinnus
Ungracefully, indecorè, inconcinnè
Ungracefulness, inconcinnitas
Ungracious, impius, improbus, pravus; (wretch), scelus, nequam
Ungraciously, sceleratè, impiè
Ungraciousness, impietas
Ungrafted, nondùm insitus
Ungrammatical, arti grammaticæ non consentaneus
To ungrapple, libero
Ungrateful, ingratus
Ungratefully, ingratè
Ungratefulness, ingratitudo
Unguarded (not guarded), incustoditus; (indiscreet, rash), imprudens, temerarius, incousultus
Unguardedly, inconsultè, temerè
Unguent, unguentum
Unhabitable, inhabitabilis
To unhallow, profano, temero
Unhallowed, profanatus, violatus
Unhandsome, invenustus, indecorus
Unhandsomely, ineleganter, turpiter
Unhandsomeness, deformitas
Unhappily, infelicitèr, improsperè
Unhappiness, infelicitas
Unhappy, infelix, inauspicatus
Unharmonious, immodulatus
To unharness, phaleras detrahere
To unhasp, resero
Unhasped, reseratus
Unhatched, nondùm patefactus
[143]

Unhealable, insanabilis
Unhealed, nondùm sanatus
Unhealthful, Uuhealthy, valetudinarius, infirmus, insalubris
Unhealthiness, insanitas
Unheard of, inauditus
Unheeded, inobservatus
Unheedful, Unheedy, oscitans, negligens
Unheediness, incuria
Unhidden, apertus, retectus
To unhinge, de cardine detrahere; (disorder), perturbo
Unholiness, impietas
Unholy, impius, profanus
Unhonoured, inhonoratus
To unhook, hamum solvere
Unhoped for, insperatus, inexpectatus
To unhorse, equo dejicere
Unhospitable, inhospitalis
Unhoused, ex ædibus exturbatus
Unhuman, inhumanus, crudelis
Unhurt, illæsus, inviolatus
An unicorn, monoceros
Uniform, uniformis, sibi constans
Uniformity, uniformitas
Uniformly, uniformitèr
Unimaginable, mente or cogitando non percipiendus
Unimpaired, non diminutus
Unimportant, levis momenti
Uninformed, parum eruditus
Uninhabitable, inhabitabilis
Uninhabited, non habitatus, vacane
Uninjured, illæsus
Uninstructed, indoctus
Unintelligible, animo non percipiendus
Uninterrupted, continuus
Unithralled, sui juris
Uninvited, invocatus
Union, unio, concordia
Unjoyous, tristis, partim alacris
At unison, concentus
An unit, monas, unitas
To unite (or join together), jungo, conjungo; (differences), lites componere; (be joined together), coaleo, coalesco
An uniting, conjunctio
Unity, unitas
Unjudged, injudicatus
Universal, universus, universalis
Universality, universalitas
Universally, universè, universìm
The universe, mundus universus
An university, academia
Of an university, academicus
Univocal, univocus
Univocally, univocè
Unjust, injustus, iniquus
Unjustice, injustitia
Unjustifiable, justitiæ non consonus
Unjustifiableness, iniquitas
Unjustifiably, iniquè
Unjustly, injustè, iniquè
Unked, Unkward, solitarius
To unkennel, è cubili excitare
Unkind, inclemens, inhospitus
Unkindly, inclementèr, inhumanè
Unkindly, inclemens, adversus
Unkindness, inclementia
To unknit, enodo, evolvo
Unknowingly, inscientèr, inconsultò
To be unknown, ignoror, lateo
Unlaboured, inelaboratus
To unlace, diloríco, exsolvo
To unlade, exonero, decapulo
Unlamented, indeploratus
Unlawful, illicitus, illegitimus
Unlawfully, illicitè

Unlawfulness, injustitia
To unlearn, dedisco
Unlearned, indoctus, illiteratus
Unlearnedly, indoctè, inerudite
Unleavened, azymus
Unless, ni, nisi
Unlighted, non accensus
Unlike, di-similis, diversus
To be unlike, differo, discrepo
Unlikely, improbabilis
Unlikeliness, improbabilitas
Unlikeness, dissimilitudo, diversitas
To unload, exonero, deonero
Unloaded, Unloaden, exoneratus
To unlock, resero, recludo
Unlocked, Unlockt, reseratus
Unlooked for, insperatus, inopinatus
To unloose, solvo, resolvo
An unloosing, solutio, dissolutio
Unlovely, inamabilis
Unluckily, infelicitèr, inauspicatò
Unluckiness (unhappiness), infelicitas, infortunium; (untowardliness), nequitia, protervitas
Unlucky (unhappy), infelix, infaustus; (untoward), nequam, improbus; (throw at dice), jactus supinus
Unmade, infectus, imperfectus
To unman, emasculo, eviro
Unmanageable, intractabilis
Unmanly, effeminatus, viro indignus
Unmannerliness, inurbanitas
Unmannerly, adj. inurbanus
Unmannerly, adv. inurbanè, rusticè
Unmanured, incultus, inaratus
Unmarried, cælebs
To unmarry, matrimonium abrogare
To unmask, larvam detrahere
Unmasked, larvâ exutus, apertus
Unmasterable, indomabilis
Unmastered, indomitus, invictus
Unmeaning, nihil designans
Unmeasurable, immensus
Unmeet, indecens, indecorus; (for), impar, impos
Unmeetness, incongruitas
Unmerciful, immitis, crudelis, atrox
Unmercifully, crudelitèr, atrocitèr
Unmercifulness, crudelitas, sævitia
Unminded, neglectus
Unmindful (forgetful), immemor; (heedless), negligens, incautus
Unmindfulness, oblivium; (heedlessness), negligentia
Unmixt, purus, non mixtus
Unmolested, imperturbatus
Unmoved, immotus
Unmourned, indeploratus
To unmuffle, focale detrahere
Being unmuffled, focali detracto
Unmusical, non modulatus
To unmuzzle, capistrum exuere
To unnail, clavum extrahere
Unnatural (void of natural affection), crudelis, inhumanus; (preternatural), portentosus, præter naturam
Unnaturally, inhumanè, crudelitèr
Unnaturalness, inhumanitas
Unnavigable, innabilis
Unnecessarily, inutilitèr, supervacuò

UNQ   UNS   UNS

Unnecessary, inutilis, inanis
To unnerve, infirmo, debilito
Unobservant, immoriger
Unobserved, non observatus
Unoccupied, incultus, inexercitatus
Unorganised, organis non instructus
Unowned, non agnitus
To unpack, fasciculum resolvere
Unpaid, insolutus
Unpainted, nondûm pictus
Unpalateable, ingrati saporis
Unparalleled, incomparabilis
Unpardonable, inexpiabilis, irremissibilis
Unpared, irresectus
Unparliamentary, consuetudine parliamentariæ dissentaneus
To unpave, lapides eruere
Unpawned, non pignori oppositus
Unpeaceable, turbulentus, turbidus
Unpeaceably, turbulentèr, turbidè
To unpeg, paxillum eximere
Unpegged, paxillo exempto
To unpeople, vasto, depopulor
Unpeopled, depopulatus
Unperceivable, sub sensum non cadens
Unperceived, minimè perceptus
Unperformed, infectus
Unperishable, incorruptibilis
Unpestered, imperturbatus
Unphilosophical, regulis philosophiæ minimè conveniens
To unpin, acicalis exemptis solvere
Unpinioned, à manicis solutus
Unpitied, cui misericordia non adhibetur
Unpleasant, injucundus, inamœnus
Unpleasantly, injucundè, infacetè
Unpleasantness, injucunditas ; (of the air), intemperies
Unpleasing, injucundus, insuavis
Unpliant, inflexibilis
Unploughed, inaratus
Unpolite, impolitus, rudis
Unpolluted, impollutus
Unpractised, inexercitatus
Unprecedented, sine exemplo
Unprejudiced (impartial), æquus
Unpremeditated, non præmeditatus
Unprepared, imparatus
Unpressed, minimè pressus
Unprincipled, scelestus, pravus
Unprofaned, non profanatus
Unprofitable, inutilis, incommodus
Unprofitableness, inutilitas
Unprofitably, inutilitèr
Unpropitious, infaustus
Unproportionable, minimè secundum justam proportionem
Unprosperous, infaustus, infelix
Unprosperously, infelicitèr
Unproved, inexpertus, non probatus
Unprovided, imparatus
Unprovoked, non provocatus
Unpruned, nondûm amputatus
Unpublished, ineditus
Unpunished, impunitus, inultus
Unpurchased, inemptus
Unqualified, inhabilis, non idoneus
Unquenched, inextinctus
Unquestionable, indubitatus
Unquestionably, indubitantèr

[144]

Unquiet, inquietus
To make unquiet, inquieto
Unquietness, inquietudo
Unrated, non æstimatus
To unravel, extrico, expedio
Unravelled, extricatus, expeditus
Unread, non rectus
Unreadily, non promptè
Unready, imparatus
Unreasonable, irrationalis; (unjust), injustus; (immoderate), immodicus
Unreasonableness, injustitia
Unreasonably, injustè, iniquè
Unrebukable, irreprehensus
Unrecompensed, non compensatus
Unrecorded, non in tabulas relatus
Unrecounted, non memoratus
Unredeemable, nullo pretio redimendus
Unredeemed, nullo pretio redemptus
Unrefreshed, non levatus
Unreguarded, neglectus, spretus
Unrelenting, inflexibilis
Unrelieved, minimè levatus
Unremediable, immedicabilis
Unremittible, inexpiabilis
Unrepaired, non reparatus
Unrepealed, minimè abrogatus
Unreproved, inculpatus, irreprehensus
Unrequited, non compensatus
Unreserved (in speech), liberè loquens
Unresisting, non repugnans
Unresolved, hæsitans, fluctuans
To be unresolved, hæsito. fluctuo
Unrestored, minimè restitutus
Unrestrained, minimè repressus
Unrevealed, minimè revelatus
Unrevenged, inultus
Unrewarded, non numeratus
To unriddle, ænigma solvere, explico
Unriddled, explicatus, expositus
To unrig (undress), vestes exuere
Unrigged (as a ship), sublatis armamentis; (as a person), vestibus exutus
Unrighteous, injustus, iniquus
Unrighteously, injustè, iniquè
Unrighteousness, injustitia
To unrip, dissuo, resuo
Unripe, immaturus, crudus
Unripeness, immaturitas, cruditas
Unript, dissutus, resutus
Unrivalled, sine æmulo
To unrivet, clavum retusum refigere
To unrol, evolvo, explico
Unroiled, evolutus
To unroof, tecta detrahere
Unruffled, imperturbatus
Unruliness, effrenatio
Unruly, effrenatus, effrænus
To be unruly, nullis legibus teneri
To unsaddle, ephippium detrahere
Unsaddled, non ephippiatus
Unsafe, intutus, minimè tutus
Unsafely, periculosè
Unsaid, indictus   [bilis
Unsailable, innavigabilis, innaUnsaleable, non vendibilis
Unsalted, insulsus, non salitus
Unsaluted, insalutatus
Unsanctified, minimè consecratus, minimè superstitiosus
Unsatisfactory, minimè satisfaciens
Unsatisfied, minimè contentus

Unsavorily, insipidè, insulsè
Unsavory, insipidus, insulsus
Unsavoriness, insulsitas
To unsay, recanto
To unscale, desquamo
Unscaled, desquamatus
To unscrew, cochleam refigere
Unscriptural, scripturis sacris non innitens
To unseal, resigno
Unsealed, resignatus, solutus
Unsearchable, inscrutabilis
Unseasonable, intempestivus
Unseasonableness, intempestas; (of weather), intemperies
Unseasonably, intempestivè
Unseasoned, minimè salitus ; (timber), humida materia
Unsecure, intutus
Unseemliness, indecorum
Unseemly, indecens, minimè decorus
It is unseemly, dedecet
Unseen, invisus, invisibilis
Unsent for, non vocatus, invocatus
Unserviceable, inutilis, ineptus
Unserviceableness, inutilitas
Unserviceably, inutilitèr
Unset, non satus, spontè natus
Unsettled (instable), instabilis ; (doubting), dubius; (not fixed), incertus; (as lees), fæculentus
Unsettledness, instabilitas
To unsew, dissuo, resuo
To unshackle, à compedibus liberare
Unshaded, apricus
Unshaled, minimè decorticatus
To unsheath, è vaginâ stringere
Unsheathed, è vaginâ strictus
Unshod, discalceatus ; (as a horse), ferreis soleis carens
To unshoe, discalceo
Unshorn, intonsus, irrasus
Unshut, apertus, disclusus
Unsightliness, deformitas
Unsightly, deformis, fœdus
Unsincere, simulatus, fucatus
Unskilful, imperitus, ignarus
Unskilfulness, imperitia
Unskilled, inexpertus, rudis
Unslain, non occisus
Unslaked, non aquâ maceratus
Unsnared, laqueo expeditus
Unsociable, insociabilis, inurbanus
Unsociably, inurbanè
Unsodden, incoctus
Unsoiled, immaculatus
Unsold, non venditus
Unsoldered, non ferruminatus
Unsolicited, minimè solicitatus
Unsolicitous, non solicitus
Unsolid, non solidus, fluidus
Unsought, minimè quæsitus
Unsoundness, putredo, insanitas
Unspeakable, ineffabilis
Unspent, inconsumptus
Unspilt, non effusus
Unspoken, intactus, indictus
Unspotted, intaminatus, impollutus
Unstable, instabilis, inconstans
Unstableness, instabilitas
Unstaid, inconstans, levis
Unstaidness, levitas   [lutus
Unstained, intaminatus, impolUnsteadily, Unsteadfastly, levitèr
Unsteadiness, Unsteadfastness, levitas
Unsteady, Unsteadfast, levis
Unstirred, immotus

UNT   UPW   USE

unstitch, dissuo, resuo
stitched, dissutus, resutus
unstop, aperio
unstring, laxo, retendo
strung, retentus, remissus
studied, non studio elaboratus
stuffed, minimè refertus
subduable, indomabilis
subdued, indomitus, invictus
successful, infaustus, infelix, improsper, sinister [prosperè
successfully, infeliciter, improsperè
successfulness, infelicitas
sufferable, intolerabilis
sufferably, intolerabilitèr
suitable, incongruens, inhabilis
sullied, intaminatus
sung, non decantatus
supportable, impatibilis
supportably, intolerabilitèr
supported, non sustentatus
sure, dubius, incertus
surmountable, insuperabilis
susceptible, haud capax
suspecting, haud suspicans
suspicious, non suspiciosus
sustained, non sustentatus
unswaddle, è fasciis evolvere
swaddled, è fasciis evolutus
sworn, injuratus
tainted, integer, intactus, intaminatus
taken, indeprehensus
tameable, non domabilis
tamed, indomitus, invectus
o untangle, extrico, expedio
tangled, extricatus, expeditus
tasted, illibatus, intemeratus
taught, indoctus, rudis
o unteach, dedoceo
tenable, non tenendus
terrified, intrepidus, impavidus
unthankful, ingratus
unthankfully, ingrato animo
unthankfulness, ingratitudo
unthawed, non regelatus
unthinking, inconsideratus
unthought of, inopinatus, inexpectatus
unthriftily, prodigalitèr, prodigè
unthriftiness, profusio
unthrifty, prodigus, profusus
to untie, solvo, recingo
until, donec, usque ad, usque dum; (now), adhuc, hactenus, etiamnum; (then), antehac, eousquè; (when?), quousque?
to untile, tegulas detrahere
untimely (unseasonable), intempestivus; (not ripe), immaturus; (ripe too soon), præmaturus, præcox
an untimely birth, abortio
untinged, non infectus
into, ad, tenus. See To
untoothsome, gustui minimè gratus
untouched, intactus, illibatus
untoward, contumax, perversus
untowardliness, pervicacia
untowardly, protervè [vicax
untractable, intractabilis, pertried, intentatus, inexpertus
untrimmed, incomptus, incuratus
untrod, Untrodden, non calcatus
untrue, mendax, falsus
untruly, falsò, falsè
to untruss, discingo
untrussed, discinctus, dissolutus
untrusty, infidus, infidelis
an untruth, figmentum, mendacium
To tell an untruth, mentior
[145]

Full of untruths, fabulosus
To untuck, recingo
Untucked, recinctus
Untuneable, dissonus
Untutored, minimè doctus
To untwine, or untwist, retexo
Untwisted, retortus, resolutus
Unvaluable, inæstimabilis
Unvanquishable, indomabilis
Unvanquished, indomitus, invictus   [tus
Unvaried, immutatus, non variaTo unveil, revelo, detego
An unveiling, patefactio
Unversed, imperitus, inexpertus
Unviolated, illæsus
Unuseful, inutilis, ineptus
Unusefulness, inutilitas
Unusual, inusitatus, insuetus
Unusually, inusitatè, rarò
Unusualness, raritas, desuetudo
Unutterable, inenarrabilis
Unwarily, incautè, improvidè
Unwariness, temeritas, imprudentia
Unwary, incautus, improvidus
Unwarrantable, minimè defendendus
Unwashed, illotus, sordidus
Unwasted, inconsumptus
Unwatched, inobservatus, incustoditus
Unwatered, non rigatus
Unwearied, indefessus, assiduus
Unweariedly, indefessè, assiduè
To unweave, retexo
Unwedded, cœlebs, conjugii exors
Unwelcome, ingratus, invisus
Unwholesome, insalubris
Unwholesomeness of the air, cœli intemperies, or inclementia
Unwieldily, torpidè, ineptè
Unwieldiness, difficultas movendi
Unwieldy, inhabilis, pinguis
Unwilling, nolens, invitus
To be unwilling, nolo
Unwillingly, invitè, ægrè
Unwillingness, repugnantia
To unwind, retrò glomerare
Unwise, insipiens, stolidus
Unwisely, imprudentèr, stolidè
Unwished for, inexpectatus
Unwithered, immarcescibilis
Unwitting, clàm; (to me), me inscio; (to any one), ignaro aliquo
Unwitting, adj. insciens, incautus
Unwittingly, inscientèr, incautè
Unwitty, illepidus, infacetus
Unwonted, insolitus, inusitatus
Unworkmanlike, infabrè, crassè
Unworn, non detritus, non gestatus
Unworthily, indignè, immeritò
Unworthiness, indignitas
Unworthy, indignus, immeritus
Unwound, retrò glomeratus
To unwrap, evolvo, explico
Unwrapped, evolutus, explicatus
An unwrapping, evolutio
To unwreath, retorqueo
Unwreathed, retortus
Unwrinkled, minimè rugatus
Unyielding, minimè concedens
To unyoke, abjungo, disjungo
Unyoked, abjunctus, disjunctus
Up (go up), ascendo; (rise up), surge; (by the roots), radicitùs; (to), tenus, usque ad; (and down), sursum, deorsum, huc illuc
To be up at play, vinco
Up on end, erectus
Uphill, acclivis, difficilis
Up, or upwards, sursum

To upbear, tollo, elevo
To upbraid, exprobro, objurgo
An upbraider, exprobrator
An upbraiding, exprobratio
To uphold, sustento, sustineo
Uphold, Upholden, sustentatus
An upholder, sustentator; (or upholsterer), lectorum fabricator
An upholding, sustentatio
Uplandish, montanus
Uplands, loca montana
Upon, à, ad, in, super, supra
Upon (the right), dextrorsùm; (left), sinistrorsùm; (my life), ne vivam si, dispeream si
Upper, superior   [gulum
The upper-leather, calcei obstraTo get the upper hand, supero
To give the upper hand, loco cedere
Uppermost, supremus, summus
Uppish, superbus, insolens
To uprise, or uprear, elevo
Upright, integer, probus; (in posture), arrectus, erectus
Upright dealing, æquitas
Uprightly, integrè, justè, æquè
Uprightness, probitas, integritas
To uprise, surgo
An uproar, turba, tumultus
To be in an uproar, tumultuor, fremo
The upshot, eventus, successus
Upside down, inverso ordine
An upstart, vir novus
To upturn, elevo, egero
Upward, sursùm
Bending upward, reclivis
With the face upward, supinus
To turn upward, resupino
Urbanity, urbanitas, comitas
An urchin, erinaceus; (dwarf), nanus, pumilus, pumilio
Ure (use), usus
The ureter, ureter
To urge, urgeo, impello, insto
Urgency, impulsus, necessitas
Urgent, importunus, vehemens
Urgently, importunè, sollicitè
An urger, stimulator
An urging, incitatio, stimulatio
An urinal, vitrum ad urinam accipiendam, matula
Urinary, urinarius, urinalis
Urine, urina, lotium
Difficulty of urine, stranguria
To urine, meio, mingo
An un, urna
With us, nobiscum
Usage, consuetudo, usus; (treatment), accipiendi ratio
Use (the using of a thing), usus; (profit), ususfructus; (custom), consuetudo; (or interest for money), usura, fœnus
Of, or in use, usitatus, consuetus
After common use, usitatè
Out of use, desuetus, exoletus
To use, utor, occupo; (often), usurpo; (one's endeavours), sedulò facere, operam dare; (exercise), exerceo; (treat), tracto, accipio; (tenderly), mollitèr habere; (genteelly), liberalitèr habere; (a tavern), frequento
To use, sueo, soleo, consuesco
To make use of, utor, fruor
To grow into use, obtineo; (out of use), desuesco, exolesco
Want of use, desuetudo
Used, usurpatus; (accustomed), assuetus, consuetus; (treated), acceptus, tractatus
Much used, usitatus

H

VAI   VAT   VEN

Useful, utilis, necessarius
Usefully, utilitèr
Usefulness, utilitas
Useless, inutilis, incommodus
Uselessly, inutilitèr
Uselessness, inutilitas
An usher, anteambulo; (serjeant), lictor; (of a school), subpræceptor
To usher, introduco
An using, usus
Usual, usitatus, consuetus
Usually, usitatè, plerumquè
Th usurer, fœnerator
Ao usurp, usurpo, invado
Usurpation, usurpatio
Usurped, iniquè usurpatus
An usurper, usurpator
Usury, usura, fœnus; (of the 100), usura quincuncialis
With usury, fœneratò
Belonging to usury, fœneratorius
To borrow on usury, fœneror
To lend on usury, fœnero
Utensils, instrumenta, vasa
Uterine, uterinus
Utility, utilitas, commodum
Utmost, extremus, summus
To one's utmost, pro viribus
Utopian, imaginarius
Utter, exterior; (total), totus, totalis, integer
To utter (speak), eloquor, pronuncio, profero; (sell), vendo
Utterable, effabilis
Utterance, elocutio, eloquium; (selling), venditio
Of good utterance, eloquens, disertus
Utter barristers, licentiati in jure
Uttered, enunciatus, prolatus
An utterer, editor, venditor
An uttering, enunciatio ; (of wares), venditio
Utterly, penitùs, omninò, fundìtùs
Uttermost (utmost), extremus
The uvula, uvula, columella
Uxorious, uxorius, uxori nimis deditus

V.

Vacancy (of place), vacuitas ; (leisure), otium, vacatio
Vacant (void), vacans, vacuus; (at leisure), otiosus, ferians ; (hours), horæ subsecivæ
To be vacant (empty), vaco
To vacate (make void), abrogo, rescindo
A vacation, vacatio, otium; (between terms), justitium
Vacillation, vacillatio
Vacuity, vacuitas, vacuum
A vacuum, vacuum
To vade, vado, evanesco
A vagabond, erro, homo vagus
A vagary, repentinus animi impetus
Vagrancy, vagatio
A vagrant, erro
Vails, lucella adventitia
Vain (idle, useless), vanus, inanis, futilis, inutilis ; (proud), superbus, arrogans ; (glorious), levis, inconstans
In vain, frustrà
To be vainglorious, superbio
Vainglory, superbia, arrogantia
Vainly, superbè, arrogantèr, inanitèr
[146]

Vain-speaking, vaniloquentia
A vaivode, præfectus
A vale, vallis
Valediction, valedictio
Valedictory, valedictorius
A valet, assecla, famulus ; (de chambre), cubicularius
Valetudinary, valetudinarius
Valiant, fortis, magnanimus, animosus
Valiantly, fortitèr, animosè
Valiantness, magnanimitas
Valid, validus, firmus, ratus
Validity, validitas, firmitas
A valley, vallis, convallis
Valorous, fortis, animosus, virilis
Valorously, fortitèr, animosè, virilitèr
Valour, fortitudo, virtus
Valuable, pretiosus, charus
Valuation, æstimatio
Value, valor, pretium
To value, æstimo, censeo, pendo ; (at a high rate), magni facere ; (at a low rate), parvi ducere, vili pendere
Of no value, vilis
To be of no value, vilesco
Of so great value, tanti
Of more value, pluris
Of less value, minoris
A valuer, censor, æstimator
A valuation, æstimatio
Valves, valvulæ
To vamp up, reficio, resarcio
A vane, venti index versatilis, triton
A vanguard, acies prima
To vanish, vanesco, evanesco
Vanity, vanitas, inanitas ; (vainglory), arrogantia
To vanquish (in combat), vinco, supero, debello ; (in debate), confuto, refello, redarguo
Vanquishable, superabilis
A vanquisher, victor, domitor
A vanquishing, expugnatio
Vantage, lucrum, additamentum
Vapid, vapidus
A vapor, vapor, exhalatio
To vapor, jacto, glorior
Vaporation, vapor, exhalatio
Vaporous, vapores emittens
Full of vapours, vaporosus
Vaporing, jactans, gloriana, ferox
Vaporish, morosus, difficilis
Variable, levis, instabilis
Variableness, levitas, inconstantia
Variance, dissidium, contentio, lis, altercatio
To be at variance, dissideo, litigo
Variation, variatio, mutatio
To variegate, coloribus variare
Variety, varietas, diversitas
Various, varius, diversus
Variously, variè, diversè
To vary (altèr), vario, muto; (disgrace), dissentio, discordo
A varlet, homo scelestus
Varnish, vernix
To varnish, polio, fuco; (disguise), dissimulo
A vase, vas speciosum
A vassal, verna, vassalus
Vassalage, mancipium
Vast, vastus, ingens, enormis
Vastation, vastatio
Vastly, vastè, valdè
Vastness, vastitas
A vat, cupa, dolium ; (for barley), ptisanarium ; (for cheese), forma casearia; (for dyeing), ahenum tinctorium

A vault, fornix, camera, testudo; (underground), crypta ; (for dead corpses), sepulchrum cameratum
To vault (cover with an arch), arcuo, fornico, camero ; (or leap over), transilio; (off), desilio; (on), insilio
A vaulter, desultor, saltator
A vaulting, desultura
Vaulting, desiliens, desultorius
A vaunt (boasting), jactatio
To vaunt, glorior, jacto
A vaunter, jactator
Vaunting, gloriosus ; (words), ampullæ, sesquipedalia verba
A vaunting, jactatio
Veal, caro vitulina
A veer, navigatio obliqua
To veer (about), circumago; (a cable), rudentem transferre, or in orbem vertere ; (the sails), sinus velorum obliquare
Veered, circumactus
Vegetable, vegetabilis
To vegetate, vegeto, germino
Vegetation, vegetatio
Vegetative, vegetativus
Vegete, vegetus, vividus
Vehemence, vehementia, vis
Vehement, vehemens, fervidus
To be vehement, ferveo
Vehemently, vehementèr, valdè
A vehicle, vehiculum
A veil, velum
To veil, velo, obnubo
A vein, vena; (in writing), stylus ; (of wit), lepor, facetiæ; (of poetry), facultas poëtica; (of silver, &c.), molybdæna
In a pleasant vein, lepidus, salsus
Veiny, venosus
Vellication, vellicatio
Vellum, pergamena, membrana
Of vellum, membranaceus
Velocity, velocitas, celeritas
Velvet, velvetum
Venal, venalis
To vend, vendo, vendito
Vendible, vendibilis, mercabilis
A vending, venditio
A vender, venditor
Veneficial, veneficus
Venerable, venerabilis, venerandus, colendus
Venerably, augustè
To venerate, revereor, colo
Veneration, veneratio, reverentia
Venereal, venereus
Venery, res, or libido venereæ ; (hunting), venatio
Venesection, venæ sectio
Vengeance, ultio, vindicta
To take vengeance, ulciscor
With a vengeance, diras imprecando
Vengeful, ultionis cupidus
Venial, venialis, veniâ dignus
Venison, caro ferina
Venom, venenum, virus
To venom, veneno inficere
Venomous, venenosus, virosus
Venomously, perniciosè, malignè
A vent, spiraculum, exitus; (sale), venditio
To vent (sell), vendo, vendito ; (give vent to), spiraculum aperire; (passion), iram effundere
To take vent, patefio, evulgor
Having vent, respirans
To ventilate, ventilo
Ventilation, ventilatio
The ventricle, ventriculus
A venturing (undertaking), an-

VES

sum, inceptum; (chance), sors; (hazard), alea, periculum
At a venture, temerè, periculosè
To venture, periclitor, experior; (a wager), pignus deponere; (or dare to do), audeo
A venturer, audax
Venturesome, Venturous, audens, audax
Veracity, veracitas, veritas
A verb, verbum
Verbal (derived of a verb), verbalis; (verbally), verbo tenus
Verbatim, ad verbum, verbatim
Verbose, verbosus
Verdant, virens, viridis
Verdegrease, ærugo
To pass a verdict, sententiam ferre
Verdict, sententia, opinio; (of a jury), veredictum, judicium, juratorum sententia
Verdure, viriditas
The verge (limit), limes, ambitus; (instrument), fascis lictoria
To verge, vergo
A verger, lictor, vergifer
Veridical, veridicus
A verifier, confirmator
To verify, confirmo, ratum facere
A verifying, confirmatio
Verily, quidem, equidem, verè, certè, reverà; (yea verily), imò, maximè
Verity, veritas
Veritable, verus, certus
Verjuice, omphacium
Vermicular, vermicularis
Vermiculated, vermiculatus
Vermilion, minium
Of vermilion, miniaceus
To paint with vermilion, minio
Marked, &c. with vermilion, miniatus
Vermin, vermis, pediculus
Full of vermin, verminosus
Vernacular, vernaculus
Vernal, vernus, vernalis
Versatile, versatilis
A verse, versus, carmen; (in verse), oratio numeris stricta; (short), versiculus; (of a chapter), versus, incisum
Well versed, peritus, edoctus
A versicle, versiculus
A versifier, versificator
To versify, versifico, versus con- [dere
A versifying, versificatio
A version, versio
Vertical, verticalis, in vertice; (point), zenith
Verticity, rotatio
A vertigo, vertigo
Vertiginous, vertiginosus
Vervain, verbena
Very (true, even, self, &c.), verus, merus, ipse
A vesicatory, vesicatorium
A vesicle, vesicula
Vespers, preces vespertinæ
A vessel, vas; (ship), navigium, navigiolum, navicula
A vest, vestis, vestimentum
To vest with possession, possessionem dare; (with an office), inauguro
Vestal, vestalis
Vested (in office), inauguratus
A vestige, vestigium
A vesting in office, inauguratio
A vestment, vestimentum
vestry (room), vestiarium, sacrarium; (parish meeting), parœciæ concilium; (keeper),
[147]

VIL

æditunus, sacrista; (man), in parœciæ concilium cooptatus
A vesture, vestitus, vestis
A vetch, vicia, ervum
Of vetches, viciarius
A veteran, veteranus
To vex, vexo, inquieto
To be vexed, affligor, angor
Vexation, vexatio, mœror
Vexatious, molestus, acerbus
Vexationally, acerbè, ægrè, infestè
Vexed, Vext, vexatus, iratus
A vexer, vexator, interpellator
Vexing (causing vexation), molestus; (grieving), mœrens, dolens
A vexing, vexatio, perturbatio
A vial, phiala
Viands, cibaria, cibus; (dainty), dapes, cupediæ
To vibrate, vibro, agito
Vibration, vibratio, agitatio
A vicar, vicarius
A vicarage, vicariatus
A vicarship, vicarii munus
Vicarius, vicarius
A vice-admiral, legatus classiarius; (chamberlain), vice cubicularii fungens; (chancellor), vice cancellarius; (gerent), legatus; (roy), prorex
Vicinage, Vicinity, vicinitas
Vicissitude, vicissitudo
A victim, victima, hostia
A victor, victor, superator
Victory, victoria, palma
To get the victory, vinco, supero
Victorious, victor, victrix
Victoriously, victoris instar
Victuals, victus, res cibaria; (for an army), commeatus
To victual, cibaria suppeditare
Victualled, cibariis suppeditatus
To sell victuals, cauponor
Belonging to victuals, cibarius
To buy victuals, obsonor
A victualler, caupo
A victualler's trade, cauponaria
A victualling-house, caupona, popina [popinor
To frequent victualling-houses,
To vie with, contendo, æmulor
A view, visus, conspectus; (of a place), prospectus
At first view, primâ specie
To view (the situation), exploro, lustro; (the posture of an enemy), specular copias hostium; (take a view of), lustro, inspicio, circumspicio; (examine), investigo, indago, scrutor, exquiro; (narrowly), inspicere propius
In one view, uno aspectu
In view of the world, palàm
To have in view, prævideo
Under one's view, sub aspectum
Having viewed, intuitus
A viewer, inspector, speculator
Viewing, intuens, speculans
A viewing, inspectio, speculatio
A vigil, vigilia, pervigilium
Vigilance, Vigilancy, vigilantia
Vigilant, vigilans, vigil, diligens
Vigilantly, vigilantèr, diligentèr
To be vigilant, vigilo, excubo
Vigour (of body), robur, vigor; (of mind) firmitas animi
Vigorous, validus, vigens, strenuus, acer, vegetus, valens
Vigorously, strenuè, acritèr
Vigorousness, robur, vigor
Without vigour, enervatus, enervis
Vile (mean), vilis, abjectus; (fil-

VIS

thy), fœdus, sordidus, obscœnus, spurcus, impurus; (wicked), sceleratus, pravus, flagitiosus, perditus
Vilely, vilitèr, pravè, fœdè
Vileness, pravitas, fœditas
To vilify, vitupero, calumnior
A vilifying, vituperatio
A villa, villa, diversorium
A village, vicus, pagus [tha
Village by village, vicatim, pagaA villager, vicanus, paganus
A villain (bondman), mancipium; (rogue), sceleratus, nequam
Villainy, scelus, flagitium
Villainage, clientela
Villainous, sceleritas, sceleatus
Villainously, nefariè, inhonestè
Villainousness, scelus, flagitium
Villous, villosus, hirsutus
Vimineous, vimineus
Vincible, vincibili-, superabilis
To vindicate, vindico, defendo
Vindicated, vindicatus, defensus
A vindicating, Vindication, defensio
A vindicator, vindex, defensor
Vindictive, ultionis cupidus
A vine, vitis; (wild), labrusca; (branch), palmes, sarmentum
A vine-planter, vitiator; (dresser), pampinator, vinitor; (leaf), pampinus
To prune a vine, pampino
Of a vine-leaf, pampineus
Full of vine-leaves, pampinosus
Of a vine, vinearius, vinealis
Vinegar, acetum, vinum acidum
A vineyard, vinetum, vinea
Vinous, vinosus
A vintage, vindemia
A vintager, vindemiator
Belonging to a vintage, vindemiatorius
A vintner, vinarius
A viol, fides, lyra, cithara
Violable, violabilis
To violate, violo, rumpo, temero
Violated, violatus, temeratus
Not violated, inviolatus
A violating, Violation, violatio
A violator, violator, ruptor
Violence, violentia, vis
With violence, violentèr, per vim
Violent, violens, vehemens, acris
To lay violent hands on one's self, mortem sibi conasciscere
Violently, violentèr, gravitèr
A violet, viola
Of, or like violets, violaceus
A violin, fides minor
A viper, vipera, echidna
Viperous, viperinus, viperius
A virago, virago
A virgin, virgo
Of a virgin, virgineus
Virgin, adj. purus, optimus
A virginal, clavecymbalum
Virginity, virginitas, castitas
Virgo, signum virginis
Virile, virilis, masculus
Virility, virilitas, fortitudo
Virtual, insitus
Virtually, vi insitâ
Virtue (piety), virtus, pietas, probitas; (efficacy), virtus, proprietas, via
Virtuous, pius, probus
Virtuously, piè, religiosè
A virtuoso, curiosus indagator
Virulence, acerbitas, asperitas
Virulent, virulentus, asper, mordax
Virulently, aspèrè, acerbè
The visage, facies, vultus, os
H 2

VOL

Sour-visaged, torvus, tetricus
Viscid, viscidus
Viscosity, viscositas
A viscount, vicecomes
Viscous, viscosus, viscidus
A viser, or visor, cassidis, buccula
Visibility, visibilitas
Visible, visibilis, aspectabilis; (manifest), conspicuus, clarus, manifestus, perspicuus
Visibly, apertè, manifestè
The grand visier (vizier), summus imperatoris Turcici consiliarius
A vision, visio; (phantasm), spectrum, phantasma
Visionary, ad visionem pertinens
A visit, officiosus aditus
To visit, visito, viso, inviso
A visitor, salutator
A visiting, or visitation, visitatio; (inspection), inspectio
Visored, personatus
Visual, opticus
Vital, vitalis
Vitality, vitalitas
Vitally, vitalitèr
The vitals, vitalia
To vitiate, vitio, depravo, corrumpo
A vitiating, depravatio
Vitious, vitiosus, pravus
Vitiously, vitiosè, pravè, nequitèr
Vitiousness, pravitas
Vitreous, vitreus
To vitrify, in vitrum mutare
Vitriol, vitriolum
To vituperate, vitupero
Vivacious, vivax, vitalis
Vivacity, vivacitas, vitalitas
A vivary, vivarium
Vivid (lively), vividus
Vividly, vividè
Vivific, vivificus
To vivify, vivum facere
Viviparous, viviparus
A vixen, femina rixosa
A vizard, or visor, larva, persona
A vocabulary, vocabularium
Vocal, vocalis; (music), vocum cantus
Vocation, vocatio, genus, or institutum vitæ
Vocative, vocativus; (case), vocandi casus
Vociferation, vociferatio
Vociferous, clamosus
Vogue, fama, æstimatio
To be in vogue, invalesco
A voice, vox; (vote), suffragium
With a good voice, benè vocalis
A giving one's voice, suffragatio
Void (empty), expers, inanis, vacuus; (of no authority), invalidus, cassus
A void space, vacuum
To void (or go from), cedere de; (cast out), egero, excerno
To be void, vaco
To make void, evacuo; (a law), legem rescindere
Voidance, evacuatio; (in law), vacatio beneficii
Voided, evacuatus
A voider, cophinus ad analecta colligenda
A voiding, excretio
Voidness, inanitas, vacuitas
Volatile, volatilis, volaticus
Volatility, inconstantia
Volery, avium volatus
Volition, voluntas
A volley (about), acclamatio; (of shot), emissa tela
Volubility, volubilitas
Voluble, volubilis, lubricus
[148]

WAG

A volume, volumen, tomus
A portable volume, manuale
Voluminous, magnus, crassus
Voluntarily, ultrò, spontè, libentèr
Voluntary, voluntarius
Volunteers, volones, milites voluntarii [tuosus
Voluptuous, Voluptuary, voluptuously, luxuriosè, jucundè
Voluptuousness, luxuria
Volutation (rolling), volutatio
A vomit, vomitus
To vomit, vomo; (again), revomo; (often), vomito; (out, or up), evomo, ejicio
To be like to vomit, nauseo
Ready to vomit, nauseans, nauseabundus
A vomiting, vomitio
Belonging to vomiting, vomicus
Vomitive, Vomitory, emeticus
Voracious, vorax, gulosus
Voracity, voracitas
A votary, voto obstrictus
A vote, suffragium, sententia
To vote, suffragium ferre
To vote for, suffragor
To vote against, refragor
A voting, suffragatio
Votive, votivus
To vouch, affirmo, assero
A voucher, assertor, vindex
A vouching, assertio, vindicatio
To vouchsafe, dignor, concedo
Having vouchsafed, dignatus
Vouchsafement, donum
A vow, votum
To vow, voveo
To bind by vow, devoto
A vowel, litera vocalis
A vowing, votum, devotio
A voyage, iter per mare, navigatio
To go a voyage, navigo
A volcano, mons ignitus
Vulgar, vulgaris, communis, humilis, abjectus, tritus, sordidus
The vulgar, vulgus, plebs, populus
Vulgarity, mores vulgi
Vulgarly, vulgò, abjectè
Vulnerable, vulneri obnoxius
Vulnerary, vulnerarius
A vulture, vultur
Of a vulture, vulturinus
To vye, æmulor, certo

W.

To wabble, motu vacillare
Wad, stibium
A wad, fascia, fascis
Wadded, panno suffarcinatus
Wadding, pannus villosior
To waddle, incessu vacillare, provolvo
To wade, in aquâ incedere; (over), per vadum transire, vado
A wafer (made of meal), crustulum farinarium tenuissimum; (for sealing letters), crustulum signatorium
The wafer (consecrated by the Romish priest), hostia
To waft (shake), vibro; (convey), deduco, defero; (or carry over), trajicio
Waftage, vectatio
A wag, homo lepidus, salaputium
To wag, agito, vibro; (neut.) vacillo, nuto, trepido; (the tail), ceveo, caudâ blandiri

WAN

To wage, pignore certare; (law), litigo; (war), bellum gerere
To lay a wager, pignus opponere
A wager, pignus, sponsio
Wages, stipendium, salarium; (of a sailor), naulum; (of a day), diarium
Serving for wages, stipendiarius
Belonging to wages, stipendiarius
Waggery, dicacitas
A wagging, vacillatio
Waggish, procax, petulans
Waggishly, lascivè, jocosè
Waggishness, petulantia
A waggon, rheda, plaustrum
A waggoner, rhedarius
To wail, deploro, defleo [dus
To be wailed, lamentabilis, ingenA wailing, luctus, ploratus
A wain, plaustrum; (load), vehes; (driver), plaustrarius
The wain of the moon, decrementum [corporis
The waist, cinctura, media pars
A waistcoat, subucula
To wait (for), expecto, præstolor, opperior; (upon), inservio, famulor; (upon, or accompany), comitor; (upon, or visit), inviso, visito; (for, or lie in wait), insidior, insidias struere; (stay), maneo
A lier in wait, insidiator [cens
Lying in wait, insidians, insidiBy lying in wait, insidiosè
A lying in wait, insidiæ
Waited on, comitatus
A waiter, assecla, minister
A waiting for, expectatio
A waiting man, pedissequus; (woman), pedissequa
The waits, spondaulæ
To wake, act. suscito, expergefacio; neut. expergiscor
To be wakened, expergefio
Wakeful, vigil, insomnis
Wakefulness, vigilantia
Wakes, paganalia
A walk, ambulacrum, ambulatio
To walk, ambulo; (about), circumambulo; (the streets), incedere per vias; (back), redambulo; (forth), prodeambulo; (abroad), expatior; (through), perambulo
A walker, ambulator, ambulatrix
Walking, ambulans
Of walking, ambulatorius
A walking, ambulatio; (abroad), deambulatio; (place), ambulacrum; (about), obambulatio; (stick), scipio
A night-walker, noctivagus
A wall (of a town), murus, mœnia; (of a house), paries; (mound), maceria
Of a wall, muralis
To wall, muro cingere, munio
Walled about, muro cinctus
A wall-flower, parietaria
A wallet, pera, mantica
To wallop, ebullio
To wallow, act. voluto; neut. volutor; (in pleasures), voluptatibus se addicere
Wallowing, volutans
A wallowing, volutatio
A wallowing-place, volutabrum
A walnut, juglans
Wan, pallidus, luridus
To be wan, palleo, expalleo
To grow wan, pallesco
A wand, virga, rudis
To wander, vagor, erro; (about), pervagor, oberro; (from), ab-

WAR   WAS   WAX

erro; (over), pererro; (under), suberro; (up and down), evagor
Wandered over, pererratus
Having wandered, vagatus
A wanderer, erro
Wandering, vagus, erraticus; (on hills), montivagus; (alone), solivagus; (about), circumforaneus; (much abroad), multivagus
A wandering, erratio, vagatio; (through), peragratio
The wane, decrementum
Wanness, pallor, luror
Want, egestas, inopia, indigentia, defectus, desiderium; (of knowledge), inscientia, ignorantia; (of money), pecuniæ inopia; (of corn), annonæ difficultas; (of parents), orbitas
To want (desire), desidero; (or be in want), egeo, indigeo, careo; *seul.* deficio, desum, absum
In want, egens, egenus
Wanting, egens, deficiens
A wanting, indigentia, inopia
Wanton, petulans, procax, lascivus
To make wanton, emollio
To grow wanton, nimis efferri
To play the wanton, lascivio
Playing the wanton, petulans
Wantonly, procaciter, molliter
Wantonness, procacitas, lascivia
War, bellum, arma
A man of war (military man), bellator; (ship), navis bellica
To war, bellum inferre, *or* gerere
To serve in war, milito
To warble, modulor
Having warbled, modulatus
A warbler, modulator
Warbling, modulans, canorus
A warbling, modulatio
A ward (guard), custodia; (one under ward), pupillus, pupilla; (part of a city, &c.), regio, tribus; (of a lock), serræ ferramenta clathrata
Of the same ward, tribulis
Ward by ward, tributim, curiatim
To ward (guard), custodio, tueor; (against), caveo; (off), depello
Warded, custoditus, defensus; (off), depulsus, repulsus
A warden, custos
A warder, vigil, speculator
A wardmote, wardemotus
A wardrobe, garderoba, armarium
A wardship, tutela
Of wardship, tutelaris
Ware, merx; (small), mercium particulæ; (earthen), vasa fictilia; (cutlers'), instrumenta cultraria; (turners'), toreumata
A seller of wares, tabernarius
A warehouse, repositorium; (man), solidarius
Ware (beware), cave!
Warfare, bellum, militia
Warfaring, bellicus, militaris
Warily, cautè, providè, prudentèr
Wariness, cautio, cautela
Warlike, bellicosus, bellicus
Warm (not hot), calidus, tepidus; (ardent), ardens; (in temper), acris, vehemens, iracundus
To warm, calefacio; (often), carefacto
To be made warm, tepefio
To be warm, tepeo, caleo
To grow warm, calesco
To keep warm, foveo, focillo

[149]

Warmed, tepefactus, calefactus
A warming, calefactio; (pan), thermoclinium
Warmly, calidè, tepidè; (ardently), ardentèr, iracundè, vehementèr
Warmth, Warmness, calor, tepor
To warn, moneo; (privately), submoneo; (aforehand), præmoneo
To be warned, commonefio
A warner, monitor
A warning, monitio, monitum; (notice), notitia
To give warning, moneo
The warp, panni stamen
A warp (at sea), helcium
To warp (a woof), telam ordiri; (as wood), eurvor, contrahor
Warped (as wood), incurvatus
A warping, incurvatio
To warrant, warrantum, cantio
A warrant, securum præstare, protego; (in law), fidejubeo
Warranted, legitimus, genuinus
Unwarrantable, non defendendus
Warrantably, legitimè, justè
Warranted, ratus, firmatus
A warranting, auctoritas
A warren, vivarium, warenna; (of hares), leporarium; (keeper), vivarii custos, warrennarius
Warring, bellum gerens
A warrior, miles, homo bellicosus, bellator
A wart, verruca
Warty (full of warts), verrucosus
Wary, cautus, prudens, providus; (thrifty), parcus, frugalis
To be wary, caveo, prævideo
I was, eram
A wash (or marsh), æstuarium; (or washing), lavatio; (for hogs), sorbitio; (for the skin, &c.), compositio ad lavandam
To wash, luo, lavo; (about), circumluo; (away, *or* off), abluo; (between), interluo; (all over), perluo, diluo; (gargle), gargarizo
To be washed, lavor
Not washed, illotus, immundus
A washer, lotor; (woman), lavatrix, lotrix
A washing, lotio, lavatio; (away), ablutio; (gargling), gargarizatio
A wash-house, lavacrum; (ball), smegma; (bowl), labrum
Washy, humidus
A wasp, vespa
Waspish (tetchy), morosus, difficilis
Waspishly, morosè, perversè
Waspishness, morositas, perversitas
Waste (spoil), vastatio; (loss), damnum; (place), ager incultus; (or loose papers), adversaria
The waste (of the body), media pars corporis; (of a ship), laterum navigii septa
Waste (useless), inutilis
To waste (spend), consumo; (riotously), prodigo, profundo; (or pine away), tabesco, decresco; (lay waste), vasto, depopulor, spolio
Wasteful, profusus, prodigus
Wastefully, profusè, prodigè
Wastefulness, prodigalitas
A waster, depopulator, vastator, nepos, prodigus
Wasting (pining away), tabescens
A wasting (or pining away), tabes; (prodigally), profusio, prodigentia; (spoiling), spoliatio, vastatio
A watch, automatum loculo portandum, *or* manuale
A watchmaker, automatopœus
Watch and ward, excubiæ
To watch, vigilo, evigilo; (observe), observo, exploro; (for opportunity), capto, aucupor; (all night), pervigilo; (and ward), excubo
A watcher (lier in wait), insidiator; (observer), observator
Watchful, vigil, vigilans
Watchfully, vigilantèr
Watchfulness, vigilantia
Watching (being on the watch), in excubiis stans; (all night); pernox; (all day), perdius; (for), captans, aucupans
A watching (observing), observatio; (all night), pervigilatio, pervigilium; (and warding), excubatio
A watch-candle, lucerna lucubratoria
A watch-man, excubitor, vigil; (word), tessera, symbolum; (tower), specula, pharus
Water, aqua; (river), amnis, fluvius, flumen
A fall of water, cataracta
Living in water, aquatilis; (by land and water), amphibius
Of the water, aquaticus, aquatilis
Spring water, aqua fontana
The springing of water, scaturigo
Standing water, lacus, stagnum
High water, plenis maris æstus
Low water, maris refluxus
To water, rigo, irrigo, humecto; (take in fresh water), aquor, aquatum ire; (hemp), maceraro cannabem aquâ
To make water, meio, mingo
To water cattle, aquatum agere
A taking in fresh water, aquatio
A water-bailiff, aquarius; (bank), ripa; (bearer), aquator; (beetle), scarabæus aquaticus; (course), aquæductus; (course, at a mill), gurges molaris; (gruel), pulmentum; (hen), fulica; (horse), hippopotamus; (lily), nymphæa; (fall), cataracta; (ers)
A waterman's trade, navicularia
A water-snake, natrix; (trough for beasts), aqualiculus
Watered, riguus, irriguus; (steeped in water), aquâ maceratus
A watering, irrigatio; (steeping), in aquâ maceratio
Watery, aquosus, humidus
To wattle, cratio, contexo
A wave, unda, fluctus
To wave (play up and down), fluctuo, vacillo; (toss up and down), jacio, agito; (omit), omitto; (waft), trajicio
Wave-offerings, dona agitationis
Waved (tossed), jactatus, agitatus, vibratus; (in waves), undulatus; (omitted), omissus, prætermissus
To waver, fluctuo, ambigo
Wavering, fluctuans, inconstans
A wavering, fluctuatio
Waveringly, inconstantèr, dubiè
Full of waves, undosus, fluctuosus
Like waves, undatim
A waving (tossing), jactatio; (omitting), omissio
Wax, cera

H 3

WEA

Of wax, cereus
Covered with wax, inceratus
Of wax-colour, cerinus
A wax-chandler, cerarius
To wax (do over with wax), incero, cero; (grow), cresco; (become), fio; (old), senesco, caneo; (fat), pinguesco
Waxed, *or* waxen (done over with wax), inceratus; (become), factus
Waxing (growing), crescens
A waxing (increasing), incrementum, augmentum
A' way, via, iter; (passage), aditus, meatus; (beaten), callis, via trita; (broad), platea, via lata; (by), diverticulum, via devia; (foot), semita; (horse), actus; (high, *or* public), via regia, *or* publica; (great), longè; (cross), trivium; (direct), via recta
By the way, obitèr, præter propositum; (in a journey), in viâ, per viam
In the way, obviàm, obvius
By way of, causâ
A way (of life), consuetudo; (manner), ratio, modus
A way out, exitus
Both ways, in utramque partem
This way, hâc; (that), illàc; (every), quaquaversùm; (another), aliò
Which way soever, quacunquè
A long way about, circuitus
Out of the way, devius, avius
To be out of the way, à viâ aberrare; (be absent), absum
On the way, in itinere
Leading the way, prævius
Many ways, multifariam
All ways, omnifariam
A wayfaring man, viator
To waylay, insidior
A waylayer, insidiator
Wayward, morosus, perversus
Waywardly, protervè
Waywardness, protervitas
We ourselves, nosmet ipsi
Weak, debilis, imbellis; (in judgment), fatuus
To be weak, langueo
To weaken, debilito, frango
A weakening, debilitatio
Weakly, *adj.* infirmus; *adv.* imbecilitèr, infirmè, debilitèr
Weakness, debilitas, impotentia; (of constitution), infirmitas valetudinis, corporis languor; (of age), ætatis imbecillitas; (of courage), animi debilitatio; (of mind), mentis debilitas
Wealth, opes, divitiæ
Wealthiness, opulentia
Wealthy, opulentus, dives
To wean, ablacto, à lacte depellere; (from pleasures), à voluptatibus abstinere
Weaned, à lacte depulsus
A weaning, à lacte depulsio
A weanling, à mammâ nupèr depulsus
A weapon, telum, ferrum
Weapons, arma, tela
Bearing weapons, telifer
Weaponless, inermis
A wear (floodgate), cataracta; (for catching fish), nassa piscatoria
To wear away, *or* out, tero; (be, worn out), atteror, decresco (in flesh), tabesco
To wear clothes, vestior
[150]

WEE

To wear out land, agrum effœtum reddere; (out patience), patientiâ abuti, patientiam exhaurire; (out of use), desuesco; (out of mind), è memoriâ elabi
A wearer, tritor
Not wearied, indefessus
Cannot be wearied, indefatigabilis
Weariness, lassitudo
A wearing (away), attritus; (out of use), desuetudo
Wearisome, molestus, fatigans
Wearisomeness, tædium
Weary, lassus, fessus
To be weary, defatigor
To grow weary, lassesco
To make weary, fatigo, lasso; (with toil), laboribus frangere
Weary of, pertæsus
The weasand, gurgulio
A weasel, mustela
Weather, tempestas, cœlum
To weather (a cape), promontorium præternavigare; (a storm), tempestatem eludere; (dangers), pericula magno animo sustinere
Weatherbeaten, tempestate actus
A weathercock, triton
A weatherglass, thermometrum
Weatherwise, tempestatis præscius
Weathered, latus, sustentus
Weathering, ferens, sustinens
To weave, texo; (together), contexo; (throughout), pertexo
Weaved, textus, textilis
A weaver, textor, textrix; ('s trade), texendi ars; ('s shop), textrina; ('s beam), jugum textorium; ('s shuttle), radius textorius; ('s slay), pecten textoris
A weaving, textura; (together), contextura
A web, tela, textum
Webbed, Webfooted, palmipes
To wed, nubo
A wedding, nuptiæ, conjugium
Of a wedding, nuptialis
A wedding-ring, annulus sponsalis; (song), epithalamium
A wedge, cuneus; (of metal), massa, *or* lingula metalli
Cleft with a wedge, discuneatus
Like a wedge, cuneatìm; *adj.* cuneatus
To wedge in, vi perrumpere
Wedlock, conjugium, matrimonium
Wednesday, feria quarta
A weed, herba inutilis
Sea-weed, alga
Weed, *or* weeds (dress, *or* garment), habitus, vestis; (mourning apparel), vestis pulla, *or* lugubris
To weed, sarrio, eranco
Weeded, à noxiis herbis liberatus
A weeder, sarritor, runcator
A weeding, sarritura, runcatio; (hook), sarculum, marra
A week, hebdomada, septimana; (day), dies profestus
Weekly, singulis hebdomadis
A weel (trap for fish), nassa; (whirlpool), gurges
To ween, autumo, opinor
To weep, fleo, lachrymo; (like a woman), ea lamentis muliebritèr dedere; (for), defleo, deploro; (greatly), in lacrymas solvi

WEP

Ready to weep, lachrymabundus
Weeping, flens; (much), lachrymosus
Weepingly, lachrymosè
A weesel, mustela
A weevil (insect), curculio
Weftage, textura
A weir, beatia erratica
A weigh (of cheese, 256lb.), pondus casei continens 256 libras
To weigh, pendo, appendo, pondero, libro; (consider), penso, pensito, pondero, æstimo; (anchor), anchoram solvere; (up), tollo, levo; (down, *or* more), præpondero, degravo, prægravo; (*or* sink down), deprimo
A weigher, librator, pensator
Weighing, ponderans, pensans; (down in a scale), gravans
A weighing, ponderatio, pensitatio; (down), depressio
A weight, pondus; (even), æquilibrium; (great), moles; (authority, *or* interest), auctoritas
A matter of weight, magni momenti
Over-weight, additamentum
Weightily, gravitèr
Weightiness, gravitas
Weights, trutina
Weighty, gravis, ponderosus
To grow weighty, gravesco; (more weighty), ingravesco
To be more weighty, præpondero
A Welchman, Cambrobritannus
Welcome, gratus, optatus
To welcome, liberalitèr accipere, gratulor
Welcoming, gratulans
A welcoming, gratulatio
Welfare, incolumitas, salus [sum optimè; (exceeding), imprimìs, benè; (as), æquè, tam
The welkin, æther, cœlum expansum
Well, benè, probè, rectè; (very),
Well! age! (aday!) eheu! (done!), euge! bellè! (nigh), penè, ferè
Well, *adj.* (in health), sanus, validus, viribus integer; (in years), ætate provectus; (in one's wits), compos animi; (to pass), locuples, opulentus, dives; (safe), salvus; (advised), consultus; (beloved), carus, dilectus
Well met, optato advenis
A well-wisher, amicus
A well, fons, puteus
Of a well, fontanus
A well-digger, putearius; (mouth), fontis crepido, *or* margo; (head), scaturigo
To be well (in health), valeo, benè se habere; (to pass), opibus satis abundare
To live (*or* fare well), opiparè epulari; (*or* uprightly), piè vitam agere
The welt (of a garment), limbus; (of a shoe), lacinia
To welt, limbum assuere
Welted, prætextus, subsutus
To welter, volutor
A weltering, volutatio
The wem, abdomen, pantex
A wen, struma, scrofula
Full of wens, Wenny, strumosus
A wench (young woman), puella; (servant-maid), ancilla
To wench, scortor
A wencher, scortator
Wept for, ploratus, deploratus
To be wept for, flebilis

WHE	WHI	WHO

Were it not that, nisi, si—; (as it were), quasi, ceu, tanquàm
The west, occidens, occasus; (wind), zephyrus, favonius; (west-south-west), africus, libs
Western, Westerly, occidentalis
Westward, occidentum versus
Wet, humidus, madidus, madens; (with dew), roscidus
To wet, humecto; madefacio
To begin to wet, humesco
To be wet, madeo
To be thoroughly wet, permadeo
To be wet with dew, roresco
Wet, Wetness, humiditas, humor
A wether-sheep, vervex
A bell-wether, dux gregis
Wether-mutton, caro vervecea
Of a wether, verveceus
Wetting, humectans
Wettish, humidulus
Of a whale, cetaceus
A whale, balæna, cetus
A wharf, fluminis portus
Wharfage, portorium
A wharfinger, portûs custos
What, subst. quid; adj. qui, quis, qualis; (that which), quod
To what place, quò; (soever), quocunque, quâcunquè
In what place, ubi; (soever), ubicunque
By what place, quâ; (means soever), quibuscunque modis
At what time, quandò; (soever), quandocunquè
For what cause, quamobrem
Whay, serum lactis, succus lactis
Whay-coloured, albidus
Whayish, serosus
A wheal, pustula, tuberculum
Full of wheals, pustulatus
Wheat, triticum; (flour), pollen; (cake), farreum; (plum), prunum cereum
Wheaten, triticeus, frumentaceus
Of fine wheat flour, siligineus
To wheedle, pellicio, allicio
A wheedler, delinitor
Wheedling, pellax, blandiloquus
A wheedling, blanditia
A wheel, rota; (lathe), tornus; (for torture), equuleus; (of a pulley), trochlea
To wheel about, circumago
A wheelbarrow, vehiculum unâ rotâ instructum
A wheelwright, faber rotarum
Wheeled, rotatus, circumactus
A wheeling, rotatio; (round), circumactio
To wheeze, irraucesco
Wheezing, asthmaticus
A wneezing, raucitas, ravis
To whelm, tego, obtego
A whelp, catulus, catellus; (lion's), scymnus
Of a whelp, catulinus
To whelp, catulos edere
When? quando? (at what time), quandò, cùm, quum, ubi, postquam, inter; (as), quum, quando, quandoquidèm; (soever), quandocunquè; (just), simul ac
Whence, or from whence, unde, ex quo; (soever), undecunquè; (you will), undelibet
Where, ubi, ubinam; (or whereas), cùm, quòd; (about), ubi, ubi, loci; (at), quo, ad quod; (by), quo, per quod; (ever), ubicunquè, ubi ubi; (fore), cur, quarè, quamobrèm; (in), in quo, in quibus, in quâ parte;

(into), in quod, in quæ; (of), cujus, quorum, de quo; (ou), super quod, in quo; (on), super quod, in quo; (soever), ubicunque, ubi ubi; (to, or unto), cui, ad quod; (upon), ex quo, unde, inde, exinde; (with, or withal), quo, quibus
A wherry, scapha, cymba
Whether, seu, sive, utrùm, an, anne, num, ne; (of the two), uter
A whet, incitamentum
To whet, acuo, exacuo
A whetting, exacutio
A whetstone, cos
Whey, serum. See Whay
Which, quis, uter; (a relative), qui; (way), quâ; (way soever), quomodocunquè, quocunquè
A whiff, halitus, flatus
To whiffle, vacillo, hæreo
A whiffler (or shuffler), homo futilis, inconstans, or levis; (to clear the way), viator
A whig, libertatis populi assertor
While, or whilst, dum, cùm, quoàd; (until), donèc, dùm
A while, or little time, paulispèr, paramper, aliquantispèr; (after), paulò pòst, aliquantò pòst, interjecto tempore; (ago, or since), nupèr, pridèm
A good while, jamdudum
After a while, brevi, mox
For a while, ad quoddam tempus
The mean while, interim, intereà
To while, otior
Whilst that, donèc, quoàd
Whilom, olim, aliquandò
A whim, repentinus animi impetus, nugæ
A whimwham, næniæ aniliæ, fabula
To whimper, obvagio
Whimsical (flighty), inconstans, levis; (uncommon), non vulgaris; (ingenious), ingeniosus
A whin, genista spinosa
To whine, gannio, vagio
A whiniard, gladius falcatus
A whining, querela, gemitus
Whining, queribundus, queritans
To whinny, hinnio; (after), adhinnio
A whip, flagellum, scutica
To whip, flagello; (stitch), prætexo; (or run up and down), curaito, discurro; (or snatch up), arripo, corripio; (out of doors), forâs se proripere; (a top), turbinem agere
To be whipped, vapulo
A whipper, flagellator, verberator
A whipping, flagellatio, verberatio
A whirl, verticillum; (about) vertigo
To whirl about, torqueo, roto
Whirling about, circumagens
The whirling of a stream, vortex
A whirlbat, cæstus
A whirligig, rhombus
A whirlpool, vortex, gurges
A whirlwind, typhon, turbo
Full of whirlwinds, turbineus
Whirring, stridulus
A whisk, scopæ vimineæ, scopula
To whisk (dust), scopulè purgare; (about), celeriter circumagere
The whiskers, mystax
A whisking about, vertigo
Whisking (swinging), magnus;

(a whisking lie), mendacium magnum
To whisper, submissè loqui; (in the ear), in aurem dicere, susurro
A whisperer, susurro; (tale-bearer), gerro, susurrator
A whispering, susurrus, susurratio
Whist! (hush!) tace! au! st!
To whistle, ore fistulare; (as birds), cantillo; (as wind), crepito
A whistle, fistula
A whistler, fistulator
Whistling, fistulâ canens
A whistling (to a horse), poppysma; (wind), ventus stridulus
With a whistling sound, stridulè
A whit, aliquantulum
Every whit, omninò, prorsùs
Never a whit, ne hilum
White, albus, candidus, albens; (as milk), lacteus; (as snow), niveus; (as ivory), eburneus; (lead), cerussa; (livered), invidiosus
A white, album; (of an egg), albumen; (of the eye), albor; (to shoot at), alba meta; (spot, or speck in the eye), albugo
The whites, albæ fluxiones
In white, candidatus, albatus
A white friar, frater Jacobinus
To white, or make white, dealbo
To be white, albeo, candeo
To grow white, albesco, candesco; (or pale), pallesco; (white with age), canesco, incanesco
White with age, canus
Whitely, candidè
To whiten, candefacio, dealbo; (clothes), insolo; (grow white), albeo, albico, albesco
Whiteness, albor, albedo; (of hair), canities; (shining), nitor, candor
A whitening, dealbatio; (of clothes), insolatio
A whiting (fish), alburnus
Whitish, exalbidus; (with frost), pruinosus; (with age), canus
To grow whitish, canesco
Whither, quò, quonam
Any whither, usquam, quopiàm
Some whither, aliquò
Any whither, alicubi
No whither, nusquam
Whithersoever, quocunquè
A whitlow, ulcus digitale
A whitster, dealbator
Whitsuntide, pentecoste
A whittle (knife), cultellus
To whittle, cultello resecare
To whizz, strido, strideo
Whizzing, stridulus
A whizzing, stridor
Who? (interrogative), quis? quæ? quid? (relative), qui, quæ, quod; (indefinite), quis, quæ, quid; (ever, or soever), quisquis, quilibet, quicunque, quæcunque
Whole, solidus, integer; (all), totus, universus; (in health), sanus, validus
Made whole, sanatus
The whole, summa totalis
To be whole (in health), valeo
To make whole, sano, curo
Wholesale, in solidum
A wholesale-man, solidarius
Wholly (altogether), prorsùs, omninò
Wholesome, saluber, salutaris; (very), saluberrimus

WIL — WIN — WIP

Wholesomely, salubritèr
Wholesomeness, salubritas
Whom (of who), quem, quam
Of whom, de quo, de quâ
With whom, quîcum, quibuscum
Whomsoever, quemcunque, quemlibet
A whoop, clamor
To whoop, clamo, vociferor
Whooping, vociferans, clamosus
A whooping, clamatio, vociferatio
A whooping-cough, tussis ferina
A whore, meretrix, scortum; (pocky), meretrix ivusta lue venereâ; (common), prostibulum
To whore, scortor, meretricor
Whoredom, meretricium
A whoremonger, or whoremaster, mœchus, scortator, ganeo
A whoring, scortatus
Whoring (given to whores), stuprosus
Whorish, meretricius
Whorishly, meretricè
Whose, cujus, a, um; cujus, quorum, quarum; (soever), cujuscunque, quorumcunque [qua
Whosoever, quicunque, quæcun-
To whur (as a dog), ringo
Why, cur, quarè, quamobrèm; (not), cur non, quid ita non, quin, quidni; (so?), quid itâ? quamobrèm?
Wicked, impius, flagitiosus, nefastus, nefarius, pravus, scelestus
A wicked rogue, scelus
Wickedly, impiè, scelestè, nefariè
Wickedness, nequitia, scelus
Full of wickedness, nequissimus
A wicker, vimen
Made of wickers, vimineus
A wicket, ostiolum
To widdle-waddle, vacillo
Wide, spatiosus, latus, amplus; (open), patulus, propatulus; (very), perlatus
Widely, latè, amplè, laxè
To widen, amplio, dilato
Wideness, Width, latitudo
A widow, vidua, mulier relicta
A widower, viduus
Widowhood, viduitas
A widow's estate, bona dotalia
To wield (or handle), tracto; (brandish), vibro; (govern), guberno
A wife, uxor, marita, conjux, sponsa, matrona
The son's wife, nurus
An old wife, anus, vetula
A wife's father, socer
A wife's mother, socrus
Belonging to a wife, uxorius
A wig (cake), libum; (for the head), capillamentum
A wight, homo, animal
Wild (untamed), indomitus, ferus; (mad), demens, insanus, furiosus; (flighty), inconstans, levis; (uncultivated), silvestris; (absurd), impertinent), absurdus, insulsus, ineptus; (untaught), indoctus; (hair-brained), dissolutus
A wild beast, fera
Wildfire, malleolus
Wild-fowl, volucres palustres
To make wild, effero
To grow wild (as trees), silvesco
A wilderness, desertum, deserta, solitudo, eremus
Wildly (fiercely), ferocitèr, dementèr; (impertinently), ineptè, absurdè

Wildness, ferocitas, insulsitas
A wile, dolus [tumax
Wilful, pervicax, perversus, contumax
Wilfully, pertinacitèr, obstinatè
Wilfulness, pertinacia, contumacia
Wilily, astutè, versutè, dolosè
Wiliness, astutia, calliditas
Wily, vafer, astutus, dolosus
The will, voluntas; (desire), votum; (pleasure), arbitrium, libido; (command), jussum, mandatum; (intention), propositum, intentio, consilium
A will, or last will, testamentum
Good-will (kindness), benevolentia; (for a house, shop, &c.), premium
To bear good-will, benè velle
With a good will, libentèr
Of mere good-will, gratuitò, gratis
Ill will, invidia, livor
Against one's will, invitus
With an ill will, invitè, ægrè
Of one's own will, spontè, ultrò
To will, volo; (command), jubeo, mando
Not to will, nolo
To make a will, testor
A will-maker, testator, testatrix; (writer), testamentarius
Without a will, adj. intestatus; adv. intestatò
Of a will, testamentarius
Willed (by will), legatus; (desired), optatus, exoptatus
Self-willed, obstinatus
Will-with-a-wisp, ignis fatuus
Sweet-willed, armenia
Willing, libens, volens
Willingly, libentèr; (and wittingly), sciens prudensque
Not willingly, invitè
Willingness, desiderium
A willow, salix
A place planted with willows, salictum
Of a willow, salignus
A wimble, terebra, terebrum
To bore with a wimble, terebro
A wimple, peplum
To win, lucror, lucrifacio; (a battle), victoriam adipisci; (by assault), expugno; (one's favour), gratiam conciliare; (by conquest), vinco, supero, domo; (by entreaty), exoro; (a prize), palmam reportare; (obtain), potior, consequo, obtineo
To wince, or winch, calcitro
A winch (tool), trochlea
Wincing, calcitrosus
A wincing, calcitratus
The wind, ventus; (equinoctial east), eurus; (equinoctial west), zephyrus, favonius; (due north), septentrio; (due south), meridies; (north-east), aquilo, boreas; (south-west), caurus, argestes; (south-east), euronotus, vulturnus; (south-west by west), libs, africus
Windbound, vento adverso detentus
A wind-fall (apple), pomum caducum; (unexpected luck), lucrum insperatum; (gall), intertrigo; (cholic), flatus hypochondriacus
To take wind, or breath, respiro, animam recipere; (become known), patefio, evulgor
To wind (or turn about), verto, circumverto; (or roll about), circumvolvo; (or twist about),

torqueo; (in), intorqueo; (into bottoms), in glomos glomerare; (off), devolvo; (up a clock), filum horarii torquere; (up a discourse), orationem concludere; (a horn), cornu inflare
Long-winded, animæ prælargus; (discourse), oratio nimis longa; (piece of work), opus diuturni laboris   [eus
Short-winded, anhelus, asthmaticus
A winder, tortor, contortor
Windiness, ventositas
Winding, tortilis, flexilis
A winding (bending), flexus
Winding in and out, flexuosus, sinuosus
With windings, flexuosè
The winding of a path, anfractus; (of a river), flexus, sinus; (of a rope), spira; (of vine-twigs), funetum
A winding-sheet, linteum ferale
Winding stairs, scalæ cochlides
A windlace, or windlass, trochlea; (of a crane), grus, sucula
The windpipe, gurgulio
A window, fenestra
Having windows, fenestratus
Of windows, fenestralis
Windward, ventum versus
Windy, ventosus; (expressions), amplus
Wine, vinum; (new), mustum; (neat), merum; (muscadel), ex uvâ Apianâ; (old), vetustum
Tempered with wine, vinolentus
Wine and water, vinum aquâ dilutum
Like wine, vinosus
Belonging to wine, vinarius
A winebibber, vinolentus
A wine-cooper, vietor
A wine-glass, vitreum vinarium
A wine-press, torcular vinarium
A wine-vault, œnophorum
A seller of wines, œnopola, vinarius
A wing, ala, penna; (of an army), ala, cornu; (of a building), ala, latus
Belonging to wings, alaris
A wink, nictus, obtutus
To wink, nicto, conniveo; (at, or upon), alicui adnictare; (or connive at), tolero, permitto; (with one eye), collineo
Winked at, toleratus, permissus
Winking eyes, oculi conniventes
A winking at, conniventia
A winning, lucrum
Winning (engaging), alliciens
To winnow, evanno, ventilo
Winnowed, ventilatus
A winnower, ventilator
A winnowing, ventilatio
Winnowings, gluma
Winter, hyems, bruma
In depth of winter, summâ hyeme
Winter quarters, hiberna
Of winter, hyemalis
To winter, hyemo, hyberno
It is winter, hyemat
A wintering, hyematio
Wintry, hyemalis, brumalis
Winy, vinosus, vinolentus
A wipe (jeer), sanna, dicterium
To give one a wipe, ludificor, derideo, mordeo, illudo
To wipe (clean), tergeo, extergeo; (off, or away), abstergeo, detergeo; (the nose), nares emungere; (out), deleo, erado, expungo
A wiping, purgatio, emunctio

[165]

Wire, metallum nitum
To wiredraw, metallum nere; (spin out, or prolong), protraho; (sift, or search out), exquiro, scrutor
A wizard, veneficus, hariolus
Wisdom, sapientia, prudentia
Wise, sapiens, prudens, consultus
To be wise, sapio; (again), resipisco, resipio
In any wise, quoquo modo; (nowise), nequaquam, nullo modo, nullatenùs; (this wise), sic, ita, hoc modo, in hunc modum
A wiseacre, insulsus, plumbeus
Wisely, sapientèr, consultò
Wiser, sapientior
Wisest, sapientissimus
A wish, votum, optio
To wish, opto, exopto; (one joy), gratulor, congratulor; (rather), malo, præopto; (well unto), benè velle, fausta præcari, alicui favere
To have one's wish, optato potiri, voti compos fieri
Wished for, optatus, expetitus
A wishing, optatio
A wisket, corbis
A wisp (brush), scopula; (little cushion), pulvillus; (of straw, &c.), manipulus; (in the eye), inflammatio
Wist (known), notus
I wist, novi, intellexi
Wistful, expetens, intentus
Wistfully, oculis intentis
Wit, ingenium, solertia, lepor, sales
To wit, videlicet, nempè, scilicèt
In one's wits, mentis compos
To be out of one's wits, insanio, desipio
At wits' end, ad incitas redigi
A witch, saga, venefica
Witchcraft, veneficium, magia
Of witchcraft, magicus
An user of witchcraft, magus
With, cum
With a good will, libentèr
With ill will, invitè; (all speed), quamprimùm, primo quoque tempore; (one another), inter se, mutuò; (much ado), ægrè, vix
One with another, promiscuè
Together with, simul, unà cum
Withal (with which), quocum, quibuscum, quo, quibus; (besides), ad hæc, præterea
With child, gravida, prægnans
To withdraw (draw away, or from), avoco, abstraho, seduco; (retire), recedo, secedo; (from business), à negotiis se removere; (alienate), alieno, averto, deduco
A withdrawing (or drawing away, or from), subductio, seductio; (retiring), secessio, recessio, recessus; (room), secretum, recessus
To wither, exaresco, flaccesco, marceo
Withered, flaccidus, marcidus
Withering, marcescens, caducus
A withering away, tabes, languor
To withhold, detineo, retineo
A withholding, detentio, retentio
Within, intùs, intrò; prep. cis, in, intra; (a while), propediem, brevi; (a while after), paulo post, haud multò post; (a few days), paucis diebus; (a little), ferè, propè, penè, fermè
[163]

Without (not with), sine, absque, extra, ultrò, citra; (not within), foris, extra, extrinsecùs; (unless), ni, nisi
To be without (or destitute of), egeo, vaco
Not without cause, meritò
Not without much ado, ægrè, vix
To withsay, contradico
To withstand, obsisto, obnitor, resisto, repugno, obluctor
Withstanding, repugnans
A withstanding, repugnantia
A withy, salix, vimen
A witness, testis, arbiter; (testimony), testimonium
To witness, testor, testificor
A witnessing, testatio
A witticism, argutum dictum
Wittily, argutè, acutè, scitè
Wittiness, sagacitas
Wittingly, scientèr
Witless, stultus, insipiens
Witty, acutus, sagax; (sayings), facetiæ, argutiæ
A witwal (bird), vireo
Wives, uxores
A wizard, veneficus, magus
Wo, calamitas, miseria
Wo, interj. væ!
Woad, glastum, isatis
Woful, ærumnosus, miser, calamitosus, tristis
Wofully, miserabilitèr, miserè
Wofulness, miseria, calamitas
A wolf, lupus; (she), lupa; (dog), lycisca; (disease), phagedæna
Wolfbane, aconitum
A wolf-catcher, luparius
Wolfish, lupinus
A woman, mulier, femina; (little, or mean), muliercula; (young), adolescentula; (grave), matrona; (prating), linguaca; (working), operaria; (manly), virago; (new married), sponsa; (servant), ancilla, famula
Of a woman, muliebris
Womanish, Womanly, muliebris, femineus
Like a woman, effeminatus
Womanly, effeminatè
Womanly (sober, staid, grave), matronalis
The womb, uterus, matrix
Of the womb, uterinus
Won (of win), lucrativus; (by assault), expugnatus
A wonder, miraculum, prodigium, portentum, res mira
To wonder at (admire), miror, admiror; (be astonished at), stupeo, obstupesco
To be wondered at, mirandus
A wonderer, mirator
Wonderful, Wondrous, mirus, mirabilis, admirabilis, prodigiosus
Wonderfully, mirabilitèr, mirè
Wonderfulness, mirabilitas
Wondering, mirans
A wondering, admiratio
Wonder-working, thaumaturgus
A wont, or custom, consuetudo, mos
To be wont, soleo, consuesco
As men are wont, humanitùs
Wood (timber), lignum, materia
Made of wood, ligneus
Full of wood, lignosus
A wood, sylva, nemus, saltus; (sacred to a deity), lucus
Woody, sylvosus, nemorosus
Brush-wood, cremium
Seared wood, ramale

Great fire-wood, lignum
Great timber-wood, materia
To grow to wood, sylvesco
A woodcock, gallinago
A sea woodcock, trochilus
A wood-pigeon, palumbes; (lark), galerita arborea; (louse), cimex; (man), arborator; (monger), lignarius; (ward, or forester), saltuarius; (worm), cossis
A woodpecker, picus martius
Wooden, ligneus
To woo, procor, ambio
A wooer, procus, amasius
Wooing, ambiens, solicitans
The woof, trama
Wool, lana
A wool-seller, lanarius
A wool-carder, lanifica
A wool-pack, or sack, lanæ fascis
Woollen, laneus, lanarius
A woollen-draper, lanarius
Woolly, lanatus, lanaris
A word, vox, dictum, verbum, vocabulum, sermo
Big words, ampullæ
Opprobrious words, convicia
A word (promise), promissum; (command), jussum, mandatum, præceptum
The word (or watchword), tessera, symbolum
By word of mouth, vivâ voce
Word for word, ad verbum
In a word, brevitèr, brevi
In word only, verbo tenus
Not a word, imper. tace
To word, verbis exprimere
Well worded, elegantèr dictus, or scriptus
Full of words, adj. verbosus; adv. verbosè
A work, opus, opera; (trouble), turba, tumultus; (checker), opus tessellatum
Works (buildings), ædificia, opera; (fences), munimenta
To work, operor, laboro; (fashion), fabrico, fingo; (as liquors), fermentor; (as physic doth), alvum movere; (upwards), vomitionem ciere; (downwards), purgo; (as an artificer), elaboro; (needlework), acu pingere; (into favour), in gratiam insinuare; (upon), persuadeo, suadeo
A workman, opifex, artifex
A workhouse, ergastulum
A workshop, officina, fabrica
A working, operatio
A working-day, dies negotiosus
Working, operans, laborans; (boisterous), intumescens
Workmanlike, affabrè, elegantèr
Workmanship, opificium
The world, mundus, orbis; (affairs of the world), res, res humanæ
Little world, microcosmus
A world of, magnus, infinitus
Worldliness, avaritia
A worldling, avarus
Worldly (belonging to the world), mundanus, terrenus; (covetous), avarus; (pleasures), voluptates corporeæ
A worm, vermis, lumbricus
Worm-eaten, vermibus erosus
A breeding of worms, verminatio
Infested with worms, vermiculatus
Full of worms, verminosus
To be worm eaten, vermiculor
H 6

APPENDIX.

A LIST OF WORDS IN THE ITALIAN AND FRENCH LANGUAGES WHICH ARE DERIVED FROM THE LATIN.

I. ITALIAN WORDS.

Italian.	Latin.	Italian.	Latin.
abbeverare	ad-bibere	brache	braca
abito	habitus	brieve	brevis
abrostino	labruscum	brina	pruina
acceggia	accia	brobbrio	opprobrium
addietro	retro	budello	botulus
aggiustare	ad-juxtare	bufalo	bubalus
Agosto	Augustus	buono	bonus
allegrezza	alacer	cacio	caseus
allegro	alacer	cagliare	coagulare
alna, auna	ulna	cagna	canis
ambiadura	ambulatura	caldo	calidus
ambio	ambulatura	calogna	calumnia
ammanto	mantellum	camicia	camisia
anari	naris	cammino	caminus
annegare	necare	campione	campus
appio	apium	canaglia	canalis
approcciare	adpropiare	canzone	cantio
aragna	aranea	carbonajo	carbonarus
arpa	harpa	carbonchio	carbunculus
aspruma	asper	carrota	carrus
assai	ad-satis	carrozza	carrus
augello	aucella	cascio	caseus
avanti	abante	cassa	capsa
avere	habere	castagna	castanea
avoltojo	vultur	cattivo	captivus
avventura	adventura	cavaliero	caballarius
babbaccio	baburrus	cavallo	caballus
babbeo	baburrus	cavolo	caulis
babbuino	baburrus	cedrato	cedrus
bacciocco	baceolus	cenere	cinis
bagno	balneum	ceppo	cippus
bajo	badius	cercare	quæricare
bambino	bambalio	cerchio	circulus
bambo	bambalio	cervello	cerebellum
battaglia	battualia	cheto	quietus
battere	batuere	chiamare	ciamare
belva	belua	chiambra	camera
berbice	vervex	chiassato	classicum
bévere	bibere	chiasso	classicum
biasimo	blasphemare	chiave	clavis
biasmare	blasphemare	chiavica	cloaca
bichiére	bacarium	chiesa	ecclesia
blasphème	blasphemia	chiesi	quæso
bocca	bucca	chioma	coma
boccone	bucca	cicala	cicada
boldone	botulus	cielo	coelum
bolla	bulla	cinghiale	singularis (scil. porcus)
bollire	bullare	cinghiare	singularis
bontà	bonitas	cipolla	cepulla
bosso	buxus	città	civitas
bottega	apotheca	ciurmaglia	turmalis (turmalia)
bottiglia	buticula	civaja	cibaria
bove	bos	coda	cauda
bracciata	brachium	cofano	cophinus
braccio	brachium	collina	collis

[156]

APPENDIX.

Italian.	Latin.	Italian.	Latin.
colonna	columna	Giácomo	Jacob
coltello	cultellus	giammai	jam magis
compagnia	companium	giglio	lilium
compagno, compagnone	companium	giocolare, gullare	joculator
congedo	commeatus	giogo, jugo	jugum
congegnare	concinnare	giornale	diurnalis
coniglio	cuniculus	giorno	jornum (diurnus)
consiglio	consilium	giovane	juvenis
conte	comes	giove-di	Jovis dies
coppa	cupa	Giudeo	Judæus
coppia	copula	giudice	judex
coprire	co-operire	giuggiare	judicare
corazza	coratium	giunare, digiunare	jejunare
corcare	collocare	giungo	jungere
coro	chorus	giuoco	jocus
correre	currere	giuso and già	deosum (deorsum)
corso	cursus	golpe	vulpes
corte	cohors	gomito	cubitum
cosa	causa	gonfiare	conflare
coscia	coxa	gotta	gutta
coscino	culcitinum	governale, governaglio	gubernaculum
costare	con-stare	gracchio	graculus
covare	cubare	grasso	crassus
cresima	chrisma	grasia	gratia
crespo	crispus	greggo	grex
cresta	crista	grembo	gremium
croce	crux	grieve	gravis
cucchiajo	cochlear	grosso	crassus
cucina	coquina	gru	grus
cugino, cugina	cosinus	grugno	grunnire
culmo	culmen	guadò	vadum
cuocere	coquere	guascóne	Vascones
cuojo	ecorium	ieri	heri
cuore	cor	innantimente	manu tenens
daino, daina	dania	inalzare	inaltare
dangiero	damniarium	inchiostro	encaustum
dannaggio	damnaticum	indi	inde
detta	debitum	intermezzo	inter-medius
devere and dovere	debere	inveggia	invexia
di	dies	io (old form, eo)	ego
dieci	decem	isola	insula
dietro	deretro	labbro	labrum
dimostrare	demonstrare	laccio	laqueus
dio	deus	ladrone	latro
dire	dicere	lago	lacus
discorso	discursus	lagrima	lacrima
dito	digitus	laguna	lacuna
doge	dux	lardo	laridum
doglio	dolere	lasciare	laxare
dolce	dulcis	latta	lac
dolsore	dulcor	lattuga	lactuca
domani	de mane	lavoro	labor
donde	deunde	leale	legalis
donna	domina	lecere	licet
donzella, damigella	dominicilla	legame	ligamen
doppio	duplus	legge	lex
dotta	dubitare	leggere	legere
dove	deubi	legno, legna	lignum
dozzina	duodeni	lembo	limbus
drappo	drappas	lettera	litera
dunque, dunche	tunc	levriere	leporarius
duomo	domus	licorno	uni-cornis
edera, ellera	hedera	lieto	lætus
eguale	æqualis	lieve	levis
elice, elce	ilex	lira	libra
erede	heres	luogo	locus
erpice	irpex	macchia	macula
fagiano, fagianetto	phasianus	macina	machina
fagiuolo	phaselus	Maddalena	Magdalena
faro	Pharos	madre	mater
fra	infra	maestria	magisterium
fráte (monk)	frater	maéstro, mastro	magister
fratello	frater	maggio	majus
fregio	Phrygius	maggiore	major
gabbia	cavea	magro	macer
gaggia	cavea	mai	magis
gastigare	castigare	mancare	mancus
gatto	catus	mandola	amygdala
geloso	zelosus	mangiare	manducare
Gennajo	Januarius	maniglio, amaniglio	monile
gesso	gypsum	mansione and magione	mansio
gettare	jacére	mantenere	manu tenere
già (di già)	jam	martedi	Martis dies
giaccio	jacére	maschéra	masca

[157]

APPENDIX.

Italian.	Latin.	Italian.	Latin.
maschio	masculus	onore	honor
mattino *and* mattinata	matutinus	ora	hora
meco	mecum	orciuolo	urceolus
meglio	melius	orecchio	auricula
megliore, migliore	melior	ortica	urtica
menare	minare	orto	hortus
meno	minor	ortolano	hortulanus
mercoledì	Mercurii dies	orvieto	urbs vetus
mesa	mensa	orzo	hordeum
mese	mensis	osceno	obscoenus
mescolare *and* mischiare	misculare	oscuro	obscurus
messaggio	missaticum	ospitale	hospitalis
mestiero	ministerium	ospitio	hospitium
méttere	mittere	osso	os, ossis
mezzo, mezzodì	medius	ostaggio	obstaticus
mica	mica	ostare	obsto
midollo	medulla	oste, ostello, osteria	hospes
miele	mel	ottanta	octoginta
miétere	metere	ottantesimo	octogesimus
miglio	milium	ottavo	octavus
migliorare	meliorare	otto	octo
mio	meus	ove	ubi
mio scentre	me sciente	óvunque	ubicumque
mila *and* miglio	mille	ovviare	obviare
minaccia	minaciae	padrino	patrinus
minaglio	minaculus	padella	patella
miraviglia	mirabilis	padiglione	papilio
misurare	mensurare	padre	pater
mò	modo	padule	palus
moda	modus	paése	pagensis
moggio	modius	paglia	palea
moglie	mulier	pane pagnotta	panicum
molcere	mulcere	pajo	par
molo	moles	paladino	Palatinus
mondo	mundus	palafreno	parafredus
montagna	montaneus	palanca	planca
mormorio	murmur	palazzo, palagio	Palatium
mostrare	monstrare	Palermo	Panormus
mulino	molinus	palese	palam
mùngere	mulgere	panatica, panaggio	panaticum
muovere	movere	pannocchia	panniculus
muraglia	muralis	paolo	paulus
naso *and* nasone	nasus	parecchio	pariculus
naviglio	navicula	parete	paries
nepote et nipôte	nepos	pargoletto	parvus
nerbo	nervus	Parigi	Parisii
nero	niger	paroco	parochus
nespolo	mespilum	parola	parabole
nessuno	nec ipse unus	paura	pavor
nettare	nitidare	pavone, paone	pavo
neve	nix	pedone	pedes
nido *and* nidio	nidus	peggiorare	pejorare
niego	negare	pellere	pellere
niente	nec ens	pelliccia	pellicius
ninfa *and* sninfa	Nympha	pelo	pilus
no et non	non	pena, penare	poena
nocchio	nucleus	pennacchio	penna
noce	nux	pensito	pensare
noi	nos	pentire	poenitentia
nome	nomen	pensolo, pendolo	pendulus
notte	nox	per	pro
nove	novem	pero	pirum
novero	numerus	personaggio	personaticum
nozze	nuptiae	pertugio	pertundere
nuócere	nocere	Perugia	Perusia
nuora	nurus	pesce	piscis
nuovo	novus	peschia	apicula
nuvolo *and* nugôlo	nubilus	peso	pensum
obbliare	oblitare	peato	pinsere
oca	anca	pettorale	pectoralis
occasione, cagione, cagioncella, cagionare	occasio	pettoresco	pictor
occhio	oculus	pévere	piper
oggeto	objectus	pezzo, pezza	petium
oggi, oggidì	hodie	piacere	placere
ogni	omnis	piagare	plagare
oglio	oleum	piaggia	plagia
oltra, oltre	ultra	piangere	plangere
oltraggio	ultragium	piano	planus
ombelico, bilico	umbilicus	pianto	planctus
ombreggiare	umbra	pianezza	planitia
omero	humerus	piato	placitum
ondato	undo	piede	pes
onninamente	omnino	piego	plicare
		pieno	plenus

[158]

APPENDIX.

Italian.	Latin.	Italian.	Latin.
pietra	petra	ragghio	rugire
piggione	pipio	ruota	rota
pigliare	pilare	rusco, brusco	ruscum
pigrizia, pigrezza	pigritia	ruspare	ruspari
pillola	pilula	saetta	sagittarius
pioggia	pluvia	saggio	sapius
piombaggine	plumbago	salazzare	solatiari
piombo	plumbum	salcete	salictum
pioppo	populus	salmo	psalmus
piòvere	pluere	salsiccia	salsicea
piuma	pluma	sanguigno	sanguineus
Po	Padus	santo	sanctus
poco	paucus	sapore, savore	sapor
podesta	potestas	sarchiellare	sarritare
poggio	podium	sasso, sassolino	saxum
poi	post	Sassone	Saxones
pollastro	pullastra	savere, sapére	sapere
polvo, polvere	pulvis	scalfire	scalpere
popolazza	populaceus	scapigliare	discapillare
poppa	puppis	scarafaggio	scarabeus
portiere	portarius	scemare	semis
poscia	post	scempio	simplus
posore	pausare	schernire	carinare
potére	possum	scialiva	saliva
poto	putare	scimia	simia
povero	pauper	sciringa	Syrinx
pozzo	puteus	scoglio	scopulus
preda	præda	scolare	scholaris
preghiera	precaria	scolpire	sculpere
presso	pressus	scorza	cortex
priego	precor	scrigno	scrinium
prigione	prehensio	scrivo	scribere
primiero	primarius	scudo	scutum
proda	prora	scuola	schola
prossimano	proximus	scure	securis
prugno	pruneus	se, sed	si
pruova	proba	secco	siccus
pruovo, provare	probare	segala	secale
pulce	pulex	segare	secare
punto	punctum	seggia	sedes
puto	putere	seggiola	sella
putto	putus	seggo, seggio, siedo, sédere	sedere
quandunque	quandocumque		
quattordici	quatuordecim	segnacolo	signaculum
quanto	quantus	segno	signum
quattro	quattuor	sego	sevum
quello	eccillos (eccillum)	segugio	segusius
quercio	quercus	segreto	secretus
questo	ecc'iste	seguire	sequi
quinci	eccu'-hincce	sei	sex
quindici	quindecim	selva	silva
rabbia	rabies	selvaggio	silvaticus
racimolo, gracimolo	racemus	sembiante	simulans
raggio, rai, and razzo	radius	sembro	simulare
ragione	ratio	seme	semen
ragnatella	aranea	seno	sinus
ragunare, raunare	readunare	sentiero	semitarius
rame	æramina	senza	sine
ranocchio	ranunculus	sera, serata	serus
rapa	rapum	serbare	servare
ratto	rapidus	serbatojo	servatorium
re	rex	sergiento	serviens
reale	regalis	sermento	sarmentum
recére	reicere	serraglio	serra
reina, regina	regina	servizio, servigio	servitium
remiggio	remigare	sessanta	sexaginta
restio	restivus	sessantesimo	sexagesimus
ricoverare	recupero	setenta	septuaginta
riedo	redire	sette	septem
rio, reo	reus	settina	septeni
rio	rivus	sezzo	secus
ritroso	retrorsum	sicuro	securus
riviera	riparia	siero	serum
rivolo	rivalus	signore	senior
roccia	rupea	singhiottire	singultire
roggio	rubens	smeraldo	smaragdus
rogo	rubus	smerlo	merulus
rompere	rumpere	smergo, mergo	mergus
rondine	hirundo	soave	suavis
rosso	rursus	soffice	supplicamentum
rovina, rovinare	ruminari	soglio	solium
rozzo, rude	rudis	sognare	somniare
rubello	rebellare	solicchio	soliculus
ruggiada	roa	soma	sagma

[159]

APPENDIX.

Italian.	Latin.	Italian.	Latin.
somaro	sagmarius	tortore, tortora	turtur
sommità	summitas	tosco	toxicum
sonaglio	sonaculus	tra	intra
sonno	somnus	traere	trahere
sonnolento	somnulentus	traino	tractus
soperchio	superculus	traliccio	trilix
sorbire	sorbere	travaglio	trabs
sordo	surdus	tre	tres
sorgo, sorcio	sorex	tremolare	tremulus
sorta, sorte	sors	trenta	triginta
sospizione	suspicio	triaca	theriacus
sostanza	substantia	tribolare	tribulare
sottile	subtilis	Trieste	Tergeste
sotto	subtus	triplice	triplex
sovente	subinde	trota	tructa
sovra	supra	tuono	tenus
sovrano	supernus	tuorlo	torulus
spada	sparus	tutto	totus
spasimo	spasmus	ubbidienza	obedientia
specchio, speglio	speculum	ubhidire, obbedire	obedire
spesso	spissus	uccello	ancella
spezie	species	uccidere	occidere
spiaggia, piaggia	plaga	udire	andire
spoglia	spolium	ulire, olire	olere
sposo	sponsus	uliva, ulivo	oliva
spuma	spuma	umido	humidus
staffa	stapia	umile	humilis
stagione	statio	undici	undecim
stagno	stannum	unghia	ungula
stelo	stilus	uomo	homo
sterpo, sterpigno	stirps	uopo	opus
stoja	storea	uovo	ovum
stoppa	stuppa	uquale	aequalis
storia	historia	usare	utor
strambo	strabo	uscio	ostium
strega	striga	vaglio	vallus
stregghia and streglia	strigilis	vago, vaguccio	vagus
stretto	strictus	valenza	valentia
stria	stria	valére, vaglio	valere
striscia	strix	vantare	vanitare
stroppolo	struppus	vasallo	vassus
strozzule	stragulus	vecchio, vechiotto, veglio	vetulus
successo	successivus	vedere	videre
suggello	sigilla	vedova	vidua
sugo, succo	succus	vedovo	viduus
suocero	socer	vegliare	vigilare
suolo	solum	venagione	venatio
suono	sonus	veneno, veleno	venenum
suore	soror	vengiare	vindicare
svaliare, svariare	variare	ventaglio	ventaculus
svegliere, sverre	vellere	verde	viridis
svolazzare	volare	verga	virga
tafano	tabanus	vergine	virgo
tagliare	taleare	vergogna	verecundus
tavolo	tabula	vergognarsi	verecundor
teglia, tegghia	tegulae	vermiglio	vermiculus
temere	timere	verno	hibernus
tempia	tempora	vescica	vesica
tenerezza	teneritas	vesco	viscum
tensone	tentio	vetro	vitrum
tepo	talpa	viaggio	viaticus
terzo	terracea	vieto	vetare
terno, terzina	terni	vigna	vineus
tesauro, tesoro	thesaurus	vilano	vilanus
teso	tendere (tensum)	villegiare	villicare
téssere	texere	vilta	vilitas
testimone	testimonium	violetto	viola
tetto	tectum	viorne	viburnum
tiglio	tilia	vipistrello, pipistrello, vespertillo	vespertilio
tingere, tignere	tingere	vittore, vincitore	victor
tinto	tingo (tinctus)	vo	vado
tirannizare	tyrannus	voi	vos
tisana	ptisana	volontiero	voluntarius
titolo	titulus	vostro	vester
tizzone	titio	zambuco, sambuco	sambucus
tonare, tronare	tonare	zeppa	cippus
tondo	rotundus	sinfonia	symphonia
torcere	torquere	Zolpho	sulfurans
toro, tauro	taurus		
torre	turris		

APPENDIX.

II. FRENCH WORDS.

French.	Latin.
abeille	apicula
abreuver	ad-bibere
ache	apium
agréer	gratus
aider	adjūtare
aïeul	avolus
aigle	aquila
ail	allium
ailleurs	aliorsum
airain	æramina
aisselle	axilla
ajuster	adjuxtare
allégresse	alacer
alleu	allodium
amande	amygdala
amble	ambulatura
âme	animus
améliorer	meliorare
amer	amarus
amertume	amaritudo
ami	amicus
amorce	admorsus
ancêtres	antecessor
ange	angelus
août	Augustus
approcher	ad-propiare
âpre	asper
araignée	aranea
arrière	ad-retro
assez	ad-satis
assourdir	absurdescere
aube	albus
aujourd'hui, i. e. au jour d'hui	hodie
aune	alenus
auparavant, i. e. aupar- avant	abante
autel	altaria
autre	alter
autrui	alter
avant	abante
aventure	adventura
avoine	avena
avoir	habere
bachelier	baccalaureus
bai	badius
baie	baja
bain	balneum
baleine	balæna
barbier	barbarius
bataille	battualia
battre	batuere
beau	bellus
bel	bellus
bêler	balare
bellâtre	bellus
besace	bisaccium
bête	bestia
bien	bene
bilan	bi-lanx
bissac	bisaccium
blâme	blasphemare
bœuf	bos, bovis
boire	bibere
bombasin	bombycinus
bombe	bombus
bon	bonus
bougré	bona gratia
bonheur	bona hora
bonté	bonitas
bouche	bucca
bouchée	bucca
boudin	botulus
bougre	Bulgarus
bouillir	bullare
boule	bulla
bouleverser	bulla
bouteille	buticula
boutique	apotheca

[161]

French.	Latin.
boyau	botulus
bras	brachium
brassard	brachium
brassée	brachium
brayes	bracæ
brebis	vervex
bref	brevis
brefet	brevis
brief	brevis
bruire	rugire
brusque	ruscum
buffle	bubalus
buis	buxus
buisson	buxus
cabane	capanna
cabinet	cabana
cage	cavea
cailler	coagulare
caillou	calculus
caisse	capsa
calcul	calculus
calomnie	calumnia
canaille	canalis
canevas	cannabis
campagne	Campania
car	qua-re
carotte	carrus
carte	charta
casse	quassus
casser	quassare
cédrat	cedrus
cendre	cinis
cent	centum
cep	cippus
cercle	circulus
cerfuil	cærefolium
cerise	cerasus
certain	certanus
certes	certus
cervelle, cerveau	cerebellum
cet, ce (Prov. cest)	ecc'iste
ceux (old Fr. cels)	eccillos (eccillum)
chaine	catena
chair	caro
chaise	capsus
chaleur	calor
châloir	calere
chambre	camera
champ	campus
Champagne	Campania
champart	campi pars
champêtre	campester
champion	campus
chandelle	candela
change	cambire
changer	cambire
chanson	cantio
chant	cantus
chanteur	cantor
chantre	cantor
chape	cappa
chapelain	capellanus
chapelle	capella
chapitre	capitulum
char	carrus
charbon	carbo
charbonnier	carbonarius
charité	caritas
charme	carmen
charte	charta
chat	catus
châtaigne	castanea
château	castellum
châtier	castigare
chaud	calidus
chaudière	caldaria
chaux	calx
chemin	caminus
cheminée	caminus

APPENDIX.

French.	Latin.	French.	Latin.
chemise	camisia	croître	crescere
chêne	casnus	croix	crux
chêne	quernus	croyable	credibilis
chenil	canile	cru	cradus
cheneau	quercuetum	cruel	crudelis
chenu	canutus	cuiller	cochlear
chercher	quæricare	cuir	corium
chétif	captivus	cuire	coquere
cheval	caballus	cuirasse	coratium
chevalier	caballarius	cuisine	coquina
cheveu	capillus	cuisse	coxa
chèvre	capra	cure	cura
chevron	capro	daim, dame	dama
chez	casa	dame	domina
chœur	chorus	danger	damniarium
chose	causa	dauphin	delphinus
chou	caulis	dauphiné	delphinatus
chrétien	Christianus	décheveler	discapellare
chien	canis	déchoir	decidere
ciboule	cæpulla	décider	decidere
ciel	cœlum	défaire	deficere
cierge	cera	degré	gradus
circonstance	circumstantia	déjà (old Fr. ja)	jam
cire	cera	déjeûner	jejunare
cité	civitas	demain	de mane
clameur	clamare	demeure, demeurer	demoror
clef	clavis	demoiselle	dominicilla
cloître	claustra	démontrer	demonstrare
clou	clavus	dent	dens
clorre or clôre	claudere	dénier	denegare
cocu	cugus or cucus	dépéri	deperitus
cœur	cor	dépit	despectus
coffre	cophinus	dépouille	spolium
coin	cuneus	depuis	depost
colère	cholera	députer	deputare
collier	collare	derrière	deretrò
colline	collis	désavouer	disadvocare
colonne	columna	désert	desertum
comble	cumulus	dessous	desubter
compagnie	companium	dessus	desuper
compagnon	companium	dette	debitum
concurrence	concurrentia	deuil	dolere
condamner	condemnare	devant	de-abante
confiture	confectura	devenir	devenire
congé	commeatus	devoir	debere
conjugaison	conjugatio	dieu	deus
connoître	cognoscere	dire	dicere
conseil	consilium	discours	discursus
conte	comes	dix	decem
coquin	coquinus	doigt	digitus
corbeau	corvus	dommage	damnaticum
corbeille	corbicula	dome	domus
corps	corpus	dompter	domitare
côte	costa	donc	tunc
côté	costa	dont	deinde
coteau	costale	dorénavant	de-hora-in-ab-ante
cou	collum	dos	dorsum
coucher	collocare	double	duplus
coudé	cubitum	douaire	dotarium
coudre	corylus	douceur	dulcor
coudrier	corylus	doute	dubitare
couleur	color	doux	dulcis
coupe	cupa	douzaine	duodeni
couple	copula	drap	drappus
cour	cohors	duché, ducat	ducatus
courbe	curvus	duel	duellium
couronne	corona	échandole	scandula
cours	cursus	écluse	inclusura
courir	currere	école	schola
cousin, cousine	cosinus	écolier	scholaris
courtine	cortina	écorce	cortex
coussin	culcitinum	écrin	scrinium
couteau	cultellus	écrire	scribere
couter	costare	écrit	scriptum
coutume	costuma	écrivain	scribarius
couver	cubare	écu	scutum
couvrir	co-operire	écueil	scopulus
craindre (old Fr. cri-embere)	tremere	écuelle	scutella
		égal	æqualis
crême	crema	église	ecclesia
crêpe	crispus	émeraude	smaragdus
crépu	crispus	empêcher	impedicare
crête	crista	empereur	imperator
croire	credere	employer	implicare

APPENDIX.

French.	Latin.	French.	Latin.
en	inde	hurler	ululare
encourrement	incurrimentum	île	insula
encontre	in-contra	ivre	ebrius
encre	encaustum	jaloux	zelosus
endosser	in-'dorsare	jamais	jam magis
enfer (Prov. enfern)	infernus	Janvier	Januarius
engin	ingenium	Jaques	Jacob
enseigne	insignis	je (old Fr. ieo, ie)	ego
enseigner	insinuare	jetter	jacêre
entre	inter	jeudi	Jovis dies
envie (Prov. enviea)	invidia	jeu	jocus
environ, virer	ingyrare	jeune (old Fr. jovene)	juvenis
épais	spissus	joindre	jungere
épée	sparus	jongleur (old Fr. jongiere)	joculator
épice	species		
éponge	spongia	joug	jugum
épousailles	sponsalia	jour	jornum (diurnus)
époux	sponsus	journal	diurnalis
éprouve	probare	juge	judex
escalier, échelle	scalæ	juger	judicare
escarboucle	carbunculus	Juif	Judaeus
esclandre	scandalum	jusque	usque
espèce	species	labeur	labor
espiègle	speculum	labourage	laboragium
essai	exagium	lac	lacus
essarter	sarritare	lacet	laqueus
estomac	stomachus	lache	laxus
estrope, étrope	struppus	lagune	lacuna
étain	stannum	laisser	laxare
état	status	lait	lac
éteindre	stinguere	laitue	lactuca
étinceler	scintillula	lambeau, dolabrer	lamberare
étoile	stella	lambruche	labrusca vitis
étoupe	streppa	lange	laneus
étreindre	stringere	langouste	locusta
étrenne	strena	lard	laridum
étrille	strigilis	larme, larmier	lacrima
étroit	atrictus	larron	latro
éventail	ventaculus	lavange	labina
faisan	phasianus	lé (old Fr. les)	latus
fascolé	phasilus	lettre	litera
gaine	vagina	levrier	leporarius
Gascon	Vascones	lézard	lacerta
gésir, gire, git (Prov. jacère jaser, jazir)		liaison	ligatio
gire	gyrus	licorne	uni-cornis
glas	classicum	lierre	hedera
gonfler	conflare	lieu	locus
goupillon	vulpes	lièvre	lepus
goût	gustus	linge	lineus
goutte	gutta	lion	leo
grâce	gratia	lien	ligamen
graille	graculus	lire	legere
grain	granum	lis	lilium
grand	grandis	livraison	libratio
gras	crassus	livre	liber
grave, grief	gravis	loi	lex
gré	gratus	loisir	licet
grêle	gracilis	louer	laudare
grenouille	ramicula	loyal	legalis
grillon	gryllus	luire (old Fr. luisir)	lucere
grogner	grumire	Lyonnais	Lugdunensis
gros	crassus	mâcher	masticare
habit	habitus	maçon	maciare
hamegon	hamus	Madeleine	Magdalena
hante	hasta	Mai	Majus
harpon	harpa	maigre	macer
haut	altus	maigreur	macror
hennir	hinnire	maille	macula
herse	irpex	main	manus
heure	hora	maintenant	manu tenens
hier	heri	maintenir	manu tenere
histoire	historia	maire (old Fr. majeur)	major
hiver	hiberuus	mais	magis
homme, on	homo	maison	mansio
honneur	honor	maître (old Fr. maistre)	magister
hôte	hospes	maîtresse	magistrissa or tressa
hôtel	hospitalis	malade	male aptus
huile	oleum	mâle	masculus
huis, huissier	ostium	malheur	mala hora
huit	octo	maligne, malin	malignus
huitante	octoginta	manche	manica
huitre	ostrea	manger	manducare
humble	humilis	manquer	mancus

[163]

APPENDIX.

French.	Latin.
manteau	mantellum
marbre	marmor
marchand	mercans
mardi	Martis dies
marge	margo
marin	marinus
masque	masca
matin *and* matinée	matutinus
mauvais	malus
médecin (*old Fr.* miege)	medicinus
meilleur	melior
mêler (*old Fr.* mesler)	misculare
mendier, mendiant	mendicare
ménace	minaciæ
méner (*old Fr.* mesuer)	minare
menton	mentum
menu	minutum
mercredi	Mercurii dies
mère	mater
mer (*old Fr.* mers)	mare
merveille	mirabilia
message	missaticum
métier	ministerium
mettre	mittere
midi, *from* mi-di	medius dies (meridius)
mie	mica
miel	mel
mien, mon	meus
mieux (*old Fr.* mels)	melius
milieu	medius locus
mille	mille
minuit	media nox
miroir	miratorium
mode	modus
moelle	medulla
mœurs	mos
moi	me
moindre *and* moins	minor
mois	mensis
moitié	medietas
monceau	monticellus
monde	mundus
montagne	montaneus
montrer	monstrare
mordache	mordax
mortel	mortalis
motif	motivus
mouchoir	mucatorium
mou, molle (*old Fr.* mol)	mollis
moucher	mucare
moudre (*old Fr.* molre)	molere
mouline	molinus
mourir	moriri
mousse	muscus
mouvoir	movere
moyen, moyenner	medianus
muer	mutare
muet	mutus
muid	modius
mûr (*old Fr.* meúr)	maturus
muraille	muralis
muscle	musculus
nager	navigare
nain	nanus
maître (*old Fr.* maistre)	nascor
nappe	mappa
natif et naïf	nativus
naturel	naturalis
naucher et nocher	nauclerus
naulage	naulagium
néant	nec-ens
nèfle	mespilum
neige	niveus
net	nitidus
nettoyer	nitidare
neuf, neuve (*old Fr.* nuef, nueve)	novus
neuf (*old Fr.* nuef)	novem
neveu	nepos
nez	nasus
ni (*old Fr.* ne)	nec
niais	nidensis
nice	nescius
nicher	nidificare

French.	Latin.
nid	nidus
nièce	neptis
nier	negare
niveau	libella
noble (*old Fr.* nobles)	nobilis
noces	nuptiæ
nœud	nodus
noël	natalis
noir	niger
noircir	nigrescere
noise	nausea
noix	nux
nom	nomen
nombre	numerus
nombril	umbilicus
nonchalant	noncalens
nonante	nonaginta
nonnain	nonna
note	nota
notifier	notificare
nôtre *and* notre (*old Fr.* nostre)	noster
nouer	nodare
nourrir	nutrire
nous (*old Fr.* nos *and* nus)	nos
nouveau, nouvelle	novellus
novice	novicius
noyau	nucalis
noyer	necare
noyer	nucarius
nu, nue	nudus
nue et nuage	nubes
nuire	nocere
nuit	nox
nul, nulle	nullus
obéir	obedire
obéissance	obedientia
obituaire	obitarium
obit	obitus
obscurcir	obscurare
obsèques	obsequiæ
œil	oculus
œuf	ovum
œuvre	opera
oie	auca
oindre	ungere
oignon	unio
oiseau	aucella
oisif	otiosus
ombre	umbra
on, homme	homo
oncle	avunculus
ongle	ungula
onze	undecim
opiniâtre	opiniaster
oreille	auricula
orge	hordeum
orme, ormeau	ulmus
orphelin	orphanus
ortie	urtica
ôter	hostire
où	ubi
ouaille	ovicula
oublier	oblitare
ouir	audire
outrage	ultragium
outre	ultra
page	pagina
paillasse	paleaceus
paille	palea
pain	panis
pair	par
paisible	pacibilis
paisseau	paxillus
paître	pascere
palais	Palatium
pâle	pallidus
palfroi	parafredus
paon	pavo
pape	papa
papillon	papilio
pâque	pascha
paraître	parêre

[164]

APPENDIX.

French.	Latin.	French.	Latin.
parc	parcus	poussin	pullicenus
pareil	pariculus	poutre	poledrus
paresse	pigritia	pouvoir	possum
parole	parabole	pré, préau	pratum
parrain	patrinus	prêcher	præ-dicere
partie	partitio	prefix	præfigere
pas	passus	premier	primarius
passereau	passer	prendre	prehendere
paternal	paternalis	près	pressus
pauverté	paupertas	présence	præsentia
pauvre	pauper	présent	præsens
payen	paganus	presser	premere
payer	pacare	présumer	præ-sumero
pays	pagensis	prêt	præstare
pécher	peccare	prêtre	presbyter
pécheresse	peccatrix	preuve	proba
pécheresse	piscatrix	prévoyance	providentia
peindre	pingere	prie	precari
peiner	pœna	prière	precaria
peintre	pictor	prince	princeps
pelisse	pellicius	prison	prehensio
pencher	pendicare	privé	privare
pensée	pensare	prix	pretium
perche	pertica	prochain	proximus
perdrix	perdix	proche	propior
père	pater	proie	præda
péril	periculum	prompt	promptus
personnage	personaticum	prône	præconius
peu	paucus	propre	proprius
peuple	populus	provençal	provincialis
peuplier	populus	prune	prunum
peur	pavor	prunier, prunellier	pruneus
physicien	physicus	pseaume	psalmus
pièce	petium	puce	pulex
pied	pes	pucelle	pulchellus or pulcellus
piége	pedica	pudeur	pudor
pierre	petra	pudique	pudicus
piéton	pedes	puer	putere
pigeon	pipio	pui or puy	podium
pignon	pinna	puis	post
piller	pilare	puissant	potens
pin	pinus	puits	puteus
pinceau	penicillum	pur	purus
place	platea	putain	putus
plage	plagia	quadruples	quadruplus
plaie	placitum	qualité	qualitas
plaie	plaga	quand	quando
plaindre	plangere	quant	quantus
plaire	placere	quatorze	quatuordecim
planche	planca	quatrain	quaterni
plantage	plantago	quatre	quattuor
plein	plenus	quel	qualis
plenier	plenarius	quelconque	qualiscunque
pleurer	plorare	querelle	querela
pleuvoir	pluere	quérir	quærere
plie, ploie	plicare	questionner	quæstio
plomb	plumbum	queue	cauda
plombagine	plumbago	quiconque	quicunque
pluie	pluvia	quinze	quindecim
poêle	parella	quitte	quietus
poids, pèse	pensum	racine	radicina
poignard	pugnalis	rage	rabies
poil	pilus	raire	radere
poindre	pungere	rais	radius
poing, poignée	pugnus	raisin	racemus
pointe	punctum	rame	remus
poire	pirum	rançon	redemptio
poison	potus	ration, raison	ratio
poisson	piscis	rauque	raucus
poitrail	pectoralis	ravage	rapagium
poivre	piper	rave	rapum
pomme	pomum	ravir	rapere
pommier	pomarius	rayer	radiare
ponce	pumex	recevoir	reciprocatio
pondre	ponere	règne	regnum
populace	populaceus	reine	regina
populaire	popularis	remorquer	remulcum
portier	portarius	renoncer	renunciare
possible	possibilis	reparer	repatriare
pouce	pollex	rétif	restivus
poudre	pulvis	rets, ret	rete
poulain	pullanus	rez	rasus
pour	pro	Rhône	Rhodanus
pourceau	porcus	rien	rem

APPENDIX.

French.	Latin.	French.	Latin.
rire	ridere	soif	sitis
ris	risus	soir, soirée	serus
rive	ripa	soixante	sexaginta
rivière	riparia	soleil	soliculus
roche	rupea	somache	salmacidus
rognon	renes	somme	sagma
roi	rex	sommeil	somniculus
roide	rigidus	son	sonus
rôle	rotula	songe	somnus
romain	Romanus	sonnaille	sonaculus
rompre	rumpere	sonner	sonare
rond	rotundus	sorcier	sortiarius
rosace	rosaceus	sorte, sort	sors
rose	rosa	sortir	sortior
rosée	ros	soudain	subitaneus
rosier	rosarius	soudre	solvere
rôter	ructare	soufre	sulfurans
roue	rota	soulager	solatior
rouge	rubeus	soupçon	suspicio
roure, rouvre	robur	souple	supplicamentum
route	rupta	sourd	surdus
roux, rousse	russus	souris	sorex
royal	regalis	sous	subtus
royaume	regalimen	souvenir	subvenire
rude	rudis	souvent	subinde
sachet	saccus	souverain	supernus
sade	sapidus	soyer and seier	secare
sage	sapius	spectacle	spectaculum
sailler	salire	splendeur	splendor
sain	sanus	stile	stilus
saint	sanctus	stupeur	stupor
salace	salax	stupide	stupidus
saluer	salutare	subit	subitò
salut	salus	subtil	subtilis
samedi	sabbatidies	succès	successivus
sang	sanies	suer	sudare
sanglier	singularis (scil. porcus)	sueur	sudor
sans	sine	suc	sucus
sapin	sapinus	suivre	sequor
saucisse	salcicea	supplier	supplicare
sauf	salvus	sur	supra
sauge	salvia	sûr	securus
saule	salix	table	tabula
saussaie	salictum	tailler	taleare
saut	saltus	taire	tacere
sauveur	salvator	tandis	tamdiu
sauvage	silvaticus	taon	tabanus
savoir	sapere	tapis	tapete
Saxon, onne	Saxones	taupe	talpa
scarabée	scarabeus	taureau	taurus
scel, sceau	sigilla	teiudre	tingere
sec	siccus	tel	talis
sèche	sepia	témoin	testimonium
sécher	siccare	tempête	tempestas
sécheresse	siccitas	temps	tempus
second	secundus	tendre	tener
seigle	secale	tendresse	teneritas
seigneur, sire	senex	tenir	tenere
sein	sinus	terrasse	terracea
seine	sagena	tête	testa
sel	sal	tiède	tepidus
selle	sella	tiers	tertius
semble	simulare	timbre	tympanum
semblant	simulans	tintin	tintinnare
semence	semen	titre	titulus
sens	sensus	titre	texere
sentier	semitarius	toise	tendo (tensum)
seoir	sedere	toit	tectum
sept	septem	ton	tonus
serge	Seres	ton, tien	tuus
sergent	serviens	tondre	tondere
serie	series	torche	tortus
serment	sacramentum	tordre	torquere
sermonner	sermonor	tort	tortus
seul	solus	tour	turris
sève	sapa	tourment	tormentum
siècle	seculum	tourner	tornare
siége	sedes	tourtre	turtur
siffle	sibilus	tout	totus
signe	signum	traille	traha
singe	simia	train	tractus
singulier	singularis	traire (to milk)	trahere
six	sex	travail	trabs
sœur	soror	treille	trichila

[166]

APPENDIX.

French.	Latin.	French.	Latin.
treillis	trillix	vergogne	verecundus
trembler	tremulus	vermeil	vermiculus
trente	triginta	verrat	verres
tresse	tricameratum	verre	vitrum
trésor	thesaurus	verrou, verrouil	veruculum
treuil	torculus	verrue	verruca
tribouiller	tribulare	vers	versus
triple	triplex	vert	viridis
trois	tres	vertu	virtus
tronçon	truncus	verve	verva
troubler	turbulare	vessie	vesica
troupe	troppus	vêtir	vestire
truite	tructa	veuve	vidua
un	unus	vide, veuf	viduus
user	utor	vieillard, vieil	vetulus
vache	vacca	vierge	virgo
vaguer	vagor	vigne	vineus
vain, en vain	vanus	vilain	villanus
vaincre	vincere	violet	viola
vais, vas, va	vadere	vœu	votum
vaisseau	vascellus	voie	via
valoir	valere	voile	velum
vanter	vanitare	voir	videre
vassal	vassus	voisin	vicinus
veau	vitellus	volage	volaticus
veiller	vigilare	volaille	volatilis
veine	vena	voler (*to steal*)	(in) volare
venaison	venatio	volontiers	voluntarius
vendange	vindemia	vôtre	vester
venger	vindicare	vouer	votare
venin	venenum	vous	vos
ventouse	ventosus	voyage	viaticus
verd	viridis	vrai	verus
verger	virga		

THE END.

WORKS
PUBLISHED BY JOHN WEALE,
59, HIGH HOLBORN.

In morocco, tuck, price 6s.,

THE ENGINEER'S AND CONTRACTOR'S POCKET BOOK,
REVISED.

In One large Vol. 8vo, Third Edition, revised and enlarged by H. LAW, C.E., with engravings, price 21s. in strong half-morocco,

MATHEMATICS FOR PRACTICAL MEN:

being a Common-place Book of Principles, Theorems, Rules, and Tables, in various departments of Pure and Mixed Mathematics, with their application especially for the use of Civil Engineers, Architects, and Surveyors.

By OLINTHUS GREGORY, LL.D., F.R.A.S.

The plates are folded in the book, but spaced out for reference whilst reading any part of the work, and consist of

1 to 5. Geometrical diagrams.—250 figures.
6. Details of a breast water-wheel.
7. Fenton, Murray, & Co.'s steam-engine.
8. A six-horse engine constructed by Thos. Middleton, London.
9. A six-horse engine, slides, cylinder, &c.
10. Longitudinal section of locomotive engine.
11. Transverse section of do.
12. Sections of the cylinders of Woolf's engine, Cornish engine, and Atmospheric engine.
13. Isometrical perspective.

In One small Volume, with many plates and wood-cuts, Third Edition, corrected and improved, neatly bound. Price 5s., the

OPERATIVE MECHANIC'S WORKSHOP COMPANION,
AND
THE SCIENTIFIC GENTLEMAN'S PRACTICAL ASSISTANT;

containing a great variety of the most useful Rules in mechanical science, divested of mathematical complexity; with numerous Tables of practical data and calculated results for facilitating mechanical and commercial transactions.

By WILLIAM TEMPLETON, Author of several useful Practical Works.

In 18mo, in boards, comprising 390 pages, price 5s.,

A SYNOPSIS OF PRACTICAL PHILOSOPHY,

alphabetically arranged, containing a great variety of Theorems, Formulæ, and Tables, from the most accurate and recent authorities in various branches of Mathematics and Natural Philosophy; with Tables of Logarithms.

By the Rev. JOHN CARR, M.A., late Fellow of Trinity College, Cambridge.

WORKS PUBLISHED BY MR. WEALE.

ELEMENTS OF MECHANISM

ELUCIDATING

THE SCIENTIFIC PRINCIPLES

OF

THE PRACTICAL CONSTRUCTION OF MACHINES.

FOR THE

USE OF SCHOOLS AND STUDENTS IN MECHANICAL ENGINEERING.

WITH

NUMEROUS SPECIMENS OF MODERN MACHINES,

REMARKABLE FOR THEIR UTILITY AND INGENUITY.

BY T. BAKER, C.E.,

Author of "Railway Engineering," "Land and Engineering Surveying,"
"Mensuration," "Principles and Practice of Statics and Dynamics,"
"Integration of Differentials," &c. &c.

ILLUSTRATED BY TWO HUNDRED AND FORTY-THREE ENGRAVINGS.

Price 2s.

WORKS PUBLISHED BY MR. WEALE.

GREEK AND LATIN CLASSICS.

In Preparation, and will be Issued Monthly,

Price 1s. per Volume,

(Except in seven instances, and those are at 1s. 6d. or 2s. each),

VERY NEATLY PRINTED ON GOOD PAPER,

A SERIES OF VOLUMES

CONTAINING

THE PRINCIPAL

GREEK AND LATIN AUTHORS,

ACCOMPANIED BY

ENGLISH NOTES ON A UNIFORM PLAN,

AND COMPRISING

all those Works that are essential for the Scholar and the Pupil, and applicable for use at the Universities of Oxford, Cambridge, Edinburgh, Glasgow, Aberdeen, and Dublin,—the Colleges at Belfast, Cork, Galway, Winchester, and Eton, and the great Schools at Harrow, Rugby, &c.,—also for Private Tuition and Instruction, and for the Library.

Vol. 1—Introductory to the Latin Series—will appear July 1st, and the Greek Introduction, August 1st. The publication of the Classical Authors will commence November 1, and be regularly continued on the 1st of each succeeding month.

EDITED BY HENRY YOUNG,
Second Master of the Royal Grammar School, Guildford.

In One Large Volume Octavo, Eleven Hundred Pages, with numerous
Engravings, price 1*l.* 8*s.*,

A GENERAL TEXT BOOK,

FOR THE

CONSTANT USE AND REFERENCE OF

ARCHITECTS, ENGINEERS, SURVEYORS, SOLICITORS, AUCTIONEERS, LAND AGENTS, AND STEWARDS,

IN ALL THEIR SEVERAL AND VARIED PROFESSIONAL OCCUPATIONS;

AND FOR THE

ASSISTANCE AND GUIDANCE OF

COUNTRY GENTLEMEN AND OTHERS

ENGAGED IN THE

TRANSFER, MANAGEMENT, OR IMPROVEMENT OF
LANDED PROPERTY:

CONTAINING

THEOREMS, FORMULÆ, RULES, AND TABLES

IN GEOMETRY, MENSURATION, AND TRIGONOMETRY; LAND MEASURING, SURVEYING, AND LEVELLING; RAILWAY AND HYDRAULIC ENGINEERING; TIMBER MEASURING; THE VALUATION OF ARTIFICERS' WORK, ESTATES, LEASEHOLDS, LIFEHOLDS, ANNUITIES, TILLAGES, FARMING STOCK, AND TENANT RIGHT; THE ASSESSMENT OF PARISHES, RAILWAYS, GAS AND WATER WORKS; THE LAW OF DILAPIDATIONS AND NUISANCES, APPRAISEMENTS AND AUCTIONS, LANDLORD AND TENANT, AGREEMENTS AND LEASES.

TOGETHER WITH EXAMPLES OF VILLAS AND COUNTRY HOUSES.

BY EDWARD RYDE,
Civil Engineer and Land Surveyor, Author of several Professional Works.

TO WHICH ARE ADDED SEVERAL CHAPTERS ON

AGRICULTURE AND LANDED PROPERTY.

BY PROFESSOR DONALDSON,
Author of several Works on Agriculture.

WORKS PUBLISHED BY MR. WEALE.

CONTENTS

CHAPTER I.—ARITHMETIC. 1. Notation—2. Proof of the First Four Rules—3. Vulgar Fractions—4. Decimals—5. Duodecimals—6. Powers and Roots—7. Properties of Numbers—8. Logarithms and Mathematical Tables.

II.—PLANE AND SOLID GEOMETRY. 1. Definitions—2. Of Angles and Right Lines, and their Rectangles—3. Of Triangles—4. Of Quadrilaterals and Polygons—5. Of the Circle, and Inscribed and Circumscribing Figures—6. Of Planes and Solids—7. Practical Geometry.

III.—MENSURATION. 1. Comparison of English and French Weights and Measures—2. Mensuration of Superficies—3. Mensuration of Solids.

IV.—TRIGONOMETRY. 1. Definitions and Trigonometrical Formulæ—2. General Propositions—3. Solution of the Cases of Plane Triangles.

V.—CONIC SECTIONS.

VI.—LAND MEASURING. Including Table of Decimals of an Acre—Table of Land Measure, by dimensions taken in yards.

VII.—LAND SURVEYING. 1. Parish and Estate Surveying—2. Trigonometrical Surveying—3. Traverse Surveying—4. Field Instruments, the Prismatic Compass; the Box Sextant; the Theodolite.

VIII.—LEVELLING. Levelling Instruments, the Spirit Level; the Y Level; Troughton's Level; Mr. Gravatt's Level; Levelling Staves—Examples in Levelling.

IX.—PLOTTING. Embracing the Circular Protractor—The T Square and Semicircular Protractor—Plotting Sections.

X.—COMPUTATION OF AREAS. The Pediometer—The Computing Scale—Computing Tables.

XI.—COPYING MAPS. Including a description of the Pentagraph.

XII.—RAILWAY SURVEYING. 1. Exploration and Trial Levels; Standing Orders.—2. Proceedings subsequent to the Passing of the Act; Tables for Setting out Curves; Tables for Setting out Slopes; Tables of Relative Gradients; Specification of Works to be executed in the construction of a Railway; Form of Tender.

XIII.—COLONIAL SURVEYING.

XIV.—HYDRAULICS IN CONNECTION WITH DRAINAGE, SEWERAGE, AND WATER SUPPLY.—With Synopsis of Ryde's Hydraulic Tables—Specifications, Iron Pipes and Castings; Stone-Ware Drain Pipes; Pipe Laying; Reservoir.

XV.—TIMBER MEASURING. Including Timber Tables, Solid Measure, Unequal Sided Timber; Superficial Measure.

XVI.—ARTIFICERS' WORK. 1. Bricklayers' and Excavators'—2. Slaters'—3. Carpenters' and Joiners'—4. Sawyers'—5. Stonemasons'—6. Plasterers'—7. Ironmongers'—8. Painters'—9. Glaziers'—10. Paper Hangers'.

XVII.—VALUATION OF ESTATES. With Tables for the Purchasing of Freehold, Copyhold, or Leasehold Estates, Annuities, and Advowsons, and for Renewing Leases for Terms of Years certain and for Lives.

XVIII.—VALUATION OF TILLAGES AND TENANT RIGHT. With Tables for Measuring and Valuing Hay Ricks.

WORKS PUBLISHED BY MR. WEALE.

CONTENTS (*continued*):—

XIX.—VALUATION OF PARISHES.
XX.—BUILDERS' PRICES. 1. Carpenters' and Joiners'—2. Masons'—3. Bricklayers'—4. Plasterers'—5. Ironmongers'—6. Drainers'—7. Plumbers'—8. Painters'—9. Paper Hangers' and Decorators'—10. Glaziers'—11. Zinc Workers'—12. Coppersmiths'—13. Wireworkers'.
XXI.—DILAPIDATIONS AND NUISANCES. 1. General Definitions—2. Dilapidations by Tenants for Life and Years—3. Ditto by Mortgagee or Mortgagor—4. Ditto of Party Walls and Fences—5. Ditto of Highways and Bridges—6. Nuisances.
XXII.—THE LAW RELATING TO APPRAISERS AND AUCTIONEERS. 1. The Law relating to Appraisements—2. The Law of Auction.
XXIII.—LANDLORD AND TENANT. 1. Agreements and Leases—2. Notice to Quit—3. Distress—4. Recovery of Possession.
XXIV.—TABLES. Of Natural Sines and Cosines—For Reducing Links into Feet—Decimals of a Pound Sterling.
XXV.—STAMP LAWS.—Stamp Duties—Customs' Duties.

EXAMPLES OF VILLAS AND COUNTRY HOUSES.

ON LANDED PROPERTY, BY PROFESSOR DONALDSON.

I.—Landlord and Tenant—their Position and Connections.
II.—Lease of Land, Conditions, and Restrictions; Choice of Tenant and Assignation of the Deed.
III.—Cultivation of Land, and Rotation of Crops.
IV.—Buildings necessary on Cultivated Lands—Dwelling Houses, Farmeries, and Cottages for Labourers.
V.—Laying-out Farms, Roads, Fences, and Gates.
VI.—Plantations—Young and old Timber.
VII.—Meadows and Embankments, Beds of Rivers, Water Courses, and Flooded Grounds.
VIII.—Land Draining, Open and Covered,—Plan, Execution, and Arrangement between Landlord and Tenant.
IX.—Minerals—Working and Value.
X.—Expenses of an Estate—Regulations of Disbursements—and Relation of the appropriate Expenditures.
XI.—Valuation of Landed Property; of the Soil, of Houses, of Woods, of Minerals, of Manorial Rights, of Royalties, and of Fee Farm Rents.
XII.—Land Steward and Farm Bailiff: Qualifications and Duties.
XIII.—Manor Bailiff, Woodreve, Gardener, and Gamekeeper—their Position and Duties.
XIV.—Fixed days of Audit—Half-Yearly Payments of Rents—Form of Notices, Receipts, and of Cash Books, General Map of Estates, and of each separate Farm—Concluding Observations.